Seventeenth-Century Art & Architecture

Seventeenth-Century Art & Architecture

Ann Sutherland Harris

Laurence King Publishing

For Neil and my students—
past, present, and future

Published in 2005 by Laurence King Publishing Ltd
71 Great Russell Street
London WC1B 3BP
United Kingdom

Tel: + 44 20 7430 8850
Fax: + 44 20 7430 8880
e-mail: enquiries@laurenceking.co.uk
www.laurenceking.co.uk

Copyright © 2005 Ann Sutherland Harris

All rights reserved. No part of this publication may be reproduced or transmitted in any form or by any means, electronic or mechanical, including photocopy, recording or any information storage and retrieval system, without prior permission in writing from the publisher.

A catalogue record for this book is available from the British Library.

ISBN 1-85669-415-1

Printed in China

Editor: Richard Mason
Picture Researcher: Susan Bolsom
Design: Ian Hunt
Typesetting: Marie Doherty

Front cover: Michelangelo Merisi da Caravaggio, *Bacchus*, 1595–96. Oil on canvas, 37⅜ x 33½ ins (94 x 85 cm). Uffizi, Florence.

Back cover: Jules Hardouin-Mansart & Louis Le Vau, Galerie des Glaces, Versailles, 1678.

Frontispiece: Gerrit Berckheyde, *The Market Place and the Grote Kerk at Haarlem* (detail), 1674. Oil on canvas, 20⅜ x 26⅜ ins (51.8 x 67 cm). National Gallery, London.

CONTENTS

Preface viii

INTRODUCTION xi

Politics, Religion, and Art xi
The Economics of Art xii
Geography, Cosmology, and Astronomy xiii
Concepts of the Body, Ancient and Modern xv
Education and Literacy xvi
Artists' Changing Status and Training xvii
New Subjects, New Genres xviii
Transforming the Renaissance and "Baroque" Art xxi

1 ITALY 1

The Decline of Mannerism 3
Architecture and City Planning in Rome, 1585–1625 4
Bolognese Painting: The Carracci Reform 7
Painting in Rome, 1585–1610 21
    Annibale Carracci in Rome, 1595–1609 24
Michelangelo Merisi da Caravaggio 34
Caravaggio's Italian Followers 50
The Carracci Succession in Rome and Bologna 56
Architecture and City Planning in Rome, 1625–1680 78
Italian Sculpture 85
    Gian Lorenzo Bernini's Early Career 86
    Bernini, Algardi, and the Portrait Bust 91
    The Competition: Alessandro Algardi and Francesco Duquesnoy 94
    Bernini and Urban VIII 99
    Algardi and Bernini during the Papacy of Innocent X 108

Painting in Rome, 1623–1680   113
    Pietro da Cortona   113
    Andrea Sacchi   120
    Pietro da Cortona in Florence and Rome   123
    Carlo Maratta   125
    Giovanni Battista Gaulli (Il Baciccio)   127
Painting in Naples   134

2 FLANDERS   143

Peter Paul Rubens   145
    Rubens in Italy, 1600–1608   148
    Rubens in Antwerp, 1609–1622   152
    Rubens, Diplomat and Artist, 1622–1630   165
    Rubens's Last Decade, 1630–1640   169
Anthony van Dyck   174
    Van Dyck in England and Italy, 1621–1627   176
    Van Dyck's Second Antwerp Period, 1627–1632   180
Jacob Jordaens   182
Still-Life Genre Painters   186

3 SPAIN   195

Spanish Architecture   196
Spanish Sculpture   197
Spanish Painting, 1600–1650   200
    Jusepe de Ribera   201
    Francisco de Zurbarán   208
    Diego Velázquez in Seville   217
    Velázquez in Madrid, 1623–1648   220
    Velázquez in Italy, 1648–1651   228
    Velázquez in Madrid, 1651–1660   228
Spanish Painting, 1650–1700   232
    Bartolomé Esteban Murillo   232
    Juan de Valdéz Leal and Claudio Coello   239

4 FRANCE   243

Architecture and City Planning   244
    Paris: The Pont-Neuf, Palais du Luxembourg, and Hôtel de la Vrillière   244
    Expansion under Louis XIV; The Louvre and Versailles   248
French Sculpture   254
    Pierre Puget   255
    François Girardon and Antoine Coysevox   256
French Painting and Printmaking   258
    Simon Vouet   260
    Valentin de Boulogne   263
    Georges de la Tour   264
    Simon Vouet's Successors   267

    Philippe de Champaigne 269
    Nicolas Poussin in Paris and Rome 273
    Poussin after 1630 279
    Poussin and Landscape Painting 289
    Poussin's Last Works 292
    Claude Lorrain and French Landscape Painting 295
    Charles Le Brun and the Academy 303

5 THE DUTCH REPUBLIC 311

Haarlem and the Creation of a Dutch National Style 313
    The Haarlem Mannerists 313
The Utrecht "Caravaggisti" 315
Frans Hals and Dutch Portraiture 319
Town Planning and Architectural Developments in Haarlem and Amsterdam 327
Painting in Amsterdam 333
Rembrandt van Rijn and his School 334
    Rembrandt's Early Years in Leiden 334
    Rembrandt in Amsterdam, 1627–1639 336
    Rembrandt's Self-Portraits 341
    Rembrandt in Amsterdam, 1639–1642 344
    Rembrandt's Landscape Prints and Drawings 346
    Rembrandt after 1642 348
    Rembrandt's Artistic Heirs 354
Dutch Genre Painting before 1650 356
    Judith Leyster 358
Dutch Genre Painting after 1650 361
    Johannes Vermeer 366
    Jan Steen 374
Landscape Painting before 1650 378
    Early Tonal Landscape Painting 378
Landscape Painting after 1650 380

6 ENGLAND 387

English Painting 388
    Van Dyck in England 388
    Later Portrait Painters 393
Palladianism and Architectural Planning in London 396
    Inigo Jones 396
    Christopher Wren 398

EPILOGUE 404

Notes 407
Timeline 408
Bibliography 412
Picture Credits 416
Index 417

PREFACE

This book is written as an introduction to the most significant artistic developments in Western Europe in the seventeenth century. It is intended to inform students of art and the interested reading public about a period that encompassed the careers of many of the best-known artists of European history. The text privileges painting over sculpture and architecture. Far more painting than sculpture was produced because the latter is an expensive medium and fewer artists took it up. Dutch, Flemish, and English patrons usually imported sculptors or sculpture from France or Italy, so their own sculpture is not covered here. French, Spanish, and Italian sculpture is covered with an emphasis on Gian Lorenzo Bernini, the transformative genius of this medium in the seventeenth century.

The achievements of Europe's architects and builders could easily have dominated everything else in the book. Because architectural history is usually taught separately in American colleges (except in introductory survey courses), this text focuses on a few key architects and monuments, and on city planning in Rome, Paris, and London. Those readers whose main interest is architecture of this period will find books such as the Pelican *History of Art* (Yale University Press) and *Baroque* (Könemann; ed. Rolf Toman) readily available sources of supplementary information.

This book focuses on the six countries whose art and architecture is usually taught in courses on European Baroque art — Italy, Flanders, Spain, France, the Dutch Republic, and England. There is no chapter on artists from eastern or central Europe (what remained of the Holy Roman Empire), because the turmoil of the Thirty Years' War, finally ended by the Treaty of Westphalia in 1648, did not allow any cities in these countries to provide steady patronage for native artists for most of the seventeenth century. The Habsburg court of Emperor Rudolf II in Prague, where he ruled from 1576 until 1612, attracted painters, engravers, and sculptors from Antwerp, Amsterdam, Frankfurt, Basle, and Milan. Their sophisticated style became the final fling of Mannerism. The court moved to Vienna in 1620. Most ambitious young artists born in the territories now called Germany, Austria, and the Czech Republic left for Flanders or Italy, ostensibly to train, but many never returned; among those were the painters Adam Elsheimer, included here in the chapter on Italy, and Johann Liss from Oldenburg, who died in Venice.

The first and longest chapter is devoted to Italy. In the sixteenth century Italy became a magnet for artists from the Netherlands and France, while Italian artists were sought by courts in Spain, France, and England. The influence of Raphael, Michelangelo, and their successors soon reached Antwerp, Madrid, and Fontainebleau outside Paris. Thus, the logical place to begin our story is Italy, specifically Bologna and Rome where the Carracci and Caravaggio began the stylistic revolution that deposed an international Mannerist style and replaced it with other styles based on renewed life study and a respect for Renaissance artists least affected by *maniera*. The Counter-Reformation Church offered so many opportunities for artists in Rome that the city became the most important center of artistic production in Europe. Its only rivals in Italy were Bologna and Naples, the former too small to offer serious competition (although its artists were enjoying their greatest period of achievement), the latter controlled by the Spanish monarchy. Venice produced no worthy successors to Titian, Tintoretto, and Veronese until the eighteenth century. Thus Rome remained the most important European city for ambitious artists until Paris gradually replaced it in the nineteenth century.

The next chapters discuss Flanders and Spain, whose developments were most directly affected by Italian art. Both were Catholic countries and Flanders (the Spanish Netherlands) was still part of the dwindling Spanish Empire. The seven northern provinces of the Netherlands had effectively been ceded to the Dutch by 1609. The economic decline that resulted from their control of sea trade in Northern Europe meant that artistic production in the Spanish Netherlands gradually declined after the deaths of Peter Paul Rubens and Anthony van Dyck in the 1640s. There was not another influential Flemish artist until Antoine Watteau (1684–1721), who was born in Valenciennes (which had passed to France in 1677). There were no major architects or sculptors working in Flanders (Francesco Duquesnoy spent his working life in Rome), so these arts are mentioned only in passing.

While Spain also experienced a drastic contraction of its economic resources after 1600, the Church and the Court continued to provide substantial opportunities for painters, sculptors, and architects, notably in Madrid and Seville, and the careers of Francisco de Zurbarán and Bartolomé Esteban Murillo carry the story well into the second half of the century. Velázquez made two visits to Italy but this was not typical of Spanish artists, who were less likely than their peers elsewhere to spend their formative years abroad. They usually learnt about foreign developments from prints or an occasional visit to Madrid where, if they were lucky, they might have access to the art collections of Philip IV, in which Titian and Rubens were especially well represented. Unlike their European peers, Spanish sculptors and architects paid less attention to the models offered by ancient Greece and Rome. The results are idiosyncratic and, in the case of church buildings, often spectacularly original.

The next three chapters move north from France to the Dutch Republic and finally to England. Before 1600 French artists had been strongly influenced both by the work of their Flemish contemporaries and also by that of Italian visitors working at Fontainebleau. The earlier part of the book has thus prepared the reader to understand these connections and to appreciate the evolution of a distinctive French style in painting, sculpture, and architecture during the seventeenth century. The transformation of Paris into a modern city began around 1600, so it is vital to pay some attention to its planning and major monuments.

With one exception—the new Town Hall of Amsterdam—the social and political structure of patronage in the Dutch Republic did not demand monumental buildings, and it gave few opportunities for ambitious sculptors. Printmakers and painters, on the other hand, found a huge new market among the middle classes, many of whom had enough discretionary income to form art collections. Thus, the chapter on the Dutch Republic emphasizes painting, with some attention to prints and a brief section on the Dutch adaptation of Palladian architectural models for their new churches and fancier residences.

The last chapter is devoted to England. Anthony van Dyck's presence at the court of Charles I for a decade (1632–42) transformed court portraiture by raising standards and offering a more flattering and relaxed image of the aristocracy than the stiff formulas that had prevailed before. The English continued to depend on imported talent, however, long after the death of van Dyck, except in the special field of the miniature portrait. Patronage for any other kind of painting—decorative, historical, or religious themes, landscapes or genre scenes—was slow to develop until the end of the century. The sculptors working in England tended to be foreigners too, and not of impressive originality. Only in the field of architecture did English artists emerge as rivals to their continental peers. Thus, the emphasis here is on Inigo Jones, who introduced English patrons to the work of Andrea Palladio and forever changed the appearance of British architecture, and Christopher Wren, who designed and built St. Paul's Cathedral, the largest church erected in Western Europe in the seventeenth century.

There is no simple relationship between artists' personalities and the character of their art, but knowing something about artists' lives and reading their own statements about their tastes and intentions can create empathy for work that may seem at first inaccessible. The contrast between Caravaggio's violent temper and the profound religious sentiment that he could conjure up on canvas immediately engages both specialists and the general public. Both Rubens and Poussin were serious students of the visual and intellectual culture of the Italian Renaissance and its ancient roots, but Rubens was an extrovert involved in the major diplomatic and religious issues of his time while Poussin lived quietly in Rome, working steadily except when taking a walk in the Borghese Gardens with learned friends. The differences in their personalities partly explain the differences between their paintings. Issues of competition, conflicting ambitions, and rivalries play a role in every chapter of this book. That many artists felt the need both to outdo their peers and the great names of the previous century had a visible effect on many of the works discussed here.

Whether an artist is part of the popular canon or not, this text has longer analytical descriptions of the works illustrated than is typical of introductory books. Looking long and carefully at a particular work is a skill not mastered during a survey course; a slow examination of any visual image invariably yields deeper understanding. One may well puzzle over some fascinating details in these artworks. Why does van Dyck's Christ (see Fig. 2.39) hold a bulrush instead of a stick? Why does Murillo's beggar boy (see Fig. 3.39) have scorpions around him? Why is the table between Christ and the Virgin so large in Zurbarán's *Virgin and Christ in the Holy House of Nazareth* (see Fig. 3.19)? Why does Vermeer's servant (see Fig. 5.56) wear clothes of such beautiful colors? The interpretations offered here may be disputed, but they will at least open a dialogue with inquiring readers.

The introduction that follows reminds readers of the persistence after 1600 of certain medieval beliefs ranging from the shape of the world to those about the way in which the human body works. Little education was available to the majority of the populace, even in urban centers. Background knowledge of this kind, including the gradual changes brought about by scientific discoveries and the mapping of the world by intrepid sailors, navigators, and map makers, is also vital to understanding the arts. The seventeenth century is a watershed between the medieval and modern world. Fundamental religious beliefs were challenged as Europe's rulers, intellectuals, and artists faced constant tensions and warfare, while the hegemony of the Roman Catholic Church was undermined. Artists responded magnificently by presenting space, light, and human experience in revolutionary ways that changed art forever.

Acknowledgments

Many people encouraged me to write this book and kept my spirits up when the task seemed overwhelming. First in line is Cass Canfield, Jr., who long ago suggested that I do a book on the "baroque", although he also wanted the "rococo". Once persuaded that the art and architecture of seventeenth-century Europe needed a book of its own, he spoke up for me at crucial points while supporting my editors' requests that my huge draft manuscript be reduced. I am also deeply grateful to Laurence King for his faith in this project and to the editors who have worked with me over five years as the text took shape: Lee Greenfield, Kara Hattersley-Smith, and Richard Mason. My text benefited enormously from their expertise and that of the following reviewers: Kelly Donahue-Wallace, University of North Texas; Heidi Hornik, Baylor University; Julie Anne Plax, University of Arizona; and Wendy Roworth, University of Rhode Island. Sue Bolsom enterprisingly pursued the best images for the text.

Authors in the bibliography deserve thanks for making it possible for me to produce what I hope is a reliable survey of artistic developments in all six countries covered. As a scholar of Italian and French painting, drawing, and sculpture, I depended particularly on the *Grove Dictionary of Art* for leads to recent scholarship, as well as the volumes of the *Pelican History of Art* covering Spain, Belgium, the Dutch Republic, and England. The revised volumes of Jonathan Brown on Spanish painting and Seymour Slive on Dutch painting were especially helpful, as were exhibition catalogues published by the Metropolitan Museum of Art, New York, and the National Gallery, Washington, D.C.

The text was read in various drafts by friends, colleagues, and students, whose thoughtful critiques and enthusiasm were more important than they may realize. Special thanks go to Peter Bell, Deborah Blocker, Sarah Cantor, Wayne E. Franits, Barbara Haeger, Patricia Howard, Hector Huertas, Rebecca Long, Peter Machamer, Jennifer Montagu, Claire Pace, and James Wilkinson. Additionally, John Beldon Scott lent me an important photograph. Evelyn Blue kept my house in order and my son Neil provided the kind of encouragement every author needs, as did many other colleagues and friends. To all my heartfelt thanks and a glass of good wine the next time we meet!

Ann Sutherland Harris
Pittsburgh, February 14, 2004

INTRODUCTION

THE BEST KNOWN of the many outstanding painters, sculptors, and architects who were working in seventeenth-century Europe include Bernini, Borromini, Caravaggio, Claude, Hals, Poussin, Rembrandt, Rubens, van Dyck, Velázquez, Vermeer, and Wren. This book seeks to explain why so many exceptional artists emerged and transformed the visual arts at that time. Was there a seismic shift in the relationship between artists and patrons that fostered innovation rather than reiterated convention? Did the training systems available to promising young artists change? What role did the visual arts play in the self-definition of the new nations formed in the seventeenth century? It is also important to ask why Florence, Antwerp, and Venice declined as centers of artistic significance, whereas Rome, Paris, and Amsterdam expanded, and why certain seventeenth-century artists praised by some were reviled by others. Why did some women artists have successful careers for the first time since antiquity? And what is "the Baroque", the word usually applied to the arts of this era? This book addresses such questions. It will show how the visual arts reflected developments in religious beliefs, political systems, economic fluctuations, cultural change, and the scientific discoveries that ushered in the modern era.

Politics, Religion, and Art

The disintegration of the Holy Roman Empire in the seventeenth century produced major shifts of power and territory in Western Europe. Holland, Belgium, Spain, and France began to settle into the geographical boundaries that they occupy today, although Eastern Europe remained a complex patchwork of warring principalities, bishoprics, and kingdoms. The Italian peninsula, despite being a geographical unit whose residents shared a common language, was still a divided land. The pope in Rome controlled a Z-shaped band of territory in the center. Spain ruled most of Italy south of Rome, including Sicily, and exercised *de facto* control over Milan and the northern port of Genoa. Venice still had its Republic while a few smaller principalities survived in Northern Italy. England and Scotland became, if not happily, one country under James I in 1603. By mid-century, most of Ireland, Scotland, and Wales were controlled by Parliament too.

The religious wars between Protestants and Catholics that began in the sixteenth century continued in the seventeenth, although some countries were more affected than others. Henry VIII had already declared himself head of the Church of England in 1534, but the status of those who wished to remain loyal Catholics, including the French wife of Charles I, kept alive hopes of Britain's return to the Roman Catholic fold long after 1600. Religious wars kept the territories now called Germany, Switzerland, and Austria, then controlled by the emperor's heirs, minor princes, and bishops, in a constant state of turmoil until 1648. Only the court of Rudolf II in Prague (1576–1612) supported a talented group of Flemish, German, and Italian artists. Otherwise, little artistic production of significance emerged in Eastern Europe until later in the century. Particular circumstances resulted in the division of the Netherlands into the Dutch Republic, which tolerated religious dissent, and the Spanish Netherlands, which did not. The rich agricultural land surrounding Antwerp and Brussels sustained a limited degree of prosperity after warfare ended, but the collapse of Antwerp's economy after the Dutch blockaded its port meant that the southern Netherlands could no longer serve as Spain's "cash cow." This was one of many reasons for Spain's steady economic decline after 1600.

Neither the pope nor the Spanish kings and their regents in Brussels accepted the loss of Britain and the Seven Provinces to Protestant rulers; the French were barely more tolerant of Protestants than the Spanish. The political machinations undertaken to try to reverse these political and religious changes of power sometimes involved artists, among them Peter Paul Rubens, Anthony van Dyck, Diego Velázquez, Gian Lorenzo Bernini and Charles Le Brun. The political propaganda created in Rome on behalf of a militant Catholic faith was also a rich source of artistic patronage, while the suppression of Catholicism in the Dutch Republic produced other challenges and opportunities for their artists. The Church, Catholic and Protestant, was a major catalytic force in the visual arts.

The Economics of Art

Art flourishes where there is wealth.
CAREL VAN MANDER, 1604[1]

The creation of impressive art requires considerable disposable income. The enormous number of architecturally significant buildings, major sculptural monuments, and large-scale paintings produced in Western Europe in the seventeenth century are eloquent proof of the improved economic conditions after 1600 in most of the countries discussed in this book. The economic decline of Spain did not, however, prevent the Crown or the Church from building new palaces and churches, and decorating them lavishly afterwards. The relative lack of disposable income among its aristocracy and merchant classes meant, however, that there were fewer private collectors there than elsewhere, and fewer artists. Around 1650, for example, roughly 850 artists are recorded in the Dutch Republic while only about 150 were active in Spain.

Economic factors are not the only ones affecting the production of visual art in these years: established traditions were powerful factors too. The shortest chapter here covers the art and architecture of England, yet its economy, although slackened by the Civil War in the middle of the century, had recovered and overtaken that of the Dutch Republic by 1700. The dissolution of the monasteries, their destruction and the confiscation of Church property by the Crown in the 1530s, wiped out the most substantial source of artistic patronage in England, Scotland, and Wales for all the arts, major and minor. The recovery from that artistic disaster took centuries. Despite the examples of Hans Holbein (1497/8–1543), who spent twelve years in London, and Anthony van Dyck, who worked for the court of Charles I from 1633 until his death, locally trained painters rarely rose above the level of journeymen. Imported artists, usually Dutch, filled the gap. Not until the eighteenth century did British artists dominate artistic production in all media. Even then, most patrons wanted only portraits; those with more adventurous tastes went to the Continent to add to their collections. The money was there but the taste and inclination were not.

The economic situation of Italy was not impressive yet its strong artistic traditions sustained its achievements in many centers. Its population declined in the seventeenth century, as did that of Spain. Venice began to lose trade to Genoa and Naples as other sea routes were discovered and more ships carried more goods to Northern Europe than had previously been landed there. Urban VIII (r. 1623–44), Maffeo Barberini, drained the Church's treasury in order to decorate Il Gesù (Fig. 0.1), the interior of St. Peter's, and his family's properties, and then to fight the futile War of Castro over a small hill town north of Rome that belonged to his hated rivals, the Farnese family. When famine struck in the early 1640s, the papal treasury could not afford to buy sufficient grain to alleviate hunger. As a result, Urban was hated by the Roman

0.1 Andrea Sacchi & Jan Miel, *Urban VIII Visiting Il Gesù, Rome*, 1639-41. Oil on canvas, 11 ft × 8 ft 2 in (3.36 × 2.47 m). Galleria Nazionale di Arte Antica, Palazzo Braschi, Rome.

populace when he died. His successor, Innocent X (r. 1644–55), Giambattista Pamphili, was known for his parsimonious spending on art and all other matters but Alexander VII (r. 1655–67), Fabio Chigi, spent lavishly to improve the city of Rome. The papacy and its court remained the most significant source of artistic patronage in Italy but the artistic traditions of Florence, Bologna, Genoa, Milan, Venice, and Naples were maintained throughout the century.

France emerged from a disastrous series of squabbles over royal succession and religious affiliations in the later sixteenth century to settle down under Henry IV and Louis XIII. It was always potentially the richest country in Western Europe thanks to its extensive areas of fertile terrain and its many well-placed rivers, the interstate highways of their day. Still, warfare persisted along its borders with modern Germany. Jacques Callot's engravings documenting the cruelties of warfare in Lorraine testify to the price paid by the rural inhabitants of eastern France (see Fig. 4.18). Both Louis XIII and his son, Louis XIV, benefited from the services of brilliant administrators—Cardinal Richelieu for Louis XIII and Colbert for Louis XIV. They enriched the royal treasury and themselves while setting up national and local governing systems that enabled many cities besides Paris to build new town halls, courts of justice, and churches. Towards the end of the century, Louis XIV added to his territories by waging war against the Spanish Netherlands and Dutch Republic, though he did not always manage to keep what he captured. His victories were recorded by Charles Le Brun on the ceiling of the Galerie des Glaces at Versailles (see Fig. 4.10). Unlike Philip II, Louis XIV could afford to wage war and spend lavishly on art at the same time.

Geography, Cosmology, and Astronomy

And new Philosophy calls all in doubt,
The Element of fire is quite put out;
The Sun is lost, and th'earth, and no man's wit
Can well direct him where to look for it.
And freely men confess that this world's spent,
When in the Planets, and the Firmament
They seek so many new [...]
'Tis all in pieces, all coherence gone;
All just supply, and all Relation.
                                JOHN DONNE, 1611[2]

Political and religious conflicts were a constant feature of European history but were not the only forces with profound impact on people's lives. Developments in navigation, cartography, and astronomy in the sixteenth and seventeenth centuries revealed new worlds to Europeans, while astronomical discoveries were found to be even more disturbing. The exploration of the world beyond Europe by brave voyagers such as the Portuguese Vasco da Gama, who sailed around Africa to Calcutta in 1497, Amerigo Vespucci, who reached Brazil in 1499, and Cristoforo Colombo, who had reached America a few years earlier, led to revolutionary concepts about the place of man and the earth within a larger universe. If at the start of the fifteenth century all believed that the world was a flat circle hovering in a crystal sphere, with God in heaven overhead and hell somewhere below, by 1500 a few realized that the world was round and hell at least had to be imagined elsewhere. As mathematicians struggled to reconcile their observations of the paths of the planets with their trajectories as plotted by Ptolemy in the second century AD, some began to question their supposedly circular paths around the earth and to propose other explanations. It was Johannes Kepler (1571–1630) who discovered the three laws of planetary motion, proving what Nicolaus Copernicus (1473–1543), among others, had argued, that the sun and not the earth is at the center of the planetary system. Copernicus still believed that the planets moved in circles, however, and at uniform speeds. Kepler demonstrated that their paths are elliptical and that their speeds vary depending on their distance from the sun. He also worked out how to calculate the time it takes each planet to make its journey round the sun. He did all this although he did not know the law of gravity: that was Sir Isaac Newton's great contribution later in the century.

John Donne's poem reveals how unsettling such pronouncements were at the time. Both Calvin and Luther denounced heliocentrism long before Copernicus finally published his conclusions in 1543. The Roman Catholic hierarchy also believed that the foundations of their doctrines were challenged by these conclusions. Galileo Galilei's forced public recantation of heliocentrism at the Vatican before Urban VIII in 1633 is famous, along with his muttered retraction—"Epur si muove!" (but still it [the earth] moves!). Galileo's published observations of the surface of the moon seen through his telescopes had already been used by Ludovico Cigoli for a fresco of the Immaculate Virgin (Santa Maria Maggiore, Rome, 1610–12), and Adam Elsheimer had correctly shown the Milky Way as an irregular band of tiny stars instead of some mysterious cosmic vapor in his moonlight *The Flight into Egypt* of 1609 (see Fig. 1.56). Protestantism was not the only challenge to the hegemony of the Roman Catholic faith; now mathematics and astronomy were conspiring to challenge essential biblical texts. Kepler, however, still believed in astrology, and so did Urban VIII, though he had to keep secret the fact that he consulted astrologers because the Catholic Church was officially opposed to their practice.

Maps of the world had to be redrawn constantly as new coastlines were mapped. The Dutch cartographers and boat builders were the best in the world; Dutch lens grinders and instrument builders produced the finest telescopes, quadrants, and astrolabes. Equipped with these tools, their sea captains traveled beyond India to Malaysia, establishing colonies in Sumatra, Java, and the Moloccos (Spice) Islands, even reaching China. Silks, rare spices, and sea shells, Chinese porcelain and other luxuries were brought back to Amsterdam, as well as new plants, exotic animals, and slaves, though not yet in large numbers.

Curiosity about these new worlds and the desire to record, map, and explain their fauna, flora, and inhabitants meant a ready market for books describing travelers' experiences. Artists and botanists traveled too and brought back drawings of new plants and animals from Asia, Africa, and also South America. Frans Post (*c.* 1612–1680) did good business in Haarlem with views of Brazil and its inhabitants after returning from an extended stay at the Dutch colony there in 1637–44. Maria Sibylla Merian (1647–1717) spent three years in the Dutch colony of Surinam before returning to Amsterdam in 1701 to prepare the third of her publications on the life cycles of insects and their plant hosts (Fig. 0.2), *Metamorphosis Insectorum Surinamensium*. Artists marched hand in hand with scientists to map the fauna and flora of the old and new world in the seventeenth century.

0.2 Maria Sibylla Merian, *Cassava Plant with Caterpillar and Butterflies*, from *Metamorphosis Insectorum Surinamensium*, 1705. Handcolored engraving, 17¾ × 13 in (45 × 33.5 cm). Private collection.

Concepts of the Body, Ancient and Modern

Around 1600 everyone thought that health depended on the harmonious balance among the four humors and their manifestation within human bodies in the form of four liquids—blood, phlegm, yellow and black bile. The belief in the humors and their temperaments—sanguine, phlegmatic, melancholic, and choleric—had originated with Galen, a physician practicing in Asia Minor in the second century AD. Artists and intellectuals believed that they suffered from marked melancholic tendencies; some had themselves portrayed with a solemn expression, their head propped up on one hand (see Fig. 1.55). These four elements were also gendered—earth and fire were male; water and air, female. Not until 1628 did doctors begin to understand how blood circulated through the body or the role of the heart and lungs in this process. In that year William Harvey (1578–1657) published his proof that blood circulates through the heart to both veins and arteries in one, not two separate systems, as was thought previously. This discovery soon led to the questioning of other ancient beliefs about human physiognomy, but belief in the four humors remained unchallenged long after 1700.

Devastating outbreaks of the bubonic plague, the so-called Black Death, persisted in Western Europe, with especially severe cases occurring in 1629 and 1656. The only solutions were isolation of the infected, quick burial of the dead in common graves, and the incineration of the clothes of the deceased. Some cities commissioned votive paintings dedicated to local patron saints (see Fig. 1.67) and to St. Roch and St. Sebastian, whose aid had long been sought in this situation. The main diagnostic tool of sickness not identified by spots and sores was the visual examination of urine in a clear glass. The standard remedy was blood-letting to drain the body of its "choleric fluids" or purging with pungent herbal concoctions. Despite more accurate renderings of human anatomy in textbooks by Vesalius (1514–64) and others, and more dissections for medical students (see Fig. 5.26), many doctors still believed that a woman's womb moved around inside her body unless anchored in place by a fetus. Unsanitary practices during childbirth made it a dangerous event for the mother as well as the baby (and so it remained until the twentieth century). Thus in many ways life in seventeenth-century Europe had changed little since ancient times. Still, some skepticism existed about doctors' claims: a number of prints and paintings of quack doctors were made in the sixteenth and seventeenth centuries in the Netherlands.

As well as the four humors, everyone was believed to have a soul. Its presence was manifested by the poses, gestures, and facial expressions that revealed that person's mood—happy, sad, puzzled, angry, and so on. The modern term "body language" roughly coincides with the Italian term "affetti" as it was used in the seventeenth century. Artists had of course conveyed their protagonists' moods in narrative scenes before 1600 but the intensity, variety, and subtlety of facial expressions, and supporting poses and gestures, became far greater thereafter. Raphael's *Baldassare Castiglione* (Fig. 0.3) was

0.3 Raphael, *Baldassare Castiglione*, c. 1514–15. Oil on canvas, 32¼ × 26⅜ in (82 × 67 cm). Louvre, Paris.

praised in 1515 by the sitter for being so alive that he seemed on the verge of speech. Bernini, Frans Hals, and others made portraits of sitters in mid-speech (see Fig. 1.91), the muscles tensed round their mouths, their eyes focused on an imagined presence which, when set beside the Raphael, make it look quietly self-contained. Another memorably captured incident is Adriaen Brouwer's picture of a man reacting to a bitter drink (see Fig. 2.56). Narrative scenes by Caravaggio and Rembrandt can convey a sense of inner life that makes earlier interpretations of the same story seem stiff and naïve. Artists' study of nature thus comprised far more than accurately drawn human bodies and settings: intense observation of minute changes in facial expression and empathy for the significance of a slight shift of weight, the angle of a head, the placing of a hand give seventeenth-century narrative painting a new power to connect with the spectator centuries later.

Education and Literacy

The invention of printing and movable type in the mid-fifteenth century by Johann Gutenberg is rightly hailed as a milestone in the creation of modern society. Literacy rates did not, however, instantly escalate. There was no universal system of elementary education even for boys in Western Europe in the early seventeenth century, though gradually schools, both free and fee-based, were opened in the major cities. Rural communities remained almost completely illiterate. Even parish priests in Italy and France often knew only what they had learnt by rote during their training. Protestants encouraged universal literacy because they wanted everyone to be able to read the Bible, so free elementary schools were established earlier in the Dutch Republic and Britain than elsewhere. European literacy rates at this time rarely exceeded 30 per cent for men in major cities, and were far lower for women, maybe 10 per cent, for only fathers wealthy enough to hire private tutors could educate their daughters as properly as they wished. The growth of free schools in the Dutch Republic helped literacy rates there to improve much faster than elsewhere in Europe, though they were still well below those of Europe today.

A high degree of literacy was thus a marker of high social status. This fact explains why a literary education was strongly encouraged by those who wanted to elevate the social standing of artists to that of other professions that required fluent Latin and extended book learning of their practitioners. The kind of education that Rubens received before training to become a painter was exceptional among artists. Boys entering craft professions, which is how painting and sculpture were still regarded, usually left school between the ages of eight and twelve. Unless their fathers intended them to become notaries, lawyers, or clerics, they will not have learnt more Latin than the common prayers recited in church. Any book learning that followed will have been on the students' own initiative. Most books were expensive: artists with large private libraries were rare, though some accessed the libraries of patrons.

Paintings with complex allegorical programs always depended on extensive discussions between the artist and the learned adviser of the patron. Even the patrons may not have been aware of all the subtleties of meaning in a major fresco cycle or history painting resulting from such collaborations. The publication of Cesare Ripa's *Iconologia* in 1593, however, and its first illustrated edition in 1603, made available to artists and patrons the attributes of hundreds of allegorical figures beginning with Abundance and ending with Zeal. Here anyone who could read Italian could learn how to represent the seven virtues and vices, countries and continents, months and seasons, and qualities such as Prudence, Temperance, and Fortitude. Some of the allegories would have been familiar because images of the theological virtues and vices, for example, had appeared in many works of art since the Middle Ages. Others were culled from ancient sources or invented by the author. The prefaces of the first edition, which contained only a hundred allegories, suggested that poets and writers would find the book helpful; the expanded illustrated edition was recommended to painters and sculptors too. It was frequently reprinted in Italy. A Dutch edition came out in 1645 and was used by Vermeer for his *Art of Painting* (see Fig. 5.61). English, French, and German editions were also published before 1700. The book remains an essential reference work for scholars of European art and literature.

Artists' Changing Status and Training

Painters, sculptors, and architects are generally supposed to have gained higher social status during the Renaissance, gradually exchanging their status as humble craftsmen for that akin to practitioners of learned professions such as the law and literature. It is true that some artists joined courts or became wealthy enough to afford the clothes and residences of a wealthy merchant or scholar. Some even acquired titles and thus permission to wear a sword, then an important status symbol. These were the exception, but their social and financial success was noted by their less fortunate peers and acted as a spur to achieve similar status. Artists did not, as some do today, advertise their outsider status by wearing less conventional clothing than other professionals. Even those attending a life-drawing session in the seventeenth century are shown wearing smart clothes as they sit around sketching the posed model (Fig. 0.4).

Artists continued to receive their training as they had since the Middle Ages—as apprentices in the studios of the artists they admired and hoped to emulate. The system gave matriculated artists some steady income and assistance with studio chores in exchange for instructing their pupils in practical matters as well as the techniques of the artists' chosen specialty. Though artists' academies had been founded in Florence (1563) and Rome (1593), with the goal of providing regular instruction in life drawing as well as educational lectures from artists and humanists, their members joined after receiving their basic training, so these activities were never more than an irregular supplement. The founding of the Royal Academy in Paris in 1648, and its support after 1660 by Louis XIV as a fully funded training system for artists and craftsmen, inspired other academies to emulate its example in the late seventeenth and eighteenth centuries. When Carlo Maratta became the Principal of the Accademia di San Luca in Rome in 1663, he held regular meetings and established the first reliable schedule of life-drawing sessions. He also instituted a program of lectures and offered prizes to the most promising young artists, which his successors at the Accademia managed to maintain. Young artists still began their training in individual studios, because the Roman Academy's classes supplemented rather than replaced apprenticeships.

0.4 Michael Sweerts, *A Drawing Academy*, c. 1650. Oil on canvas, 30⅛ × 43¼ in (76.5 × 110 cm). Frans Hals Museum, Haarlem.

New Subjects, New Genres

The most important change in artistic production in the seventeenth century was the dramatic growth in the production of paintings that did not depict scenes from the Bible, ancient history, or mythology. Portraiture was well established at all the major European courts in the sixteenth century, and in some places among the merchant classes too, but it had become a commonplace among prosperous middle-class families throughout Europe by 1700. It was by some distance the preferred genre in Britain, and the French were almost as enthusiastic as the Dutch and the Flemish about preserving their likenesses for posterity. Many of these images are pedestrian, but the greatest artists of this genre—Rembrandt, Hals, and van Dyck—not only made memorable portraits of single sitters in a far greater variety of poses and settings than before, but also transformed the wedding portrait, the family portrait, the group portrait, and court portraiture. The self-portrait also became an increasingly ambitious category raising self-promotion and self-awareness to new levels. Rembrandt created more self-portraits than anyone else, but many artists made highly original images of themselves, none more so than Velázquez in *Las Meninas* (see Fig. 3.38).

Landscapes, scenes of daily life, and still-lifes were all produced in the previous century but in relatively small numbers by a few artists, most of whom worked north of the Alps. After 1600 the popularity of these genres grew exponentially, especially in the Dutch Republic (Fig. 0.5), where the destruction or removal of all religious imagery from churches converted to Protestant use forced artists to turn to other subjects that would appeal to private clients. Statistics compiled from inventories of art collections in Amsterdam and elsewhere show the percentage of religious and history paintings declining and that of landscapes growing. By 1650 the latter were the most popular type of painting, followed by portraiture. Still-life and genre scenes were less so, the former because they required a meticulous technique, which meant that they could not be produced quickly and were thus always expensive. The salacious content of many genre scenes made before 1650 probably limited their audience.

The consequences of this expansion of the art market from the elite few to the many was as revolutionary as the expansion of the categories of imagery that appealed to this new clientele. The endless discussions about what does or does not constitute art originated in the seventeenth-century expansion of visual themes. Art could now be a picture of a colander with artichokes (see Fig. 2.53), men playing cards (see Fig. 1.38), women having their fortune told (see Fig. 4.20), flat fields beneath a gray sky (see Fig. 5.67), or a maid pouring milk onto bread in the sunny corner of a kitchen (see Fig. 5.56). None of these images now seems in any way offensive or unacceptable but, according to the academicians of Rome and Paris who upheld the doctrine of the "hierarchy of the genres," these subjects were beneath the dignity of serious artists. Great art narrated morally uplifting stories from the Bible, ancient history, or mythology. It depicted men and women with exemplary behavior, not drunk and disorderly. In 1660 the painter Andrea Sacchi wrote to a friend in Bologna complaining about the high prices paid to artists who portrayed people getting lice removed from their hair.

0.5 Gerrit Dou, *The Young Mother*, 1658. Oil on canvas, 29 × 21⅞ in (73.5 × 55.5 cm). Royal Cabinet of Paintings, Mauritshuis, The Hague.

Dutch painters in Rome found a ready market for scenes of street peddlers selling food or people enjoying drinks at outdoor taverns. Sacchi, who lacked patrons, resented their success.

Portraiture was officially ranked below genre scenes, whether of good or bad behavior, because it was believed to require less imaginative effort on the part of the artist who did not have to transform the model into an actor in a larger composition. Hence an artist who specialized in portraiture, as van Dyck and Hals did, were likely to be judged by critics as not of the same stature as artists such as Raphael or Rubens for whom it was a sideline. Rembrandt, who produced more portraits than anything else, painted a wide range of other subjects and drew far more comment, positive and negative, than most of his peers. Van Dyck painted sufficient numbers of religious and mythological works to be counted a serious artist by the Italian critic Giovanni Pietro Bellori; his portraits were also mainly of the nobility. Hals, on the other hand, rarely painted anything except portraits of middle-class patrons standing against a blank wall. If Bellori had known them, he would not have been impressed and, like Sir Joshua Reynolds in the eighteenth century, might well have complained about the lack of "patience in finishing what he had so correctly planned."

Landscapes without any figures and still-life images were ranked at the bottom of the hierarchy, landscapes being slightly more highly regarded. The still-life painter, like the portraitist, was regarded as merely an able recorder of selected objects. Landscape paintings, on the other hand, were often based on trips made to study particular kinds of scenery that had to be re-created in the studio using sketches made on the spot. This process, which resembled that used by artists for history paintings, required both judgment (*giudizio*) and invention (*invenzione*), and so elevated landscape's status above still-life. Bellori, also a noted antiquary, librarian of Queen Christina of Sweden and author of an important volume of lives of a select group of painters, sculptors, and architects (published in 1672), wrote of Annibale Carracci:

> One should not omit praise for the landscapes of this master, which today serve as a model for the choice of sites, for the most part delightful views of pastoral villages. His landscape paintings and drawings surpass those of all other painters, except Titian, who is the best (primo) at this sort of imitation.

This statement comes at the end of Bellori's long life of Annibale, one of his heroes, just after a description of a painting of the *Rest on the Flight into Egypt*, in which he also notes a "veduta di paese vaghissimo" (a very beautiful landscape setting). Bellori lists without comment Annibale's large lunette landscape with the Virgin, Child, and St. Joseph calmly leaving Egypt, which has become one of his most frequently reproduced works (see Fig. 1.37). Since Bellori's aesthetic views favoring the idealizing art of the Carracci, Domenichino, and Nicolas Poussin over that of vulgar realists such as Caravaggio were crucial to establishing the reputations of these artists in subsequent historiography, and since Annibale's lunette is now regarded as a key work in the history of "ideal" landscape, Bellori's lack of interest in this aspect of Annibale's artistic achievement now seems astonishing. He did not grasp the significance of Poussin's landscape painting either. For Bellori, landscape could never be more than the setting for the human drama, the proper subject of art.

Northern artists had been employed in the sixteenth century as landscape specialists to provide backgrounds and settings for figure compositions by Italian artists. As Carel van Mander noted in 1604: "our backgrounds are done particularly well; it is in this field that the Italians employ us though we are foreigners, for they consider the Netherlanders excellent landscape painters [though they] maintain they are superior in figure painting." By 1600 Northerners were doing more than paint backgrounds. Paul Bril's little landscapes on copper (see Fig. 5.66) were sought after by many influential private collectors in Rome, and his mural landscapes in both sacred and secular settings there opened up important new possibilities for artists. Adam Elsheimer also played a key role despite rarely making a painting in which landscape dominates the figures (see Fig. 1.56). Foreigners dominated landscape production in Rome (and thus in Italy) throughout the seventeenth and well into the eighteenth century. A succession of Dutch painters traveled south, made brilliant drawings that captured the quality of Italian light on trees and ruins, and returned

0.6 Juan de Valdéz Leal, *Finis Gloriae Mundi*, 1670–72. Oil on canvas, 7 ft 3 in × 6 ft 9 in (2.2 × 2.1 m). Church of the Brotherhood of Charity, Seville.

home to paint a southern paradise for clients who had never crossed the Alps. The two greatest landscape painters in Rome were also immigrants, Nicolas Poussin and Claude Lorrain. The best Italian landscape artist, Salvator Rosa, who could sell every landscape he painted, yearned only to be a history painter. In Luigi Salerno's encyclopedic survey of landscape painting in Rome in this period, only thirty-eight of the 173 artists covered are Italian, and many of these are artists for whom landscape was, as with Annibale Carracci, a small part of their overall artistic production.

Still-life brought up the theoretical rear of artistic subject matter, but the enormous popularity of this genre throughout Europe once it was launched proves that most art collectors paid little attention to critics or theorists. Artists who were working in Milan, Rome, Naples, Seville, Antwerp, Haarlem, Leiden, Frankfurt, and Paris produced different kinds of still-life images that provide a fascinating record of European material culture. The objects shown may be as common as artichokes (see Fig. 2.53) or as exotic as parrots (see Fig. 2.55). Artists' skills at recording the features of a great variety of plants, animals, insects, and shells contributed to the scientific study of species long before their classification by the noted Swedish biologist Carolus Linnaeus. Neapolitan painters celebrated their superb local fish as well as their abundant harvests of grapes, pomegranates, and melons. In Florence the interest in scientific classification of species supported by the powerful Medici court gave employment to Giovanna Garzoni in the 1640s when she painted many kinds of fruit and flowers on vellum using a distinctive stippled technique. The court also commissioned Bartolomeo del Bimbo to decorate two of their country villas with large canvases depicting all known species of cherries, figs, pears, and lemons. Genoa had its animal specialists, while Bergamo produced Evaristo Baschenis, who mainly painted musical instruments, most memorably a lute with finger marks in the dust on its back. Simple earthenware pots, plucked fowl, root vegetables as well as more costly seasonal delicacies, all found their way into the paintings decorating Italian dining rooms in the city and country retreats.

While the brilliant illusions of Clara Peeters (see Fig. 2.53) or Pieter Claesz can be enjoyed simply for their own sake, most still-life paintings conveyed additional messages to their owners. Flower paintings inevitably represent the transience of all life, because they fade so quickly once cut and displayed in a vase (see Fig. 5.48). Fresh fish, dead fowl, and produce waiting to become a banquet (see Fig. 2.54) will also not last long. Some artists acknowledge this by adding a butterfly hovering on a leaf, a common symbol of the human soul, or a fly on the counter to represent sin, or a peach, one of the fruits of paradise. One type of still-life drives this lesson home insistently—the *Vanitas*—a specialty of painters in Leiden but produced elsewhere in the Dutch Republic as well as in Flanders, France, and Spain (Fig. 0.6). The example by Claesz (see Fig. 5.44), who was born in Westphalia but worked in Haarlem, has the classic elements displayed on a table set at the edge of the temporal world: a skull weighting down some large scholarly tomes, a fancy watch in a gold case, an empty overturned glass and an oil lamp whose flame has just been extinguished. A wisp of smoke rises heavenwards, a poignant metaphor of a life just ended. The restrained color scheme of browns, fawns, and dull cream might reflect the words "ashes to ashes, dust to dust" from the Christian burial ceremony. Only the blue ribbon attached to the watch case brings a slight hint of color to this almost monochrome image. Claesz painted the skull so tenderly, bathing it in a filtered, warm light, that viewers are compelled to absorb the uncomfortable message of their own mortality so easy to ignore before a sumptuous bouquet of prize blooms.

Transforming the Renaissance and "Baroque" Art

The word "Baroque" is used sparingly in this book and the reader deserves an explanation. The simplest one is that no one used that word in the seventeenth century. As a term applied to seventeenth-century visual arts, it was used pejoratively in the later eighteenth century by supporters of the rules of classical architecture who saw Francesco Borromini's imaginative transformation of its forms as distortions of long-established perfection. Instead of a perfectly spherical pearl, Borromini offered the equivalent of a distorted one; the French term "baroque" is derived from the Portuguese "barrocco", meaning a pearl of irregular shape. What began as an insult has become a more positive word associated with energy, emotion, drama, even extravagance, qualities believed to be especially characteristic of the arts of seventeenth-century Europe. Thus the word is often adopted to embrace all seventeenth-century art, whether or not it exemplifies these qualities.

Not all seventeenth-century art and architecture has the exuberant qualities now associated with the term "Baroque". Art that is more restrained and more closely based on Greek and Roman models tends to be labeled "classical" but such art also, by implication, lacks those splendid positive characteristics of the Baroque. Thus the term privileges certain kinds of artistic achievement over others and implies divisions along aesthetic lines that are much clearer to us than they were then to artists or patrons. Terms such as "Baroque classicism" have been invented to accommodate artists who seem less Baroque than Rubens and Bernini but not as "classical" as Poussin and Philippe de Champaigne. Thus, "Baroque" becomes the antithesis, the anti-classical style. As discussed below, Bernini, the archetypal "Baroque" sculptor, profoundly admired the paintings of Poussin, the archetypal "classical" artist. Rubens, another pillar of Baroque art, was one of the most learned scholars of ancient visual culture and literature of his time, and Pietro da Cortona, whose richly complex ceiling frescoes epitomize "Baroque" decorative painting, fills his work with quotations from Roman art and architecture. In brief, both "Baroque" and "classical" artists admired ancient art and used it in their own work, though in quite different ways. They all participated in and continued the revival of ancient Greek and Roman culture associated with the term "Renaissance".

Even the most "classical" seventeenth-century artists cannot be confused with their Renaissance predecessors. The simple reason is the greater realism thrust into the increasingly sterile artistic environment of late sixteenth-century Rome by Caravaggio and his many followers, who carried his vision to the rest of Europe's artistic centers. Even his critics could not resist the challenge presented by Caravaggio's dramatic illusionism and pungent observations of real life inserted into the heart of Christian narrative. Bellori, whose decision to write the biographies of only a select number of artists made him the most influential art critic of the century (his predecessors, from Giorgio Vasari onwards, had aimed to be comprehensive), included Caravaggio, acknowledging his achievements while warning against the dangers they posed if artists followed his approach uncritically. Thus to see the arts of the seventeenth century as broadly comprising two opposing styles and aesthetic philosophies inevitably results in distorting caricatures of a complex artistic revolution that combined deep respect for the achievements of ancient art and architecture and for their revival in Italy during the Renaissance with a desire to surpass these achievements and create original work of their own. By avoiding labels except to note some of the artists and monuments often associated with these terms, this book aims to present a nuanced account of the many ways in which seventeenth-century artists created an original visual language to express the ideas, values, and desires of their patrons and contemporaries, and (increasingly) of themselves.

1 Italy

Michelangelo Merisi da Caravaggio, Entombment of Christ, 1603–4. Oil on canvas, 9 ft 9 in × 6 ft 7 in (3 × 2.03 m). Pinacoteca, Vatican Museums, Rome.

THE GEOGRAPHIC AND LINGUISTIC unity of Italy was not reflected in its government. Control of the peninsula in 1600 was divided between Spain, the papacy, and the Florentine and Venetian republics (Fig. 1.1). A few cities still belonged to the aristocratic families that had ruled them previously but all were soon absorbed by or allied with more powerful neighbors. Genoa, Milan, and Naples were either ruled by Spanish vice-regents or controlled by financial dealings with Spain's rulers; Bologna, Florence, and Venice retained a degree of autonomy. All of these cities produced significant contributions to the visual arts in the seventeenth century but this survey focuses on Rome, where papal patronage and the Church offered the greatest opportunities. Many were due to the efforts of the Roman Catholic Church to reassert its authority after the emergence of Protestantism in Northern Europe in the sixteenth century.

Politics, religion, and the arts were inextricably linked in Italy during the Renaissance and remained so in the seventeenth century. The Catholic Church responded to the attacks on corrupt Church practice made by Martin Luther, John Calvin, and others from 1517 onwards by initiating its own reforms, or Counter-Reformation. It issued catechisms for the instruction of the laity and improved education of parish priests, who were often barely literate. The pope took control of the dissemination of doctrine to his bishops throughout Europe. Tribunals for examining heretical beliefs, originally created in the thirteenth century, were revived by Paul III, Alessandro Farnese, in 1540. The first List of Prohibited Books appeared in Milan in 1538 and was soon followed by others; the first Roman list came out in 1554. Even famous texts such as Giovanni Boccaccio's *Decameron* and Niccolò Machiavelli's *The Prince* were banned for a time.

These censorious attitudes affected the visual arts primarily when artists were believed to have treated religious subjects frivolously or in ways that offended Catholic dogma. Indecency—primarily defined as nudity—was condemned to greater or lesser degrees depending on the personal views of the reigning pope. Michelangelo's travails are well known. He had filled both the ceiling frescoes and his later *Last Judgment* on the altar wall of the Sistine Chapel with male nudes whose genitalia were not covered. Paul III, during whose papacy the latter was completed, had no complaints but Pius IV, who was pope in 1555–9, found this an intolerable breach of decorum and had drapery added by Daniele da Volterra though the nudes on the ceiling were left alone. The attempts of the Inquisition in 1573 to make Veronese eliminate figures regarded as distractions in his monumental canvas depicting the *Last Supper* are also well known. As a Venetian, Veronese was protected by the independence of that city-state from serious prosecution by the Church authorities. He merely changed the title

1.1 Map of Europe in 1648.

of his painting to the *Feast in the House of Levi* (Accademia, Venice) but left the painting as it was.

When, after meeting for almost twenty years (1545–63), the Council of Trent finally concluded its affairs, it issued many recommendations intended to strengthen Church practice, a few of which concerned the visual arts. Not only must religious images conform to official Church doctrine but they must also communicate it in a straightforward manner easy for the faithful to understand. Intricate symbolism and overwrought compositions were to be avoided. Cardinal Gabriele Paleotti, the Archbishop of Bologna, who wrote a *Discourse on Images, Sacred and Profane* in 1582, reflected these concerns when he wrote:

> *everyday one sees [. . .], especially in churches, pictures so obscure and ambiguous that while they should, by illuminating the intellect, encourage devotion and touch the heart, their obscurity confounds the mind, distracting it in a thousand ways, and keeping it occupied in trying to decide which figure is what.*[1]

Later he summed up the duties of a good Catholic artist in three Latin words, *docere, delectare, movere* (to teach, to delight, to move), which could serve as the motto for many of the finest artists of the seventeenth century.

The Decline of Mannerism

Maniera means both style and manner in Italian, but sixteenth-century writers did not use it as we do today. The term is currently applied to works of art in which the artists' desire to impress the audience with their skills at drawing foreshortened figures, creating bizarre juxtapositions of scale and color, and highly refined treatment of materials privilege artistic achievement over subject matter. It was a pan-European phenomenon, affecting all the arts by the mid-sixteenth-century in many forms, if less popular in some places than others. In the 1580s, however, a few Italian painters working in Bologna and Florence began to abandon its artificial elegance, its excessively complex poses, bizarre spatial settings, and artificial colors for images that were more natural. The artists credited with initiating this stylistic revolution are three members of the Carracci family in Bologna and Caravaggio, a Milanese-trained painter who moved to Rome soon after 1590. All four of them looked for inspiration to North Italian artists of earlier generations who had never succumbed to the siren charms of *maniera*.

Michelangelo was the prime source of inspiration for *maniera* art in Rome, Florence, and Bologna. His ceiling frescoes (1508–12) and *Last Judgment* (1536–41) in the Sistine Chapel in the Vatican and his sculptures of *Night* and *Day*, *Dawn* and *Dusk* on the tombs of Giuliano and Lorenzo de' Medici in the New Sacristy, San Lorenzo, Florence (Fig. 1.2), were copied and adapted by many artists. They adopted the

1.2 Michelangelo Buonarotti, *Tomb of Giuliano de' Medici*, 1519–33. Marble, height of seated figures 5 ft 10 in × 5 ft 8 in (1.77 × 1.72 m). San Lorenzo, Medici Chapel, Florence.

superhuman perfection of his male figures and then tried to outdo him by giving their figures more bulk and putting them into ostentatiously difficult poses. Pellegrino Tibaldi's *Adoration of the Shepherds* (Fig. 1.3) is a characteristic example of overreaction to Michelangelo's impressive male nudes. Twisted, unnatural poses such as those of the shepherd in the right foreground, and the affected hand of his equally muscular companion above him, draw attention away from the Virgin and Child, who seem comparatively small; her pose and hand gesture are as artificial as theirs. After 1563 the Roman Catholic Church discouraged such self-absorbed imagery. Nevertheless it was twenty years before Italian artists began to produce paintings that fulfilled Paleotti's precepts.

1.3 Pellegrino Tibaldi, *Adoration of the Shepherds*, 1549. Oil on canvas, 61¾ × 41⅜ in (157 × 105 cm). Borghese Gallery, Rome.

Architecture and City Planning in Rome, 1585–1625

Here I am in Rome, and yet I cannot find the Rome I knew: so great are the changes in the buildings, the streets, the piazzas, the fountains, the aqueducts, the obelisks, and the other marvels with which the glorious memory of Sixtus has beautified this old and ruinous city that I cannot recognize nor find, so to speak, any trace of that old Rome I left ten years ago.

ABBOT ANGELO GRILLO, 1585[2]

This was the reaction of a contemporary to the papacy of Sixtus V (1585–90), Felice Peretti. Although elected as a caretaker pope, he proved to be a dynamic administrator, financial manager, and builder. He repaired the only Roman aqueduct still functioning and insured a reliable supply of water to the city. He was a "law and order" ruler who filled the Roman jails with robbers and other miscreants: the heads of executed leaders of robber gangs were displayed on pikes near Castel Sant'Angelo to deter others pondering a life of crime. He filled the papal treasury by selling Church offices for higher prices than his predecessors, issuing bonds and taxing both luxuries and basic commodities. Even after lavish spending on new buildings and street paving, there were 4.5 million scudi in the papal treasury when he died.

Sixtus V's contributions to Roman city planning were especially important. He began construction on new roads radiating out from Santa Maria Maggiore that, when completed, made it much easier for pious visitors to reach the other six main pilgrimage churches of Rome on its outskirts. Sixtus restored the columns of Trajan and Marcus Aurelius in the center of Rome and put statues of St. Peter and St. Paul at their summits, thus symbolically converting these monuments celebrating the military conquests of Roman emperors to the cause of Christianity. The dome of the New St. Peter's was finally completed and an ancient Egyptian obelisk moved and re-erected in Piazza San Pietro. Both were considerable feats of engineering but the latter caused a bigger stir. Domenico Fontana (1543–1607), the architect responsible for designing the machinery that managed to shift the huge obelisk without mishap, became a celebrity and was knighted. Both columns and the obelisk were exorcised and given inscriptions to ensure that the populace understood that these monuments had been drained of all pagan significance.

The restoration of Rome had been a piecemeal affair before 1585. Abandoned by the papacy for long periods from the twelfth century onwards, most famously between 1309 and 1377, when the popes and their court lived in Avignon, Rome became "a shrunken nut within her shell of antique walls."[3] Its population in 1400 was only about 25,000. It was little more than a market town with some impressive ruins. The efforts of Martin V (1417–31), and Nicolas V (1447–55), to repair the decaying fabric of Old St. Peter's and improve the Vatican palace initiated a haphazard sequence of building, restoration, and repair continued by some of their fifteenth-century successors. Julius II (1503–13) was far more ambitious. He hired Bramante to make plans for new buildings around St. Peter's and made the radical decision to replace the frail Constantinian basilica of Old St. Peter's with a new church. Under his successor, Leo X (1513–21), Bramante's plans for a centrally planned church were modified by Antonio da Sangallo the younger, but it was Michelangelo who was primarily responsible for the executed design of the dome and crossing area (1546–64).

The area around and inside the New St. Peter's (Fig. **1.4**) was a construction site throughout the sixteenth century and in the early seventeenth. A small building erected over the site of the high altar protected it but it was rarely used for services. These were conducted instead in the last five bays of the old church nave, sealed off with a brick wall in 1538. The new nave was eventually vaulted in 1607 and the façade completed in 1612, both in the papacy of Paul V (1605–21), Camillo Borghese, as his proud inscription across the center of the façade proclaims. Both were

1.4 Giovanni Battista Piranesi, *View of the Piazza and Basilica of St. Peter's*, c. 1751. Engraving, 17⅞ × 27½ in (45.5 × 70.1 cm).

Architecture and City Planning in Rome, 1585–1625

1.5 Carlo Maderno, Santa Susanna, façade, Rome, 1593–1603.

designed by Carlo Maderno (c. 1556–1629), Domenico Fontana's nephew, who became architect in charge of St. Peter's in 1603 and was succeeded by Bernini.

The New St. Peter's was the most important symbol of the invigorated Roman Catholic Church in Catholic Europe. The decoration of its vast interior took the rest of the century and gave opportunities to many of the finest sculptors and painters in Rome. During the papacy of Alexander VII (1655–67), Fabio Chigi, the great oval piazza with its colonnaded perimeter designed by Bernini around the obelisk set up by Fontana was added, completing the majestic ensemble. Meanwhile construction began on three new churches to accommodate the crowds attracted by the eloquent preachers of the new religious orders founded by the Jesuits, the Theatines, and the Oratorians. The Gesù was the first, designed and built by Giacomo Barozzi da Vignola in 1568–75 (the façade is by Guglielmo della Porta). It was followed by Santa Maria in Vallicella, also known as the Chiesa Nuova (new church), built for the Oratorians between 1575 and 1605 (see Fig. 1.83) and the Theatines' church, Sant'Andrea della Valle, begun in 1591 and completed in 1625. Maderno contributed important parts of the last of these, including the design of the dome, the largest in Rome after that of St. Peter's. All three churches have a domed crossing and broad barrel-vaulted naves that enabled large crowds to hear the sermons.

Maderno's most influential commission was that for the façade of Santa Susanna (Fig. **1.5**), completed the year he was appointed architect of St. Peter's. While none of the basic elements of its design were new to Rome—a two-tier plan with bays articulated with pilasters and columns, niches containing statues on both levels in the side bays, emphasis on the central bay, and a triangular pediment at the summit—Maderno gave his interpretation new grandeur by making his design progressively thicker as it progresses from the sides to the center. On the ground floor the five bays are separated by a pilaster, then by a column, and finally by a pair of engaged columns that frame the central doorway. The cornice above, which projects forward more than usual to create deep shadows, advances in steps to accommodate each thickening of the wall below. This progression is continued above with single pilasters on the outside and paired pilasters flanking the central bay filled with a wide niche whose design echoes that of the doorway below; both have segmental rather than triangular pediments so that the contrast between the crowning triangular pediment at the summit over a smaller segmental pediment below is repeated on both levels. Even the center of the crowning pediment is thicker above the central bay than at the sides. The pediment is finished with a balustrade that supports giant candelabra on each side and a cross at the summit. The thickening of many elements means that the façade catches the Roman sunlight and reads more like a sculptural relief than a wall. The principles it embodied were understood, adopted, and elaborated by later architects, including Bernini and Pietro da Cortona.

Chapter 1: Italy

1.6 Annibale Carracci, *Study of Reclining Boy*, c. 1580. Red chalk on paper, 13⅞ × 15⅜ in (35.3 × 39.2 cm). Nationalmuseum, Stockholm.

Bolognese Painting: The Carracci Reform

The art of Ludovico Carracci (1555–1619) and his slightly younger cousins, Agostino (1557–1602) and Annibale Carracci (1560–1609), made a clear break with the *maniera* style popular in Bologna when they were growing up. This new vision emerges first in works made around 1580–85 in their shared workshop. According to their biographers, in addition to copying the drawings and paintings of the local art establishment, they drew from life, working from the model in their studio and sketching people in the street and at home. Annibale's impressive red chalk study of a boy (Fig. **1.6**) and Ludovico's touching drawing of beggars (Fig. **1.7**) help confirm these accounts.

The Butcher's Shop of about 1580 (Fig. **1.8**) by Annibale is remarkable not only for the genre

1.7 Ludovico Carracci, *Family of Beggars*, c. 1580. Pen and ink on cream paper, 13⅜ × 10⅛ in (34 × 25.8 cm). Louvre, Paris.

subject but also for its size. Four men are at work: the man on the left with a surprisingly clean apron is weighing a cut of meat for the halberdier on the left, who reaches into his purse for money; an older man behind the counter reaches up to get something for the old woman waiting behind him; a man on the right is handling a side of beef; and a young man in the middle foreground is about to slaughter a sheep. Annibale makes the rough impasto of the paint mimic the texture of bone, fat, and sinew, a technique utterly unlike that of *maniera* art, whose surfaces were so smooth that its critics described them as licked. Annibale's skill at depicting the figures is less impressive. The man weighing meat is the most successful, but the foreshortening of the upper body of the man behind the counter and the one hauling meat are not convincing. Annibale was only about twenty when he did it and was evidently still learning his craft. The odd torsion of the halberdier may be, as Charles Dempsey suggested, a deliberate mocking of the kind of affected poses used by *maniera* painters, and the emphasis on the meat a manifesto of the Carracci's intentions to work "assolutamente da viva carne" (absolutely from living flesh), to quote their Bolognese biographer, Carlo Cesare Malvasia. The exceptional size of the picture—almost 9 feet (2.7 m) wide—also suggests that Annibale had ambitions beyond a vivid record of a scene that he knew well: Ludovico's father was a butcher.

In 1582 the Carracci established an academy later named the Accademia degli Incamminati or "of those who have set forth," presumably on the path to artistic greatness. It began as a room where they and other like-minded artists could meet and share the cost of hiring a model and practice life drawing. Later Agostino's contacts among the *letterati* of Bologna brought artists and local humanists together at the academy to discuss art and literature and listen to musical

1.8 Annibale Carracci, *The Butcher's Shop*, c. 1580. Oil on canvas, 6 ft 4 in × 8 ft 9 in (1.90 × 2.71 m). Christ Church College, Oxford.

performances. This activity was intended to enhance the artists' education and their social standing in a city whose university was the oldest in Europe. When Agostino died in his mid-forties, members of the academy staged a spectacular funeral on his behalf. The book recording that event is the best source about the academy, which did not survive long without his leadership.

The shared workshop of the Carracci and their determination to blend their styles in collaborative commissions for which they sought equal credit has proved a challenge to art historians seeking to define the particular artistic personality of each. The two primarily active as painters, Ludovico and Annibale, have quite distinctive styles, and their work would probably not have been as often confused had it not been for their shared surname. Ludovico's early career is poorly documented, making it seem as if his younger cousins were more innovative than he was. His first dated altarpieces were made in 1587–8; Annibale's feisty *Crucifixion with Saints* had been installed in Santa Maria della Carità four years earlier.

Ludovico was at his best with dramatic subjects such as *The Conversion of St. Paul* (Fig. **1.9**), painted for the Zambeccari family chapel in San Francesco. The most famous treatment of the subject was Michelangelo's fresco in the Pauline Chapel in the Vatican (Fig. **1.10**), which inspired later painters to invent their own variants on his dazed figure of the saint on the ground and the fleeing men and horses around him. In these, true to Mannerist artists' desire to intrigue and challenge the viewer, it is often difficult to locate the saint amid the tangle of limbs around him. Ludovico rejects affectation in a design that marries clarity and drama to brilliant effect. An X marks out the main lines of the composition. Saul (as he was known before his conversion) fills the central foreground of the painting, his limbs rimmed with light, his red military garb the only strong color note in the picture. He seems to have just landed, bracing his body with his right arm while looking toward the vision with eyes that can no longer see. His left leg is still airborne, his left arm lifted in a gesture that combines defense with acknowledgment. The faithful who came to pray before this powerful image will have remembered the words heard by the saint at the moment of his conversion on the road to Damascus, "Saul, Saul, wherefore dost thou persecute me?" A counter-diagonal pulls our eyes back up to the sky, where streaks of lemony light against thunder-dark sky direct our attention to the vision to begin the circuit again.

Nothing by Annibale achieves this high level of dramatic impact. Annibale preferred gentler light effects to the bold chiaroscuro typical of Ludovico's paintings and drawings; his male figure types are also less plebeian than those of his cousin. In 1585 Annibale painted a *Pietà with Virgin and Saints* (Fig. **1.11**), whose idealized figures are not at all like those of *The Butcher's Shop*. They are arranged to form an arch that surrounds the dead Christ and focuses the viewer's attention on him. The event has been imagined as a vision of St. Francis of Assisi, the founder of the Franciscan Order, and St. Clare, founder of the sister order of Poor Clares. Franciscans were devoted to images of the crucified Christ because their founder had a vision of Christ on the cross who transmitted his wounds, or stigmata, to the saint's own body. His kneeling pose on the left in this painting allows us to see the wounds in his feet and hands beside those in Christ's limp body. Even in death, Christ's right arm seems to reach toward the saint, who looks out at us, beseeching us to meditate on the meaning of this sacrifice. St. Clare holds her usual attribute, a small monstrance containing a host (bread blessed during Mass). The Virgin Mary, who is seated behind her son, has fainted with grief but her right hand still curls protectively near Christ's head, as if to prevent it from falling further. Two angels look at her anxiously, as does St. John on the right, the youngest apostle and favorite of Christ, who leans over a wall built at the mouth of the cave where Christ will be entombed. On clouds overhead angels support a large wooden cross that gives additional emphasis to the Franciscan devotional content of this altarpiece. St. Mary Magdalene fills the right foreground, gorgeously attired in a dark ocher brocade cloak over a violet dress whose folds flow onto the ground, almost touching the white shroud of Christ that fills the center of the painting below his body. The contrast between the simple brown woolen robes of St. Francis, a reminder of his vow of poverty, and the sumptuous garments of the Magdalene must be intentional. While she is shown here adoring Christ, thus after her conversion, she is still wearing the luxurious clothes she wore before that event. The decision to show her this way means that the viewer will recall her sinful past before she became the Church's favorite example of penitence.

The influence of Correggio is especially evident in Annibale's *Pietà*, which was made for the high altar of the Franciscans' church in Parma. Annibale had written a letter to Ludovico from Parma in 1580 full of enthusiasm for this artist: "the little putti of Correggio breathe, live, and laugh with a grace and truth that compel us to laugh and to feel happy along with them." Both the physical type of the adolescent angel who holds the cross and the way angels and clouds meld so easily together come from Correggio's depictions of similar visions in the pendentives of Parma Cathedral. The violet and ocher colors worn by the Magdalene are also typical of Correggio, as are the forms of her drapery. The

1.9 Ludovico Carracci, *The Conversion of St. Paul*, 1587–89. Oil on canvas, 110 × 67⅜ in (278 × 170 cm). Pinacoteca Nazionale, Bologna.

1.10 Michelangelo Buonarotti, *Conversion of St. Paul*, 1542–45. Fresco. Cappella Paolina, Vatican, Rome.

1.11 Annibale Carracci, *Pietà with Virgin and Saints*, 1585. Oil on canvas, 12 ft 3 in × 7 ft 9 in (3.74 × 2.38 m). Galleria Nazionale, Parma.

softness of the modeling of Christ's carefully observed ribcage and the sfumato transitions from half light into shadow across the painting also recall Correggio. The subdued lighting in the background completes the somber mood. It is difficult to imagine a better solution to the patrons' need for an image that would focus the worshipers' attention on the central mysteries of the Catholic faith and their significance for the Franciscan Order. There is enough realism to make the vision believable but enough idealism to remove it from the mundane. It fulfills admirably Cardinal Paleotti's desire for art that would teach, delight, and move.

An altarpiece that depicts the Virgin and Child with accompanying saints had by now a long

1.12 Titian (Tiziano Veccellio), *Pesaro Altarpiece*, 1519–26. Oil on canvas, 15 ft 11 in × 8 ft 10 in (4.85 × 2.69 m). Santa Maria Gloriosa dei Frari, Venice.

1.13 Ludovico Carracci, *Madonna dei Bargellini*, 1587. Oil on canvas, 9 ft 3 in × 6 ft 2 in (2.82 × 1.88 m). Pinacoteca Nazionale, Bologna.

history in Italian art. Since the thirteenth century, the saints had been arranged in strict symmetry around a centrally placed Virgin and Child enthroned. In Titian's *Pesaro Altarpiece* (or *Virgin and Child with Saints and Members of the Pesaro Family*) (Fig. **1.12**), however, the throne is shifted, changing the viewer's relationship to the scene from front and center to one side. Annibale did this too in his *Madonna with St. Matthew* (see Fig. **1.16**), placing his Madonna, however, on the left. Ludovico adopted a similar arrangement for his *Madonna dei Bargellini* (Fig. **1.13**). They were not the first artists to follow Titian's lead—Veronese had done so in his magnificent *Mystic Marriage of St. Catherine* (c. 1565; Accademia, Venice)—of which Agostino Carracci made an

Bolognese Painting: The Carracci Reform 13

1.14 (left) Agostino Carracci, *Mystic Marriage of St. Catherine*, 1582. Engraving after Paolo Veronese, 19⅞ × 13½ in (50.5 × 34.4 cm). Library of Congress, Washington, D.C.

1.15 (right) Annibale Carracci, *Mystic Marriage of St. Catherine*, c. 1586. Oil on canvas, 63 × 46½ in (162 × 118 cm). National Museum of Capodimonte, Naples.

engraving (Fig. **1.14**), but so few artists chose or patrons wanted this eccentric arrangement that its use by Veronese and, over two decades later, by Annibale and Ludovico Carracci amounts to a belated tribute to Titian's bold departure from convention. It was then taken up by many other artists in the seventeenth century.

The *Mystic Marriage of St. Catherine* now in Naples (Fig. **1.15**) was probably painted a year or two after the *Pietà*. It allows us to have a closer look at Annibale's technical accomplishments at this stage because it is a much smaller painting made for private devotion. The composition is roughly divided along a diagonal that puts the Virgin and Christ in one half and the saint and her escort angels in the other. Mary seems comfortably seated but there is no throne, only clouds to support her; those behind her head contain the dim forms of cherubim. Mary holds the baby Jesus, whose extended right arm is supported by the angel who embraces the saint gently as she holds up her hand to receive a wedding ring

from Christ. All this conforms to a vision of the saint, a legendary princess from Alexandria who survived various tortures, including attempts to stretch her on the wheel (her usual attribute) before she was finally beheaded. Annibale has given her a sumptuously embroidered costume and golden hair beneath a coronet tipped with pearls. The Virgin's clothes are instead simple—a plain red dress and blue cloak, neither edged nor embroidered. Mary is shown absorbed in her own thoughts as she tenderly holds the child whose fate she already knows. Long in possession of the Farnese family in Parma, from whom the artist was to receive his major commissions in Rome, the painting may have been among their first acquisitions from the artist.

Annibale's *Madonna with St. Matthew* of 1588, made for the Merchants' Chapel of San Prospero in Reggio Emilia (Fig. **1.16**), is a brilliant fusion of Correggio, Titian, and Veronese. St. Matthew, who is standing on the left, looks to the Virgin and Child for inspiration as he steadies a

14 *Chapter 1: Italy*

writing board and ink pot in his left hand. The angel (his usual attribute) is seated on the ground, holding a scroll of text and looking out at us. On the right St. Francis kisses the Christ Child's foot while St. John the Baptist looks out at us too and directs our attention to the majestic figure of the Virgin and her lively Child. Behind her a fluted column rises up beyond the frame and baby angels lift up heavy swags of brocade hangings. Sky and trees open up the pictorial space on the right.

Titian's *Pesaro Altarpiece* is installed on the left wall of the huge Franciscan Gothic church in Venice, not within a chapel enclosure, so that the spectator sees it first from the side. Annibale's San Prospero altarpiece was also originally

1.16 Annibale Carracci, *Madonna with St. Matthew*, 1588. Oil on canvas, 12 ft 7 in × 8 ft 4 in (3.84 × 2.55 m). Staatliche Kunstsammlungen, Dresden.

Bolognese Painting: The Carracci Reform 15

1.17 (left) Ludovico Carracci, *Madonna degli Scalzi*, c. 1590. Oil on canvas, 86¼ × 57 in (219 × 114 cm). Pinacoteca Nazionale, Bologna.

1.18 (right) Raphael Sanzio, *Sistine Madonna*, 1515–16. Oil on canvas, 8 ft 9 in × 6 ft 7 in (2.69 × 2.01 m). Staatliche Kunstsammlungen, Dresden.

placed along the outer wall of the nave, which may account for its asymmetrical composition. Ludovico's *Madonna dei Bargellini* altarpiece (see Fig. 1.13) was, however, placed in a chapel, since destroyed. His design is closest to that of Titian in that the Virgin is placed on the right with two columns on the left that symbolize the "gateway to heaven." It is easy to imagine that a competitive atmosphere ruled in their studio as Annibale and Ludovico worked on these commissions simultaneously. Annibale's work exudes a majestic calm; Ludovico's somewhat smaller altarpiece makes a more human connection: his Virgin looks down at us from her lofty seat and the baby Christ seems to shrink back against her protective arms as he gazes at St. Francis and the kneeling donor in the foreground. There are few real colors—blue in the sky, indigo over rose for the Virgin's robes, and a burnt orange over ruby red for the Magdalene in the right foreground.

Otherwise all the colors are neutral—brown, gray, black, and white. Annibale's painting is more brightly and evenly lit and spreads gold, red, blue, and green around the foreground figures, a color range like that of Veronese. Both works are masterly interpretations of a subject with a long visual tradition.

Ludovico's *Madonna degli Scalzi* (Fig. **1.17**), made for the Bentivoglio family chapel in the Church of the Madonna degli Scalzi, is a prescient image of a young and beautiful Virgin poised on a crescent moon, made twenty-five years before it became standard for depictions of the Immaculate Conception. Ludovico's primary source here was Raphael's *Sistine Madonna* (Fig. **1.18**), then still on the high altar of San Sisto in nearby Piacenza, for which it was made in 1512–14. It shows the Virgin standing on clouds, flanked by two saints and holding in her arms a Christ Child in a relaxed pose that only an adult

16   *Chapter 1: Italy*

would adopt. The kneeling St. Sixtus on the left looks up at her, his left hand on his heart, his right gesturing to the imagined worshiper in the church below. The right edge of his heavy cope falls away from this arm and extends his physical presence almost to the ledge along the bottom of the canvas where his miter rests and two cheeky baby angels regard what is happening above them with barely concealed boredom. Balancing St. Sixtus on the right is St. Barbara, who looks down at the two infant angels with tolerant sympathy. Because her robes do not sweep down toward us, her kneeling form seems to be set above that of Sixtus although their heads are level. The two putti below are also unevenly positioned, one lower than the other, so that the eye keeps moving to the left, up along the cope of Sixtus, following his glance to the Virgin and Child, to be swept out then by her billowing veil to St. Barbara before starting this clockwise route again. This astute play of balanced asymmetries was understood and adapted by Ludovico, whose standing Virgin is also flanked by two saints. They are placed at slightly different levels and distances from the picture plane. St. Jerome fills the left corner of the canvas, looking up at Mary, like Sixtus, and like him, also placed closer to the viewer than St. Francis on the right, who is a little higher up and who extends his right hand to embrace the tiny hand of Christ. The neat oval face of the Virgin is Ludovico's idea of perfect female beauty, as is Raphael's smoothly rounded facial type. A pale yellow haze radiates from the head of Ludovico's Virgin. Within it is a circle of twelve stars that hovers over her head. Music-making angels are dimly visible in the haze to either side. The somber palette and freely brushed handling of the male saints recalls Tintoretto; the torso of St. Jerome, however, reminded Malvasia of Michelangelo.

Annibale painted easel pictures of mythological and religious subjects in Bologna as well as an occasional portrait and landscape. All three Carracci also made witty drawings which opened the way to the invention of caricature and eventually to the political cartoon. Made spontaneously and often destroyed soon after the joke had been appreciated, few certainly attributable to any of the Carracci are known today. A page of ink sketches probably by Annibale of heads,

most facing to the left, one scratched out, another obscured by a blotch of ink, gives some idea of the informal technique that they used when making these comic studies (Fig. **1.19**). A smug lady with a vast ruff (center), a beak-nosed cleric (lower right), and a bearded man with a bulbous nose like that of a circus clown (upper right) can be picked out amid other less distorted or less finished heads. Scholars have located the roots of such images in books comparing the physiognomy of men and animals, a subject that already fascinated Leonardo, and in sixteenth-century attempts to codify the beautiful and the ugly. The playful and informal approach of the Carracci was new. Maybe Annibale (or Agostino) had a particular priest in mind when he drew this man with his long nose and pointed beard, but the history of caricatures of known sitters begins with Bernini. Only an artist of his stature could get away with making a pope look like a grasshopper, as he once did![4]

1.19 Annibale Carracci, Caricature heads, c. 1590. Pen and ink on buff paper, 76¼ × 53⅛ in (195 × 135 cm). The Trustees of the British Museum, London.

1.20 Annibale Carracci, *The Resurrection of Christ*, 1593. Oil on canvas, 85½ × 63 in (217 × 160 cm). Louvre, Paris.

Annibale's *The Resurrection of Christ* (Fig. **1.20**), now in the Louvre, made for a private family chapel in Bologna, presents a dramatic story in the restrictive vertical format of an altarpiece. A forceful diagonal splits heaven and earth. Christ's left foot marks the divide between dark and light zones as he hovers above the tomb whose illuminated mass creates a vertical line that anchors the entire picture field. A soldier lies asleep on the lid; the seal fastened to the end of the tomb is unbroken. A soldier in the middle distance points out the seal to a turbaned spectator. How did Christ escape, we are meant to ask, if not through a divine miracle? Other soldiers turn and flee on the left and right, but one remains comfortably asleep in the foreground, his back to us, his head cradled in his right hand. Angels manipulate the clouds, as if they had some substance, to clear a path to heaven for the Savior.

Resurrection paintings usually show the heavy lid of the tomb lifting up unaided or already removed as Christ rises heavenwards. Whether it was Annibale or his patrons who suggested the novel approach of a sealed tomb is not known. Despite the dramatic action and fleeing figures, the design retains an essential symmetry appropriate for an altarpiece of a subject of great doctrinal importance. After noting that Annibale's figures of the fleeing soldier on the left, and the other on the ground who turns round to

18   *Chapter 1: Italy*

see what has happened, were inspired by the figures in Titian's *Martyrdom of St. Peter Martyr* (destroyed but then in SS. Giovanni e Paolo, Venice), and then noting that the sleeping soldier on the tomb lid seems to him a judicious blend of qualities found in the work of both Parmigianino and Veronese, Malvasia concluded: "The well-understood poses, the fine sequencing of planes, the refinement of every part, the harmony of the hues, the judgment, the knowledge, the discretion—all these are abundantly displayed here and make for an unsurpassed and triumphant performance."[5]

Malvasia's words were published in 1678, long after the painting was made. Critics writing around 1900, however, dismissed the Carracci and their successors as eclectics, that is artists lacking original ideas and overly dependent on the compositions, poses, and techniques of admired predecessors. Ludovico's *Madonna degli Scalzi* is, however, no simple copy of Raphael; nor were Annibale's *Madonna with St. Matthew* and Ludovico's *Madonna dei Bargellini* mere imitations of Titian's *Pesaro Altarpiece*. Further, the Venetians admired by the Carracci had never inspired the artists who filled Bolognese churches with altarpieces before the Carracci launched their careers. Even Raphael's influence was far less evident than that of Michelangelo. The Carracci had a true painter's understanding of the achievements of Correggio, Titian, Veronese, and Tintoretto and the abilities to transform what they admired into paintings utterly unlike those being produced when they were training. Indeed, they are credited with establishing Correggio's reputation as one of the great artists of the sixteenth century.

The Carracci collaborated on the decoration of several rooms with friezes for the Palazzo Fava in the 1580s and, around 1590, on a much larger frieze in the reception room of Palazzo Magnani in Bologna, depicting the *Story of the Founding of Rome* (Fig. 1.21). The patron, Lorenzo Magnani, had just built the family a new home in 1589 and, in 1590, after a long campaign, managed to get the Magnani restored to the ranks of Bologna's ruling families by achieving the status of senator, which they had lost some seventy years before. This achievement was confirmed by the pope himself from Rome, hence, it appears, Lorenzo's choice of subject, one that implies that the family's status was justified by millennia of distinguished ancestry. The skillful fusion of large narrative scenes with complex framing elements using architectural motifs, figures painted to look like stone sculpture with other "real" figures,

1.21 Annibale Carracci, *Story of the Founding of Rome*, c. 1590. Fresco. Palazzo Magnani, reception room, Bologna.

garlands of fruit and flowers, and a great variety of grimacing masks, made an irresistible ensemble. All three Carracci collaborated on this important commission. In the first scene on the left wall (Fig. **1.22**), Ludovico shows the wolf suckling Romulus and Remus in a vast landscape; the next scene by Annibale shows Remus battling cattle thieves; the third scene was painted by Agostino. Annibale brought all this experience with him to Rome where, between 1595 and 1600, he created the two works which set him apart from his brother and cousin as an artist of greater ambition and synthetic power. In the opinion of some critics, they made him a worthy successor to predecessors such as Raphael and Michelangelo.

While Agostino assisted with the frescoes in Palazzo Fava and Palazzo Magnani, he produced very few independent paintings between 1585 and 1595, devoting his time primarily to the production of prints, notably some influential reproductive engravings after the work of Correggio, Tintoretto, and Veronese (see Figs. 1.14, 2.16). He did, however, produce one altarpiece, the *Last Communion of St. Jerome* (Fig. **1.23**), which provoked a debate about the degree to which an artist could follow an earlier model without being accused of plagiarism (see Fig. 1.59). Agostino's painting was part of a major renovation and decoration of the Certosa di San Girolamo just outside the city walls (it is still Bologna's most important cemetery). Agostino is said to have struggled to finish his canvas and even considered abandoning it. The composition presents the viewer with a closely packed frieze of figures backed by an arched opening flanked by Corinthian columns with a landscape view beyond. Just left of the center in the foreground, a priest wearing a blue chasuble bends forward as he holds up the host which he is about to give to the kneeling saint. According to the legend, St. Jerome refused to receive his last communion in bed but insisted on being helped to his knees by his companions, thus demonstrating his humility before Christ. The symmetry of the composition is relieved by two baby angels flying over the arch to the left and by a slight diagonal movement that leads from the left foreground to the kneeling saint. The more brightly lit figures of Carthusian monks on the left, however, tend to pull the eye away from the saint on the right, much of whose body is in shadow. Even his red robe seems subdued next to the blue and gold chasuble of the priest with its flash of crimson lining. The

1.22 Ludovico Carracci, *Story of the Founding of Rome*, detail of Romulus and Remus, c. 1590. Fresco. Palazzo Magnani, reception room, Bologna.

Painting in Rome, 1585–1610

The frescoes and altarpieces commissioned to decorate Rome's large new churches gave major opportunities to many artists. The interior decoration of Santa Maria in Vallicella (Chiesa Nuova) offers a particularly splendid ensemble. The high altar was provided by Rubens (see Fig. 2.13). Federico Barocci and Giuseppe Cesari d'Arpino painted the transept altarpieces, Barrocci painted another one for a side chapel. Caravaggio painted his powerful *Entombment* for the Vittrici Chapel (see p. xxii). Reni and Maratta contributed altarpieces too. Pietro da Cortona painted the ceiling fresco in the sacristy in the 1630s above its carved altarpiece by Algardi (see Fig. 1.95) and, in the 1650s, covered the entire ceiling of the church with frescoes and stucco framing elements celebrating St. Philip Neri, the founder of the Oratorian Order, and the Virgin Mary, their heavenly patron. These are only the most celebrated works in a church that has retained most of its seventeenth-century decoration and thus offers a splendid introduction to Roman religious painting of this time.

The transept altarpieces (see Figs. 1.24, 1.25) were painted by artists of quite different stylistic persuasion. Barocci, the older artist, had retreated to his home town, Urbino, after training in Rome and beginning his career there in the 1560s. His artistic fathers were Raphael, also a native of Urbino, and Correggio, whose soft contours and delicate tonal transitions Barocci adopted, adding a distinctive palette of his own. Though often called a Mannerist painter, his work lacks its salient characteristics. His compositions are clear and legible; his numerous preparatory drawings testify to intense study from life before he began to paint.

Cesari's training is not well documented. He seems to have made his way up the ranks of young apprentices helping Niccolò Circignani to decorate the Vatican Loggie in the 1580s. Though now regarded as a painter of modest talent, he was hugely successful, garnering major commissions in St. Peter's and elsewhere from Clement VIII (1598–1605), Ippolito Aldobrandini. Cesari never altered his Mannerist style even after everyone else had abandoned it. His flat draperies with knife-edge folds, his limited

1.23 Agostino Carracci, *Last Communion of St. Jerome*, c. 1590. Oil on canvas, 12 ft 4 in × 7 ft 4 in (3.76 × 2.24 m). Pinacoteca Nazionale, Bologna.

reaction and response of each of the twelve figures who witness this touching scene have been carefully differentiated—and the artist's conscious efforts to do this were much appreciated by later critics—but the result now seems calculated rather than deeply felt. The final effect is somber but static.

Ludovico did not join his cousins in Rome. Annibale's move there effectively ended their collaboration and set up, at least in the eyes of their admirers after their deaths, intense debate about Annibale's Roman period among his Bolognese admirers. Malvasia argued that Annibale did his best work before going to Rome and also loyally supported the achievements of Ludovico, who outlived Annibale by ten and Agostino by seventeen years. By surviving them, Ludovico became the founder of the new school of painting in Bologna. All the best artists of the next generation were either trained by him or deeply affected by his art. Of these, the most notable were Guido Reni, Domenichino, and Giovanni Francesco Barbieri, il Guercino. Before considering them, however, we must follow Annibale to Rome (see p. 24).

repertoire of hand gestures and his unvaried facial types with large, deep-set shadowed eyes and large straight noses appear in his first identifiable frescoes and persist until his death in 1640. He still had occasional commissions in the 1630s, proof of the conservatism of some patrons.

Barocci took ten years to produce the *Presentation of the Virgin at the Temple* (Fig. 1.24). According to *The Golden Legend*, the Virgin ascended fifteen steps unaided at the age of three. Barocci finessed this detail, letting us imagine a few more steps in the foreground and others behind the priest who sprinkles holy water on the kneeling figure of Mary, who is also older than three. Her parents, exuding pride and amazement, watch on the left. Country folk bringing doves, a ram, and a calf to the temple watch from the foreground. The empty steps in the center lead our eyes to Mary and the priest, as does the pose and gaze of the young man holding the ram by a horn. Other figures on either side of the priest react with quiet pleasure to the miracle. The colors are restrained: dark blue for the Virgin; salmon-rose for her mother, St. Anne; golden yellow for the priest and the woman in the left foreground; and a subtle range of warm neutral hues for the rest of the work. The painting was received with ecstatic praise—Barocci's

1.24 Federigo Barocci, *Presentation of the Virgin at the Temple*, c. 1594. Oil on canvas, 12 ft 6 in × 8 ft 1 in (3.83 × 2.47 m). Chiesa Nuova, Rome.

dilatory behavior was tolerated because his work was so widely admired then and later by innovative painters such as Lanfranco and Sacchi.

Cesari received his first payment for the *Coronation of the Virgin* (Fig. 1.25) late in 1592 but, busy with bigger commissions, made no progress. His patrons decided in 1614 that they no longer wanted the picture for which they had waited twenty-one years. Spurred on by rejection, Cesari produced the altarpiece the following year. Stiff, conventional, and austere compared with Barocci's *Presentation*, Cesari's painting has the Virgin in an almost central position, with Christ closer to the right edge as he holds the crown over her head. Her red dress and blue cloak are the strongest colors in the work with Christ's white garments and the golden sky behind them. Cesari's treatment of form and texture is bland. Skin is not differentiated from cloth, cloth from clouds or feathers, unlike comparable elements in Barocci's work. Almost all the principal figures' hands are in the same position. The putti above and angels below have mechanically repeated poses. Still, the patrons did not refuse it. Cesari's career shows that talent and success did not always march in unison and that a variety of styles coexisted in Rome. He was also less controversial than Caravaggio.

1.25 Giuseppe d'Arpino Cesari, *Coronation of the Virgin*, 1592–1614. Oil on canvas, 12 ft 4 in × 6 ft 8 in (3.73 × 2.12 m). Chiesa Nuova, Rome.

Painting in Rome, 1585–1610

Annibale Carracci in Rome, 1595–1609

Annibale moved to Rome in 1595 at the invitation of Cardinal Odoardo Farnese, the younger son of Duke Alessandro Farnese. The Farnese family traced their roots back to the twelfth century and controlled extensive territory in Emilia, including the towns of Parma and Piacenza. Their influence was at its peak when Cardinal Alessandro Farnese became Pope Paul III in 1534. During his long reign (he died in 1549), he commissioned Michelangelo to paint the *Conversion of St. Paul* and the *Crucifixion of St. Peter* in the Pauline Chapel in the Vatican and to complete the family palace, begun in 1519 and finished forty years later. Palazzo Farnese is still the largest private palace in Rome, occupying an entire city block (Fig. **1.26**). Apart from frescoes by Francesco Salviati and Taddeo Zuccaro depicting the achievements of Paul III in the main salon, the only interior decoration in 1595 consisted of carved wooden ceilings and handsome fireplaces. The family's important collection of antiquities was installed in the courtyard and gardens behind the palace as well as in its reception rooms: the Farnese *Hercules* stood in the center of the courtyard façade facing visitors as they entered (Fig. **1.27**). The scale and quality of these possessions radiated immense wealth and power.

In February 1595 Cardinal Odoardo wrote to his brother, Duke Ranuccio, in Parma declaring his intention "to have the *sala grande* of this palace painted with the deeds of the Duke our father of glorious memory by the Bolognese painters, the Carraccioli [*sic*], whom I have accordingly taken into my service and whom I had come to Rome some months ago."[6] In order to do this, the cardinal requested that his brother send him a book with drawings representing their father's most glorious moments for the artists' use. By emphasizing their father's victories on behalf of the Catholic faith, his sons hoped to maintain their influence with the current pope, Clement VIII, a goal that was furthered, after extensive negotiations, by the marriage of his niece, Margherita Aldobrandini, to Duke Ranuccio in 1600. Annibale and Agostino did not, however, paint a cycle of frescoes glorifying the heroic accomplishments of Duke Alessandro

1.26 Antonio da Sangallo the Younger and Michelangelo Buonarroti, Palazzo Farnese, façade, Rome, 1530s–1550.

in the biggest room of the palace. Instead Annibale painted the ceiling of a much smaller room, the so-called Camerino, that served as Cardinal Odoardo's private study (1595–7), before beginning work on the Galleria.

The Camerino (Fig. 1.28) is rarely accessible to members of the public today but the canvas made for the central space, *The Choice of Hercules* (Fig. 1.29), can be seen in Naples, along with many other masterpieces from the Farnese collections. Its original setting contributes to its message of virtuous choice in a world of temptations. The coved ceiling of the rectangular room has a complex form, interrupted along its long and short sides by lunettes that create curved triangular shapes connecting them to the adjoining ceiling surfaces. Annibale unified these shapes by outlining them with gilded plaster frames that clarify the shape of the ceiling. He then filled them with beautiful grisaille decorations imitating carved reliefs of scrolling vegetal forms, satyrs, putti, ignudi, Farnese lilies, and circular reliefs illustrating four of Hercules' twelve labors. In the four lunette fields, Annibale painted Ulysses and the Sirens, Ulysses and Circe, Perseus beheading the Medusa, and the Catanian brothers rescuing their parents from a volcanic eruption. Two additional spaces above and below the central image portray Hercules carrying the weight of the world on his shoulders and

1.27 Hendrick Goltzius, Farnese *Hercules*, 1617. Engraving, 16 × 11½ in (40.5 × 29.4 cm).

1.28 Annibale Carracci, *Camerino*, 1595–97. Fresco, 15 ft 7 in × 30 ft 9 in (4.8 × 9.4 m). Palazzo Farnese, Rome.

1.29 Annibale Carracci, *The Choice of Hercules*, 1597. Oil on canvas, 65¾ × 93⅓ in (167 × 237 cm). National Museum of Capodimonte, Naples.

Hercules pondering the riddle of the Sphinx. Most of these subjects had long been used as inspiring examples of virtuous behavior. The entire ensemble was intended to guide the young cardinal through life. (He was only twenty-two when Annibale began planning the design.)

As the younger son of Duke Alessandro, Odoardo entered the Church not as its committed servant but rather as an obedient scion of an ambitious family furthering itself by placing a member close to the seat of papal power. He became a cardinal at the age of eighteen. The librarian of the Farnese family, Fulvio Orsini, a passionate scholar of classical art and literature and himself a collector of antiquities, who had been grooming Odoardo for his destiny, was the author of the program used for the Camerino ceiling. Not only are its literary sources from antiquity; its visual sources depend on them too—Farnese gems and cameos, reliefs and statues have all been spotted as models adapted by the artist.

The Choice of Hercules anchors the entire scheme. Hercules is seated in the center, a position emphasized by the sturdy trunk of a palm tree above his head, by the vertical mass of his right leg, and the rock on which he is seated. His raised leg, his right arm embracing the length of his enormous club, and his slightly averted head make a barrier between him and the image of Virtue on the left who looks at him while pointing to the winged horse Pegasus awaiting him at the summit of a rocky mountain. The left side of his body seems more open to the seductive charms of Vice on the right, though there is more space between her and Hercules than between him and Virtue. Her skimpy garments float around her body as if stirred by a light breeze. She has theatrical masks and musical instruments nearby but the woods that she faces lead nowhere. Hercules is tempted, resisting for a moment the stern path of duty that lies ahead. The light falls from the direction of duty; gloomy shade behind temptation underlines the dangers awaiting those who are seduced by her charms.

That Annibale should have begin to study ancient art once he reached Rome is not surprising but the speed with which he absorbed and understood its relevance to the Camerino is impressive. The Farnese Hercules in the palace courtyard provided the physiognomy of Annibale's hero and suggested the position of the arm cradling the club, but Glycon's statue is standing and his torso is much broader and more muscular than that of Annibale's Hercules. The head of Annibale's hero seems based instead on a portrait bust of Caracalla in the Farnese collections. Thus Annibale created his own Hercules while borrowing from ancient precedents. The Galleria frescoes make even more extensive use of ancient sculptural and architectural sources and in addition take their basic structure from two ceilings by the most prestigious artists of the High Renaissance in Rome, the Loggia of Psyche by Raphael and Michelangelo's Sistine Chapel ceiling. Annibale expected his audience to recognize these sources and to compare his work with theirs. The Galleria was, among other things, a bold claim by an artist from North Italy to be seen as the equal of, if not better than, the greatest artists of the Tuscan-Roman tradition.

Annibale's design turns the plain barrel vault of the Galleria's ceiling into a collection of paintings of various sizes with fancy frames that exactly fit its surface (Fig. **1.30**). They depict the loves and resulting mishaps and tragedies

1.30 Annibale Carracci, Galleria Farnese, Palazzo Farnese, 1595–1600. Vault and ceiling fresco.

Painting in Rome, 1585–1610

of the pagan gods and goddesses of Mount Olympus. His principal literary source was Ovid's *Metamorphoses*. There is no single viewpoint: the visitor must move around the room to see all four sides and study the many scenes and lively accompanying cast of putti, handsome young men, statues supporting the central elements, and grimacing masks amidst garlands of fruits and vegetables. A large rectangular scene that fills the center depicts the triumphal progress of Bacchus and Ariadne (Fig. **1.31**). Starting here with their backs to the window wall, spectators can grasp the overall scheme and see the maximum number of narrative scenes correctly oriented. Two smaller rectangular pictures are attached to the top and bottom of the central scene, creating an arch of pictures that seem to be supported by the main cornice. Painted by Agostino, they represent Cephalus and Aurora above and, maybe, Thetis and Peleus below. Two vertical picture fields with sphinxes in the corners of their lavish frames are attached to each side of the central scene. In these Pan is tempting Diana with a beautiful wool fleece and Mercury is bringing the golden apple to Paris, who awarded it to Venus in his famous "judgment" that launched the Trojan War. At the outer edges of these scenes, the viewer discovers an attic space that appears to continue behind the central band of images of Pan, Bacchus, and Mercury. Two satyrs are perched in these spaces on either side of smaller scenes that bridge the gap between the central band of paintings and the two large scenes that dominate either end of the gallery. In one the teasing Galatea on her dolphin-shell craft drifts by the one-eyed giant Cyclops, who has fallen in love with her and serenades her on a set of pipes. At the other end, having discovered her in the embrace of her lover Acis, Cyclops hurls a boulder at the fleeing couple, who will be killed.

The next layer of decoration is a frieze running along both long sides just above the cornice, as if

1.31 Annibale Carracci, "Galleria di Carracci," Palazzo Farnese, Rome, 1595–1600. Frescoes.

1.32 Annibale Carracci, *Jupiter and Juno* (detail), "Galleria di Carracci," Palazzo Farnese, Rome, 1595–1600. Fresco.

continuing behind the two scenes by Agostino. The frieze alternates scenes of lovers in full color (Jupiter and Juno, Diana and Endymion, Hercules and Iole, and Venus and Anchises) with bronze roundels patinated green with age on which additional mythological scenes appear (Fig. 1.32). These, together with the handsome pairs of youths seated below them manipulating the cloths attached to the heavy garlands of produce, make direct reference to the Sistine ceiling, imitating but never copying the seated ignudi there who hold ribbons threaded through openings in bronze medallions and cope with bundles of acorns and oak leaves. Behind Annibale's seated youths are herms and more young men, this time standing and painted to seem like statues that help the herms support the cornice that runs along the edges of the central band of narratives. These statues twist and turn, hiding their heads in swathes of drapery, eyeing us and each other, rejecting their assigned role as caryatids and behaving instead like real men. Pairs of adorable babies (and one infant satyr) cavort in the tiny triangular spaces between the upper edges of the bronze discs and their square frames; masks below fall asleep, yawn, grimace, smile, and look astonished, inviting us to respond to what we can see better than they can. In the four corners the frieze ends and we can glimpse blue sky beyond a balustrade on which pairs of putti are tussling over palm branches, a flaming torch, and a floating laurel wreath. Here, if nowhere else on the ceiling, some sort of moral allegory seems intended, maybe the struggle between Eros and Anteros—Love given and Love returned.

The mood of the ceiling is established by the central scene where the dignity of the procession of Bacchus and his bride Ariadne, each in their own chariots pulled by leopards and goats, quickly disintegrates into a noisy rout. On the right fauns struggle to keep the obese and tipsy Silenus from falling off his donkey. Women clash cymbals and rattle a tambourine; men blow horns and pipes and the donkey brays. Airborne putti carry a golden vase and saucer with which the married couple can drink more wine, perhaps supplied by the huge wineskin carried by the excited satyr on the right edge of the picture. An elephant brings up the rear. If the Camerino preached restraint, the Galleria seems to celebrate excess and all the pleasures of the flesh from which the brooding Hercules is just deciding to abstain. How did Cardinal Odoardo justify these visions of pagan love nearby? Were they really commissioned simply for the pleasure of visitors who could enjoy these colorful images of the ancient world brought to life after strolling through rooms filled with the Farnese antiquities? Do these mythologies contain hidden messages about the ambitions of the Farnese family or more virtuous moral conceits like those of the Camerino?

Scholars are still puzzling over the patron's motives. For a while it was believed that the decorations of the Galleria were created in the spirit of an ancient epithalamium or wedding chamber designed to inspire erotic thoughts and so to encourage the fertility of a newly married couple, in this case Duke Ranuccio and Margherita Aldobrandini. The ceiling was started well before the marriage was certain to take place and its progress halted when the engagement was announced, so that the Sala Grande could be prepared for the ceremonies. Still, neither the cardinal nor Orsini could have given Annibale permission to do whatever he wanted. Other Roman families had ceiling frescoes with entertaining mythological themes, notably those by Raphael and assistants that the banker Agostino Chigi ordered for his mistress's villa across the Tiber from the Palazzo Farnese (Fig. **1.33**). The villa (now the Villa Farnesina) had since been acquired by the Farnese, who planned to make a bridge over the Tiber connecting the two buildings with a new structure in their garden where works of art were to be displayed. The themes portrayed in the Galleria, which faces the garden and looks across to Chigi's former residence, would link these frescoes. Raphael's Loggia ceiling with the story of Cupid and Psyche also played with illusion and reality by showing some scenes as tapestries fastened overhead on a pergola of fruit and flower garlands while others appear to be "real" figures visible against the sky behind the structure of the pergola. The visual and thematic connection would even associate the cardinal with the brilliant artistic patronage of his predecessor. When plans for the ambitious wall frescoes honoring Duke Alessandro in the Sala Grande fell through, Annibale and Agostino must have proposed a substitute that would keep them employed. Thus it is possible that Annibale himself proposed the scheme for the Galleria and the essential outlines of its program, working with his better educated brother and Orsini. The final result could never have been imagined, let alone proposed, by anyone but an artist aware of the visual traditions woven into its sophisticated design, for the web of artistic meaning is far more complex than its mythological content.

Annibale created an extraordinary amalgam of ancient and modern art, blending painting, sculpture, and architecture in a rich ensemble that is, among many things, as eloquent a testimony to the fertility of one artist's imagination as has ever been painted. There are eleven major narrative compositions, ten smaller ones, and a multitude of other figures organized into a coherent scheme that plays wittily with illusion and reality: the flat surface of the curved barrel vault is now layered with framed paintings and reliefs, open to the sky at the corners and extended above as well. Real satyrs perch on the corners of some paintings while others play with gods and goddesses in the painted scenes. Real putti

1.33 Raphael Sanzio, *Galatea*, c.1512. Fresco, 9 ft 8½ in × 7 ft 4 in (2.96 × 2.24 m). Villa Farnesina, Rome.

smile at statues that smile back. Statues behave like people and people like statues. Ovid's mood of tolerant amusement at the all too human appetites of the inhabitants of Mount Olympus has been brilliantly captured in language borrowed from Michelangelo, Raphael, and antiquity and then transformed by Annibale's empathetic portrayal of human emotion and his virtuoso grasp of human anatomy: the many surviving drawings that he made, especially for the ignudi and herms, have been celebrated among artists and collectors ever since. The patron should have been overwhelmed by Annibale's achievement but, when it came time to pay the artist, he deducted the artist's living costs for the period and then sent a servant to Annibale's room with a saucer containing 500 scudi. Not only was this a ludicrously small sum for three years of work on such an enormous and complicated fresco, but the form of presentation was also an insult, implying that the patron was not satisfied. No payments have been traced to prove or disprove this act of meanness, but it is repeated by all the artist's biographers and may well be true.

Annibale's Galleria frescoes opened a new chapter in the history of Italian ceiling decoration. It can be seen as the last truly Renaissance masterpiece for, like the Camerino, it openly emulates literary and visual models from antiquity while transforming them with the artists' passionate study of real life and the finest art of the preceding century. It has also been called the first Baroque ceiling decoration, a phrase that conjures up images of ceilings covered with a rich mixture of illusionistic architecture and figures that combine narratives and allegories that pay tribute to their patrons, sacred and secular. No one undertook such commissions after 1600 without studying Annibale's fresco carefully. Most artists chose a diluted version of its complexities. Few were able, as Cortona was, to present an even more formidable synthesis of the three sister arts on an even larger scale.

The scenes below the main cornice in the Galleria were completed by Annibale's studio using his designs in 1603–4 with subjects such as *The Virgin and the Unicorn* (see Fig. 1.57) painted by Domenichino, that counteract somewhat the erotic messages of the scenes above.

Annibale began working for other patrons, notably Tiberio Cerasi, the pope's treasurer, for whom he made the *Assumption of the Virgin* for his chapel in Santa Maria del Popolo (Fig. 1.34), for which Caravaggio painted the *Crucifixion of St. Peter* and the *Conversion of St. Paul* (see Fig. 1.45) for the side walls. Annibale's style became hard, so unlike the painterly, textured surfaces of his Bolognese years that Malvasia argued that Annibale was a better painter before he came to Rome—if one ignores the frescoes in Palazzo Farnese.

1.34 Annibale Carracci, *Assumption of the Virgin*, 1601. Oil on cypress wood, 8 ft ½ in × 5 ft 1 in (2.45 × 1.55 m). Cerasi Chapel, Santa Maria del Popolo, Rome.

Painting in Rome, 1585–1610

Annibale's rate of production dropped but he still produced some masterpieces. Among these is the somber *Pietà*, perhaps made for a chapel in the Palazzo Farnese at Caprarola around 1599–1600 (Fig. **1.35**). The juxtaposition of the dead Christ in the lap of his grieving mother recalls these figures in the center of the Parma altarpiece of 1585 (see Fig. 1.11). The differences are significant. Christ is now a taller, more powerful man whose body seems draped over Mary's lap. She faces left, cradling his head in one hand, looking at his head, facing us, and gesturing to us to behold this sad spectacle. His body stretches out to the right; together they form a still, triangular mass with the light falling on them, leaving most of the rest of the arched pictorial space in deep shadow. Her blue robes are virtually the only color in the picture which is otherwise painted in neutral tones—sooty shadows, flesh tones, and white for the shroud in the foreground. Two massive blocks of stone in the right background are the tomb into which the body will be placed. This image is not intended to be a plausible moment in the story of Christ's Passion but rather a moment excerpted for meditation.

Mary and Christ are accompanied only by two child angels, one of whom supports Christ's right hand so that the wound is visible. Its rosy flesh tones accent the pallor of Christ's skin. The other on the right looks at us while touching the crown of thorns with an outstretched finger. As he does so, his expression appears to change from a teasing smile to pain. The gesture and expression (*affetti*) of this figure were much admired by Bellori.

Annibale is one of the founders of a new kind of landscape painting, a "classical" style that offers vistas of the countryside that idealize its features and depict its inhabitants relaxing rather than working. Its roots are Venetian, especially the landscape settings of Titian's mythological paintings and landscape prints, but Annibale substitutes ordinary people for the nymphs and shepherds that inhabit Titian's pastorals. Before 1600, however, landscape paintings were rarely made by Italians except as part of a decoration in a country villa and only Northern artists such as Paul Bril (see Fig. 5.66) specialized in it. Annibale's *Landscape with River and Bridge* (Fig. **1.36**) is an obvious confection of natural

1.35 Annibale Carracci, *Pietà*, c. 1599–1600. Oil on canvas, 61⅜ × 58⅝ in (156 × 149 cm). National Museum of Capodimonte, Naples.

and man-made elements. Across the banks of a river and partly blocking our view of a pleasant panorama of gentle hills is a group of buildings reached from a bridge whose arches raise its roadway much higher than the situation would seem to require. A couple perform a musical duet in the left foreground, men row or pole boats on the river, and other figures take a walk or watch from steps below the bridge. Apart from the pollarded willow and a grape vine attached to the trunk of a tree on the right, the trees are generic.

The wide horizontal format emphasized by the riverbanks, the bridge, and the flat terrain beyond create a calming effect. The painting was never intended to be taken as a serious work of art but rather as an image that would evoke the pleasures of a relaxing summer day in the country.

The most famous landscape by Annibale is a large lunette, the *Landscape with the Flight into Egypt*, one of six with New Testament subjects painted for a chapel in Palazzo Aldobrandini in Rome (Fig. **1.37**). While the role of the studio

1.36 Annibale Carracci, *Landscape with River and Bridge*, c. 1595. Oil on canvas, 31½ × 56⅓ in (80 × 143 cm). Gemäldegalerie, Berlin.

1.37 Annibale Carracci, *Landscape with the Flight into Egypt*, 1603–4. Oil on canvas, 48 × 90½ in (122 × 230 cm). Galleria Doria Pamphili, Rome.

Painting in Rome, 1585–1610

is acknowledged to be substantial in most of them, this perfectly composed panorama with the Holy Family walking across its foreground is judged too authoritative in its placing of intersecting land masses and too beautifully executed to have been designed and painted by anyone except Annibale. The figure of Mary carrying the infant Christ may, however, have been painted by Domenichino, Annibale's favorite student and assistant. The buildings in the middle distance fit comfortably into the contours of the hillside, unlike the somewhat awkward relationship between buildings and terrain in the Berlin *Landscape with River and Bridge*. Their mass above the figures of Mary and Joseph emphasizes their importance. The spacious vista invites us to imagine their journey—if they have just been ferried across the river by the boat on the right, then they may have traveled miles from the distant violet hills on the right to the river shore below the flock of grazing sheep. Only a pair of camels on the brow of a hill on the left, which look like a last-minute addition, suggest that this is Egypt: other artists usually included one palm tree and sometimes a pyramid. A gentle progression of slanting land masses lures the viewer out to the vistas on either side of the buildings which anchor the composition, echoing its semicircular format. Blues, some violet, olive and dark greens, and browns provide a subdued backdrop for the brighter colors of the Holy Family and their donkey with its red saddle cloth. This may have been Annibale's last completed painting.

Annibale left Palazzo Farnese for simpler living quarters around 1605. Whether because his pride was hurt or because he was worn out by the mental and physical effort required to paint the Galleria, he became seriously ill and virtually gave up painting himself, though he supervised his studio, encouraged his best assistants, obtained good commissions for them, and even provided them with drawings. The symptoms described by a doctor who examined him sound like severe depression. After a desperate trip to Naples in 1609, where the air was supposed to be especially healthy, Annibale returned to Rome in mid-July and died a few days later. He was buried in the Pantheon near Raphael at his own request. He was only forty-eight.

Michelangelo Merisi da Caravaggio

Caravaggio's real name was Michelangelo Merisi (1571–1610) but he is now always known by the name of the small town near Milan where his family lived. His father, who died when Michelangelo was six, was the household administrator of Francesco Sforza, Marchese of Caravaggio and a descendant of the powerful family for whom Leonardo had worked in the 1480s. He continued to help the family after 1577 so Caravaggio was not born into poverty, nor to a family of artists, though a grandfather may have been an architect. In 1584 he was apprenticed for four years to Simone Peterzano, a mediocre Milanese painter who made much of the fact that he had once studied with Titian. Caravaggio's unconventional painting techniques and his rebellious character have made scholars wonder if he remained in Milan until 1588 or left to travel and study on his own. The paintings of Girolamo Savoldo, Moretto da Brescia, Lorenzo Lotto, and G. B. Moroni in Bergamo and by Titian and Tintoretto in Venice all had more visible impact on his work than did his teacher. Documents prove that Caravaggio was home in 1589–90 when the family estate was settled after his mother's death. His inheritance was sufficient to support him for a few years if used carefully. He probably left for Rome in 1592–3, preceding Annibale Carracci there by two or three years.

Caravaggio reached Rome as an unknown painter from Milan with few connections; Annibale arrived in 1595 at the invitation of the Farnese family after more than a decade of success in Bologna. While the latter was confined to Palazzo Farnese working on his frescoes, Caravaggio was living by his wits. He received no public commissions until 1598 and survived by painting works sold to dealers and by assisting in Giuseppe Cesari's workshop. His inheritance was quickly spent, perhaps on a nice sword, as he liked to wear one while walking Rome's streets at night. Eventually his work caught the eye of Cardinal Francesco Maria del Monte, an astute patron of younger artists, who invited him to join his household, providing room and board at his palace near Piazza Navona and a small stipend in return for his pick of the work that Caravaggio produced. His first acquisition may have been *The Cardsharps* (see Fig. 1.38). His collection eventually contained eleven works by the artist.

The small canvases that Caravaggio painted before 1598 for private patrons such as Cardinal del Monte cannot be dated with precision. Some are more competent than others; his training before reaching Rome was evidently inadequate. He was not apprenticed to anyone in Rome though he could observe what went on in Cesari's studio. Caravaggio's most revolutionary and criticized decision was to skip the process of making preparatory drawings before beginning work on the canvas. Caravaggio would merely scratch a few guidelines around the principal contours of the motif into the damp priming paint and, when it had dried, start working *alla prima* (directly onto the canvas). No drawings by Caravaggio survive; there are hundreds by the Carracci and over a thousand by other seventeenth-century Italian painters. Caravaggio's lack of preparation seemed foolhardy to his peers because mistakes and changes would have to be made on the canvas, thus wasting paint and time. It also skipped the process of contemplation of models, that is, of raw nature, that would then be refined into a more idealized form suitable for a work of art, that sixteenth-century writers on art, as well as their seventeenth-century successors, regarded as essential. Simply copying what the artist had in front of him—and Caravaggio was believed always to work from models—was, they argued, a process that required no discrimination, only the ability to reproduce in paint what the eye sees. Theorists and many artists were also motivated by concern for the status of the visual arts, which they wanted to see ranked with the canonical seven liberal arts. Manual effort was unavoidable but the emphasis was put on the intellectual effort required to create the imagery rather than on its execution. Caravaggio's way of working, which effectively bypassed what was regarded as the most intellectual stage in the creation of a work of art, was seen as corrupting art, and Caravaggio himself therefore as a dangerous example. His critics' worst fears were fulfilled as his style and methods were adopted by many admirers (he had no pupils). Drawings by his followers are also rare.

The Cardsharps (Fig. 1.38) brings three figures together around a table but was probably painted two or three years earlier than the *Bacchus* (see

1.38 Michelangelo Merisi da Caravaggio, *The Cardsharps*, c. 1594. Oil on canvas, 37 1/16 × 51 9/16 in (94.2 × 130.9 cm). Kimbell Art Museum, Fort Worth, TX.

Fig. 1.39), which has only one. The former unites three figures who occupy the front plane (to the right), the next plane (to the left), and a third plane (in the middle). The lighting is comparatively bright with an arc of shadow on the wall behind the two smartly dressed cardsharps who are about to defeat the naïve, soberly dressed youth on the left pondering his next move. The older man just behind him signals to his accomplice, who slowly removes a card from behind his back while making sure his move goes undetected. The viewer takes in both gestures, feeling the tension before the resolution of this vividly captured moment. The stiffly composed figures betray Caravaggio's inexperience but in compensation there are wonderful details to observe—the expertly drawn right hand removing the spare card, the patterns on the shark's dark yellow brocade waistcoat with its fashionable black stripes and blue sleeves, the hole in the finger of the raised gloved hand of his accomplice and the deep burgundy velvet of the victim's outfit.

Caravaggio's familiarity with the Lombard portrait tradition created by Lorenzo Lotto and G.B. Moroni informs the precise, almost pedantic, description of fabric, skin, and facial features. The lines in the forehead of the cardsharp in the middle recur in many of Caravaggio's later paintings of older men.

This painting was a huge success: over thirty copies are known! Other artists in Rome began to paint gaming and gambling scenes, a theme that originated in Flanders as an adaptation of the parable of the prodigal son wasting his inheritance. Even Caravaggio's *The Cardsharps* can be read as a warning not to waste time playing cards and backgammon, especially not with expert cheats. His *Fortune Teller* (Louvre, Paris) of a year or two later carries a similar message, for the conceited young man shown there wearing the latest fashions is about to lose a ring from his finger to the gypsy reading his palm. It also inspired many later pictures of this subject (see Fig. 4.20).

The *Bacchus* (Fig. **1.39**) is the most polished of several half-length pictures of young men that Caravaggio painted in the 1590s. Unlike most of his other early works, it was never copied. This is no conventional smiling Bacchus surrounded by drunken companions. This androgynous youth with his bright red lips and absurd garland of vine leaves on his mop of black hair gazes at us knowingly, offering us a beautiful Venetian goblet of red wine while fingering the black bow at his waist. If he were a girl, we would get the seductive message immediately. But who is Bacchus seducing? Is it a homoerotic come-on, as Donald Posner suggested? This interpretation could explain why the painting was hidden away, perhaps by Maddalena d'Austria, the pious and censorious widow of Grand Duke Cosimo II de' Medici, who died in 1621. The pale skin and ruddy hands of the artist's model have been faithfully recorded; an idealizing artist such as Annibale would have unified the skin tones. Caravaggio's failure to do so makes us wonder if this is really Bacchus or just a young man dressed up and playing the role, like the Bacchus in Velázquez's later painting (see Fig. 3.28). The carafe has just been set down, the liquid in it still moving with bubbles around the edge. The heaped dish of fruit in the foreground attracts

1.39 Michelangelo Merisi da Caravaggio, *Bacchus*, 1595–96. Oil on canvas, 37⅛ × 33½ in (94 × 85 cm). Uffizi, Florence.

our admiration until we see that some of the fruit is rotten. The painting is more than a provocative image of Bacchus: it is also a warning about the transitory delights of lust and gluttony. Annibale's *The Choice of Hercules* (see Fig. 1.29) shows us the alternative to a life of voluptuous pleasures. Caravaggio's attitude toward such vices is ambiguous, hence more provocative.

Caravaggio's first religious painting may be the *Penitent Magdalene* and the next his *Rest on the Flight into Egypt* (Fig. 1.40), both now in Palazzo Doria Pamphili in Rome. Bellori's reaction to the first was that the artist had simply posed a young woman drying her hair and then added the Magdalene's attributes—a carafe of oil and the jewelry discarded after her recent conversion—to convert a genre picture into a religious image. She is wearing contemporary clothing, unlike most earlier Italian pictures of this saint; the bowed head, closed eyes, the tear on her cheek, and her self-protective gesture with her arms in her lap convey a mood of sad meditation about the meaning of this new life she has chosen.

The *Rest on the Flight* is a far more ambitious painting containing four figures of different ages and, for the first time, an extensive setting—barren stones in the left foreground and green plants in the right foreground, an oak tree in the center and a river landscape seen beyond bulrushes on the right. The terrain looks like the Lombard plains from which Caravaggio came; there is no token palm or pyramid to suggest Egypt. The Virgin bows her head over the plump sleeping Christ Child in her lap; her relaxed right hand tells us that she has dozed off. Joseph is utterly absorbed in holding up music for an angel playing a viol who fills the central foreground. Their donkey standing just behind Joseph studies the angel too. Joseph looks ill at ease, one foot

1.40 Michelangelo Merisi da Caravaggio, *Rest on the Flight into Egypt*, c. 1594–5. Oil on canvas, 52½ × 65½ in (133.5 × 166.5 cm). Palazzo Doria Pamphili, Rome.

drawn up over the other like a shy child. The provocative adolescent angel has his back to us. His white drapery flows past his buttocks and cascades round his knees to the ground. It does not, apparently, cover his genitalia, whatever they are (angels are officially sexless). Rural calm is disturbed by the angel's well-lit forms and elegant *contrapposto* that split the painting into two halves and distract the viewer's attention from the Holy Family.

Caravaggio's first public works—two paintings of events in the life of St. Matthew for the Contarelli Chapel in San Luigi dei Francesi—created a sensation (see Figs. 1.41–1.44). The French patron, Matteu Cointrel (Matteo Contarelli in Italian), had contracted with Girolamo Muziano, a fine Venetian painter then working in Rome, to decorate his new chapel in 1565; thirty years later, however, nothing had been done. Cointrel died in 1585 and so never saw the masterpieces for which he paid. His heirs took over and in 1591 hired Giuseppe Cesari. He frescoed the vault and made drawings for the scenes on the side walls, but, distracted by bigger commissions, also failed to complete the task. Probably Cardinal del Monte, in whose household Caravaggio was then living nearby and who knew Cointrel's heirs, proposed Caravaggio's name. He signed a contract in June 1599 that retained the subjects chosen over thirty years earlier for Muziano; the two side paintings were finished and installed in July 1600. The altarpiece took longer.

Caravaggio had never before painted anything as large as these two canvases. Roughly ten feet (3 m) square and requiring many figures, whose actions and setting are specified in some detail in the contract, they were an enormous challenge, especially to an artist who shunned the normal procedures of working out the design on paper, getting it approved by the patron, and then squaring up the design to a full-scale "cartoon" for transfer to the primed canvas. The relatively static *The Calling of St. Matthew* (Fig. **1.41**)

1.41 Michelangelo Merisi da Caravaggio, *The Calling of St. Matthew*, 1599–1600. Oil on canvas, 10 ft 6½ in × 11 ft 2 in (3.8 × 3.4 m). Contarelli Chapel, S. Luigi dei Francesi, Rome.

came together on the canvas with only minor changes to the poses of Christ and St. Peter on the right but the *Martyrdom of St. Matthew* (see Fig. 1.42), which has more figures and shows some in motion, drawing away from the act of execution in horror and fleeing, was completely revised after a false start.

The first thing to which the eye is pulled in *The Calling* is the diagonal shadow that divides the wall behind the figures into light and dark, skimming Christ's head, emphasizing his extended arm and pointing finger and leading us to Matthew, seated in the midst of four men around a table on the left. He points to himself with his left hand as if to say "Me?" His right hand is stopped in the act of counting change; the angle of his legs below the table suggests that he will rise from the table to follow Christ. His four companions react with amazement, incomprehension, or—in the case of the two men on the left absorbed in counting money—complete indifference. Christ's feet, which do not point in the direction of his upper body, are only dimly visible. He has just turned around to call Matthew to follow him. His companion, probably St. Peter, is moving toward the table while shielding much of Christ from our view. He was added later, and Christ's pose was changed too. His gesture recalls the limp hand of Adam in Michelangelo's *Creation of Adam* on the Sistine Chapel ceiling, the first of several prominent quotations by Caravaggio from the work of his famous namesake.

The setting is both spare and ambiguous: are they outside or inside? Shutters on windows were then, as now in Italy, used both indoors and outdoors but the partial curtain over the right panes would be likely only on an indoor window. The window over the altarpiece in the Contarelli chapel is above and to the right of this canvas, whose lighting is oriented toward it but does not replicate it. The fall of light is symbolic, coming from the direction of Christ, "the way of light, the way of truth," to which only Matthew at this moment is receptive. The setting is both the Capernaum of Christ, where this event took place, and the Rome of Caravaggio, for Matthew and his companions wear modern dress similar to that in *The Cardsharps* and the *Fortune Teller*. The bravo seated with his back to us has a sword hanging from his belt, the weapon that will kill the saint. The window and furniture suggest a modern Roman room too. Christ is made vividly present in Caravaggio's own world, entering Matthew's office to command him to leave his profession for an unknown future. Like Annibale's Hercules (see Fig. 1.29), Matthew is about to make a choice between vice and virtue, and, like Hercules, he will clearly do the right thing.

Matthew's call to follow Christ begins his story; his martyrdom on the right wall ends it, but it is the first scene that visitors see as they walk up the left aisle toward the last chapel on that side of the nave (Fig. **1.42**). A half-naked man leans back into the lower right corner; a fleeing child just above him looks back over his shoulder as he rushes away from something terrifying. Then we see the executioner, naked except for a loincloth, holding Matthew's right wrist in his left hand, his raised sword casting a shadow on his leg as he peers at his victim to see if he has done the job properly. *The Golden Legend* says that the deed was done from the back as Matthew was celebrating Mass but here it seems the saint has been stabbed from the front. The cross on the front of the altar is visible in the shadows just above the saint's raised right hand. Blood has begun to seep into his robes. His arms are spread out, a gesture which recalls the crucified Christ and tells us that the saint welcomes his fate. A naked angel whose buttock is tactfully concealed by shadow leans acrobatically over a cloud bank above them to offer the saint his martyr's palm.

In the gloom on the left a jumble of figures react in various ways to the central event. The loincloths worn by the men in the left and right foreground identify the executioner's accomplices, but these men cringe and retreat from an event that seems to horrify them. Other men on the left wear contemporary clothing: a young bravo with a feather in his hat is carrying a sword and making off with another smartly dressed companion; the raised leg of another fleeing man just below that sword reveals another departing coward; and, just above him in the middle distance, a man looks back with an expression of concern. This is the artist himself, who had already included himself as a witness to the

40 *Chapter 1: Italy*

capture of Christ (National Gallery of Ireland, Dublin) and will do so again. The "signature self-portrait" was a well-established tradition by now but, unlike his predecessors, Caravaggio shows himself as more than a passive witness.

The most respected older artist then working in Rome, Federico Zuccaro (1540–1609), is reported to have come to see the chapel after the side wall paintings were installed in 1600 and to have declared, "What's all the fuss about? This is nothing but warmed over Giorgione."[7] The comment might refer to the fact that Giorgione was also believed to work without making drawings and used chiaroscuro to conceal his flawed draughtsmanship. Either way, Zuccaro's views were those of the old guard who rightly suspected that Caravaggio's ability to create such powerful, realistic images of events, described in one short sentence in the Bible, could only be a threat to their own work.

The altarpiece of the Contarelli Chapel had already caused the donors grief. The original commission went to a sculptor, Jacob Cobaert, who by 1602 had finished the statue of St. Matthew but not that of the angel required by the contract. The statue was installed in January 1602 and was quickly rejected. In February Caravaggio was commissioned to paint an altarpiece with an image of St. Matthew with the angel on the right dictating the gospel to him; *The Inspiration of St. Matthew* was to be finished by May 26 (see Fig. **1.43**). This he did but it too was rejected. What happened is known not from the documents, which show only that Caravaggio was paid once in 1602 for an altarpiece then in place, but from his biographers. A rival painter, Giovanni Baglione (c. 1573–1644), who wrote a set of lives of artists working in Rome from 1572 to 1642, declared that no one liked Caravaggio's *The Inspiration of St. Matthew*. Bellori offered a more nuanced explanation: "After he had finished the [. . .] St. Matthew and installed it on the altar, the priests took it down, saying that the figure with its legs crossed and its feet rudely exposed to the public had neither decorum nor the appearance of a saint." Marchese Vincenzo Giustiniani took the rejected altarpiece and paid for a replacement, the picture on the altar to this day. The marchese's version perished in 1945 during the fall of Berlin.

The first version (Fig. **1.43**) does indeed show St. Matthew with his legs crossed in such a way that the visible sole of his left foot projects beyond the picture plane and, installed on the altar, would be level with the host at the most sacred moment of the Mass when the priest elevates it and declares, "This is my body; do this in remembrance of me." The saint seems illiterate. He does not even know how to hold a pen and stares in disbelief as the nubile young angel, its body barely concealed by thin white draperies, leans across to guide his hand across the page to create beautiful Hebrew script. Caravaggio's intent was to show that the Gospel of Matthew was divinely inspired, but the priests may also have thought that the saint looked like a village idiot and that the angel's close physical presence was inappropriate. Caravaggio did not know

1.42 (opposite) Michelangelo Merisi da Caravaggio, *Martyrdom of St. Matthew* (right), Contarelli Chapel, S. Luigi dei Francesi, Rome, 1599–1602.

1.43 Michelangelo Merisi da Caravaggio, *The Inspiration of St. Matthew (St. Matthew and the Angel)*, 1st version, 1602. Oil on canvas, 7 ft 4 in × 5 ft 10 in (2.23 × 1.88 m). Destroyed, formerly Gemäldegalerie, Berlin.

Hebrew. He must have had expert advice from theologians who could read the language in which God was believed to have communicated the words of the Bible. His learned consultants did not apparently find the half-finished painting objectionable. Only when it was installed did the awkward position of the saint's foot behind the elevated host become apparent.

The second version (Fig. 1.44) carefully avoids these problems. The saint is taking dictation like an expert as the airborne angel ticks off points to be noted. Matthew's feet are well away from the picture plane but Caravaggio could not resist playing tricks with the division between his painted world and the viewer's. The stool on which Matthew is kneeling balances precariously on the edge of the platform, casting a shadow beyond the picture plane, as did the saint's foot in the original altarpiece. Finally, this St. Matthew has the same features as the saint in the two side paintings. The first St. Matthew looks curiously like Socrates and not at all like his image in *The Calling* and *Martyrdom*. Quite how Caravaggio expected that anomaly to be overlooked is not clear. He may just have been arrogant enough to think that his dazzling performance would sweep away all objections. The huge white wings of the angel in the lost version look especially beautiful. They were painted from swan's wings that Caravaggio later lent to another painter.

Other public commissions were soon offered to Caravaggio despite the initial rejection of the first altarpiece for the Contarelli Chapel. The first of these was for two paintings on the side walls of Tiberio Cerasi's chapel in Santa Maria del Popolo. The contract, dated September 24, 1600, specifies that the *Conversion of St. Paul* and the *Crucifixion of St. Peter* were to be painted on cypress panels and that the artist was to supply a sketch of his designs for approval before starting work (if he did, it is lost). The ceiling of the chapel had already been painted by members of Annibale Carracci's studio to his designs and he had finished an *Assumption of the Virgin* (see Fig. 1.34) for the altar—at least it is believed that it was in place (no contract for Annibale's work has been found). The chapel thus brings together the two artists now regarded as the most gifted and original then working in Italy. The patron, who is not otherwise known as an art patron, probably hired them on the advice of the artists' supporters, maybe Cardinal Pietro Aldobrandini for Annibale and Cardinal del Monte and Marchese Giustiniani for Caravaggio. Cerasi, the wealthy treasurer of Clement VIII, died before Caravaggio's two pictures were finished, so he too, like Contarelli, never saw the works for which he paid.

Although Caravaggio's contract required that he use cypress wood for his pictures, which Annibale did for his *Assumption*, Caravaggio's paintings are on canvas. Another painting by Caravaggio of the *Conversion of St. Paul* on cypress wood, whose measurements would fit

1.44 Michelangelo Merisi da Caravaggio, *The Inspiration of St. Matthew (St. Matthew and the Angel)*, 2nd version, 1602. Oil on canvas, 9 ft 8 in × 6 ft 5 in (2.96 × 1.95 m). S. Luigi dei Francesci, Rome.

the frame in the Cerasi Chapel, seems to be the rejected first version. The chief difference between the two compositions is the economy of the final design. Competing with a Bolognese artist who had mastered both fresco and oil painting, Caravaggio packed four figures close to the picture plane as well as a large horse and a landscape vista into his meticulously rendered first version. In the final canvas (Fig. **1.45**), St. Paul lies on his back, his head close to the viewer, his arms flung wide to receive the light his sealed eyes cannot see. His horse, who fills the rest of the canvas, lifts his right foreleg, treading carefully to avoid hurting his owner. A groom standing behind its head holds the bit at its mouth. The scene seems to be taking place in a dark stable rather than in the open on the road to Damascus. The drama no longer emphasizes physical action, as do all earlier depictions of this subject, including that of Ludovico Carracci (see Fig. 1.9), but rather the inner psychological turmoil of a man at the moment of his conversion to Christianity. In neither version did Caravaggio try to incorporate the light of the chapel itself, which comes from a lunette window above the altarpiece and would fall from the upper left onto the figures. Instead the light comes from the upper right, effectively from the church transept which gives access to the chapel.

The concentrated drama of the second version of the *Conversion* must be in part Caravaggio's response to the style of the altarpiece which it was to accompany. Annibale's *Assumption of the Virgin* (see Fig. 1.34) differs from the warm-toned, neo-Venetian altarpieces of his Bolognese period. The roughly square panel is organized around a triad of figures: the central Virgin, shown rising from the tomb, fills most of the upper half of the picture; below, St. Peter and St. Paul, who gaze up at her, occupy the foreground. The bright primary colors worn by the Virgin (blue over red) and Peter (yellow over blue) and the traditional red and green of Paul's robes dominate the front picture plane as do the hard, almost sculptural forms of their limbs and drapery. Into the remaining space Annibale has crammed nine other apostles, seven of them on the right (Judas is missing). Of some only the back of their heads is visible. The stiffened forms and crowded composition in Annibale's painting have been interpreted as a conscious shift to a "hyper-idealized manner" that rejects the warmth and painterly qualities of his Bolognese period for a style indebted to ancient sculpture and to Raphael. Still, neither ancient reliefs nor Raphael crowded their pictorial fields in this way. Others have read its claustrophobic character as a sign of the impending mental breakdown that severely reduced Annibale's ability to work in his last years. Whatever Annibale's intentions, it seems likely that Caravaggio found Annibale's composition too crowded, which would explain why he decided to eliminate all but the most essential figures in his two paintings.

Caravaggio now had steady patrons for both public and private commissions, the latter larger and more ambitious than the simple designs with which he had first attracted patrons. Marchese Giustiniani eventually owned thirteen works, the largest group assembled by a private collector

1.45 Michelangelo Merisi da Caravaggio, *Conversion of St. Paul*, c. 1601. Oil on canvas, 7 ft 6 in × 5 ft 8 in (2.3 × 1.75 m). Sta. Maria del Popolo, Rome.

then or since. Among them is the cheeky *Victorious Cupid*, or *Amor Vincit Omnia* ("Love Conquers All") (Fig. **1.46**) made for the marchese in 1602, which was described in the inventory of Giustiniani's collection taken after his death in 1638 as follows: "A picture of a laughing Cupid, who shows his contempt for the world, which lies at his feet in the guise of various instruments, crowns, scepters, and armor; known, because of its fame, as the Cupid of Caravaggio." Cupid is "played" by a mischievous boy on the verge of adolescence, his skin smooth, his arms still skinny, his legs just beginning to acquire the muscular strength of adulthood. The tip of one gray wing rests on his thigh and seems to point at his genitals, which are the focal point of the painting. Directional lines created by his legs, the arrows in his right hand, the slanting forms of the lute and violin with its bow on the left, and the crisp white drapery on which he sits all pull the eye to his shamelessly exposed pudenda, and his knowing, tilted gaze tells us that he is fully aware of our failure to look away. The concealed position of his left arm and hand make the erotic content even more blatant. Joachim von Sandrart, a German painter who was in Rome around 1630, says that he told the marchese to cover the painting with a curtain and to reveal the Cupid only after visitors had seen every other work in his collection. Its degree of artistic skill could well

1.46 Michelangelo Merisi da Caravaggio, *Victorious Cupid (Amor Vincit Omnia)*, c. 1602. Oil on canvas, 60⅝ × 43⅓ in (154 × 110 cm). Staatliche Gemäldegalerie, Berlin.

have diminished the visitor's appreciation of the rest of the marchese's collection. Still, its teasing eroticism was probably not considered appropriate for every visitor, especially women.

The *Victorious Cupid* seems an open declaration of warfare on the dry academicism of Mannerists like Cesari and Federico Zuccaro. "If it is so easy to copy nature, let's see if you can do it and do it better," is one of the work's messages to its Roman audience. It is also, as Hibbard notes, the work which "most clearly exhibits [Caravaggio's] confrontation with Michelangelo's achievement, a compound of admiration and almost childish rebellion." The latter had used a similar seated pose with one leg extended, the other bent back, for a statue of *Victory* (Palazzo della Signoria, Florence) as well as for one of the ignudi on the Sistine Chapel ceiling and St. Bartholomew in the *Last Judgment* nearby on the altar wall (Fig. **1.47**). Some scholars have seen the Cupid as a deliberate parody, intended to mock the elevated visual language of Michelangelo and to expose that artist's sublimated homosexuality. It is certainly no simple image of Love conquering all. By using an apparently unmediated realism for a subject usually cloaked in idealizing fictions, in which Cupid is a phenomenally agile baby rather than an adolescent boy, Caravaggio extracts the theme from its husk of visual tradition and almost turns it into a genre scene. Almost but not quite—once we try to imagine this tableau as actually happening, its fictions reassert themselves. "Fiction and reality are poised as delicately [. . .] as the feather against the boy's leg," wrote Charles Dempsey, "and it is this balance that gives the painting still its extraordinary power to shock."

Caravaggio's criminal records began in 1600, just as his public career in Rome was taking off, and were to culminate there in a murder charge. His initial minor offenses included carrying a sword without a permit and throwing artichokes at a waiter in a restaurant when he thought the waiter was being rude. In 1603, however, he was imprisoned for libel, which seems excessive punishment for a non-violent civil offense. The libeled party was Giovanni Baglione, who had been given an important commission in the Gesù that Caravaggio would have liked to have had himself. When Baglione's *Resurrection of Christ*

(lost) was unveiled, obscene comments about the artist's character and art, some of them in verse, started circulating. Baglione sued Caravaggio, believing not unreasonably that he and his friends had composed the insulting doggerel. However trivial the case, the trial records documented Caravaggio's only recorded opinions about the art of his contemporaries and the role of an artist: he had met and was on civil terms with Annibale Carracci but not with Cesari, Baglione, or Orazio Gentileschi; he regarded all but Orazio as good painters. Further, he declared that a good painter knows his art and how "depenger bene et imitar bene le cose naturali" (to paint well and to imitate well natural things). This sounds like the perfect motto for a realist but it was by now a commonplace and artists of widely varying styles all believed that they were doing exactly that. Imitating nature was a goal that could be interpreted in many different ways.

1.47 Michelangelo Buonarotti, *St. Bartholomew*, detail from *Last Judgment*, 1536–41. Fresco. Sistine Chapel, Vatican, Rome.

Caravaggio's next public commission, the *Death of the Virgin* (Fig. **1.48**), created a real stir. Rejected by its patrons, it is regarded as one of the artist's supreme achievements. The chapel in the newly completed church of Santa Maria della Scala, for which the work was intended, belonged to Laerzio Cherubini, a papal lawyer not known as an art patron; the artist signed the contract in June, 1601. The subject was not common after 1400. Caravaggio followed tradition in showing the Virgin fully dressed in bed, but abandoned it by not having the bedclothes pulled up to her chest and her arms folded as if she had just fallen asleep while praying. The grieving apostles, who arrived miraculously to attend her last moments, are gathered around her. In some earlier images, Christ himself comes to receive his mother's soul; a heavenly vision above the apostles is also very common. The Magdalene, prominently placed here in the right foreground, is rarely included and never with such emphasis. The church, which belonged to Discalced (barefoot) Carmelites, ministered in particular to "fallen" women. Thus the bare feet of the apostles, and even of the Virgin, may allude to them, and the Magdalene, whose legend identified her as a reformed prostitute, must be there as inspiration for her Roman counterparts.

Eleven apostles are present here behind the narrow cot on which Mary's body is laid out. Grouped to left and right in shadow, their spacing gives prominence to two in the center whose bald heads catch the light and lead us in a falling diagonal to Mary. Two of the apostles closest to her are kneeling and weeping openly. The pool of light on Mary holds our attention as we examine her limp hands and peaceful expression. The Magdalene may have started to wash the body before the apostles arrived (a copper basin with a cloth sits on the floor in front of her). She bows her head and mops her tears with the edge of her sleeve. A large red drapery pulled up by cords fills the upper third of the high-ceilinged room in which everyone has assembled.

Whether it was the church authorities or the patron who rejected the painting is not known but by April 1607 Rubens, who was then in Rome, had persuaded the Duke of Mantua, Vincenzo I Gonzaga, to buy it. What did some viewers find objectionable about the work? Caravaggio shows Mary flat on her back on a bed so short that her feet extend beyond its end; her skirt has been pulled up, immodestly exposing her feet. This detail certainly challenged standard decorum. Mary's hair is uncombed and her arms have not even been folded across her chest. She is not dressed in the soothing blues and wine reds of tradition and also seems considerably younger than the Virgin in the *Entombment*. Caravaggio may have intended to show her at the moment of death before anyone had attended to her body but the effect is to suggest both that she did not die in a state of grace and that no one cared enough to treat her corpse afterwards with the proper respect. This, in short, is the death bed

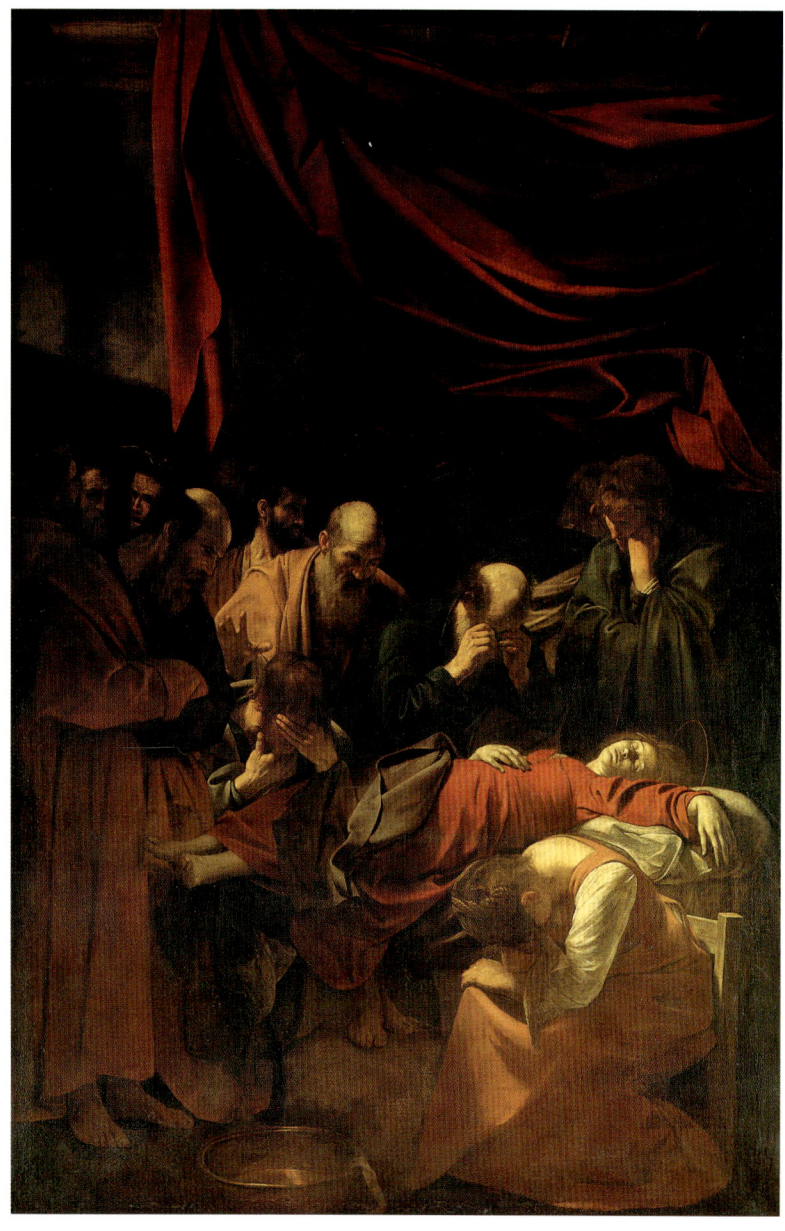

1.48 Michelangelo Merisi da Caravaggio, *Death of the Virgin*, c. 1601–2. Oil on canvas, 12 ft 1 in × 8 ft (3.69 × 2.45 m). Louvre, Paris.

of an ordinary woman, not that of the mother of Christ. It was rumored that the model for the Virgin was the artist's mistress or a whore who had drowned in the Tiber. After its purchase by the Duke of Mantua, the artistic community insisted that the painting be exhibited in Rome for a week before it was shipped north because so few people had seen it. By then Caravaggio had fled Rome to escape imprisonment after killing an opponent over a lost bet in a tennis match, and so missed this moment of triumph.

The most important altarpieces then being commissioned in Rome were for St. Peter's. Caravaggio had to make do with one of the dark side chapels in Santa Maria in Vallicella for which he painted his *Entombment of Christ* in 1603–4 (p. xxii). The church did not yet have its high altarpiece by Rubens and only one of the two altarpieces by Federico Barocci had been installed (the *Visitation*, also in a side chapel, finished in 1586). The Vittrici Chapel, which was dedicated to the Pietà, promised those who prayed there a papal indulgence for their sins, a benefit of the donor's close friendship with Gregory XIII (1572–85). It was redecorated in 1602–4 when the existing altarpiece was removed and another artist painted a small fresco of the Pietà in the vault above the altar. Whether because the down-to-earth piety of St. Philip Neri's followers was in close sympathy with Caravaggio's art or whether the artist decided to play it safe, the *Entombment* was not controversial then or later. It was even praised by Baglione and Bellori. The six figures are arranged in an irregular descending arc that we follow once our attention has been caught by the upraised arms of the Magdalene. We understand that they are lowering Christ's body into the tomb in the darkness beneath the stone slab that projects into our space. St. John supports Christ's upper body; his fingers both cradle the torso and lead our eyes to the wound in Christ's side. Nicodemus wraps his arms around Christ's knees and gazes absently outward. Mary and John both study Christ's peaceful face. Except for the Magdalene, all the emotions shown are restrained. This time a priest raising the host to bless it during the Mass would find a dignified, powerfully realized image of Christ just above it, reinforcing the meaning of that ritual.

There are many earlier Italian paintings depicting various moments after Christ's body was lowered from the cross but before it was placed in the tomb; Caravaggio used none of them. The *Pietà* by Michelangelo in St. Peter's offered a challenge that was taken up by Caravaggio, however, especially the hanging right arm and ideal male body of Christ. One telling detail is Christ's left hand with its awkwardly contracted fingers frozen by *rigor mortis*; Mary's right hand in the controversial *Death of the Virgin* has a similar position (see Fig. 1.48). Caravaggio's painting presents the body of Christ not as an abstracted icon of the grieving mother alone with her dead son but as a subject for meditation: a stopped moment in the story of his execution and burial. Thus the painting is often called an "entombment," despite the chapel's dedication to the Pietà, and despite the fact that Christ's body cannot be lowered into the tomb shown here without the help of others standing below to receive it. Once again, Caravaggio's painting is less real than it seems.

Caravaggio's last four years were spent on the move—first to Naples, where he spent the last months of 1606 and part of 1607. Two public commissions painted there escaped destruction in earthquakes and warfare: the *Flagellation* (now kept at Capodimonte) and the *Seven Works of Mercy* for the church of the Pio Monte della Misericordia. By July 1607 he was in Valletta, Malta, where he painted his largest picture, *The Beheading of St. John the Baptist* (see Fig. 1.49), for a chapel attached to the Co-Cathedral of St. John. It was well received: he was made a Knight of St. John in July 1608, but in October, perhaps for attacking another knight, he was imprisoned once more. He soon escaped and fled to Sicily, where he landed at Syracuse and painted the *Burial of St. Lucy*; by December 1608 he was in Messina, where he painted the *Resurrection of Lazarus* and an *Adoration of the Shepherds*, then traveled to Palermo and back to Naples in October 1609. His supporters had been trying to obtain a pardon so that he could return to Rome, and hearing that it was forthcoming, he set off by boat, landing at Port Ercole on the coast, just outside the papal territories. He was arrested but released two days later. The boat with his possessions had sailed. He tried to catch up with

1.49 Michelangelo Merisi da Caravaggio, *The Beheading of St. John the Baptist*, 1608. Oil on canvas, 11 ft 9 in × 17 ft (3.61 × 5.2 m). Oratory of S. Giovanni Battista, Co-Cathedral of St. John, La Valletta, Malta.

it, running along the seashore in the summer heat, became ill, and died on July 10. Baglione gloated, reporting that Caravaggio died "as miserably as he had lived." Other reports, however brief, nevertheless mentioned that he was a "most famous painter and most excellent in coloring and imitation of nature." He was thirty-eight.

The masterpiece of Caravaggio's last years is the huge *The Beheading of St. John the Baptist* (Fig. **1.49**). It fills the end wall of a large chapel, attached to the left wall of the cathedral and lit by windows in its left wall. Like almost all the Sicilian commissions that followed, the pictorial space occupied by the figures is reduced and, as Howard Hibbard put it, the rest is "powerful emptiness." The scene takes place in front of a wall pierced by a large arched doorway framed by dressed stones and a barred window through which two men peer. The main group on the left forms a lunette—Salome bending over from the left to receive the head of the Baptist, still not fully severed from his neck, and the executioner bending over from the right, his left arm holding back the Baptist's hair as he takes a dagger from his belt to finish his task. Between them stand Herodias, her head in her hands, finally shocked at this turn of events, and a jailor who calmly points and issues instructions. The only real color in the painting is the red of the Baptist's cloak. Caravaggio's signature is written in the blood dribbling from the saint's neck in the foreground, or so the viewer is meant to believe. The horror of the event is tempered by the stillness of the figures and the somber tones of the painting. Caravaggio's contemporaries were all too familiar with public executions; modern audiences who realize what is happening in this scene may well find it unbearable.

Caravaggio's ability to empathize with such subjects was enhanced by the knowledge that he too might be executed, either in a revenge killing or after being brought to justice in Rome. The subject of death, especially by decapitation, drew him several times, most strikingly in *David with the Head of Goliath* (Fig. **1.50**), where the artist himself plays the role of the dead victim. The painting is first recorded in the collection of Cardinal Scipione Borghese, which implies that Caravaggio painted it before fleeing from Rome in 1606, but most authorities believe that it was painted much later and may be one of his last works. A boy, much younger than the figures of *David* by Donatello, Michelangelo, or Bernini (see Fig. **1.88**), emerges from deep shadow and

Chapter 1: Italy

offers us the head of Goliath. The right side of his body is invisible but the end of his sword resting against his thigh lets us imagine the arm holding it. His left arm comes out toward us, the fist grasping the hair of a huge head, twice the size of his own. David looks down at his conquered foe with compassion. Goliath's mouth hangs open yet does not seem fully relaxed although his eyes no longer focus. Blood drips from his freshly severed neck. Caravaggio does not spare us from any of the gory facts of decapitation and forces us to pay close attention by putting himself in the role of the villain. No other image of this subject, painted or sculpted, gives so much emphasis to the punished enemy. In doing so and in declaring his identification with Goliath, Caravaggio seems to admit his own guilt and his pessimism about his chances of salvation. David, whom the Church identified as a prefiguration of Christ, seems disposed to forgive his enemy, and thus perhaps the artist himself. It is an unforgettable image that is both simple and complex, moving and repellent. Its contradictions mirror the life of the troubled genius who painted it and whose art profoundly affected the course of subsequent European painting.

1.50 Michelangelo Merisi da Caravaggio, *David with the Head of Goliath*, c. 1609–10. Oil on canvas, 4 ft 2 in × 2 ft 11 in (1.25 × 0.9 m). Borghese Gallery, Rome.

Caravaggio's Italian Followers

The Carracci had students but Caravaggio had followers. He was a temperamental loner whose admirers imitated his final products without being involved in their creation, as was the case with young apprentices in daily contact with the master in a studio. Few of Caravaggio's most gifted followers knew him personally or even met him. During the decade after his death, however, Italian, Dutch, French, Flemish, and Spanish artists all paid him the sincerest form of flattery by imitating both his style and his working methods. They adopted his floodlit figures set against nondescript dark backgrounds. They based their characters, sacred and profane, on ordinary-looking models. Paintings of fortune tellers, cardsharps, and music parties proliferated, especially by Northern artists. They featured young men wearing the same kinds of fashionable clothes with striped sleeves as those seen in Caravaggio's early genre scenes, while adding other characters and complicating the narrative. Simon Vouet's *The Fortune Teller* (see Fig. 4.20) and Valentin de Boulogne's *The Four Ages of Man* (see Fig. 4.22) are outstanding examples.

One of the few artists affected by Caravaggio during his lifetime was Orazio Gentileschi (1563–1639), the son of a Pisan goldsmith who went to Rome around 1577–8 after some training as a painter in Florence. His first Roman works are nondescript essays in conservative *maniera*, utterly unlike his mature work. He seems to have been transformed by seeing what Caravaggio could do by working from models. In 1603, when Orazio was already forty, Caravaggio testified in the libel suit brought by Baglione that he had not seen Orazio for three years and did not regard him as one of the better painters in Rome. This was fair comment, for Orazio never had a good grasp of anatomy and his compositional structures can be awkward. His color schemes reject Caravaggio's somber monochromes relieved by some red drapery in favor of blues, violets, grays, golden yellow, lapis blues, rose pinks, even greens. The meticulously observed surfaces of materials like brocades, feathers, and polished metals in his mature works have an almost Flemish precision that can seem to be the entire point of the painting. His works are saved from being trivial exhibitions of virtuoso technique by an affecting, if sometimes naïve, approach to narrative.

Orazio's *The Rest on the Flight into Egypt* (Fig. **1.51**) owes its touching humanity to Caravaggio's treatment of this subject (see Fig. 1.40). As Orazio's painting is much larger, however, his figures are monumental by comparison. Instead of a landscape, the space behind the reclining figures of Joseph and Mary is screened off by a ruined wall, behind which appears the oversize head of their donkey and a cloud-streaked sky. Showing Joseph dozing as he receives the message that the family must flee was traditional, but to show him so utterly exhausted that he would fall asleep in this uncomfortable position was Orazio's own invention. The Virgin breastfeeds Christ, who is no newborn (the family may be returning to Egypt rather than fleeing). His chunky body has been studied from life but the relationship between him and his mother is awkward: her breast is too high; and a feeding child needs to be closer to the mother. Her limbs are also enormous compared with her small head. Mary's outsize scale may be deliberate, to indicate her symbolic role as Ecclesia (the Church); another possibility is that Orazio had difficulty working on such a big canvas. He repeated this composition at least three times, making minor changes. Only this version, which

1.51 Orazio Gentileschi, *The Rest on the Flight into Egypt*, c. 1610. Oil on canvas, 69½ × 86¼ in (176.6 × 219 cm). Birmingham Museums and Art Gallery, Birmingham, England.

1.52 Orazio Gentileschi, *The Finding of Moses*, 1633. Oil on canvas, 7 ft 11 in × 9 ft 3 in (2.42 × 2.81 m). Prado, Madrid.

is probably the first, includes the ruined wall, the donkey, and the cloud-streaked sky.

After working outside Rome in Fabriano (the Marches), Orazio spent the years 1621–3 in Genoa; he then went to Paris before settling permanently in London in 1626. His seductive mixture of naturalism and refined execution and his exquisite color sense was thus seen by artists in all these cities: French painters in particular appreciated his work. George Villiers, Duke of Buckingham, had already acquired two paintings from Orazio, one of them a version of the *Rest on the Flight* (Kunsthistorisches Museum, Vienna). In London Orazio also enjoyed the support of Charles I, whom he advised about his art collection.

Orazio often repeated his own compositions with minor variations and some changes in the colors of clothing. Drapery fold patterns were repeated exactly. To do this he must have kept detailed drawings or full-scale cartoons of the principal figures from paintings first made in Italy, then reproduced in France and England. His daughter Artemisia (whose work is discussed below) probably began her training by helping Orazio to make these autograph variants. Most ambitious artists shunned this practice, however, and prided themselves on never repeating themselves. Patrons who wanted an example of his beautifully rendered silk draperies apparently did not mind getting a copy in different colors as long as it was painted by Orazio himself.

A spectacular example of Orazio reworking an important commission when he had an opportunity to do so for another prestigious client is *The Finding of Moses*, sent by the artist as a gift to Philip IV of Spain in 1633 (Fig. **1.52**). It takes over all but two of the figures in an earlier version, now in a private collection, made for Queen Henrietta Maria, with minor improvements in their poses. The two eliminated women are replaced with the woman in a shot silk dress of plum red and violet just behind Moses; she looks down at him and raises her right hand in a gesture that conveys both surprise and respect. The group of women is now more coherent. There is more space too for a beautiful landscape on the right with pink and violet clouds; the river, so distant in the earlier version, is now closer. The position of the woman in gray-blue satin who presents the basket to the pharaoh's daughter is echoed by that of the kneeling girl on the left, who is Miriam, the sister of Moses, who had kept watch after their mother had exposed Moses amid the bulrushes. Behind Miriam is her mother, whom the pharaoh's daughter is about to hire as a wetnurse. Their clothes are much plainer, though the brilliant crimson outer garment of Moses' mother hints at her importance. The pharaoh's daughter, who wears Orazio's favorite yellow over white satin, points to the boy's genitalia, here concealed by his raised leg but exposed in the first version. The gesture is important to the recognition of Moses as a Jewish baby but here carries further significance. Both paintings have recently been connected by Weston-Lewis with the birth of royal heirs—the Prince of Wales (later Charles II) in 1630 and Prince Baltasar Carlos, the heir to the Spanish crown, in 1629.[8] The delay of a few years from the happy event might seem to preclude such a connection but so many babies, even in the best families, died within a few months of birth that dynastic hopes became secure only once the child had survived those dangerous first years. Orazio's sumptuous painting was hung prominently in the Alcázar and Philip IV was so pleased that he sent the artist 900 ducats. Orazio had hoped for something else as well, namely a good word with the Grand Duke Ferdinand de' Medici in Florence, for he wanted to go home. He even signed the painting ORATIO GIENTILESCHI FIOREN. He was now seventy, but the invitation he hoped for never came. He remained in England until his death, comforted at the end by his daughter Artemisia who joined him in 1638 to assist him and remained to complete his commissions.

Artemisia Gentileschi (1593–1652/3) is currently better known than her father. The subject of two substantial monographs, two novels based on her life, several exhibitions, and even a movie, she has become a celebrity woman artist. The presence of the Bolognese painter Lavinia Fontana (1552–1613), who had had a long and productive career in Bologna before arriving in Rome in 1603, may well have encouraged Orazio to train his daughter. Her mother died when Artemisia was twelve. Confined to the house by custom (an unmarried woman could not leave the house without a chaperone), and minimally educated (only boys received free elementary schooling), assisting her father in the studio may have seemed welcome relief from her monotonous daily routine. Only occasionally when her father took her to private collections or escorted her on visits to Roman churches could she see the work of other artists.

In 1610, when she was only seventeen, she signed and dated an ambitious *Susanna and the Elders* (Fig. **1.53**). Featuring a full-length female nude accompanied by two men, only partly visible, the painting has a convincing, if shallow, setting in an elegant stone enclosure with a pool of water and a cloud-streaked sky behind. As noted, her training would have been limited to what her father could teach her, and, while he had a gift for rendering fabrics, he was not a strong draughtsman and had difficulty with human anatomy. Furthermore, women could not attend life-drawing classes attended by male students at the Academy of St. Luke or in artists' studios, for which only male models were hired. Had she hired a man to pose for her, Artemisia would have caused a scandal, yet she had to master human anatomy if she was to be considered a serious artist. Her solution was to study the female body and to choose subjects that allowed her to flaunt her first-hand knowledge of women's anatomy.

The central figure in *Susanna and the Elders* looks like a real woman. Her skin looks soft and smooth rather than hard and muscular. Her visible breast has the right shape, and an aureole

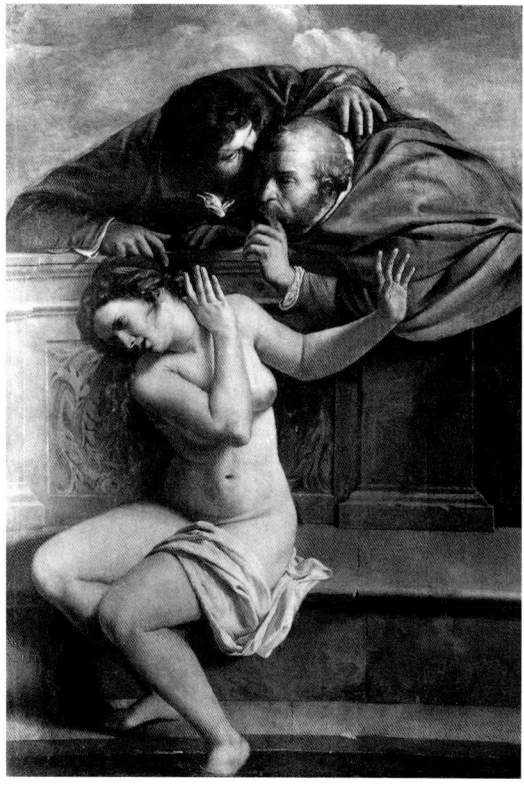

1.53 Artemisia Gentileschi, *Susanna and the Elders*, 1610. Oil on canvas, 66.9 × 47.6 in (170 × 121 cm). Count Schönborn Kunstsammlungen, Pommersfelden.

as well as a nipple, a detail almost always omitted by male artists. Orazio did not paint a female nude for several more years, and when he did, he was far less successful, a fact that argues against giving him any credit for this figure; it is therefore not hard to believe that Artemisia painted the rest of the picture. A few weaknesses—a failure to suggest the bulk of the elders' arms and shoulders beneath their drapery, the too smooth contours outlining their forms—also argue for her responsibility, even if her father will certainly have been watching and critiquing her progress. He was immensely proud of her, declaring in a letter written in 1612 that "having been active in the profession now for three years, [she] has learnt so much that I can dare to say that there are few equal to her, and that some major painters of our time cannot match her skills."[9]

Artemisia's *Susanna and the Elders* has attracted much comment. The story concerns a woman threatened with rape by two old men. Unless she gives in to them, they will publicly accuse her of adultery with a young man, which would result in her death. Susanna refused and her innocence was eventually proved. Those who see Artemisia as a proto-feminist argue that she identified with the apocryphal heroine's distress (some male artists have Susanna welcoming the advances of the elders), even though the painting predates her unfortunate affair with Agostino Tassi. Others see Artemisia as an ambitious young artist who does not identify with Susanna's plight but chose the subject as a way of showing off her ability to paint a convincing female body in a complex narrative. Significantly, Artemisia's Susanna has more of her body exposed than in any other artist's treatment of this subject produced in Rome before 1610, which suggests that stressing the protagonist's virtue was not her chief aim.

The only Caravaggesque element in this painting is its naturalism. Susanna is so close to the picture plane that we can touch her. A print by Annibale Carracci of *Susanna and the Elders* and another by Marcantonio Raimondi after Michelangelo's *Expulsion of Adam and Eve* on the Sistine Chapel ceiling both contributed to the twisting pose and gesture of rejection used by Artemisia for her heroine. Artemisia also knew that Cesari, Annibale Carracci, Domenichino, Rubens, and others had painted this subject in the past decade. Thus Artemisia's choice of the subject seems a calculated challenge to her male peers and an implied criticism of their inability to paint a convincing female figure.

In later works, Artemisia used Caravaggio's dark, impenetrable settings and flashes of light on figures in the front plane to tell dramatic stories effectively. Her two pictures of Judith decapitating Holofernes (Capodimonte, Naples; Uffizi, Florence) (well known and so not reproduced here) are modeled on his gory rendition (Palazzo Barberini, Rome) and make clear her admiration for his work and her willingness to be compared with him too. She also painted less violent moments in the apocryphal story of the Jewish heroine's life, including *Judith and her Handmaid with the Head of Holofernes* (Fig. 1.54). The figures are almost life-size. The deed has been done: the Assyrian general's head has been tucked into the sack and the two women pause, listening to see if the guards have been alerted, before they make their escape. The event took place at night, so the enveloping darkness is justified, but Artemisia decided, as many of Caravaggio's Northern followers did, to explain the light source. She shows a candle on the table to the left whose small flame could not have shed such strong light on Judith and her kneeling companion, especially on the latter's white turban. Both here and in her earlier treatments, the maid is a young and attractive woman; in Caravaggio's version, by contrast, she is a wrinkled crone, a foil for her mistress's beauty, reminding all women of their loss of beauty as they age.

Caravaggio made all artists think about light by eliminating most of it in his mature work. Night pictures are not unknown in earlier European art but they are rare—the best-known examples including works by Geertgen Tot Sint Jans, El Greco, and Correggio. Light—natural and artificial in all its infinite variety, dawn and dusk, indoors and outdoors, early morning and late afternoon as well as night—was explored by many artists after the shock treatment applied by Caravaggio. An important pioneer in this regard was the German painter Adam Elsheimer (1578–1610), who went to Rome in 1600 from Frankfurt via Venice and spent the rest of his short life there. He never received a public

commission and always painted on small silvered copper panels. He was nevertheless greatly admired by artists and surprisingly influential, given how difficult it was for most people to see his work in the original. News of his death at the age of thirty-two reached Rubens in 1611. He was distressed by this "most cruel news [. . .] which was very bitter to me." Rubens then declared:

I shall never regard with a friendly eye those who have brought him to so miserable an end. I pray that God will forgive Signor Adam his sin of sloth, by which he has deprived the world of the most beautiful things, caused himself much misery, and finally, I believe, reduced himself to despair; whereas with his own hands he could have built up a great fortune and made himself respected by all the world.[10]

He then told his correspondent that he wished he could afford the painting *The Flight into Egypt* that Elsheimer's widow was trying to sell off for 300 crowns.

That Elsheimer was reduced to penury in his last years is touchingly documented by a recently discovered drawing (Fig. **1.55**) that shows an artist seated at a cluttered table, his head in his hands as his children cry and search an empty cupboard for food. A pet dog sits on his haunches beside the distraught artist, patiently waiting for a table scrap but on the table there are only books, a globe, and a small statue of Mercury. The work that his widow was trying to sell, which is signed and dated 1609 on the back, is now Elsheimer's most famous and frequently reproduced painting (Fig. **1.56**); that he should have died without managing to sell it seems a cruel fate. It was taken to Holland by Count Hendrick Goudt, probably the person who "brought [Adam] to so miserable an end," who made a superb engraving of this painting and six others by Elsheimer. Whatever his dealings with the artist during his lifetime, Goudt's prints made his compositions and nocturnal light effects far more widely known and influential than would have been the case otherwise.

Elsheimer's *The Flight into Egypt* is above all a night landscape illuminated by the moon, stars, and the Milky Way, by the burning twigs carried by Joseph guiding the donkey with its precious cargo in the central foreground, and by a fire throwing sparks up into the sky on the left where

1.54 (opposite) Artemisia Gentileschi, *Judith and her Handmaid with the Head of Holofernes*, c. 1625. Oil on canvas, 72½ × 55¾ in (184 × 141.6 cm). Gift of Mr Leslie H. Green. Detroit Institute of Arts, MI.

1.55 Adam Elsheimer, *Destitute Artist with His Family*, c. 1605. Pen and ink drawing, 7⅛ × 7⅝ in (18.2 × 19.5 cm). Staatliche Graphische Sammlung, Munich.

1.56 Adam Elsheimer, *The Flight into Egypt*, 1609. Oil on copper, 12¼ × 16⅛ in (31 × 41 cm). Alte Pinakothek, Munich.

a shepherd family and their animals are sheltering. Great rounded masses of trees silhouetted against the deep blue sky recede into the distance on the right, where the still water of a small lake reflects the moon and the trees at its edge. This diagonal movement into depth from left to right is accented by the band of stars of the Milky Way, here depicted for the first time a year before Galileo published his observations proving that it is not some sort of heavenly steam but is entirely composed of stars. Elsheimer's night sky is not, however, scientifically correct. Such a bright moon would make the Milky Way invisible, and, were the moon just rising, as seems likely, the Milky Way would not be in this position either. Even that most familiar of constellations, the Great Bear in the upper right, is misplaced. None of this matters to the enchanted spectator of this nocturnal world through which the Holy Family is slowly traveling. Can they cross the water and shelter with the animals around the fire or will they continue their journey? Like Annibale Carracci's much larger panorama setting of the same story (see Fig. 1.37), the landscape lures our thoughts away from the figures to ponder their message for the world.

The Carracci Succession in Rome and Bologna

After 1600, Annibale's Roman workshop also attracted young Bolognese painters, already trained and even launched with a public commission or two in Bologna, who collaborated with him and, as his energies failed, assumed the major responsibility for executing his commissions. Of these, the most important was Domenico Zampieri, always known as Domenichino (1581–1641), who arrived in 1602 after starting his training with the ill-tempered Flemish artist Denis Calvaert, whom he left around 1595–6 to join the Accademia degli Incamminati on the advice of Agostino Carracci, a good friend of his father. There he became friendly with Francesco Albani (1578–1660) and Guido Reni (1575–1642), whose careers had followed a similar path, though Reni, a little older than they were, left the academy after a dispute with Ludovico in 1598 and never collaborated with Annibale. Domenichino had by 1603 made a few small easel pictures for Cardinal Pietro Aldobrandini and Monsignor Giovanni Battista Agucchi, both patrons with powerful connections (Cardinal

Pietro was a nephew of Pope Clement VIII and Agucchi was his *maggiordomo* or chief administrator). Agucchi became an especially important patron and supporter of Domenichino.

Domenichino first assisted Annibale by painting some of the small scenes in the decoration of the walls beneath the Galleria vault after its completion in 1600–01 using drawings by Annibale. The *Virgin and the Unicorn* over the central doorway (Fig. **1.57**) has the immediately recognizable facial type of Domenichino's women: a neat oval face with eyes that tilt up slightly at the outer edge, a straight nose, a small mouth, and hair pulled back from a central parting to give her forehead an inverted V at the hairline. When the gestures permit, he paints hands with the fingers carefully separated, as here in the hand caressing the unicorn's back. The beautifully realized landscape setting reveals Domenichino's sympathy for this genre. Some of his most appealing early works are small landscape paintings, some with genre themes (figures crossing a ford), some with a familiar religious subject such as the flight of the Holy Family. Other fresco commissions soon followed, notably the entire decoration of the Founders' Chapel at the abbey of Grottaferrata near Rome, for which Cardinal Odoardo Farnese's payments were as stingy as those to Annibale for the Galleria.

Most of Domenichino's later production was in fresco, always regarded as the most challenging medium for a painter, though he made altarpieces, easel paintings of mythological and religious subjects, occasional landscapes, and portraits on canvas as well. He quickly absorbed Annibale's Roman style, deliberately imitating it at first by making copies or close variants of a number of Annibale's later works. He understood how to pace and vary a large crowd of figures in a dramatic narrative, how to draw the viewer's attention to the important figures without destroying the overall unity of the composition, and how to make the particular state of mind of each participant clear. His arrangements of buildings or landscape elements behind the figures are tactfully scaled and placed to emphasize key figures. These might seem skills required of any competent painter, yet the ageing conservative

1.57 Domenico Zampieri Domenichino, *The Virgin and the Unicorn*, 1603–4. Fresco. Galleria, Palazzo Farnese, Rome.

Mannerists did not have them and Caravaggio mastered only some of them late in his career.

Domenichino was Caravaggio's artistic opposite, preparing every figure in his paintings almost obsessively: almost two thousand of his preparatory drawings have survived. Everything was planned before he started to paint. Domenichino studied his figures from models yet his characters never really seem as real as Caravaggio's always do. Instead he blends his studies from life with his knowledge of Roman reliefs, Raphael, and, above all, Annibale. His figures have a physiognomy peculiar to him, and, once familiar, they are as recognizable as those of Botticelli or Mantegna. Sometimes the same model can be recognized in different paintings by Caravaggio but when he changed models for roles such as old male saint or ugly executioner, their physiognomy changes too.

The commission that Domenichino received in 1612 to decorate the Polet Chapel in San Luigi dei Francesi, across the aisle from the Contarelli Chapel by Caravaggio, was his first opportunity to show his mature skills to a Roman audience. Except for the altarpiece, supplied by Reni, Domenichino did not share the commission with anyone. He provided a ceiling fresco of St. Cecilia ascending to heaven and, above the two large side wall paintings, small scenes of her coronation with St. Valerian, her newly converted

1.58 Domenico Zampieri Domenichino, *St. Cecilia Distributing Alms*, 1612–14. Fresco, 11 ft 2 in × 11 ft 2 in (3.40 × 3.40 m). S. Luigi dei Francesi, Rome.

spouse, and her refusal to sacrifice to pagan idols. The left-hand wall shows her martyrdom, a slow death in her own house after Roman soldiers botched her beheading. *St. Cecilia Distributing Alms* (Fig. **1.58**) fills the right wall. The saint is giving away clothes that had belonged to the recently martyred Valerian and his brother Tiburtius. A large crowd has gathered around a raised terrace with a simple balustrade where a crush of figures reach up to get the garments. Two boys collaborate, one climbing on the other's back in order to get their share. Small children are trying on adult clothes while their parents and grandparents watch fondly. Two boys fight in the foreground as their mother, handicapped by a baby in one arm, tries to stop them. Another woman seated in the foreground wants to exchange her garment with one held by a man on the left, whose hand gestures indicate that the exchange will take cash as well. The crowd is arranged in a roughly triangular shape that reaches almost three-quarters of the height of the fresco. A wall behind the figures, whose upper ledge is even with the upper edge of the terrace on which the saint stands, provides a stabilizing horizontal across the full width of the painting; there are other horizontal lines made by the steps on which the poor are assembled and the roof of a Roman temple just visible above the wall. The pagan gods on its pediment have their backs to the saint. The terrace provides the only emphatic vertical geometry in the composition. This grid not only allows us to understand the space occupied by this busy crowd and even to draw a ground plan of the walled enclosure where this scene is taking place; it also sets limits to their actions, subliminally calming what may at first seem a confusing rabble. Unlike Caravaggio's *Martyrdom of St. Matthew* (see Fig. **1.42**), however, every figure can be made out and their responses to the saint clearly understood. The measured clarity of the whole design, and even more so of the scene of Cecilia's martyrdom opposite, seem intended to show up the mystifying darkness and confusion of Caravaggio's *Martyrdom*.

When Domenichino was commissioned to paint the *Last Communion of St. Jerome* for San Girolamo della Carità in 1612 (Fig. **1.59**), he painted what is in effect a respectful critique

1.59 Domenico Zampieri Domenichino, *Last Communion of St. Jerome*, 1614. Oil on canvas, 13 ft 8 in × 8 ft 4 in (4.19 × 2.56 m). Pinacoteca, Vatican Museums, Rome.

of Agostino's altarpiece (see Fig. **1.23**). He had returned to Bologna in 1612 for a visit, so his memories of Agostino's interpretation were fresh. A decade later, Domenichino's altarpiece provoked a rival to accuse him of copying Agostino rather than inventing his own composition. At first glance, it seems to be a retread in reverse of Agostino's altarpiece, but an important difference between them is immediately apparent: Domenichino's painting has far fewer figures. This is, in fact, partly an illusion. The crowd of spectators looks much smaller but there are still eight figures to Agostino's eleven, pushed out to the sides, however, or half hidden in a central pool of shadow in order to give more emphasis to St. Jerome and the priest in his golden chasuble. By moving St. Jerome into the light and keeping the space between him and the priest a dark void that draws attention to the white spot of the sacred wafer, the psychological and formal focus of the painting, Domenichino creates a dramatic tension that is absent from Agostino's crowded composition. The angels in the upper right (four to Agostino's two) create an arc of movement

The Carracci Succession in Rome and Bologna

that also leads the eye to the saint, who seems to summon all his failing strength to remain upright as he receives the host. The shadowed profile and straight back of the young acolyte kneeling beside the priest convey his rapt attention. A second priest behind him lowers his head too, watching and waiting to offer a sip of wine to St. Jerome from a chalice.

A wide, tall arch behind the figures relieves the claustrophobic compression of the earlier painting by allowing a wider landscape vista beyond. There is even room for St. Jerome's faithful lion, whose snout and claws just make it into the right edge of Agostino's canvas. Domenichino's first Roman altarpiece is proudly signed and dated in the foreground. It was greatly admired and frequently copied, despite Lanfranco's attempts to denigrate it in the 1620s by circulating a print by François Perrier of Agostino's version of the composition. This move was intended to make Domenichino look like a plagiarist unworthy of the commission to decorate the apse of Sant'Andrea della Valle. Lanfranco succeeded only in getting the commission to paint the dome (see Fig. 1.63), but not the apse or pendentives below of the four evangelists. Domenichino took great pains to make these powerfully effective figures, much easier to read from the ground than those in the distant heaven of Lanfranco.

Domenichino rarely painted mythological subjects after assisting in the Farnese Galleria but two major commissions from the Aldobrandini family—a cycle of frescoes about Apollo for their country villa at Frascati and, for their Roman palace, a painting of the *Archery Contest of Diana and her Nymphs* (Fig. 1.60)—gave the artist two important opportunities around 1615. The frescoes from the Sala di Apollo (National Gallery, London), long detached from their damp original home in a garden grotto, have majestic landscape settings that later inspired both Claude and Poussin. The huntress and her companions, however, dominate this ambitious painting, which shows them engaged in an archery contest. The target is a bird tethered to a pole on the right. One archer has lodged an arrow at the top of the pole, another has severed the string holding the bird, and the winner has shot the poor creature through the head. Diana lifts her own bow and scabbard in a gesture of triumphant praise, glancing at the victor, who wears a crimson stole over her peach pink skirt. The eleven lightly dressed nymphs who surround them react in various ways to this outcome. Other nymphs

1.60 Domenico Zampieri Domenichino, *Archery Contest of Diana and her Nymphs*, 1616. Oil on canvas, 7 ft 4 in × 10 ft 6 in (2.25 × 3.2 m). Galleria Borghese, Rome.

in the distance wrestle, run, and blow a horn. In the foreground one nymph undresses, preparing to join two others in the water, one of whom floats fetchingly on the surface, eyeing us instead of paying attention to the archery contest. A large hunting dog, which has detected the pair of spying shepherds in the bushes on the right edge, is restrained by a nymph in the center of the picture. Another dog drinks the water.

None of the myths about Diana mentions such an event. Moreover, if Diana and her companions were shown near water, it was when the unfortunate Actaeon stumbled on them bathing. Diana changed him into a stag for intruding into their private domain, and his own dogs devoured him. Despite the fig-leaf explanation of all pictures of beautiful women as metaphors for both art and beauty, the story of Actaeon was clearly a pretext for a painting full of exposed female flesh for the delectation of male patrons. Furthermore, it was a popular enough subject that the sophisticated visitors to this collection would, on seeing Domenichino's picture, have recalled such works immediately and wondered what the artist was trying to do by inventing this fictitious contest and clothing most of the nymphs. Was it intended as a discreet image of beautiful women—all of them sworn to remain chaste—suitable for a cardinal's house? It was to join Titian's rambunctious *Bacchus and Ariadne* (now National Gallery, London) and *Bacchanal of the Andrians* (see Fig. 1.118) in the Aldobrandini collection, but Cardinal Scipione Borghese stepped in, pulled rank as the papal nephew, and took it for his own collection.

The *Archery Contest* was a work to which the artist attached great significance, as is indicated by its size (over ten feet [3 m] wide), the invention of a new subject for a familiar goddess, and the large number of figures. Agucchi probably suggested using the description of a tethered bird shooting contest in Book V of Virgil's *Aeneid* as the focus of the nymphs' activities. The nymphs usually loll around a forest pool and react in mock horror to the arrival of Actaeon. Here they engage in a serious athletic contest. *Invenzione* is displayed not only by the theme but by the variety of poses, costumes, and features of the women. Domenichino's ability to handle *colore*, the forte of Venetian painters, would have been considered too had his canvas been displayed beside Titian's *Bacchanals*. The tempered eroticism and subdued color scheme are enlivened by a few brilliantly colored clothes worn by Diana and the most important nymphs.

Domenichino next went to Fano to decorate a chapel in the cathedral, and then to Bologna, where he painted two enormous altarpieces and some private commissions. He returned to Rome when the Bolognese Gregory XV, Alessandro Ludovisi, was elected pope in 1621, as did several other Bolognese artists, knowing that they would get the first pick of new commissions. He was succeeded only two years later by Urban VIII, whose family was Florentine. Some Bolognese artists left for home but Domenichino had commissions and remained.

The decoration of the apse and transepts of the Theatines' new church was begun as soon as construction was completed in 1623. Lanfranco began the dome in 1625 and finished it in 1627 (see Fig. 1.63). Domenichino had made plans for a dome fresco before he lost the job to Lanfranco but the area assigned to him nevertheless was extensive (Fig. **1.61**). It was his most important Roman commission and occupied him from 1625 to 1628. He treated the section over the choir as a broad horizontal band with one large rectangular picture field in the center, and then divided the apse into wedges, yielding three large but irregularly shaped picture fields on concave surfaces. These four frescoes show the Baptist pointing out Christ in the distance to Sts. Peter and Andrew (choir fresco); Christ calling Peter and Andrew from their fishing boat to be fishers of men (the central apse image); the flagellation of Andrew before his martyrdom (the left picture field in the apse); and St. Andrew kneeling to adore the cross on which he will be martyred (right field). The saint's ascent to heaven is shown in the small semicircular space at the summit of the apse where it joins the choir. The scenes are framed by broad bands of gilded stucco decoration with plaster statues of herms who seem to support the U-shaped bands of classicizing decoration that frame the scene of Andrew's ascent to heaven. The spaces beside the three apse windows are filled with illusionistic depictions of six theological virtues, among them the unusual Voluntary Poverty, who overturns a vase of coins that seems

1.61 Domenico Zampieri Domenichino, *Vault of the Tribune*, 1625–28. Fresco. S. Andrea della Valle, Rome.

to spill into the viewer's space. She was chosen to emphasize the Theatines' strict vows of poverty, which denied them any personal possessions. The entire decoration is well proportioned for its setting and easy to understand. The narrative scenes are all *quadri riportati*, that is, no adjustment is made in them for the spectator's low point of vision. Only the saint ascending to heaven is foreshortened slightly but not to the degree that Lanfranco used for his figures in the dome.

The *Calling of Sts. Peter and Andrew*, which can be seen at the lower center of the apse view here, shows Christ standing on the shore with his right arm extended toward the boat which a young man with an oar is maneuvering. His pose is momentarily precarious but safe, if he steps back into the boat. St. Andrew is stopped in midflight as if he was running forward when Christ's message struck him. St. Peter must have been climbing out of the boat to pull in his nets when he too was stopped. Andrew's arms are spread wide as he welcomes Christ's message but Peter has his right hand on his chest like St. Matthew in Caravaggio's *The Calling* scene (see Fig. 1.41) as if still unsure that this message is meant for him.

The quietly commanding figure of Christ echoes his counterpart in the Contarelli Chapel too. Preparatory drawings show that Domenichino began with a different design: the two saints were seated in the boat, in no danger of falling into Lake Galilee; these active yet frozen poses were deliberately chosen to emphasize the miraculous conversion of the two fishermen to Christ when he asked them to follow him.

Domenichino moved to Naples in 1631, where his skills as a fresco painter were employed in the Cathedral of San Gennaro, despite the jealousy of Neapolitan artists, who did not then have a strong school of their own fresco painters. Lanfranco was also working there then, so their rivalry persisted for another decade. According to his widow, Domenichino's death in 1641 was from poisoning; he left his wife and their daughter a considerable sum of money. He was almost sixty. His last unfinished altarpiece for the cathedral was replaced with one by Ribera (see p. 194). Many writers, past and present, prefer Domenichino's work before 1630 to his Neapolitan phase. These later frescoes lack the clarity of his Roman work for he apparently felt pressure to add more figures to keep up with Lanfranco, who was more skillful at weaving a web of airborne figures together. At all events, it was Domenichino's work in Rome that earned him the reputation as Annibale's true successor who passed on the baton of classicism to Poussin and Maratta. He remained in the canon of artists who should be studied by all serious painters well into the nineteenth century, though John Ruskin despised him and the Carracci, even declaring that "there is no entirely sincere or great art in the seventeenth century."[11] By 1901, when Mary Cassatt sought out his work in Rome, she wondered to her travel companion, the collector Louisine Havemeyer, that he was so little known.

Giovanni Lanfranco, Domenichino's great rival in the 1620s and 1630s, was born in Terenzo near Parma in 1582. He is first recorded working with Agostino Carracci for Duke Ranuccio Farnese in July 1600 in the Palazzo del Giardino, Parma. Correggio's dome frescoes in Parma proved crucial to Lanfranco's artistic formation. When Agostino died in 1602, Lanfranco went to Rome and joined Annibale's workshop. Apart from a short spell in Piacenza after Annibale's death, his subsequent career took place mainly in Rome until 1633–4, when he moved to Naples. There his talents as a ceiling fresco painter found expression in the Certosa di San Martino, the cathedral, and elsewhere. He returned to Rome in 1646, hoping finally to paint the Benediction Loggia ceiling in St. Peter's, for which he had prepared ambitious designs during the papacy of Paul V (1605–21), but he died the following year. He completed one more heavenly vision in the apse of San Carlo ai Catinari in Rome, sealing his reputation as Correggio's true successor and a key figure in the development of illusionistic ceiling frescoes, among the most spectacular and characteristic creations in Italy in the seventeenth century.

Lanfranco's altarpieces are well designed for viewing from a distance with strong lighting that looks both natural and miraculous. His backgrounds are not as dark as those of Caravaggio, nor is his lighting as patchy and haphazard as that of Guercino. The *Virgin and Child with Saints Charles Borromeo and Bartholomew* (Fig. **1.62**), painted for San Lorenzo, Piacenza, around 1616, displays Lanfranco's characteristic luminosity. It brightens the left side of St. Charles and the right side of St. Bartholomew but leaves the two small angels between them mainly in shadow. One of them points to the knife and skin of the saint lying on a stone with a carved decoration, an allusion to his martyrdom by being flayed alive after his refusal to worship pagan idols. The airborne Virgin and Child on their cloud bank above are lit from the left but silhouetted by the yellow radiance of heaven behind them. This lighting is illogical but pictorially effective, keeping the viewer's attention on the two saints who point to heaven and demonstrate the appropriate devotional response. The pose of St. Charles Borromeo is inspired by that of St. Dominic in Ludovico Carracci's *Madonna dei Bargellini* (see Fig. 1.13), while the Madonna and Child with angels recall Correggio's frescoes. The saints are natural without being plebeian, the Virgin beautiful as she gazes affectionately at Christ.

1.62 Giovanni Lanfranco, *Virgin and Child with Saints Charles Borromeo and Bartholomew*, c. 1616. Oil on canvas, 93¾ × 58¼ in (238 × 148 cm). National Museum of Capodimonte, Naples.

As explained above, Lanfranco had taken the commission to paint the *Assumption of the Virgin* (Fig. **1.63**) away from Domenichino. It became his most famous work. He located the Virgin near the lower edge of the drum so that she can be seen by worshipers as they move up the aisle. Photographed from directly beneath, as this work usually is, the figures shrink and become impossible to disentangle but in the church itself, the viewer who stands back and moves in a circle can follow the compositional flow and pick out some saints and apostles in the lowest register of figures. The design ingeniously incorporates the interruption of the domed surface by the lantern at its summit through the painted garland around its perimeter, which makes it seem to float in space below the rest of the figures that recede behind it. Cortona used this solution for his dome fresco in the Chiesa Nuova in the 1650s. The cloud banks supporting unevenly spaced groups of figures receding into the empyrean combine both the casual formations of actual clouds with enough compositional order hinting at receding rows to give the design some structure. Few of the figures are easily identified from the ground but the general effect is impressive. Bellori compared the result to a harmonious choir and even thought the stylistic contrast between it and Domenichino's forceful pendentives enhanced the final result to the benefit of both painters.

Guido Reni (1575–1642), who reached Rome from Bologna in 1601, was older than either Domenichino or Lanfranco, and he never joined Annibale's studio there. His father, who directed the choir in the cathedral, hoped that his son would also become a musician but Guido must have displayed artistic talent early and began his training in Denys Calvaert's shop around 1590. Like Domenichino, Reni found Calvaert difficult and left him to join Ludovico's studio around 1595. He carried out his first public commission in 1596 and competed successfully against Ludovico and others for a commission in 1598 to provide decorations for Bologna during a visit by Clement VIII.

Reni's first public commission, a *Coronation of the Virgin with Four Saints* of 1596, is closely

1.63 Giovanni Lanfranco, *Assumption of the Virgin*, 1625–28. Fresco. S. Andrea della Valle, Rome.

modeled on Raphael's *Vision of St. Cecilia* (both Pinacoteca Nazionale, Bologna), his only work in Bologna. When Reni left Bologna in 1601, he took a copy of Raphael's altarpiece with him, and his first patron in Rome, Cardinal Sfondrato, installed it on the altar of the Polet Chapel in San Luigi dei Francesi, where it remains below Domenichino's frescoes (see Fig. 1.58). Reni's early affection for Raphael was strengthened by the experience of seeing his frescoes in the Vatican as well as more altarpieces and works by him in private collections. He found in Raphael's paintings a perfect model for an art that strove to represent an ideal based on nature but not on unmediated reality. So intent was he on creating beautiful people that his devils and executioners are as handsome as other artists' saints. He soon became known for images of young women—female saints, the Virgin, and an occasional Cleopatra or Lucrezia—their eyes raised to heaven, as he himself later boasted, "in a thousand different ways."[12]

One of Reni's first public commissions in Rome was a *Crucifixion of St. Peter* (Fig. **1.64**), painted three years after Caravaggio's treatment in the Cerasi Chapel. Reni's version also reduces the cast of characters to three men raising the saint on his cross, illuminates them dramatically, and suggests that the event is taking place on a dark night, so the influence of Caravaggio seems undeniable. Caravaggio thought so too, supposedly accosting Reni and accusing him of stealing his ideas. Nevertheless, the moonlit clouds behind the figures suggest space unlike his rival's blank background. Reni also gives his executioners more dignified poses than those in Caravaggio's painting.

Reni gradually shed the influence of Ludovico for that of Raphael and the antique. By 1607–8, he was painting frescoes in the Vatican for Cardinal Scipione Borghese, and, in 1609–12, an entire chapel dedicated to the Annunciation for the pope in the Palazzo Quirinale. The altarpiece of *The Annunciation* (Fig. **1.65**) exemplifies in its simplicity, symmetry, and serenity the ideal visions of angels and young Virgins for which Reni became famous. The semicircle of hand-holding baby angels who fill the summit of the painting and accompany the dove of the Holy Spirit on its mission from heaven are beautifully choreographed and lighten the mood of this otherwise somber interpretation. The ceiling frescoes above the altarpiece, especially the dome where the Virgin ascends to heaven, show that Reni, unlike Lanfranco, was not comfortable with this kind of assignment. After one more attempt in Bologna (the *Glory of St. Dominic* in San Domenico, 1613–15), which was criticized for its inadequate foreshortening, he avoided ceilings and frescoes for the rest of his career.

1.64 Guido Reni, *Crucifixion of St. Peter*, 1604–5. Oil on canvas. Pinacoteca, Vatican Museums, Rome.

The Carracci Succession in Rome and Bologna 65

1.65 Guido Reni, *The Annunciation*, 1609–11. Oil on canvas, 6 ft 6 in × 11 ft 6 in (2 × 3.5 m). Cappella dell'Annunziata, Palazzo del Quirinale, Rome.

One of Reni's most famous and admired paintings is, however, a ceiling fresco, the *Aurora* (Fig. **1.66**), completed in 1614 for Cardinal Scipione's summer house in the garden of his palace across the road from the Palazzo Quirinale. Here Reni made no attempt to suggest that Apollo and his chariot are passing overhead. Instead the scene is given an elegant gilded plaster frame and isolated in the center of an otherwise plain ceiling, the most literal example of a *quadro riportato* produced in seventeenth-century Rome. The horizon level places the viewer at roughly knee level of the dancing women: the viewer can just see the belly of the nearest horse. Imagine Cardinal Scipione reclining on a daybed below: he could have gazed up at the nicely rounded forms of the Hours who dance alongside the chariot as it slowly rises into the sky following Aurora as she floats ahead of them, scattering flowers in their path. Although Reni's Hours seem inspired by the pure classicism of the Parthenon friezes, Greek monuments were still hardly known in Italy at this time. His classical sources were Roman derivations of Greek reliefs. Reni himself later insisted fervently to some admirers, who believed that he simply pulled his images from his imagination, that he had studied ancient sculpture assiduously for eight years in order to distill the concepts of beauty on which his art was based. If we look at ancient reliefs and then back again at Reni, his women look wonderfully robust and energetic. Even the most "classical" of seventeenth-century art is also based on a solid grasp of the human body and of chiaroscuro. As a result, the figures of Reni and his fellow devotees of antique models have far more substance than those of their Renaissance predecessors.

By 1615 Reni had moved back to Bologna and by 1620 he was the most sought after painter in Europe, with patrons from Genoa, Ravenna, Naples, and Rome, and soon from Madrid, Paris, and Warsaw as well. Three commissions—a major altarpiece, a large mythological painting, and a full-length portrait—carried out around 1630 show him at his best. The *Pala della Peste* was made for the city of Bologna in the aftermath of a devastating outbreak of bubonic plague in 1629–30 (Fig. **1.67**). Made for San Domenico, it was to be carried in procession every year on

1.66 (above) Guido Reni, *Aurora*, 1614. Fresco. Casino Pallavicini Rospigliosi, Rome.

1.67 (below) Guido Reni, *Virgin and Child with Patron Saints of Bologna (Pala della Peste)*, 1631. Oil on silk, 12 ft 6 in × 7 ft 10 in (3.82 × 2.42 m). Pinacoteca Nazionale, Bologna.

The Carracci Succession in Rome and Bologna **67**

December 10, the Feast of the Rosary, as a means of protecting the city from further outbreaks. Every patron saint of the city appears below the Virgin, who is seated on a cloud bank that has settled on a moonbow. The city's bishop saint, Petronius, wearing a magnificent embroidered golden cope, fills the lower left foreground, looking up to heaven and gesturing to the city below where, beneath gray skies, bodies are being carried out of the city for burial. St. Dominic echoes St. Petronius's actions on the right. The other saints include the two founders of the Jesuit Order, Ignatius of Loyola and Francis Xavier, with St. Francis in the center between Petronius and Dominic, and two local warrior saints, Florian and Proculus.

The *Pala della Peste*, which is over 13 feet (4 meters) high, is painted on a heavy silk cloth. It is one of Reni's most carefully executed and best preserved works. The vertical picture field is divided into heavenly and earthly zones, united by a background of various grays that suggest an approaching thunderstorm, a metaphor for the plague that decimated the city's population (and that of many other Italian cities). A contemporary reported that "every street held funerals, and every house was filled with weeping and fear. [. . .] entire families perished [. . .] the city seemed a widow, desolated."[13] The light blue and rose pink garments of the Virgin set against a warm yellow haze offer the faithful the promise of heavenly release from this grim reality. The Virgin on her cloud bank and the symmetrical grouping of the patron saints below are both arranged to create a V shape so that we can imagine her descending into the space left between Sts. Petronius and Dominic. There is little real color used for the saints—a little rose on the lining of Ignatius's chasuble and Petronius's beautiful golden cope, and on St. Francis Xavier's stole. Otherwise Reni limited himself to white, grays, black, and flesh tones. The subtly varied symmetry of the saints' positions and poses and their carefully graduated degrees of importance reflect two centuries of experimentation by Italian artists making altarpieces uniting the Virgin with the men and women whose lives seemed exemplary to the Catholic Church. Reni knew that tradition well, acknowledged it, and here surpassed all but the finest examples of the *sacra conversazione* altarpiece in a work that the citizens of Bologna have admired ever since. In the eighteenth century, it was replaced in the church by a copy so that the original could be more easily appreciated in the Palazzo Pubblico in the city center.

Reni rarely painted portraits but when called on to do so for an important patron, could produce a spectacular image. While the full-length portrait was a format originally reserved for royalty (although the Lombard nobility had used it in the sixteenth century), and even the popes had kept to a simpler knee-length format since Raphael used it for Julius II in 1513, two

1.68 Guido Reni, *Cardinal Bernardino Spada*, 1630–31. Oil on canvas, 89⅓ × 57⅝ in (227 × 147 cm). Galleria Spada, Rome.

1.69 Guido Reni, *The Abduction of Helen*, 1631. Oil on canvas, 8 ft 4 in × 8 ft 7 in (2.53 × 2.65 m). Louvre, Paris.

cardinals commissioned full-length portraits from Reni, the first in 1625 (*Cardinal Roberto Ubaldini*, Los Angeles County Museum), and the other in 1630–31, *Cardinal Bernardino Spada* (Fig. **1.68**), who succeeded Ubaldini as Papal Legate to Bologna in 1627. Reni was famous for his depiction of drapery, a skill displayed to great effect here. Both show the subject seated in a velvet-padded, straight-backed chair beside a table with hints of palatial splendor behind them. Cardinal Spada's study is furnished with silk and velvet hangings and a wall unit of small cubicles for storing documents. Pausing during the writing of a letter, he regards the viewer calmly. He is in complete control of his life and utterly sure of his position in the world. Both portraits have spectacular color schemes: that of Spada has pinks and whites set against gray-rose, while that of Ubaldini has stronger pinks and crimson backed by wine and dark plum; the crimson biretta (the cardinal's hat) is painted in the pure color played out in light and dark variations throughout both canvases. The looser, more spontaneous paint handling of van Dyck's full-length portrait of *Cardinal Guido Bentivoglio* (see Fig. 2.42), another symphony in clashing reds, offers a revealing contrast in styles for an identical commission.

Cardinal Spada was instrumental in persuading Reni to complete *The Abduction of Helen* (Fig. **1.69**), commissioned for Philip IV by the Spanish Ambassador to the Vatican, Conde Onate, when Reni made a brief visit to Rome in 1627. Onate had also ordered an *Immaculate Conception* (Metropolitan Museum, New York) for the Infanta but Reni had retired in a huff to Bologna with the picture after Onate had pressured him to finish, then dragged out the

The Carracci Succession in Rome and Bologna 69

1.70 Guido Reni, *The Archangel Michael*, 1635. Oil on silk, 9 ft 7 in × 6 ft 7 in (2.93 × 2.02 m). Sta. Maria della Concezione, Rome.

payments. When Spada posed for his portrait, he would praise the *Helen*, urging the artist to finish it for the honor it would do the profession and Italy. Thus gently encouraged, Reni completed what instantly became a celebrated picture. Malvasia reported that "the applause with which it was viewed was, we can only say, little less than adoring. Entire groups converged [...], even from surrounding cities." Sonnets were even written in its honor but it was not sent to Spain. It was shipped instead to Paris because Marie de' Medici hoped to acquire it. By the time the painting reached Paris, however, she had gone into exile. It was acquired instead by Louis Phélipeaux de la Vrillière, one of the richest men in Paris. Recently cleaned, the painting can be appreciated in all its cool splendor and restrained elegance.

Given that Helen is being abducted—an event that other artists showed her protesting strenuously—Reni's staging of the event is strangely tranquil. Paris grasps her limp left hand as they walk toward the shore as if going for a stroll. Three women accompany her, one carrying a small chest of jewels, another a tiny dog, while a young black servant with a marmoset on a leash gazes up at her blonde beauty. Pietro da Cortona is said to have mocked another mythological painting by Reni, calling it "il quadro della processione" (the procession picture), an insult appropriate to the surprising decorum of this abduction. Reni was famously misogynist. While the various ways in which his repressed sexual nature is reflected in his work is a complex subject recently explored by Richard Spear, it is apparent that Reni avoided erotic themes if possible and, when he could not (as on this occasion when the commission came from a king), found ways to diffuse the sexually charged nature of such stories.

Urban VIII and his nephews Cardinals Francesco and Antonio Barberini had long sought a major work from Reni. The pope had offered him the chance to paint a large altarpiece in St. Peter's of Christ giving the keys to St. Peter. Despite the singular importance of the location—the space now occupied by Bernini's *Cattedra Petri* (see Fig. 1.110)—Reni gave up this chance when he left Rome in 1627. A new opportunity soon came when the Capuchins' new church, Santa Maria della Concezione, paid for by the Barberini, was ready for decoration in 1630. They ordered altarpieces from Lanfranco, Domenichino, Andrea Sacchi, Pietro da Cortona, and others. Reni was commissioned to paint *The Archangel Michael* (Fig. **1.70**) for the first altar on the right. Knowing that it would be compared with works by a younger group of painters then enjoying great success in Rome, and that Michael was the pope's patron saint, Reni took special pains with this work, for which he again chose a silk canvas.

Raphael had painted *St. Michael* (Louvre, Paris) toward the end of his career in 1518 for Francis I. Raphael's painting, whose design was known in Italy, shows a powerful young man balanced like a dancer with his right leg planted on the back of the cowering devil and with a spear held in both hands ready to plunge downwards. The saint seems in mid-flight, his stability momentary. Reni's saint has landed and is in full control, his right foot set on a smooth rock, his left planted on the devil's head. He holds chains in his left hand and an unsheathed sword pointing downwards in his raised right hand. His muscular torso is encased in a skin-tight blue body armor *all'antica* and draped in a salmon pink stole that sweeps around him. The head attached to this magnificent body is surprisingly small, young, and sweet. The devil is a balding lout with the build of a wrestler. The intentional contrast between pure good and pure evil is depicted in exemplary fashion. Still, some of Reni's contemporaries found the archangel effeminate.

After delivering his *St. Michael*, Reni wrote to the chamberlain of Urban VIII that he wished he had had:

an Angel's brush or forms from Paradise when creating the Archangel, and to have seen him in heaven, but I could not reach such heights and I sought him in vain on earth. So I depended instead on forms whose Idea I had established for myself. One may also find the Idea of ugliness, but that I leave to the Devil to bring out because I myself flee it even in thought, nor do I care even to occupy my mind with it.

It is indeed difficult to find anything that might be called ugly in Reni's work, even the devil depicted here. Curiously, his splayed foreshortened left hand repeats that of Caravaggio's Holofernes as he is being beheaded by Judith (Palazzo Barberini, Rome). Did Reni mean viewers who knew both works to see in his not only Good conquering Evil but Good Art subduing Bad Art?

Reni's *Ecce Homo* (Fig. **1.71**) is a fine example of his smaller devotional paintings made in his late years for private patrons; the finish,

1.71 Guido Reni, *Ecce Homo*, c. 1640. Oil on canvas, 44½ × 37⅜ in (113 × 95.2 cm). Fitzwilliam Museum, Cambridge, England.

1.72 G.F. Barbieri (Il Guercino), *Guiseppe Gaetano Righetti (?) Presented to the Virgin by Four Saints*, c. 1616–17. Oil on canvas, 10 ft 2 in × 6 ft 3 in (3.09 × 1.92 m). Musées Royaux des Beaux-Arts de Belgique, Brussels.

while not as densely worked as before, is resolved throughout. A somber mood is created by the brown background which is relieved only slightly by the rays of light emanating from Christ's head and a faint aura of light along his left shoulder. His muted rose cloak provides the only color in what would otherwise be a cream and brown monochrome. Christ faces right in three-quarter view, holding a bamboo staff with a broken tip in his left hand and fingering the cloak with his right hand, in both cases with gestures that seem effortless and so communicate his passive response to the cruel mocking that just preceded

this moment. This is not, however, a narrative picture. The story of Christ's Passion has no such moment because he was constantly surrounded by soldiers and spectators. Reni painted a vision of Christ come to earth to face believing viewers and remind them of his sacrifice. He seems exhausted and absorbed in his own thoughts. His torso is hardly marked by the soldiers' ropes; only a few drops of blood from the thickly woven crown of thorns can be seen on his face, neck, and shoulders. Reni's blend of the ideal with the real is here perfectly resolved.

The last of the artists born north of the Apennines and formed by the Carracci studio in Bologna before making his name in Rome was Giovanni Francesco Barbieri (1591–1666), always known by his nickname Guercino (squint-eyed). This malady did not prevent him from developing a wonderfully idiosyncratic blend of Ludovico Carracci's dramatic chiaroscuro and the dark, saturated colors of Jacopo Tintoretto and Jacopo Bassano. Guercino's figures do look more like peasants than noblemen in his early works, though this aspect of his style, as well as his juicy colors and brilliant contrasts of light and dark were considerably muted in his later paintings. Born in the small town of Cento, which lies halfway between Bologna and Ferrara, he was trained locally by artists who could teach him little except basic knowledge of materials. It was the work of Ludovico Carracci that was crucial to his early artistic formation. In the year of Guercino's birth, Ludovico sent his altarpiece the *Virgin and Child with Saints Joseph and Francis* to a church in Cento. Guercino later referred to it as his artistic mother ("la sua Cara cinna"), words that are not only assonant with Carracci but mean wetnurse. He studied the work of Ferrarese artists and then sought out Ludovico in Bologna. There is no formal record of Guercino's apprenticeship but he was clearly familiar with the master's paintings and drawings. Ludovico praised Guercino in a letter to an agent in 1617 as "a great draughtsman and an felicitous colorist: he's a freak of nature, and a miracle who astonishes all who see his work. I'll say nothing more: he'll make the finest painters look like fools; you'll see when you return."[14]

In 1616 Guercino began an altarpiece for Sant'Agostino, Cento, the *Guiseppe Gaetano*

Righetti (?) Presented to the Virgin by Four Saints (Fig. **1.72**). It demonstrates both his gifts as a colorist and his mastery of the Carracci reform of the *sacra conversazione* altarpiece. St. Augustine's red cloak on the right captures the viewer's attention first: the Virgin looks down at him too. He looks at her and points at the elegantly dressed (unknown) donor kneeling in the foreground. Just behind him kneels St. Joseph, probably the donor's name saint. Behind Joseph is St. Louis, who directs our attention back to heaven, and St. Francis, seen behind St. Augustine, the only person apart from the young donor who is absorbed in prayer. In the shadows behind St. Louis is a thick column more like those in Titian's *Pesaro Altarpiece* (see Fig. 1.12) than the slimmer ones in Ludovico's *Madonna dei Bargellini* (see Fig. 1.13), suggesting that Guercino must have been to Venice by now. The arrangement of the saints and donor shows awareness of other models by the Carracci, yet the grouping looks so fresh and informal in Guercino's painting that the similarity of gestures seems more accidental than borrowed. It is the dramatic chiaroscuro and particular palette of Guercino that declare his independence and originality. Here this "felicissimo coloritore" uses indigo blues, plum and ruby red, a gray that seems tinged with violet, and a dark ocher, all accented with white. Transitions from light to dark are blurred with patches of *sfumato* so that the transient lighting—a sort of dappled patchwork of chiaroscuro that suggests it was made by small clouds scudding past on a windy day—enlivens the entire picture surface. Like Caravaggio's extreme contrasts of light and dark, Guercino's lighting is impossible to explain as it resembles neither daylight nor the available sources of artificial light. All the key figures are, however, picked out with patches of light, especially their heads and hands.

While most of Guercino's paintings are religious, he did produce a few mythological and poetical subjects. For Marcello Provenzale of Cento Guercino painted *Erminia Discovering the Wounded Tancred* in 1618 (Fig. **1.73**), a popular subject from Tasso's epic poem *Gerusalemme Liberata*. The Christian knight lies

1.73 G.F. Barbieri (Il Guercino), *Erminia Discovering the Wounded Tancred*, 1618. Oil on canvas, 57 × 73⅝ in (145 × 187 cm). Galleria Doria Pamphili, Rome.

wounded, his page Vafrino hovering over him as his distraught lover, Erminia, rushes to his side, her skirts and scarves rippling out behind her. Guercino has used his favorite indigo blue-plum-chocolate palette with patchy lighting that spotlights Erminia's gesture of alarm and the blood on Tancred's bare chest. Much of his head is in shadow, as is hers. The head of her horse peers out from the right. Like Caravaggio, Guercino pushed the figures close to the viewer, almost blocking out the world beyond them, though clouds, sky, and a few trees are visible. Erminia is a robust but striking woman with dark hair, very different from the classical beauties in Reni's paintings; Tancred too is a muscular hero with powerful legs whose bulging contours look nothing like the slender limbs of the Apollo Belvedere. Poussin later treated the same subject very differently (see Fig. 4.37).

Soon Guercino began receiving commissions from patrons in Ferrara and Bologna. In 1617–18 Guercino painted a number of easel pictures for Cardinal Alessandro Ludovisi, including a *Susanna and the Elders* (Prado, Madrid), and others for Cosimo II de' Medici in Florence and Cardinal Jacopo Serra, the papal legate in Ferrara, who invited the artist to work there. Serra had been Rubens's most eloquent advocate in Rome, helping him to obtain the commission to paint the high altar of the Chiesa Nuova. That he should have admired Guercino's work and encouraged him is thus of particular interest.

When Cardinal Alessandro Ludovisi became Gregory XV in 1621, many Bolognese artists moved to Rome, knowing that the pope and his nephew, Cardinal Ludovico Ludovisi, would turn to them first for major commissions. Guercino joined the exodus and was not disappointed. He was awarded one of the largest altarpieces in St. Peter's, a ceiling painting for San Crisogono in Trastevere, and the decoration of two ceilings in Cardinal Ludovisi's garden retreat near the Porta Pinciana. Cardinal Ludovisi knew Reni's *Aurora* (see Fig. 1.66), finished seven years earlier for Cardinal Scipione Borghese's Casino. When he commissioned Guercino to paint the same subject in his new Casino (Fig. **1.74**), both artist and patron knew that comparisons would be made. While both patrons probably chose the theme to suggest the dawn of a new era, Cardinal Scipione did not have this bit of mythological propaganda created until his uncle's papacy was almost a decade old. Ludovisi lost no time ordering an Aurora for his garden house immediately after acquiring it in June 1621. Agostino Tassi, a specialist in *quadratura* (illusionistic architectural settings for narrative frescoes by other painters), received his first payment a month later and the whole fresco was finished that year.

Reni's *Aurora* is a close to flawless *quadro riportato*, while the ceiling by Guercino and Tassi demonstrates how *quadratura* and a *di sotto in su* viewpoint can work together to suggest that the ceiling above has vanished and been replaced with a parade of figures passing overhead. Tassi provided a substantial entablature supported by piers that flank imaginary openings in front of and opposite the ideal viewpoint that match doorways in the wall below. Aurora is placed with her chariot and horses in the center of this expansive opening, surging ahead on a dusky cloud bank, chasing away the darkness. In the painted niche below the entablature on the left wall is a young boy holding aloft a torch to represent the Day. Aurora leaves her elderly lover Tithonus behind and will now awaken Night, who dozes beneath a ruined arch on the right wall along with a sleeping child, an owl, and a bat. Apollo and his well-schooled chorus of Hours, who are the center of attention in Reni's fresco, are nowhere to be seen. Using tempera instead of true fresco, Guercino was able to produce some of the strongly contrasted tonal values that he preferred, and which would not have been possible using true fresco. The rainbow pastels of Reni's *Aurora* are absent. Below Aurora is a view of the Casino itself and some trees. Opposite on the wall is another garden vista of tall cypresses where four cupids cavort happily. In the room directly above, which has a ceiling of identical dimensions, Guercino painted Fame trumpeting the arrival of the Ludovisi papacy accompanied by figures of Honor and Virtue. Here the allusions to the new papal administration are more blatant but it is the fresco below that has captivated audiences while making artists aware that a new kind of painting had arrived in Rome.

Gregory XV died in July 1623 and was succeeded by Urban VIII, whose family had

Florentine connections so that Florentine artists arrived in Rome looking for support. Guercino went back to Cento. He was now famous enough to attract a steady stream of clients and was more comfortable there, it seems, than in Bologna, where his active studio would have presented a more open commercial and stylistic challenge to the hegemony of Guido Reni and his supporters. Guercino's style gradually changed over the next decades of his long and productive career. The brilliant contrasts of light and dark were eliminated and the overall lighting made to resemble filtered daylight instead of some surreal zone where flashes of light pierce inexplicable gloom. Crimson red replaced wine and maroon, lighter blues the indigo blue, and golden yellow the murky ocher he had favored before 1623. His women assume features like those of ancient Athenas and Venuses, his men lose their peasant clumsiness. Was it the experience of Rome, where he finally saw the work of Raphael, the Roman frescoes and altarpieces of Annibale, and a great deal of Roman statuary, that persuaded him to modify his robust naturalism? Was this a change encouraged by Monsignore Agucchi, the learned friend and supporter of Domenichino, when he met Guercino in 1621? Did the immense popularity of Guido Reni's beautiful, classically inspired figures affect Guercino when he returned north?

Guercino's contemporaries were also puzzled by his switch from a vibrant *colore* to a restrained *disegno* aesthetic. Francesco Scannelli, whose *Microcosmo della pittura* was published in 1657 during Guercino's lifetime, reportedly

1.74 G.F. Barbieri (Il Guercino), *Aurora*, 1621. Tempera. Casino Ludovisi, Rome.

The Carracci Succession in Rome and Bologna

interviewed the artist, who explained that he had responded to:

the taste of the majority [. . . as] he had often heard complaints from those who possessed works of his first manner that in these the eyes, the mouth, and other members were hidden (so they said) in dark shadows and that as a result they could not consider certain parts as fully executed [. . .]. So, in order to satisfy the majority [. . .] and especially those who paid money for the requested work, he had executed the paintings in a lighter manner [modo più chiaro].[15]

Even if this dialogue was invented by Scannelli, it records one contemporary response to Guercino's dark early paintings. At all events, the change of style was not sudden. Guercino's Roman experiences certainly made him more self-conscious about the various styles and modes then being used by other artists than he was before. Just as he had been open to the painterly achievements of Tintoretto and Ludovico Carracci in his formative years, now he was anxious to blend what he had already mastered with a more refined human physiognomy and less assertive presentation of his narratives that also conformed to changes in taste due to Reni's popularity. Two private commissions of the same subject, *The Mystic Marriage of St. Catherine*, painted thirty years apart, make this dramatic stylistic shift apparent. The first one (Fig. **1.75**), of 1620, is a small vertical image which shows the standing Christ Child on the right supported by the Virgin, who looks down at St. Catherine and steadies her ring finger while the infant Christ watches, holding the ring he will soon place on it. While the two women are only partially visible, there are enough details to make the story clear: the fur collar and jeweled border of the saint's robe, for example, hint at her legendary status as a

1.75 G.F. Barbieri (Il Guercino), *The Mystic Marriage of St. Catherine*, 1620. Oil on canvas, 34⅝ × 27½ in (88 × 70 cm). Gemäldegalerie, Berlin.

princess. There is a faint glow behind the heads of Mary and Jesus, and they are the most fully lit parts of the picture, the brightest patch of all being the baby's white garment, lifted to expose his genitals. Most of Catherine's profile is in shadow, a device Guercino used elsewhere when depicting someone having a vision. The ocher yellow of her robe and the almost invisibly dark blue of Mary's garment are colors typical of his early years.

The version of 1650 (Fig. **1.76**) has a horizontal format. This time the Virgin and St. Catherine are shown half-length facing each other. Mary supports the standing Child, who places the ring on the saint's left ring finger without assistance. The Virgin is turned slightly toward the viewer. St. Catherine is in a profile that draws attention to the classical purity of her features and to her elegant hairdo, with her coronet attached to the back of her head. The three primary colors that dominate the color scheme radiate with a quiet glow—the dense, pure ultramarine blue of Mary's outer garment over a soft rose-pink dress, and the golden sleeve and soft red wrap of St. Catherine on the right. Only Christ has a halo glow round his head.

Both pictures are beautiful interpretations of the subject. So different are they, however, that were the documentation of Guercino's career not so extensive, they might well have been attributed to different artists. That Guercino was emulating Reni's idealism while finding his own version of this popular style seems undeniable. His contemporaries were certainly aware of his dramatic change of style. Some patrons preferred his early work and asked him to use it in works he made for them but he could not reproduce his former manner at will. After committing himself to a style based on classical models and classical rhetoric for twenty years, he was by the 1640s irrevocably a convert to the camp of those for whom Raphael and the antique were the supreme exemplars of perfection. The results were far more conventional than his early work but he remains a "felicissimo coloritore" to the end, blending his pure hues with a blurred shimmer of light and dark that is as distinctively personal as the patchy chiaroscuro of his early years.

1.76 G.F. Barbieri (Il Guercino), *The Mystic Marriage of St. Catherine*, 1650. Oil on canvas, 45¼ × 59⅞ in (115 × 152 cm). Galleria Estense, Modena.

The Carracci Succession in Rome and Bologna 77

Architecture and City Planning in Rome, 1625–1680

The restoration of the dilapidated ancient and medieval city that began under a succession of Renaissance popes continued throughout the seventeenth century. The pope who made the greatest contribution to city planning was Alexander VII (1655–67). Unlike his predecessors, he did not concentrate on his families' residences and the spaces near them. The great oval piazza in front of St. Peter's (see Fig. 1.4) is only the largest and most expensive of the many projects that he initiated and supported. He widened and straightened the Corso, the street leading from Piazza del Popolo to Piazza Venezia (then Piazza San Marco), and proposed and closely monitored the new façade of Santa Maria della Pace and its little forecourt piazza as well as two new churches in Piazza del Popolo to greet pilgrims entering the city. He also encouraged the completion of unfinished church façades along the Corso and of Sant'Andrea della Valle. He was in almost daily contact with Bernini, who was usually involved, directly or indirectly, in every architectural and sculptural commission that Alexander undertook. The pope had his own views, however, and did not simply do what Bernini wished. He appreciated the architectural talents of Pietro da Cortona, giving him several opportunities, even relishing the jealous reactions of Bernini. He also refused to patronize Borromini, regarding him as difficult and his style as problematic, bizarre, and Gothic, by then a pan-European term of abuse.

In 1656 Pietro da Cortona produced a brilliant design combining a new façade for the Renaissance church of Santa Maria della Pace with an enlarged trapezoidal piazza in front that created a space like a theater with the church façade as the stage set (Figs. **1.77, 1.77a**). A semicircular portico on the ground floor projects into the piazza, its paired columns leaving spacious openings for pilgrims seeking the protection of the Madonna of Peace then being invoked against another outbreak of the plague. The upper story has a convex profile whose vertical divisions marked by columns and pilasters rhyme with the columns below. A smaller segmental pediment inserted into the main triangular pediment at the summit drops below the cornice with a rectangular extension that emphasizes the center of the façade and creates space for the papal coat of arms. Concave extensions behind the façade provide a counterpoint while screening nearby buildings from view. The whole ensemble is a delightful interruption amid the narrow streets surrounding it.

Long straight avenues are now taken for granted in modern cities but they do not occur naturally. They could be created in old city centers only by rulers with the economic means to exercise eminent domain, tear down structures blocking the pure geometry of straight lines and symmetrical vistas, and then rebuild according to a bold vision of an elegant urban environment that enhanced their image and political goals. Sixtus V, followed by Alexander VII, began the process of breaking through the labyrinth of medieval Rome, replacing "barbarous irregularity" with straight roads which are still in use. Their example was imitated by other European rulers for the next three centuries.

While Gianlorenzo Bernini and Pietro da Cortona both made outstanding contributions to the architecture of seventeenth-century Rome, only Francesco Borromini (1599–1667) is regarded as a genius. He was the most original and arguably the most influential architect not only in Rome but in all of seventeenth- and eighteenth-century Europe. Unlike Bernini and Cortona, he worked exclusively as an architect. Bernini hired Borromini in 1619, soon after his arrival from Milan, where he had trained in the workshop of the cathedral, a late Gothic extravaganza still under construction. Its masons employed a medieval system of proportion based on triangles that Borromini adopted rather than the Renaissance system of modules used in the rest of Italy. He had a phenomenal grasp of mathematics and geometry. He was also a brilliant draughtsman. His beautiful working drawings with their smudged passages of chalk testify to his mastery of this old system of spatial planning when devising his complex interior spaces and curved façades. He had even less respect for the rules of ancient Roman architecture than did Michelangelo. Modern viewers see in Borromini's work only a richly imaginative use of space and innovative decorative forms but some of his

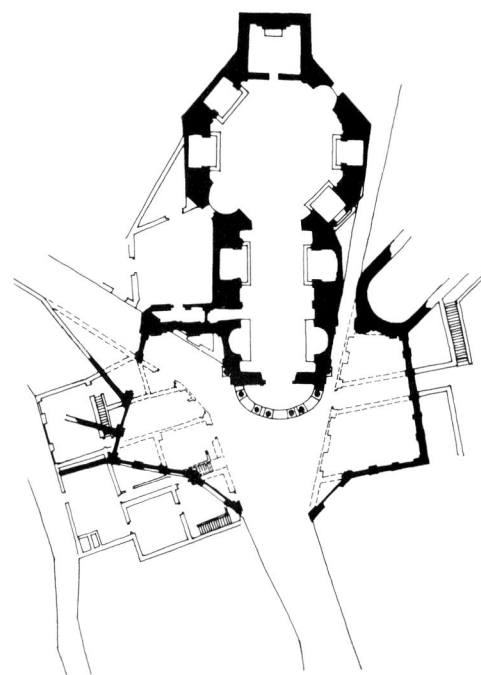

contemporaries found it strange. He eventually became as celebrated for heresies against the norms of classical architecture as Caravaggio was for basing his art on raw nature rather than on Raphael. A complicated man whose relations with his patrons were not always easy, he eventually committed suicide.

Borromini's family connections enabled him to find employment at St. Peter's under a distant relative, Carlo Maderno, the architect in charge of the completion of St. Peter's. Soon realizing his gifted assistant's potential, Maderno gave Borromini opportunities to design and execute iron grilles and carved stone door frames in St. Peter's as well as making fair copies of his own plans. In 1624 Bernini used him in similar ways when he began work on the immense Baldacchino (see Fig. 1.103), a bronze canopy to be placed over the high altar in St. Peter's.

1.77 (above) Pietro da Cortona, Santa Maria della Pace, Rome, 1656. Engraving.

1.77a (below) Pietro da Cortona, Santa Maria della Pace, Rome, plan, 1656.

Architecture and City Planning in Rome, 1625–1680   79

Borromini carved the papal coats of arms on the base of the columns and may also have contributed to the final design of some details. The plans for the expansion and renovation of Palazzo Barberini (Fig. **1.78**) are a blend of ideas by Maderno, Bernini, and Borromini, but Borromini's distinctive style emerges in details like the window frames on the third floor of the façade to either side of the huge double arcade of windows that illuminates the Salone. Adapted from the square attic windows of Michelangelo at St. Peter's that Maderno had used in modified form on its façade, their square shape is enlivened by a pediment that angles forward at the sides before curving over an inverted scallop shell in the center. Stylized garlands looped through stone channels hang down either side like ears. Borromini had taken the most original idioms of Michelangelo and made them his own. The dynamic interaction of both plane and right angle are characteristic: if Borromini could modulate a flat surface or eliminate a corner with a curve, he did.

Borromini's most celebrated commission is the little church of San Carlo alle Quattro Fontane (Figs. **1.79, 1.79a**), built between 1638 and 1641. The façade, also by him, was added in 1665–7. Its undulating façade and interior walls offer such a neat example of the mythical "Baroque" architect's preference for curves over flat surfaces and complexity over simplicity that it has become the canonical example of a "Baroque" church. It was not, however, the first Italian church with an oval ground plan and it did not initiate a trend that gradually eliminated more traditional rectangular church plans in Italy and elsewhere. These were retained for large churches; it was new plans for small churches that began to resemble San Carlo. It was, however, uniquely complex for such a small church and is full of

1.78 Carlo Maderno (with G.L. Bernini and Carlo Borromeo), Palazzo Barberini, entrance façade, Rome, 1628–33.

original features, only some of which can be described here. It was the architect's first independent commission in Rome and he wanted to show the Roman art world what he could do when not under Bernini's control.

Here and elsewhere Borromini worked with limitations of space and budget that Bernini never faced. His patrons were Spanish Discalced (barefoot) Trinitarians, a poor order that collected money to free Christians captured by Moors. Borromini laid out the various components of their new monastery in the small plot of land on the corner of two busy streets with great ingenuity, fitting the church, sacristy, refectory, library, and dormitory as well as a small cloister into slightly under half of the trapezoidal lot, leaving the rest free for a garden. The cloister is no mere parade of columns supporting a cornice around a rectangular space. Pairs of columns at the angles flank convex protrusions of the walls that buttress an arched opening at each end. There are two similar arched openings along each side. Smaller columns support the upper walkway with its ingenious balustrade whose vase-shaped balusters are alternately inverted. This creates a rhythmic ripple of interest in an otherwise austerely simple design of unadorned surfaces. The same ingenious design was used for the balustrade on the façade (see Fig. 1.79).

The basic contour of the church's oval plan is indented by two convex intrusions in the long sides. The entrance and main altar face each other on the long axis; two more altars fill the concave centers of the long sides. The corner spaces created by the distortions of the oval form contain a staircase leading to the lower church and the belfry and a corridor connecting the church to the other rooms of the monastery. The other two corners contain small chapels in hexagonal spaces. Four pairs of columns partly embedded in the walls flank the entrance and the three altars and support the undulating cornice that runs around the entire interior (Fig. 1.80). The oval dome (Fig. 1.81) is supported on four semi-domes—two small ones at each end, two larger ones at each side—that create pendentives filled with irregular ovals containing stucco reliefs depicting events in the life of St. Charles Borromeo, to whom the church is dedicated. The dome is decorated with a complex design of

1.79 (above) Francesco Borromini, San Carlo alle Quattro Fontane, façade, 1638–67, Rome.

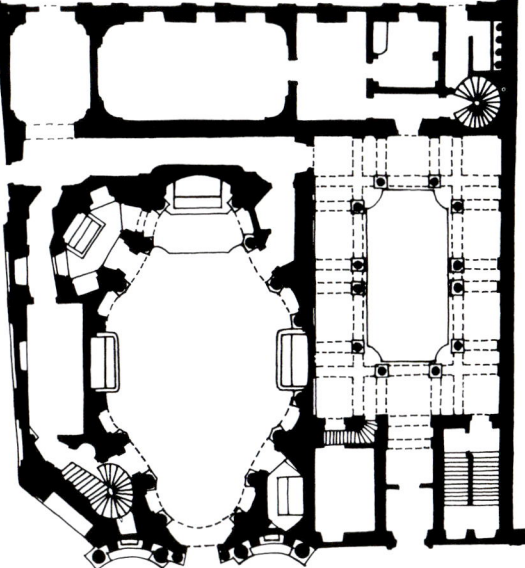

1.79a (below) Francesco Borromini, San Carlo alle Quattro Fontane, plan, 1638–67, Rome.

Architecture and City Planning in Rome, 1625–1680

1.80 (above) Francesco Borromini, San Carlo alle Quattro Fontane, interior, 1638–67, Rome.

1.81 (below) Francesco Borromini, San Carlo alle Quattro Fontane, dome, 1638–67, Rome.

interlocking crosses, octagons, and hexagons of diminishing size that make it seem taller than it is. At its summit in the lantern is a triangle containing an image of the dove of the Holy Ghost. The triangle refers to the Holy Trinity, for whom the order is named.

This description barely covers the main structural elements of the interior. Anyone familiar with the conventions and rules of Roman architecture can, however, pick out Borromini's departures from them by looking closely at decorative details. No capital is quite Ionic or Corinthian; all borrow knowingly and wittily from the traditional forms, altering them, adding appropriate symbols such as a cross where the Romans would put a rosette. Shell niches sprout points or have exotic trilobe forms. The rosettes in the coffers are not uniform but have a variety of floral forms. The façade repeats the undulating concave-convex-concave form of the interior walls but combines giant order columns with smaller ones on both levels. Two angels whose wings create a frame flank a central niche with a statue of St. Charles Borromeo by Antonio Raggi (1624–86) over the central door. The patrons were delighted with the result. Their Procurator General declared that "in the opinion of everybody nothing similar with regard to artistic merit, caprice, excellence and singularity can be found anywhere in the world."[16] Copies of the plans were requested, he reported, by people from throughout Europe, and even from India.

Borromini's other church commission over which he had complete control is Sant'Ivo alla Sapienza, fitted into a square space at the end of an existing rectangular cloister (Figs. **1.82, 1.82a**). Construction began in 1642 and was finished by 1650 but the west façade and interior decoration took longer. Work was completed in the papacy of Alexander VII (1655–67), which explains why his coat of arms was incorporated into the decoration. The view from the entrance to the cloister shows how skillfully Borromini inserted his highly original centrally planned church into its conservative sixteenth-century setting. By carrying both levels of the arcades of the cloister across his concave façade, he blended the old and the new. The arches are filled in, however, with smaller arches and windows, except the central ones which contain the main door

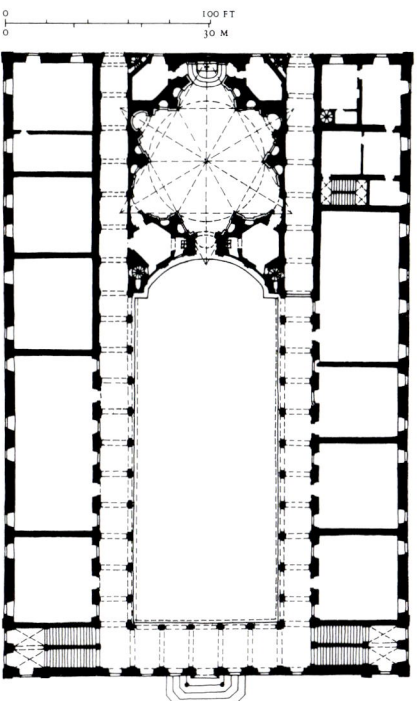

1.82 (left) Francesco Borromini, Sant'Ivo alla Sapienza, facade and cloister, 1642–50, Rome.

1.82a (above) Francesco Borromini, Sant'Ivo alla Sapienza, plan, 1642–50, Rome.

and a large window above. At the next level a low concave wall containing oval openings filled with an eight-pointed star partially screens the lower level of the drum of the dome. At either end the Chigi coat of arms—six mountains with an eight-pointed star at the summit on circular bases ringed with more stars—frames the small, dome-like small turrets. Above it rises the six-lobed form of the drum containing the dome whose interior design alternates concave and convex sections that become concave imperceptibly as they rise to the lantern level. The execution of designs of such complexity required craftsmen of the highest intelligence and dexterity: their anonymous contributions to Borromini's buildings should not be forgotten.

The outer dome roof rises in stages like that of the Pantheon, though these steps are smaller and curved to conform to the interior design. Above it all is a cupola with six pairs of small columns lined up with the six ribs of the dome. The composition is completed with a spiral ramp edged with small flames rising to a crowning element of wrought iron with a globe and cross at its summit. It is the most original dome in Rome, never forgotten once seen and a bravura challenge to the placid cylinder and half circle of the Pantheon's venerable dome and interior nearby. The recently restored interior is even more spectacular. To be noted is the symbolism of its plan based on a six-pointed star representing wisdom (that is, "sapienza") which appears as well on the interior of the dome in rows alternating with the eight-pointed star of the Chigi.

Borromini faced a different situation when he won a competition to complete the Casa dei Filippini adjacent to the Chiesa Nuova in 1637. The huge block of land occupied by the Oratorian

Architecture and City Planning in Rome, 1625–1680 83

1.83 Fausto Rughesi, Chiesa Nuova, façade of Oratory and church (Borromini), 1575–1605.

fathers' residence had already been intelligently laid out by Paolo Maruscelli and construction started before he was dismissed. Borromini had to conform to those basic plans. His design for the oratory, where famous musical concerts were given, gave him the chance to articulate its rectangular interior in his own inimitable fashion, and then to design a façade for the exterior wall of the oratory that would complement Fausto Rughesi's church façade to the right without competing with it (Fig. **1.83**). The result is one of the most appealing urban vistas in Rome. The contrast in style, materials, and proportions between the two buildings enhances both, one a fine example of the respectful use of classical and Renaissance architectural forms, the other an elegant display of original variations on the traditional elements beside it.

Borromini's façade for the oratory is built of rose-pink brick with decorative elements executed in stone. Once again Borromini coaxed marvels from his craftsmen using cheap materials. His bricklayers had to build a façade with a concave plan across its main five bays crowned by a pediment combining curves and straight lines in its silhouette. The central bay on the ground floor, however, is convex while the bay above it is a deep concave niche. The two flanking bays on either side are flat and finished with rusticated outer edges. The cornices and capitals of the pilasters on the ground floor are not connected but the eye tends to read them as a band of alternating flat inverted V forms and Ionic scrolls and stars. The balustrade of the central niche above the main cornice uses Borromini's alternating inverted baluster motif once more. The stone frames of the windows on all three levels are full of sophisticated variations on themes first used by Michelangelo but with slenderer profiles. The carving of wreaths, palm leaves, garlands, and stars is meticulous throughout.

The buildings by Carlo Maderno, Pietro da Cortona, and Borromini discussed here offer only a brief introduction to the architecture and city planning of seventeenth-century Rome. Cortona's most important building, Santi Luca e Martina (1635–50), has been omitted although the location and funds enabled him to produce one of the most impressive new churches of the seventeenth century. Bernini's ingenious design for Sant'Andrea al Quirinale (1658–70) also deserved an extensive discussion. Their contributions with those of many other less famous architects transformed Rome and fulfilled the desire of a succession of powerful popes to make the city worthy of the religious beliefs to which, for all their worldly ambitions, they had dedicated their lives.

Italian Sculpture

The difference between Mannerist painting and the more realistic styles that replaced it is easily grasped. For sculpture, however, the story is not so simple. Sixteenth-century sculptors did not try to rival the more bizarre manifestations of contemporary *maniera* painting. As a result, the stylistic differences between Bernini's marbles and those of his predecessors are not as marked as those between Caravaggio and Pellegrino Tibaldi, and can seem simply a difference of skill rather than of aesthetic attitudes.

The cost of making sculpture from marble and bronze fostered conservatism. Artists could not expect to get commissions for large-scale works in these costly materials if the patron was shown sketches or models that departed too far from accepted conventions. The bread-and-butter commissions—repairing antiques, making portrait busts for tombs, and providing small religious statues for private devotions—were also not tasks that allowed for much expression of idiosyncratic artistic temperament. Thus, far more than painting, sculpture tended to be dominated by a few artists whose superior skills and imaginations garnered them the support of kings, dukes, and popes, the only patrons with the resources to employ a major sculptor on major works for an extended period of time. Other sculptors might be hired by them to help with important commissions or to carry out smaller works for less prestigious patrons as part of their workshop. On the other hand, the success of bronze statuettes by Jean de Boulogne or Giovanni da Bologna, usually called Giambologna, encouraged the taste for such objects at courts throughout Europe long after his death. Similarly, Bernini's enormous success dominated the production of sculpture in Rome and helped to create a new market for ambitious tombs, fountains, memorials, and portrait busts among a range of ecclesiastical and lay patrons who had rarely commissioned such monuments to their posthumous fame in the sixteenth century.

Giambologna (1529–1608) was the most important sculptor working in Italy after the death of Michelangelo in 1564. A Fleming who went to Italy in 1550 and settled in Florence, he worked almost exclusively for the Medici. His mastery of both marble carving and bronze casting and finishing made him the most versatile and influential sculptor working in Europe in the last decades of the sixteenth century. His first major commission was unveiled in Bologna in 1566, hence his Italian nickname. He created the magnificent free-standing fountain of Neptune in the center of the city supporting an enormous bronze statue of the sea god (Fig. **1.84**). It is set in a broad street between two palaces facing Piazza Maggiore and the façade of San Petronio, the huge red-brick Gothic church dedicated to the city's patron saint. Neptune displays all of Giambologna's artistic gifts—his mastery of the male nude, his sympathetic understanding of appropriate antique models, and his impeccable sense of rhythm in a pose. The god stands in a classic *contrapposto* position with his weight on his left leg but his right resting on the back of a small dolphin, which lifts it up and creates a sense of slightly unbalanced movement to the right. His head is turned sharply to the right too, while his left arm is extended outwards, as if he has just heard something. His huge trident rises vertically from behind his right arm, echoing the stable vertical of the left leg. Lively putti at the angles of the upper section of the pedestal and harpies spouting water from their breasts below provide visual entertainment on all sides, though the front and right sides are the principal viewpoints.

Neptune is not only a powerfully realized image of an athletic male god, perfectly cast and finished, in itself a considerable achievement on this scale; he is also posed so that the movement of his turned head, raised arm, and bent leg makes contact with the much larger space in front of San Petronio. His pose makes the spectator want to walk around the statue to look into Neptune's gaze before exploring the other sides. This is true of all of Giambologna's statues, even those that are not free-standing. His popular table bronzes can be turned in the hand and his *Rape of the Sabine Woman* (Fig. **1.85**) in the Loggia dei Lanzi, Florence, can be studied from all sides.

Bernini did not design his sculptures to have a sequence of equally satisfactory viewpoints that flow into each other as the viewer moves around

1.84 (left) Giambologna (Jean de Boulogne), Neptune Fountain, 1566. Bronze and stone. Piazza Nettuno, Bologna.

1.85 (right) Giambologna (Jean de Boulogne), *Rape of the Sabine Woman*, 1580–82. Marble. Loggia dei Lanzi, Florence.

the work. Instead, his statues have one principal viewing position in which the facial expression, gestures, and composition created by the pose and drapery forms all act in concert for maximum psychological effect. Giambologna makes the three-dimensionality of sculpture essential to the viewer's experience of his work; part of the sense of wonder (or *meraviglia*, to use a favorite term of contemporary critics) it inspires lies in the unfolding of a sequence of compositions, each beautiful and revealing a little more about its subject. Bernini, on the other hand, provided all the vital information from the front view, as in his group *Aeneas, Anchises, and Ascanius* (Fig. **1.86**). The facial expressions of all three figures (father, grandfather, and son) are visible as they walk toward the viewer, and their differing physiognomies too. Viewers who expect Bernini's statues to be equally rewarding from all sides, however, will be disappointed.

Gian Lorenzo Bernini's Early Career

The group of *Aeneas, Anchises, and Ascanius* (see Fig. **1.86**) was the first of a spectacular series of marble sculptures that Bernini carved for Cardinal Scipione Borghese between 1618 and 1624. These works established Bernini as a sculptor of such imaginative power that only

1.86 Gian Lorenzo Bernini, *Aeneas, Anchises, and Ascanius*, 1618–19. Marble, height 7 ft 3 in (2.2 m). Borghese Gallery, Rome.

Michelangelo could rival him. His stature was further enhanced by his achievements as an architect and city planner, a gifted painter who never bothered to make a serious foray into that profession, a playwright and stage designer, and a close friend and counselor of two of the most important popes of the century, Urban VIII and Alexander VII. Hibbard called Bernini "the last of the dazzling universal geniuses who had made Italy the artistic and intellectual center of Europe for more than three hundred years."

Gian Lorenzo Bernini was born in Naples in 1598, the son of a Florentine sculptor, Pietro Bernini (1562–1629), and a Neapolitan mother. Pietro moved the family back to Rome in 1605–6 to work on the Pauline Chapel in Santa Maria Maggiore for Paul V. By 1618, when Bernini was twenty, he had already made three portrait busts for tombs, a tiny marble bust of Paul V as well as three almost life-size marble statues. Such precocity is rare in the visual arts generally and even rarer for sculptors because the mastery of marble carving takes much greater physical strength than painting and is more difficult to learn. There are also far fewer sculptors than painters, for the economic reasons already discussed, thus fewer possible masters to train students. Growing up in the workshop of his father helped Gian Lorenzo,

Italian Sculpture 87

for Pietro had a reputation for such effects as making marble look like sheep's fleece and clouds. He soon recognized, however, that his son was a more gifted sculptor than he was and began assigning commissions for portrait busts to him.

Bernini's *Rape of Proserpine* was made between June 1621 and the summer of 1622, by which time Bernini was fully in control of his craft (Fig. **1.87**). The illustration shown here is of the principal viewpoint in front of the striding figure of Pluto, who grasps the resisting woman round her waist and hips, balancing her on his left hip. She arches her body away from him, pushing up the skin at the side of his face with the heel of her right hand as she struggles to escape. Two tears streak down her face; her mouth is open as if she will scream for help. Her right arm reaches out behind her uselessly. The unequal battle between brute male physicality and tender female flesh had never been conveyed so vividly before by either a sculptor or a painter—and

1.87 Gian Lorenzo Bernini, *Rape of Proserpine*, 1621–22. Marble, 7 ft 5 in (2.25 m) high. Borghese Gallery, Rome.

Bernini certainly intended his interpretation of these myths to be compared with painters' efforts to treat such themes. Proserpine seems real as Pluto's huge hands dig into the soft flesh of her thigh and waist, while her delicately carved hair and plaited locks fly out behind her. Pluto's curly hair and beard convey a rippling erotic energy (he merely smiles at her feeble efforts to escape). Behind them serving as a stabilizing base is the three-headed dog Cerberus guarding the mouth of the underworld, their destination. His body is covered with ridges that expertly mimic the typical starburst pattern of hair on a dog's chest as well as the rest of his furry coat.

Such specific texturing of marble to imitate a range of surfaces had never been done before with such assurance and virtuosity. The goatskin robes and tousled hair and beard on Pietro Bernini's statue of St. John the Baptist (Sant'Andrea della Valle, Rome) look identical from a normal viewing distance. Even Michelangelo's meticulously polished and finished *Pietà* (St. Peter's, Rome) keeps the surface textures uniform. Bernini was enormously sensitive to the way that light reacts to marble when left rough or smoothed out, kept matte or worked to various degrees of glossy polish with oil and sand. He used these varied textures in his earliest works but they have a degree of refinement by 1622 that very few later sculptors would ever rival. Some of these details are more easily studied by viewers who move from the front of the piece to look at the side views but, when they do so, they will find the powerful thrust of Proserpine's body against Pluto's is diminished and their facial expressions are no longer clearly visible. The work is fully finished on all sides but, like all of Bernini's statues in this collection, was originally displayed on a base set against a wall. Thus the viewer who approached them from the sides initially would have been intrigued by what was portrayed but could only understand the work properly by studying it from the front. Today all are shown in the center of the rooms on the ground floor of the gallery, inviting the visitor to walk around and inspect them from all sides, but the back view adds nothing to the meaning of the piece.

Bernini worked on his *David* (Fig. **1.88**) and *Apollo and Daphne* (Fig. **1.89**) simultaneously in 1623–4. The former has become one of the

1.88 Gian Lorenzo Bernini, *David*, 1623–24. Marble, height 5 ft 7 in (1.7 m). Borghese Gallery, Rome.

Italian Sculpture

1.89 Gian Lorenzo Bernini, *Apollo and Daphne*, 1623–24. Marble, 8 ft (2.43 m) high. Borghese Gallery, Rome.

canonical works used to define the Baroque, set against Donatello's indolently sensuous bronze *David* (c. 1430, Bargello, Florence) contemplating the huge head of his dead enemy at his feet and Michelangelo's colossal *David* (1505, Accademia, Florence) cradling the sling and planning his attack. Michelangelo shows David before, Donatello after; Bernini depicts David launching the stone. Both his predecessors' works are static, meditative icons of the divinely aided young warrior. Bernini's statue comes alive with energetic force as David approaches that instant when the whirling sling will send forth its deadly stone to its target. Spectators standing in front may well feel that they should duck to avoid getting hit. Even more than with *Aeneas* and the *Rape of Proserpine*, Bernini has succeeded in capturing a stopped moment in time in a medium that would not seem capable of doing that. Indeed, the biographer G.B. Passeri has claimed that to suggest so much movement in a statue was inappropriate because the Latin word for a statue, *statua*, comes from the verb *stare*, meaning to stand. He was no doubt reflecting the jealous comments of rivals who could not conceive, let alone carry out, a work of comparable bravura.

Bernini's *David* and the *Apollo* group have antique sources of inspiration. The Borghese Warrior, now in the Louvre but then in the Cardinal's collection, shows a man with a spear striding with an open-legged pose that has something in common with the extended reach of Bernini's *David*, but the warrior has stopped; David will continue this motion by twirling his body round to give the sling the momentum it needs. Bernini's *Apollo* rethinks the Belvedere Apollo, taking him off his pedestal, obliterating the dignified hauteur of that self-aware pose and turning him into a beautiful mortal who has just caught up with his prey, touched Daphne's waist, and felt the bark creep between him and her desired flesh. His perfect features are openly adapted from this source, as is the complex knot of hair over his forehead. Neo-classical critics disliked this transformation, of course, but to everyone else, then and now, this statue is one of the *meraviglie* of seventeenth-century art. Here more than in any other commission Bernini sought to outdo painting by doing things in stone that had never been done before, thus demonstrating the superiority of sculpture. The figures are running, not still. Daphne is turning into a laurel tree as we watch, the bark racing up her thighs, roots springing from her toes and branches with leaves from her hair and fingers at the very moment she has called out to her father to save her. Bernini has even provided a setting—some rocks, some plants at her feet, and a few pebbles on the ground behind Apollo. Spectators can complete the picture by imagining the sky behind them as they contemplate this miraculous event captured in a miraculous work of art.

Unlike Bernini's other figure groups in the Galleria Borghese, *Apollo and Daphne* has its ideal viewpoint somewhat to the right of the long side of its rectangular block. From this position, we can just see the tips of Apollo's fingers on Daphne's stomach and his facial expression on the verge of transition from joy to puzzlement. This viewpoint was chosen because the work was visible at this angle from the doorway of the room in which it is still shown, though it is now in the middle of the room. Moving to the left also provides a beautifully composed view of the two running figures, and a move slightly to the right reveals the bark keeping Apollo at bay. The back is fully carved and almost as finished as the main views but the whirl of drapery and arms makes little sense. According to an unfriendly source (Passeri once more), Bernini was assisted in finishing the work by the young Giuliano Finelli, who may have helped with the hair and leaves because Bernini was preoccupied by designing the Baldacchino for St. Peter's in 1624. Still, the *concetto* and most of the execution were Bernini's alone. The *Apollo* is rightly regarded as Bernini's most spectacular demonstration of his technical prowess. Never again did he make his own genius such an obvious element of his work. Having shown the world that he could outcarve anyone, ancient or modern, he set about using those gifts to convey the messages of the invigorated papacies of Urban VIII and his successors. He never made another mythological statue for a private patron.

Bernini, Algardi, and the Portrait Bust

Bernini's earliest work was a portrait bust of *Antonio Coppola* (San Giovanni dei Fiorentini, Rome) for which his father signed the contract in 1612; Gian Lorenzo was then fourteen. He produced tomb designs with busts as well as independent portrait busts steadily from 1615 onwards; his first papal bust, of *Pope Paul V* (Fig. **1.90**), was followed by one or more of every succeeding pope, with a half figure of *Clement X* unfinished in Bernini's studio at his death in 1680. Most of his busts of other sitters, however, were made before 1630. Apart from a lost bust of Charles I of England and one of Cardinal Richelieu, both patrons with considerable political clout, Bernini's non-papal commissions included a portrait of a Spanish cleric, Pedro de Foix Montoya (made for his tomb around 1622), which Urban VIII proclaimed was more alive than the man himself, and two busts of *Cardinal Scipione Borghese*.

While the portrait busts that Bernini carved in his teens are not impressive, by 1620 his powers of observation and skills enabled him to transform a moribund convention into images of astonishingly life-like presence. Bernini declared that he wanted to create a "speaking likeness," and that the ideal moment to portray was either just before or after someone has spoken. His first bust of *Cardinal Scipione Borghese* (Fig. **1.91**)

1.90 (left) Gian Lorenzo Bernini, *Pope Paul V*, c. 1618. Marble, height 13⅝ in (35 cm). Borghese Gallery, Rome.

1.91 (right) Gian Lorenzo Bernini, *Cardinal Scipione Borghese*, 1632. Marble, 30¾ in (78 cm) high. Borghese Gallery, Rome.

shows how Bernini achieved this goal. Bernini would have the sitter continue to converse while he drew the head from various angles, capturing the subject in a series of quick sketches. The only surviving example (Fig. 1.92) shows the cardinal in profile with his mouth open but with no unflattering muscular tension around it. The bust itself avoids the awkward sense of presenting a man sliced off across the upper chest by making the cut follow the contours of the cardinal's cape and making the expanse of torso deep enough to give the bust some weight. The sitter's head is turned slightly to our left and tilted slightly too, as is his biretta, whose central fold is angled slightly to our right. All of these subtle shifts from perfect symmetry keep the viewer's eyes in play, as does the light reflecting off the creases and folds of his cape. The cardinal almost seems to shift position as we look at him. The eyeballs are not blank spheres but have been carved to create the illusion of a pupil and iris. The cardinal comes alive because we can imagine him looking out across the room as if reacting to a comment coming from someone in our viewing space with a witticism of his own.

The informal, spontaneous character of Bernini's bust of Cardinal Scipione Borghese reflects the long friendship between the artist and a man better known for the pursuit of pleasure than for his intellectual prowess. For grander, more powerful sitters, Bernini had several ways of marking their elevated social status and political power. As described below, around 1635–6 Anthony van Dyck sent Bernini a portrait of *Charles I in Three Positions* (see Fig. 6.4) so that Bernini could produce a bust of the king with the cut disguised by a sash knotted on one shoulder. He used this motif to even greater effect for his bust of *Francesco d'Este, Duke of Modena* in 1652–53 (Fig. 1.93), and in 1665 for that of *Louis XIV* (Versailles). The drapery gives these busts a dramatic swirl of movement that serves as a sort of framing device separating them from us while hinting at dynamic personalities and splendid possessions. While all of Bernini's subjects turn their heads to one side, thus avoiding a static symmetry, the gaze is averted more obviously when the subject is a king or powerful aristocrat. Charles I and Louis XIV both look up and away from us, avoiding any direct eye contact with spectators standing near them. Similarly Francesco d'Este looks sharply to our left without betraying any reaction to whatever has attracted his attention. This averted gaze creates a barrier then believed necessary between men of high rank and humbler folk. The bust was carved in Rome using three painted views of the duke's features. Bernini never met Francesco d'Este and swore afterwards that he would never again carve a bust without the subject himself having posed. Nevertheless, the duke—who was described by his own secretary as "a feckless, vain princeling"—is here captured as a supremely self-confident ruler, even if all he controlled was a small area of North Italy. The carving of his cascade of ringlets, his delicately textured lace collar, polished armor, and the drapery that moves like jagged lightning around his left shoulder is of superb quality, perhaps the most virtuoso display of Bernini's incomparable carving skills since

1.92 Gian Lorenzo Bernini, *Cardinal Scipione Borghese*, 1632. Graphite and red chalk on cream paper, 9¹⁵⁄₁₆ × 7¼ in (25.3 × 18.4 cm). Pierpont Morgan Library, New York.

Apollo and Daphne (see Fig. 1.89). The duke was extremely grateful: he sent Bernini the enormous sum of 3,000 scudi for his pains.

The sculptor Alessandro Algardi (1598–1654) devoted much of his career to portraiture, whether busts for display in the home of the client or on memorials and tombs in churches. He was fully aware of Bernini's innovations—the irregular cut of the bust, the suggestive turn of the head, the slight hint of disorder in the drapery that gives the marble a hint of lived reality—and used them all with a technique of remarkable subtlety that gives his portraits a convincing realism. He did not exaggerate the hollows on the surface of a face or drapery to create deep shadows, as Bernini did, to make his busts legible from a distance. The eye sockets of Algardi's sitters have a carved pupil but it is not deeply incised. Except in close-up, the eyeball reads as a blank and the sitter seems absent. The *contrapposto* between head and shoulders is also less marked in his busts. Finally, their lips are sealed: Algardi did not try to emulate Bernini in creating a "speaking likeness."

Algardi's bust of *Donna Olympia Maidalchini* (Fig. **1.94**), Innocent X's formidable sister-in-law, displays both the delicate refinement of Algardi's technique and his ability to suggest character when the opportunity presented itself. Serving as a greedy guardian of access to the generally vacillating pope, she accumulated great wealth in that role, though when Innocent died in 1655, neither she nor any other member of the family stepped forward to bury him. The pope's former butler, who had been sacked, paid for a modest coffin so that Innocent could be interred after his body had lain in state for three days in St. Peter's and had then been moved to a side room infested with mice. The set of her jaw and slightly pursed lips suggest a character so unpleasant that it is surprising she allowed this bust to survive. The veil attached to her forehead, the traditional garb of a widow, makes her look like a hooded cobra. Algardi's sensitive carving of the fabric descending from the widow's peak to her shoulders, where it lies over her collar, testifies to his considerable technical skills with marble, something he had had to wait a long time to demonstrate to the Roman public after arriving there from Bologna in 1625.

1.93 (above) Gian Lorenzo Bernini, *Francesco d'Este, Duke of Modena*, 1652–53. Marble, 3 ft 3 in (1 m) high. Galleria Estense, Modena.

1.94 (below) Alessandro Algardi, *Donna Olympia Maidalchini*, c. 1650. Marble, height 27½ in (70 cm). Palazzo Doria Pamphili, Rome.

Italian Sculpture

The Competition: Alessandro Algardi and Francesco Duquesnoy

Algardi, who was exactly the same age as Bernini, trained in Bologna in the studio of Ludovico Carracci and with a local sculptor, Giulio Cesare Conventi, becoming both a polished draughtsman and a skillful modeler in clay and stucco, the usual materials of sculptors in a city with no easy access to marble. Around 1620 Algardi went to Mantua to work for the Gonzaga court, making small works in precious materials such as gold and ivory and repairing antiques, which would have required some skill in carving marble. Thus when he reached Rome in 1625 he was a versatile sculptor but had yet to receive any substantial commissions. He intended only to study the works of sculptors, ancient and modern, before returning to Mantua, but when Duke Vincenzo II Gonzaga died in 1627 and the city was sacked, Algardi decided to settle in Rome.

By 1625, Bernini was firmly established in papal favor. There were few opportunities outside his workshop at a time when Bolognese contacts at court no longer had the resources and opportunities they had enjoyed during the brief papacy of Gregory XV. Still, some Bolognese patrons of the arts remained, including Gregory's nephew, Cardinal Ludovico Ludovisi, who continued to enlarge his collection of art and antiques. Algardi repaired the Athena Ludovisi for him and made stucco statues of *St. Mary Magdalene* (see Fig. 1.100) and *St. John the Evangelist* for a chapel in San Silvestro al Quirinale frescoed by his compatriot, Domenichino, who helped him obtain the commission in 1629. In 1634, when the tomb of Leo XI was commissioned for St. Peter's (see Fig. 1.96), Algardi was at last able to work in marble; it was not completed and installed until 1644. Before its completion, however, Algardi was invited to carve a statue of *St. Philip Neri* for the altar in the sacristy of Santa Maria in Vallicella (Fig. **1.95**). The statue was finished by 1638, though the entire sacristy was not dedicated until 1640. The bills were paid by Pietro Buoncompagni, a fellow Bolognese.

The statue is straightforward in presentation: the saint stands in classic *contrapposto* gazing heavenwards, his right hand raised in a gesture of acceptance, his left marking the place in a large book supported by a kneeling angel whose presence seems normal rather than miraculous. No strong visual currents of movement are created by drapery. The saint's chasuble is partly pushed aside by the angel but otherwise its broad surface covers the saint's body with flat forms. It is decorated with a lightly incised embroidered panel of acanthus scrolls, extending from the saint's shoulders to the hem. Below it the cascading lace-edged hem of his surplice is visible. The Latin text from Psalms 118:23 is one read during services on St. Philip Neri's feast day: "I will run

1.95 Alessandro Algardi, *St. Philip Neri with an Angel*, 1638. Marble, 9 ft 9 in (3 m) high. Sacristy, Sta. Maria in Vallicella, Rome.

94   Chapter 1: Italy

1.96 Alessandro Algardi, *Tomb of Leo XI Medici*, 1634–44. Marble. St Peter's, Rome.

the way of thy commandments, when thou shall enlarge my heart." Algardi provided a beautiful setting for this dignified image of a man whose handsome and kindly features were still remembered by people who had known him (he died in 1595 at the age of eighty). The angel's wing, the saint's right hand, and the lily, one of this saint's regular attributes, all emerge from the niche into our space but quietly, almost imperceptibly. In its own way, the work exemplifies the "bel composto" usually associated only with Bernini, for the colors of the setting add a hint of painting to the architectural and sculptural elements.

Algardi did receive one major commission for St. Peter's during Urban VIII's papacy, namely that for the tomb of Pope Leo XI (Fig. **1.96**), the Medici pope who had ruled for less than a month in 1605. Only because of this family's power was his brief reign commemorated in Carrara marble in an aisle of St. Peter's. The site is narrow, unlike those occupied by Bernini's papal clients, but Algardi used the same formula—a seated effigy on a sarcophagus flanked by two female allegorical figures, here representing Magnanimity and Liberality. They are turned toward visitors arriving from the entrance, as is the pope, who extends his right arm in a gentle gesture of blessing very different from the commanding arm of Urban VIII (see Fig. 1.108). The relief on the sarcophagus shows Henry IV of France kneeling at the pope's feet, returning to the Catholic faith and submitting to its authority: on the right, they confer amicably around a table. This unassuming but beautifully carved and proportioned

and other decorative elements on the giant bronze columns of the Baldacchino. He did get one small commission in 1629 for the tomb of Andrien Vryburch in Santa Maria dell'Anima, the church of the Flemish community in Rome (Fig. **1.97**). Here Duquesnoy first showed the public his ability to carve touchingly realistic babies, a specialty for which he was so admired that many later sculptors and painters kept casts of them in their studios.

His best-known work is the statue of *Sta. Susanna* (Fig. **1.98**) for Santa Maria di Loreto, a small church near the Forum. This was one of only two full-size figure sculptures that he carried out in Rome but so perfectly does it exemplify the

1.97 (left) Francesco Duquesnoy, *Vryburch Monument*, 1629. Marble, height c. 5 ft (1.5 m). Sta. Maria dell'Anima, Rome.

1.98 (right) Francesco Duquesnoy, *Sta. Susanna*, 1629–33. Marble, height 90½ in (230 cm). Sta. Maria di Loreto, Rome.

monument was far more influential than Bernini's dramatic tombs, as will be evident to any visitor who examines the later papal monuments made in St. Peter's.

Several other sculptors carried out substantial commissions in Rome in the early seventeenth century but the one who cannot be omitted here is the Fleming François Duquesnoy (1594–1643), usually dubbed Il Fiammingo (the Fleming) in Italy. Trained in Brussels by his father, Jerôme Duquesnoy, François arrived in Rome in 1618. He had some difficulty establishing his career against the local competition and the Flemish community, from which he could hope for patronage, was not large. Duquesnoy survived on minor commissions including work on the putti

96   *Chapter 1: Italy*

aesthetic of artists who sought their inspiration in ancient art that it has assured his fame ever since. Duquesnoy transformed a Roman virgin into a Christian saint who gently urges us to turn our attention from her to the high altar. Her toga-like drapery and absence of Christian attributes means that she looks like a young Roman matron who has strayed into the church (the martyr's palm branch once resting on her left arm is missing). Recalling Guido Reni's idealized women, the figure's poise and beauty are similarly based on those of Raphael. Her drapery reveals yet conceals her body in almost teasing fashion. This statue is always compared with Bernini's *Sta. Bibiana* (Fig. **1.99**), finished in 1626 for the high altar of the little church dedicated to that saint, and Algardi's stucco *St. Mary Magdalene* (Fig. **1.100**), installed in San Silvestro nearby in 1629, just as Duquesnoy began his statue. Both envelop their women with drapery weighted in strong folds. The simplicity of *Sta. Susanna* looks instead presciently neo-classical, a style that did not emerge clearly until the next century. Poussin, Duquesnoy, and the collectors who supported them were the first to try to distinguish between Greek and Roman art and to perceive the former as purer and more beautiful than the latter. In this context, both Algardi and Bernini look "Baroque" and Duquesnoy looks "classical."

1.99 (left) Gian Lorenzo Bernini, *Sta. Bibiana*, 1624–26. Marble, lifesize. Sta. Bibiana, Rome.

1.100 (right) Alessandro Algardi, *St. Mary Magdalene*, 1629. Stucco, over lifesize. S. Silvestro al Quirinale, Rome.

Italian Sculpture

1.101 Stefano Maderno, *Sta. Cecilia*, 1600. Marble, lifesize. Santa Cecilia in Trastevere, Rome.

1.102 (below) Stefano Maderno, *Laocoön*, 1630. Terracotta model after antique, 28 in (71 cm) high. Hermitage, St. Petersburg.

Almost as famous as *Sta. Susanna* is the *Sta. Cecilia* by Stefano Maderno (c. 1576–1636), made for the high altar of the church dedicated to her in Trastevere (Fig. **1.101**). Cecilia does not stand but lies on her side in a black marble niche, her head turned away from us so that we can see a cut on her neck, her arms extended as if they were once bound together. She is a beautiful corpse, a martyr carved in the position in which her well-preserved body was supposedly found when the foundations of the church were excavated in the late sixteenth century.

Maderno's superb technique enabled him to make a touching masterpiece whose image of a vulnerable young woman killed for her faith resonated with Romans who had just witnessed the tragic fate of Beatrice Cenci, the beautiful daughter of an abusive, wealthy father who had imprisoned her with her mother in a mountain fortress. After killing her father with the aid of a brother in order to escape such cruelty, she had been arrested, condemned, and publicly beheaded in the center of Rome in September 1599. Her exemplary behavior during her execution led to widespread sympathy for her and a belief that she too was a martyr, the victim of papal greed and politics (the family property was confiscated by Clement VIII).

Maderno, like Duquesnoy, also admired classical sculpture and made some beautiful small replicas of famous works such as the *Farnese Hercules* and *Laocoön* (Fig. **1.102**; see also the drawing after it by Rubens, Fig. 2.8). Accurate, meticulously finished, signed, and dated, Maderno made the Laocoön and similar works not as student exercises but for private collectors who could not afford the more expensive bronze replicas.

Bernini and Urban VIII

Cardinal Maffeo Barberini was elected Pope Urban VIII on August 4, 1623. One of his first acts was to call Bernini into his chambers and to declare: "It is your great good luck, Cavaliere, to see Maffeo Barberini Pope; but we are even luckier in that Cavaliere Bernini lives in the same time of our Pontificate."[17] They were already friends. Maffeo reputedly held a mirror up so that the sculptor could study his own features as he grimaced to get the expression he needed for *David* hurling the stone to crush the giant Goliath and later provided appropriate verses to go on the base of *Apollo and Daphne*. As pope, however, he could monopolize Bernini's talents for the greater glory of the Roman Catholic Church and his own family.

The most important task was the decoration of the New St. Peter's, whose nave had been completed in 1609. Urban VIII and Bernini had to devise a new structure to draw attention to the high altar that otherwise would be reduced to insignificance by the vast size of the new crossing area. The new structure had to do this without hiding the altar or overwhelming it, connecting the viewer's awareness of the enormous interior spaces of the new church, the most important of the Roman Catholic faith, with the high altar. There the central mystery of the Mass would be celebrated by the pope himself over the tomb of St. Peter, designated by Christ as his first bishop according to Roman Catholic tradition.

Bernini's Baldacchino (Fig. **1.103**) adapted the traditional altar canopy made of marble by using bronze and increasing its size to a monumental scale. Because the worshiper can see through the columns to the apse while standing in the nave or from one transept to the other, the Baldacchino draws attention to what it protects without interrupting the spatial flow of the vast interior. The dark bronze contrasts with the pale gray giant order pilasters that flank the niches in the piers of the crossing and the arches that give access to the side aisles. The bronze flaps of the canopy are decorated with Urban VIII's ubiquitous personal symbol, a trio of bees, alternating with the heads of cherubim. Other Barberini symbols—suns and laurel leaves—are used too, the laurel festooned around the columns with bees and baby angels and the sun on the outer sides of the impost block above the capital of each column. On the canopy four huge volute scrolls, seemingly supported by angels, curve upward from each corner to support a crowning element with a gilded ball surmounted by a cross, symbol of the world united under Christ. An image of the Holy Ghost appears under the canopy over the altar.

The Baldacchino is many things: a canopy to protect the pope and the body of Christ miraculously present at every Mass; a fabulous confection of gilded bronze that honors the

1.103 Gian Lorenzo Bernini, Baldacchino, 1624–33. Bronze and gilt, 93 ft 6 in (28.5 m) high. St. Peter's, Rome.

memory of St. Peter buried below; and a work of art whose powerful presence seems itself a symbol of the invigorated Post-Tridentine Church. Hibbard called it "the first Baroque monument of world significance [. . . freely combining] natural, architectural and decorative forms." The twisted columns are based on eight antique examples supposed to have come from the Temple of Solomon in Jerusalem and now incorporated into the niches of the balconies in the crossing piers. Like the Egyptian obelisks and Roman victory columns topped with Christian symbols during the reign of Sixtus V, the use of these legendary columns in the design of the baldacchino was another way of asserting the dominance of Christianity over all other religions.

The four huge niches in the piers of the crossing that face the Baldacchino and the balconies above them were also enlarged and decorated according to Bernini's designs and three sculptors were commissioned to make statues of *St. Helena* (Andrea Bolgi), *St. Veronica* (Francesco Mochi), and *St. Andrew* (Duquesnoy) (Fig. **1.104**). Bernini himself contributed the statue of *St. Longinus* (Fig. **1.105**), the Roman centurion who was converted to Christianity when he thrust his spear into Christ's side. All were ordered in 1629 and finished roughly a decade later. Relics of each of these saints are housed in the niches behind balconies on the second story above the statues. St. Veronica, just visible on the left edge of the illustration of the Baldacchino reproduced here (see Fig. 1.103), is shown rushing to wipe Christ's

1.104 Francesco Duquesnoy, *St. Andrew*, 1629–40. Marble, height c. 14 ft 5 in (4.4 m). St. Peter's, Rome.

brow with the veil that later preserved a perfect imprint of his face. St. Helena, partly visible to the right, stands in a quieter pose, holding the cross that, according to her legend, was the true cross on which Christ was crucified and which she recognized and preserved. St. Andrew embraces and displays the X-shaped cross on which he was martyred (his skull is preserved in the reliquary above). Both he and St. Longinus face the Baldacchino and look up at its summit. The whole space around the high altar and the Baldacchino is thus intended to remind pilgrims of different moments in the narrative of Christ's Passion and the founding mysteries of their faith.

Duquesnoy's *St. Andrew* and Bernini's *St. Longinus* have almost identical poses with upturned gazes, outflung arms, and bare chests, their weight carried on their left legs. Bernini may even have required Duquesnoy to adopt this pose, which is also used by Bolgi for his *St. Helena*, to create a uniform effect broken only by Mochi's rushing, almost hysterical *St. Veronica*. The first important difference to note is the firm stance of Longinus and the implied motion of St. Andrew. The latter, while holding a massive, rough-hewn cross, seems about to step to the right. His garments fall in long, flowing folds that respond logically to gravity and to the saint's limbs beneath them. The huge swathe of drapery knotted on Longinus's hip and the piece of cloth cascading down from his right shoulder have a life of their own that denies reality and suggests instead the internal drama of the saint's moment of conversion. His arms look as if he has just

1.105 Gian Lorenzo Bernini, *St. Longinus*, 1629–38. Marble, 14 ft 5 in (4.4 m) high. St Peter's, Rome.

Italian Sculpture 101

flung them apart; St. Andrew's are in a static pose that he sustains as he embraces the cross on which he will shortly be killed for his faith. Duquesnoy's quieter, more introverted artistic persona was better suited to portray a saint nobly accepting martyrdom; Bernini was the appropriate artist to portray a sudden conversion.

Long before pilgrims entered St. Peter's in the seventeenth century, their route was dominated by urban planning and sculptural decoration designed by Bernini. The bridge opposite Castel Sant'Angelo has ten statues of angels carrying the symbols of Christ's Passion, executed to Bernini's designs between 1667 and 1671. After walking a short distance, the pilgrim finally has a clear view of St. Peter's, including the magnificent dome of Michelangelo. The vast piazza (see Fig. 1.4) was designed by Bernini and built during the papacy of Alexander VII (1655–67). The colonnades, which shelter pilgrims from the summer heat and winter rains, support the scores of statues of saints and martyrs set over each massive column in the front row, all of them designed by Bernini (every able sculptor then working in Rome was employed to carve them). Because the colonnades and the extensions attached to each side of the façade of St. Peter's are only half the height of the façade itself, the façade appears taller and more majestic than it did before this addition. Thus Bernini created a vast exterior space where pilgrims would feel embraced by the Church and could meditate on the sacrifices and exemplary behavior of scores of saints and martyrs before entering the place of worship.

Behind the façade is a portico with a marble relief by Bernini over the main entrance: it shows Christ telling St. Peter to "Feed my Sheep!" (*Pasce Oves Meas*), that is, to minister to the flocks of Christians then and for ever. To the right is Bernini's equestrian monument to Constantine the Great (1654–70), installed on a landing of the Scala Regia (1663–6) (Fig. **1.106**). Constantine, the first Christian emperor, is shown at the legendary moment of his conversion when the *Chi-Rho* sign of Christ appeared in the sky before the Battle of the Milvian Bridge, which Constantine went on to win. Once inside the vast interior, whose scale equals that of the grandest Roman ruins still standing, the pilgrim would be pulled toward the high altar and Bernini's Baldacchino, though he or she might notice Michelangelo's *Pietà*, one of the few monuments from Old St. Peter's reinstalled in the new church. There are four more major monuments by Bernini—his tombs of Urban VIII and Alexander VII (see Figs. 1.108, 1.109), the altar and ciborium in the Chapel of the Most Holy Sacrament (1673–4), and the extraordinary monument that fills the apse, the *Cathedra Petri* (Fig. **1.110**). The long time taken to complete two of these works hints at the complex practical and political problems they presented. Bernini's skill at resolving them,

1.106 Gian Lorenzo Bernini, *The Vision of Constantine*, 1654–70. Marble, with painted stucco curtain. Scala Regia, St. Peter's, Rome.

and his ability to inspire a team of artists to carry out his ideas for him as he aged, were no less remarkable than his capacity to find powerful and original solutions for traditional commissions (the papal tombs) and for unique situations for which he had no precedents to emulate or reject (the Cathedra).

Urban VIII, as anxious as his predecessors to ensure that his tomb would be completed soon after his death to maintain public memory of his reign (and hoping that it would be placed in St. Peter's and not elsewhere), had Bernini submit ideas for its design only three years after his election, though the tomb took another twenty years to complete. He was well aware of Michelangelo's vicissitudes with the tomb of Julius II, originally planned as a vast free-standing structure in St. Peter's and finally erected, in a much reduced form, as a wall monument in the church of San Pietro in Vincoli. Urban's tomb is installed in the niche to the right of the central apse niche now filled by the *Cathedra Petri*. The niche to the left of the *Cathedra* contains Guglielmo della Porta's tomb of Paul III, moved there by Bernini from its previous location in one of the piers of the crossing in 1626 (Fig. **1.107**). Thus the sixteenth-century papal tomb and Bernini's interpretation of this type of monument now flank his largest and most complex artistic creation.

The tomb of Paul III was originally envisaged in 1549 as a much larger structure inspired by Michelangelo's original free-standing scheme for Julius II. The monument installed in the niche in 1626 kept only the seated bronze effigy of the pope and two of the four allegorical figures that had adorned the tomb in its previous location. They represent Justice and Prudence (Peace and Abundance were taken to the family palace in

1.107 Giacomo della Porta, *Tomb of Paul III*, 1549–75. Bronze and marble. St. Peter's, Rome.

Italian Sculpture 103

1.108 (opposite) Gian Lorenzo Bernini, *Tomb of Urban VIII*, 1628–37. Marble and bronze. St. Peter's, Rome.

Rome). Thus Bernini's tomb for Urban VIII, which also consists of a seated bronze effigy of a pope set on a high podium above two allegorical female figures, repeats its basic elements, but with utterly different results (Fig. **1.108**). For Paul III's gentle blessing gesture such as might be given to a child, Bernini substituted a commanding raised arm and forceful outward gaze that speaks to the entire tribune area. Guglielmo's passive, reclining women echo Michelangelo's allegories of the times of day in the Medici Chapel rather than embodying the qualities that they represent. Bernini's standing allegories of Charity and Justice act out their roles and mirror the imagined grief of the spectator contemplating the papal tomb. Charity (or Divine Love) cradles a child sleeping after a satisfying meal at her breast (originally exposed, now covered) and turns to comfort the hungry baby squalling at her side and reaching up for attention. Metaphorically of course, Charity reaches out to the faithful who seek Divine Love as desperately as her baby cries for sustenance. Justice meditates instead, her head resting on her right hand and raised to heaven for divine guidance. One of her two babies supports—if barely—her bound *fasces*, a traditional attribute of her authority, while his companion, hiding in her skirts, plays with the scale pans of Justice. These majestic, allegorical figures are well over life-size but the sympathetic interaction of Charity with her babies and Justice's tolerance of hers humanize both of them and make the qualities that they represent more than noble abstractions.

Between Charity and Justice is a massive bronze sarcophagus whose lid is made from two scrolled volutes that leave a gap in the center from which emerges a winged bronze skeleton. It inscribes Urban VIII's name in a huge book with black marble pages. Three bees wander over the tomb, one on the sarcophagus and two on the podium below the pope, as if so distracted by his death that they no longer know what to do. Bernini transformed every passive element of the traditional tomb into an active drama paying tribute to the deceased pope. The tomb is further enlivened by the use of various colors of marble in the base, podium, and niche, all unified by Bernini into a design that does not flatter the disconnected elements in the pendant monument to Paul III. Knowledge that the Farnese family, the opponents of the Church in the futile War of Castro in the final years of Urban VIII's papacy, helped to drain the papal treasury in a time of famine and thus to ruin the reputation of the Barberini pope, adds a final irony to our appreciation of these monuments. The artistic war was won by Urban VIII, however, with the aid of Bernini, as astute a politician as anyone in the pope's inner circle. Urban's tomb guarantees him eternal fame and a favorable reception by those who know little or nothing about his papacy.

Bernini's tomb of Pope Alexander VII has the same basic components as those used for Urban VIII, but in dealing with an awkward location over a doorway Bernini found a compelling solution (Fig. **1.109**). This pope kneels facing toward the high altar (actually hidden from his view by one of the crossing piers), absorbed in prayer and unaware of the skeleton emerging from beneath the sumptuous drapery of mottled red *diaspro di Sicilia* and waving an hourglass at him. Now that his allotted time on earth is over, Alexander VII is ready to accept his destiny. Charity on the left leans forward, supporting a contented, sleeping baby while looking up at the pope in adoration. Truth on the right cradles a sun, the source of light and truth, and looks down without making eye contact with the viewer, perhaps because to do so would have seemed provocative. Originally naked, except for the parts covered by the red jasper cloth, her body had drapery added later. In the back of the niche are two more allegorical women—Justice behind Charity and Prudence behind Truth. Still, it is the skeleton of Death lifting up the huge drapery folds who steals the show, animating the otherwise meditative ensemble of figures and incorporating the doorway into the *concetto* of the whole monument. Death transforms it into the earthly tomb from which the pope will ascend to his heavenly reward.

Bernini designed the tomb of Alexander VII and supervised its execution but the only part of the work on which he may have worked himself is the portrait head of the pope. The figures on Urban's tomb, however, were designed and carved by Bernini himself. The difference is apparent to anyone who inspects both monuments closely. Bernini's ambitious projects required the constant collaboration of carpenters,

1.109 Gian Lorenzo Bernini, *Tomb of Alexander VII*, 1671–78. Marble. St. Peter's, Rome.

plasterers, marble carvers and polishers, and bronze casters. As a brilliant administrator, Bernini communicated his ideas to his teams of assistants so coherently that few people notice the lack of Bernini's personal touch in some of his most famous commissions. This is especially true of the *Cathedra Petri*, the monumental structure that fills the apse of St. Peter's and completes the sequence of works by Bernini seen by pilgrims and visitors.

Every cathedral is both the actual and symbolic seat of a bishop; his chair in the apse represents his authority even in his absence. St. Peter's is the mother church of the Roman Catholic faith, the "Regina delle Basiliche" (Queen of Basilicas), as Filippo Baldinucci put it. *Cathedra Petri*

106 *Chapter 1: Italy*

means the Chair of Peter in Latin; thus the huge chair now held aloft by four Fathers of the Latin and Greek Church (Fig. **1.110**) in the apse of St. Peter's is first of all a symbolic throne for St. Peter, the first bishop of the Roman Catholic Church. It is also a gigantic reliquary for inside it is an old chair made of wood and ivory believed since the late Middle Ages to be the actual chair of St. Peter (it is now dated by experts to AD 875). In the 1630s Bernini had installed this relic in a chapel near the entrance, where it remained until Alexander VII decided to move it to the most important site still awaiting decoration and the most logical one for this venerated object.

Bernini decided that the first scheme presented to the pope was too modest to have a suitable impact even though it filled the large niche below the great window of Michelangelo. He then set about enlarging the design by incremental stages between 1657 and 1660; he did not foresee that the end result would be twice the size of his original design. The niche is completely hidden by the chair, its volute legs, the gilded stucco clouds that embrace it, and the majestic figures of the four Church Fathers, who have emerged from the niche into the space of the tribune. Instead of a static monument in a niche surmounted by one airborne figure, Bernini has imagined the chair itself in motion, arriving miraculously through the window, which is transformed by a framework of gilded plaster clouds full of angels and cherubim. It is settling gently to earth guided by the four theologian saints who had most forcefully presented the case for the primacy of the Roman Catholic faith over all competitors.

The huge bronze chair weighs so little, it seems, that the Fathers can support it and guide it into position using loops of ribbon around one

1.110 Gian Lorenzo Bernini, *Cathedra Petri*, 1657–66. Marble and bronze. St. Peter's, Rome.

Italian Sculpture 107

finger. St. Ambrose on the left turns inwards, directing our attention to the chair while St. Augustine on the right, who supports a massive tome on his left hip, looks out with a stern expression toward the Baldacchino. Behind them are the two fathers of the Greek Church, Athanasius and John Chrysostom, whose heads are bare and who wear robes with crossed stoles. A relief on the back of the chair shows Christ again giving the command to St. Peter, "Feed my Sheep!"—the theme of Bernini's earlier marble relief over the main entrance. The antique chair, wrapped in protective layers of silk, must be imagined through the decorative grille below the seat of its ceremonial container.

The incorporation of Michelangelo's window into the final design, which looks so logical, was such a late decision that bronze angels intended for a smaller, lower *Gloria* had to be fitted into the mass of plaster clouds and angels that now surrounds what is left of the original opening. It is the only window with tinted glass in St. Peter's. When the late afternoon sun pours through its orange and yellow panes, the miraculous arrival of the *Cathedra Petri* seems reenacted once more. It is Bernini's most dazzling "bel composto," whose splendor celebrates the distant roots of the Catholic faith and personifies the post-Tridentine Church's energetic defense of that faith against its Protestant competition.

Algardi and Bernini during the Papacy of Innocent X

Algardi's most prestigious commission in St. Peter's was the enormous relief, over 25 feet (8.58 meters) high, depicting *Pope Leo I Driving Attila from Rome* (Fig. **1.111**). So generous was his fee—10,000 scudi, larger than any given to Bernini for a single work—that Innocent X evidently wanted to show that Algardi was the greater sculptor whose worth was finally recognized. The site behind a crossing pier was not ideal because it is less visible than those in the tribune, apse, and crossing area. Nevertheless Algardi grasped the opportunity to display his talents in the one type of sculpture for which he had a special affinity and which Bernini avoided.

The subject, based on a historical event of AD 452, was painted by Raphael in the Vatican Stanze on a large lunette-shaped wall. He showed the calm pope advancing on horseback below the airborne figures of Sts. Peter and Paul, causing Attila and his troops to turn back from the city walls in confusion. The vertical format of the space allotted to Algardi meant that he had to reduce the composition to its main figures, whom he shows dismounted, the pope vigorously gesturing to the heavenly apparition above and Attila turning away to begin his retreat. The space between them, which effectively splits the composition in half, emphasizes the drama of their encounter. Algardi carved Attila's figure so completely that he seems ready to step out of the marble. The pope and his kneeling companion who holds back the edge of his cloak are similarly carved almost free of the block while other figures blend gradually into the background, where the forms of clouds, horses, lances, and leaves can be seen. Algardi did not work his surfaces with Bernini's variety of textures, but controlled the fall of light in other ways, creating pools of shadow where needed to emphasize key gestures and movement. This relief was greatly admired and revived interest in Rome in carved altarpieces: none had been commissioned since Pietro Bernini unveiled his turgid *Assumption of the Virgin* for the baptistery in Santa Maria Maggiore in 1611.

During Innocent X's papacy, when Bernini was out of favor, he was hired by the enterprising Cardinal Federico Cornaro, a member of one of the most distinguished families of Venice, to create a family chapel dedicated to St. Teresa of Avila in the left transept of the small church of Santa Maria della Vittoria (Fig. **1.112**). William Barcham has argued that Cardinal Cornaro had papal ambitions (his father had been a Doge of Venice) and that the commission was undertaken to draw attention to himself, which it certainly did. Cornaro was also sympathetic to the Discalced Carmelites, the order founded by St. Teresa and affiliated with this church in Rome. St. Teresa had been canonized in 1622 with three other Spanish saints—Isidore of Seville, Ignatius of Loyola, and Francis Xavier—but while they had all been honored with churches named for them, St. Teresa had until then not even had a chapel dedicated to her. Bernini was on his mettle to prove that he was an artist it would be foolish to ignore and Cornaro was happy to

1.111 Alessandro Algardi, *Pope Leo I Driving Attila from Rome*, 1646–53. Marble, 28 ft 1 in (8.58 m) high. Vatican, St. Peter's, Rome.

indulge him in an opportunity to make his point. The result is one of Bernini's best-known works; the artist called it "his least bad work."

For his 12,000 scudi—an enormous sum of money, more than Borromini had at his disposal for San Carlo alle Quattro Fontane—Cardinal Cornaro had a tall, wide but shallow space upholstered with magnificent marble veneers up to the level of the cornice where the vault begins. The vault contains scenes of the saint's life painted to look like gilded bronze reliefs and a ceiling fresco of clouds, angels, and a radiance surrounding an image of the Holy Ghost that seems to descend into the chapel, concealing some of the scenes and even casting a shadow on them. Most visitors never glance upwards, so mesmerized are they by the altarpiece that shows the saint falling back in a trance as a beautiful young angel lifts the edge of her garment and prepares to stab her with an arrow. The carved group is set behind a massive architectural frame whose broken pediment swells outwards as if the forces that sustain the saint on a cloud bank of rough marble and bring heavenly light on to her from a hidden source were forcing the stone to expand.

1.112 (left) Gian Lorenzo Bernini, *Ecstasy of St. Teresa*, 1645–52. Marble. Cornaro Chapel, S. Maria della Vittoria, Rome.

1.113 (right) Gian Lorenzo Bernini, *Ecstasy of St. Teresa* (detail), 1645–52. Marble, 11 ft 6 in (3.5 m) high. Cornaro Chapel, S. Maria della Vittoria, Rome.

Two openings in the side walls at the same level as the altarpiece serve as private oratories for deceased members of the Cornaro family, who are shown as if they were alive, reacting to this vision. Only the cardinal patron, who is in the group on the right, makes eye contact with us. He is also the first one to be seen by the visitor walking up the nave toward the chapel. Gesticulating skeletons decorate the pavement below; a gilded bronze relief of the Last Supper covers the front of the altar table. An elegant marble balustrade allows kneeling worshipers to meditate on the lessons of St. Teresa's piety.

The chapel surrounding this famous sculpture helps to envelop the spectator in a visionary experience. Bernini made a shallow box-like extension in the outside wall of the chapel, with a window glazed with yellow glass inserted on top that casts a golden light on the figures in the altarpiece (Fig. **1.113**). The saint is shown experiencing "transverberation" from an angel who, according to her own description of this vision, plunged an arrow with a flaming tip into her heart and entrails again and again.[18]

When he pulled it out, I felt that he took them with him and left me utterly consumed by the great love of God. The pain was so severe that it made me utter several moans. The sweetness caused by this intense pain is so extreme that one cannot possibly wish it to cease, nor is one's soul then content with anything but God.

The parallel with sexual union was noted in the eighteenth century by the President de Brosses, who is said to have remarked: "If that is divine love, I have known it!" Bernini evidently did not intend a lascivious interpretation as he covered Teresa's body with layers of heavy drapery so that only her face, one limp hand, and her feet can be seen. Her unfocused eyes and open mouth convey her absorption in this miraculous experience. The angel's drapery is made of finer material so that the folds resemble flames flickering around his body. His beatific smile projects both joy and sympathy.

Bernini's *Four Rivers Fountain* (Fig. **1.114**) in Piazza Navona was also carried out during the papacy of Innocent X. Fountains were not merely decorative embellishments to the city. For most people, they were the only source of water, which had to be collected from the fountain, whose steady supply depended on the repair of the ancient aqueducts that can still be seen in the countryside beyond the city limits. The popes were responsible for their maintenance, and the fountains, decorated with their coats of arms and inscriptions, were permanent reminders of their civic generosity. Bernini had finished the *Triton Fountain* (Fig. **1.115**) in the piazza to one side of Palazzo Barberini towards the end of Urban VIII's reign. It took up the idea of an animated union of animal and human forms used by Giacomo della Porta for the Fountain of the Turtles nearby, where young boys support the basin and help turtles to drink its water, but transformed it into something far more dynamic. Four twisting dolphins use their tails to support a huge open scallop shell straddled by a triton who lifts a conch shell like a trumpet to his lips and blows out water. The pulse of energy coursing upwards from the basin of water through the dolphins to the conch shell, where it bursts forth, is sensed by every spectator who feels refreshed and recharged.

Bernini had not been invited to compete for the commission for the Four Rivers fountain design and only won it by subterfuge. The artist had a supporter place an ambitious model for a fountain where the pope would see it. He is said to have remarked after being waylaid by the model: "Those who do not want to employ Bernini should not look at his work."

1.114 Gian Lorenzo Bernini, *Four Rivers Fountain*, 1648–51. Travertine and marble figures, granite obelisk, Piazza Navona, Rome.

1.115 Gian Lorenzo Bernini, *Triton Fountain*, 1642–43. Piazza Barberini, Rome.

The program devised by Bernini in collaboration with the Pamphili for their fountain in Piazza Navona is more ambitious than usual. Piazza Navona derives its name from a corruption of the ancient *platea in agone*, and its extended oval shape from the race course it contained in Roman times (foot races were called *agones*). The Pamphili had built themselves a splendid new palace along its south-west flank in 1644–50, and next to it the church of Sant'Agnese in Agone with the Collegio Innocenziano. Borromini, Algardi, and others had already been invited to submit ideas for a fountain base for an obelisk then lying in fragments in the Circus Maximus but which Innocent X wanted to restore and erect to the greater glory of his family in the middle of "their" piazza.

Bernini's proposal was bolder, more dramatic, and far more expensive than anything the competition had dared to propose to a family not given to extravagance or bold art patronage.

The *Four Rivers Fountain* now in Piazza Navona resembles a mountain hollowed out along its main axes but still robust enough to support the Egyptian obelisk and its substantial base. The contrast between its linear geometry and the almost playful freedom of the roughly carved travertine peaks and crevasses below is just part of this surprising monument's perpetual charm. Four river gods representing Europe (the Danube), Africa (the Nile), Asia (the Ganges), and America (the Plata) recline and gesticulate on their perches at the four outer corners of the sprawling rock formation, framing the views through the hollows excavated through its center. Europe, who is closest to the Pamphili residence, leans back to touch the papal insignia. America, who has African features, looks up at the summit of the obelisk as if experiencing conversion. The Nile of Africa tugs at covers on his head, not because he cannot stand the sight of Borromini's church façade nearby, as tour guides like to tell tourists, but because the source of the Nile was then unknown. The attributes traditionally associated with the continents cavort in the water and decorate the rocky precipices—a crocodile, an armadillo, a large palm tree, cactuses, a lion, a sea serpent, jars of coins, and, at the summit on the north and south sides, the Pamphili coat of arms is surmounted by the papal tiara and keys. At the top of the pagan obelisk carved with hieroglyphs, whose meaning was bravely interpreted but completely misunderstood at the time, is a bronze dove with a palm branch in its beak. This is another Pamphili symbol, but, placed here above water gushing from various cunningly hidden pipes, recalls the flood that once covered the world and from which only Noah, who listened to the Lord, was saved. The good news came to him from a dove with an olive branch in its beak.

This commission required Bernini to make intriguing vistas from all sides and tantalizing partial views that would make the visitor keep moving around the large circular pool from which the mountain emerges. He began with designs showing two main views (from the far ends of the piazza), then one with four views (two distant and two from the sides where the spectator is closer to the fountain), and finally created a design that reads well from all angles. The fountain dominates the piazza without overwhelming it and is understandably a favorite with Romans and tourists. When it was almost finished, Innocent X came to see it and asked if the water could be turned on. Bernini explained that it was not yet possible, but as the pope turned to leave, gave a signal to his engineer and the water began to gush forth. The pope was momentarily shocked but then delighted. He is supposed to have said that Bernini took ten years off his life, but it was worth it. The populace were less pleased. Many people were still suffering from the bad harvests of the 1640s and complained: "Pane, pane vogliamo, e non guglie!" (We want bread, bread, not obelisks!).

Algardi died in 1654; Bernini lived on for another twenty-six years, working until the end, though less and less on the final marble product himself. By 1655 he had become the administrator of a vast enterprise that provided jobs for many sculptors and craftsmen who collaborated in the execution of Bernini's designs for organ covers, nave and dome decorations, and for the tabernacle of the Holy Sacrament in St. Peter's, to mention only some of the kinds of tasks he carried out for Alexander VII and his successors. Often quoted was the awed response of John Evelyn after seeing an opera in Rome "wherein [Bernini] painted the scenes, cut the statues, invented the engines, composed the music, writ the comedy, and built the theatre."[19] Bernini's successors mined his work for ideas, but they also found patrons willing to follow Algardi's lead and make sculptured altarpieces instead of the far cheaper and more usual painted canvases. Later papal tombs look more like Algardi's monochrome monument to Leo XI than the polychromatic splendor of those Bernini made for Urban VIII and Alexander VII. The subsequent history of Italian seventeenth-century sculpture is well worth further study even if it generated no more artists to vie with Bernini and Algardi. Bruce Boucher's compact account of developments throughout Italy carries this story well into the eighteenth century; it is warmly recommended to those seeking an introduction to these later developments.

Painting in Rome, 1623–1680

Pietro da Cortona

The most important artist to emerge after Urban VIII had become pope was the versatile Pietro Berrettini, now usually called Pietro da Cortona (1597–1669). Born in Cortona (southern Tuscany), a town that looked north to Florence for artistic direction, he became a major architect as well as a brilliant painter, above all of large-scale decorative frescoes. His father was a stone mason but he began his studies in Florence around 1610 with a painter, Andrea Commodi (1560–1638), with whom he went to Rome in 1612. Once there, the city became his most important teacher. Cortona made numerous studies after Trajan's Column and other famous Roman reliefs and statues, many commissioned by Cassiano dal Pozzo, the scholarly secretary of Cardinal Francesco Barberini who employed many young artists to make drawn copies after every surviving scrap of Roman art for his Museo Cartaceo (Paper Museum). Pietro also painted copies after works by Raphael and Titian.

Cortona's first Roman public commission was for scenes from the life of St. Bibiana in the nave of the little church by Bernini dedicated to her. *Sta. Bibiana Refusing to Sacrifice to Pagan Idols* (Fig. 1.116) has a sophisticated architectural setting, though based on Renaissance rather than ancient Roman forms, and accessories such as altars and costumes loosely derived from ancient models. The freedom with which Cortona interpreted antiquity separates him from his close French contemporary, Nicolas Poussin, who, like Cortona, plunged himself into studying every aspect of Roman art to which he had access. Poussin would follow his chosen Roman model of a tripod or cithera, for example, as drawn but Cortona would not. His furnishings and costumes contain elements found in ancient art but transformed into something more sculptural and decorative than their sources. Cortona's idea of respect obviously did not mean slavish imitation but, like Borromini, an original interpretation of the visual culture of antiquity.

Most of Cortona's work of the 1620s was made for the Sacchetti family. They were wealthy Florentines who had moved to Rome in the sixteenth century. Marchese Marcello Sacchetti

1.116 Pietro da Cortona, *Sta. Bibiana Refusing to Sacrifice to Pagan Idols*, 1626. Fresco. Santa Bibiana, Rome.

became Urban VIII's treasurer in 1623, an appointment that reflected not only their shared Florentine roots and long friendship but also their deep interest in the arts. Marcello hired Cortona to decorate his seaside villa at Castelfusano (1626–9) with religious scenes in the chapel and mythological scenes in the long Gallery. He also painted some easel pictures for the Marchese, among them a large *Triumph of Bacchus* (Fig. **1.117**). It reveals his admiration for Annibale's central fresco in the Galleria Farnese and Roman sarcophagus reliefs but also suggests that he had studied Titian's so-called *Bacchanals*. These three large paintings (the *Bacchanal of the Andrians* and the *Worship of Venus*, both now in the Prado, Madrid, and *Bacchus and Ariadne*, National Gallery, London) had been confiscated in 1598 and brought to Rome from Ferrara with the rest of the Este collections by Clement VIII. Only Annibale and Domenichino seemed aware of them before 1620, but when Titian's *Bacchanal of the Andrians* (Fig. **1.118**) and *Worship of Venus* were acquired by the Ludovisi in 1621, they must have been more accessible for many artists including, as will be seen, van Dyck, Poussin, Sacchi, and Cortona, who copied or made paintings inspired by them in the 1620s.

Unlike religious commissions for altars or church decorations, which inevitably placed certain limits on artistic flights of imagination, mythological themes allowed both painters and sculptors to demonstrate their powers of artistic imagination with fewer restrictions, as is clear from such works as Annibale's Galleria Farnese series (see Figs. 1.30–1.32) and Domenichino's *Archery Contest of Diana and her Nymphs* (see

1.117 Pietro da Cortona, *Triumph of Bacchus*, c.1626–29. Oil on canvas, 56⅝ × 80⅞ in (144 × 205 cm). Capitoline Museums, Rome.

1.118 Titian (Tiziano Vecellio), *Bacchanal of the Andrians*, 1523–25. Oil on canvas, 68⁹⁄₁₆ × 75¹⁵⁄₁₆ in (175 × 193 cm). Prado, Madrid.

Fig. 1.60). Then there was the challenge posed to painters by Bernini's spectacular *Rape of Proserpine* (see Fig. 1.87) and *Apollo and Daphne* (see Fig. 1.89). Was there a painter in Rome equal to that challenge? Cortona seems to have decided in 1630 that he was ready and produced the masterpiece of his early maturity, the *Rape of the Sabine Women* (Fig. **1.119**).

The legend, as told by Plutarch and others, describes how young Roman men captured women from a neighboring settlement as a means of increasing the population of their city. Cortona's choice of subject would mean that his painting would inevitably be compared with sculpture, not only with Bernini's early groups but also with Giambologna's *Rape of the Sabine Woman* (see Fig. 1.85). The rich pictorial surface—crammed with temples, columns, trees, clouds, primary and secondary figure groups—seems in itself a declaration of painting's superiority to sculpture, stressing its polychrome reality in contrast to the other's monochrome simulacra. A crisscross of surface rhythms keeps the spectator's eye shifting from one group to another, effectively conveying the sense of confusion that would have been part of the historical event. The positions of the main figure groups are, however, carefully planned to compose a triangular mass on the right with a diagonal opening between these protagonists and the struggling pair on the left. The gap allows us to see Romulus seated between the columns on the left giving the order to his men to seize the woman of their choice: only unmarried women were to be picked, but one married woman was taken by mistake, a detail recorded by Cortona who shows her protesting child crying on the left.

None of the poses replicates those of Cortona's predecessors or rivals exactly: indeed, it would have been a point of honor to create new ones, especially in a work that was bound to be compared by knowledgeable connoisseurs with its precedents. What Cortona did not achieve is much sense that real human beings are caught up in this drama. His characters are heroic types—virile soldiers, fertile women—

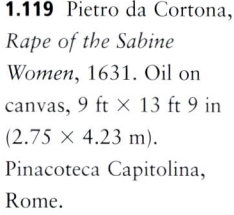

1.119 Pietro da Cortona, *Rape of the Sabine Women*, 1631. Oil on canvas, 9 ft × 13 ft 9 in (2.75 × 4.23 m). Pinacoteca Capitolina, Rome.

are lit by the heavenly light emanating from the Virgin and by a second light source on the left. The latter casts shadows from the cherubim playing with the cardinal's hat on the left and from the folded front edge of his cloak on the larger fold behind, which is especially effective in suggesting the weight and mass of his robes. A wilderness retreat appropriate to this order, whose members withdrew to meditate in solitude, can be seen in the background.

Cortona's altarpiece of the *Martyrdom of St. Lawrence* (Fig. **1.121**), made for the high altar of a restored medieval church on the edge of the

1.120 (left) Pietro da Cortona, *St. Peter Damian Offering the Rule of the Camaldolese Order to the Virgin*, 1629. Oil on canvas, 57⅞ × 44½ in (147 × 113 cm). Toledo Museum of Art, Toldeo, OH.

1.121 (below) Pietro da Cortona, *Martyrdom of St. Lawrence*, 1646. Oil on canvas, 10 ft 7 in × 5 ft 10 in (3.25 × 1.8 m). S. Lorenzo in Miranda, Rome.

whose gestures are conventional rather than freshly observed. In this respect, Bernini outclassed Cortona for his Daphne is both beautiful and very moving in her vulnerability, and his Proserpine seems genuinely afraid as she uselessly pushes against Pluto's cheek with her hand without affecting his expression of delighted anticipation of his conquest.

Cortona's steady production of handsome, lushly painted religious altarpieces helped to establish his style with a generation of painters who started out as apprentices in his studio before launching their own careers. By the 1640s the "Cortoneschi," as they were dubbed, were dominating painting in both Rome and Florence. A characteristic example of Cortona's religious work is *St. Peter Damian Offering the Rule of the Camaldolese Order to the Virgin* (Fig. **1.120**). Its composition was a familiar type by then: the Virgin appears in a vision on the upper left to a kneeling saint on the lower right; Cortona's figures, however, dominate the picture surface more than usual. The Virgin arrives before St. Peter Damian on a thick cloud that fills much of the left side of the canvas. She is a majestic figure with deep-set, dark eyes who wears a somber blue wrap over her crimson dress. Her head is framed by a golden radiance. The saint wears the white woolen robes of his order; they

Painting in Rome, 1623–1680

Forum, is a spectacular interpretation of a subject treated in numerous earlier images, most notably in two altarpieces by Titian. St. Lawrence died a martyr's death in Rome in 258 after refusing to hand over money from his church's treasury to Roman soldiers. According to legend, he was roasted alive on a grid, which became his identifying attribute. He had always been shown stripped except for a loincloth as soldiers force him down on the grid and poke at the fire beneath him. In Cortona's version, the saint wears a richly embroidered chasuble pulled aside to reveal an intricately pleated and lace-edged surplice tumbling over the logs below the grid. The clothed St. Lawrence probably reflects the decision by the ecclesiastical authorities to emphasize the saint's role as a deacon rather than Cortona's desire to display his skills at depicting such rich fabrics. A soldier on the right grimaces and brandishes flaming twigs as if intending to set fire to the saint's garments. Another on the left pulls at the saint's shoulder, trying to make him lie down. Neither act disturbs Lawrence's rapt meditation. He opens his arm and gazes up at two plump cherubim bringing him the martyr's crown and palm. His robes are almost distractingly beautiful, pulling our eyes away from his ecstatic gaze and thus diluting the message intended for the faithful. This may be the most spectacular exhibition of Cortona's skills as a painter in oils. The spontaneity of his brushwork combined with his skillful manipulation of tonal contrasts and subdued neutral colors surrounding passages of richer hues is used to even greater effect in his ceiling frescoes.

By 1633, when Cortona began work on the vast ceiling of the Salone in Palazzo Barberini (Fig. **1.122**), he was an experienced fresco painter but not yet on this scale. In every case, he had divided up the expanse of ceiling into small units of *quadri riportati* surrounded by a decorative framework that combined architectural forms with garlands of fruits and vegetables or reliefs inspired by ancient models. He also delegated parts of these commissions to others, which the clear divisions between narrative scenes and decorative framework made it easy to do. The *Allegory of Divine Providence* in Palazzo Barberini leaves behind such conservative schemes and melds the painted architecture and sculpture of the framework with overlapping elements of the narratives that seem to escape from their boundaries to join up with the triumphant imagery in the long, central section. Everything seems to flow like currents of energy from the corners up to the figure of Divine Providence and the Barberini symbols overhead. The result is a complex union of all three arts, a "bel composto," that benefited enormously from Cortona's brief visit to Venice in 1637. There he saw for the first time the ceiling canvases set into heavy gilded wooden frames by Veronese in the Doge's Palace. Cortona was impressed by Veronese's systems for depicting figures overhead without using too much distorting foreshortening and his vivid characterization of the allegorical women celebrating the city of Venice. Documents and study of the ceiling confirm contemporary accounts that tell us Cortona was not satisfied with the virtually completed fresco after returning from Venice, and that he destroyed or painted over a substantial portion in 1638–9. When it was finally unveiled, Urban VIII was ecstatic, comparing it with Raphael's frescoes in the Vatican Stanze, which celebrated the papacies of Julius II and Leo X.

The ceiling, whose subject is the triumphal reign of Urban VIII guided by Divine Providence, is divided into five main units. The upper part of the central rectangular area contains a huge laurel wreath held up by the theological virtues of Faith, Hope, and Charity, while above them Rome supports the papal tiara and Religion the crossed keys of the papacy at the summit of the wreath. In its center are three golden bees, the most distinctive of many Barberini symbols, flying in close formation like small aircraft. While viewers tend to accept that these elements are hovering overhead, they are not much affected by foreshortening except for a putto holding the wreath between Charity and Faith. We do look up into the interior of the papal tiara but the bees are flying upside down (we see their backs) and the allegorical women are hovering overhead in positions that place them almost parallel to the ground. Below these colossal figures and attributes supporting the Barberini family symbols is the smaller figure of Divine Providence set at the tip of a triangle formed by Saturn devouring his children and the Three Fates. Their

1.122 (opposite) Pietro da Cortona, *Glorification of the Reign of Urban VIII*, 1633–39. Fresco. Palazzo Barberini, Rome.

cloud bank spills out over the richly ornamented stone entablature that frames the central rectangle and which is held up by lavishly decorated piers that rise to support it from the four corners of the coved ceiling.

This framework creates two picture fields on either end and two longer ones along the sides of the central field. Cortona split it into two sections whose central division is marked by more allegorical women who seem to float in front of the narratives and rise up toward the central area. Among them are Prudence, Dignity, Power, and Fame (on the left) and Chastity, Divine Assistance, Moral Knowledge, and Piety (on the right). Below Divine Providence, Minerva chases the giants (that is Heresies) away from this heavenly ensemble of Christian virtue. Some of the giants are shown in dramatic foreshortening as they tumble out of their world into ours; many artists, including Cortona, thought such distortions were more appropriate to evil than to good characters. At the other end (and seen only by spectators who have turned their backs to the rest of the ceiling) Hercules, assisted by Authority and Abundance, expels Harpies (symbols here of renegade princes who defied papal authority) and protects the granaries needed to feed the families in the foreground.

Identifying the main figures—and this description has only partly done that—hardly begins the work of interpreting the meaning of these mythological characters in a papal context. What is Venus doing lolling in her lush garden retreat, where she is receiving some abuse from Chastity? Why does Piety regard the drunken orgy of Bacchus and Silenus so benignly? Does the pope reject the vices of lust and gluttony represented so appealingly here but with a merciful understanding of the sins of those who cannot follow his good example? The forge of Vulcan is easier to interpret as the mythological equivalent of the defense budget, for the popes then had to wage war periodically. On the other side the women representing appropriate virtues (Prudence, Power, Fame, Peace) close the doors to the temple of Janus (or War) as Gentleness controls Fury.

In general terms the message of this propaganda is clear: evil will be overcome by Wisdom, Strength, and so on. As the Fates spin out the lifeline of this papacy, food will be abundant and life will be delightful as this perfect pope, divinely appointed, blessed with Divine Providence, and guided by all the appropriate virtues, enacts his policies and guides the Church forward in a reign of peace and prosperity. The result will benefit the Church and give Urban VIII Immortality: she is present carrying a crown of stars just below the airborne papal *stemma*. Even in the seventeenth century, most visitors could not grasp more than the essential pro-Barberini message unless they were given a tour by a member of the Barberini household, one of whom was enterprising enough to publish a useful small pamphlet. Only the more learned cardinals and intellectuals attached to the papal court would have grasped the intricate references woven into this lavish pictorial spectacle. Cortona's own diffidence regarding the subjects he was commissioned to paint means that he must have worked closely with advisers such as the poet Francesco Bracciolini, whose ode to Maffeo Barberini on his elevation to the papacy uses the figure of Divine Providence: vices like Self-Interest, seeking to defeat the election of Urban VIII, are ultimately defeated by the figure of Religion after a temporary setback caused by Drunkenness. Still, the artistic vision was Cortona's own; no literary adviser could have imagined such a gorgeous union of the arts on behalf of the Barberini papacy.

Andrea Sacchi

Another allegorical ceiling celebrating the Barberini was finished just before Cortona began work on his vast fresco. Its author, Andrea Sacchi (1599–1661), had emerged from obscurity in Rome in the late teens, his talent spotted by Cardinal del Monte, for whom almost all his first works were made, including an altarpiece for St. Peter's. The illegitimate son of a father from Fermo, who was adopted by a painter, Benedetto Sacchi, Andrea studied with both Giuseppe Cesari and Francesco Albani, with whom he traveled to Bologna after 1615. Thus he was exposed to the Carracci and their successors in Bologna before settling in Rome, where he worked for the rest of his life. Sacchi was a subtle colorist who appreciated both Correggio and Barocci. He was also a sensitive observer of human psychology. When del Monte died in

1626, Cardinal Antonio Barberini the Younger became Sacchi's chief patron.

Sacchi's *Allegory of Divine Wisdom* (Fig. **1.123**) was painted in 1629–30 in a square room with a much lower ceiling than the two-story Salone of Cortona's *Divine Providence*. It is the largest of a series of connected rooms in the family quarters installed in the old wing of the Sforza palace incorporated into the new palace designed by Maderno, Bernini, and Borromini. Most importantly, it serves as an extension of the small family chapel, to which it gives access. Visitors standing beneath Sacchi's ceiling look straight up at an expanse of sky and cloud where eleven women are casually arranged around a golden throne on which is seated the figure of Divine Wisdom. In the sky above her to the left a winged young man with a golden arrow rides a bounding lion; to the right another youth aims a silver arrow at a hare. The center of the ceiling around Divine Wisdom glows with yellow light. She points her scepter at the globe of the earth, positioned to show Italy in the center of the most brightly illuminated section. Sirens hold up Barberini suns in each corner. Barberini bees can be found at the top of the throne of Divine Wisdom and in the framing frieze that runs between the sirens.

The clue to the meaning of this heavenly ensemble is provided by a text in the Barberini archives. It explains that Divine Wisdom rules the world aided by her divine archers, who

1.123 Andrea Sacchi, *Allegory of Divine Wisdom*, 1629–30. Fresco. Palazzo Barberini, Rome.

Painting in Rome, 1623–1680 121

motivate us with love for wisdom (the youth on the lion) or fear of its absence (the youth with the hare) to seek it in prayer. Each of the women standing or seated around her represents one of her qualities: Nobility with her crown; Justice with the scales; Eternity in green, holding a snake with its tail in its mouth; Strength just below her with a club; Suavity with a lyre; Divinity with a triangle; and Beneficence with an ear of wheat, who also squeezes milk from her breast. To the right of Wisdom's throne are Holiness with the flaming altar, Purity with the swan, Perspicacity with the eagle, and Beauty holding golden hair (the locks of Berenice). Each attribute is also a constellation and is marked with a few golden stars, though not in the actual formation in which they appear in the sky. These allude to the verses in the book of Wisdom (VII, 29–30), from which these attributes are drawn, where Divine Wisdom is said to be "more beautiful than the sun and above all the order of stars: being compared with the light, he is found before it. For after this cometh night: but vice shall not prevail against Wisdom." Divine Wisdom herself shares attributes with the Virgin of the Immaculate Conception—the sun behind her and on her chest, the spotless mirror which she holds, and her blue and white garments. Her throne with the lions at its base is the Throne of Solomon.

Sacchi's *Divine Wisdom* used to be dismissed as an unsuccessful example of a *quadro riportato*, mainly because writers based their reactions on photographs taken from directly beneath rather than from the spectator's actual viewing position. Sacchi's beautiful fresco is now appreciated for its originality in dispensing with any framing *quadratura* architecture. The room is to be imagined as literally open to the heavens, that is, to the realm of Divine Wisdom herself, who is not hovering directly overhead but rather above the chapel. Having understood her message, viewers should then enter and pray for her guidance. The huge globe is a prominent feature of the fresco where it is displaced from the center of this universe by the sun. Galileo's support of the heliocentric theories of Copernicus were receiving some support from Urban VIII when the fresco was painted, though Galileo had to submit to the Church's demand that he abandon this position soon afterwards. Sacchi's first patron in Rome, Cardinal Francesco Maria del Monte, who was also Caravaggio's first major supporter, was in close touch with the scientific circles in Florence supporting Galileo's research. Through him, Sacchi was more aware of these matters than might be expected of an artist of modest origins. Despite Galileo's forced denial of his view that the earth moves around the sun, Sacchi's fresco was not destroyed as having heretical content. Indeed, according to John Beldon Scott, it also contains astrological prognostications, which the pope practiced privately while denouncing it publicly. Thus this simple gathering of beautiful women encompasses a fascinating range of meanings, sacred, scientific, and political.

1.124 Andrea Sacchi, *Death of St. Anne*, 1649. Oil on canvas, 14 ft 2 in × 7 ft 6 in (4.3 × 2.3 m). S. Carlo ai Catinari, Rome.

Sacchi carefully differentiated these allegorical women not only physically but through their attributes. The powerful back and long limbs of Strength are as suited to her as the discreet nudity of the golden-haired blonde representing Beauty. Perspicacity rests her head on her chin and stares right at the sun, as an eagle, her attribute, was believed to be able to do without harming its vision. The women lean toward one another, conversing quietly or, in a few cases, glancing down at us. Sacchi's quiet artistic personality was better suited to this commission than to the grand scale of the Salone ceiling. He was not a fluent decorator but preferred to paint altarpieces and smaller easel paintings where his perceptive observations of human reactions to miracles and tragedies could be seen and appreciated.

When Cardinal Antonio Barberini the Younger fled to Paris after the death of Urban VIII in 1644, Sacchi lacked steady patronage, though he still received public commissions until the mid-1650s. A fine example of Sacchi's thoughtful religious imagery from his later career is his *Death of St. Anne*, installed on the left transept altar in San Carlo ai Catinari in 1649 (Fig. **1.124**). It is Sacchi's largest canvas. Now that it has been cleaned, its subtle chromatic harmonies can be appreciated and Bellori's enthusiasm for the artist's abilities as a Roman painter equal to Correggio be understood. The Christ Child held by Mary blesses his dying grandmother but with open arms that suggest he is welcoming her to heaven. He anchors the center of the painting. St. Anne, lying back against her pillows, looks past him to the enormous archway in the left background where blue sky is visible. The moment shown is called "death" in English but "transito" in Italian, which conveys the idea of the soul being transported from body to heaven. St. Anne is surrounded by her family, with cherubim hovering overhead supporting a cloth of honor. So close is the composition to Caravaggio's *Death of the Virgin* (see Fig. 1.48), which left Rome for Mantua when Sacchi was a child, that he must have seen a copy of this painting which, though never engraved, had attracted some notoriety for its lack of decorum and subsequent rejection by its patron. The line of heads that leads our eyes to Christ and the dying woman, the grieving figure seated, the jug and basin waiting to be used to prepare the body for burial, and the figure of St. Anne herself lying parallel to the picture plane in the center of the canvas, are all elements found in Caravaggio's painting. There the Virgin looks dead, but Anne is still alive. Her feet are covered and her arms rest comfortably on or beside her body. Sacchi would seem to be saying that the passage of Mary or Anne to the next world should be portrayed with dignity and restraint, for believers know that eternal life awaits them.

Sacchi's range of hues is subdued: cream and brown for Joachim seated beside his dying wife; russet red for the curtain held over St. Anne; some blue in the sky and on the Virgin; and some pink, sage green, and brown on the other figures. His much admired painting, the *Dream of St. Romuald* (1631, Pinacoteca Vaticana) depicts a group of monks, all wearing white woolen robes, listening to the founder of their order describe his vision of them ascending to heaven. Whether in half shade or in the sunlight, each monk is a fully realized character with different features and reactions. Whether conveyed with Sacchi's sensitivity or Cortona's power, the portrayal of feelings, ranging from inner reflection to outward hatred or anger, gathered momentum after 1600. To call Sacchi "classical" and Cortona "Baroque," as they are usually labeled, is one way of recognizing their different artistic temperaments but it also exaggerates them. Their contemporaries would have believed them to have more in common with each other than Caravaggio and Annibale did.

Pietro da Cortona in Florence and Rome

The success of Cortona's *Divine Providence* ceiling in Palazzo Barberini led to other opportunities for him to create ceiling frescoes glorifying the Medici in Florence in the 1640s and then the Pamphili in Rome in 1651–4. The five large rooms in Palazzo Pitti in Florence, each one dedicated to one of the planetary gods—Venus, Jupiter, Mars, Apollo, and Saturn—show an increasingly complex interweaving of the framework and the painted areas, though the painted world never breaks through the boundaries of the frame. In the first room executed, the Sala di Venere (Room of Venus), the framework is kept out of the main picture field, which is rectangular, but with rounded corners, allowing it to be photographed isolated from its setting (Fig. **1.125**). The principal scene has one main viewpoint, which places spectators with their backs to the windows. In the other rooms Cortona used oval boundaries that leave empty corners filled in with smaller frescoes whose themes relate to the main scene. He also gave the other ceilings multiple viewpoints that require the spectator to move around the rooms' four walls to appreciate all the figure groups. The allegories celebrate the Medici family as divinely appointed and divinely guided rulers.

The main scene in the Sala di Venere begins the story. It shows a young, blond Medici prince being taken with obvious reluctance from the realm of Venus by Pallas Athena, who lifts him up toward the waiting figure of Hercules, who will guide the next stage of his education. This young man is not abandoning pleasure lightly but looks back longingly at Venus, who reaches out to him from her bower with red velvet hangings. A blond and a brunette putto hold up the red velvet overhead; a blond and brunette nymph peer out from behind Venus. A winged blond putto tugs at the princeling's orange drapery trying to keep him back; another winged putto hovers near Hercules with a crown of laurel leaves decorated with a white ribbon, ready to inspire him to strive to become a worthy member of the Medici clan. These two babies are Eros and Anteros, prototypical embodiments of the contradictory nature of desire. More delicious young women watch from the left, where Pan plays his pipes but one putto plays with a shield, a hint at the more serious duties awaiting the heir to the leadership of the Medici family. In the next room Hercules and the heir, now several years older and presumably somewhat wiser, float toward the throne of Jupiter as the other residents of Mount Olympus watch approvingly. The Medici youth may represent Cosimo III, who was born

1.125 Pietro da Cortona, *Medici Prince Taken from Venus by Minerva*, 1641–42. Fresco. Sala di Venere, Palazzo Pitti, Florence.

in 1642, but he can also stand for all past and future male heirs to the political power and prestige of this family.

Cortona has treated the picture space on the ceiling as Sacchi did in the *Divine Wisdom* fresco, imagining that the room is open to the sky and that spectators look up to see a scene taking place above and slightly ahead of them. The corner of an entablature visible on the left establishes our location well below the women lolling about on it, as does the view of Venus's parked chariot in the center in which putti are playing. The reclining woman on the left edge of the fresco is not seen from such a low viewpoint, however. We seem to be level with her rather than well below her, though we are below the young heir as he is lifted toward his destiny. This compromise allows the artist to stage his scene in the sky without distorting the main characters with too much foreshortening. This was Veronese's solution: Cortona had already used this combination of sharply foreshortened architectural elements and less foreshortened figures in Palazzo Barberini. Most spectators will not stop to dissect the mechanics of Cortona's illusions but will accept what is presented as an enchanting fiction of Venus's heavenly abode and the young man's rapture from her arms to the stern duties of leadership. Seldom has the arrival of puberty been celebrated with such splendid pictorial language. The French artists who stopped here on their way to study in Rome in the seventeenth and eighteenth centuries found plenty of inspiration for their political and erotic mythologies, whether destined for ceilings or walls. Rudolf Wittkower aptly noted that "the 'style Louis XIV' owes more to the decorations of the Palazzo Pitti than to any other single source."[20]

In 1647, on returning to Rome from Florence, Cortona was commissioned to fresco the apse, dome, and nave of Santa Maria in Vallicella, the largest commission of this kind ever given to one artist in Rome and the most significant since Domenichino and Lanfranco shared the decoration of the apse and dome of nearby Sant'Andrea della Valle in the 1620s. Though plagued by gout and the demands of other commissions, he soldiered on, finishing the nave fresco depicting a miracle of St. Philip Neri only in 1665. Still, like Bernini and Rubens, Cortona was an excellent administrator who hired the best available collaborators. In all three commissions, the surrounding gilded stucco framework, which adds significant elements of both architecture and sculpture to the whole ensemble, reveals the fertility of Cortona's artistic imagination as well as his wide-ranging familiarity with his predecessors' tricks of the trade.

Carlo Maratta

Cortona's studio produced many painters able to mimic his fluent brushwork and to copy the physiognomy of his buxom women, handsome men, and plump babies. Ciro Ferri (1628/34–1689) was the best of them, and there has been some understandable confusion between their work. Sacchi, however, produced one pupil of distinction, Carlo Maratta (Maratti) (1625–1713), who left Ancona to join an older brother in Rome in 1635, when he was ten. By 1645 he was carrying out frescoes using drawings and cartoons supplied by Sacchi, whose own rate of production dwindled in the 1650s, affected, like Cortona, by gout, but also, to judge from his biographers' accounts, by failing confidence in his own abilities. On Sacchi's death in 1661, Maratta took over unfinished commissions and oversaw the settling of the artist's estate, including his drawings, many of which came into his possession and later passed, with many of his own, into the collections now at Windsor Castle and in Düsseldorf.

Maratta was an assiduous draughtsman throughout his career and, judging by the many artists he trained who mimic his manner, an extremely effective teacher. When he was elected president of the Accademia di San Luca in 1664, that institution finally became the training school that its founders had envisioned but which it had rarely managed before then. Drawing sessions before posed models monitored by experienced masters took place on a regular basis. Artists gave a work to the academy when elected and paid dues regularly. Prizes were distributed for the best drawings of set subjects and talks were delivered to aspiring artists on such themes as "L'Idea del Bello" (The Idea of the Beautiful). This was, in fact, the title of Bellori's discourse of 1664, printed as the preface to his influential set of artists' lives published in 1672. He and

Maratta were close friends and shared the same artistic values—intense study of the best models from earlier art, ancient and modern, and close study of nature, especially the male body. Both men also believed that a good literary education was necessary to enable artists to understand the subjects they were depicting and to discuss them with the scholars who advised their patrons.

Maratta, like Sacchi, was not a decorator by temperament. His one major commission of this type—*The Triumph of Clemency* in the Salone of Palazzo Altieri painted for Clement X—is a dignified exercise in allegorical flattery confined by its gilded frame to a rectangular picture field with semicircular extensions at each end (Fig. **1.126**). The surrounding ceiling was left white, although other allegories were planned for the spandrels of the vaulting surrounding it. Like Sacchi, Maratta was more comfortable with altarpieces, usually variations on that staple, the *sacra conversazione*, on which Maratta could ring compositional changes with ease. An impressive example, *St. John the Evangelist Explaining the Doctrine of the Immaculate Conception to Sts. Gregory, Augustine, and John Chrysostom* (Fig. **1.127**), is still in the Cybo Chapel in Santa Maria del Popolo, where it was installed in 1686. Cardinal Alderano Cybo, a fervent supporter of this doctrine, had undertaken a lavish redecoration of the entire chapel in 1682, hiring the architect Carlo Fontana to design the new interior, and several other artists to fresco the dome and paint side altars. The Chigi Chapel across the aisle, whose sixteenth-century decoration was completed with two statues by Bernini for Alexander VII in the 1650s, has a dome mosaic designed by Raphael. Maratta was well aware of the proximity of this major work by his artistic hero as well as Cybo's desire to create a family chapel of comparable splendor, and took immense pains over this commission.

Maratta's altarpiece exemplifies his well-schooled talent and his enormous respect for the artists he believed set the standards of perfection. Raphael's *Disputation on the Holy Sacrament* of 1510 (Stanza della Segnatura, Vatican), which shows four Church Fathers beside an altar engaged in an animated discussion about the doctrine of transubstantiation, provided all the basic elements of Maratta's composition. He adapted the horizontal fresco to a vertical format with only one main figure in the sky instead of the spacious semicircular grouping of saints and angels in his model. His four saints considering the doctrine of Mary's sinless nature echo the four Church Fathers in Raphael's fresco fervently discussing the nature of the host displayed on the altar beside them. Maratta made a prodigious number of composition and figure studies before resolving the final design. All of them guide the viewer's eye from figure to figure, from side to

1.126 Carlo Maratta (Maratti), *The Triumph of Clemency*, 1673–75. Fresco, Palazzo Altieri, Rome.

1.127 Carlo Maratta (Maratti), *St. John the Evangelist Explaining the Doctrine of the Immaculate Conception to Sts. Gregory, Augustine, and John Chrysostom*, 1686. Oil on canvas. Cybo Chapel, Sta. Maria de Popolo, Rome.

side, before leading us up to the figure of the Virgin, whose seated pose comes from Raphael's *Madonna di Foligno* (Pinacoteca Vaticana), then still in Santa Maria in Aracoeli in Rome. The design invites the viewer to consider the arguments in defense of the Virgin's sinless nature advanced by each of the saints in her presence. It is not an approach that will move spectators unfamiliar with the theological debates into a deeper understanding of the doctrine. This is art for an intellectual elite that seeks persuasion through rational argument rather than appeal to its senses.

Giovanni Battista Gaulli (Il Baciccio)

For altarpieces and frescoes that combined exuberant painterly talents with some passion and dramatic effects that could impress and persuade the average worshiper, patrons could turn instead to Giovanni Battista Gaulli (1639–1709). Bernini spotted him soon after he reached Rome from Genoa around 1660. Gaulli was familiar with the sensuous painterly effects that Rubens and van Dyck produced in their portraits for Genoese patrons after their close study of Titian. Gaulli had also studied Genoese, Venetian, and Bolognese ceiling and dome decorations. He quickly found patrons for his brilliantly realized bust-length portraits among the College of Cardinals. Altarpieces and fresco commissions soon followed. Gaulli in turn discovered Bernini. The physiognomy of Gaulli's figures adopts the elongated, leggy bodies, cascading curly hair, convoluted drapery forms, and almost serpentine hands of Bernini's mature figure style.

Painting in Rome, 1623–1680

Gaulli was far more than the docile executor of Bernini's ideas. Only a painter of enormous gifts could have absorbed the visual language of Bernini, Rubens, van Dyck, Annibale Carracci, and Correggio and transformed it into new images of seductive beauty and powerful drama. The Virgin's hands and Christ's white loincloth in Gaulli's *Pietà* of 1667 (Fig. **1.128**), for example, recall Bernini, but the composition pays tribute to Annibale Carracci's *Pietà* (see Fig. 1.35). Gaulli reversed the pose of Christ and Mary, but retained her somber blue and violet robes, the dark setting, and the two mourning cherubim who here draw our attention to the wound in Christ's right hand instead of playing with the crown of thorns. Gaulli's Christ is thinner and is thus a more vulnerable-looking figure than Annibale's Savior. A very notable difference between the two works, however, is the way Gaulli has made the white cloth draped around Christ seem to glow with an inner light. The result is a vibrant shimmer to passages of drapery and limbs in well-lit areas of his paintings that makes the work of many of his peers look dull and flat.

Gaulli's special handling of light can be seen on the red velvet cape and hat in his portrait of *Clement IX* (Fig. **1.130**). No less effective is the rendering of the delicate features of the elderly pope and his blessing hand that seems to emerge from the pictorial space into ours. Clement IX, Giulio Rospigliosi, was pope for only two years (1667–9). He was so frail that he fainted several times when posing for Maratta's more conventional three-quarter-length seated image of him (Fig. **1.129**). The lips seem just about to part in Gaulli's sympathetic portrayal as he gazes kindly at the viewer in this exceptionally intimate image. This is Gaulli's interpretation in paint of Bernini's "speaking likeness" portrait busts. It is, despite its small scale, a masterpiece, as affecting as any papal portrait ever painted. Not even Raphael's introspective portrait of *Julius II* (National Gallery, London), made at the end of his reign when he was exhausted by military campaigns, lifts the official façade to reveal the vulnerable man behind it to a similar degree.

Gaulli did not owe his entire career to Bernini but the latter helped him to obtain his most important commission, the decoration of the

1.128 (opposite) Giovanni Battista Gaulli (Il Baciccio), *Pietà*, 1667. Oil on canvas, 72⅝ × 57⅝ in (185 × 147 cm). Palazzo Barberini, Rome.

1.129 (left) Carlo Maratta (Maratti), *Portrait of Clement IX Rospigliosi*, 1669. Oil on canvas, 11 × 63¾ in (254 × 162 cm). Pinacoteca Gallery, Vatican Museums, Rome.

1.130 (right) Giovanni Battista Gaulli (Il Baciccio), *Clement IX*, 1667–68. Oil on canvas, 29½ × 24¼ in (75 × 61.5 cm). Galleria Nazionale d'Arte Antica (Palazzo Barberini), Rome.

Painting in Rome, 1623–1680

Gesù, against strong competition. He also recommended Gaulli to the Jesuit fathers who commissioned him to paint the *Death of St. Francis Xavier* (Fig. **1.131**) for a chapel in Sant'Andrea al Quirinale, which Bernini designed and built for the Jesuit Noviciate between 1658 and 1670. Gaulli's painting was finished in 1676. Clutching a crucifix given to him by St. Ignatius, St. Francis Xavier had died alone in 1552 on an island within sight of the Chinese coast; after a decade spent spreading the Christian faith in Goa (Portuguese India), Ceylon (now Sri Lanka), and Japan, he had intended to do the same in China, a country then forbidden to foreigners. His only protection from the elements is a simple hut made of wood and straw. Gaulli's artistic inspiration seems to be Rubens's visionary lighting in his *Circumcision* (Sant'Ambrogio, Genoa) and the fluent compositions and expressive brushwork of the Genoese painter G.B. Castiglione (1609–63/4). The heavenly apparitions in the golden sky seen through billowing clouds, and the Berninesque angels and cherubim witnessing the saint's passage to heaven echo the heavenly apparition in the upper part of Bernini's *Cathedra Petri* (see Fig. 1.110). The saint's gaunt features, his almost skeletal hands, his black robes, and the dark landscape behind him make the glorious vision of heaven all the more incandescent.

1.131 Giovanni Battista Gaulli (Il Baciccio), *Death of St. Francis Xavier*, 1676. Oil on canvas, 8 ft 9 in × 5 ft 11 in (2.71 × 1.82 m). S. Andrea al Quirinale, Rome.

Before Gaulli undertook his extensive fresco campaign at the Gesù, he completed four large pendentives below the dome of Sant'Agnese in Agone, the imposing church that the Pamphili family had begun in 1652 in Piazza Navona. On its completion in 1665, Bernini recommended to Prince Camillo Pamphili that Gaulli be commissioned to paint the pendentives (Ciro Ferri painted the dome). Gaulli approached this important commission with some caution, preparing many sketches and, in 1669, making a study trip to Parma and Modena so that he could look at Correggio's frescoes before starting work. Each pendentive illustrates one or more virtues; in *Temperance and Chastity* (Fig. **1.132**), for example, a beautiful woman dressed in pale violet and white holding a branch of lilies is crowned with white roses by Fame. A putto above her to the right holds a horse's bit and reins, her standard attribute. She looks down at two winged putti, Eros and Anteros, that is sacred and profane love. Eros, crowned with laurel leaves and carrying a torch, is restraining his blindfolded and ruddier-fleshed companion. The woman in the middle distance on the left with a unicorn is Chastity. The distraught woman lying over the curved lower frame is Avarice, who clutches some jewelry and coins visible on the right. None of the figures projects beyond the picture plane to cast shadows on the frame, but the space is opened up behind the figures by the sky and clouds. This vista adds to the sensation that the figures that fill the front plane are floating masses of cloud and drapery. Indeed, the figures of Temperance and Fame seem to rise up from the right as if on the point of moving up and out of the framed space to the heavens behind them.

Gaulli's achievements should have assured him the commission to paint the ceilings of the Gesù without opposition, but several artists coveted

1.132 Giovanni Battista Gaulli (Il Baciccio), *Temperance and Chastity*, 1666–71. Fresco. S. Agnese in Agone.

Painting in Rome, 1623–1680 131

this important opportunity, including Ciro Ferri and Maratta. Bernini, a close friend of Padre Paolo Oliva, the Father General of the Jesuit Order, not only made sure that Gaulli obtained the commission; he also helped him to design some areas, among them the key figures in the dome. Gaulli began with the dome where God the Father and the dove of the Holy Spirit greet Christ and the Virgin amid a throng of saints, apostles, and the blessed (1672–5). He then completed the pendentives (1675–6) before taking up the challenge of the nave with the central fresco, *The Glorification of the Holy Name of Jesus* (Fig. **1.133**). This vast area took him and his assistants four years to complete. The flat barrel vault presents an uninterrupted surface except for four triangular wedges over window openings along each side. Gaulli followed Cortona's example in the Chiesa Nuova in providing a richly decorative architectural framework made

1.133 Giovanni Battista Gaulli (Il Baciccio), *The Glorification of the Holy Name of Jesus*, 1676–79. Nave fresco (post-1999 restoration). Il Gesù, Rome.

132 *Chapter 1: Italy*

of gilded plaster. Twin bands of rosette-filled coffers line up with the double pilasters in the nave below and edge the frame around the central picture field. He gave the windows elaborate frames and placed angels and allegorical figures around them too. Antonio Raggi, a sculptor who regularly assisted Bernini, was responsible for the sculptures, and a team of experienced craftsmen prepared the gilded stucco setting for the central fresco.

While the shape of the frame surrounding the fresco is clear—a rectangle extended by half-circles at each end—the actual shape of the fresco field is not. Gaulli extended it to accommodate the Damned pouring out of the clouds at the bottom and the Blessed rising up from the sides to join the heavenly vision surrounding the IHS sign of Christ glowing in the upper center of the picture field. The area of the painted fresco is thus an irregular shape that overlaps and breaks through the frame and seems to cover up a considerable part of the architectural decoration. Gaulli employed many clever devices to make the nave look open to the sky, with hosts of saints and angels floating up to heaven to adore the symbol of Christ while vices are thrust from heaven, tumbling into the space below. Many of the figures are painted in extreme foreshortening, thus strengthening the impression of being overhead. The gilded coffers are also glazed with brown to suggest shadows cast by the arc of clouds that breaks the frame on either side.

The notion of a vision arriving from heaven to earth was partly inspired by Bernini's *Cathedra Petri* (see Fig. 1.110), which Gaulli saw being completed in the mid-1660s to universal praise. Gaulli's work on the nave of the Gesù is far more than a painted echo of Bernini's sculpture. It is rightly seen as one of the greatest achievements by an Italian painter in the seventeenth century. It is also one of the works most frequently used to define "Baroque" art: it blends painting, sculpture, and architecture; it blurs the boundaries between the world created by the artist and the world of the spectator; it is full of color, movement, light, and drama; and it is intended to persuade all who see it of some essential truth by disarming viewers of rational argument. Gaulli provided a powerful and inspiring model for many later illusionistic ceilings in churches, old and new, especially in southern Germany in the eighteenth century. Its only rival was Padre Andrea Pozzo's later ceiling fresco in the nave of Sant'Ignazio nearby, painted in 1691–4, which celebrates the *Triumph of the Missionary Efforts of the Jesuits*. Its spectacular effect depends on the most extensive use of *quadratura* of any ceiling painted in seventeenth-century Italy.

Floating at the summit of Gaulli's fresco is a loop of ribbon on which appear a few words from a verse in the Epistle of St. Paul to the Philippians: "Wherefore God hath also highly exalted him, and given him a name which is above every other name: that at the name of Jesus every knee should bow, of things in heaven and things in earth and under the earth." This text is the message of the nave fresco. It is nothing less than the Church Triumphant spreading the faith throughout the world and conquering all heresies, vices, and alternative belief systems in the process. The Jesuits, as the brief account of the death of St. Francis Xavier given above makes clear, placed particular emphasis on carrying the Catholic faith beyond Europe to Asia and to Africa and America as well. This "propagation of the faith" was an important component of the Church's campaign to counteract the spread of Protestant sects, especially in the seventeenth century. A Vatican office dedicated to this goal, the Propaganda Fide, was established in the center of Rome. It is also the message behind Bernini's *Four Rivers Fountain* (see Fig. 1.114). None of the new orders had been more successful in doing this than the Jesuits; the Gesù, the mother church of the order, was an appropriate place to celebrate their achievements and inspire their young priests to continue these successes.

Gaulli's later work, especially that produced after the death of Bernini in 1680, is more restrained, probably to accommodate taste for the more conservative eclecticism of Maratta's art, which was promoted by the Accademia di San Luca and his numerous, well-schooled pupils. Gaulli continued to produce luminous altarpieces and frescoed the vault of SS. Apostoli in 1707, but had no real successors. Maratta's intelligent synthesis of the classicizing tendencies of earlier Roman painting had, however, one outstanding representative in the next century, namely Pompeo Batoni (1708–87).

Painting in Naples

This account has concentrated on developments in Rome. It has largely ignored what was happening elsewhere in Italy, although Bologna's contribution to the new styles has been covered up to mid-century. It has mentioned Rubens's and Van Dyck's works for Genoese patrons, but it has omitted the subsequent emergence of an important school of painters in Genoa. Milan, Venice, and Florence all had some excellent artists with distinctive stylistic traits that reflect their local traditions and new influences, and Bologna continued to produce first-rate painters of both decorative frescoes and easel paintings after the deaths of Reni and Guercino. No city except Rome, however, can offer the depth and continuity of artistic achievement in the seventeenth-century found in Naples.

Ruled from Madrid by viceroys, Naples was the largest and most prosperous city in the Italian peninsula in the seventeenth century, and offered opportunities for major commissions that drew artists there from Bologna and Rome and from Spain itself. Bombing during World War II as well as earlier earthquakes and later economic decline have taken a greater toll of important monuments in Naples than elsewhere in Italy. Nevertheless, much remains from the seventeenth century, and recent conservation efforts have restored such monuments as the Certosa di San Martino and the cathedral to much of their former splendor.

Caravaggio was in Naples from the autumn of 1606 until July 1607 and returned briefly in 1609. Two of the four public commissions that Caravaggio carried out there were destroyed in 1798 but two remain, a *Flagellation*, now moved from San Domenico to the museum at Capodimonte, and the *Seven Acts of Mercy*, still in the church for which it was made. His *The Crucifixion of St. Andrew* (Fig. 1.134) was also made there for the Conde de Benavente, the viceroy who took it back to Spain when he left in 1610. Caravaggio's art had an immediate impact on the local painters. Giovanni Battista Caracciolo (1578–1635), who was trained in the local Mannerist idiom, produced his *Immaculate Conception with Sts. Dominic and Francis of Paola* for Santa Maria della Stella in 1607. By then he had taken over the most distinctive traits of Caravaggio's late style, preferring, however, a sooty chiaroscuro and a cool silvery light on the key figures. His angels look like Caravaggio's adolescents, his male saints and his Virgin as if real people posed for them. Caracciolo went to Rome in 1614, where as well as Caravaggio's earlier work he could study that of his Roman followers, of whom Orazio Gentileschi most impressed him. Until Ribera settled in Naples in the 1620s, Caracciolo was the best painter working there and the most cosmopolitan in his artistic education. He was even capable of working in fresco, a medium few local artists up to then were comfortable using and which Caravaggio's followers generally avoided.

Caravaggio was not the only visitor to make an impression in Naples. Simon Vouet sent two handsome altarpieces to Naples in the 1620s and Reni also found patrons there. Domenichino and Lanfranco both moved to Naples in the 1630s to execute major fresco cycles for which the ecclesiastical authorities refused to hire Neapolitan painters. Local artists finally had to come to terms not only with the Roman schools' professional expertise with such commissions but also with Domenichino's refutation of Caravaggesque realism and somber lighting and Lanfranco's ability to create impressive visions of airborne saints and angels overhead. Nevertheless the dense shadows and brilliant lighting of Caravaggio's admirers persisted longer in Naples than elsewhere in Italy, primarily thanks to Ribera's brilliant continuation of Caravaggio's art, which he never abandoned. Even the exuberant Neapolitan school of still-life painting, which celebrates the splendid fish, fruit, vegetables, and flowers available there, owes its initial inspiration and taste for dark backgrounds to the still-lifes of Caravaggio and his circle.

Bernardo Cavallino (1616–c. 1656) who worked in Naples in the 1640s and 1650s, blended Ribera's intensely observed realism with a more idealizing conception of humanity. His life and career are poorly documented; he died in the plague. While his style shows an awareness of van Dyck and Rubens, who were both represented in local collections, and with the later Italian works of Vouet, Cavallino's figures have elongated proportions that are closer to a *maniera* aesthetic than to those seen in work by his contemporaries. His only public commission is also his only dated work, the *St. Cecilia in Ecstasy* of 1645 (Uffizi, Florence), made for Sant'Antonio da Padova in Naples. No other artist in Naples succeeded in suggesting the sensuous textures of silk, velvet, soft skin, and fine hair as well as he did; his color choices and handling of chiaroscuro effects are also exceptionally subtle. He is best known for small, cabinet-scale paintings with narrative subjects, although he also portrayed single figures, often beautiful young women playing the role of musician, saint, and the Virgin.

In his stunning rendering of *Judith with the Head of Holofernes* (Fig. **1.135**), the heroine is isolated from the narrative and presented as an icon of virtue who appears to address us while resting her elegant right hand on the Assyrian general's severed head. The luscious and alluring color scheme uses golden yellow for her blouse, rich lapis blue for her skirts, and dark green for the curtain behind her, draped to create a lively contour along the division between its dark folds and the lighter beige background. Yet the image is disturbing, for the hand which has just killed a man with a sword now tenderly caresses his head. Are the words we cannot hear her speak justifying her violent deed? The story has always been open to various interpretations: Judith, ostensibly an example of virtue courageously conquering vice, can also be seen as a beguiling woman who used devious schemes to achieve her aims. Judith's beauty, which enabled her to gain access to Holofernes and defeat him, is vividly present in Cavallino's image, which can be read both as a warning to the male sex to beware of dark-eyed women and as a tribute to Judith's piety and bravery. Her left hand holds her sword but mimics the gesture of a Venus *pudica*. This undercurrent of erotic appeal can be found in Cavallino's images of female saints, whose seductive gazes contradict the uplifting spiritual messages that they are meant to convey.

Mattia Preti (1613–99), like Caravaggio, was only a bird of passage in Naples but his arrival in 1656 coincided with the outbreak of the plague that killed about 60 per cent of the population, including Cavallino and Massimo Stanzione (1585–1656). Ribera had died four years earlier. Preti thus played a vital role in the revival of painting in Naples after 1656. He enjoyed a long career that involved travel throughout the peninsula, from his birthplace in Calabria to Rome, probably in the 1640s, then to Venice and Modena, and back to Rome in 1649. Having spent four years in Naples, he returned to Rome and then moved to Malta, where he settled for the rest of his life. Preti's brief presence in Naples was important because his mature work was a sophisticated blend of Venetian, Lombard, and Roman art that nevertheless employed the strong contrasts of somber shadows and dramatic highlights popular in Naples much later than elsewhere in Italy. He thus introduced them to innovations from other artistic centers in a form that made them appealing to local painters.

Among Preti's first commissions were votive frescoes commemorating the plague of 1656

1.134 Michelangelo Merisi da Caravaggio, *The Crucifixion of St. Andrew*, 1607. Oil on canvas, 6 ft 7 in × 5 ft (2.02 × 1.52 m). Cleveland Museum of Art, Cleveland, OH.

Painting in Naples

1.135 Bernardo Cavallino, *Judith with the Head of Holofernes*, c. 1650. Oil on canvas, 46 ½ × 37 in (118 × 94 cm). Nationalmuseum, Stockholm.

commissioned by the city authorities for the seven city gates. The frescoes have long since disappeared but the designs for two of them are recorded by preparatory *bozzetti* (Fig. **1.136**). These show Preti's ease when composing on a large scale, relating figures suspended in the air with others sprawled on the ground below in a skillful balance of shifting diagonals anchored by the majestic vertical figure of the Virgin placed at the summit. Preti was a brilliant draughtsman who could draw the human figure from any angle and who was as comfortable designing paintings to go overhead as on the walls. He was also a great narrative painter whose figures have naturally expressive body language and facial expressions that convey the essential emotional message of each story. His *The Feast of Herod* (Fig. **1.137**), one of a number of banquet subjects that he painted in Naples, shows his abilities as a dramatic painter to the full.

A superb late painting by Rubens on the same subject (Fig. **1.138**) was then in the collection of Ferdinand van den Einden in Naples, who almost certainly commissioned the *Feast of Herod* from Preti—another case of an artist spurred on to compete against a famous predecessor, knowing that his efforts would be compared with theirs. Both pictures fill the foreground with a table

1.136 Mattia Preti, *Virgin and Child with Sts. Francis Xavier and Rosalia*, 1656–59. Bozzetto for lost votive fresco for city gate. Oil on canvas, 50¼ × 30⅓ in (129 × 77 cm). National Museum of Capodimonte, Naples.

Painting in Naples 137

placed parallel to the picture plane, but Rubens left room for Salome to stand in front of it as she presents the Baptist's head to her parents. Only her father draws back from the sight; Herodias, wearing golden yellow, might as well be presenting him with a roast goose, so cheerful does she seem. Salome, standing in the central foreground in her crimson dress, dominates the picture. Preti's treatment is cool and restrained by comparison. His table is set at the edge of the picture plane, bringing the viewer close to Herodias, seated in the center, with Salome and Herod at either end of the table. Herodias touches her hand to her chest as if she is feeling ill and seems to gaze past the head presented to her by a very young Salome. Herod, wearing the turban and brocade robes of a Turkish potentate, seems calm, making a gesture with his right hand that seems to ask: "Is this what you two women wanted?" Viewers will find themselves looking from one side of the picture to the other, seeking to understand the expressions of this family group who have had a man killed to satisfy a whim. The figures behind the protagonists stare at the head of St. John the Baptist with a mixture of curiosity and awe. The color scheme is somber. This is a far more subtle psychological reading of the story than Rubens's colorful drama.

Luca Giordano (1634–1705) stepped into the breach left by the plague and Preti's departure for Malta. The son of a painter, he studied first with Ribera, who made an indelible impression on the young artist. His early pictures of saints and philosophers come astonishingly close to those of his teacher, including their somber palette, meticulously observed bodies of old men, and patchy illumination. When Ribera died in 1652, Luca went north to see what artists in Rome, Florence, and Venice had achieved. Titian, Veronese, and Pietro da Cortona made the biggest impression and soon Luca had lightened up his palette, mastered Venetian colorism, and (though this took longer) the fluent compositional dynamics

1.137 Mattia Preti, *The Feast of Herod*, c. 1665, Oil on canvas, 70 × 99¼ in (177.8 × 252 cm). Toledo Museum of Art, Toledo, OH.

1.138 Peter Paul Rubens, *The Feast of Herod*, c. 1639. Oil on canvas, 81¼ × 103 in (208 × 264 cm). National Gallery of Scotland, Edinburgh.

of Cortona's great frescoes in Rome and Florence. Luca's first public commissions were made for churches in Venice in 1653, when he was only nineteen. He continued to study the works of other artists after his return—Preti in particular—and his style can seem to fluctuate as he chose different modes depending on the subject matter. Enormously productive, he acquired the nickname "Luca, fa presto!," supposedly from his father urging him on to paint more quickly and bring in more money.

Giordano's major decorative commissions include that for the abbey at Montecassino, painted in 1677–8 (destroyed 1944), and those in Santa Brigida and San Gregorio Armeno in Naples immediately afterwards. Arguably his masterpiece in fresco, however, was the *Galleria* in the Palazzo Medici-Riccardi, Florence, made for the Medici in 1682–5 (Fig. **1.139**). Its long, narrow shape made it impossible to create one climactic vista. Instead, taking a cue from Cortona's experience with a similar long, narrow ceiling in Palazzo Pamphili in Rome, Luca created a series of incidents taking place along the edges of the Galleria ceiling that entice the viewer to walk slowly along each side while looking across to the other, savoring each moment before continuing to the next group of allegorical events. He dispensed with any painted or stucco framing elements, as Cortona did in the Sala di Marte in Palazzo Pitti, Florence, so that the ceiling seems opened up into one unified space of sunny skies, verdant meadows, and, to accommodate Neptune and his denizens, some lightly tossed waves. The current members of the Medici clan are shown in one central cloudburst as happy residents of Mount Olympus welcomed by Zeus, Mars, Minerva, and Mercury. The mood is

1.139 Luca Giordano, *Galleria*, 1682–85. Fresco. Palazzo Medici-Riccardi, Florence.

light-hearted with even more gorgeous blondes and plump putti than in Cortona's frescoes in Palazzo Pitti.

The patron of Luca's splendid *St. Michael Vanquishing the Devil* (Fig. **1.140**) is not known. Luca knew Guido Reni's elegant interpretation in Rome (see Fig. 1.70) but the pose of his saint is much closer to the dancing conqueror of Raphael's late version. Luca's St. Michael looks back over his shoulder at a monstrous creature whose screaming mouth and huge nostrils serve to emphasize the saint's serene beauty. Following Ribera, Luca used the pinks, blues, and whites worn by St. Michael to represent heaven, while the russet skin tones, chocolate-brown shadows, and strong chiaroscuro of the fallen angels' setting symbolize both earth and hell. The highlights on St. Michael are cleverly distributed to accent the movement of his pose—one wing in full light, the other in shadow except for its upper rim, and his cloak too in shadow on his left side except for a patch on its hem.

Luca Giordano was summoned to Spain by Charles II and spent the decade 1692–1702 working for the court, producing major frescoes in the Escorial, the Palazzo del Buen Retiro, and the sacristy of Toledo Cathedral as well as many canvases for churches and private collectors.

He was only seventy-one when he died, worn out, it seems, by the efforts required to produce such an enormous body of work. His ceiling frescoes were especially influential in the eighteenth century, affecting not only Italians like Corrado Giaquinto (1703–65) and G.B. Tiepolo (1676– 1770), who both followed him to Spain, but Spain's greatest painter of the next centuries, Francisco Goya (1746–1828). Luca painted fast but he also painted exceptionally well as he carried the history of Baroque ceiling decoration into the eighteenth century.

1.140 Luca Giordano, *St. Michael Vanquishing the Devil*, c. 1663. Oil on canvas, 78 × 57⅞ in (198 × 147 cm). Staatliche Museum, Berlin.

2 Flanders

Jan Brueghel, the Elder, *Still-Life with Bouquet of Flowers*, c. 1607. Oil on canvas, 8⅞ × 7⅛ in (22.6 × 18.2 cm). Städelsch Kunstinstitut, Frankfurt.

The territorial boundaries that divide Belgium from Holland today did not exist in the sixteenth century, but elements of the political and religious conflict that would lead to the separation of the seven northern provinces of the old Burgundian-Hapsburg territories from its southern provinces were already in play (see Fig. 1.1). In 1554 Emperor Charles V had ceded control of the Netherlands to his son, Philip II, King of Spain. Then the most densely populated part of Europe, the Low Countries (so called because the terrain was flat, and in the north, partly below sea level) were a valuable gift. Ludovico Guicciardini's *Descrittione di Fiandra* (Description of Flanders) of 1567 provides some impressive statistics, among them that there were 200 walled cities and 12,000 villages. The land was fertile enough to feed all its citizens and yield surplus grain for export to Spain. The court of Charles V and his successors was established in Brussels, which became the administrative center of the Netherlands, but the most dynamic city was Antwerp.

Antwerp dominated Europe's financial markets. Its port, which had replaced Bruges as the busiest in the Netherlands at the end of the fifteenth century, attracted Portuguese ships with spices from Indonesia, English ships with linen and wool for finishing, and precious materials from Spain's new colonies in South America for Antwerp's skilled craftsmen to turn into luxury objects for wealthy collectors throughout Europe. Guicciardini reported that Antwerp had more artists than butchers or bakers. International trade resulted in a cosmopolitan atmosphere while generating the wealth that supported the court, and the city's bankers, merchants, tradesmen, and flourishing artistic community. The publishing house founded there by Christopher Plantin in 1555 was as productive as any of its rivals in Paris and Venice. Antwerp's well-educated elite not only filled their reception rooms with works of art in many media and precious objects, man made and natural, but they also supported a number of *rederijker kamers* (chambers of rhetoric) where they performed plays and read poetry. A new town hall, finished in 1566, whose width spanned a city block and whose style firmly rejected Gothic forms for the latest in Italian Renaissance architectural vocabulary (Fig. **2.1**), was a proud symbol of Antwerp's powerful economy, modern outlook, and civic pride.

Within a decade, this flourishing, sophisticated, and relatively tolerant culture began to disintegrate as Philip II forbade all forms of Christian worship except Roman Catholicism. He had appointed Margaret of Parma Regent of the Netherlands in 1559 when he returned to Madrid. She and her advisers were reluctant, however, to follow the king's orders. The merchant classes were also opposed to the suppression of Calvinism as bad for business. When the king issued edicts that required even penitent

2.1 Cornelis Floris, Town Hall, Antwerp, 1561–66.

heretics to be put to death, those likely to be persecuted in addition to those opposed to such fanaticism began to leave the Spanish Netherlands. Trade with England had been interrupted in 1563, resulting in severe unemployment among the craftsmen who finished wool. An especially severe winter in 1565–6 produced famine conditions and unrest. Calvinist preachers began to attract large crowds. The iconoclastic riots that broke out in August 1566 were sparked both by hatred of Spanish intervention in local affairs and by anger directed against corrupt Catholic clerics whose lavish households aroused the jealousy of a populace under increasing economic stress. Antwerp, a Calvinist stronghold, suffered extensive damage.

In August 1567 the Duke of Alba, with the support of Pope Pius IV and Philip II, arrived from Italy with an army to enforce the Edicts of the Council of Trent, issued in 1564 but never promulgated by Margaret. He imposed new and severe taxes, which were hated and resisted. He arrested the Counts of Egmont and Horn, both Knights of the Golden Fleece, condemning them for allowing Calvinist preachers to spread their heretical teachings, and had them executed in Brussels the following summer. Over 12,000 other people were arrested for heresy and hundreds were executed. The population of the Spanish Netherlands declined by 2 per cent during the Duke of Alba's reign of terror. The population of Antwerp dropped even more dramatically, however, declining from over 100,000 in 1568 to 42,000 by 1589. Many artists, both Catholic and Calvinist, were among the refugees. Rubens's father moved his family to Cologne, that of Frans Hals to Haarlem. It was a commercial and cultural diaspora from which the cities that had created the artistic Renaissance in Northern Europe never fully recovered.

When Peter Paul Rubens returned to Antwerp from Italy in 1608, the city had begun to repair the damage caused by the riots. Its economy slowly improved, although trade from its port was reduced by tariffs imposed by the Northern Provinces. The Twelve Year Truce, signed in 1609, brought an end to territorial skirmishes over the borders between North and South. The Catholic Church commissioned altarpieces to replace those destroyed by the riots, and some new churches were built, notably by the Jesuits, who had arrived in Flanders in 1562. Archduke Albert and his wife, the Infanta Isabella, while firm supporters of the Catholic faith, allowed the Calvinists who remained or resumed their faith to practice it in private. Compared with the situation there before 1554, however, or with that in the Dutch Republic throughout the seventeenth century, the economy of the Spanish Netherlands was anemic and support for the visual arts was thus limited. By the later seventeenth century, attacks by Louis XIV on its southern borders imposed more financial and human hardships. These economic circumstances help to explain why the range and depth of artistic production in Flanders in the century of Rubens, van Dyck, and Jordaens, cannot rival those of the previous two centuries, or those of the Dutch Republic, which had the most robust economy in Europe in the seventeenth century.

Peter Paul Rubens

Given the economic and political conditions of his country during the forty years of his activity, the career of Peter Paul Rubens (Fig. 2.2) is astonishing. The only recent attempt to provide a complete list of paintings executed primarily by the artist himself or in collaboration with his large studio contains over 1,400 items. While roughly a third of these are small oil sketches or reduced versions of final designs made for a patron's approval, the total is nonetheless extraordinary. On Sundays he made frontispiece designs for his friend Balthasar Moretus, who ran the Plantin Press in Antwerp. Rubens's life was by no means confined to painting. He conducted a lively correspondence with scholars who shared his intellectual interests and with owners of works of art that he wanted to acquire for his own collection. In the 1620s he was actively engaged in politics on behalf of the Spanish court, attempting to bring the Northern Provinces and England back into the Roman Catholic fold. Furthermore, he was twice happily married, and the proud father of seven children. His faith, his politics, his intellect, and his family all played an important role in his art.

Peter Paul Rubens was born on June 28, 1577, in Siegen, Westphalia, the youngest of five children. His father Jan, a lawyer with Calvinist sympathies, had moved the family to Cologne in 1568 to escape the persecutions that followed the arrival of the Duke of Alba in Brussels in 1567. Both Jan Rubens and his wife came from families whose level of education and wealth were above that of most artists. He had lived in Italy for five years while studying law in Padua and was fluent in Latin and Italian, the international language of diplomacy. Exiled in 1570 to Siegen after his affair with the wife of William of Orange, Jan supervised the education of both Philip (b. 1573) and Peter Paul, teaching them Italian as well as Latin before his death in 1587. The family then returned to Antwerp and to the Catholic faith. The adult Rubens was so familiar with the writings of classical authors such as Cicero, Seneca, Horace, and Juvenal that he could quote appropriate passages from memory in his letters. Only in 1591, when he was fourteen, did he abandon the studies that would have enabled him to follow his father's career and start training to be a painter.

By the standards of most sixteenth- and seventeenth-century painters, who left school before their teens, Rubens had an exceptional education, which continued for the rest of his life. His library contained over three hundred books when he died. His close knowledge of ancient mythology and philosophy and of Catholic doctrine meant that, unlike most of his peers, he did not

2.2 Peter Paul Rubens, *Self-Portrait*, 1638–40. Oil on canvas, 43⅛ × 33½ in (109.5 × 85 cm). Kunsthistorisches Museum, Vienna.

2.3 Peter Paul Rubens, *The Judgment of Paris*, 1599. Oil on oak panel, 52¹¹⁄₁₆ × 68¹¹⁄₁₆ in (133.9 × 174.5 cm). National Gallery, London.

need to have literary or theological consultants at his elbow while composing his designs. His family's good social standing gave him the confidence needed to deal with powerful patrons. After brief service as a page in the household of Countess Marguerite de Lalaing d'Arenberg in 1591, Rubens left to begin his studies with the landscape painter Tobias Verhaecht (1561–1631), then joined the studios of Adam van Noort (1561–1641) and Otto van Veen (1556–1629). The latter had spent eight years in Italy, returning to Brussels in 1583 as painter to Alessandro Farnese before moving to Antwerp in 1593. In Rome, van Veen had met Federico Zuccaro, whose disciplined, conservative style owed much to Michelangelo but avoided the more extreme aspects of Italian Mannerism. Van Veen gave Rubens a solid technical education and inspired him to see for himself the statues and frescoes of Michelangelo and other Italian Renaissance masters and the famous antiquities of Rome.

Few paintings made by Rubens before 1600 survive to show us how much he had learnt before reaching Italy. One of them is *The Judgment of Paris* (Fig. **2.3**), which was inspired by Marc'Antonio Raimondi's engraving after Raphael's composition of the same theme (Fig. **2.4**). This print is familiar because the river gods and nymphs on the right are the source of Edouard Manet's *Déjeuner sur l'herbe* (1863, Musée d'Orsay, Paris). In 1600 it was admired as one of Raphael's most ambitious print designs and Raimondi's best engravings. Rubens did not stick closely to his source. The three goddesses awaiting the verdict of Paris fill the center of Rubens's painting and Venus, the winner, faces us instead of Paris, though she looks at him. He has his back to the viewer, whose presence is implied by the frontal poses of Venus and, just behind her, Juno. Minerva's back view helps us to imagine all three women in the round. Most of the subsidiary figures in the print have been eliminated. In addition to Mercury, only a river god and a nymph watch from the right and, on the left, a pair of lusty satyrs, Rubens's only addition to the original cast. The cool flesh tones and equally cool palette for the landscape—icy blues, dark greens, and chocolate browns—are typical of the Antwerp school at this date. Rubens probably finished this painting just before he left for Mantua. More than thirty years later he produced another interpretation of the same subject (Fig. **2.5**). The warm colors—rust and plum reds, golden yellow, olive greens, and creamy flesh tones accented with cinnabar—and the sketchy, visible brushwork make the second *Judgment of Paris* look like the work of a different artist, which in a sense it is. We will now explore the evolution of Rubens's style and his narrative language between these two works, that is, from 1600 to 1635.

Some characteristic traits can be followed throughout Rubens's career. His admiration for the art of the past, ancient and modern, and his incorporation of borrowed motifs, poses, and compositional devices into his own art is an important component of his artistic makeup. The relaxed adaptation of Raphael's figures in the *Judgment of Paris* already hints at Rubens's mature working methods: a single work may contain many such borrowings. Rubens would have expected his fellow artists and more sophisticated patrons to recognize his adaptations of motifs from Michelangelo, Raphael, and Titian and to appreciate their suitability to each context, just as they did his citations from learned authorities in his letters. Rubens believed that such knowledge, combined with mastery of human anatomy, was essential for any artist hoping to make his name and rival the achievements of the past.

From the beginning of his career, Rubens's patrons were drawn from the ruling classes of Europe. The first of these was Vincenzo Gonzaga,

Duke of Mantua, to whose court Rubens traveled in May 1600 to work as both painter and diplomat. He went on to work for Archduke Albert and his consort, the Infanta Isabella, Regents of the Spanish Netherlands, for Kings Philip III and IV of Spain, for Charles I of England, and for Marie de' Medici, second wife of Henry IV of France and regent after his assassination, to name only his most powerful

2.4 Marc'Antonio Raimondi (after a design by Raphael), *The Judgment of Paris*, c. 1517-20. Engraving.

2.5 Peter Paul Rubens, *The Judgment of Paris*, c. 1635. Oil on panel, 57 × 76¼ in (144.8 × 193.7 cm). National Gallery, London.

Peter Paul Rubens 147

employers. Italian artists during the Renaissance had struggled to be accepted as practitioners of intellectual, not craft professions, and as the social equals of gentlemen. Rubens's perfect manners, his well-furnished mind, abundant artistic imagination, and the complex, exuberant art that it produced brought him not only commissions from the most powerful families in Europe but also acceptance as a social equal at every European court with which he came into contact. Knighted by Charles I and by Philip IV, Rubens accomplished a rare feat, namely to be seen simultaneously as a gentleman, a great craftsman, and a great intellect.

Rubens in Italy, 1600–1608

The time that Rubens spent in Italy was to have a lasting influence on his painting. During his eight years based there, he left only once, to go to Madrid in 1603–4 to take gifts from Vincenzo Gonzaga to Philip III. The first of Rubens's surviving letters informs the Mantuan duke that the gifts had arrived safely, but also complains tactfully of his need for money. He did the first of his equestrian portraits in Madrid for the Duke of Lerma, who is shown as if riding out of the canvas toward us (Fig. 2.6), a bold departure from the traditional profile view. Eventually Rubens's need for money made him seek commissions from other patrons in Italy. The most important of these was the high altar of the new church of the Oratorian Order in Rome, Santa Maria in Vallicella, finished in 1608. He painted three large panels for the chapel of St. Helena in Santa Croce in Gerusalemme, one of the seven churches visited by every pilgrim to Rome, as well as altarpieces for other patrons in Genoa and Fermo. Besides religious and mythological works for private patrons, he also painted portraits in Rome, Mantua, and Genoa. Before he returned to Antwerp, he had lived for extended periods in those three cities, also visiting Parma, Venice, Bologna, and Florence. His Italian was fluent; it was to be his preferred language for corresponding with scholars and diplomats throughout Europe.

Rubens was twenty-three when he first arrived in Mantua but acted as if his studies had only begun. He drew constantly both to understand the achievements of ancient sculptors and Italian artists better and to have records of these works to hand after he returned to Antwerp. He drew the Laocoön, the Belvedere torso, and the Farnese Hercules, analyzing their proportions and making detailed studies of the expressive heads for later use. His drawing of the head of the Farnese Hercules in profile (Fig. 2.7) exudes authority appropriate for later images of commanding male figures. He made at least ten studies after the prophets, sibyls, and ignudi on the Sistine ceiling, and must also have made similar studies after Michelangelo's *Last Judgment*: individual figures as well as adaptations of the whole composition appear in his later work. In Florence he made several drawings after sculptures by Michelangelo. The use of chalks rather than pen and ink with toned washes made the stone surfaces seem soft and life-like, an important consideration as we know from Rubens's own words:

> *I am convinced that in order to achieve the highest perfection one needs a full understanding of [ancient] statues, nay a complete absorption in them; but one must make judicious use of them; and before all avoid the appearance of stone.*[1]

2.6 Peter Paul Rubens, *Portrait of the Duke of Lerma*, 1603. Oil on canvas, 9 ft 3 in × 6 ft 6 in (2.83 × 2 m). Prado, Madrid.

The Laocoön by Maderno (see Fig. 1.102) looks almost lifeless beside Rubens' drawing (Fig. 2.8) because Rubens copied freely, adding naturalistic anatomical details missing in the original and giving the embracing snakes more girth and more sinuous, energetic positions.

The collections in Mantua included important groups of work by Giulio Romano, Correggio, Parmigianino, Tintoretto, and Veronese, as well as Mantegna's extraordinary evocation of ancient Rome, his *Triumphs of Julius Caesar* (Royal Collection, Hampton Court). Nearby in Venice he could study the altarpieces of Titian and Paolo Veronese and Jacopo Tintoretto's vast cycle of Old and New Testament subjects in the Scuola di San Rocco. The latter especially impressed Rubens—the strong chiaroscuro and dramatic light effects, unusual viewpoints for familiar scenes, and surging currents of movement in crowd scenes—all were understood, recorded in notebooks, and incorporated into his own work.

He probably also bought prints, including some of Agostino Carracci's superb engraved reproductions after works such as Veronese's *Mystic Marriage of St. Catherine* (see Fig. 1.14), Antonio Correggio's *Madonna of St. Jerome* (Galleria Nazionale, Parma) and Tintoretto's *Crucifixion* in the Scuola di San Rocco (see Fig. 2.16).

Rubens's obvious borrowings in his Italian period testify to his desire to incorporate the best of earlier art, as he saw it, without prejudice to Italian views about the superiority of Raphael and Michelangelo to Titian and Tintoretto (if you were Florentine), or vice versa (if you were Venetian). Rubens found poses and compositions easier to master than Venetian and Lombard color and technique. Compared with his later works, his early Italian paintings can seem murky; after his return North, his colors become lighter and warmer and his brushstrokes more visible. Although he was in his twenties while in Italy, he was still finding his way, revealing

2.7 (left) Peter Paul Rubens, *Head of the Farnese Hercules*, 1606–08. Black chalk heightened with white chalk drawing, 14⅓ × 9⅝ in (36.3 × 24.5 cm). Courtauld Institute of Art Gallery, London.

2.8 (right) Peter Paul Rubens, Study after *Laocoön*, 1600–5. Black chalk, 17⅓ × 11 in (44 × 28 cm). Biblioteca Ambrosiana, Milan.

Peter Paul Rubens

2.9 Peter Paul Rubens, *The Transfiguration*, 1605. Oil on canvas, 13 ft 4 in × 21 ft 11 in (4.07 × 6.7 m). Musée des Beaux-Arts, Nancy.

2.10 Peter Paul Rubens, *Marchesa Brigida Spinola Doria*, 1606. Oil on canvas, 60 × 38¼ in (152.4 × 98.4 cm). National Gallery of Art, Washington, DC.

his models openly, though never without altering and transforming them. His *The Transfiguration* (Fig. **2.9**) takes Raphael's famous vertical altarpiece (Pinacoteca Vaticana, Rome) and turns it into a horizontal design invested with all the chiaroscuro drama of a Tintoretto. Blending the work of an artist exemplifying Roman *disegno* with that of a Venetian exponent of *colore* was surely a deliberate tactic, a brazen challenge to the provincial boundaries drawn between the styles associated with Venice and Parma, Florence and Rome by their supporters during the Renaissance. Rubens was never ashamed to admit his admiration for earlier artistic achievements. We need to appreciate his encyclopedic visual education and the ways in which he weaves that knowledge into his own highly distinctive amalgam of Greek, Roman, Renaissance Italian, and Flemish traditions if we are to understand his artistic achievements.

Portraits were a sideline for Rubens but he excelled in this genre throughout his career. The evolution of European portraiture can be traced from several prototypes of his invention that were later adopted by Anthony van Dyck and others. Rubens's equestrian *Portrait of the Duke of Lerma* (see Fig. 2.6) launched a motif taken up several times by van Dyck. Even more influential was that of *Marchesa Brigida Spinola Doria* (Fig. **2.10**). Originally full-length, the canvas now shows the elegant young aristocrat only to her knees: we must imagine her white silk wedding dress reaching the ground. A more spacious setting for the picture was eliminated when the picture was cut down on all sides in the nineteenth century. Its original format is known from a drawing by Rubens (Fig. **2.11**).

Full-length portraits were a novelty in the sixteenth-century. Titian used the format only for Philip II of Spain and Charles V, the Holy Roman Emperor, although a few aristocratic North Italian families commissioned them too. This format retained its connotations of high rank and power well into the seventeenth century and the Genoese preferred it. Brigida Spinola's marriage in 1605 at the age of twenty-one united two of the most distinguished families in Genoa, whose aristocrats were known for their exceptional formality (detractors called them "the stiff-necked Genoese"). The young marchesa regards us from her elevated position, further cut off from us by her splendid ruff, neither smiling nor solemn, confident of her place in society. The foreshortened architecture behind her indicates that our heads are well below hers, and, by implication, our rank as well. The architecture also tells us that she lives in a palace with immense rooms; the jewels in her hair and on her dress further emphasize her wealth and standing. This is a portrait about rank and status; it reveals virtually nothing about her own character and personality. It was a success, becoming a model for other full-length portraits of Genoese sitters that adopted the outdoor setting with some ostentatious architecture as well to buttress the stiffly posed sitters.

Rubens's success in obtaining public commissions was exceptional for a foreign artist. Italian artists resented them going to outsiders and Italian patrons were usually loyal to the artists of their own territories. His powerful contacts at the courts of Mantua and Milan played a role, as did his diplomatic skills. His most important commission was for the high altar of the Chiesa

2.11 Peter Paul Rubens, *Study for Portrait of Brigida Spinola Doria*, 1606. Pen and brown ink with wash over black chalk, 12⅜ × 7⅓ in (31.5 × 18.5 cm). Pierpont Morgan Library, New York.

2.12 Martino Longhi the Elder, Chiesa Nuova, nave and choir, Rome (apse fresco by Pietro da Cortona), 1575–1606.

Nuova in Rome, awarded in 1607 thanks to the support of Jacopo Serra, the papal treasurer. The painting had to be replaced with a second version on slate when it proved difficult to see the original because of the reflections on its surface (Fig. 2.12).

The commission required Rubens to incorporate into his design a small painting of the Virgin and Child (the "Madonna di Vallicella") that was believed to have miraculous powers. In both versions, a framed image of Mary and the infant Jesus appears in the upper part of the tall canvas, while six saints—Gregory, Maurus, Papianus, Domitilla, Nereus, and Achilleus—are shown below, either looking out at the spectator or gazing heavenwards. The image of the Virgin is mounted on a separate support, which on special occasions can be lowered behind the main picture to reveal the much older sacred image it conceals. The saints, apart from Gregory the Great, are obscure, legendary early martyrs to the Christian cause. Gregory is the central and dominant figure in the first version (Fig. 2.13), in which he is flanked by a valiant Christian soldier (Maurus) and a devout virgin martyr (Domitilla). In the second version, the six saints were shifted to two separate paintings installed on either side of the choir, St. Gregory dominating the group on the left and Domitilla that on the right. The sacred image thus became the principal focus of the composition with its rows of adoring angels and exuberant putti flying round the oval frame, but the size of the image over the high altar was reduced, and thus its impact too. The gorgeous white silk robes worn by St. Gregory in the first version, which may have been judged a distraction from the small holy image above, have been toned down in the second version in which he wears an ocher yellow cloak over a white surplice. Domitilla's icy gray and pale blue garments of the first version have been subdued with shadows in the second version. Rubens relished the opportunity to contrast an old man with a young woman, and military figures with toga-wearing companions, both to avoid monotony for the viewer and to demonstrate his artistic range. He hoped that his Mantuan patron, Duke Vincenzo, would acquire the first version, but he did not; and when Rubens failed to find a buyer in Rome, he shipped it back to Antwerp. He later installed it in the funerary chapel of his mother in the abbey of St. Michael. She had died in October 1608 before he could reach her bedside.

Rubens in Antwerp, 1609–1622

Rubens's first letters to friends in Rome reveal his regret at leaving and his desire to go back as soon as possible. Still, he returned to Flanders at a fortunate moment, for the signing of the Twelve Year Truce between the Seven Provinces and the Spanish Netherlands brought a welcome respite from intermittent warfare. Rubens was treated royally on his return. After finishing official portraits of Archduke Albert and Infanta Isabella in August 1609, Rubens was rewarded with a gold chain, and one month later was appointed their court painter. The archduke did not insist that the artist move his studio to Brussels, made few requests of him, and in addition gave him a dispensation from the rules normally enforced by the Antwerp Guild of Painters regarding assistants. He even exempted Rubens from paying taxes.

2.13 Peter Paul Rubens, *St. Gregory (Pope) Surrounded by Saints, Worshipping the Miraculous Image of the Virgin and Child*, 1606–7. Oil on canvas, 15 ft 5 in × 9 ft 2 in (4.7 × 2.8 m). Musée de Grenoble.

An advantageous marriage was arranged in 1609 with Isabella Brandt, the beautiful seventeen-year-old daughter of Jan Brandt, a distinguished humanist and lawyer, as Rubens's father had been. Public commissions quickly followed—a *Disputation on the Sacrament* for St. Paul's, an *Adoration of the Magi* for the town hall (Prado, Madrid) and an *Annunciation* for the Jesuits (Kunsthistorisches Museum, Vienna), all finished in 1609. A decade of intense activity followed as Rubens settled into a new home, built himself an impressive studio inspired by the palace architecture he had studied in Genoa (see Fig. 2.20), and painted altarpieces, mythological paintings, private religious commissions, and portraits, both official and intimate, of his influential patrons, and of his adored wife and children. His fame as an artist and humanist were quickly established. He became, according to many critics, then and now, "the greatest and most influential figure in Baroque art in Northern Europe."

Rubens celebrated his marriage to Isabella Brandt in 1609 with a magnificent full-length double portrait showing himself seated with her in front of a honeysuckle bower, an allusion to the garden of love (Fig. **2.14**). She is seated on a low stool; he is placed slightly above her. Both of them look directly at the viewer: he is alert; she has a slight smile. While she dominates the foreground, his slightly elevated position hints at the traditionally dominant role of husband. His right hand cradles hers palm down on his wrist, a formal gesture also alluding to their recent marriage. Rubens went to immense pains to record their expensive clothes: note the embroidery on his vest and his lace collar; her delicately pleated ruff, figured cream stomacher, and padded black jacket with bands of mat and shiny silk. They are among the finest illusionistic passages in his work. His right foot is placed so that her wine-red silk skirt cascades over it, hinting at their intimate relationship. Only those who know that the husband is Rubens would know that this is a self-portrait and not simply a picture of a prosperous happy couple.

Among the works singled out in even the briefest accounts of Rubens's career in this decade are two enormous triptychs that represent the moments just before and immediately after the crucifixion of Christ. The *Raising of the Cross* of 1610–11, painted for the high altar of St. Walburga (Fig. **2.15**), and the *Descent from the Cross* of 1611–12, made for the altar of the Guild of Longbowmen in Antwerp Cathedral (see Fig. **2.18**), are now both displayed in the cathedral. The mayor of Antwerp, Nicolas Rockox, helped Rubens obtain the commission of the *Descent*, and Cornelis van der Geest, a wealthy merchant and art collector, that for St. Walburga. In these works Rubens employed everything that he had learnt in Italy to make his mark as a master painter in his home town. Although the original setting of the *Raising of the Cross* no longer exists—St. Walburga was torn down in 1817—we know that the choir was twenty steps above the level of the nave. This meant that worshipers saw the picture from well below eye level. The original frame had an image

2.14 Peter Paul Rubens, *Self-Portrait with Isabella Brandt*, 1609–10. Oil on canvas, 5 ft 9 in × 4 ft 5 in (1.78 × 1.36 m). Alte Pinakothek, Munich.

of God the Father above the central image flanked by carved angels at which the crucified Christ gazed in devout concentration. At the summit of the entire work was a carving of a pelican feeding her young with her own blood, a symbol of Christ's sacrifice for mankind's salvation. There were also predella scenes below. It has been estimated that in its original form the altarpiece was 35 feet (10.66 meters) high. When open, the triptych measures 21 feet (6.4 meters) across; it is 15 feet (4.57 meters) high. It is Rubens's largest single composition.

While the subject of Christ's body being taken down from the cross after his death inspired several ambitious altarpieces in sixteenth-century Italy, no one had ever painted the moment when the cross was elevated with the living Christ on it until Rubens made an awkward attempt on one of the three panels he painted for Santa Croce in Gerusalemme in 1601. Rubens may well have decided to depict this moment himself.

His inspiration was Tintoretto's huge horizontal *Crucifixion* in the Scuola di San Rocco (Fig. 2.16). Instead of showing the two thieves already attached to their crosses erected on either side of Christ, as was the custom, Tintoretto showed one thief lying on his cross on the ground while executioners bind him to it as the other thief is lifted upright on his cross, enabling the viewer to imagine more clearly this cruel method of execution. The emotional impact generated by this narrative device was understood by Rubens, who shows Christ himself being raised upright by men whose muscular backs rival anything by Michelangelo or from antiquity. Even Christ is a far more athletic male figure than usual. His pose and facial expression are modeled on that of the father in the Laocoön group with alterations only to the left arm and right leg. The forceful chiaroscuro that mixes fully lit figures with others silhouetted against light ground is also inspired by Tintoretto, as is the way that contours of lighter

2.15 Peter Paul Rubens, *Raising of the Cross*, 1610–11. Oil on canvas, central panel 15 ft 2 in × 11 ft 2 in (4.62 × 3.51 m); wings 15 ft 2 in × 4 ft 11 in (4.62 × 1.5 m). Antwerp Cathedral.

Peter Paul Rubens 155

2.16 (and opposite) Agostino Carracci, *Crucifixion* (left), 1589. Engraving on three sheets, after Jacopo Tintoretto (right): 20 × 15⅝ in (51 × 39.7 cm); 20⅛ × 15⅞ in (51.1 × 40.1 cm); 20⅜ × 15⅝ in (51.8 × 39.9 cm). Library of Congress, Washington, D.C.

forms against a light ground are emphasized with a darker contour line.

The three sections of the open triptych are composed as if they were one continuous pictorial space but with the figures carefully arranged so that nothing of importance is cut by the two vertical seams. The strong diagonal thrust of the cross and Christ's twisting torso are balanced by the wedge of women and children anchoring the left wing and the counter-thrust of the diagonal created by the mounted soldiers in the right wing. Despite the originality of the subject and the complexity of the central action, the fact that this is Christ being crucified is never in doubt. His strongly lit form pulls all eyes to him. He wears the crown of thorns; the inscription identifying him as "King of the Jews" has been pinned above his head. Had the entire altarpiece survived intact, his gaze and left arm would have directed the viewer's gaze up to the image of God.

The women in the lower left foreground, where viewers familiar with crucifixion scenes would expect to find the Virgin Mary, the Magdalene, and St. John, are unidentifiable women of different ages weeping openly. Their anguish is echoed by the barking springer spaniel in the lower left corner of the main panel, who seems to protest in his own fashion this cruel punishment of the Savior. In contrast, the Virgin and John, standing behind the women and in shadow, are sad yet calm witnesses of an event they understand as inevitable. They are the only still figures in the entire painting.

Nine men struggle to erect the cross (Fig. 2.17). Their presence is symbolic, proof of the weight of their burden, for this is no ordinary man that they lift up. It is worth disentangling them to see how carefully Rubens the dramatist has thought out every detail of the action. At the foot of the cross an old man guides its foot into the hole. In front of him and thrust into the viewer's space is a man with curly hair and a blue garment who braces his feet on the ground while grasping the cross with his arms to pull the cross toward him as others pull it up with ropes or push it with their backs. This man looks up at Christ, though only to make sure that everything is under control. The bald man, whose brawny chest touches that of the victim, juxtaposes his ruddy skin tones with the ivory pallor of Christ and his excessive musculature with Christ's ideally proportioned figure, an image of evil

Chapter 2: Flanders

Showing Christ as worshipers might expect to see one of the thieves depicted was not only potentially confusing but also risky. Was the artist more interested in his own prowess than in creating a powerful religious image? While Rubens certainly used this commission as an opportunity to display his artistic mettle, he was a devout Catholic and his sincerity should not be doubted. He may have been inspired by reading the *Spiritual Exercises* of St. Ignatius, which required readers to try to imagine every moment of Christ's trial and subsequent physical torture and death. By doing so, the faithful would gain renewed appreciation of Christ's sacrifice and thus strengthen their own faith.

next to one of perfect goodness. Neither he nor the man opposite him wearing red look at Christ, while the soldier in armor on the left not only looks at Christ, but seems affected by his plight. This must be the centurion Longinus who, according to legend, was converted to Christianity when he thrust his spear into the crucified Christ's side. Rubens has thus imagined that the process of conversion began at this moment. This soldier's face is the only one of the group whose expression is easily legible; his gleaming suit of contemporary armor (not Roman costume) is a further point of attention. His features even resemble those of the artist, as one scholar has noted, an identification that does not preclude his role as Longinus. Rubens wanted us to make these discoveries, for he and other seventeenth-century painters expected their audiences to take the time to examine their paintings carefully, indeed to "read" them, as Poussin would later instruct a patron.

Rubens's *Raising of the Cross* is now so familiar that it is hard to appreciate its originality. To depart from the traditional static upright image of Christ on the cross and substitute an incidental moment in the story was extremely daring.

2.17 Peter Paul Rubens, *Raising of the Cross* (detail), central section, 1610–11. Oil on canvas, 15 ft 2 in × 11 ft 2 in (4.62 × 3.51 m). Antwerp Cathedral.

Peter Paul Rubens 157

2.18 Peter Paul Rubens, *Descent from the Cross*, 1611–12. Oil on canvas, 13 ft 9 in x 20 ft 3 in (4.21 × 6.17 m). Antwerp Cathedral.

The triptych with the *Descent from the Cross* (Fig. **2.18**) as its central scene is not much smaller than the *Raising of the Cross*, but the *Descent* occupies only the central unit (the flanking wings depict the *Visitation* and the *Presentation at the Temple*). It never had the crowning elements and predella scenes of its companion and is thus complete, although no longer in its original frame. The outer wings, seen when the triptych is closed, depict St. Christopher and St. Anthony Abbot. Christopher was the patron saint of the Guild of Longbowmen, who commissioned the altarpiece. St. Anthony Abbot is shown lighting the way for the saint, an act that inevitably recalls Diogenes searching for an honest man, that is, for the truth. The Greek roots of Christopher's name mean "Christ bearer," a theme illustrated by the saint with the Child on his shoulders and all the scenes on the interior of the triptych: in the *Visitation*, Jesus is carried in Mary's womb; in the *Presentation*, he is held by Simeon; and in the *Descent* he is supported by six of the eight figures surrounding him. The patrons may have originally requested a picture of St. Christopher until Rubens convinced them to accept the more complex and ambitious Christ-bearing imagery of the executed design.

While the main diagonal of the *Raising of the Cross* rises from left to right, the *Descent* falls from upper right to lower left, so that it now balances its companion in the cathedral as if they had always been intended to be shown together. Its mood is somber, as is appropriate. Instead of a wedge of muscular men tugging at the miraculous weight of the living Christ, the limp body of the dead Christ is the subject, sliding down the white shroud, barely prevented from falling to the ground by the hand of the man at the top right, who grasps Christ's left arm, and the sustaining arms of St. John. No longer a burden requiring nine strong men to support it, this body is comparatively weightless. John's crimson robe emphasizes the pallor of Christ's flesh tones; so do the ruddy arms of the two men helping to lower his body and those of the Magdalene at his feet. The three women at the foot of the cross—the Virgin Mary in dark blue, the flaxen-haired Magdalene in violet gray, and a companion—are all painted in subdued colors that will not distract the viewer from the white shroud, the pathetic body of Christ, and the blood-red robe of St. John. Many steadying horizontal and vertical elements interrupt the descent and encourage contemplation.

Chapter 2: Flanders

While the *Raising of the Cross* was a novel subject, that of the dead Savior's body being lowered from the cross was not. It had already inspired a succession of challenging interpretations by Italian sixteenth-century painters, beginning with Rosso Fiorentino in 1521. Those of the 1540s by Daniele da Volterra in Rome, of 1568–9 by Federico Barocci in Perugia and Ludovico Cigoli (1559–1613) in Florence have long been recognized as Rubens's principal sources of inspiration, together with the Laocoön. From it came the pose of the man on the right standing on the ladder, which quotes that of the son to the right of Laocoön. Christ's pose has been related to that of the other son, but it is so transformed that the source no longer seems relevant. Rubens's composition can in fact be read as a critique of those by Daniele da Volterra and Barocci, which both contain many more figures and thus confuse the viewer looking for Christ. By contrast, the disciplined clarity of Ludovico Cigoli's painting, completed just before Rubens left Italy in 1608, made a strong impression (Fig. **2.19**). Only two men support the dead Savior, whose lowered head and extended arms are taken over by Rubens together with the emphatic red of John's cloak. The pose of the man on the upper left of Cigoli's picture, reaching down to support the corpse, is echoed by the man in the same position in Rubens's painting. In Cigoli's picture, the white shroud attracts attention away from Christ and pulls spectators' eyes down to the kneeling Magdalene, who faces Him with open arms, and to Mary, seated behind her, who faces us and gestures weakly at what is happening. In Rubens's painting, the winding sheet is displayed like washing behind Christ's body and lit as if by lightening: the slow progression of comprehension orchestrated by Cigoli has become a dramatic flash of insight.

Rubens bought the land for his house, garden, and studio in 1611 and built a Flemish-style house on one side of the courtyard and a palatial studio in Italian style on the other (Fig. **2.20**). Its main room was tall enough to accommodate large altarpieces with additional workspace for the simultaneous production of other smaller commissions by himself and his assistants. It even had a musicians' gallery so that they could be entertained while they worked. Rubens attracted many pupils who were put to work preparing his commissions by scaling up his designs from the *modelli* approved by patrons to full-scale canvases or panels that Rubens would then completely rework or merely retouch, depending on the price to which the prospective patron had agreed. Rubens also collaborated with other artists whose gifts complemented his own. Of these the most significant was Jan Brueghel the Elder (1568–1625), the youngest son of Pieter Brueghel the Elder (c. 1535–69), who died when Jan was a year old. The delicacy of Jan's technique earned him the nickname "Velvet Brueghel." He was a spectacular painter of flowers (see p. 142) and landscapes into which Rubens on occasion contributed figures.

Frans Snyders (1579–1657), who was known for his skills with animal and still-life subjects (see Fig. 2.54), was also a regular collaborator. When Rubens painted Prometheus chained to a rock, his liver eternally renewed to be consumed

2.19 Ludovico Cardi, called Cigoli, *Descent from the Cross*, 1608. Oil on wood, 10 ft 6 in × 6 ft 7 in (3.21 × 2.06 m). Palazzo Pitti, Florence.

2.20 Peter Paul Rubens, A view of his house and garden, 1684. Engraving. British Museum, London.

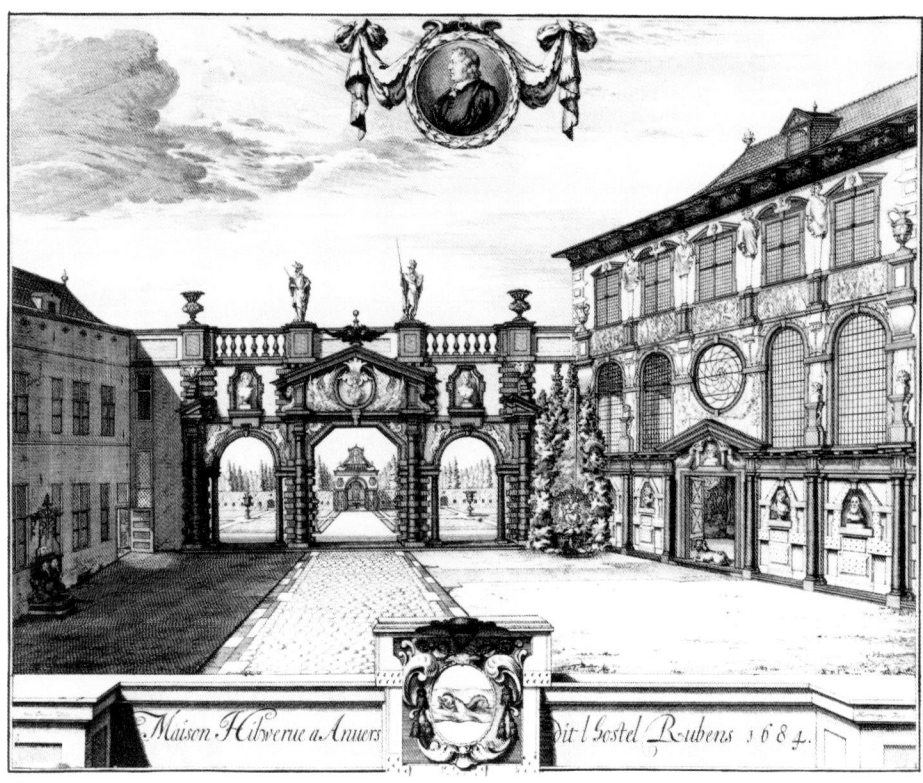

by an enormous eagle, he had Snyders paint the bird (Fig. **2.21**). His role is documented in a letter of 1618 from Rubens to Sir Dudley Carlton, the English Ambassador to The Hague, to whom Rubens hoped to sell twenty-three paintings in exchange for a collection of antique statues. Rubens told Sir Dudley that he himself, not an assistant, had painted the lions in *Daniel in the Lion's Den* (National Gallery of Art, Washington), which indeed do not look like those by Snyders. Rubens offered Sir Dudley pictures "entirely by my hand," such as the *Daniel*, and others partly by assistants, including one with "a most beautiful landscape, done by the hand of a master skillful in that department," probably Jan Brueghel. Other paintings on the list were described as laid in by a studio assistant and then completely reworked by Rubens, thus giving the patron a work whose visible surface was completely autograph but which was less expensive than a work by Rubens alone. If Sir Dudley purchased those that were entirely by assistants, Rubens would retouch them. The collaboration of artists of the caliber of Brueghel and Snyders was valued above that of less established assistants and would cost the patron as much as a painting by Rubens himself.

Rubens's honesty about the degree of his own role in the paintings he offered Sir Dudley was not rewarded. With few exceptions, including the *Prometheus*, his patron chose only the completely autograph works and wanted tapestries worth 3,000 guilders before he would agree to sell his statues. (At this stage, Rubens had neither seen nor even had a descriptive list of the statues.) Rubens managed to persuade Sir Dudley to accept further paintings for another 1,000 guilders, with tapestries worth the remaining sum to close the deal. The letters document not only Rubens's studio practices but also his negotiating skills—even if Sir Dudley was ultimately the winner. As Rubens himself wrote in a later letter, "in exchange for marbles to furnish one room, Your Excellency receives pictures to adorn an entire palace, in addition to the tapestries."[2]

Rubens, like Bernini, Cortona, and Rembrandt, was an excellent administrator. He could not have produced as much as he did without assistants, some of whom, such as Anthony van Dyck and Jacob Jordaens, became major artists in their own right. Delegating as much as possible, once his reputation was established, freed Rubens to negotiate the contracts, prepare the designs for approval, and to work on commissions for major patrons or that had particular appeal to him. The result is a wide range of quality in paintings properly associated with his name. Rubens did not believe in wasting his time painting details in areas that would never be examined closely once a work was installed, even on important commissions. Thus a Madonna in heaven in a large painting may be largely studio work, while Rubens's own hand may be detected below in silk draperies and flesh painting in the foreground. His touch is so lively and nuanced that the flatter, more monotonous areas carried out by his less gifted assistants can easily be detected. Nevertheless, to judge from the artist's dealings with Sir Dudley Carlton, patrons knew what they were getting, and if they wanted a painting by Rubens himself, all they had to do was pay the higher fee and wait.

Rubens's technique matured and changed during his second decade of activity. The cool colors and black shadows of his early Roman years were gradually replaced by a brighter, warmer palette, with his flesh painting, for which he is justly famous, becoming increasingly suggestive. He used creamy, almost opalescent colors for women's skin, the blood beneath the surface suggested by gray lines for veins that read as blue beneath a thin layer of flesh color. The shadows and contours of flesh areas are accented by touches of rust red; they can be found at the corners of mouths and eyes, in nostrils, at a shadowed point at a wrist bone. If there is any red drapery nearby, and there often is, then reflected red shadows appear on the skin too. His men follow the convention of having darker skin tones than women. The illusion of real skin taut over bone and muscle is as convincingly suggested for them as are the softer bodies of his goddesses and nymphs. All share superhuman proportions for they are Rubens's conception of an ideal humanity, the men as chunky as cart horses, the women muscular as well as smooth.

2.21 Peter Paul Rubens, *Prometheus Bound*, 1618. Oil on canvas, 95½ × 82½ in (242.6 × 209.5 cm). Philadelphia Museum of Art, Philadelphia, PA.

2.22 Peter Paul Rubens, *Allegory of the Four Corners of the World*, c. 1615. Oil on canvas, 82⅓ × 111⅞ in (209 × 284 cm). Kunsthistorisches Museum, Vienna.

An outstanding painting from this decade that displays Rubens's ideal men and women is the *Allegory of the Four Corners of the World* (Fig. **2.22**). The splendid snarling tiger protecting her young from the crocodile in the foreground may attract the eye first, but the back of the river god reclining on a superb classical vase draws the viewer toward four men and four women, two pairs well lit and two in shadow. The god with the vase embraces an African woman in his right arm. Together with the crocodile, they represent the Nile and thus Africa. Behind and above them is Europe (the river Danube holds a rudder). On the right the river god relaxing with crossed legs just above the tiger and with a blonde resting amicably on his shoulder represents Asia. The remaining pair behind them must be America, although neither figure looks like a native American. The woman who represents Europe has the powerful arms and shoulders and tiny breasts seen on many of Rubens's women. These often appear to be a male-female hybrid, in part because Rubens (and other artists of his time) could not regularly make drawings after nude female models, either in private or in public academies. Long study of the male body, even when supplemented by study of antique images of Venus and glimpses of their wives and mistresses, meant that it was the only human form that male artists knew properly. To convert it into a woman meant adding breasts (usually placed too high) and filling out the hips and stomach but otherwise making few, if any, correct adjustments to the skeletal frame and degree of muscular development. Rubens's women are anatomically correct only in the most superficial sense but the powerful physiques of the "Mr. Universe" males who surround them are hardly more realistic. They are all actors playing roles; their overdeveloped bodies are costumes appropriate to the parts they have been given. As long as we expect them to look like us, we will be disappointed by Rubens and other seventeenth-century artists who used idealized images of humanity for their art.

Rubens depicted Christian and pagan themes in steady, simultaneous production in the 1610s.

His devotion to the Catholic Church is as heartfelt as his pleasure in an imagined world of pagan gods and goddesses, his young men serving equally well as Adonis and St. Sebastian, his young women as nymphs and martyr saints. His patrons were mainly Flemish merchants but some altarpieces went to German Catholic aristocrats, and his first set of tapestry designs illustrating the story of Decius Mus (1616–18) was made for a Genoese patron. Not until the 1620s, however, did he begin to work steadily for patrons outside Flanders—in France, Spain, and England.

In 1617 the Jesuits in Antwerp commissioned twin high altarpieces honoring their founding saints, Ignatius of Loyola and Francis Xavier, and in 1620 ceiling paintings for the upper and lower aisles of their recently completed church. A fire badly damaged the nave in 1718. The altarpieces survived, but the rest of the decoration is known only from Rubens's preparatory sketches. Excluding the altarpieces, the commission required thirty-nine designs for which Rubens was to supply the sketches and *modelli* for members of his studio to carry out and for him to retouch. Much of his future activity followed this pattern of multiple sketches for a series of paintings whose execution would be supervised but only partly executed by Rubens himself. He responded energetically to this opportunity to decorate the first church in the modern Italianate style built in the Spanish Netherlands (Fig. 2.23). The challenge of taking so many familiar biblical subjects and seeing them afresh from below reveals Rubens at his creative peak, happily composing figures in strong foreshortening (Fig. 2.24). Correggio, Tintoretto, and Veronese had all portrayed figures on ceilings tilted enough to convince spectators of an overhead illusion without rendering gestures and facial expressions illegible: Rubens had learned his lessons well.

2.23 Pieter Huyssens, St. Charles Borromeo, Antwerp, west façade, 1615 (interior destroyed by fire, 1718).

2.24 Peter Paul Rubens, *St. Gregory of Nazianus*, 1621. Oil on wood panel, 19¾ × 25¾ in (50.16 × 65.4 cm). George B. Mathews Fund, 1952. Albright Knox Gallery, Buffalo, NY.

The two huge altarpieces, each 17 feet (5.35 meters) high, alternated on the high altar. Both depict posthumous healing miracles attributed to the two founders of the Jesuit Order, one indoors (Ignatius of Loyola), and one outdoors (Francis Xavier); both show the saints making similar gestures as devils leave the possessed in one and the lame and blind are healed in the other (Fig. 2.25). Francis Xavier wears black and stands in a sea of color and light; St. Ignatius wears a richly colored brocade chasuble but is flanked by members of his order in somber black. The settings, reminiscent of Tintoretto and Veronese, add grandeur and depth to the spaces where the miracles occur. The foreground figures quote from Raphael's tapestries and Vatican frescoes, Tintoretto's *St. Mark Liberating a Slave*, and Federico Barocci's *Madonna del Popolo*. Most of those who prayed before these images were unaware of Rubens's Italian Renaissance sources, nor did they need to be in order to be affected by the portrayal of miracles in which the calm demeanor of the saints and other believers is contrasted with the astonished emotions of those experiencing or witnessing the same moments.

Rubens, Diplomat and Artist, 1622–1630

The end of the Twelve Year Truce in 1621 meant the resumption of efforts on the part of Spain to regain control of the Seven Provinces. While Archduke Albert favored the prolongation of the truce rather than the resumption of hostilities, the Spanish authorities did not; after his death in July 1621, his widow, the Infanta Isabella (they had no son to assume power) could do little to intervene. While warfare did not break out until 1625, it eventually involved much of Europe. The results were dire for Antwerp and Flanders, as Rubens himself recounts in a letter of May 28, 1627:

> *we find ourselves rather without peace than at war; or, to put it better, we have the inconvenience of war without the advantage of peace. This city, at least, languishes like a consumptive body, declining little by little. Every day sees a decrease in the number of inhabitants, for these unhappy people have no means of supporting themselves either by industrial skill or by trade.*[3]

Rubens's letters show that he was fully informed about diplomatic initiatives by England, Spain, France, and Holland, as well as the various military tactics and the outcomes of battles and sieges. He was personally involved in negotiations between Holland and Flanders, to no avail, and, in 1629, between Spain and England, with little more success. His diplomatic gifts were further tested in the decade when his commissions brought him into contact with all the political leaders of Europe except the pope. Rubens used them too when working on his single most important commission, two cycles of twenty-four paintings celebrating the life of Marie de' Medici of France and her husband, Henry IV, for which he signed the contract in July 1622. He delivered nine of the paintings in May 1623, and the remainder two years later. The cycle honoring the king was never finished.

Marie de' Medici (1573–1642) has generally been held in poor regard. She was patronized in her lifetime by the French as a foreigner with a reputation for being manipulative, ambitious beyond her station, and jealous of the power of her son, Louis XIII. Much has been made of the obvious contrast between the facts of her life and their flattering presentation by Rubens. Henry IV, whom she married in 1600, was a popular king who brought some stability to France after a long period of weak rulers. His assassination in 1610 one day after her coronation was a tragedy. She could not become Queen of France and rule, as Elizabeth I ruled England, because French Salic law forbade succession through the female line, but she had considerable power as regent until Louis XIII forced her out in 1617, banishing her to Blois. He had her favorite adviser, Concino Concini, murdered, and his wife, who had been Marie's best friend since childhood, condemned to death for witchcraft. The cycle barely alludes to these events: one scene shows the queen proudly watching her son steer the ship of state (that is, attaining his majority); another shows her escaping her confinement at Blois at night, which she did in 1619; another shows her being reconciled with her son in 1620. Earlier scenes emphasize the status she was accorded by Henry before his death, especially his bestowal of the power of regency on her, and her coronation in May 1610.

2.25 (opposite) Peter Paul Rubens, *Miracles of St. Francis Xavier*, 1618–19. Oil on canvas, 17 ft 6 in × 13 ft (5.35 × 3.95 m). Kunsthistorisches Museum, Vienna.

2.26 Peter Paul Rubens, *The Education of Marie de' Medici*, 1622–25. Oil on canvas, 12 ft 11½ × 9 ft 7 in (3.94 × 2.95 m). Louvre, Paris.

The fact that this cycle, celebrating Marie's life from birth to assumption of regal status, was commissioned from the most renowned painter in Europe soon after the events themselves, and was intended for display in the palace the queen had built for herself in the center of Paris, proves that Marie was still trying to assert her right to be Queen of France. She clearly conceived this role as requiring more than the production of a male heir. Rubens's contract states that the choice of subjects will be hers (*selon l'invention de la Majesté*). Thus we must assume that their discussions involved not only the choice of biographical events to be depicted but the allegorical language to be used. For Rubens, the commission was an extraordinary opportunity to demonstrate his inventive capacities as well as his stamina when faced with so many large compositions that would draw on his full intellectual and artistic repertoire of knowledge and abilities. He apparently believed in Marie's right to rule and took her side against Cardinal Richelieu and Louis XIII as they worked to isolate her from real power. Louis tolerated her presence in Paris until 1631, when she was confined to a chateau in Compiègne. She soon moved to Brussels, where she remained until her death.

All the narrative scenes, with the exception of three large, horizontal canvases in the middle of the cycle, are vertical canvases just under 13 feet (4 meters) high and 10 feet (3 meters) wide. In their original setting, they would have been hung between windows. This would have affected their visibility by forcing viewers to see them against the light (or in reduced light if shutters or curtains screened out the daylight). They are now in a special gallery in the Louvre with top lighting and gray walls that do not compete with the paintings for attention. The contract called for Rubens to paint them entirely himself, but scholars agree that assistants contributed their share, which Rubens retouched. One scene, the *Felicity of her Reign*, was painted in Paris to replace one depicting the queen's expulsion from Paris, which Cardinal Richelieu and others found offensive; it is entirely autograph.

The cycle skillfully blends historical fact and allegorical fiction. The first narrative scene (it is preceded by an allegory of her destiny) represents Marie's birth. The infant is delivered to a woman representing Florence, Marie's birthplace. A river god representing the Arno reclines in the foreground and embraces the lion of Florence. Above hover the Hours along with the *Genius natalis* of Marie, whose cornucopia is filled with crowns, a sceptre, a palm, and the hand of Justice. In the next (Fig. **2.26**), her education is supervised by Minerva, goddess of wisdom, by the Three

2.27 (right) Peter Paul Rubens, *Henri IV Receives the Portrait of Marie de' Medici*, 1622–25. Oil on canvas, 12 ft 11½ × 9 ft 7 in (3.94 × 2.95 m). Louvre, Paris.

Chapter 2: Flanders

Graces, and by Mercury and Apollo, who with various attributes represent a liberal arts education with lessons in deportment and statecraft. The campus is a grove near Parnassus. Marie's lonely childhood and superior education resembled this scene only in the broadest metaphorical sense. In scene four, Henry IV is depicted gazing intently at a portrait of Marie held up for him by Hymen and Amor, while France gently urges him to follow his heart (Fig. **2.27**). In fact Henry enjoyed the company of various mistresses—he sired six illegitimate children—and was in no hurry to marry. Thus a marriage arranged to provide an heir and prop up the faltering finances of the French crown with the dowry of a woman from one of the richest families in Europe becomes a fiction of love-at-first-sight. In the sky above, Jupiter and Juno hold hands and look down approvingly, an image of the marital union that we know will follow (with Henry displaying some of Jupiter's philandering habits). A full account of the cycle and its symbolism would fill a long book. The commission is a prime example of art in the service of monarchical, political, and intellectual values shared by both patron and artist, a blend of self-interests openly expressed and characteristic of official art in the seventeenth century.

The most popular scene shows Marie arriving in France, walking down the gangplank at Marseilles where she is greeted by France, who wears a blue velvet cloak decorated with fleur-de-lis, and the city of Marseilles, who has a turreted hat (Fig. **2.28**). The three wildly gyrating sirens in the foreground appealed to later artists such as François Boucher (1703–70) and Eugène Delacroix (1798–1863). Rubens probably enjoyed painting them more than the dignified procession taking place above their heads. Below, Neptune calms the waves (the actual voyage had been rough), and Fortune stills the rudder of this tiny ship of the Medici state (their coat of arms decorates the awning, all that would appear to have protected them on their sea journey from Livorno). Above them flies Fame, trumpeting the good news of the arrival of this beautiful young woman destined to rule France. Henry was not in Marseilles to meet his bride but caught up with her a few days later in Lyons when she was eating supper. This encounter in Rubens's retelling becomes a heavenly encounter with Marie as Juno and Henry as Jupiter. Below, the chariot of the city of Lyons is pulled by lions bearing cupids carrying marriage torches. The metaphorical consummation of the French royal marriage thus brings with it auguries of future peace. The birth of Louis XIII (the next scene), which in fact occurred ten months later, assured the continuity of the royal line and the stability of Henry's reign.

Three scenes have horizontal canvases over twice the width of the other scenes and mark the middle of the cycle (and accommodated a different architectural setting in their original location). They depict the *Coronation of Marie*, the *Death of Henry IV and the Proclamation of Marie de' Medici as Regent* (Fig. **2.29**) and the

2.28 Peter Paul Rubens, *Marie de' Medici, Queen of France, landing in Marseilles, 3 November 1600*, 1622–25. Oil on canvas, 12 ft 11½ × 9 ft 7 in (3.94 × 2.95 m). Louvre, Paris.

2.29 Peter Paul Rubens, *Death of Henry IV and the Proclamation of Marie de' Medici as Regent*, 1622–25. Oil on canvas, 12 ft 10 in × 23 ft 10 in (3.94 × 7.27 m). Louvre, Paris.

2.30 Peter Paul Rubens, *Adoration of the Magi*, 1624. Oil on canvas, 14 ft 7 in × 11 ft (4.47 × 3.36 m). Musée Royal des Beaux-Arts, Antwerp.

Council of the Gods or the *Government of Queen Marie de' Medici*. Were this music, one would hear the full orchestra at high volume proclaiming the grief of a nation at Henry's untimely death and its faith in his spouse to carry on his wishes with the divine guidance of all the residents of Mount Olympus. Earlier scenes make clear Henry's desire for her to serve as regent should he die before Louis XIII reached his majority. Rubens's visual precedents come from images of Roman emperors, and Marie's confident assumption of a role until then reserved for men in France is underlined by the next vertical canvas, which features a military equestrian portrait of the queen in classical armor mounted on a splendid white horse celebrating the only military victory during her reign, the capture of Juliers (in eastern France).

The last scenes deal with the unhappy years of conflict between mother and son, her banishment to Blois (we are shown her escape rather than her dismissal from power), their reconciliation at Angoulême (Mercury advances toward her with an olive branch), and the establishment of peaceful relations, which lasted only six years after the completion of the commission. Members of the court philosophically opposed to women in positions of power must have found the entire cycle intolerable propaganda for the queen's cause. Its proto-feminist content may also explain what otherwise has long puzzled art historians, namely the lack of artistic influence emanating from this masterpiece by Rubens in the heart of Paris. Not until the "Rubenistes" came to his defense against the "Poussinistes" in debates in the French Academy in the early eighteenth century, by which time Antoine Watteau and others had finally discovered it, did the cycle visibly affect a generation of French painters.

The completion of this huge undertaking did not prevent Rubens from accepting other important commissions in the mid-1620s. For the high altar of St. Michael's in Antwerp, the church where his mother was buried, he then painted a magnificent *Adoration of the Magi* in 1624 (Fig. 2.30). The Virgin stands to present her child to the three kings, who normally worship in order of seniority, with the youngest king shown as an African to represent all non-European nations. Rubens's preparatory oil sketch follows this tradition, but in the painting, the oldest king stands on the right, erect and dominant in a splendid red cloak as he stares out as if to challenge anyone who would doubt that this baby is the Messiah. It is the middle-aged king who kneels before Christ to present his gift of frankincense, which is being used in the censer that he swings respectfully before the Child. His garments resemble those of a priest, as does his gesture, and scholars have read this change in the normal iconography as a way of making a deliberate allusion to the ceremony of the Mass, when the blessed host is believed to become the body of Christ. The Child is displayed on a bed of wheat, a reference to the unleavened wafer of bread used in the Mass. The changes between sketch and final work imply that it was the abbot of the church who proposed this unusual variation on a familiar theme.

Balthasar, as the black king came to be named, watches transfixed in the center of the painting. Behind the kings are soldiers on horseback, other exotically clothed spectators, and two enormous camels with their drivers. The wooden beams of the high-ceilinged stable recall Tintoretto's stable in his *Nativity* in the Scuola di San Rocco. Among them is a broken spider's web which represents the defeat of the devil and heresy by the light of Christian truth filling the sky.

The single fluted Corinthian column on the left quotes Veronese, who also painted several impressive altarpieces of this scene, but it also adopts a Flemish symbolic tradition found in depictions of this subject since the fifteenth century. There and here it represents the birth of a new religion amid the ruins of an old one, the Christian Church replacing the Jewish Synagogue. The warm colors and sympathetically characterized kings and spectators are typical of Rubens, who controlled nuances of facial expression as well as any of his greatest contemporaries, not excluding Rembrandt.

Rubens was pressed into service by the infanta and by Philip IV in 1628, undertaking a trip to Spain in August where, after carrying out his diplomatic duties, he studied the numerous works by Titian in the royal collection and made free copies of several. He also met Velázquez; the young Spaniard was impressed both by Rubens's relatively freely handled paint, and by the titles and honors accorded him by Philip IV. Rubens returned to Antwerp in the spring of 1629, visiting Brussels and Paris before going to London, where he again combined diplomacy with artistic activity, helping to negotiate peace between Spain and England. His allegory of *Minerva Defending Peace from Mars* (Fig. 2.31) was painted in London without any shop assistance. Even the fruit and animals are by Rubens himself. The painting expresses the artist's own views about the futility of violent solutions to political quarrels in typical allegorical form. In his new capacity as Secretary of the Private Council of Flanders, Rubens presented it to Charles I as if to plead his cause in pictures as well as words. The king was delighted with both the diplomat and the artist, and knighted Rubens, even presenting him with the sword used for the ceremony. He also commissioned ceiling paintings from Rubens celebrating the life of his father, James I, for the new Banqueting House in London designed by Inigo Jones. These Rubens executed with studio help after his return to Antwerp.

Rubens's Last Decade, 1630–1640

Although Rubens wished to return to painting undistracted by diplomatic duties, the infanta had come to trust him above all her advisers since the death of her husband and was reluctant to let him retire from public life completely. When Marie de' Medici was imprisoned in Compiègne by her son, she appealed to the infanta for help, and Rubens, who had been given his most important commission by the queen, could hardly refuse to come to their assistance. Time-consuming

2.31 Peter Paul Rubens, *Minerva Defending Peace from Mars*, 1629. Oil on canvas, 80⅛ × 117 5/16 in (203.5 × 278 cm). National Gallery, London.

negotiations were required involving Spain, from which the queen hoped to get financial as well as diplomatic assistance. Rubens thought that, with Spanish help, his *bête noir* Cardinal Richelieu might be ousted, but to no avail. The queen settled in Brussels until her death. Only when the infanta died in 1633 was Rubens free to paint undistracted by political duties.

The Ildefonso Altar of 1630–32 (Fig. **2.32**) is the last major altarpiece that Rubens painted himself. It was made for the chapel of the Confraternity of St. Ildefonso in the church of St. Jacob in Caudenberg, the parish church of the court in Brussels; the patron was the Infanta Isabella, for whom Rubens had worked since the beginning of his career. She and her deceased husband, the Archduke Albert, are shown with their respective patron saints, Albert and Elizabeth of Hungary, in the outer wings of the open triptych. Both wear the full trappings of royalty—he in armor, she in white silk; both wear gold cloaks lined with ermine. They flank the image of the Virgin in the central panel who presents a chasuble to St. Ildefonso as a reward for his passionate defense of the doctrine of her virginity. With the outer wings closed, the image becomes the Holy Family under an apple tree visited by the young St. John the Baptist and his parents (Fig. **2.33**). That composition is carefully designed to avoid placing any of the figures in the middle (both parts were removed from the back of the wings and permanently joined in the early eighteenth century; a central vertical division is still visible).

Rubens's technique changed considerably after 1610. His brushstrokes are visible everywhere in the Ildefonso triptych, most visibly in the foreground of the outer wing, which looks unfinished next to the glossy precision of his work of the second decade. His study of Titian's works in the Spanish royal collections in 1628 was certainly partly responsible for this change. Passages like the ruffs of the donors and their jewelry, which seem quite carefully painted from a distance, become suggestive blobs and dashes of paint when seen close up, effects that Titian used in his late work. Rubens's color range is strikingly warm—reds, golden yellows, and creams set off

2.32 Peter Paul Rubens, The Ildefonso Altar open, 1630–32. Oil on oak panel, central scene 11 ft 5 in × 7 ft 8 in (3.52 × 2.36 m); wings 11 ft 5 in × 3 ft 6 in (3.52 × 1.09 m). Kunsthistorisches Museum, Vienna.

by some blue, gray, and brown in the open triptych, and a similar range for the two holy families, though the landscape requires some olive greens. Red is always an important and emphatically present color in Rubens's work but, instead of being confined to one cloak or dress as is the case in earlier works, reds escape such boundaries here and add their glow throughout the picture—in the red drapery behind the donors, in the velvets covering their prayer stands, in the Virgin's dress, and in the shadows of flesh painting throughout.

The genres of portrait and landscape paintings play an especially important role in Rubens's last decade, when he retreated from the hectic pace of a double life as a diplomat and painter, remarried (Isabella Brandt had died in 1626), and started a new family. His second wife, Hélène Fourment, was sixteen when they married in December 1630; he was fifty-three. He seems to have been blissfully happy for he painted eight portraits of her alone or with their children, and her features appear frequently in his other paintings. The wedding picture (Fig. **2.34**) is devoted to her alone wearing a splendid gold and white brocade dress with black velvet overskirt and a delicate collar spread like a fan behind her head. A muted red velvet drapery behind her screens the base of a massive column, hinting at a palatial residence very different from their Flemish house in the center of the city. This is the first full-length portrait painted by an artist of his wife (with the exception of the double portrait of Rubens with Isabella Brandt). As noted earlier, this format began as the exclusive property of royal patrons and it kept those elevated associations long after wealthy bourgeois patrons had adopted it, which they did in both Flanders and Holland in the seventeenth century. Hélène Fourment is presented as his queen as well as his bride.

In Rubens's most appealing portraits, the sitters are shown at their ease in appropriate settings and engage the viewer with both gaze and gesture. They also seem to exude Rubens's own energy. The preacher Michiel Ophovius regards us graciously as he makes his point (Mauritshuis, The Hague). Ludovicus Nonnius, a doctor, points to a book held lightly in his lap as he engages us in conversation (National Gallery, London). Simple head and shoulder portraits of important

2.33 (above) Peter Paul Rubens, *Holy Family with the Young St. John the Baptist and his Parents* (formerly exterior of wings on closed Ildefonso altarpiece), 1630–32. Oil on oak panel, 11 ft 6 in × 8 ft 5 in (3.52 × 2.56 m). Kunsthistorisches Museum, Vienna.

2.34 Peter Paul Rubens, *Hélène Fourment in her Wedding Dress*, 1630–31. Oil on canvas, 64⅜ × 53⅞ in (163.5 × 136.9 cm). Alte Pinakothek, Munich.

Peter Paul Rubens

sitters, for example, that of *Thomas Howard, 2nd Earl of Arundel and Surrey* (Isabella Stewart Gardner Museum, Boston) echo the understated presentations of Titian's portraits. Rubens's portraits were closely studied not only by van Dyck but by other Flemish artists including Jordaens and Cornelis de Vos (1581–1651).

Although Rubens turned to landscape painting only intermittently before 1630, when he did the results were impressive, and he took up this genre with enthusiasm in the 1630s. He fully appreciated the innovations of Pieter Brueghel the Elder, especially the panoramic vistas of his *Seasons*, but Rubens's genre figures never look like peasants. His farmers, shepherds, and hunters have the proud bearing and healthy physiques of his mythological and religious characters. None of his landscape paintings is dated, so scholars differ about their chronology, but several are placed in the second and third decades of his career. The large *Landscape with Philemon and Baucis* (Fig. 2.35) depicts a mythological version of the flood in Genesis: Jupiter and Mercury come to earth disguised as travelers to see who will offer them hospitality. No one will take them in until they come to the home of an elderly couple, Philemon and Baucis, who receive the strangers and offer to kill their pet goose to feed them. As a reward, they are saved when the great flood cascades over the world that has treated the gods so poorly. The elderly couple huddle on the right as Zeus commands the heavens to open and unleash their watery powers. Most viewers will find it hard to look at anything but the burst of light and rain in the center of the sky, though Rubens has planned a slower entry into the drama along a path from the right, where the figures are placed: the eye is led left and then zigzags across the uneven terrain to the horizon. The flood has started, swelling the stream in the foreground, where a cow has already been swept off her feet. The theme of the biblical flood had attracted earlier artists periodically (and would be included by Poussin in his late quartet of *Seasons* (Louvre, Paris), but none created such a mesmerizing spectacle as this.

Rubens acquired his country estate, Het Steen, in May 1635 and moved there in November. His *Landscape with a View of Het Steen in the Early Morning* (Fig. 2.36), like the *Philemon and Baucis*, was in his possession when he died, along with another large horizontal vista, *The Rainbow Landscape* (Fig. 2.37), which is often discussed as its pair. They are the same height, but the

2.35 Peter Paul Rubens, *Landscape with Philemon and Baucis*, c. 1625. Oil on oak panel, 57½ × 82 in (146 × 208.5 cm). Kunsthistorisches Museum, Vienna.

2.36 (above) Peter Paul Rubens, *Landscape with a View of Het Steen in the Early Morning*, c. 1636. Oil on wood, 51⅝ × 90¼ in (137 × 229.2 cm). National Gallery, London.

2.37 (below) Peter Paul Rubens, *The Rainbow Landscape*, 1636–37. Oak panel, 51⅝ × 93¼ in (137 × 237.2 cm). Wallace Collection, London.

2.38 Anthony van Dyck, *Portrait of an Elderly Man*, 1618. Oil on wood, 42⅛ × 29⅛ in (107 × 74 cm). Collections of the Prince of Liechtenstein, Vaduz Castle, exhibited at the Liechtenstein Museum, Vienna.

Rainbow is a bit wider than the view of the *Steen*, and they are lit from opposite sides. They would have made a splendid effect hung together so that the light seems to emanate from the center of the landscape frieze that they create, the panorama buttressed by the trees on the outer edges of each panel. The direction of the light and the ripe brambles in the foreground of the *Steen* show that this is a fine autumn morning. Peasants are setting out for market in the cart watched by elegantly dressed figures in the left background; a hunter in the foreground is creeping up on the partridges in the field on the right. The strong right-left diagonal made by the stream is crossed by a left-right line that starts with the hunter and pulls the eye along a progression of trees right out to the far horizon. It is an exhilarating vista but not one that ordinary people could have seen by standing in the foreground. The viewer is in fact some thirty feet above the ground.

Rubens was still working for kings in his last decade, supervising and retouching the canvases for the ceiling of the Banqueting House in London for Charles I and also producing many sketches of mythological subjects for the Hunting Lodge of Philip IV. His hand is evident above all in the preparatory sketches for commissions, and in the landscapes and family portraits made for his own pleasure. He also painted tributes to Titian—variations on Titian's *Bacchanals* for the Este family that he had seen in Rome but somehow recalled and re-created after seeing many other works by him in Madrid. He knew his health was failing (his right hand was paralyzed with gout for a month in the spring of 1640). He painted a moving self-portrait in 1638–9 (see Fig. 2.2) and an altarpiece for his funerary chapel in his parish church (*Madonna and Child with Saints*, St. Jacob, Antwerp). When he died in May 1640, he was only sixty-three. Isabella outlived him by another thirty-three years.

Anthony van Dyck

Anthony van Dyck was the seventh child and second son of a wealthy Antwerp cloth merchant whose trade took him to Paris, Cologne, and London. Anthony left school at ten, unusually early for someone of his social class, to become a

pupil of the painter Hendrick van Balen. He was precocious: his first surviving dated painting was made when he was fourteen. Had he died in 1620, he would still be remembered for the works he produced in his teens. At some point between joining the studio of Hendrick van Balen in 1609 and registering as a master in the Guild of Painters in 1618, van Dyck joined Rubens's workshop, although not apparently as an apprentice. There he would have had access to Rubens's library, print collection, and his drawings after ancient and modern Italian art as well as his growing art collection. Van Dyck learnt Italian and took note of Rubens's princely lifestyle. Rubens entrusted him with important tasks—working up the cartoons for the tapestries illustrating the Life of Decius Mus from Rubens's *modelli* in 1618, and, two years later, helping Rubens to fulfill his contract to provide thirty-nine ceiling paintings for the Jesuits' new church dedicated to St. Ignatius by 1621.

Van Dyck's earliest works shows his virtuoso skill: the collar in his first *Self-portrait* (Akademie der Kunst, Vienna), made when he was sixteen, is drawn with one stroke of white paint. The *Portrait of an Elderly Man* (Fig. **2.38**), painted when the artist was nineteen, captures the sitter's character in convincing three-dimensional terms, using only varying tones of black and gray for most of the picture. The brilliantly lit head, looped ruff, clenched hands, and sketchily painted tooled leather chair back stand out from this austere setting and, with the sitter's erect posture and steady gaze, suggest that this was a man who knew what he wanted. He may have asked Rubens to paint him but Rubens refused most bourgeois sitters, passing them on to members of his studio. The only other artist capable of creating an image of such presence with such limited means at this date was Frans Hals.

Van Dyck began producing religious commissions and portraits for his own clients while still collaborating with Rubens. These show the young artist quickly mastering Rubens's hard-won stylistic achievements, even the sensational flesh painting, muscular male physiques, and magnificent horses. This early Rubensian phase is almost aggressively forceful, yet certain traits emerge that distinguish van Dyck from his mentor. He preferred canvas supports to panels, employed a rougher impasto and cooler palette than Rubens, and often elongated hands and faces. An early masterpiece, *Christ Crowned with Thorns* (Fig. **2.39**), painted around 1620 for an

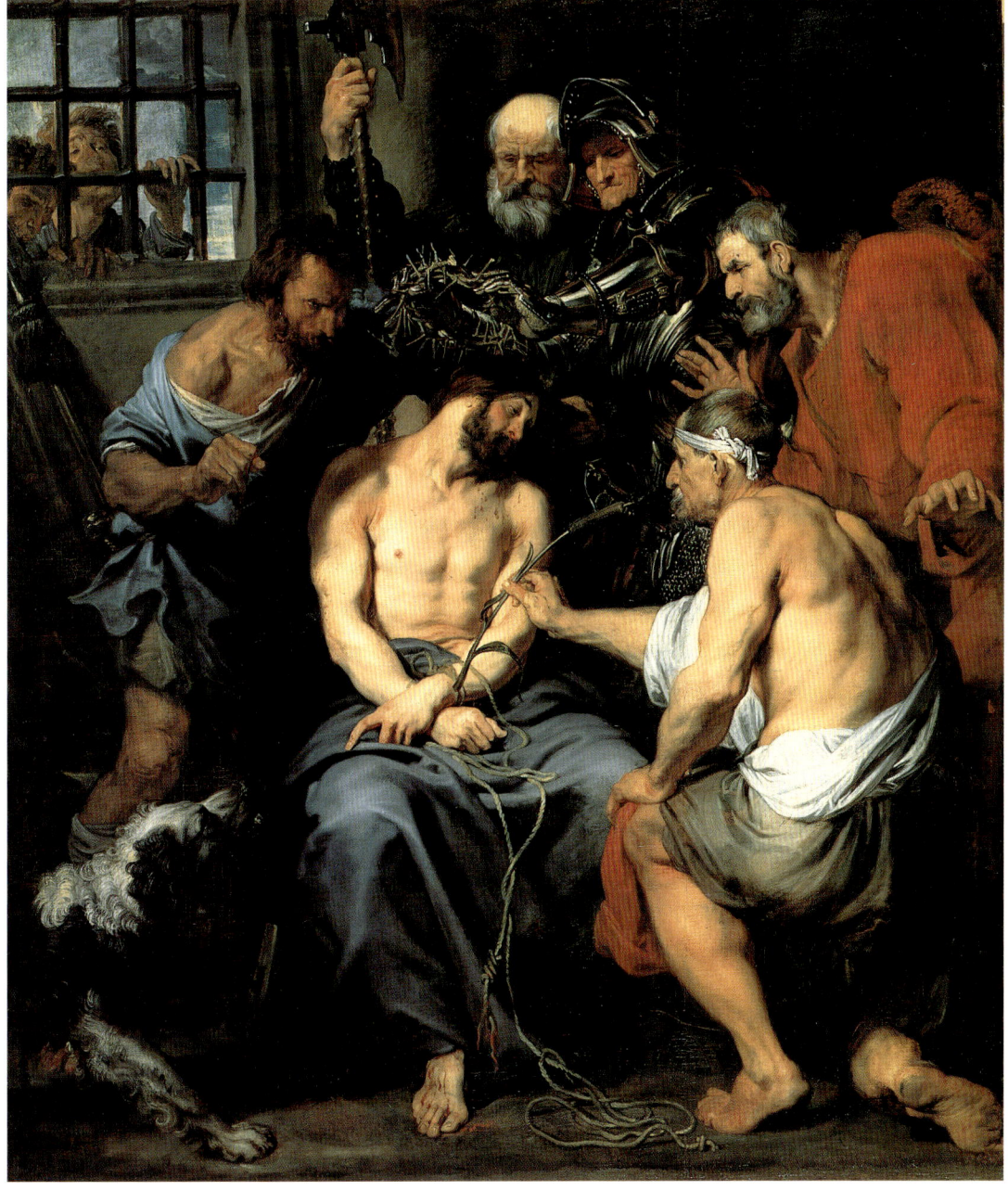

2.39 Anthony van Dyck, *Christ Crowned with Thorns*, c. 1620. Oil on canvas, 87⅞ × 77⅛ in (223 × 196 cm). Prado, Madrid.

Anthony van Dyck

2.40 Titian (Tiziano Vecellio), *Crowning with Thorns*, c. 1542–24. Engraving. Barber Institute of Fine Arts, University of Birmingham, England.

unknown patron, shows how completely van Dyck had mastered Rubens's style while evolving his own artistic persona. Christ is seated facing the viewer in the middle of this large canvas (the figures are almost life-size), sad yet composed, surrounded by five men whose role in this story is to personify evil. Van Dyck has presented a cast of five men in various attitudes of mocking respect, but, like Guido Reni, he finds it hard to portray a truly ugly human being. The kneeling man on the right presents Christ with a bulrush as a scepter, but without thrusting it at him or betraying disdain in his facial expression; the dirty sole of his right foot is probably meant to do this. The man in red above him opens his arms in a manner that suggests wonder and admiration rather than aversion, and he seems to hesitate, wondering whether he will present Christ with the object he has found to stand in for an orb. The thug on the left also seems frozen in mid-punch. Only the figure in modern (not Roman) armor acts aggressively, pulling down Christ's head by his hair as he lowers the crown of thorns over his head. The snarling spaniel, a quote from Rubens's *Raising of the Cross* (see Fig. 2.15), reinforces the element of threat. An arc of dark shadow surrounds Christ, as if to protect him from these half-hearted bullies.

These somewhat ambiguous gestures convey a more complex theological message than that usually encoded in depictions of Christ's torturers, including Titian's *Crowning with Thorns* (Fig. 2.40), which van Dyck knew from prints. The bulrush, which grows in muddy water, was both a symbol of humility and the plant associated with Moses, who was found amidst them as a baby and saved. Moses was therefore interpreted by Christian theologians as a prefiguration of Christ and thus a symbol of salvation. The men, who do not understand the deeper meaning of the bulrush, just as they do not recognize Christ, unwittingly tell educated believers that Christ is their savior. Van Dyck may have wanted to suggest that even these sinners are dimly aware that Christ is no ordinary man and thus can be saved from eternal damnation. The artist came from a devout family—two sisters and his brother entered religious orders. He was certainly aware of the implications of every gesture and symbol in this moving painting.

Shortly before he left for Italy, van Dyck painted portraits of Rubens's wife, *Isabella Brandt* (National Gallery, Washington), and the painter *Frans Snyders* and his wife, *Margaretha de Vos* (Frick Collection, New York). He portrays Snyders as a tall, handsome man who seems both introspective and reserved, and whose long fingers look boneless, incapable of producing the vigorous images of eagles, tigers, swans, lobsters, and luscious fruit for which he is known. This characterization of his hands and the omission of any clues to his profession are deliberate, allowing one artist to portray another, whom he knew well, as a gentleman rather than as a manual worker. The cool color scheme, which includes flesh tones, is by now characteristic of van Dyck. The relaxed hand and bent wrist occur frequently in his portraits of male sitters.

Van Dyck in England and Italy, 1621–1627

Before leaving for Genoa, van Dyck made a brief visit to London at the invitation of Thomas Howard, Earl of Arundel, whose agent reported in 1620 that "Van Dyck is still with Signor Rubens and his works are hardly less esteemed than those of his master." By November 25, van Dyck was in London and on February 26, 1621, he was paid £100 by the royal treasury "by way of reward for speciall service for his Majesty." Two days later, he had a pass to leave England "to travaile [work] for 8 months" and he sailed for Antwerp. Eight months later he reached Italy and soon joined Lady Arundel in Venice. He had wanted to go there after seeing Arundel's impressive collection of works by Venetian painters including Titian, Tintoretto, and Veronese. Titian became van Dyck's favorite artist. He filled sketchbooks with rapid pen studies of every Titian that he saw in Italy, in both public and private collections. He only once drew an ancient statue and he never drew anything by Michelangelo.

Van Dyck, unlike Rubens, had no powerful aristocratic protector waiting to provide him with lodging and a steady income. He went first to the house of friends in Genoa, Cornelis and Lucas de Wael, painters, engravers, and art dealers from Antwerp (see Fig. 2.45), who gave him introductions to prospective patrons. Van Dyck visited Rome and Venice in 1622, Turin, Florence, and Rome in 1623, and Palermo in Sicily in 1624, until an outbreak of the plague that year made him return to Genoa. He remained there until his return to Antwerp in 1627.

Van Dyck was in demand as a portraitist from the beginning of his career but only after he reached Italy in 1621 were his exceptional abilities in this genre fully employed. A guidebook to Genoa of 1780 lists ninety-nine works by him; seventy-two were portraits. He painted one major altarpiece, the *Madonna of the Rosary* (Fig. **2.41**),

2.41 Anthony van Dyck, *Madonna of the Rosary*, 1624–26. Oil on canvas, 13 ft × 9 ft 2 in (3.97 × 2.78 m). Oratorio del Rosario, Palermo.

Anthony van Dyck 177

an image intended to invoke the protection of the Virgin and local saints against the outbreak of the plague in Palermo in 1624. The circumstances of its commission parallel precisely those of Guido Reni's *Pala della Pesta* (see Fig. 1.67): the contrasts between their styles—gorgeous painterly effects in van Dyck, more somber tonalities in Reni's interpretation—are instructive. The opportunity to study Titian's work at first hand in Venice and elsewhere had an important effect on van Dyck, for Titian was not only a great history painter, he was also the finest and most influential portrait painter of the sixteenth century. His portraits appear to present the sitter with unaffected simplicity and instinctive sympathy for the nuances of character revealed by slight hints of facial expression and body language. Van Dyck adopted Titian's formats and warm tones but used a greater variety of poses. His technique was more fluid than Titian's and his portrayal of the sitters' states of mind less restrained.

Most of van Dyck's Italian sitters wear black costumes. Cardinal Guido Bentivoglio not only wore red, he seated himself beside a table covered with a plum-red velvet cover with a matching red velvet curtain filling the background (Fig. 2.42). The cardinal had been papal legate in Flanders until 1617 and thus knew Rubens and possibly had met the young van Dyck before returning to Rome. Shortly afterwards, he acquired Guido Reni's *Aurora* (see Fig. 1.66) and other frescoes when his family bought the palace from Cardinal Scipione Borghese in 1619. He and his brother Ezio soon filled it with other works, including some of the first paintings commissioned from Claude Lorrain.

Cardinal Bentivoglio is seated in a chair set at an angle to the picture plane marked by the diagonal strips of lighter stone in the paved floor. Thus he faces slightly left while turning to look to the right, giving his pose a discreet *contrapposto* and a reversed S movement. The document held loosely in his elegant hands seems about to slip as the cardinal, lost in thought, stares off to the right. His lips are closed, his face immobile; he is both perfectly at ease and fully aware that this image will outlive him. The wide lace fringe of his cassock cascades like froth from a wave over the swirl of red silk drapery that covers his legs. One can almost hear it rustle as he shifts his position.

Perhaps because the format hinted too clearly at worldly power, popes and cardinals had rarely commissioned full-length portraits before van Dyck used it in 1623. Raphael, Titian, and even Velázquez for his famous portrait of *Innocent X* (see Fig. 3.36) had used the three-quarter-length design invented by Raphael for his portrait of *Julius II* (National Gallery, London). Titian had experimented with a full-length image of Pope Paul III with his nephews, but never finished it (Fig. 2.43). Van Dyck saw it in the Palazzo Farnese in Rome along with Titian's more traditional three-quarter-length portrait of *Paul III*, seated in a wooden chair upholstered in dull-red velvet and wearing a matching red velvet cape (both now Museo di Capodimonte, Naples). Van Dyck's cardinal has exactly the same pose as the pope in Titian's unfinished portrait, though

2.42 Anthony van Dyck, *Cardinal Guido Bentivoglio*, 1622–27. Oil on canvas, 77⅛ × 57 in (196 × 145 cm). Palazzo Pitti, Florence.

She eyes us warily, somewhat aloof. She wears black, an austerely luxurious taste much favored in Spain and by the ruling classes of territories under its control. Even her ruff looks as if it is lined with gray fabric so that it blends with her dress and does not distract us from her head. She carries a sprig of orange blossom, a traditional attribute of brides. The date of her marriage is not recorded; the portrait is usually dated 1623, soon after van Dyck's nine months in Rome. The textured strokes that highlight the servant's ocher costume and the cloudy sky behind the figures reveal close study of Veronese, as does the fluted Corinthian column, which only he used rather than the smooth Doric order common in the sixteenth century.

2.43 (left) Titian (Tiziano Vecellio), *Portrait of Pope Paul III Farnese and his Nephews*, 1545. Oil on canvas, 78⅝ × 50 in (200 × 127 cm). National Museum of Capodimonte, Naples.

2.44 Anthony van Dyck, *Elena Grimaldi, Marchesa Cattaneo*, 1623. Oil on canvas, 96⅞ × 68⅛ in (246 × 173 cm). National Gallery of Art, Washington, DC.

he sits up straight instead of hunching over with a cautious expression directed at the nephew approaching from the right. Van Dyck's range of subdued red velvets rivals those in Titian's finished portrait of *Paul III*. Van Dyck surely intended his *Cardinal Bentivoglio* to establish his reputation in Rome, where portraits of such fluent execution and psychological insight were unprecedented. Guido Reni's full-length *Cardinal Bernardino Spada* (see Fig. 1.68), painted just two years later, seems intended not only to emulate but also to surpass van Dyck.

Van Dyck's Genoese portraits are mainly full-length images of a single sitter, sometimes accompanied by a child or servant, inhabiting a world of wealth, status, and power. Most Genoese patrons chose to be shown indoors amid columns and swags of sumptuous fabrics that are symbolic stage settings rather than portraits of their palaces. Rubens's *Marchesa Brigida Spinola Doria* (see Fig. 2.10) provided the basic formula—full-length with a low viewpoint and some hints of majestic architecture behind the subject in formal dress. Van Dyck's *Elena Grimaldi, Marchesa Cattaneo* (Fig. **2.44**) takes that formula and loosens it up. Rubens's marchesa is stationary. Van Dyck's walks slowly from her palatial dwelling to take a walk along a terrace that offers a splendid vista, her pale face sheltered from the sun by her young African servant who holds a red parasol above her head.

2.45 (left) Anthony van Dyck, *Cornelis and Lucas de Wael*, 1621–22. Oil on canvas, 47⅜ × 39⅓ in (120 × 100 cm). Capitoline Museum, Rome.

2.46 (right) Anthony van Dyck, *Virgin and Child with Sts. Paul, Peter, and Rosalie*, 1629. Oil on canvas, 9 ft × 6 ft 8 in (2.75 × 2.10 m). Kunsthistorisches Museum, Vienna.

Van Dyck's range as a portraitist in Italy is immense. There are touching portraits of aristocratic children, of his friends and acquaintances, and a parade of Genoese nobility, female as well as male. Their formality contrasts with the relaxed mood of the portrait of *Cornelis and Lucas de Wael* (Fig. 2.45). This is a "friendship" portrait, another type invented by Raphael in his so-called *Self-Portrait with his Fencing Master* (Louvre, Paris), which van Dyck has adopted and wittily recast. In both paintings, two men fill the picture space, one placed in front of the other, implying that the sitter in the foreground outranks his companion. In Raphael's painting, it is the artist who stares at the viewer from the left background while his companion gestures outwards with his right hand, turning his head as if to look back at Raphael, thus implying that the artist is more important than he is. Van Dyck reverses the glances: the foreground sitter in black (probably the younger brother Lucas) looks directly at us while his older brother in white looks off to the left to unseen viewers and gestures with his right hand toward his brother. The foreground brother's informal pose, sitting sideways on a chair, his left arm draped over its angled back, gives the image a snapshot flavor. It is easy to imagine that they spent many convivial evenings together in the de Wael household. Perhaps the picture was a parting gift of thanks for their hospitality when van Dyck left Genoa for Antwerp.

Van Dyck's Second Antwerp Period, 1627–1632

During van Dyck's absence in Italy, his father and one of his sisters had died. Anthony's return meant that his father's estate could finally be settled. He made a will in 1628 and, having no family of his own, asked to be buried beside his recently deceased sister. His property was to be divided between the two sisters still living as beguines (lay nuns); when they died, the estate was to be divided between the poor of Antwerp and the church of St. Michael. He also joined the Confraternity of Bachelors recently started by the Jesuits. Further evidence of his devotion to the Catholic faith is provided by the splendid altarpiece that he painted for the confraternity's

chapel in San Carlo Borromeo, the *Virgin and Child with Sts. Paul, Peter, and Rosalie* (Fig. **2.46**).

The composition once again honors Titian, whose *Pesaro Altarpiece* (see Fig. 1.12) had launched the asymmetrical *sacra conversazione* into Italian painting on its completion in 1526. Veronese and Annibale Carracci had also absorbed this revolutionary idea, and van Dyck's altarpiece makes use of all these sources. The architectural setting, with a massive unfluted column disappearing into clouds and the angled steps in the foreground, is derived from Titian, as is the triangular grouping of the main figures, but van Dyck moves the Virgin closer to the center of the picture and to the viewer. She wears a white cloak over a light gray dress, not the usual red dress and blue cloak of tradition. St. Peter behind her wears deep lapis blue. The greatest concentration of color in the picture is reserved for St. Rosalie, who wears a wine-red silk dress with a brocade cloak of dull ocher and plum red. She was given a prominent position because the church had recently acquired a relic associated with her. The superb still-life of the skull on the steps, its neck opening facing us, was not only an attribute of the saint who retreated to meditate in a cave, where she died alone, but also a vivid *memento mori* for all who prayed before this picture.

Mythological themes from ancient and modern literature did not play such an important role in his work as religious subjects and portraiture did, but during his second Antwerp period van Dyck depicted several familiar stories from Ovid, Virgil, and Tasso. His *Rinaldo and Armida* (Fig. **2.47**), painted for Charles I in 1629, portrays the moment in Tasso's epic poem *Gerusalemme liberata* when the sorceress Armida falls in love with the sleeping Christian knight, Rinaldo, on whom she had cast a spell, intending then to kill

2.47 Anthony van Dyck, *Rinaldo and Armida*, 1629. Oil on canvas, 7 ft 8 in × 7 ft 4 in (2.36 × 2.24 m). Jacob Epstein Collection. Baltimore Museum of Art, Baltimore, MD.

him. The king, who had his copy of an English translation with him in prison in 1649, may have proposed the subject to van Dyck, though it was already popular in Italy. A sweeping diagonal divides the lower left-hand half of this almost square canvas from the upper right section. The lower one contains the main figures, the upper is filled with sky, trees, and the billowing rose-red cloak of Armida. She occupies the center, the rest of her cloak flowing down her back and legs in a reverse S curve that enhances the sense of movement as she reaches behind Rinaldo to garland him with roses. Cupid snickers behind her back at the success of his magic arrow while another putto prepares to fire a second arrow from the sky. A naked water nymph serenades the lovers. She is all delicious temptation until our eyes reach her thighs, covered in fish scales. Unlike Rubens's female nudes, she is neither muscular nor heavy. Instead she is so convincingly natural that the stories of van Dyck's mistresses become believable: her body can only have been painted by someone who had studied and drawn women from life. Once more Titian provided inspiration—his so-called *Bacchanal of the Andrians* (see Fig. 1.118) for the pictorial stage, his *Danae* (Capodimonte, Naples) for the pose of Rinaldo, among other figures. The result is an enchanting visualization of the poetic imagery and one that rivals Titian in capturing a fleeting yet significant moment in the narrative.

Van Dyck's last decade of activity was mainly spent in London in the service of the court of Charles I. It is discussed in Chapter 6.

Jacob Jordaens

Jacob Jordaens was the first truly Flemish painter of the seventeenth century. He never traveled further than Amsterdam and worked almost exclusively for Flemish patrons. His clients were bourgeois merchants with fewer social pretensions than the aristocrats and courtiers who employed Rubens and van Dyck. Instead of their sophisticated artistic language honed by years of study in Italy, Jordaens offered one that was mainly indigenous in form and content. His figures are almost aggressively plain, and can seem vulgar, even caricatured, when set beside the suave elegance of van Dyck or the heroic humanity of Rubens. Outliving them both by almost forty years, he became heir to the market Rubens had created for powerful religious altarpieces of Counter-Reformation themes, for private images of both biblical and historical themes, and for lush tapestry designs. He did paint some fine portraits but usually left that genre to other specialists trained in Rubens's shop such as Cornelis de Vos (1584–1651). His most original and successful work portrays traditional festivals, proverbs, and fables that have no equivalent in the production of Rubens or van Dyck.

Jordaens was born in Antwerp on May 20, 1593, the son of a successful linen merchant. His mother had inherited money so Jordaens always lived well, eventually building a house with an attached studio like that of Rubens. He was apprenticed to Adam van Noort in 1607 and married his daughter in 1616, having joined the Guild of St. Luke the previous year as a *waterschilder*, that is a painter of watercolors on canvas or paper that were used as substitutes for tapestries. While his teacher had little influence on his work, Rubens did, even though Jordaens did not join the studio or collaborate on commissions until the 1630s. Jordaens soon began to sell works painted in oil on canvas, producing *waterschilders* throughout his career as well as designs for woven tapestries. His career was launched by 1616, the date on his *Adoration of the Shepherds* (Metropolitan Museum, New York) but there are relatively few dated works, especially for his early years, when most of his paintings were made for private homes. Enough documented work exists to allow scholars to chart the broad outlines of his stylistic evolution during his long and productive career.

Jordaens was impressed by the massive physiques, glossy surfaces, and rich colors of Rubens's work during the decade after his return to Antwerp in 1609. He also admired the first major painting by Caravaggio to cross the Alps. His *Madonna of the Rosary* (Kunsthistorisches Museum, Vienna) arrived in Antwerp around 1620, having been bought by a consortium of artists, including Rubens, and was installed in the Dominican church. Jordaens used its piled-up figure composition with the Virgin and Child at the summit and adopted its shallow pictorial stage and plebian figure types. The way in which the Child with a fat belly stands almost casually on his mother's lap while looking at the viewer appears in several early paintings, including the *Holy Family with St. John the Baptist* (Fig. 2.48). Mary holds Christ under his arms so that his baby fat is pushed toward us; his rotund belly and rolls of fat on his legs all seem carefully observed from life. He gazes off into the distance, but St. Joseph, the Virgin, and the young St. John in the lower left corner all look straight at the viewer, the adults solemnly, the Baptist with mischievous enthusiasm. Joseph has his mouth open and shaped as if urging us to worship this beautiful baby with a rosary draped tactfully in front of his genitals. The rich chiaroscuro that gives the baby an almost sculptural reality was inspired by both Rubens and Caravaggio; the slightly inappropriate humor of St. John is typical of Jordaens.

Around 1618 Jordaens painted *The Calling of Sts. Peter and Andrew* (Fig. 2.49) for the church

2.48 Jacob Jordaens, *Holy Family with St. John the Baptist*, c. 1620. Oil on oak panel, 48⁷⁄₁₆ × 36¹⁵⁄₁₆ in (123 × 93.9 cm). National Gallery, London.

2.49 Jacob Jordaens, *The Calling of Sts. Peter and Andrew*, c. 1618. Oil on canvas, 82⅛ × 93⅛ in (208 × 235 cm). St. Jacob's Church, Antwerp.

Jacob Jordaens

of St. Jacob in Antwerp. Patterns of light and shade divide the painting diagonally into four quarters. The apostles crowd around Christ as he tells St. Peter that he will become "a fisher of men." They are compressed into a rectangle of figures that echoes the picture format and leaves only a narrow space in which to depict the Sea of Galilee and fishing boats. All eyes are on Christ except for a man on the right edge, who is excluded from the group and looks out at us. He is seated on an upturned basket with his legs crossed so that his left foot is thrust out of the picture plane. Jordaens must have seen a copy of Caravaggio's first rejected altarpiece for the Contarelli Chapel (see Fig. 1.43), in which St. Matthew is similarly posed. Even the upper half of Jordaens's figure, who turns around to look up at Christ, resembles the upper half of the St. Matthew that Caravaggio painted to replace the rejected version (see Fig. 1.44). The powerful physiques of Peter and his companions show how closely Jordaens had studied Rubens, and how well he could emulate him, even his opalescent flesh painting.

Jordaens's reputation for vulgarity stems partly from his many pictures illustrating the feast of Twelfth Night ("The King Drinks") (Fig. 2.50). They show a large family celebrating the Feast of the Epiphany, the Church festival that commemorates the arrival of the three kings to worship the infant Christ. The king, chosen by lot in the traditions of the time, is always an old, obscenely fat, red-faced man, so grotesque that some scholars believe that he must represent Herod, King of Judea rather than Caspar, Melchior, or Balthasar. Other figures enjoy playing the fool, the wine steward, the cook and taster, all traditional roles at this event. On the wall behind is a Latin inscription that translates: "There is nothing more like a lunatic than a drunk." These enormous paintings celebrate the pleasures of food, wine, and good company while including an image of excess to warn against it.

Other family values are inculcated by his pictures illustrating the proverb, "As the old sing, so the young pipe" (Fig. 2.51). These have less crowded compositions with members of one family feasting and misbehaving—drinking a bit too

2.50 Jacob Jordaens, *The King Drinks*, c. 1655. Oil on canvas, 7 ft 9 in × 9 ft 9 in (2.4 × 3 m). Kunsthistorisches Museum, Vienna.

much, letting the family dog get at the food, and the baby stuff a toy into its mouth, but nothing extreme. Jan Steen would illustrate the same moral with a far more elaborate catalogue of the dire consequences of indulgence in alcohol (see Fig. 5.63). Behind this family in a niche on the left is a vase of flowers and a half-used candle, both common symbols of the transience of life. The barn owl perched quietly on the chair of the old woman serves as a symbol of wise restraint while she boisterously joins in singing "Een nieu liedeken van Callo," a "new song" to celebrate the victory of the Cardinal Infante Ferdinand at Callo in 1638. The artist himself plays the pipe in the center; the child below imitating him may be one of his children too. "Set a good example for your children," "have fun but don't overdo it"— these are his messages.

Shortly before 1650, Jordaens was accused of being a practicing Calvinist; in 1674 he allowed members of his church to use his house for worship. He continued, however, to paint altarpieces for Catholic clients after his change of faith, for example the *Adoration of the Shepherds* of 1657 (Fig. **2.52**). The piled-up composition, while typical of Jordaens, in this case owes something to Rubens's magnificent *Adoration of the Magi* of 1624 (see Fig. 2.30). The palette in this and other later paintings is cooler than before, with an emphasis on blues, cream, and gray instead of the reds, gold, and greens of his early maturity. Joseph and Mary are more dignified versions of their predecessors in the *Holy Family* of around 1620 (see Fig. 2.48); the Child is tiny, almost doll-like, instead of the plump, realistic baby of the earlier painting. The donkey beside him is eating the straw from the manger, the kind of informal touch that makes viewers smile and which Rubens would never have permitted. Jordaens suggests a friendly Church, one where all could approach the Lord and where laughter was as acceptable

2.51 Jacob Jordaens, "*As the Old Sing, so the Young Pipe,*" c. 1640–45. Oil on canvas, 57⅜ × 85⅞ in (145.5 × 218 cm). National Gallery of Canada, Ottawa.

2.52 Jacob Jordaens, *Adoration of the Shepherds*, 1657. Oil on canvas, 106¼ × 81 in (270 × 205.7 cm). Gift of John Motley Morehead. North Carolina Museum of Art, Raleigh, NC.

as prayer. Despite the plethora of figures, there is no confusion about who are the principal figures or doubts about the devotion of the peasants crowding round the infant Christ.

Jordaens was eighty-five when he died. Although he was the most admired artist in Flanders from 1640 until his death and had many assistants to help him keep up with his immense production, he had no successors. By 1680 political and economic power was seeping away from Flanders as the French king Louis XIV attacked from the south and even captured parts of the Spanish Netherlands in victories celebrated in paintings by Charles Le Brun on the vaults of the Galerie des Glaces at Versailles. This impressive century of Flemish art was drawing to a close.

Still-Life and Genre Painters

Rubens, van Dyck, and Jordaens were not the only painters of distinction working in Flanders in the seventeenth century, but the others who produced altarpieces, history paintings, and portraits must here give way to those who took up different subjects. Flemish landscape painters rarely produced innovative work after 1630, and the only masterpieces in this genre were painted by Rubens. There were several outstanding still-life painters, however, two of whom—Frans Snyders (1579–1657) and Jan Brueghel the Elder (1568–1625)—have already been mentioned as collaborators with Rubens (see Fig. 2.21). Painters of scenes of daily life, or genre subjects, were also popular. They expanded the boundaries of what art could represent: the life of the haute bourgeoisie in "courtly company" scenes and that of the drunken poor quarreling in taverns over cards; summer country festivals (the *kermesse*) and the indoor festivities of winter such as Twelfth Night (see Fig. 2.50). One type of genre scene was unique to Flanders, the "art collection" painting, which portrays an actual or imaginary gallery of paintings and other works of art with the owner present showing his treasures to fellow connoisseurs.

Jan Brueghel was famous for his technical finesse as a flower painter, the most highly praised kind of still-life, probably because artists could provide collectors with a permanent image of a collection of rare, perfect flowers that did not bloom simultaneously. Brueghel made some huge flower paintings that contain hundreds of blooms, veritable encyclopedias of every variety then cultivated. The work shown here is one of his small *Wunder* bouquets that offers a close-up view of his technical accomplishments (see p. 142). Against a dark ground he has depicted a selection of spring blooms: a snowdrop and a yellow crocus, several kinds of narcissi, two rare white tulips whose petals are tinged with pink and blue, a wild rose, a marigold, forget-me-nots, flax flowers, three cyclamen with their distinctive heart-shaped leaves, a tiny pansy, and a few sprigs of rosemary—all carefully arranged in a glass vase set on a dark surface. Beside it to the left is a sprig of forget-me-not with a butterfly and on the right a fragment of rosemary. The color scheme, much quieter than usual in Brueghel's work, emphasizes white and yellow with a few accents of blue and red.

These pictures offer owners more than a display of the artistic virtuosity required by the genre and the reflected status of the connoisseur able to hire a famous artist to create such mesmerizing illusions of floral perfection. All flower paintings would remind Christians of both the infinite creative power of God and the brevity of human life. Tulips were especially associated with mortality for they do not last long as cut flowers. The cyclamen, which is emphasized by appearing both in the vase and beside it, was associated with the Virgin, as were lilies, irises, and roses, so owners inclined to read further meanings into such a painting could easily do so. The coins and jewelry in the foreground of other examples serve as reminders of worldly goods that have no value in the next life.

Some of the earliest dated still-life paintings made in Antwerp are signed by Clara Peeters, about whom, despite many attempts to trace her in archives, almost nothing is known. She may have been born in 1594; her dated works span the years 1607 to 1621, although she probably continued to work for another decade. If that baptismal record is hers, she was even more precocious than van Dyck. Her most impressive works display her ability to depict reflected light on a variety of surfaces—gilt bronze, German stoneware, Chinese porcelain, wheels of cheese, curls of butter, wet fish, feathers, and glass. Her four pictures in the Prado illustrate all the main categories of still-life produced by later Flemish and Dutch artists: the fish piece, the game piece, the dessert piece, and the breakfast piece. Three of them are dated 1611, when the artist may have been only seventeen.

The *Still-Life with Colander and Artichokes* (Fig. 2.53) is among the masterpieces of early seventeenth-century still-life painting in Europe. On a surface set close to the picture plane Peeters has arranged several species of fish as well as crabs and a few shrimps, one of whose whiskers trails over the edge of the counter to tempt us

2.53 Clara Peeters, *Still-Life with Colander and Artichokes*. 1613. Oil on panel, 19⅝ × 28⅜ in (50 × 72 cm). Prado, Madrid.

to test her illusion. A magnificent metal colander with a strainer fills the center of the composition and holds two artichokes. A vegetable grown only in warm climates, artichokes must have been imported and, like the oranges and lemons often featured in later Dutch still-lifes, were expensive luxuries. The Venetian goblet on the left and intricately worked stoneware tankard on the right are also objects that would have been found only in a wealthy household. They would not have been lying around in the pantry beside the raw ingredients for a stuffed, roasted fish recipe awaiting preparation by the cook of this prosperous household. Unlike contemporary still-life painters in Haarlem, Peeters does not use a symmetrical arrangement of the objects shown, nor does she use a high viewpoint that isolates each object on the table. The viewer's eye level is just above the colander, which is partly concealed by the earthenware dish in front of it holding a carp and some smaller fish. Both colander and dish are set slightly off-center so that the composition becomes one of overlapping ellipses rhymed by the candlestick, the glass, the strainer, and the tankard. She handles the foreshortening of these difficult forms to perfection and balances their odd shapes, too, so that the composition seems natural rather than contrived. Each object has been meticulously observed and recorded.

Frans Snyders's still-life paintings fulfill the stereotype of Baroque art—abundant, exuberant, painted with verve, full of movement and drama, and utterly unlike the measured, careful arrangements by Peeters. Her clients were probably seduced away from her precise images by the luscious, more colorful still-life paintings of Snyders, which were cheaper too because he could paint them quickly. When that happened, she may have moved to Amsterdam, where local tastes favored more restrained art. His paintings mock the adjectives "still" or "dead" (the French for still-life is *nature morte*). They often include living people and animals—monkeys, cats, and dogs stealing some of the raw materials for a banquet guarded by servants, who do not always catch the thieves. These "kitchen" scenes imply wealthy owners who can afford delicacies like peacocks, pheasants, and wild boar. An upended white swan with an open wing, its long neck touching the floor, provides the bright focal point in the ostentatious display of produce in Snyders's *Still-Life with Poultry and Venison* (Fig. 2.54). The swan's head, which rests on some small songbirds in the foreground, draws our attention to a live hen and cock nesting together in the lower right corner. In the far distance in the center of the canvas a man approaches a woman with courteous deference, removing his hat as he walks towards her. Will they too become a happy couple like the poultry pair? Are the peacocks, pheasants, and other luxury meats the raw materials of a future wedding feast, or are they gorgeous *memento mori*? Is it better to be a humble hen than a peacock? The careful placing of the animal and human pair in contrasting yet marked zones suggests that contemporaries were meant to connect them and draw some moral from them.

The traditions created by Peeters, Snyders, and others in Antwerp were continued by other still-life artists. The finest local exponent of flower painting after the death of Jan Brueghel was Jan Davidsz de Heem (1606–83/4), who was born in Utrecht and trained there before moving to Antwerp, where his family had roots. His earliest works use a limited range of cool colors to depict such objects as a goblet of white wine, a pewter dish, some herring, a corkscrew of lemon peel, or a napkin. Then gradually he transformed these restrained images into sumptuous displays of rare foods and utensils (*pronk stil-leven* or "showy still lives"), a type that became popular throughout the Netherlands by 1650 (Fig. 2.55). In all these categories de Heem's inventiveness of composition and technical polish set a standard that few of his contemporaries could equal.

The most admired genre painter in Antwerp before 1650 was Adriaen Brouwer (*c.* 1605–38), who was probably born in Oudenarde just south of the border of Flanders. Records are sketchy but he is recorded in both Amsterdam and Haarlem in the 1620s and either trained with Frans Hals or knew his work well enough to derive his own distinctive "rough brush" style from it. He joined the Guild of St. Luke in Antwerp in 1631 and spent the rest of his brief life there, dying perhaps of the plague in 1638. Brouwer nearly always worked on small oak panels. None of his known works are dated and few are signed. He usually painted peasants in taverns drinking too much, fighting over cards, smoking, and propositioning the old women who serve food and drink to these ill-tempered louts. While amusing their middle-class or elite owners, these scenes also affirmed their higher social status by attributing such behavior to crude stereotypes of the lower classes. Brouwer did not invent such subjects—similar scenes occur on Hieronymous Bosch's *Table Top with the Seven Deadly Sins* (Prado, Madrid) and were then further developed by Pieter Bruegel the Elder (*c*. 1535–69) and his followers—and he never tackled more ambitious subjects like the large peasant festivals painted by several of his contemporaries. Despite the small scale and limited range of subject matter, he was admired by other artists as well as collectors. Rembrandt owned six of Brouwer's works, Rubens had seventeen, and van Dyck included his portrait with those of the other distinguished artists and collectors in his *Iconography*, a set of engraved portraits compiled between 1627 and 1641.

Brouwer's *Bitter Drink* (Fig. **2.56**) is the most original depiction of the sense of taste made in seventeenth-century Europe. The victim either of a practical joke or of a quack's prescription of some ill-tasting medicine gasps in shock at the foul taste in his mouth. Brouwer, like Hals, has captured a vivid instant of life. The only colors are a range of browns and flesh tones. The paint has been laid on quickly and efficiently, as if the artist saw the man retch and recorded it immediately. His ungainly features—a bulbous nose, unshaven chin, and matted haircut—are realistic without being cruel. David Teniers the Younger (1610–90) followed Brouwer in producing scenes of brawling peasants, but his are more refined and less effective. He also painted religious subjects and pictures of the art collection of the Archduke Leopold Wilhelm of Austria.

The "art collection" paintings of Jan Brueghel, Willem van Haecht (1593–1637), and David Teniers the Elder and Younger were unique to Flanders. They usually show a large room, the back and right walls of which are filled from floor to ceiling with rows of paintings. There is often a tall window in the left wall of the room to illuminate these treasures and a table or two laden with such objects as bronze statuettes, rare shells, prints, drawings, and scientific instruments. The owner may be present with visiting connoisseurs

2.54 Frans Snyders, *Still-Life with Poultry and Venison*, 1614. Oil on canvas, 61⅜ × 85⅞ in (156 × 218 cm). Wallraf-Richartz Museum, Cologne.

Still-Life and Genre Painters

2.55 (opposite) Jan Davidsz de Heem, *Still Life with Parrots*, 1640–45. Oil on canvas, 59¼ × 46¼ in (150.5 × 117.5 cm). The John and Mable Ringling Museum of Art, Sarasota, FL.

2.56 Adriaen Brouwer, *Bitter Drink*, c. 1630. Oil on oak, 18¾ × 14 in (47.5 × 35.5 cm). Städelesches Kunstinstitut, Frankfurt.

looking on appreciatively as he tells them about his possessions. Van Haecht's *Picture Gallery of Cornelis van der Geest* of 1628 (Fig. **2.57**) is one of the finest examples and one whose interest is increased by the presence of known paintings and portraits of identifiable individuals. Archduke Albert and Infanta Isabella are seated on the left. Rubens helps van der Geest by supporting one corner of Quentin Massys's *Madonna and Child*; as its owner, Rubens points to it and touches his chest, indicating that this is a particular favorite of his. Van Dyck stands just behind him. The woman who holds the next work to be shown to the royal visitors, a still-life of exotic fruit with monkeys by Frans Snyders, was van der Geest's housekeeper (he was not married). Snyders's elegant features can be seen looking out at us on the right edge of the painting. In front of his still-life is a little painting of Danaë by van Haecht himself, who is believed to be the man in the doorway on the right. Further to the right is Jan Wildens's picture of a man returning from the hunt with his dogs on a wintry day. Some space on the right wall has been reserved for copies of famous Roman marbles, including the Medici Venus, the Apollo Belvedere, and the Farnese Hercules. Among the other paintings is Rubens's *Battle of the Amazons* (on the end wall next to the window), Adam Elsheimer's *Ceres Mocked*, and Jan van Eyck's *Woman at her Toilet* (just above the Medici Venus), a work now known only from copies such as this one. There are landscapes, seascapes, architectural perspectives, mythologies, genre scenes, and portraits in

Still-Life and Genre Painters

2.57 Willem van Haecht, *Picture Gallery of Cornelis van der Geest*, 1628. Oil on panel, 39 × 51 in (99 × 129.5 cm). Rubenshuis, Antwerp.

addition to works with religious, historical, and mythological subjects by artists from three centuries, comprising a collection whose range, depth, and quality would make it coveted today by any major museum.

While the painting looks at first like a convincing picture of an actual gallery, it is not. No private homes in Antwerp, even those of a wealthy man, had such large rooms. Trees are in leaf in the courtyard seen through the door, yet everyone is wearing layers of clothing, some fur-lined. Van Haecht has also changed the sizes of known paintings—the lost Jan van Eyck was much smaller than it appears here, as was Elsheimer's *Ceres*. Inventories prove that van der Geest and other Antwerp art collectors kept their art in many different rooms: these "galleries" are imaginary, ideal spaces where the taste of a particular collector can be celebrated and admired. They honor both the owner and the artists, past and present, who created the collection, and the knowledgeable appreciation of this art by *liefhebbers der schilderyen*, as lovers of painting were called in writings of the day.

David Teniers the Younger (1610–90) produced a dozen or more pictures of the collection of Archduke Leopold-Wilhelm in Brussels between 1651 and 1653. In this example (Fig. **2.58**), the owner is shown walking around with the artist, who became his curator in 1651, surveying his latest acquisition—fifty-one pictures from the collection of the Duke of Hamilton. Their display in rows—edge to edge, floor to ceiling—with others propped up on the floor, did not conform to their actual hanging, but it allowed Teniers to depict all of the paintings in the archduke's possession. Many are now in the Kunsthistorisches Museum in Vienna, among them famous works by Titian, Giorgione, Raphael, Veronese, Bassano, and Tintoretto. The archduke sent these paintings to other princes with fine collections, obviously proud of his own hoard, which was indeed one of the finest of its day.

During his lifetime Rubens single-handedly incorporated Flemish art into the European mainstream. His many students and collaborators continued to work in his style and idiom for another generation or two, but the early death of van Dyck (who outlived Rubens by only a year, dying at forty-two) deprived Flanders of its most gifted heir to Rubens's artistic inheritance. Jacob Jordaens vulgarized the heroic forms of Rubens and created from them a provincial version that was popular in the Spanish Netherlands for the rest of his long life. Even after the Treaty of Westphalia was signed in 1648, the economy continued to decline. There were fewer opportunities for Flemish artists than elsewhere, so some moved to England and France in search of work. The next major Flemish painter was Antoine Watteau (1684–1721). Born in Valenciennes six years after the Flemish government ceded it to France, he considered himself (as did his contemporaries) Flemish. Flanders became an artistic backwater until the twentieth century, when its architects designed some of the finest *art nouveau* buildings and James Ensor began his extraordinary career creating art that harks back to Bosch rather than to Rubens.

2.58 David Teniers, *Archduke Leopold-Wilhelm in his Gallery in Brussels*, 1651. Oil on canvas, 50 × 64 in (127 × 162.6 cm). Kunsthistorisches Museum, Vienna.

Still-Life and Genre Painters

3 SPAIN

Jusepe de Ribera, *San Gennaro Emerging Unharmed from the Furnace*, 1641–43. Oil on silvered copper, 11 ft 7 in × 7 ft 3 in (3.55 × 2.2 m). Cathedral of San Gennaro, Naples.

SPAIN'S PAINTERS, SCULPTORS, AND WRITERS of the seventeenth century were so distinguished that the period is known as the country's "Golden Age." Miguel de Cervantes (1547–1616) wrote *Don Quixote*, a picaresque novel that remains a classic. The playwrights Lope de Vega (1562–1635) and Pedro Calderón de la Barca (1600–81) are both considered to have embraced a range of human experience that vies with that of Shakespeare's dramas. The paintings of Diego Velázquez, Jusepe de Ribera, Francisco de Zurbarán, and Bartolomé Murillo, and the sculptures of Juan Martínez Montañés, were equally innovative. During this century, however, Spain became the poorest nation in Western Europe. It was also the most corruptly administered and least tolerant of unorthodox religious beliefs. The three successors who ruled Spain between Philip II's death in 1598 and 1700, have received little positive press from modern scholars, apart from Philip IV's passionate art collecting and his patronage of Velazquez. Nowhere in Europe was the disparity greater between the wealth of a few and the poverty of the majority. The kings' chief ministers were self-seeking and corrupt, the monarchy constantly on the verge of bankruptcy despite punitive levels of taxation from its possessions. Spain may have had nominal control over parts of South America, India, and large areas of Europe in 1600 but real control and satisfactory tax revenues to fuel the ambitions of the monarchy were another matter. The defeat of the Spanish Armada by the English in 1588, which halved the Spanish fleet and reduced Spain's control of its trade routes, is only the most famous of their losses. When the English sacked Cádiz in 1596, they finished off the remaining fleet in the harbor and then destroyed the fortress and town. Philip II was then sixty-nine. Wearied by constant travel and warfare, he began to limit his ambitions to those that his ill-equipped son might be able to handle. He gave control of the Spanish Netherlands to his daughter Isabella and her husband, Archduke Albert, though on condition that the territory revert to Spain if they had no heirs.

Plans to install as the King of France a Catholic ruler sympathetic to Spanish interests were thwarted when Henry IV of Navarre, a Protestant, succeeded Henry III after his assassination in 1588. The stability that Henry IV brought to France after roughly fifty years of civil unrest should have been welcomed by Philip II as a respite from the turmoil that prevailed before. Henry even became a Catholic in 1593, but the Spanish were always suspicious of converts: the "new Christians" or *moriscos*—Spanish Muslims who had converted to the faith to avoid persecution—were expelled from Spain in 1610; Jews had been expelled in the fifteenth century. Despite increasing the *alcabala* (a sales tax on manufactured goods) from 10 to 25 per cent to pay for the Armada, and adding a stiff tax on food, Philip was still deep in debt. The silver mines of Mexico and Peru no longer produced the steady income they had when first discovered. The burden thus fell on the merchant and agricultural classes (the nobility were excused from taxation), who became less and less able to support the king's imperial ambitions. In 1596 Philip had to declare official bankruptcy for the third time during his reign. When he died two years later, he left a debt of 100 million ducats to his heir, Philip III.

Spanish Architecture

The architecture of this period is less known outside Spain than its Moorish and medieval monuments. Between the building of El Escorial by Philip II (1563–84) and the career of Antonio Gaudí (1852–1926) there was—it would seem—little but derivative, provincial variations on basic church designs supplied by the Jesuit Order with bizarre encrustations to facades. Barbara Borngässer challenged this bleak assessment in an eloquent essay with superb photographs, which alone should convince sceptics that some impressive buildings were constructed in Madrid, Valladolid, Salamanca, and Granada after 1600. There was, however, little city planning to compare with that in Rome, Paris, Amsterdam, or London, and almost all major buildings were for ecclesiastical patrons.

The severe classical idiom used by Juan Batista de Toledo (d. 1567) and Juan de Herrera (1530–97) for El Escorial, dubbed the *estile desornamentado (unornamented style)*, was soon adopted. Walls were articulated only by simple string courses or pilasters with the plainest of capitals, but the elegant proportions transmitted by Herrera, who had spent twelve years in Italy and brought back a substantial library, were well understood by his collaborators and students. They designed a number of handsome churches with original touches expertly blended into Italian models. The Plaza Mayor in Madrid (1617–19), designed by Juan Gomez de Mena (1586–1648), adopted the unified house facades of the Place Royale (des Vosges) in Paris: the Plaza is too large for the scale of its repetitive design, however, and so is a less successful example of coordinated civic design than its prototype.

The example shown here of Spanish adaptation of Italian Renaissance forms is the façade of the cathedral of Granada (Fig. **3.1**) by Alonso Cano (1601–1667), an artist whose achievements in painting and sculpture are discussed later. The new cathedral was designed and begun in 1523 by Diego de Siloé (c. 1490–1563), but it had not progressed beyond the transept and east end at the time of his death. Building was only resumed in the 1660s.

Cano had to work with the basic proportions of the nave and side aisles, and maybe even conform to Siloé's (lost) design. Nevertheless, within the tripartite division, he proceeded to create one of the most original church facades in Spain. It looks at first sight like the Arch of Constantine on stilts—that is, a large central arch flanked by smaller arches—but the arches are supported by piers, not columns, and the side arches are

3.1 Alonso Cano, Granada Cathedral, façade, Granada, 1601–67.

only a little lower and narrower than the central one. They are also deep, like porches, a feature that recalls both Spanish medieval precedents and Leon Battista Alberti's San Sebastiano in Mantua.

The structure has two stories, the upper one smaller than the main one, separated by an emphatic continuous cornice. The arched design is echoed below by the three doorways and elaborated with pairs of circular windows above the side doors and the circular relief above the main door, as well as circular motifs in the arched spaces at the top. The central oval window contains an eight-pointed star. As an arresting variation on traditional church facade design that blends Spanish and Italian precedents, the overall effect is both bold and subtle. Cano died a few months after his design was accepted and so he never saw it executed.

Spanish Sculpture

Spain did not have a Bernini, that is, a sculptor of such originality and technical accomplishment that he revolutionized the art of sculpture. The rest of Europe did not either, although it produced many accomplished sculptors who emulated Bernini's inventions and adapted them to local needs. Spanish sculptors, however, had to work within a conservative tradition controlled by a Church that was suspicious of iconographical and formal experiments; their sculptors must be situated in that context if their achievements are to be appreciated. Like painters, Spain's sculptors were mainly employed in producing religious imagery, often as part of the huge *retablos* that filled the apse end of the church or major chapel with a multi-storied structure that combined architecture, sculpture, and painting in one elaborate ensemble. Other statues, known as *pasos*, were made to be carried in religious processions on feast days. Almost all Spanish sculpture was first carved from wood and then polychromed in an elaborate process that was delegated to painters. Some artists—Alonso Cano is the best known example—worked as both sculptors and painters. To viewers used to the monochrome marble and bronze images favored in the rest of Europe, Spanish painted statues can look like waxworks or folk art, the forms obscured by layers of gesso, undercoat, and paint that imitates skin, hair, and fabric.

While the Church employed only Spanish artists, the court went to Italy for certain kinds of commission, above all for monumental works in marble and anything cast in bronze. Leone Leoni (1509–90) had provided bronze portrait busts of the Emperor Charles V and of his sisters Mary of Hungary and Eleonora of France based on studies made from life in Brussels in 1549. Leoni next cast a more ambitious full-length bronze statue of Charles V restraining Fury (1551–63), and made others of the Empress Isabella and Mary of Hungary in bronze and marble (all Prado, Madrid). Then with the assistance of his son Pompeo Leoni (c. 1533–1608), who settled in Madrid in 1572, he made twenty-seven bronze statues for the high altar of the Capilla Mayor of the Royal Basilica at the Escorial near Madrid, which were finished in 1591. Next Philip II ordered life-size kneeling bronze portraits of Charles V and himself with their respective wives, past and present, and other members of their immediate family for the Escorial, which were completed in 1598. Pompeo spent a good deal of time at the Escorial and in Valladolid finishing these and other major commissions, and trained Spanish assistants to finish and gild bronze, although the casting process remained an Italian monopoly. Bronze was the most expensive medium from which to make sculpture. These extravagant commissions were undertaken at a time when the emperor and Philip II were constantly on the edge of bankruptcy; for their own images at a site that would perpetuate their fame for posterity, however, no expense was spared.

Philip III and Philip IV did not indulge in expensive imported sculptures to the same degree as their predecessors but both commissioned an equestrian monument from Pietro Tacca (1577–1640). Like all of its predecessors reaching back to the Marcus Aurelius monument in Rome, Philip III's statue (1606–16), now in the Plaza Mayor, Madrid, shows the horse slowly pacing forward. Tacca proceeded to design a similar statue for Philip IV in response to a request of 1634 from Olivares, but this was not, it emerged, what Philip IV had in mind. The painted equestrian portraits of Rubens and

3.2 Ferdinando Tacca, *Equestrian Statue of Philip IV*, 1634–40. Stone. Plaza de Oriente, Madrid.

Velázquez showed the king on a horse rearing up on its hind legs and this was what he now requested, unaware of the immense technical difficulties that the casting of such a model presented. Backed by the considerable experience of his Florentine workshop, founded by Giovanni da Bologna in the 1560s, Tacca made the first equestrian monument with a rearing horse and rider (Fig. **3.2**). It was installed in the gardens of the Buen Retiro but now stands in the Plaza de Oriente before the Palacio Real built in the eighteenth century. The king could contemplate himself perfectly balanced on his splendid steed, one hand holding the reins, the other his baton of command, a powerful symbol of military strength, control, and restraint.

No Spanish sculptor received such lavish commissions as Leone and Pompeo Leoni, and Tacca, either from the court or from ecclesiastical patrons. Still, several achieved considerable stature in their home towns. The sculptor who dominated production in Spain's largest city, Seville, was Juan Martínez Montañés (1568–1649), who spent most of his life there, collaborating with Pacheco, Alonso Cano, and others who finished the surfaces that he had carved. He was born in a small town on the main road from Córdoba to Granada, the son of an embroiderer, and began his training in Granada with Pablo de Rojas, probably around 1580. There he could have studied tombs and altarpieces in the Capilla Real by both Italian and Spanish sculptors while learning his craft from his teacher, who seems to have had little impact on his gifted pupil. He qualified for admittance into the local sculptors' guild in 1588, when he was only twenty. He had married the year before in Seville and settled there soon after in order to take advantage of its greater opportunities.

The dominant style of the sculptors then working in Seville was derived from that of Alonso Berruguete (*c.* 1488–1561), who had spent his formative years in Italy working as a painter. After settling in Toledo around 1518, however, he worked mainly as sculptor; his greatest achievement is the carving on the choir stalls of Toledo Cathedral (1539–43). Often compared with those of El Greco, Alonso's twisting, dramatic forms demonstrate his admiration for Michelangelo's art and for the Hellenistic statue of the priest Laocoön and his sons discovered in Rome in 1506. The self-conscious display of assiduous study of the athletic male body, of ancient models, and of difficulties overcome are hallmarks of the Mannerist style. Montañés was the artist who shifted Spanish sculpture from *maniera* to the more natural visual language that gradually replaced it. His figures depend on intensely observed renderings of human anatomy and drapery for their effect. Even the most conventional of subjects become fresh in his hands, thanks to psychologically telling nuances in poses and facial expressions, as well as his exceptional facility in carving. His brilliance as a wood carver was so admired in Seville that he was dubbed "El Dios de la Madera" (the god of wood).

Montañés's first documented commissions were all small works such as bulk orders for images of the Virgin of the Rosary for export to Chile. A relief in stone and an ivory crucifix to be mounted on an ebony cross are both lost. His *Christ of Clemency* survives in Seville Cathedral (Fig. **3.3**) and shows how completely he had mastered his craft and how beautifully he fused his understanding of nature with the requirements of his patrons for an idealized image of expressive power. The theme gave the artist little scope for originality because every detail was rigidly controlled by theological requirements: whether

Christ was shown still alive or dead; whether three or four nails were used to fasten him to the cross; whether his legs were crossed or not; whether his feet were supported by a small ledge or not, and so on.

It was commissioned by an archdeacon who gave the artist quite precise instructions: Christ was to be shown "alive, before He had died, with the head inclined to the right side, looking to any person who might be praying at the foot of the crucifix, as if Christ Himself was speaking to him and reproaching him because what He is suffering is for the person who is praying; and therefore the eyes and the face must have a rather severe expression, and the eyes must be completely open."[1] Also significant is the artist's own statement in the contract that he wanted to make a beautiful crucifix that would not be sent abroad but would stay in Spain "to the renown of the master who made it for the glory of God." He promised that it would be worth 500 ducats, but that the bill would be for only 300. The surface was painted by Pacheco. The finished work hung in a chapel of Santa María de las Cuevas until that monastery was closed, when it was moved to the cathedral.

Christ's head does hang to his right and his expression fulfills the patron's request in every detail. Pacheco would have had expressive control only over the position of the pupils and the amount of blood on Christ's brow. The deeply set eyes and slightly exaggerated lower eyelids, visible only in a photographic detail, help to make Christ's facial expression legible from a distance. His slim arms and relaxed hands seem held up with a dancer's effortless poise, while his slim torso seems a little stretched by the weight of his body, but the overall impression is that Christ floats rather than hangs on the cross. The precise observation of the muscles around the armpits, the veins on the upper arms, the details of the ribcage, knees, and feet prove that Montañés had thoroughly studied the male body before starting work and may even have had life casts of body parts beside him as he carved. He had also seen a small bronze crucifix, supposedly designed by Michelangelo, of which Pacheco had made a number of copies for friends in Seville. Montañés's sculpture more than holds its own against this model. Only the whorls of drapery used for the loincloth seem a little fussy, a relic of earlier styles that valued virtuosity over significance. Zurbarán (see Fig. 3.15) was one of many later Spanish artists who found Montañés's statue a source of both spiritual and artistic inspiration. Velázquez certainly remembered it when he painted his *Crucified Christ* in 1630 (Prado, Madrid).

Montañés's relief sculptures look somewhat old-fashioned next to the finest of his free-standing figures because the backgrounds he provided lack convincing renderings of spatial recession. This mixture of conservative conventions with more advanced artistic language is typical of Spanish religious art, and seems especially characteristic of religious sculpture. The collaborative nature of the workshops that produced these ensembles also blurs the role of the supervising master whose hand becomes hard to detect. Thus some of the work that came from Montañés's shop is of a disappointing level of quality but this is not because he had ceased to be able to carve as skillfully as he did when he was younger. The high quality of *The Penitent St. Jerome*, a statue

3.3 Juan Martínez Montañés, *Christ of Clemency*, 1603–6. Gesso and tempera on wood. Chapel of St. Andrew, Seville Cathedral.

Spanish Sculpture 199

backed by an exquisitely carved tree and a large, docile lion in the central niche on the lower level of the retable made for San Isidoro del Campo at Santiponce (Fig. **3.4**), reflects the requirements of the contract that Montañés carve it himself.

Montañés was not the only sculptor of distinction working in seventeenth-century Spain but there is not space here to explore the work of contemporaries such as Gregorio Fernández en Alava (1566–1635), the major figure in Castile; Pedro de Mena (1628–88), who worked in Granada and Málaga; Alonso Cano (1601–67), active in both Seville and Madrid; or Pedro Roldán (1624–99) of Seville and his daughter, Luisa (1652–1706), whose small painted terracotta statues of subjects like the Holy Family were popular at court. Spanish museums are beginning to restore, catalogue, and exhibit their sculptures, a part of their heritage that has not had as much attention as the achievements of their painters. No Spanish sculptors will ever achieve the renown of Ribera, Zurbarán, Velázquez, and Murillo, but they produced many remarkable and beautiful devotional images that deserve to be more widely known, and which will reward visitors to Spanish museums and churches.

3.4 Juan Martínez Montañés, *The Penitent St. Jerome*, 1609–13. San Isidoro del Campo Monastery, Santiponce, near Seville.

Spanish Painting, 1600–1650

Spanish monarchs were astute patrons and collectors of the best Flemish art in the fifteenth and sixteenth centuries. As a result Spanish art became a provincial branch of the Netherlandish art favored by the Crown. Masterpieces of Flemish fifteenth-century painting such as Rogier van der Weyden's great *Deposition* were sent to Spain in the sixteenth century, as also were Hieronymus Bosch's two huge triptychs, the *Hay Wain* and the *Garden of Earthly Delights* as well as the table top depicting the *Seven Deadly Sins*, all acquired by Philip II and now in the Prado, Madrid. The first recorded owner of Jan van Eyck's *Arnolfini Wedding Portrait* (National Gallery, London) was a Spanish nobleman, Don Diego de Guevara (d. 1520), who gave it to Margaret of Hungary, Regent of the Netherlands, from whom it passed into the Spanish royal collection.

The impoverished state of Spain during much of the seventeenth century affected the development of the visual arts in many ways. Since there was not a substantial middle class with discretionary income, unlike those of Holland and France, artistic patronage was largely confined to its traditional twin pillars of support—the Church and the Crown. The consequence was conservative patronage that mainly required religious commissions for public and private use. Mythological and historical themes, even allegories, were rarely commissioned from Spanish painters in the seventeenth century. Portraiture was a staple at court for the royal family and their adherents, and was also commissioned by officials of the wealthier religious orders. Scenes of daily life and landscapes, two genres that flourished elsewhere in Europe, attracted little patronage, even in Madrid. Only still-life painting enjoyed some favor, especially in Naples, a city under Spanish control through its viceroys. Genre scenes such as Velázquez's early *Old Woman Cooking Eggs* (see Fig. 3.24) and Ribera's *Boy with a Club Foot* (see Fig. 3.12), an image used to convey a Christian message about charity, were exceptions in these artists' careers. Murillo also painted several images of happy beggar children (Fig. 3.5). Otherwise only specialists will be able to bring to mind a genre scene by a Spanish hand. The rarest of all genres by Spanish artists, however, is landscape. Until the discovery of two spectacular horizontal landscapes by Ribera, no Spanish artist was thought to have painted a memorable landscape; few had even attempted it. Ribera's were, of course, painted in Naples.[2]

Spanish painters rarely traveled to study artistic production elsewhere, but turned instead to imported works as models and examples against which to measure their own achievements. They were also assiduous collectors of prints by their European peers. Spanish patrons followed the example of the court and gave the best commissions to Flemish artists in the fifteenth century, and to Flemish and Italian artists in the sixteenth. The restless career of Charles V, who constantly moved his court to different European capitals, also meant that no stable center of artistic production was established anywhere. Only when Philip II settled in Madrid after succeeding his father did a community of artists and craftsmen begin to grow there, though the king still favored imported talent. Failing to lure Titian from Venice to Madrid, Philip II nevertheless became his most important patron in the artist's later years, ordering a long succession of portraits, mythologies, and an occasional religious work for his collection. There they were studied by Rubens and van Dyck as well as by Velázquez and had considerable impact on their careers. Later Italian Mannerists such as Federigo Zuccaro, Luca Cambiaso, and Pellegrino Tibaldi were commissioned to paint frescoes in the Escorial but their work had little lasting impact. Caravaggism and the revival of Italian High Renaissance styles soon made the work of these late Mannerists obsolete.

Jusepe de Ribera

Jusepe de Ribera (1591–1652) was a Spanish painter whose entire career unfolded in Italy. The reason he is included in the chapter on Spanish painting, even though his art exerted considerable influence over his peers and successors in Naples, is that Naples and most of Italy south of Rome was then under Spanish rule. Many of Ribera's patrons were Spanish nobility serving the king as members of his administration there and some of them commissioned altarpieces and

3.5 Bartolomé Esteban Murillo, *Two Boys Eating a Pie*, 1665–75. Oil on canvas, 48⅛ × 40⅛ in (123 × 102 cm). Altepinkothek, Munich.

private devotional works that were sent back to Spain to their home towns and estates. The artist himself proudly added the adjective "Hispanus" to many of his signatures and on occasion the phrase "Valentinus Civitatis Seteabis" (a citizen of Valencia and Játiva) as well. Ribera was one of a select group of seventeenth-century artists whose influence was not confined to one country but was carried elsewhere by their travels, by political circumstances, and by international patronage.

Between the time of his baptism in the small town of Játiva (near Valencia) on February 17, 1591 and June 11, 1611, when he was paid for an altarpiece in Parma, there is no record of Ribera's movements. His father was a shoemaker, so he grew up in a craftsman's household, if not an artistic one. He must have showed enough talent as a child to be sent to Valencia to join his older brother. The best painter in Valencia was Francisco Ribalta (1565–1628), who settled there in 1599 after training in Barcelona and Madrid.

3.6 Francisco Ribalta, *The Vision of the Father Simon*, 1612. Oil on canvas, 83 × 43⅓ in (211 × 110 cm). National Gallery, London.

church of San Prospero, which at that time still housed Correggio's *Adoration of the Shepherds* (Gemäldegalerie, Dresden). The beautifully rendered light effects in that painting mesmerized seventeenth-century painters from Annibale Carracci onwards. Ribera, for whom brilliantly orchestrated chiaroscuro is a key element of his style, must have studied it, even if its gentle illumination projects a different artistic persona. He also visited Venice. The strong tonal contrasts of Tintoretto's work, with its palette of black, browns, and white sparked with passages of ruby red, dark blue, and gold, was especially appealing to Ribera.

Ribera's first datable paintings are a set of half-length images of men representing the five senses that Giulio Mancini, writing around 1620, says that the artist made in Rome for a Spanish patron. Scholars date them around 1615. *Hearing* is lost, known only from a copy, but the surviving four make a striking ensemble. *Sight* (Museo Franz Meyer, Mexico City) holds a telescope and regards us thoughtfully. *Touch* (Norton Simon Foundation, Pasadena) is turned away from us, holding a white marble bust whose features he strokes gently, feeling his way to knowledge of its features. *Smell* (private collection) raises a cut onion and looks at us from watering eyes. *Taste* (Fig. **3.7**) raises the glass of

His mature work features compositions of focused simplicity rendered with sensitive realism (Fig. **3.6**) but when Ribera might have studied with him, Ribalta's work was a less personal blend of current late Mannerist trends. His early compositions are well organized and his drawing crisply confident, but his treatment of textures and tones is monotonously smooth. Ribera's paintings are always meticulously prepared and finished; whoever taught him gave him an excellent technical training.

In 1613 Ribera attended a meeting of the Accademia di San Luca in Rome, so he spent at least two years in North Italy.[3] A letter written by Ludovico Carracci in 1618 reveals that "Lo Spagnoletto" (the little Spaniard), as he was called in Italy, had attracted the admiration of patrons and the jealousy of other artists during his time in Bologna. The altarpiece for which he was paid in 1611, now lost, was made for the

3.7 (right) Jusepe de Ribera, *Taste*, c. 1615. Oil on canvas, 44¼ × 34½ in (113.6 × 87.6 cm). Wadsworth Atheneum, Hartford, CT.

202   *Chapter 3: Spain*

3.8 Jusepe de Ribera, *Drunken Silenus*, 1626. Oil on canvas, 72⅞ × 90⅛ in (189 × 229 cm). National Museum of Capodimonte, Naples.

wine he has just filled from a carafe and seems to invite us to join him as he tucks into a heaping dish of squid. Each man has been given a powerful physical and psychological presence enhanced by strongly individualized portrayals that include their hands—plump for the man about to consume a meal, whose grubby light gray jacket is stretched tight across his bulky chest; neatly tapered for the beggar in tattered clothes with the onion. The still-life elements on the counter in front of each man are brilliantly rendered—a fat onion, a clove of garlic, and a sprig of jasmine for *Smell* and a paper cone of small black olives, a fresh bread roll, and a glass of red wine for *Taste*. Ribera's palette is austere—browns predominate with some gray, black, and flesh tones. There is nothing here like the lush baskets of fruit or vases of flowers in Caravaggio's early half-lengths (see Fig. 1.39). Much of Ribera's subsequent work is characterized by such browns, set off by black grounds and brilliant highlights, and by the focus on one or two figures, usually male, unless the subject included the Virgin or Magdalene. Only the smooth paint surface betrays their early date. His grasp of human anatomy was already impressive; it only improved in his many subsequent images of penitent saints in wilderness settings.

Ribera left Rome in haste, leaving behind assorted debts. By July 1616 he was working in Naples. The Viceroy of Naples, the Duke of Osuna, was among his first patrons, ordering images of Sts. Peter, Sebastian, Bartholomew, and Jerome for his own collection around 1618 that his widow presented to the Collegiata in Osuna in Spain in 1627. She also ordered a *Crucifixion with the Virgin, St. John, and Another Figure* in 1618, Ribera's largest commission to date (Patronato de Arte de Osuna, Seville). The treatment of Christ's gaunt body with its almost obsessively detailed description of his prominent ribcage offers a forceful contrast with the gently idealized Christ of Annibale Carracci in his *Pietà* (see Fig. 1.35).

Ribera painted two masterpieces in 1626, *St. Jerome with the Angel of Judgment* (see Fig. 3.9) and the *Drunken Silenus* (Fig. 3.8). The patron who commissioned the *Silenus*, one of the artist's

3.9 Jusepe de Ribera, *St. Jerome with the Angel of Judgment*, 1626. Oil on canvas, 8 ft 6 in × 5 ft 5 in (2.62 × 1.64 m). National Museum of Capodimonte, Naples.

rare mythological works, remains unidentified. Silenus is the corpulent man reclining in the foreground who turns to look up at the faun beside him filling his shell-shaped cup from a wineskin. A young faun dressed in fur seated on the left looks out at us with a mischievous grin. Behind Silenus on the right is the god Pan, the father of Silenus, whose rarely depicted attributes—a shell, turtle, and a staff—are placed in the right foreground instead of the familiar pipes. Two other figures peer at the scene from the upper right corner. In the left, a donkey brays, its muzzle silhouetted against the small patch of gray sky. Hard to see in the darkened gloom that envelops much of the painting is a large wine vat behind Silenus whom Pan crowns with vine leaves.

The unusual attributes of Pan show that Ribera or his patron consulted Vincenzo Cartari's *Imagini de i dei degli antichi* (1556). He may also have known Annibale Carracci's design for an engraved silver dish in the Farnese collections in Rome that shows a similarly plump, reclining Silenus. The fancy Latin signature of *Josephus de Ribera, Hispanus, Valentin/et academicus Romanus faciebat/partenope* on the paper that is being torn apart by a snake in the lower left corner also seems intended to draw attention to Ribera's intellectual and artistic accomplishments, yet the style of the painting flaunts its vulgar realism instead of following the examples of idealizing artists like Annibale when they depicted characters from classical mythology. Is Ribera mocking the pretensions to which he alludes or was he playing it straight, believing his earthy naturalism as appropriate for Silenus as for St. Jerome? The brilliantly realized male nude with his flabby breasts and swollen belly seems a knowing parody of the many reclining images of Venus produced in Italy in the sixteenth century, and also a challenge to Caravaggio's equally sophisticated depiction of a barely adolescent naked Cupid carelessly scattering symbols of human achievement (see Fig. 1.46). Its owner, Marchese Vincenzo Giustiniani, also patronized Ribera, who will have seen the Cupid before leaving for Naples.

Ribera painted more images of Jerome than of any other subject in his career. This example (Fig. **3.9**) was made for Santa Trinità delle Monache in Naples which was destroyed by an earthquake in 1897. St. Jerome (d. 420) was one of the most frequently painted saints in Roman Catholic art, honored as one of the Doctors of the Latin Church who translated the Bible into Latin and for his austere habits. Having rejected the pomp and trappings of official Church offices when he lived in Rome, he retreated to live with hermits in the Syrian desert for several years, and is thus often shown in the wilderness as an abject penitent. These devotional images that show him alone in a rocky setting with a skull, some religious books, and his legendary pet lion, beating

his chest with a stone or listening to an angel trumpeting warnings of his final judgment, allude to several events in his life.

Ribera certainly knew Caravaggio's *The Inspiration of St. Matthew* (see Fig. 1.44), also a vertical altarpiece. Ribera's composition has a similar simplicity and concentration on essentials but instead of the black void in which Caravaggio's saint receives his miraculous assistance, Ribera's Jerome inhabits an atmospheric setting of dark granite rocks and, in the upper left, a gray sky streaked with dingy white clouds. The bent arm of the angel supporting the trumpet is echoed by the saint's right arm raised to acknowledge the vision and its message. The saint and the angel gaze intently at each other across the space that separates them, a greater distance than the more intimate encounter portrayed by Caravaggio. The light, half-light, and shadow that passes over the bony torso of Ribera's saint seems to have been meticulously observed—the shadow cast by the raised arm that falls across Jerome's chest; the shadow of his upper body that puts his left thumb and part of his left wrist in shadow as well as much of his left torso and left arm. The light is, however, no more logical than in Caravaggio's work. Daylight would not only produce an even, bright light on the saint's rose-red and white drapery as well as on the skull and book on the right, but also shine into the cave. We can, however, see nothing in the depths of the cave behind his knees and the skull, while the sharp tonal contrasts on the saint could only be created by modern stage lighting. Ribera has used artistic license to focus our attention on the details that emphasize Jerome's self-sacrifice and dedication to the Church. The chiaroscuro is painted so convincingly, however, that the viewer is never prompted to question the truth of the artist's vision, nor that of the religious message it conveys.

For a Spanish audience, no subject evoked the glories of heaven more vividly than the Immaculate Conception. Though not proclaimed official Catholic Church doctrine until 1854, the belief that the Virgin Mary was conceived without sin in order to be pure enough to be the mother of Christ had been debated since the twelfth century. The event was first celebrated as an official Church feast day in 1476 with the

support of Pope Sixtus IV and was strongly promoted by Jesuits at the Council of Trent (1545–63) and by Spanish theologians afterwards. Ribera painted two interpretations of the theme for the convent of the Agustinas Descalzas (barefoot followers of St. Augustine) in Salamanca, a large one for the high altar of the church completed in 1635 and a smaller one for the cloistered section where it would be seen only by the nuns who lived there in seclusion; the latter is signed and dated 1637 (Fig. **3.10**). The patron was Don Manuel de Acevedo, 6th Count of Monterey and, from 1631 to 1637, Viceroy of Naples. His family's connections with Salamanca explain his patronage of institutions there during his term of office in Naples.

The most important biblical text that theologians associated with images of the Immaculata occurs in Revelation (12:1): "And there appeared a great wonder in heaven; a woman clothed with the sun, and the moon under her feet, and upon her head a crown of stars." Ribera's painting has a color scheme of gold, blue, and white that represents heaven literally and metaphorically. As in

3.10 Jusepe de Ribera, *Immaculate Conception*, 1637. Oil on canvas, 100⅜ × 69⅝ in (255 × 177 cm). Columbia Museum of Art, Columbia, SC.

nearly all Spanish images, the Virgin wears a white dress instead of the more familiar red to emphasize her purity. She stands on a crescent moon; a circlet of small stars frames her head like a halo. The dove of the Holy Ghost hovers over her. Of the many other possible artistic attributes, Ribera's painting includes only the sun on the left, and, on the right, a star, the *Stella maris* (star of the sea, the translation of Mary's name from its Jewish form, Miriam). Her pose suggests a gentle dance-like step, as does the lift to the drapery on our right. She seems to turn before our eyes, still yet miraculously alive.

Ribera never painted in fresco, and thus did not compete for the large decorative commissions in Naples craved by ambitious Italian artists. He did, however, contribute to one such commission, providing Old Testament prophets and patriarchs on canvas for the nave in San Martino between 1638 and 1643 (Fig. 3.11). The entire interior of this jewel of a church is veneered in colored marbles to designs by Cosimo Fanzago and provides a sumptuous setting for the frescoes of Lanfranco and Massimo Stanzione and Ribera's ingeniously posed Old Testament figures. The awkward triangular spaces with curved bases were treated like attic cells where these wise men manage to arrange themselves so that they can study their manuscripts or write their texts. A succession of portrait-like figures, each in a different pose and costume, none too bizarre to be convincing, testify to the fertility of Ribera's artistic imagination. Two additional figures of Moses and Elijah, finished in 1638, occupy less restricted spaces on either side of the entry wall. Elijah, who cradles a book and a small fire, is especially impressive.

One of Ribera's most affecting images is *Boy with a Club Foot* (Fig. 3.12). The boy's cheerful disposition is conveyed by his gap-toothed smile and his brave imitation of a soldier, his walking stick hoisted onto his shoulder like a musket, his enormous hat tucked under his right arm. This performance distracts the viewer momentarily from the deformity of his twisted right foot. He carries a piece of paper with a message written in the large capital letters of a semi-literate who has carefully copied the Latin: DA MIHI ELIMOSINAM PROPTER AMOREM DEI ("Give me alms for the love of God"). The low viewpoint sets the beggar above the viewer for he is no ordinary child but a messenger encouraging us to be charitable and perform good works in order to be worthy of salvation. Sullivan later noted that Pierre de Besse praised the laugh "as the most Christian of facial expressions because it shows indifference to the trials of earthly existence."[4] Ribera places us in the subservient role looking up at the beggar, a novel concept for the patron who probably saw beggars in the streets of Naples only from his carriage windows. The boy blocks our view of the heavens behind him; only when we reward him will he continue his journey and let us pass.

In 1641 Ribera was asked to paint an important altarpiece for the Treasury Chapel in the Cathedral of San Gennaro. It had been commissioned from Domenichino, who left part of the dome and two altarpieces unfinished at his death in 1641. The subject of Ribera's painting is *San Gennaro Emerging Unharmed from the Furnace* (see p. 194), one of many miraculous escapes from death experienced by the legendary fourth-century patron saint of Naples. Ribera took six years to finish it. It is an exceptional work in his career for several reasons: it is painted on silvered copper, a support never normally used for such large works; it contains more figures than any other picture by him; and its palette is sumptuously rich and bright.

3.11 Jusepe de Ribera, *Elijah*, San Martino interior, Naples, 1638. Oil on canvas, 66⅛ × 38¼ in (168 × 97 cm).

Ribera, who preferred to work with a small cast of static figures, was obliged to conform to the established character of the completed decorations by Domenichino, which both he and Lanfranco are said to have criticized for having too many figures. He took his time completing *San Gennaro Emerging Unharmed from the Furnace* but finally met the challenge with one of his most impressive paintings. He used an inverted V to mark the boundaries between heaven and earth, continuing it to make a large X to provide structure for the mass of figures. There are sixteen men and boys surrounding the saint as he steps away from the white heat of the furnace. His golden miter and chasuble piped along its edges in crimson pull our eyes to him and then, following his gaze, to the baby angels cavorting in the blue sky above him. Some figures around the saint are represented by nothing more than an eye or ear seen behind an arm; other heads emerge in the shadows, yet their various emotional responses to this miracle are all convincingly suggested. The saint's steady faith is emphasized by his calm expression and the vertical mass of his form; their panic and amazement by the jangle of limbs and the criss-cross patterns they create. Ribera knew that he would be judged against the works in the chapel by Domenichino and made certain that he would more than hold his own beside an artist whom he reputedly criticized as "not a painter, because he did not paint [*non coloriva*] from nature but was only an average draughtsman."[5] The five altarpieces on copper by Domenichino and his assistants are now in poor condition, their darkened paint flaking off their supports. Beside these sad remnants, Ribera's splendid painting glows with life and makes his case over three centuries later.

The patron who commissioned Ribera's *The Holy Family with Sts. Anne and Catherine of Alexandria* in 1648 is unknown (Fig. **3.13**). It emerged from its cleaning in 1979 as one of the masterpieces of Ribera's last years. St. Anne on the left and Joseph on the right are rendered in warm browns against a dark brown background. In front of them the three primary colors stand out in strong light and sharp relief—yellow for the outer garment of St. Catherine, lapis blue over rose for those of the Virgin. Joseph and Mary both regard the spectator with identical

3.12 Jusepe de Ribera, *Boy with a Club Foot*, 1642. Oil on canvas, 64½ × 36⅞ in (164 × 93.5 cm). Louvre, Paris.

gazes but the other three figures are absorbed in the encounter between Catherine and Jesus, who allows his hand to be kissed gently by her. St. Anne, who gazes at Christ, holds a rustic basket of fruit and a rose with a thorny stem, an allusion to the crown of thorns given to him before his crucifixion. The basket in the right foreground filled with yellow and gold cloth and a cushion may allude to the domestic sewing chores often associated with the Virgin. Both a V and an X can easily be found in the composition, with the most brightly lit areas at the center of the cross. Ribera's brilliantly rendered figures, especially the infant Christ with his pinkish toes and finger tips, argue the case for making these sacred figures as real as possible in order to sustain the faith of true believers.

Ribera was approaching sixty in 1648. He took up a delayed commission, his largest canvas, the *Last Communion of the Apostles* (13 ft 4 in [4 m] square), which he finished shortly before his death in 1652, for the monastery of San Martino.

3.13 Jusepe de Ribera, *The Holy Family with Sts. Anne and Catherine of Alexandria*, 1648. Oil on canvas, 82½ × 60¾ in (209.6 × 154.3 cm). Samuel D. Lee Fund, 1934. Metropolitan Museum of Art, New York.

It is not an entirely successful union of figures and setting, probably because Ribera had never had to provide such a grand architectural background before. A far less ambitious late work, the *St. Sebastian* (Fig. **3.14**), also made for San Martino, shows the artist to better advantage. It allows the spectator to confront the pale torso of the young saint and to admire both his fortitude in the face of painful torture and, yet again, Ribera's masterful rendering of the male body. One arrow has pierced the saint's side, another is stuck in the tree to which Sebastian has been tied, so that his beautiful torso is almost unaffected by the attempt of Roman soldiers to kill him. The elegant extension of the pose recalls Reni but neither he nor other Italian painters ever depicted body hair on male saints. Ribera's fusion of realism and idealism still retained far more of the former than any Italian artist would allow. In Naples in 1656, there was a particularly severe outbreak of the bubonic plague, when the faithful would invoke the protection of St. Sebastian. The monk privileged to have this image in his cell at San Martino must have turned to it often that year.

Ribera's impact on Neapolitan painting was extensive. Spanish artists saw far less of his work but his most characteristic subject, the penitent or martyred male saint, was soon known from imports such as the *Martyrdom of St. Philip* (Prado, Madrid), commissioned in 1639 by the Viceroy of Naples for Philip IV, and from earlier purchases. After about 1650 Ribera's hard-edged realism was replaced by the softer, more painterly styles inspired by Velázquez's art. Juan Carreño, Juan de Valdés Leal, and, above all, Bartolomé Murillo would lead the way. Ribera, had he lived longer, would have had to adapt or face poverty, which was, in fact, the fate of Francisco de Zurbarán (1598–1664).

Francisco de Zurbarán

Zurbarán and Ribera were the two greatest Spanish religious painters working before 1650, but Zurbarán remained in Spain, living most of his life in Seville. His early years are only slightly better documented than those of Ribera. His father Luis was a shopkeeper in the small town of Fuente de Cantos (Badajoz), some 200 miles north of Seville near the border of Portugal. Francisco was baptized there on November 7, 1598. By the time he was twelve, he showed sufficient potential as a painter for his father to find him a teacher, and in 1614, to pay for a three-year apprenticeship in Seville with an obscure *pintor de ymaginería* (painter of images). When the contract ended, Zurbarán may have returned to Fuente, though he is next recorded as father of a daughter born to María Páez in February 1618 in the nearby town of Llerena. In 1618 he was paid for a fountain design in Seville and a painting for the gate of a church in Llerena, both lost. His first wife died, probably in childbirth in 1623. He was remarried by 1625 to a woman whose family had the means to help him set up a more ambitious workshop and seek more important commissions, including his first surviving

documented work, *The Crucifixion* made for the oratory of the sacristy in the monastery of San Pablo Real in Seville in 1627 (Fig. **3.15**). It is a masterpiece and was immediately recognized as such by contemporaries.

The power of this image comes from its simplicity. Christ is alone on a cross that emerges from the gloom like a phantom, his loins covered with a loosely draped white cloth. The artist has suppressed everything included in most basic images of the crucifixion: neither his fainting mother, nor the griefstricken Magdalene, nor St. John appear below. There is no setting, not even a clear indication of the ground in which the wooden cross has been planted. Instead of the traditional skull marking the hill of Golgotha at its foot, there is a scrap of paper pinned to the wood with the artist's signature. Christ does not slump as if he is dead, though his grayish skin tones suggest that he must be. His lowered head implies his submission to the will of his Father. The priests who robed in the sacristy prayed to this image before entering the church to celebrate the Mass when, according to Catholic doctrine, the blessed bread becomes the actual body and blood of Christ. They would have found their minds and hearts perfectly focused on their duties. A city counselor declared soon after the painting was installed that "he is a consummate artist" and urged the city council to invite the artist to move permanently to Seville.

How did Zurbarán achieve this monumental and affecting simplicity after only three years of study in Seville with an artist of no account? What could he have seen there that could have helped an artist born in a provincial town with no artistic tradition of its own to find such powerful visual language? The iconography follows the instructions of Francisco Pacheco (1564–1644), whose *Christ on the Cross* (Fundación Gomez-Moreno, Granada) of 1614 shows Christ standing, each foot nailed separately to a small

3.14 (left) Jusepe de Ribera, *St. Sebastian*, 1651. Oil on canvas, 47⅝ × 39⅜ in (121 × 100 cm). Museo di San Martino, Naples.

3.15 (right) Francisco de Zurbarán, *The Crucifixion*, 1627. Oil on canvas, 114⅓ × 65⅛ in (290.3 × 165.5 cm). Robert A. Waller Memorial Fund. Art Institute of Chicago, Chicago, IL.

Spanish Painting, 1600–1650 **209**

platform, and a blank, flat ground. Pacheco was raised by a canon of Seville Cathedral and, while not a gifted artist himself (Jonathan Brown called his work "the triumph of tenacity over talent"), used his connections with church authorities to buttress his own views about the role of artists to communicate correct doctrine. His treatise, the *Arte de la pintura*, was published posthumously in 1649 but he had already been made supervisor of sacred images for the Inquisition in Seville in 1618. Pacheco argued that Christ was crucified with four nails, not three, and so his image became dogma to be followed in Seville. If the symbolism of Zurbarán's image can be explained by Pacheco's canvas, its luminosity cannot. The early work of Diego Velázquez (who became Pacheco's son-in-law) would, however, have helped Zurbarán, who was the same age. Velázquez was studying with Pacheco when Zurbarán was training in Seville. He matriculated in 1617 and in 1618 painted an *Immaculate Conception* (see Fig. 3.26) for the Shod Carmelites of Seville that Zurbarán must have seen. Mary floats between cloud banks against a dark sky, their white shapes glowing as if the moon was behind them. No one else then practicing in Seville could achieve such effects. When Velázquez moved to Seville in 1623 to join the court of Philip IV in Madrid, he left other examples of his precocious painterly skills in public and private collections. Zurbarán absorbed their lessons, and, maybe fearing to compete against such a gifted artist, did not consider establishing himself in Seville until some years after Velázquez's departure.

Zurbarán's *Christ Crucified* was only part of the commission he received from the Dominicans of San Pablo, but only five of the twenty-one paintings recorded in the contract survive. He received his next contract in August 1628: the monastery of the Order of Mercy (Mercedarios Calzados) ordered twenty-two paintings illustrating the life of the founder of their order, St. Peter Nolasco, who was canonized that year. Zurbarán seems never to have completed this commission; only ten scenes are known, not all from his hand. He had signed another contract in 1629 for paintings to be placed in the high altar of the church of the Trinidad Calzada and apparently one with the Franciscan College of San Buenaventura too, for he painted at least four large images of their patron saint, one of which is dated 1629. Zurbarán, then just past thirty, had a large studio to help him complete all this work. With the encouragement of the city fathers, he moved to Seville in 1630.

The *St. Serapion* (Fig. 3.16) once hung in the Sala de Profundis of the Mercedarios Calzados, where the monks who had died were laid out before burial. The monks who came to pray there would also contemplate images of past members of their order who had been martyred for their cause. Serapion had accompanied Peter Nolasco on his missions to ransom captured Christians from the Moors and was killed in 1240. Strung up between two trees, he has apparently been left to die, like Christ on the cross. In fact, his throat was cut and he was mutilated. Zurbarán's painting marries dignified simplicity with powerful forms rendered in a gentle light against a background of impenetrable darkness. The method of placing a half- or three-quarter-length figure close

3.16 Francisco de Zurbarán, *St. Serapion*, 1628. Oil on canvas, 47½ × 41 in (120.6 × 104.1 cm). Wadsworth Atheneum, Hartford, CT.

3.17 Francisco de Zurbarán, *St. Peter Nolasco's Vision of the Crucified St. Peter*, 1625. Oil on canvas, 70½ × 87¾ in (179 × 223 cm). Prado, Madrid.

to the picture plane recalls the formula perfected by Caravaggio but Zurbarán probably did not see even a copy of his work. The little red and yellow badge of Serapion's order brings a small note of color to an otherwise monochrome study in creams and browns.

A larger painting for the same patrons, *St. Peter Nolasco's Vision of the Crucified St. Peter* (Fig. **3.17**), shows how restrictive were the conditions under which Zurbarán worked and how brilliantly he transcended them. He was given an engraving of 1625 after Jusepe Martinez's depiction of this scene which had been included in the documentation submitted to Urban VIII to support Peter Nolasco's qualifications for sainthood. This small, vertical image shows Peter Nolasco kneeling on the left and regarding with raised arms a vision of his name saint, Peter, who was crucified upside down. Zurbarán also limited his painting to the two protagonists but switched their positions and tilted St. Peter so that his face and more of his body are visible. St. Peter Nolasco's white woolen robes gradually vanish into the shadows behind him. He holds his hands out in a restrained gesture of surprise as St. Peter, whom he had hoped to worship in Rome, advises him to continue his mission in Spain. The body of St. Peter was studied from a model lying on his back, with the physiognomy faithfully but not pedantically rendered. Nothing but the essential elements of the story are provided to convey the didactic message required of the image by the patrons.

The limitations of Zurbarán's artistic training become evident only when he tackled multi-figure compositions that also required a convincing indoor or outdoor setting. That for *St. Bonaventure at the Council of Lyons* (Louvre, Paris) looks like a painted stage flat behind the heads of the men witnessing the dialogue between the saint and Pope Gregory X. In another canvas in this series, Zurbarán omits the setting altogether behind the men assembled to contemplate the saint on his bier after his sudden death at the Council in 1274 (Louvre, Paris). If the artist's understanding of central-point perspective was limited, his placing of principal figures amid a crowd always gives them the prominence they require. Italian and Flemish artists would have adversely criticized Zurbarán's

3.18 Francisco de Zurbarán, *Adoration of the Magi*, 1638. Oil on canvas, 8 ft 6 in × 5 ft 8 in (2.61 × 1.75 m). Musée de Grenoble.

ability to create a convincing space around his characters: this, however, must be accepted as part of his distinctive charm, and was certainly not a problem with his patrons until the last years of his career, when his style was out of fashion. He dominated religious patronage in Seville until the mid-century. His studio also sent a good deal of work abroad to Spanish possessions in Peru and Mexico.

By 1634, Zurbarán's reputation was sufficient to garner him a major commission for Philip IV, a series of the Twelve Labors of Hercules for the Hall of Realms in the Buen Retiro Palace in Madrid then being decorated by Velázquez and a team of other painters. He was also asked to contribute two canvases to the series of political and military victories for the same location, of which Velázquez's *Surrender of Breda* (see Fig. 3.29) is the best known. Whether because Zurbarán was unsure of his ability to paint a heroic, muscular male nude or because he had to produce so many pictures quickly, he turned to sixteenth-century prints as models for several of his paintings celebrating Hercules' feats. Most modern writers find the results stiff. His *St. Peter Nolasco's Vision* shows that he could paint an excellent male nude when required to do so but his beefy Hercules looks like a peasant next to the heroic interpretations of Rubens and Annibale Carracci (see Fig. 1.29), who based their hero on the ancient Farnese Hercules in Rome.

This commission gave Zurbarán the opportunity to see the work of Velázquez as well as Italian and Flemish paintings in the royal collections but there is no visible effect on his later work. He made no concessions either to the sophisticated illusionism of Velázquez or to the painterly surfaces of Rubens and van Dyck. In 1638 Zurbarán carried out a huge multi-story altarpiece for the Carthusian church Nuestra Señora de la Defensión in Jerez de la Frontera, including an *Adoration of the Magi* (Fig. **3.18**); only its judiciously composed design might reflect his experiences at court. In this case, however, Velázquez had left a model in Seville, his somber *Adoration of the Magi* of 1619 (Prado, Madrid). In Velázquez's painting, a strong diagonal links the seated Virgin on the right holding the swaddled Child in front of her and the kneeling king in front of them on the left. It also divides the canvas in half, separating the two waiting kings behind Caspar from the viewer, who is further removed from the Virgin and Child by rocks and plants in the foreground. The kings' robes have plain fabrics and Balthazar, the black king, even lacks the large turban worn to mark him as a follower of an alien faith. Zurbarán's picture was originally displayed well above the viewer's eye level on the second story of this composite altar. Its original location explains why Zurbarán lavished attention on the gold and red brocade of Caspar, the oldest king, which fills the foreground. Its rich color would have stood out and helped the distant worshiper to identify him. His white ermine collar, white beard and hair, and the white garments and crib blanket of the infant Jesus also ensured their visibility from the ground. They make a strong diagonal dividing foreground from middle ground like the division in Velázquez's canvas; their poses come strikingly close to his too. The pink silk cloak of Balthazar and Mary's pink dress in Zurbarán's picture bracket the lighted areas in the front plane. Melchior, who has a fanciful military outfit, stands proudly in the shadowed center, his right hand on his hip. The sky behind shades from indigo to pale yellow, silhouetting the forms of a lance, a spear, and some ruined architectural elements. The spatial depth is implied by overlapping forms rather than demonstrated. It is among the artist's most successful multi-figure compositions.

All the paintings we have considered in this chapter so far were made for specific locations in churches and monasteries; none remain in their original sites. As Jonathan Brown explained, "two violent acts of history pried [Spanish art] loose and set [it] adrift in the mainstream of European art."[6] The Peninsular War of 1808–14, which gave French generals the opportunity to loot art from the towns they captured, was followed by the Secularization Act of 1835. This gave the State control of the properties of Spain's monastic orders, allowing even more dispersal of church decorations and fittings, many of which were also acquired by British and French collectors. Even if Zurbarán's paintings are now easier to see in well-lit museum rooms than they would be in their original locations, it is important to understand their intended situations of display. There they were objects of worship for church officials in such spaces as sacristies or cloisters not always accessible to the public as well as in churches where their intended audience also included the lay public. Unique to Spain were the huge, multi-story high altars (*retablos*) that filled the apses of churches with elaborate architectural structures resembling church façades. The *Adoration of the Magi* was part of an altar ensemble with five other canvases of equal size, three on two levels with smaller images on the attic above them. The exhibition of Zurbarán's work held in New York and Paris in 1987–8 provided installations that gave the visitor some idea of these lost settings while the catalogue contains helpful reconstructions of destroyed ensembles and photographs of the spaces for which they were made. Only one of Zurbarán's major commissions for an ecclesiastical patron has survived untouched, the sacristy of the Jeronymite monastery in Guadalupe (Estremadura), probably because of its isolated location.

A masterpiece by Zurbarán that illustrates his typical synthesis of observed realism and archaizing simplicity is the *Virgin and Christ in the Holy House of Nazareth* (Fig. **3.19**). Although the

3.19 Francisco de Zurbarán, *Virgin and Christ in the Holy House of Nazareth*, c. 1631–40. Oil on canvas, 65 × 85⅞ in (165 × 218.2 cm). Leonard C. Hanna, Jr., Fund. Cleveland Museum of Art, Cleveland, OH.

Spanish Painting, 1600–1650   213

work is neither signed nor dated, and its patron is unknown, its authenticity has never been questioned. It has been dated between 1631 and 1640 by different authorities. The horizontal format suggests that it was made for private devotion rather than for a public altarpiece, which normally has a vertical format. It is not a small painting, however; it is over 7 feet (2.18 meters) wide and meticulously planned to display an exceptionally large number of symbolic references to the life of Christ. The domestic setting would have made it an attractive image for a wealthy lay patron, though experts suggest that a prior or abbot kept it in his private quarters. Several copies show that it was much admired.

The Gospels of Matthew and Luke provide few real details about Christ's childhood but Apocryphal versions elaborated on them and other accounts were popular from the thirteenth century onwards. The Council of Trent permitted them as harmless from a doctrinal point of view. Pictures of the young Jesus helping his carpenter father Joseph were popular throughout Europe (see Fig. 4.25); pictures of him with his mother once he was no longer a baby are less frequent. Zurbarán's *Virgin and Christ in the Holy House at Nazareth* shows mother and child seated in a domestic interior with a heavy wooden table filling the space between them. The artist invites us to see a parallel between Christ pricking his finger on the crown of thorns he has been making and the Virgin's sewing chores, which she has ceased, absorbed in the significance of this moment, which prefigures that before his crucifixion. He looks quietly at his pierced finger; there is no indication of any pain in his facial expression. While he accepts his destiny, the Virgin, equally aware of future events, is weeping quietly.

The surface of the table implies that our viewpoint is just above Mary's head yet the ceramic bowl of water on the floor near Christ and the work basket in front of her are seen from a lower viewpoint. The space, in short, is not logically defined. The window opening above Mary makes a strict horizontal match with the picture plane and implies a back wall but its join with the floor is invisible, concealed by a gloom like that around Zurbarán's *St. Peter Nolasco's Vision* (see Fig. 3.17). Here too a wide beam of golden light leads our eyes to Jesus and to the table surface with its books and two pears still connected to a branch and leaves. This fruit was used as a symbol of Christ's love for mankind; here it must refer to both Christ and Mary, one pear being slightly larger and more mature than the other. There are three books: an open one near Christ, who has interrupted his reading to construct his crown of thorns, and two closed books near Mary, which allude to her role as *Virgo sapientissima*, the Virgin Mother of Wisdom. The roses and lilies in the vase beside the Virgin are familiar symbols of her purity and suffering. The pair of white doves recall the presentation of the infant Christ at the temple when two doves were offered in sacrifice, and the aged Simeon recognized him as the Messiah. The water in the brown bowl alludes to the sacrament of baptism.

Only the table has attracted no symbolic reading from the many scholars intrigued by this masterpiece. The assumption is that it serves only to represent the modest household of Christ's family but its central position amid such a calculated display of significant symbolism suggests that it too has a symbolic role to play. The odd detail of its half-open drawer must be significant, as is its size, too high for the stools on which Jesus and Mary are seated. The table forms a barrier between Mary and the beam of heavenly light and its surface carries symbols of prayer and meditation on holy mysteries, and of Christ's good will to humanity. It serves thus as both an altar table and as the tomb from which Christ will rise along the beam of light to heaven. This reading explains the table's prominence and its open drawer in this meditation on Christ's future martyrdom. The white cloth on which the Virgin is working represents Christ's shroud, an interpretation supported by her tears and Christ's meditation on his own death. Every element in the painting, including the spatial relationships between the figures, every inanimate object and the space in which they have all been placed, all contribute to the painting's somber message. The lapis lazuli used for the blue of Christ's robes and the soft rose of the Virgin's dress are among the most beautiful passages in Zurbarán's work.

Zurbarán also painted some portraits and an occasional still-life. One of these has become

famous, perhaps the most frequently reproduced still-life painting of the seventeenth century, though it is a design of such austerity that its popularity is puzzling (Fig. 3.20). Why is this picture of a basket of oranges crowned with orange leaves and blossom, flanked by a dish of lemons and a cup of water with a rose in its saucer, so mesmerizing? The design with a table surface parallel to the picture plane and a few isolated objects arranged along that horizontal plane is common in other still-life paintings made before 1620, among them Juan Sánchez Cotán's remarkable study of gourds and cabbages arranged in a parabolic curve in a rectangular window frame (San Diego Museum of Art, California). By 1633, when Zurbarán painted this picture, collectors favored more lavish displays that offered more visual entertainment (see Fig. 2.54). The simplicity of Zurbarán's painting is exemplary of his artistic preference for plain, almost archaic designs, while his habitual inclusion of objects with familiar religious associations as well as his preference for religious commissions suggest that this painting too has a Christian message. Its symbols are not obscure: the number three would instantly be associated with the Holy Trinity; the oranges and lemons with the fruit of paradise; the water with the sacrament of baptism; and the rose with the Virgin Mary. Their precise placement equidistant from each other across the picture plane gives these simple objects a ceremonial aura that invites contemplation. Zurbarán's depiction of the fruit and the little cup in a strong light that leaves the background dark is a surreal, even miraculous, image.

When Philip IV's chief minister, Gaspar de Guzmán, Conde-Duque de Olivares, fell from favor in 1643, Seville entered a period of serious economic decline. The city was also devastated by an outbreak of the bubonic plague in 1649 that killed half the population, leaving only 60,000 inhabitants. The city's religious foundations did not react by commissioning works dedicated to patron and plague saints, so Zurbarán had to seek commissions elsewhere. In 1649 he sent some of his work to Buenos Aires, for which he was still seeking payment in 1660. It is generally acknowledged that after the 1640s the quality of his work declined as his studio assistants played a greater role in his production.

3.20 Francisco de Zurbarán, *Still Life with Lemons, Oranges, and a Rose*, 1633. Oil on canvas, 24½ × 43⅛ in (62.2 × 109.5 cm). Norton Simon Foundation, Pasadena, CA.

3.21 Francisco de Zurbarán, *The Annunciation*, 1650. Oil on canvas, 85⅝ × 124½ in (217.5 × 316.2 cm). Philadelphia Museum of Art, Philadelphia, PA.

Zurbarán's *The Annunciation* of 1650 (Fig. 3.21) can be traced back to the sacristy of San Miguel in Penarande de Bracamonte, which received the painting in 1658 from Gaspar de Bracamonte, a leading diplomat at court. Aware of tastes in Seville and elsewhere for softer, more atmospherically rendered imagery—Murillo's career had been launched by 1650—Zurbarán made his figures slimmer than before, lightened his palette somewhat, abandoned simple drapery folds for smaller, more complex fold patterns, and even tried to suggest wind currents activating the veils and outer garments of the Virgin. The adjustments to Zurbarán's style were essentially superficial, however. The white robes of the angel still look like starched linen shining against the shadows that surround them. The eccentric perspective of the setting would not be unexpected in a fourteenth-century painting but is surprising in a work produced three centuries later. It is patently a stage on which the mystery of the Virgin's impregnation by the Holy Ghost with the future Savior is enacted.

Documents for the artist's last years suggest a difficult time. One of his sons had died in the plague of 1649, leaving two small children; others in his family may have died too. He ran up debts when his foreign patrons failed to pay him and in 1659 he had to offer paintings instead of three years of rent payments to the monastery of San Jerónimo de Buenavista, who owned the house which he shared with his wife and a daughter. He had moved to Madrid by 1658, when he testified that his friend Velázquez was worthy of a knighthood. When he died there four years later, none of the three children born since 1650 to his third wife were still alive. The inventory of his possessions suggests that he had enjoyed a decent standard of living and he did not die in debt. Still, his somber, deeply serious work was no longer in fashion, superseded by the fluent brushwork and softer, more appealing religious sentiment conveyed by Murillo's charming babies and beautiful, smiling Madonnas.

Zurbarán's finest Sevillian contemporary was Alonso Cano (1601–67), who was also active as a sculptor and architect, though he worked primarily as a painter in his early years. His style seems far more affected by trends outside Spain than that of his contemporaries but he never went to Italy and did not go to Madrid until 1638, when Olivares invited him to join his household. Still, he had access to works by Ribera in local collections and possibly also to paintings by Italians patronized by collectors in Seville. Cano's handling of three-dimensional form and space is far more assured than that of Zurbarán, as a glance at Cano's painting *St. John the Evangelist's Vision of Jerusalem* (Fig. **3.22**) reveals. He also employs a range of colors of Venetian inspiration with an acidic edge that differs sharply from the earthier hues preferred by Zurbarán and other painters in Seville. Here the clouds around the vision are lemon yellow, the angel's flying stole is emerald and grass green, its dress bronzed gold and the cloak of the saint a wine red that shades to pale pink in the light and maroon in the shadows. The swirling movement generated by the angel's wings and flying stole bring our eyes back to the head of the saint who looks, open-mouthed in wonder, at the angel who tenderly holds his hand. It is both a touching and a beautiful image. Maybe Cano's work with Montañés gave him a more complete grasp of solid form and human anatomy than is usual among Spanish painters. It is not surprising that Olivares, by now familiar with the work of Velázquez as well as with Venetians such as Veronese and Tintoretto, who favored the colors that Cano used on this occasion, realized that his talents might be useful in Madrid.

Diego Velázquez in Seville

Although the two artists were born only a year apart, the career of Diego Velázquez (1599–1660) was launched much sooner than that of Zurbáran. Because he was born in Seville, his artistic gifts, once spotted, could quickly be given the best training available. More important, he was precocious, one of the rare examples of a painter who was producing outstanding work while still only in his teens. His principal teacher (and, after 1618, his father-in-law) was Francesco Pacheco, whose intellectual attainments far surpassed his mediocre level of artistic achievement (see Fig. 3.25). Velázquez started his apprenticeship when he was only eleven, so Pacheco was responsible for the rest of his education too. Pacheco may have had little to teach his pupil about painting except basic skills but he had good relations with the cultural and aristocratic elite of Seville. His house functioned as a sort of salon, providing an environment that prepared Velázquez for his future life at court as well as completing the intellectual education that Pacheco believed was necessary for serious artistic achievement.

Seville was Spain's liveliest and most cosmopolitan city at the start of the seventeenth century. Its monopoly on trade with the Americas meant that wealthy Flemish and Italian merchants established themselves there and began to support its cultural life. Nevertheless, nobody brought anything by Caravaggio to Seville, whose first followers in Spain worked in Valladolid (Orazio Borgianni; c. 1578–1616) and Toledo (Juan Bautista Maino; 1569–1649). If Velázquez had been able to visit Italy in his late teens and thus to see originals by Caravaggio, the Carracci, and their sixteenth-century sources of inspiration, then his artistic evolution would not seem so astonishing. Velázquez did not reach Rome until 1628, however, by which time he had already developed his distinctive technique and even changed from an early style of thickly painted, sharply lit, and acutely observed forms seen against a dark background to a more atmospheric rendition of visible reality.

3.22 (left) Alonso Cano, *St. John the Evangelist's Vision of Jerusalem*, 1635–38. Oil on canvas, 32¼ × 17 in (81.9 × 43.2 cm). Trustees of the Wallace Collection, London.

Spanish Painting, 1600–1650

The only Spanish painter who had seen and absorbed the work of Caravaggio in Italy and used it on his return to Spain when Velázquez was training was Maino but his work could not be seen in Seville. After he moved to Toledo in 1611, he painted several large canvases for the Dominican church of San Pedro Martir. If Velázquez managed to travel there and see Maino's *Adoration of the Shepherds* (Fig. **3.23**), then the achievement of his first works would seem less miraculous. Amid many passages of careful observation in his almost obsessively realistic depiction of the Holy Family as ordinary folk surrounded by the rural poor, Maino's painting includes a wonderful sleeping dog, a lamb with bound feet, a muscular peasant, and a basket of eggs nestling in straw in the foreground. Once Velázquez had moved to Madrid to join the court of Philip IV, he could easily study the works of Italian and Flemish artists in the royal collection, but it is what he achieved before he had access to such sophisticated visual models that demonstrates the degree of raw talent that he brought to his profession. Still, the sculpture of Juan Montañés (see Fig. 3.3), often cited as a possible aid to the visualization of such powerful three-dimensional forms as those in the early work of both Zurbarán and Velázquez, surely helped. Montañés carved convincing figures in clothing whose folds respond to gravity rather than to artistic fancy. Thus he shared their artistic goals of achieving an elevated artistic language while grounding his forms in nature.

The *Old Woman Cooking Eggs* (Fig. **3.24**), which Velázquez painted at the age of nineteen, is one of several *bodegones* (genre scenes) from his early years in Seville, when he seems to have used such subjects to train his eye. The forms at first look hard edged, but even the contours that are fully lit are slightly blurred where light becomes dark. His sensitive observation of the fall of light on the different surfaces of clay, copper, cloth, and glass is remarkable. The translucent egg whites in broth in the brown ceramic dish, set over hot coals, seem to congeal and cook before our eyes. If the old woman and young boy are characters in a Spanish tale, no one has so far identified it. Velázquez seems to have chosen them as contrasting types—male and female, old and young—to demonstrate his skills as a painter, the purpose too of the dazzling still-life in the foreground. In yet another early *bodegone*, Velázquez portrayed an old waterseller giving a glass of water to a young boy while a third man watches from the background (Wellington Museum, London). Here the choice of men of three differing ages seems even more calculated, for the old man, who occupies most of the picture space, is shown in profile, the younger man faces us and the boy is posed in three-quarter view. Even the three containers—a huge clay pot held by the old man, a medium-size clay pot on the counter to the left and the smaller glass held by the boy—echo the sizes of the three men.

The distance between Velázquez and Pacheco is clearly shown by comparing their interpretations of that quintessential Spanish subject, the *Immaculate Conception* (Figs. **3.25** and **3.26**). Velázquez painted his for the church of the Shod Carmelites in Seville in 1618, a year after Pope Paul V had issued a decree in support of the

3.23 Juan Bautista Maino, *Adoration of the Shepherds*, 1612–13. Oil on canvas, 10 ft 4 in × 5 ft 8 in (3.15 × 1.74 m). Prado, Madrid.

3.24 Diego Velázquez, *Old Woman Cooking Eggs*, 1618. Oil on canvas, 39½ × 46⅝ in (100.5 × 119 cm). National Gallery of Scotland, Edinburgh.

3.25 (below left) Francisco Pacheco, *Immaculate Conception*, 1616–17. Oil on canvas, 62¹⁵⁄₁₆ × 42¹⁵⁄₁₆ in (160 × 109 cm). Seville Cathedral.

3.26 (below right) Diego Velázquez, *Immaculate Conception*, 1618. Oil on canvas, 53 × 40 in (135 × 101.6 cm). National Gallery, London.

Spanish Painting, 1600–1650

doctrine. Velázquez's is the first known dated Spanish painting of this theme. Pacheco, who was a member of the Inquisition that checked all religious works in Seville for doctrinal conformity, made the example shown here in 1621 for Seville Cathedral. Velázquez must have been given some verbal instructions by Pacheco, because their designs are close in many respects. While Pacheco's is a pedantic account of the various symbols associated with Mary's sinless nature, Velázquez's Virgin radiates light like a full moon on a clear night, convincing the believing viewer of her purity by her sheer visual beauty. The absence of the rich blues that can be achieved only by using expensive lapis lazuli implies that the patrons could not afford such luxurious materials.

Velázquez in Madrid, 1623–1648

Velázquez introduced himself to the court of Philip IV with his portrait of *Luis de Góngora*, which he painted in Madrid in 1622 at Pacheco's request (Museum of Fine Arts, Boston). It is a small picture that shows only the poet's head and a bit of his shoulders but, despite the modest format and the simplicity of means, the painting projects Góngora's ferocious intellect as well as the self-control required to use it to the full. Velázquez was invited back the following year to paint the king (this work is lost). Perhaps he had other work by the young Velázquez from which to judge his suitability for the kind of painting he required of a court artist, which was mainly portraiture—portraits of himself, his consort, his children, his courtiers, and his achievements. If not, Philip IV was a most astute judge of artistic talent: Velázquez was soon installed as *pintor del rey*, a title he retained until his death almost forty years later.

If a court appointment meant a steady income and decent working conditions, it also meant rules as strict as those facing Zurbarán when fulfilling the demands of his religious patrons. No European court was more traditional and status conscious than that of Madrid. The portraits that Velázquez supplied at first show that he had to follow well-established formulas for full-length images used by earlier court artists, including Titian, and most recently by Antonis Mor and Alonso Sánchez Coello. Velázquez's *Infante Don Carlos* (Fig. **3.27**) shows the king's brother facing us but with the head and body turned at a slight angle to the picture plane. His right foot (on our left) points toward us, the other to the right corner of the picture. He carries a wide-brimmed hat in his gloved hand while his other glove dangles from his right fingertips. This detail is a variation on a pan-European custom for gentlemen to wear one glove and carry the other. The Order of the Golden Fleece hangs on Don Carlos's chest together with a showy gold chain, the *fanfarone*, a fashionable accessory of the upper echelons at court. The setting is very minimal: throughout Velázquez's career it rarely consists of more than a table and a swag of drapery. The subject is expressionless, thus timeless. The color scheme is a drab monochrome.

If Velázquez had been required to produce nothing but tedious court icons like this one for the rest of his career, then the king's money and Velázquez's gifts would have been wasted. Luckily this was not the case. The king liked the artist and eventually learnt to give him much

3.27 Diego Velázquez, *Infante Don Carlos*, 1629. Oil on canvas, 82⅜ × 49⅛ in (209 × 125 cm). Prado, Madrid.

3.28 Diego Velázquez, *The Drinkers (Los Borrachos)*, c. 1628. Oil on canvas, 65 × 88½ in (165 × 225 cm). Prado, Madrid.

more latitude. He also shared with Velázquez a deep admiration for the work of Titian, lavishly represented in the royal collections thanks to the patronage of Philip II. Eventually van Dyck and Rubens, both profoundly affected by Titian's work, visited Madrid in 1628, when they met Velázquez. If only their conversations in front of Titian's canvases had been recorded! Titian's portraits seem to capture both the physical presence and the character of a sitter with a transparency unaffected by the artist's own personality. Rubens, by contrast, seems to imbue all of his sitters with his own abundant physical and intellectual energy, while van Dyck's more reserved personality seems reflected in that of his sitters. The lessons that they had learnt from studying Titian long before they reached Madrid had given warmth to their palettes and expressive texture to their brushwork. Velázquez's paint surface began to loosen up and show more scumbling and visible brush tracks, a trend that accelerated after his first trip to Italy in 1629–31.

While Velázquez breathed new life into the Spanish court portrait, he knew that his prestige as an artist would be limited if he did not produce history paintings. Philip IV, however, rarely commissioned other kinds of imagery from him. Velázquez did sometimes make a religious painting after he moved to Madrid but it was his occasional production of mythological images and other exceptional commissions that revealed his full powers. An example of his highly original take on classical mythology is *The Drinkers* (Fig. **3.28**). It shows a self-conscious young man playing the role of Bacchus, crowning a kneeling man with ivy as other men watch. That Bacchus is not the classical god himself returned to earth to carouse with some Spanish farmers is indicated by the contemporary dress worn by his companions and the forceful realism with which all are portrayed. Even Bacchus' pale skin suggests that the artist found his model among the indoor rather than the outdoor servants at court. The four men on the right, whose expressions convey their exuberant mood as well as their delight at being depicted by the artist, look like real people, perhaps men who worked in the royal gardens and vineyards. Bacchus himself has a pose close to that of Caravaggio's *Bacchus* (see Fig. 1.39), another image of a real young man acting the role rather than a heroicized portrayal of an ancient god like those in the paintings of

Titian and Rubens. No copies are known of Caravaggio's painting, however, so it seems unlikely that Velázquez knew it. Even more intriguing is the reclining, foreshortened torso of the nude youth behind Bacchus who raises a glass. This unusual pose blends that of two figures in the foreground of Titian's *Bacchanal of the Andrians* (see Fig. 1.118), then still in Rome, of which Velázquez must have seen a drawn or painted copy. It depicts the invention of wine on the island of Andros and its effects on the Andrians. Thus it was an appropriate place for Velázquez to find figures for his painting, which may be both a tribute and a challenge to Titian. The rendering of this young man's powerful physique, most of it in shadow, is superbly realized. Velázquez could justifiably believe that he portrayed nature as well as Titian did.

What was Velázquez's attitude toward the more respectful interpretation of classical mythology that he knew from works by Italian and Flemish artists in the royal collection? Here he seems to mock that tradition while demonstrating by his knowing borrowings that he respects it too. Jonathan Brown has argued that the picture is not a parody of pagan gods but represents Bacchus' gift of wine to mortals, which eases the pain of daily life. Whatever the artist intended, Philip IV evidently appreciated this sly interpretation of the ancient myth, perhaps because, as a conservative Catholic, too much respect for pagan religious heroes might seem heretical: better to mock than to admire. The painting was hung in the king's summer bedroom, where he could be amused by the vice of drunkenness, here indulged in only by members of the lowest social classes, while admiring Velázquez's ability to create form using the most subtle modulations of tone and shadow. The dull yellow leather jerkin of the kneeling man and the brown cloak of the old man behind him are virtuoso passages of painting whose effects are achieved with such simple means that it is easy to underestimate the skill required.

Between 1633 and 1635 Velázquez, Zurbarán, and others were commissioned to paint twelve

3.29 Diego Velázquez, *Surrender of Breda*, 1634–35. Oil on canvas, 10 ft × 12 ft (3.07 × 3.67 m). Prado, Madrid.

3.30 Juan Bautista Maino, *The Recapture of Bahia*, 1634–35. Oil on canvas, 10 ft 2 in × 12 ft 6 in (3.09 × 3.81 m). Prado, Madrid.

large pictures of Spanish military triumphs for the Hall of Realms in the Palacio del Buen Retiro, its most important room and thus the logical site for pro-Hapsburg propaganda. Zurbarán's pictures of the Labors of Hercules were installed above the scenes of conquest, so that Hercules' mythical achievements against great odds parallel those of the Spanish kings below. The completed ensemble was blatant propaganda for a monarchy whose victories were few and often short-lived. Indeed, the success of the Spanish siege of Breda, which led to its surrender, the event portrayed by Velázquez (Fig. 3.29), was reversed soon after the scene was painted in 1634–5. Nevertheless it inspired a masterpiece and allows us to measure his achievement against those of the other artists who also contributed to this series.

The Dutch town of Breda had surrendered in 1625 after a year's siege by Spanish and Burgundian troops. However, the town was not sacked and burned afterwards, nor was their leader humiliated. Instead Justin of Nassau, the Dutch leader, was allowed to depart with his troops watched by Ambrogio Spinola, the Genoese commander of the victorious armies. A play by Calderón performed at court in 1625, *El Sitio de Bredà*, has as its climactic moment the surrender of the keys of the city to Spinola, who said: "Justin, I receive them in full awareness of your valor; for the valor of the defeated confers fame upon the victor." This is the moment shown in Velázquez's painting, but it is not based on fact. The encounter was imagined by Calderón and portrayed by Velázquez because it emphasized the value attached to magnanimity in victory by the ideal ruler. Still, the array of vertical pikes on the right makes clear who is powerful and victorious, and the air of defeat among the companions of Justin is palpable. Brown points out that the riderless horse is also significant; it is Spinola's horse, and in another picture in this series, he is shown on his horse looking down on a kneeling, defeated commander. Thus, as Brown neatly put it, Velázquez "transformed the scene from a tableau of Spanish military power into a metaphor of Spanish moral superiority."[7]

All of the scenes of victory made for the Hall of Realms employ the same compositional device of important figures in the foreground on imagined high ground with distant panoramas behind them that refer to the event being celebrated. None succeeded, as Velázquez did, in making foreground and distance seem a unified space. Even Maino's *The Recapture of Bahia* (Fig. 3.30), among the best of the others, presents a very awkward juxtaposition between the ordinary figures on a wedge of foreground on the left, and the stiff ceremony in the middle ground on the right where the victorious commander points to a tapestry image of the king flanked by the goddess Minerva and Olivares, making clear their role in this triumph. Neither zone connects with the ships in the bay far below them. Velázquez, using engravings of the event, produced a remarkably convincing view of the distant city with smoke rising from fires seen from a high vantage point, though there were none in that river estuary that could have provided this view. Just below the central section of the distant landscape Justin approaches Spinola, offering him the key to the city while Spinola kindly touches his shoulder and makes no move to accept the symbol of Breda's defeat. Both men wear dark clothes but the expanse of Justin's white collar attracts the eye as does the patchwork of light blues behind his hand. Spinola's dark armor blends into the background, though his prominent position indicates his importance. There are many others present but only as partial figures represented by the tops of their heads or the lances they hold behind the figures on the right, concealed from full view by Spinola's horse. The defeated Dutch on the left occupy less space and are less numerous. Justin's horse is only partly visible. All of these pictorial decisions, of which the viewer is at first only subliminally aware, mark out the winners and the losers. It is an ambiguous image of conquest. After mentioning comparable images by Rubens, Cortona, and Le Brun, Brown comments that "Reticence and reserve are the words that [. . .] come to mind when confronting [this] painting. The absence of the apparatus of glory is conspicuous."

The portraits that Velázquez painted in the 1630s and 1640s after his return to Madrid from his first visit to Italy (1629–31) are much more colorful and more freely painted than the few that survive from his first period of court activity. He moved his sitters out of doors to show them on horseback or standing beside their hunting hounds with the mountains of the Sierra de Guadarrama in the distance. There is no loss of dignity despite the greater naturalism and informality. The hunting portraits especially are enlivened by the presence of dogs whose character and mood are conveyed so effectively that they are in danger of stealing the scene from their owners.

Philip IV (Fig. **3.31**) uses the warm rust reds of Titian for the curtain and table, the minimal elements of setting flanking the standing king, who wears a splendid brown wool costume embroidered with squiggles and fringes of silver lace. Only the face is carefully painted. The king's legs and shoes are barely described except as subtly modulated shapes of white and black, yet when the viewer looks at the head, the rest of the image is perfectly convincing. Our eyes keep in focus only what we are looking at; the rest of the image in our field of vision is a blur until our gaze shifts. Velázquez was fully aware of this and knew exactly how much information to provide to create a convincing illusion. Details of a mature Velázquez painting can seem incomprehensible; seen from the right distance, these daubs of paint become a hand, a sash, a cockade of ribbon on a hat.

3.31 Diego Velázquez, *Philip IV*, c. 1635. Oil on canvas, 78½ × 44½ in (199.5 × 113 cm). National Gallery, London.

3.32 Diego Velázquez, *Equestrian Portrait of Conde-Duque de Olivares*, 1638. Oil on canvas, 10 ft 3 in × 7 ft 9 in (3.13 × 2.39 m). Prado, Madrid.

The hunting portraits of Philip IV, his brother, and his son were less formal exercises than Velázquez's large *Equestrian Portrait of Conde-Duque de Olivares* (Fig. 3.32). Olivares was the most powerful man in Spain after the king, whom he served as chief minister, but he needed to assert his status constantly. His portraits hint at the fundamental insecurity even of a close and trusted minister at court by emphasizing his importance and his attributes of office far more than do those of the king. This canvas is even larger than Velázquez's equestrian portrait of Philip IV for the Hall of Realms. Olivares's massive form, encased in a suit of parade armor swathed with a huge gold-embroidered pink sash, is seated astride a glossy chestnut horse, which rears up and directs our attention to the landscape at the left edge of the canvas. A plume of smoke and some sketchily indicated troops maneuvering in the middle distance hint at Olivares's recent victory over the French at Fuenterrabia, though he was not present at that event. The careful description of his suit of armor and elaborate sword handle are all intended to convey his superior status and power, as does his condescending glance from the height of his mount to the spectator standing below.

Velázquez's portraits of the so-called fools and dwarves, who were part of this (and many other) court households from the Renaissance onwards,

Spanish Painting, 1600–1650

3.33 Diego Velázquez, *Sebastián de Morra*, c. 1645. Oil on canvas, 41⅝ × 31⅞ in (106 × 81 cm). Prado, Madrid.

now generally have more appeal than his images of social and political status. A well-proportioned dwarf, like Sir Jeffrey Hudson, the favorite of Queen Henrietta Maria of England (see Fig. 6.5), might enjoy the privileges of a luxurious life close to members of an aristocratic household. Nothing is known about their lives at the Spanish court other than what Velázquez implies in his empathetic portraits. Most are shown seated on the ground in a position that diminishes their stature but enhances their dignity by emphasizing their normally proportioned heads and torsos. *Diego de Avedo* (Prado, Madrid) is shown with books, paper, pen, and ink as he interrupts his reading to contemplate the viewer with a serious expression. *Francisco Leczano* (Prado, Madrid) seems to be preparing to deal a pack of cards and studies the viewer as he plans his strategy. *Sebastián de Morra* (Fig. 3.33) confronts us, however, with a steady gaze, the upturned soles of his shoes and his fists planted firmly on his thighs as if to say, "Yes, I have short arms and legs, but don't underestimate me." While their ungainly walking and running might have been a cause for jest at court, the artist does not show these figures as comic. He also presents them in private moments when they were not entertaining the king or his family.

The king, the queen, and the prime minister did not spend hours in the artist's studio posing for Velázquez. He would only have had time to make a finished oil sketch of the sitter's head, which would then be used as a basis for several portraits until, after a few years, he would make another. The clothes to be depicted would be brought to the studio, and there worn by a court official standing in the selected pose. Velázquez's *Philip IV (The "Fraga Portrait")* (Fig. 3.34) was painted, however, in unusual conditions: the king posed for this portrait three times during a military campaign in Fraga in the summer of 1644, when he was trying to recapture Lérida from French troops. Velázquez had to live and work in a hovel which had a new window cut to allow some light to enter. Artist and sitter stood on muddy straw as the painting was blocked out. The three-quarter-length format, unique for a royal sitter in Velázquez's production, was no doubt used because the temporary studio could not accommodate the taller canvas needed for the usual full-length image. It took Velázquez roughly a month to finish it, allowing time for it to dry before being sent to Madrid at the end of July; a few days later Lérida was back in Spanish hands.

The king wears the costume in which he reviewed his troops—a splendid sleeveless salmon-pink coat with silver trim, worn over a blond buckskin waistcoat and a jacket with silvery sleeves. The king regards us from reddened eyes, looking tired even as he maintains an upright posture with his baton of command in his right hand and his huge hat in his left. Once again, the head is more finished than the rest of the figure: the pink coat is encrusted with jabs of white and gray paint that from the correct viewing distance simulate perfectly the fall of light on its embroidered edges. Although Philip holds the baton of a commander, he does not project the authority of a true military hero. His image makes a telling contrast with the ostentation of Olivares's equestrian portrait.

For the collector and womanizer Gaspar de Haro, Velázquez painted *Venus and Cupid* (Fig. 3.35), the only Spanish seventeenth-century mythological work that depicts a naked woman. Other European painters who painted female nudes seldom used a back view. Unlike those of

Rubens, Annibale Carracci, and Simon Vouet, Velázquez's goddess was based on life study, in part because he had no classical statues and few painted models from which to derive his knowledge of the female body at second hand. The modest back view was chosen yet what could be more provocative than her soft right buttock settled against the gray-blue silk cover of her day bed? As Allan Braham proved by posing a woman in this position with a child playing Cupid with the mirror, Venus could not have seen her own reflection with the mirror at that angle, and we would have seen her crotch, unless it was concealed by drapery. Only one other life-size female nude was produced in seventeenth-century Spain, a figure of Eve in Alonso Cano's *Christ's Descent into Limbo* (Los Angeles County Museum) made around the same time. Eve also turns her back. Its treatment displays accurate knowledge on the artist's part of a real woman's body, though a heavier one than that of Velázquez's lithe model, while the bodies of Christ, Adam, and Seth (the child in front of him) also seem to have been studied from life. Cano here uses a softer, more atmospheric brushwork than in earlier years, the result of studying the work of Titian and Velázquez in the royal collections.

3.34 (above) Diego Velázquez, *Philip IV of Spain (The "Fraga Portrait")*, 1644. Oil on canvas, 51⅛ × 39⅛ in (129.8 × 99.4 cm). Frick Museum, New York.

3.35 Diego Velázquez, *Venus and Cupid (The "Rokeby Venus")*, 1648. Oil on canvas, 48¼ × 69¼ in (122.7 × 177 cm). National Gallery, London.

Spanish Painting, 1600–1650

Velázquez in Italy, 1648–1651

Velázquez made a second trip to Italy, leaving Madrid in November 1648 in order to obtain paintings and ancient statues (or, failing that, casts) for the royal collection. He went first to Venice, arriving in Rome in April 1649 and returning to Spain in November 1651. It was during this second Roman sojourn that Velázquez painted his remarkable portraits of *Innocent X* (Fig. 3.36) and *Juan de Pareja* (Fig. 3.37), his Moorish servant who was also an artist. Both sitters face right and regard us steadily, the pope seated in a high-backed chair with papal insignia on the back, Juan standing and visible only to the waist. The papal portrait, whose surface is obscured by a film of yellowed varnish, is rendered in russet, wine, crimson, and rose reds that contrast with the pope's white surplice, whose lacy fringes fall beyond the edge of the canvas. The streaks of reflected light on his cape pull our eyes to him and to his riveting gaze. The hands are blurs, the tonal modulations on the yellow-white garment slight except where the arm of the chair casts a shadow on the left. A thick impasto mimics the pleats and folds of the surplice.

The three-quarter view of a seated pope in a chair with his papal insignia was invented by Raphael for his portrait of *Julius II* (National Gallery, London) and has rarely been varied since. The adoption of a uniform design throws all the emphasis on the artist's ability to transform the ordinary into the exceptional. In his *Innocent X*, Velázquez created such a convincing illusion of reality, with a seemingly casual technique applied to a formulaic composition, that this portrait is regarded as one of the greatest ever painted. Both it and the *Juan de Pareja*, painted in a monochrome of warm grays, relieved only by the flesh tones of Pareja's face and hand and his white collar, were much admired in Rome by both artists and collectors. The latter was exhibited at the Pantheon in March 1650 at the annual show organized by the Congregazione dei Virtuosi, an artists' society to which Velázquez had been elected the previous month. That the artist could create such an arresting image with such limited means was an achievement that his peers could best appreciate.

Velázquez in Madrid, 1651–1660

On his return to Madrid, Velázquez resumed his court duties and continued to produce royal portraits, rarely of the king but instead of his new wife, Queen Mariana of Austria, whom he married in 1649, and their children, the Infanta Margarita and Prince Philip Prosper, the new male heir to the Hapsburg throne after the death of Prince Balthasar Carlos at the age of seventeen. Philip Prosper lived only four years (1657–61). Velázquez produced a particularly affecting image of the two-year-old prince (Kunsthistorisches Museum, Vienna), his crimson dress and white apron strung with good luck charms as he stands quietly, his right hand resting on the back of a small chair occupied by a little spaniel. Like many of Velázquez's dogs, this one competes with the sitter for our attention, here by resting his head slightly askew on the arm of the chair and looking at us as if waiting for a signal to play.

In the last two decades of Velázquez's life, he produced only twenty paintings. Given that they do not look as if he labored long and hard over minute detail, as, for example, Elsheimer and Gerard Dou did, Velázquez's low rate of production requires some other explanation. It had slowed down in the 1640s as his court duties increased with his appointment as *ayuda da*

3.36 Diego Velázquez, *Innocent X*, 1650. Oil on canvas, 55⅛ × 48 in (140 × 120 cm). Palazzo Doria-Pamphili, Rome.

cámera (gentleman in waiting) in 1643. These chores became even more onerous in 1651, when he was promoted to *aposentador de palacio*, which meant that he was in charge of the king's living quarters. Those at the Alcázar in Madrid as well as others at the Escorial were being refurbished as settings for the king's growing collection of paintings by Italian and Flemish artists, among which some by Velázquez were included, the only Spanish painter so honored. Some years he produced nothing at all. Whenever he was able to devote some time to his profession, however, Velázquez produced some of his greatest works.

Velázquez's most ambitious painting and almost his largest (only the *Surrender of Breda* covers a larger area, though it is not as high), *Las Meninas (The Maids of Honor)* (Fig. 3.38) was painted four years before his death. Since nothing like it had ever been produced by Velázquez or anyone else, it could not have been a commission from the king. Velázquez himself invented the concept and executed it, and the king accepted it and hung it in his summer office. This was neither a public room nor a large one where the picture would have been a dominant presence. The knowledge of its semi-private display only adds to the mystery of its intended significance.

Las Meninas is many things. It is an artist's self-portrait first of all, even if the artist has placed himself in the shadowed background on the left behind the enormous canvas on which he is working, so that the emphasis falls instead on the Infanta Margarita and her attendants. It is a group portrait, for almost everyone depicted can be identified, and a court portrait, for Philip IV and Mariana are present as reflections in the mirror, and the central figure is their daughter, the Infanta Margarita. It is a genre scene too, for no particular event is being shown, just the artist at work in his rooms at the Alcázar with various members of the court present. It captures an imagined moment in the life of Velázquez at court, and what he has chosen to imagine is that he is at work on a large painting, only about a foot (30 cm) shorter than *Las Meninas*, which is over 10 feet (3.18 m) high. Almost everyone in the picture is looking outward, even the man who has paused in the doorway and looks back at the viewer: only the maid in front of the artist, the dwarf teasing the dog on the right, and the woman behind the other maid are momentarily distracted. They are not looking out, but at the royal couple, who must be posing for their double portrait and whom the princess and her companions are entertaining during this tedious process. The modern viewer takes the place of the royal couple. Our flattered egos have surely played a role in this painting's immense popularity.

Neither Velázquez nor any other artist employed by the Spanish court ever painted a double portrait of any of their royal couples. In addition, as noted earlier, the king and queen would never have posed for an extended period of time, as they might be imagined to be doing here. Velázquez's full-length portraits of the queen are all painted on shorter canvases than *Las Meninas*. Velázquez would seem to be saying to his royal patron that he was capable of painting far more challenging works than he had been asked to do so far. Why not, indeed, a double portrait of Philip and Mariana in a setting that would reflect their status better than the abstracted spaces in which they usually stood, alone, with a table, a bit of drapery, and a gloomy distance? Done from life, the results would have been spectacular.

3.37 Diego Velázquez, *Juan de Pareja*, 1650. Oil on canvas, 32 × 27½ in (81.3 × 69.9 cm). Fletcher Fund, Rogers Fund. Bequest of Miss Adelaide Milton de Groot. Metropolitan Museum of Art, New York.

Spanish Painting, 1600–1650

3.38 Diego Velázquez, *Las Meninas (The Maids of Honor)*, 1656–57. Oil on canvas, 10 ft 5 in × 9 ft (3.18 × 2.76 m). Prado, Madrid.

How did Velázquez set about depicting himself in his own studio, including the ceiling, with so many models? What looks like a deft capturing of a moment of court life had to be meticulously laid out, observed, and painted over many sessions. The result is, as many writers have recognized, far more than a picture of Velázquez at work. The sheer scale of *Las Meninas*, combined with the provocative informality of the portraiture in the context of Spanish court etiquette, was enough to ensure its fame in Madrid. It was valued enough by Charles II for him to take the painter Luca Giordano to see it during his residence at court later in the century. Luca's reaction is famous and much quoted: "Sire, this is the Theology of Painting." It is widely accepted that, by portraying himself as an intimate of the king and his family, Velázquez intended to further his claims for the nobility of the art of painting and higher social standing for himself, for the picture was made just as his campaign to be knighted was reaching its climax. The paintings dimly visible on the wall above the mirror image of the king are copies by the artist's son-in-law, Juan del Mazo, of paintings by Rubens of the *Story of Arachne* and *Apollo and Midas*. Both myths deal with mortals who challenged the artistic achievements of the gods—Arachne challenging the weaving of Athena (she lost and became a spider) and Midas the musical talent of Apollo (who rewarded him with ass's ears). Was Velázquez asking us to compare him with Rubens and all the great artists in the royal collection? If so, he has not been given Midas' reward by posterity.

An artist who could capture life in paint, or *imitare bene il naturale*, as the Italians would say, was praised from the Renaissance onwards as the rival of nature herself, even outdoing her by making perfect images instead of the imperfect ones found in nature. In this apparently realistic image of court life, Velázquez plays the role of artistic creator in the image and is its creator. If he was seeking comparison with great predecessors such as Titian and contemporaries such as Rubens, he was doing so in a way that would make comparisons difficult, for they had never made a picture quite like it. Only Jan van Eyck's tiny *Marriage Portrait of Giovanni Arnolfini and Giovanna Cenami* of 1434 (National Gallery, London), which was then in the Spanish royal collection, offers a challenge. It too shows people posing in a domestic interior witnessed by the artist, who appears in the mirror reflection behind them and declares in his inscription that he *fuit hic* (was here). He too created an image whose meticulous record of the fall of daylight into an interior space and on various surfaces still enchants the viewer with its seeming reality, though on a miniature scale. Velázquez's huge hunting dog who ignores the foot on his rump even seems to be the artist's response to the little terrier in Jan van Eyck's picture.

To see *Las Meninas* primarily as Velázquez's propaganda for his desired knighthood and his future reputation among artists and aristocrats would be a mistake. To do so would be to overlook the significance of the Infanta Margarita, whose central position and white dress immediately and repeatedly attract the viewer's attention. In 1656, when the picture was made, she was Philip's only heir. Her brother, so hopefully named Philip Prosper, was born one year later. Her only rival, her older half-sister, had been forced to give up her right of succession. Beautifully dressed, her blond hair falling like gauze over her shoulders, and her posture as perfectly erect as that of a ballet dancer, she looks to her parents for their approval as her two ladies-in-waiting hover attentively. No doubt when she posed for her usual portraits (he painted her three other times), a scene much like this surrounded her to relieve the tedium. The king did not pose for long but a royal child could be expected to do so: the greater humanity of their portrayal also suggests that they did. The other portraits were sent to her most eligible suitor, the Austrian Archduke Leopold Wilhelm, whom she married at the age of sixteen. She outlived her brother but not by much, dying in 1671 at the age of twenty-two.

Velázquez took on the posts of *ayuda da cámera* and the more onerous one of *aposentador* as a way of advancing the status of the visual arts at court and in Spain. These positions brought him into close contact with the king on a daily basis: such privileged access was given to few at court. Velázquez knew that both Titian and Rubens were honored with knighthoods, something that no Spanish artist had yet received. He expended considerable energies during his later years seeking support from anyone who might help him: during his second visit to Rome (1649–51), he appealed to Innocent X for a letter, and his old friend Zurbarán later obliged too, but the sticking point was the difficulty of proving noble descent on both his mother's and father's side, a qualification not required of foreign artists. He did finally receive admission to the Order of Santiago, but only after the Council on Orders had initially rejected the king's request in February 1659. After two papal dispensations regarding the artist's dubious family origins had been obtained from Alexander VII, Velázquez was at last admitted on November 28, 1659. He was dead less than a year later.

His fellow artists in Madrid can have had few illusions about their status after watching Velázquez's fight for his acceptance by the aristocratic old guard at court. A campaign to have works of art exempted from the *alcabala* (sales tax), as literary works of art were, had been launched in 1626, was successful in 1633, only to be reversed in 1636, and so on for the rest of the century as the king's Council on Finance desperately sought funds to defend Spain's diminishing territories. The founding of an Academy in Madrid, where artists could get a proper training and education, did not occur until 1752; its first director was an Italian, Corrado Giaquinto. Meanwhile, the court continued to import artists from Italy for major decorative commissions. Luca Giordano (in residence 1692–1702), Corrado Giaquinto (in residence 1753–61), and Giambattista Tiepolo (in residence 1762–70) all worked in Madrid painting frescoes in various royal residences, including the new royal palace designed by Giambattista Sacchetti, another Italian, in the 1730s. Not until Francisco Goya (1746–1819) emerged in the later eighteenth century did Spain have another painter of international stature. His debt to Velázquez was enormous, as much later in the nineteenth century was that of Edouard Manet. Velázquez's son-in-law, Juan Bautista del Mazo, imitated his style well enough for some of his replicas of Velázquez's portraits to have been attributed to him instead, but neither he nor any other Spanish painter could produce painterly illusions like those that Velázquez seemed to brush onto his canvases with such casual ease.

Spanish Painting, 1650–1700

Bartolomé Esteban Murillo

Murillo (1617–1682), the finest Spanish painter of the late seventeenth century, had no serious competition after the deaths of Zurbarán and Velázquez. He was born in Seville, the fourteenth child of elderly parents, who died when he was nine. One of his sisters took him in. Her husband was a barber-surgeon, as their father had been; their mother came from a family of silversmiths and painters, and Murillo's first known teacher was one of her relatives, Juan del Castillo. He probably began his studies around 1632. Little is known of his life until 1645, when he married and received his first major commission, a cycle of paintings illustrating the life of St. Francis for the small cloister of San Francisco el Grande in Seville, completed in 1646. Murillo, then almost thirty, obtained the commission, it is believed, by offering to carry out the cycle for a modest fee, hoping thereby to launch his career, which it did. One of the larger canvases, the so-called *Angels' Kitchen* (Louvre, Paris), was especially admired. It shows a friar arriving with two lay companions to discover St. Giles hovering in mid-air, absorbed in his devotions, while angels carry out his abandoned kitchen duties. Murillo's sympathetic characterization of the young angels hints at his future success with themes that require engaging depictions of children, such as the Holy Family and the young St. John the Baptist. The female saints who attend the death of St. Clare in the other large horizontal canvas from the series (Gemäldegalerie, Dresden) are the first of many beautiful women whose images brought Murillo great success then and later.

While the majority of Murillo's paintings have religious subjects, he was also a fine portrait painter, as his *Self-Portrait* demonstrates (see Fig. 3.42). He also created a popular new type of genre subject featuring beggar children eating fruit or playing games, happy despite their torn clothes and dirty bare feet. The earliest of these images, however, is more somber (Fig. **3.39**). It shows a boy seated on the ground in the corner of a small bare room lit by a patch of sunshine pouring in from a window on the left. The painting is executed entirely in browns, beige, gray, and flesh tones. The boy is crushing fleas with his

3.39 Bartolomé Esteban Murillo, *The Young Beggar*, c. 1650. Oil on canvas, 52¾ × 39⅜ in (134 × 100 cm). Louvre, Paris.

thumbnails pressed together. Scattered on the floor around him, however, are dead scorpions, a symbol of evil associated particularly with Judas and betrayal. A large clay waterpot fills the left foreground. Behind it is a straw shopping bag on its side with some apples spilling out, one of which has a small bite on its surface.

The painting may simply be a *bodegone* painted as eye-training by Murillo: certainly the odd position of the boy's face and the confident rendering of his skinny legs and bare feet must have been studied from life. Still, the presence of the bitten apple (an allusion to the temptation of Eve and the fall of Man), the jug of water (an allusion to the sacrament of baptism, the first administered by the Church to those admitted to the Christian faith), and the dead scorpions (evil defeated) suggests that, like Ribera's *Boy with a Club Foot* (see Fig. 3.12), Murillo intended this image of abject poverty to convey a serious Christian message. The search for fleas can also be a metaphor for the desire to rid oneself of sin. The shaft of sunlight that helps the boy detect and kill the scorpions acquires the symbolic meaning of divine truth coming to assist souls struggling to overcome sin.

The popular genre scenes of children that Murillo produced in the 1660s and 1670s do not carry such serious moral messages: a young girl offers us roses held in the folds of her patterned stole; a boy refuses to share his pie with a black child carrying a water jug (both Dulwich College

3.40 Bartolomé Esteban Murillo, *Virgin of the Rosary (Escorial Madonna)*, c. 1650–55. Oil on canvas, 64½ × 43⅜ in (164 × 110 cm). Prado, Madrid.

3.41 (opposite) Bartolomé Esteban Murillo, *Immaculate Conception of the Escorial*, c. 1660–65. Oil on canvas, 81⅛ × 56⅝ in (206 × 144 cm). Prado, Madrid.

Picture Gallery, London); two boys share a pie watched anxiously by a dog, who expects to get his share (see Fig. 3.5). Despite their bare feet and scruffy clothes, these children are all attractive, idealized images of life at the lowest end of the social scale. They may be poor but most of them seem happy and they have enough to eat. The weather is never cold, there is abundant fruit and bread, and there is always someone to play with. There are hints of the need to share and to be charitable but any moral message, if intended, is conveyed quietly.

The quality of Murillo's early work is uneven. Although almost thirty, he was still experimenting with various styles, above all Zurbarán's disciplined simplicity and Cano's more cosmopolitan idealism. Works by Genoese and Milanese painters such as Gioacchino Assereto, Bernardo Strozzi, and Giulio Cesare Procaccini were finding their way into local collections as well, however, and their fluid brushwork and skillful staging of religious drama also impressed Murillo. By 1650 he had discovered how to please his audience and his patrons with gentler, more appealing treatments of familiar themes featuring the Holy Family.

In the 1650s Murillo painted several versions of an image showing the Virgin with the young Christ on her lap holding a rosary, of which one of the finest is the *Virgin of the Rosary (Escorial Madonna)* (Fig. **3.40**). Its original patron may have had Dominican connections, for that order was especially associated with reciting the prayers of the rosary, but this painting is first recorded in the Spanish royal collection in 1788. Dated by all the experts before 1658, when Murillo made his first and only documented trip to Madrid, it would seem to prove that the artist had already been there and feasted his eyes on the rich, red draperies in Rubens's *Immaculate Conception*, and, even more important, seen Raphael's *Madonna of the Fish* (both Prado, Madrid), taken from Naples for Philip IV in 1638. Where else could Murillo have found such a perfect model for the harmonious serenity of his own Madonna? His two figures make a compact diamond shape against the dark background. The deep crimson of the Virgin's dress is the principal color note surrounding the light skin tones of the naked Christ Child. Christ climbs onto his mother's lap, raising his head just above hers, while he holds one end of the rosary beads in his right hand. She has the other end as well as a small white cloth which she holds against his thigh. She is seated on a wide stone step, which seems in fact to be a sarcophagus: the space between its side and the lid is clearly visible. Both mother and child regard us solemnly, reflecting the mood conveyed by the somber setting: Christ is the Word made Flesh, flesh that will be sacrificed for sinners at his death, to which their serious expressions, the tomb on which they are seated, and the darkness surrounding them allude. The massive arms and majestic presence of the Virgin mean that she is also Ecclesia, the Church, which will guide sinners to salvation through prayer. It is a devotional image of dignified beauty as fine as anything produced in Europe in the seventeenth century.

For an artist of Murillo's gifts, the subject of the Immaculate Conception was ideal and he painted it many times; there are four versions in the Prado alone. The *Immaculate Conception of the Escorial* (Fig. **3.41**) is perhaps the most perfectly resolved of these images of a young woman dressed in blue and white who seems to float on

clouds as she ascends slowly to heaven, supported by a few baby angels and a wisp of moon. They carry some of the Virgin's attributes—a lily, palm branches, a rose, and an olive branch. Mary is, as Pacheco had instructed in his *Arte de pintura*, shown as a young girl whose hands are joined in prayer. Only the lighter tones and softer, more atmospheric paint handling reveal that this image was painted after 1650. Velázquez's young Virgin Immaculate, painted forty years earlier, stands still on her inverted half-moon, her dull rose gown framed by her indigo blue cloak (see Fig. 3.26). She looks as solid as a sculpture by Montañés while Murillo's Virgin can be imagined dissolving into the golden haze around her as she continues her ascent to heaven. An ethereal vision has replaced an image of almost palpable reality. The shift in style represented by these two paintings can stand for a broader shift from solid realism to painterly visions of heaven by artists working in both Seville and Madrid after 1660.

Pacheco had started an Academy at his house where artists, scholars, and humanists could meet for congenial conversation. It never functioned as Italian academies did, off and on, in the first half of the seventeenth century, that is as teaching institutions that sponsored life-drawing classes for students and lectures on perspective, composition, and the theory of painting. Murillo tried to fill this gap when he founded an Academia de Dibujos (Academy of Drawing) in 1660 that was to hold evening drawing sessions. Pairs of artists were appointed to function as instructors for a week at a time in turn. Murillo himself served along with Francisco de Herrera (1622–85) at the beginning, Juan de Valdés Leal 1622–90) was appointed treasurer, and other painters were assigned to other offices. The academy survived for only fourteen years, closing due to lack of funds in 1674.

Far fewer drawings survive from seventeenth-century Spain than anyone familiar with the production of drawings elsewhere during this period would have expected. The practice of drawing does not seem to have been stressed as part of all artists' initial training, as it was in Italy and

3.42 Bartolomé Esteban Murillo, *Self-Portrait*, c. 1670–75. Oil on canvas, 4 ft × 3 ft 6 in (1.22 × 1.07 m). National Gallery, London.

France, and the preservation of drawings in artists' studios seems to have been more haphazard than elsewhere too. Fewer than a hundred drawings by Murillo have been preserved; there are none known by Zurbarán and only a handful plausibly attributed to Velázquez. Those by Murillo prove that he not only used them when working out his designs and showing patrons his proposals, but that he and his patrons valued them enough to keep them afterwards. Murillo's belief in the importance of drawing is demonstrated by his elegant *Self-Portrait* (Fig. **3.42**): the artist is seen behind a carved stone oval, at the base of which are drawing materials to the left and a palette with brushes on the right. Murillo's motives for founding the Academy and his self-presentation in the portrait were the elevation of his own status as well as that of his fellow artists in Seville, who were still fighting to keep the dreaded *alcabala* from being imposed on the sale of their work. The Academia de San Fernando in Madrid, which was a fully fledged teaching institution like the Accademia di San Luca in Rome after 1660, was created almost a century later. The medieval system in which family workshops served as training schools where young apprentices paid to learn, living with the master's family, and performing menial chores until they had mastered the requisite skills, persisted longer in Spain than anywhere else in Europe.

Murillo's wife died in December 1663, leaving him with seven children between the ages of two and seventeen. He did not remarry. His oldest child, Ana Maria, probably assumed her mother's role because his wife's death did not interrupt his steady production of paintings. He finished an important cycle for Santa Maria la Blanca in 1665, and began work immediately on another for the Hospital de la Caridad as well as an elaborate *retablo* for the high altar of the Capuchins' church.

An outstanding work of the artist's later years is *The Marriage Feast at Cana* (Fig. **3.43**), first recorded in the collection of Nicolas Omazur,

3.43 Bartolomé Esteban Murillo, *The Marriage Feast at Cana*, c. 1665–75. Oil on canvas, 70½ × 92½ in (179 × 235 cm). Barber Institute of Fine Arts, University of Birmingham, England.

Spanish Painting, 1650–1700

the artist's most important patron and collector after 1660. It shows that Murillo could compose a picture with a large cast of characters in a spacious architectural setting. The bride and groom are seated in the center of the picture but in the middle distance. The light colors of their clothing, accented with golden yellow borders and crimson ribbons, as well as the expanse of white table cloth in front of the couple, are all in accord with the wedding theme. Christ, seated on the left, is wearing sober violet-gray garments, and Mary, placed behind him in even more somber colors, is watching as six large jars are filled with water at her suggestion after the wine ran out. Christ gestures toward five tall ceramic jars on the right (the sixth is just arriving on the far right) into one of which a bare-chested man is pouring water. The master of ceremonies must be the man in green standing beside the jars who looks at Christ and gestures as if to say, "Is this what you want me to do?" His black page looks up at him for further instructions. The water is changing to wine inside the jars as we watch Christ perform his first miracle, as recounted in St. John's Gospel. Nicely paced with appropriate emphasis on the major and secondary characters, enough quiet conversation among the remaining guests to keep the mood respectful as the miracle occurs, this work is perfectly designed to convey its religious message. The crimson jacket draws attention to the black page to make the point that heathens as well as Jews could be converted to the faith of the man who could perform such miracles.

Among Murillo's finest late paintings are the *Healing of the Paralytic at the Pool of Bethesda* (National Gallery, London), painted in 1668 for the Hospital de la Caridad in Seville, and *The Two Trinities*, painted around 1680 for an unknown patron (Fig. 3.44). Murillo had painted this rare subject forty years earlier but it is hard to believe that the same artist painted both pictures, so different are their styles. The theme places the young Christ Child between Mary and Joseph as an earthly trinity to complement the traditional Trinity of God the Father, who hovers overhead, and, directly below him, the dove of the Holy Ghost. The early work focuses on Mary, Jesus, and Joseph with God above painted on a much smaller scale. The paint is applied with care, the contours well defined. The slight asymmetry in the disposition of the figures in the larger later work keeps the viewer alert. God the Father and the infant Christ are placed slightly left of center with Mary closer to Christ than Joseph. In both works, Murillo shows Joseph as a handsome young man instead of the grandfather-type seen in earlier centuries. The "new" Joseph reflects theologians' arguments that he must have been an exceptional person to have been chosen by God to care for the infant Christ and the Virgin Mary. Here he is given the role of intercessor. He looks out at us and by doing so pulls us into the picture, where we follow his right hand to Christ. Mary also gestures toward her son, who looks up at the sky, though not at the dove or at God the Father. Christ stands on a slab of stone like a bench with a broken wedge of stone on the ground beside it. Once again an allusion is intended to the tomb from which Christ will rise after three days. The color scheme blends rose, violet, cream, and gold in the upper zone, contrasted with a strong crimson and deep blue on Mary below and ocher over violet, his usual colors, for Joseph. The rose garment of Christ makes a visual connection with the muted pinks in the sky, establishing him even more clearly as part of both trios. Abstract theological concepts have been transformed into a touching picture of family pride. Unlike many Spanish artists working in the later seventeenth century, Murillo understood the value of keeping a composition simple and allowing his figures room to breathe. Every element in this tall painting is perfectly placed according to its religious significance: the members of the Holy Family are just real enough to seem human as well as divine.

Murillo was only sixty-four when he died in April 1682 after falling from scaffolding. He left just over three hundred paintings, many of which are variants of his most popular themes. Like Guido Reni, he specialized in images of divine grace, rarely painting anyone who might be described as homely, let alone ugly. His images are never difficult to understand and never depart from familiar compositional formulas, although his sources were more cosmopolitan than those of his peers. Adorable babies, touchingly beautiful young women, handsome male saints, dignified old men and women—everything he painted had *grazia*. He was celebrated in the nineteenth century and the early twentieth as one of the greatest painters from past centuries. Current taste favors artists with more edge to their imagery and more drama in their lives. Murillo has gained back some of the respect he lost in recent years but may never again achieve the fame that in 1852 inspired the French government to buy his *Immaculate Conception* (the "Soult Immaculada") of 1675 for 615,000 francs, then the largest sum of money ever paid for a single painting. It was displayed at the Louvre until 1941, when it was sent back to Spain in exchange for a portrait by Velázquez. Not until the Metropolitan Museum bought Velázquez's portrait of *Juan de Pareja* (see Fig. 3.37) in 1971 did another Spanish painting of the Golden Age set a market record, when it was the first painting to cost more than a million dollars, a sum long since eclipsed by the prices paid for works by French Impressionists and Vincent van Gogh.

Juan de Valdéz Leal and Claudio Coello

Murillo was not the only successful painter working in Seville in the latter years of the seventeenth century. Juan de Valdés Leal, treasurer of Seville's short-lived Academy, was both productive and versatile. He contributed two spectacular paintings for the church of the Hermandad de la Caridad (Brotherhood of Charity) for which Murillo painted the seven acts of mercy

3.44 Bartolomé Esteban Murillo, *The Two Trinities*, c. 1680. Oil on canvas, 9 ft 6 in × 6 ft 8 in (2.93 × 2.07 m). National Gallery, London.

(1667–70) to decorate their new chapel. The patron, Miguel de Mañara (1627–79), was a wealthy man who devoted his fortune and energies to the Brotherhood of Charity, a lay brotherhood, after all members of his immediate family had died young, most recently his adored wife in 1661. Valdés Leal's canvases are still-lives but on such a large scale—more than 7 feet high (2.2 meters)—that they transcend that genre to become religious paintings.

The skeleton in one canvas – *In Ictu Oculi* – is the sole actor amid the lavish display of symbols of worldly wealth and power (Fig. **3.45**). In the other, a dead bishop's decomposing body lies in an open coffin, garbed in miter and cope, a hand still resting on his staff, filling the foreground where a scroll declares "*Finis Gloriae Mundi*". Other decaying bodies and skeletons are dimly visible in the gloom beyond it. The message is familiar but conveyed with brilliant theatricality: we are all mortal, even popes and kings. Life is extinguished "in the twinkling of an eye" (the skeleton has just extinguished the flame of a tall candle) and only those who have lived lives devoted to Christian acts of charity can hope for salvation.

Suitably chastened by these images, visitors to the chapel would then enter and see Murillo's tender paintings of charitable acts such as clothing the naked (*The Return of the Prodigal Son*, now Washington, National Gallery) and *Christ healing the Paralytic* (London, National Gallery). The contrast between these two extravagantly staged spectacles of worldly treasures and the utter simplicity of Zurbarán's little *Still-life with Lemons, Oranges, and a Rose* (see Fig. 3.20) could hardly be greater.

Spanish political fortunes did not improve after the death of Philip IV in 1665. His frail son, Charles II (1661–1700) was only four when he became king and in no position to exert any control over the intrigues of his mother, Queen

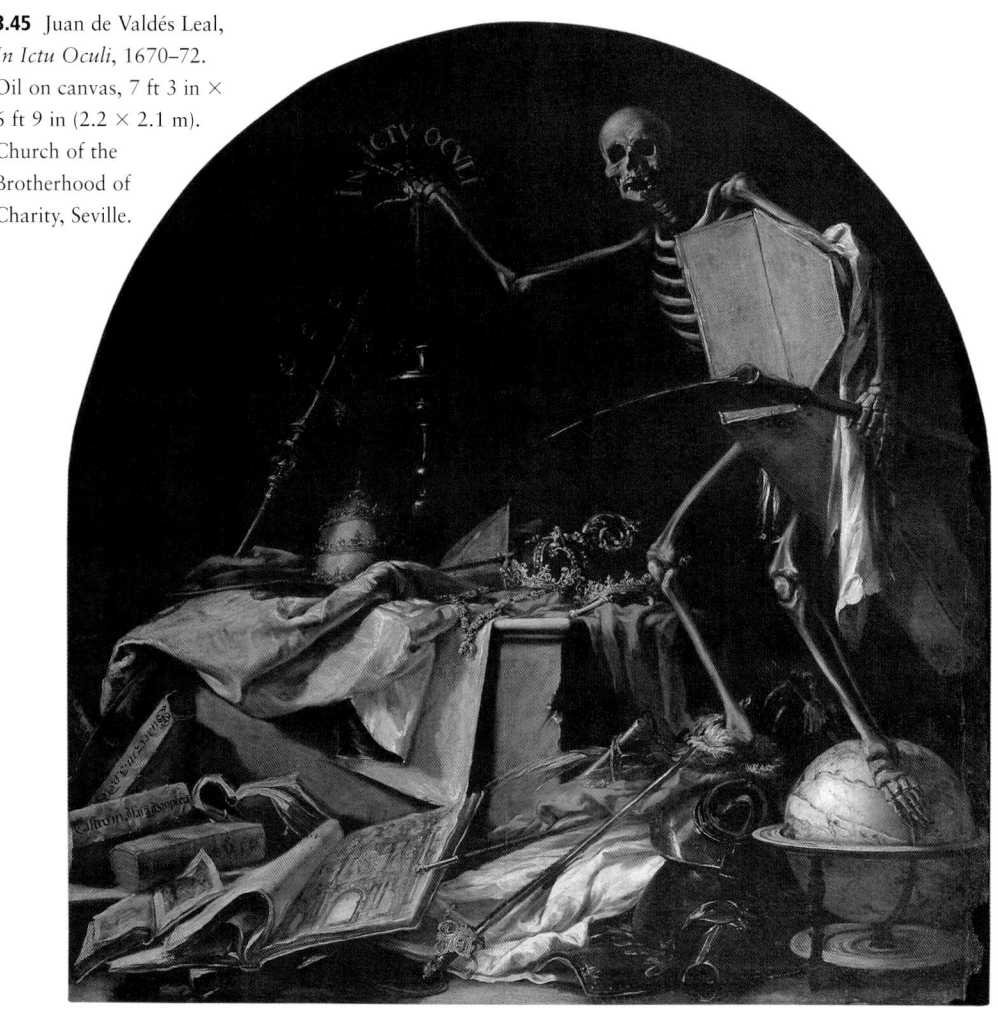

3.45 Juan de Valdés Leal, *In Ictu Oculi*, 1670–72. Oil on canvas, 7 ft 3 in × 6 ft 9 in (2.2 × 2.1 m). Church of the Brotherhood of Charity, Seville.

3.46 Claudio Coello, *La Sagrada Forma*, 1685–90. Oil on canvas, 9 ft 10 in × 16 ft 5 in (3 × 5 m). Sacristy, The Escorial, near Madrid.

Mariana of Austria or the court officials who effectively ruled over Spain's disintegrating economy, failing agricultural resources and weak army. Still, the court continued to commission plays, festivities and church decorations as well as portraits, these last by Velázquez's unworthy successor, Juan Carreño de Miranda (1614–85), who admittedly faced an insuperable task when portraying the strangely elongated face of the king, the last of the fatally inbred line of Habsburg monarchs.

Only Claudio Coello (1642–92) rose above the level of painterly competence of Carreño and his teacher, Francisco Rizi (1614–85), to earn his standing as the best Spanish painter of the late seventeenth century. His most famous surviving work, *La Sagrada Forma* (Fig. **3.46**), is "at once a documentary, a ceremonial group portrait, a religious allegory, and a statement of political propaganda all conjoined in a masterpiece of illusionistic painting".[8] This enormous canvas in the sacristy of the Escorial was commissioned after several nobles and soldiers invaded the sanctuary of the monastery to arrest Fernando Valenzuela, the Queen's favorite, who had taken refuge there after being banished. The Pope excommunicated them; a new, lavish altar in the sacristy was the price demanded for obtaining his pardon. The "Sagrada Forma" is a monstrance that bled when seized by Protestants in 1672: in the painting the officiating priest holds it up before the kneeling king and the offending grandees. Only the angels flying overhead and holding up a crimson cloth to reveal the spectacle depart from the realism of the depiction, which the spectator watches from a privileged viewpoint. The superb rendering of the white and gold brocades used for the robes of the priests and the king's *prie-dieu* and the red patterned carpet in the foreground offer a splendid coda to a century of great painting in Spain.

Spanish Painting, 1650–1700   241

4 FRANCE

Pierre Puget, *Alexander the Great with Diogenes* (detail), 1671–93. Marble relief. Louvre, Paris.

THE TRANSFORMATION OF FRANCE in the seventeenth century into a unified nation controlled by a powerful monarch, and of Paris into a modern city, began during the reign of Henry IV. He became king in 1589 but he did not subdue his opponents and solidify his power until Philip II of Spain signed the Peace of Vervins in 1598. With Spain no longer a threat, Henry could focus on the delicate issues raised by his return to the Catholic faith in 1593 (he had been a Protestant since 1576), which meant that powerful men on both sides of the religious divide distrusted him. Gradually the desire to avoid further bloody conflicts and the conversion of some of Henry's close advisers to the Catholic faith eased the situation. The Edict of Nantes, which he issued in 1598, gave some freedom of worship to Protestants while also placing them under royal control. Henry made a politically astute second marriage with Marie de' Medici, who duly produced a male heir, Louis, in 1601. Until his assassination by a Catholic fanatic in 1610, Henry was largely responsible for restoring peace and prosperity to France in general and to Paris in particular.

In the fifteenth century, the most significant French art patrons after the Church were the Dukes of Burgundy, whose territory included parts of modern Belgium as well as Dijon and Beaune in eastern France. French painters used Flemish compositional models and worked in the Flemish tradition of meticulous realism. While Italian influence became significant after 1520, artistic contacts between Brussels, Antwerp, and Paris continued to affect French artists and to provide opportunities in Paris for Flemish painters. French art and architecture were transformed by the contacts between French patrons and Italian artists resulting from the French invasion of North Italy in 1494 and their capture of Milan in 1500. Anthony Blunt called it "a reverse invasion of France by Italian taste."[1] Dazzled by the life at the North Italian courts, the French began to imitate their buildings, fashions, decorative arts, and manners. Francis I, who ruled from 1515 to 1547, emulated their example, adding wings to his castles at Chambord and Blois to make suitable quarters for the Italian humanists, writers, painters, and architects that he invited to his court. The most famous of these was Leonardo da Vinci (1450–1519), who brought the *Mona Lisa* and some other paintings with him in 1517. The king acquired them after the artist's death as well as works by Andrea del Sarto, Fra Bartolomeo, Raphael, and Giulio Romano. Only the Venetians were neglected, though the king had his portrait painted by Titian, who worked from a medal.

The decoration of Francis I's palace at Fontainebleau by the Italian artists who followed Leonardo to France had even more impact on the taste of French artists and collectors than the king's collection did. Giovanni Battista Rosso, usually called Rosso Fiorentino (1494–1540), spent the last ten years of his life working on the decorations of the Galerie François Ier there with Francesco Primaticcio from Bologna (1504/5– 70), who arrived in 1532. Both worked in a Mannerist style. Rosso's somewhat eccentric art evolved in Florence in the orbit of Andrea del Sarto, while Primaticcio and his later collaborator Niccolò dell'Abbate (c. 1510–71) were both trained in North Italy and thus influenced instead by the elongated figures and sinuous linear rhythms of Parmigianino (1503–40). They were also familiar with the Palazzo del Tè in Mantua, designed and decorated for the Gonzaga court by Raphael's most famous pupil, Giulio Romano (1499?–1546). From their varied backgrounds, these artists created a novel combination of rich decorative frames of stucco around frescoes of complex mythologies that celebrated the king's reign in allegorical form. The framing elements included figures, fruit and vegetable garlands, and strapwork, decorative bands that look like folded and cut strips of leather. It became a fad throughout Northern Europe, appearing in decorative designs on objects as varied as church pews and book bindings for the rest of the century

The complex union of painting, sculpture, and architecture made for Francis I at Fontainebleau set a standard for later decorations commissioned to celebrate the dynastic ambitions of his successors. Louis XIV's grandiose rooms and decorations at Versailles were undertaken to demonstrate his greater stature not only in relation to his French predecessors but also to other European monarchs. Rosso, Primaticcio, and Niccolò dell'Abbate needed many skilled craftsmen and artists to make the stucco decorations and to assist with the paintings. Thus by example and collaboration, these expatriates created a court style, called the First School of Fontainebleau, characterized by recondite mythological subject matter with erotic overtones and figures and settings of refined elegance. The Wars of Religion, which kept France in turmoil from 1562 until 1598, dispersed the artists who had worked at Fontainebleau for Francis I. Nevertheless they established the dominant style in France, except for portraits, until the early seventeenth century. After 1594 Henri IV and Marie de' Medici resumed the decoration of the château and even enlarged it, hiring Flemish as well as French artists to carry out their schemes (the Second School of Fontainebleau). Much of their work at Fontainebleau has been destroyed but the château and its art collections remained an important source of inspiration for French artists in the seventeenth century.

Architecture and City Planning

Paris: the Pont-Neuf, Palais du Luxembourg, and Hôtel de la Vrillière

In 1607 Henry IV wrote to a relative in Rome, proudly listing the flurry of building activity he had generated in Paris:

My cousin, I write in particular to give you news of my buildings, and about my gardens, and to assure you that I have lost no time since you left. In Paris you will find my grand gallery [in the Louvre], which reaches as far as the Tuileries, finished, the small one gilded and paintings installed. In the Tuileries, a fish pond and superb fountains, beautiful plantings and gardens; the buildings surrounding the Place Royale [. . .] three-quarters complete (the fourth to be finished next year); at the end of the Pont-Neuf a beautiful street which goes as far as the Bussy Gate finished, and the houses on both sides either ready, or they will be, by the end of next year; there are more than two or three thousand workshops here and there engaged on the decoration of the city, something you will hardly believe so great is the change.[2]

Henry invested not only considerable resources but also his personal energies in an ambitious building program intended to make Paris as impressive as any Italian city. Paris was the largest city in Europe in 1328 with a population of 220,000; by 1650 its population had doubled. One of its oldest churches is the Cathedral of Notre Dame (begun 1163), one of the first buildings in the French Gothic style; the city is also the seat of the oldest university in Europe after that of Bologna. Henry IV, unlike his predecessors, made the Louvre his primary residence and set about restoring and expanding it. At that time Paris was notorious for its narrow muddy streets fouled with garbage and horse manure; human excrement was tossed from the upper floors of houses. It was at Henry's instigation that streets were widened and equipped with gutters and drains. Edicts promoting proper sanitary practices were enforced rather than ignored. Paris gradually lost its reputation as an open sewer to assume its new image as possibly the best planned and most civilized city in Europe.

Jacques Callot's *View of Pont-Neuf, Paris* (Fig. **4.1**) shows this transformation in progress. The medieval Tour de Nesle, built in the early thirteenth century but torn down in 1663, dominates the composition. Someone living at its summit is hauling up a dripping bucket of water from the Seine, where boatmen maneuver their craft and groups of horses take a bath and a drink. On the unpaved shore to the right business is carried on in the street—merchants make deals, men carry firewood on their backs, and some soldiers investigate the inn on the right, whose new style is that favored by the king. The only woman visible is hanging something to dry on the ramshackle balustrade of her residence at the summit of the Tour de Nesle. Beyond the inn on the right the odd roof levels and types of houses represent the old Paris: the new one is rising in the middle distance on the left. Callot packed all this into an etching about 13 inches (33 cm) wide!

The arches of the Pont-Neuf span the river Seine at the western tip of the Ile de la Cité. First projected in the 1570s, it was eventually built between 1599 and 1606, the delay being caused by the Civil War. Initially resisted by Parisians who feared the additional taxes needed to pay for its construction, the "new bridge" became their favorite place to stroll in their best clothes, admiring the views of their city. The absence of houses along either side was a novelty that allowed pedestrians an unobstructed view of the Seine and the new buildings in both directions. Behind it can be seen the two rows of houses that mark the exterior of the triangular Place Dauphine, which, with the Place Royale, begun in 1605, had the first houses with uniform façades built north of the Alps. On a pedestal facing the narrow opening of the Place Dauphine is Giambologna's bronze equestrian statue of *Henry IV*, commissioned by Marie de' Medici but not installed until 1614.

The wealthy, both religious and secular, preferred to insulate themselves from the kind of people who populate the foreground of Callot's view of Paris. Safe behind stone walls and heavy doors from persistent beggars, unwanted peddlers, or—even worse—rioting mobs, they could enjoy their beautifully appointed refectories and chapels, spacious salons, paved courtyards, and enclosed gardens in peace. The king nevertheless

4.1 Jacques Callot, *View of Pont Neuf, Paris*, 1629. Etching, 5⅓ × 13¼ in (13.6 × 33.7 cm). Louvre, Paris.

encouraged the erection of uniform house façades of brick framed by quoins of cream stone, still partially preserved at Place Dauphine and the Place Royale (now the Place des Vosges), the king's biggest urban planning venture (Fig. 4.2). Here merchants and lawyers could live in comfort around an open space instead of isolated in urban fortresses set amid the jumbled housing of the poor. The king himself built two large units in the center of the north and south rows and before long the surrounding area became fashionable too. The uniform façades of the Place Royale around a shared open space were an innovation that was to have enormous impact on later city planning, not only in Paris and London, but also in Europe and the United States.

Henry's widow, Marie de' Medici, ruled as regent for young Louis XIII until 1617, and, after a two-year exile during which he and his advisers assumed control, still exerted considerable political influence until her permanent exile to Brussels in 1630. As a Florentine, she grew up exposed to outstanding art and architecture so it is not surprising that she was an astute art patron. She commissioned Salomon de Brosse (c. 1571–1626) to build her a palace across the river from the Louvre (Figs. 4.3, 4.3a). Salomon understood mass and scale, something missing in earlier French architecture that updated medieval structures with surface decoration taken from Italian sources. The queen wanted her residence to look like the Palazzo Pitti in Florence but the Palais du Luxembourg does not resemble it except in scale and its rusticated surfaces. Its original street façade (see bottom of Fig. 4.3a) is a low screen wall articulated by pilasters at regular intervals with massive three-story pavilions at either end. Inside was a spacious courtyard flanked by long wings that contained the galleries where Rubens's cycles of the lives of the king and queen were to be displayed (see Figs. 2.26–2.29). The present garden façade (see Fig. 4.3) was reconstructed and moved forward in the nineteenth century when the wings were torn down, but it follows the original design in most respects. Pairs of pavilions at each end of the main residential building contained *apartements*, sets of rooms for privileged members of the queen's court. In her own quarters in the west wing she displayed, among other works, the full-length portrait of herself by

4.2 Anonymous, *The Marriage of Louis XIII and Anne of Austria, 7 April 1612*, Place des Vosges, Place Royale, Paris. Engraving.

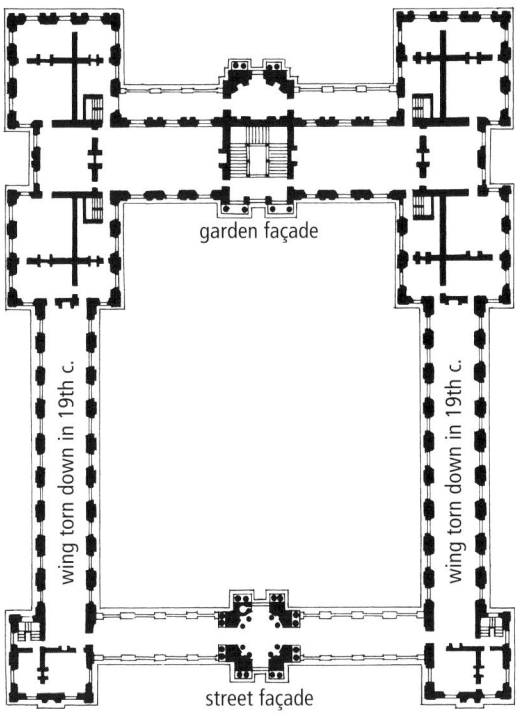

the Flemish painter Frans Pourbus the Younger (Louvre, Paris) and Orazio Gentileschi's *Public Felicity Triumphant over Dangers* (Louvre, Paris), a pointed political allegory painted for her in 1623–5. Marie was only able to occupy a part of her unfinished palace for six years before going into exile; the palace was never completed according to her plans. Around it on both sides of the river, merchants began to build more houses such as those of the Place Royale. Wealthy nobles and court officials built new town houses whose basic plan resembled that of the Luxembourg Palace on a smaller scale, with rooms surrounding three sides of an inner courtyard.

French architects showed increasing sophistication as they adapted the grammar of Italian sixteenth-century architecture to the scale of Paris and the social customs of its wealthy citizens. Without ever visiting Italy, François Mansart (1598–1666) produced buildings of great subtlety

4.3 (above) Salomon de Brosse, Luxembourg Palace, garden façade, Paris, begun 1615.

4.3a (below) Salomon de Brosse, Luxembourg Palace, plan, Paris, begun 1615.

Architecture and City Planning **247**

in both plan and surface, among them the Hôtel de la Vrillière, ingeniously fitted into a triangular piece of land (Figs. **4.4, 4.4a**). Visitors admitted through the carriage entrance to the inner courtyard with the main *corps de logis* flanked by wings would see only symmetry as they entered the circular entrance hall that gave access to the elegant garden terrace. Behind the right wing, however, were extensive quarters for servants, horses, and storage. On the left side a much smaller area was concealed from the visitor by the façade. Along the right side of the garden was the Orangerie and, over it, the Gallery of the owner, Louis Phélypeaux de la Vrillière (1598–1681), secretary of state to Louis XIII. Here he displayed the nine paintings commissioned between 1635 and 1660 to hang with Guido Reni's *Abduction of Helen* (see Fig. 1.69) which he acquired after Marie de' Medici, who had wanted it, was forced into exile in 1630. This superb ensemble of subjects from ancient history by Guercino, Pietro da Cortona, Carlo Maratta, Poussin, and others was dismantled when the hôtel became the property of the Banque de France in 1811, though the paintings remain in French museums. Marie de' Medici and La Vrillière set a pattern: other hôtels began to be designed with a long room in which the finest paintings in the owner's collection, or a group of specially commissioned ones, could be displayed with good lighting from facing windows. Copies of famous ancient sculptures might be included as private collectors began to emulate what only kings and queens had done in the sixteenth century.

Expansion under Louis XIV: The Louvre and Versailles

Rich Parisians needed country residences too and these gave architects far more scope than city houses because the sites were not hemmed in by neighboring buildings. The grandest of these new country residences is the château at Vaux-le-Vicomte built by Louis Le Vau (1612–70) for Nicolas Fouquet (1615–80), the Surintendant des Finances of Louis XIV (Figs. **4.5, 4.5a**). Erected with phenomenal speed between 1657 and 1661, the huge bulk of the château's main building

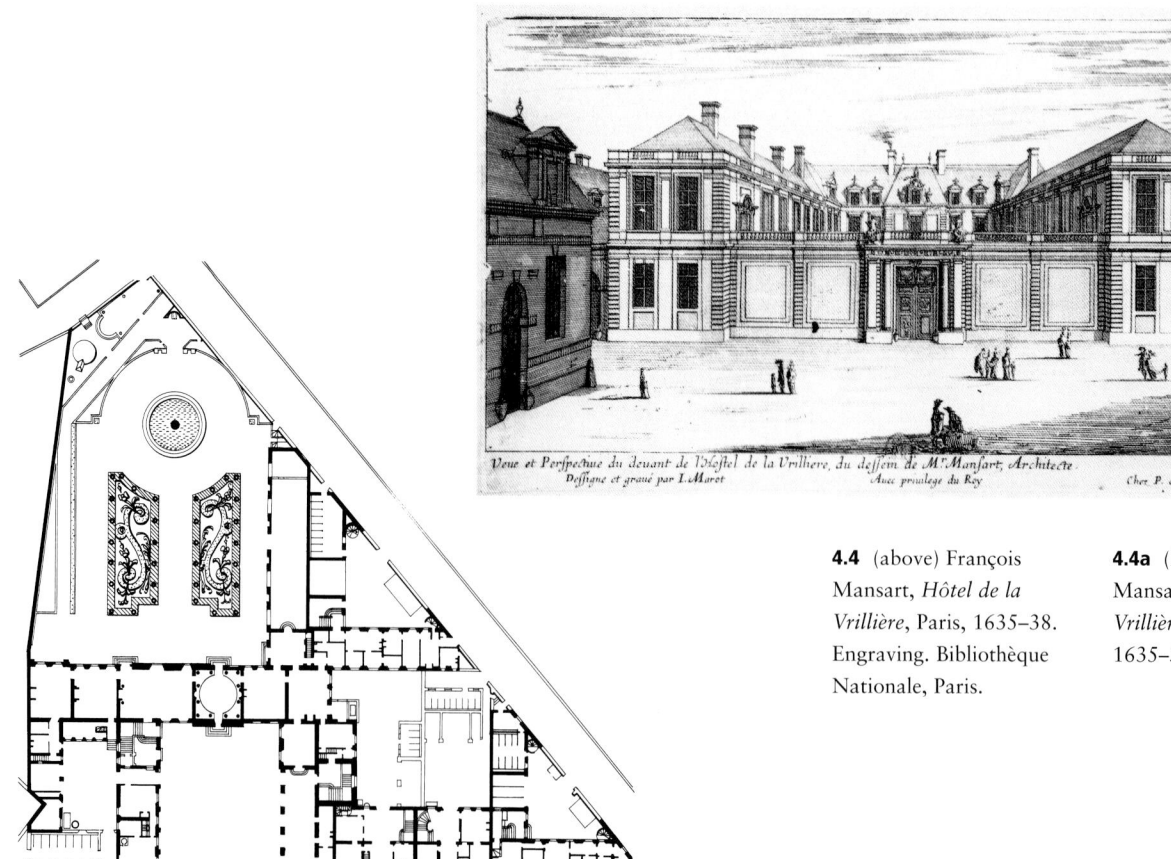

4.4 (above) François Mansart, *Hôtel de la Vrillière*, Paris, 1635–38. Engraving. Bibliothèque Nationale, Paris.

4.4a (left) François Mansart, *Hôtel de la Vrillière*, plan, Paris, 1635–38.

dominates the surrounding property from its position on a site cleared and raised to emphasize its importance. Stables, servants quarters, wine cellars, and such were housed in separate buildings to either side of the front entrance and invisible from the garden front. Flanking wings with the characteristic steep pitched roof preferred in France frame a central pavilion housing the enormous oval Grand Salon beneath its domed roof. Visitors could pass from the salon out to the splendid gardens designed by André Le Nôtre through three arched openings flanked by columns.

Le Vau's sense for the harmonious relationships of overall proportions and the correct forms of Roman architecture was not always secure. The garden entrance with two levels of columns crowned by a flattened triangular pediment looks out of scale next to the giant order pilasters used for the wings. The bulge of the

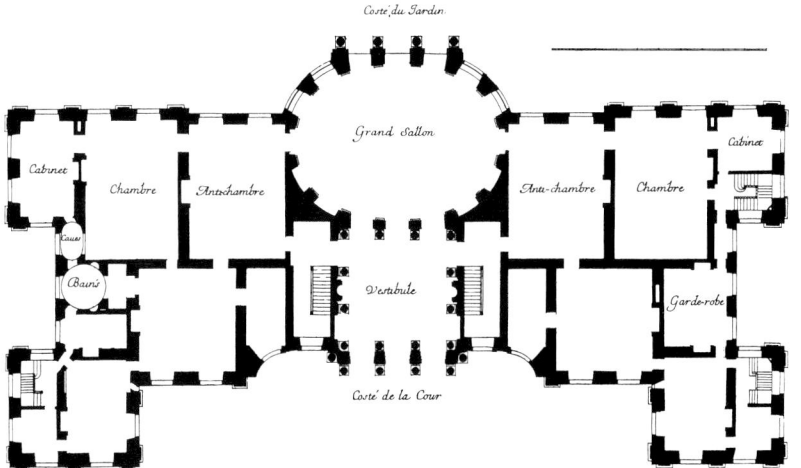

4.5 (above) Louis Le Vau, Vaux-le-Vicomte, garden front, 1657–1661.

4.5a (below) Louis Le Vau, Vaux-le-Vicomte, plan, 1657–1661.

Architecture and City Planning 249

dome also looks odd because all the other forms of the roof are rectilinear, as is most of the rest of design. Nevertheless, the whole is undeniably impressive and it is enhanced immeasurably by the symmetrical ponds, parterres, and terraces of Le Nôtre's garden plans. Le Vau's later designs for the Palais des Quatres Nations across the Seine from the Louvre and his work at Versailles are more harmoniously proportioned.

To either side of the salon at Vaux-le-Vicomte are apartments intended to be occupied by the king to the east and Fouquet himself to the west. The lavish interior decoration carried out by a team supervised by Le Brun, including the ceiling of the famed Salle des Muses (Fig. 4.6), suits the grandiose proportions of the building. Enough has survived to give visitors today a sense of the impressive ensemble that greeted Louis XIV when he attended the opening festivities on August 17, 1661. The royal party was given a banquet, a comedy-ballet by Molière with sets by Le Brun and music by Lully, followed by fireworks. In September Fouquet was arrested for embezzlement; he died in prison nineteen years later. The king was angry not because a courtier had enriched himself but because Fouquet had the gall to use his new wealth to create a château more sumptuous than all royal residences except Fontainebleau. No one should live more splendidly than Louis XIV nor try, as Fouquet also did, to accrue so much influence behind the scenes that his power rivaled the king's. Louis XIV and his trusted minister Jean-Baptiste Colbert (1619–83) took over Fouquet's offices. Significantly, one of the scenes painted by Le Brun on the ceiling of the Galerie des Glaces in Versailles was *The Assumption of Personal Rule by Louis XIV in 1661*.

Colbert wanted the king to keep his main residence in Paris at the Louvre and made considerable efforts to have the east front facing St. Germain l'Auxerrois completed with a design combining grandeur and convenience (Fig. 4.7). He ignored plans already made by Le Vau, commissioned plans from Mansart, who refused to be held to a final solution, and after having Le Vau's designs reviewed by his peers, wrote to Rome for other ideas. Both Pietro da Cortona and Bernini submitted designs featuring curves and counter-curves that were judged too exotic for French taste. Bernini was finally brought to Paris in 1665 to work on a third scheme after submitting a second. Characteristically, his third plan was much larger and more ambitious than his previous proposals and would have swallowed up the existing interior façades by Lescot, Lemercier, and Le Vau. The French resisted this obliteration of their work by an Italian outsider. Bernini did not help his cause by criticizing French architecture during his visit, especially the steep roofs (his scheme had a flat roof ornamented with a balustrade and statues).

The French were no longer meek provincials happy to accept ideas and plans from Italians.

4.6 Charles Le Brun, Vaux-le-Vicomte, Salle des Muses (entrance hall) ceiling, 1657–61.

4.7 Louis Le Vau with Claude Perrault and Charles Le Brun, Louvre, east façade, Paris, 1667–70.

The executed design, which is credited to a team consisting of Claude Perrault, Le Vau, and Le Brun, uses a flat roof line relieved by a pediment at the center and a forward projection three bays wide at each end. The colonnade of paired, fluted Corinthian columns set in front of the actual wall of the façade between these projections creates a sculptural play of voids and solids that fuses Roman grandeur with French elegance. Italian influence is most evident in the adoption of the flat roof edged with a balustrade and the confident use of the giant order, for the third level comprises two floors. When cleaned recently, the basement level was excavated to create a moat, as the architects originally intended, so that the design progresses from a massive ground level with rusticated blocks of masonry like the foundations of a fortress to a second level of smooth wall penetrated by tall windows. These windows mark the main divisions of the third colonnaded level and so help to unify the whole. The design has both strength and finesse, qualities that the king attributed to his monarchy.

In 1667 Louis XIV began the expansion of his hunting lodge at Versailles into its complex current form, employing the team of artists assembled by Fouquet at Vaux-le-Vicomte. An aerial view of the overall plan of the palace and its surrounding gardens (Fig. 4.8) gives an idea

4.8 Jules Hardouin-Mansart & Louis Le Vau, Versailles, plan, 1667.

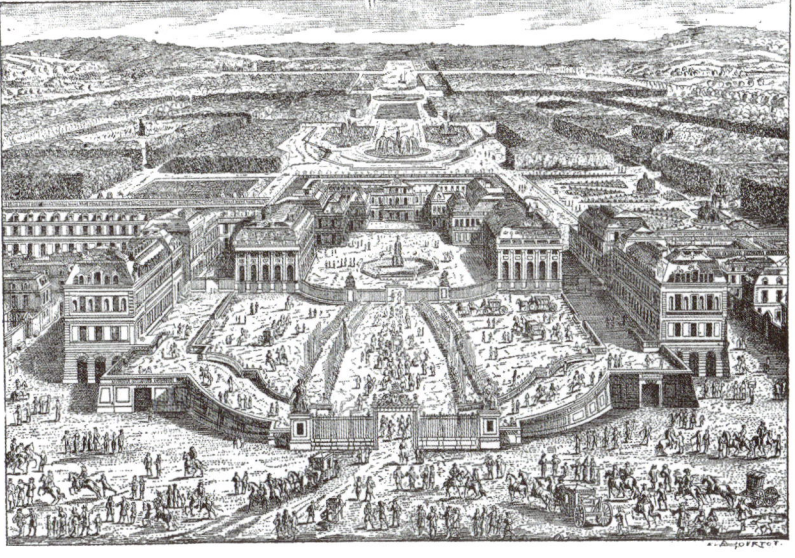

Architecture and City Planning 251

of the scale of the king's ambitions: he wanted no one to be able to challenge his rank and prestige, nor that of the nation he ruled. The symmetry extends in one axis stretching from the entrance gate to the furthest reaches of the garden beyond the palace with the king's quarters at its center. All that remains of Louis XIII's hunting lodge is the Cour de Marbre, the inner court facing the main entrance but now reached only after passing several long wings in the forecourt added by Le Vau and Jules Hardouin-Mansart (1646–1708) that make the journey to reach it on foot a good test of fitness. Each of the king's set of seven rooms was dedicated to a planet; his bedroom was dedicated to Apollo, the sun god, with whom Louis XIV identified so completely that his courtiers had to attend his rising from his bed every morning and his setting there every night after he moved permanently to Versailles in 1682.

The vast expanse of the façade that faces the gardens today (Fig. 4.9) was not meant to be an uninterrupted horizontal mass broken only by porticos with paired columns at either end and six columns in the center. The central eleven bays of Le Vau's design were set back in the original structure. After settling boundary disputes with the United Provinces and Spain to his advantage in 1678 (the Treaty of Nijmegen), the king ordered Le Vau's inset to be filled in by Jules Hardouin, thus creating the Galerie des Glaces (Hall of Mirrors) (Fig. 4.10) with the Salon de la Guerre (War) at one end and the Salon de la Paix (Peace) at the other. Two new wings behind the façade tripled its width: the scale of Le Vau's columns and pilasters was no longer inadequate. All that mattered to the king was the grandiose scale.

The length of the Galerie with its shallow barrel vault impresses the modern visitor first of all for its size—it is 240 feet (73 meters) long, over 33 feet (10 meters) wide, and 47 feet (13 meters) high—then for the long wall of arched spaces filled with panels of Venetian mirrors that reflect the sunlight flooding in from the window wall opposite. Its arched openings have windows from top to bottom, itself an innovation. The view

4.9 Jules Hardouin-Mansart & Louis Le Vau, Versailles, garden façade and lake, 1669–85.

they frame of the gardens, with symmetrical parterres of clipped box hedges and rows of chestnut trees stretching into the far distance on either side of a long reflecting pool, is intended to add to the king's prestige by making the territory under his control appear to be almost infinite.

The mirrors along one wall of the Galerie des Glaces reflect the gardens outside by day and double the light of candles and torches by night. While this might seem their principal purpose, they had another—possibly unintentional—effect on Louis XIV and his court. Mirrors were luxury items in the seventeenth century. Not even the rich owned mirrors larger than 18 inches (45 cm) square, in which only the head and shoulders can be seen easily. The Galerie des Glaces, whose walls of mirrors are assembled from many smaller ones, made it possible for the king and his courtiers to study themselves and their fine clothes at full length in good light for the first time in their lives. The sumptuous velvets and silks worn by both men and women in the later years of the king's reign, brilliantly captured in portraits by Nicolas de Largillière and Hyacinthe Rigaud (1659–1743), radiate this new self-awareness. Grandest of all was the king himself

4.10 Jules Hardouin-Mansart & Louis Le Vau, Galerie des Glaces, Versailles, begun 1678.

4.11 (left) Hyacinthe Rigaud, *Louis XIV*, 1701. Oil on canvas, 9 ft × 6 ft 3 in (2.77 × 1.94 m). Louvre, Paris.

4.12 (right) Jacques Sarrazin and Gilles Guérin, Caryatids on the Pavillon de l'Horloge, Louvre, Paris, 1641. Stone.

in his blue velvet coronation robes, studded with gold fleur-de-lis and lined with white ermine, standing beneath swathes of plum-red velvet with all his royal attributes to hand. Thus he was immortalized by Rigaud in 1701 (Fig. **4.11**). His hauteur is perfectly captured. His successors had themselves portrayed in similar garb but even Rigaud never managed to equal the assured arrogance of the original.

French Sculpture

France did not produce a sculptor with the phenomenal range of artistic, intellectual, and administrative gifts of Gian Lorenzo Bernini in the seventeenth century. Henry IV and Marie de' Medici sought out Giambologna in Florence when they wanted an equestrian monument of the king for the center of the Pont-Neuf in 1604. Other important commissions also went to Flemish or Italian sculptors until the 1630s. Not until the 1660s could France boast of sculptors who were not only fine craftsmen in bronze or marble but also skillful adapters of current Italian models, especially for the portrait bust, as well as innovative designers of free-standing tombs for important patrons.

Jacques Sarrazin (1588–1660) spent his twenties and thirties in Rome, where he worked with Stefano Maderno and also knew Pietro Bernini. The careers of Algardi and Duquesnoy had barely begun before Sarrazin left around 1627, though he could have seen Bernini's remarkable early marble sculptures made for Cardinal Scipione Borghese as well as some of his portrait busts and early tombs. Sarrazin, however, evidently absorbed little influence from Hellenistic works such as the Laocoön and Farnese Hercules. In 1641 he carved caryatids and other decorations for Lemercier's Pavillon de l'Horloge at the Louvre (Fig. **4.12**); these show an excellent understanding of earlier classical sculpture as well as details of drapery and anatomy that are convincing without being fussy.

Pierre Puget

The finest French sculptor of the seventeenth century was Pierre Puget (1620–94), who was born in Marseilles and spent much of his working life there and in Toulon. He also found strong support for his work in Genoa, where more of his work is preserved than in France, so that he is a major figure in Italian sculptural history too. He trained in Italy with Pietro da Cortona, reaching Rome in the late 1630s and travelling with Cortona to Florence in 1640, when Pietro began work on the decoration of the Sale dei Pianeti in Palazzo Pitti. Cortona rarely worked as a sculptor himself but he was an architect of distinction and a brilliant designer of decorative ensembles; Puget's versatility was fostered by his training with Cortona.

Puget returned to Marseilles in 1643 and began his career as a painter, also providing designs for the elaborately carved poops of French warships where the influence of both Cortona and Algardi is evident. His first surviving sculpture of importance was not made until 1656–7, when he designed and built the doorway of the Town Hall in Toulon (Fig. **4.13**). Its most striking feature is a pair of herms who struggle to support the heavy cornice overhead with its balcony. Their agonized faces inevitably recall the Laocoön, while the dynamic sense of upward movement and easy union of human and natural forms seem inspired by Bernini's *Triton Fountain* (see Fig. 1.115). The brilliantly proportioned whole shows Puget's mastery of architectural as well as sculptural forms. This led to his first Parisian commissions, one of which was a statue of a Gallic Hercules for Vaux-le-Vicomte (though damaged, it survives in the Louvre). Fouquet commissioned other statues for Vaux-le-Vicomte from the sculptor, who went to Genoa to order the necessary marbles from Carrara. Before they could be delivered, Fouquet was imprisoned. Luckily Genoese patrons stepped forward and Puget was soon making works for Genoese churches. He was summoned back to France in 1668, completing commissions for patrons in Genoa until the late 1670s.

In 1669 Colbert put Puget in charge of the sculpture workshop at the naval shipyard in Toulon, but the best commissions for sculptors were to be found at Versailles. For whatever reason, Colbert did not encourage Puget by commissioning statues for the gardens there. It was Puget himself who took the initiative after finding two abandoned blocks of marble from which he carved his *Milo of Crotona* (Fig. **4.14**) between 1670 and 1682. The subject is an ancient story of hubris punished. Milo, a resident of Crotona in southern Italy in the sixth century BC, was known for his great strength. When he found a tree trunk partially split apart with a wedge, he removed it and tried to pull the trunk apart with his bare hands, only to became trapped. He was then eaten alive by wild beasts. Puget's sculpture shows him caught only by the fingertips of his left

4.13 Pierre Puget, Town Hall, doorway, Toulon, 1656–57.

French Sculpture 255

hand but still unable to escape or to fight off the lion attacking him from behind. The Laocoön is a primary source: in both works man loses a battle of strength with an animal and with the superior forces of fate controlled by the gods. The *Milo of Crotona* also has some of the muscularity of the Farnese Hercules and some of the dynamic tension of Bernini's *David* (see Fig. 1.88). Puget offered the king a French challenge to two of the most famous ancient sculptures in Rome and to no less an artist than Bernini. Louis XIV was ecstatic, declaring that no sculptor anywhere could have produced anything finer; in other words, Puget was better than Bernini.

François Girardon and Antoine Coysevox

Puget's younger rivals at court, François Girardon (1628–1715) and Antoine Coysevox (1640–1720), who had the lion's share of the sculpture commissions at Versailles, were resentful of Puget's success, professing that while he was clever, he was unable to render natural forms beautifully and was no good at drapery. In 1684 Puget sent his *Perseus Liberating Andromeda* (Louvre, Paris), another ambitious free-standing statue, to Versailles; this was more justifiably criticized for making Andromeda too small. He also sent a superb relief of *Alexander the Great with Diogenes* (see p. 242), perhaps intending to seek comparison, to his own benefit, with Algardi, who specialized in relief sculpture and which Bernini avoided. Puget's familiarity with ancient relief sculpture is also apparent in this masterly interpretation of the meeting between Alexander and the cynic philosopher, who lived in a barrel, wore one simple garment, and told Alexander to get out of his light! No diplomat and always supremely confident of his gifts, Puget remained somewhat isolated in Marseilles and Genoa and was rarely well used by the king and his advisers.

Jean Warin (1604–72), who ran the royal Mint after 1646, made excellent portrait busts in bronze, for example that of *Cardinal Richelieu* (Bibliothèque Mazarine, Paris) and was an outstanding designer of medals too. Fine busts by Coysevox adapt Bernini's lively formats with their hint of a moving body beneath a swathe of drapery. Girardon's ambitious group sculpture of *Apollo tended by Nymphs* in the gardens of Versailles, and Coysevox's relief of Louis XIV on horseback trampling on his enemies over the fireplace in the Salon de la Guerre, Palace of Versailles, are only the most famous of the many works contributed by these sculptors to that grandiose enterprise.

The tombs of *Cardinal Richelieu* by Girardon (Fig. **4.15**) and *Cardinal Mazarin* by Coysevox (Fig. **4.16**) gave both sculptors a better opportunity to display their respective gifts with a major commission in a prominent site than their work at Versailles. Richelieu has a free-standing monument executed entirely in white marble, ingeniously designed for a site in the central axis of the church of the Sorbonne. (It has since been

4.14 Pierre Puget, *Milo of Crotona*, 1670–82. Marble, 8 ft 8 in (2.7 m). Louvre, Paris.

moved to a side chapel.) The cardinal reclines on the lid of his sarcophagus in the arms of Piety, whose swelling body, ornamented with crisply carved acanthus leaves at each corner, is partly concealed by a huge cloth whose border is decorated with Richelieu's coat of arms and armorial devices. Seemingly still alive but weak, Richelieu looked up toward the altar (when the tomb was in its original location) in a pose that fulfills his desire to be shown offering himself to God. Doctrine has collapsed in grief at his feet, her lap toward the altar, her body turned away from Richelieu, in a pose that recalls the grieving woman at the foot of the bed in Poussin's *Extreme Unction* (see Fig. 4.41). Visitors entering the church from the university would have seen Richelieu from the side looking toward the altar, but Girardon provided something for the viewer on the other sides as well—a better view of Doctrine on the far side and two putti with the cardinal's coat-of-arms at the back.

4.15 (above) François Girardon (based on drawings by Le Brun), *Cardinal Richelieu*, 1694. Marble. Church of the Sorbonne, Paris.

4.16 (below) Antoine Coysevox, *Cardinal Mazarin*, 1689–93. Bronze, height 55¼ in (140 cm). Institut de France, Paris.

French Sculpture

Mazarin's wall monument, now back in its original location after various moves since the Revolution, is framed by two mottled brown marble columns. The sculptor used black, white, and gray marble for the effigy and sarcophagus, and bronze for three women seated on the base below the sarcophagus. (Prudence and Fidelity on the sides are by Coysevox; Peace in the center may be by a collaborator.) In the lunette above is Mazarin's coat-of-arms flanked by figures of Religion and Charity. A black memorial tablet behind the Cardinal keeps his form from blending into the wall behind. This effigy also shows the subject as if still alive, kneeling in prayer, the left hand touching his heart, watched by a small genie supporting bound fasces. Except for the effigy, the design is completely symmetrical; it is also perfectly scaled for its setting, and beautifully carved and finished throughout. The use of bronze and marble of different colors invites comparison with Bernini's papal tombs in St. Peter's, but those incorporate red, green, and ocher marbles as well as neutral tones; Bernini's allegorical figures also react more dramatically to the impending death of the figures they accompany. Such theatrical effects were shunned in France. Both Girardon's and Coysevox's debts to classical rather than Hellenistic sculpture also mark their distance from Bernini's more theatrical aesthetic preferences. To call the French sculptors "classical" and Bernini "Baroque" in this case clarifies rather than confuses the differences between their works.

French Painting and Printmaking

France produced many outstanding etchers and engravers in this century. Most reproduced the designs of other artists; a few created their own as well. The most influential of this latter category was Jacques Callot (1592/3–1635), whose career spans the period of change from *maniera* court art to less artificial imagery. He was born in Nancy, the capital of the Duchy of Lorraine, to a family with court connections and trained there and in Rome. He worked for the Medici in Florence from 1614 to 1621 making prints of court festivals, theatrical characters, and local fairs before returning to Nancy. Callot invented a new technique, a combination of linseed oil and mastic, that produced a hard surface capable of being marked more easily than metal with a burin yet still strong enough to retain fine detail through many impressions. Brilliant tonal contrasts in the foreground and delicate tonal shadings in the distance give even his smallest compositions a sense of infinite space that belies their scale.

While some of his Florentine prints, such as the *Fan with the Festival of St. James on the Arno* (Fig. 4.17), use the exaggerated physiognomies of late *maniera*, others are filled with acute observation of human activity. Callot's most ambitious works offer a mass of detail within coherent compositional schemes. He was both versatile and productive, creating more than a thousand prints that range in size from miniatures to monumental maps of major military victories comprising many plates. His subjects are also comprehensive—theatrical subjects, records of festivals and fairs, views of Paris (see Fig. 4.1), images of the fashionable nobility of Lorraine, religious themes such as the life of the Virgin and—his most famous work—*The Great Miseries of War* (Fig. 4.18). He made two series depicting the devastation provoked by Cardinal Richelieu's efforts to combat Protestantism in the regions near Nancy during the Thirty Years War. They show the usual consequences of pitting poorly paid and undisciplined soldiers against a civilian populace without means of defense. Farms are pillaged, homes sacked and torched after their owners have been raped or murdered; even churches are set on fire. A tree strung with hanged men is Callot's most famous image from these series. Others show all the current methods of execution and torture observed by large crowds. They are the first anti-war images in western art and had no rival until Francisco Goya was moved by the horrors of the Peninsular War of 1804–14 in Spain to make his even more graphic and powerful prints, *Los Desastres de la Guerra*. Unlike Callot's prints, however, Goya's were only published in 1863, long after his death and the events that inspired them.

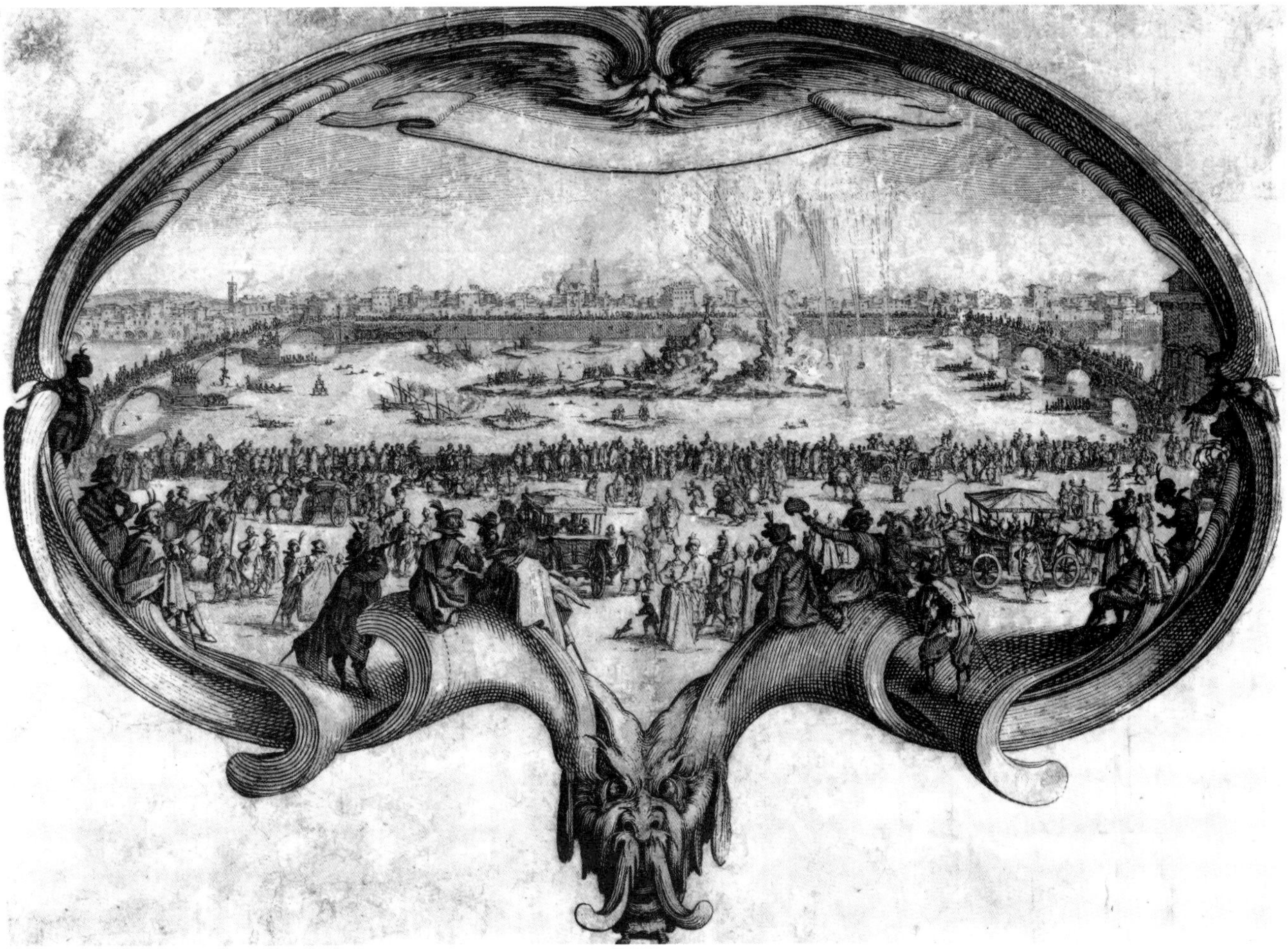

4.17 (above) Jacques Callot, *Fan with the Festival of St. James on the Arno*, 1619. Etching, 8¾ × 11⅝ in (22.2 × 29.6 cm). British Museum, London.

4.18 (below) Jacques Callot, *Pillage of a Farmhouse*, from *The Great Miseries of War (Les Grandes Misères de la Guerre)*, plate 4, 1633. Etching, 3¼ × 7⅓ in (8.2 × 18.7 cm).

French Painting and Printmaking 259

Simon Vouet

Instead of importing Italian artists, Henry IV and Marie de' Medici began sending young French artists to Italy to train. Simon Vouet (1590–1649) was among the first French painters to be given a royal pension to enable him to study in Italy, a privilege of which he took full advantage, returning home after more than a decade to achieve success in Paris working for the court and the nobility. He was also one of the founders of the French Academy in 1648, the institution that regularized such scholarships, awarded annually to painters and sculptors. Vouet was precocious, painting a portrait in London at the age of fourteen before traveling to Constantinople (1611–12) with the French Ambassador for whom he made portraits too. He was in Venice in 1612–13 and reached Rome in 1614. A rapidly sketched informal *Self-Portrait* (Fig. **4.19**) of Vouet in his twenties shows how much raw talent he had: he used an open mouth to produce a "speaking likeness" more than a decade before Bernini did. Vouet made altarpieces for St. Peter's and decorated two chapels in other churches, sent altarpieces to Naples and Genoa, and was elected *principe* of the Accademia di San Luca (1624–7), a post he held for three years instead of the usual one. His fellow artists paid him a rare tribute, thanking him for his many services, "in particular for having opened the [drawing] studio, reformed the statutes and [. . .] for [. . .] having spared neither effort nor expense to achieve what would be of public benefit."[3]

Vouet's administrative talents enabled him to run a large and efficient studio in Paris after his return in 1627. He quickly found patrons for altarpieces for Paris churches, devotional pictures for private patrons, and decorative schemes for the town houses and country retreats of the nobility. Sadly, most of his secular decorations have since been destroyed and many of his altarpieces were lost during the Revolution. His Parisian years are therefore now mainly known from the works he made for private clients—easel paintings of mythological and allegorical subjects as well as religious themes such as the Holy Family and Penitent Magdalene. His dominance of this market might have been challenged had Poussin settled in Paris instead of returning to Rome in 1642, as least so thought Louis XIII, who is said to have remarked "Voilà Vouet bien attrapé!" ("Now Vouet is caught!") after managing to lure Poussin to Paris in 1640. Still, Poussin and Vouet catered to quite different audiences, the former serious about intellectual pursuits, the latter seeking attractive rather than challenging images for their walls.

Vouet arrived in Rome just four years after Caravaggio's death when many artists, especially those from north of the Alps, were obsessed with his seductive mixture of brilliantly observed reality and dramatic chiaroscuro. Vouet succumbed as well. *The Fortune Teller* (Fig. **4.20**) of around 1620 reprises one of the genre subjects portrayed by half-length figures introduced by Caravaggio (Louvre, Paris). Vouet's characters, who stand before a dull brown wall, are lit as if by a shaft of sunlight. A second light source creates a diagonal shadow on the wall behind them, a favorite

4.19 Simon Vouet, *Self-Portrait*, 1618–19. Oil on canvas, 25⅛ × 18⅞ in (64 × 48 cm). Musée Réattu, Arles.

4.20 Simon Vouet, *The Fortune Teller*, c. 1620. Oil on canvas, 47¼ × 67 in (120 × 170.2 cm). National Gallery of Canada, Ottawa.

Caravaggio motif. Vouet has even employed a looping figure 8 on its side to link the four figures, a device Caravaggio used in early works. Caravaggio had only two characters in his portrayal—a female gypsy and her naïve young male dupe, so pleased with his appearance that he does not notice the ring being slipped off his finger. In Vouet's interpretation, the deceit of the female gypsy has been answered by having an accomplice of the couple on the left dip into the gypsy's cloak to steal her purse. The woman whose palm is being read seems fully aware of the deception, for she directs our attention to the gypsy and pays little heed to the gypsy's message. Though her wine-red silk dress suggests that she is a woman of means, such a woman would not venture into the Roman streets without an escort, so she must be the accomplice of these ruffians. The choreography of hands at the heart of the painting creates a melodrama of its own amid the exchange of glances and gazes of the perpetrators of this deception, also a metaphor for the art of painting: the viewer is deceived into accepting painted images as reality.

During the 1620s Vouet gradually abandoned the robust naturalism and dark tones of his early works for a smoother, more idealizing manner. Only the boneless hands with tapering tips seen on the lady in red appear in his later works. He began to study Annibale Carracci, Guido Reni, and Lanfranco as well as Caravaggio. He gave up the strong chiaroscuro, the dark, blank backgrounds, and earthy color range relieved by a few passages of crimson for more evenly lit scenes with proper settings and a lighter palette of muted pastels. Before returning home he stopped in Venice, where he studied Veronese's ceiling paintings and altarpieces with particular care.

Vouet's conversion to a completely different style owing nothing to Caravaggio was virtually complete by 1627. This mature style can be appreciated in his *Presentation of the Virgin in the Temple* of 1641 (Fig. **4.21**), made for the Jesuit church in Paris. Originally it was installed in an elaborate two-story frame like a church façade with an image of St. Louis, the patron saint of the church, ascending to heaven in the central space above Vouet's painting. Flanked by paired columns on the same scale as those in the painting, the altarpiece would have been far more impressive in its original setting than it is today. The majestic curved colonnade of Corinthian columns backed by a Doric arcade basking in the sunshine behind the figures is as much a tribute

French Painting and Printmaking **261**

4.21 Simon Vouet, *Presentation of the Virgin in the Temple*, 1641. Oil on canvas, 12 ft 7 in × 8 ft 3 in (3.93 × 2.5 m). Louvre, Paris.

to Veronese as the somber lighting and plebeian characters of his *Fortune Teller* were to Caravaggio. The suave color scheme and idealized figures recall Guido Reni. The steps in the foreground recall Veronese's *Mystic Marriage of St. Catherine* (see Fig. 1.14), as does the overall arrangement of the figures on a rising diagonal from lower right to upper left, where angels carry the scroll with the words of the old priest, Simeon: "Nunc dimittis servum tuum," traditionally translated as "Lord, now lettest thou thy servant depart in peace" (Luke 2:29). On the left a typical Vouet woman, plump and smooth, holds her child by the hand and watches this touching scene with an old man who kneels in front of them with his black goat, a sacrificial offering. The color scheme of blond neutrals has little bright local color. Even the Virgin's outer garment is a dull gray-blue instead of the brilliant lapis lazuli blue often found in French seventeenth-century painting. That blue was reserved for the cloak of St. Louis in the painting once installed above the *Presentation* (now Musée des Beaux-Arts, Rouen).

Valentin de Boulogne

Among the other French artists who settled in Rome in the 1610s having discovered Caravaggio was Valentin de Boulogne (1591–1632). Only his last decade is documented with payments and dated commissions: he benefited, as Poussin did, from the Barberini papacy's preference for those with French connections. In 1629 Valentin was commissioned to paint one of the altarpieces in the New St. Peter's, namely, the *Martyrdom of Sts. Processus and Martinian* (see Fig. 4.35). This was the most prestigious public altarpiece commission then available, and one rarely given to foreigners, especially an artist still using the dramatic chiaroscuro and naturalism of Caravaggio. Installed in the right transept beside Poussin's more colorful and daylight depiction of *The Martyrdom of St. Erasmus* (see Fig. 4.34), Valentin's altarpiece was immediately compared with that of his French compatriot, and judged as fine, if not finer in some respects.

Valentin's *The Four Ages of Man* (Fig. 4.22), an allegory, is a departure from his usual genre scenes of fortune tellers, drinkers, and musical

4.22 Valentin de Boulogne, *The Four Ages of Man*, c. 1620. Oil on canvas, 37⅞ × 52⅞ in (96 × 134 cm). National Gallery, London.

parties, though not in format or color. Four figures are arranged around a block of stone that serves as a table: a child in the center foreground has let a bird escape from a cage; a fashionably dressed youth on the left plays a lute; an old man sits lost in thought before a pile of coins, a glass of wine in one hand, a flask in the other; and, on the right, a man in armor with a laurel wreath on his head has dozed off while reading a book about military fortifications. Only the musician looks at us. Melancholy pervades the scene. Is the child sad because his pet bird has escaped, the youth because his serenades are ignored by his lover, the old man because he is facing death after a wasted life? Is the soldier dreaming of fame and glory through military pursuits? The theme is the brevity of human life and the futility of earthly pursuits. Finely observed and beautifully painted details include the hands of the four characters, the wine flask, and bird cage, all evidence of Valentin's grasp of form, anatomy, tonal values, and light. No drawings by Valentin have been identified; apparently, like most of Caravaggio's followers, he rarely drew after his student days. His death, probably from the plague, cut short the production of an artist at the peak of his powers.

Georges de La Tour

The other French painter of distinction whose encounter with the art of Caravaggio was crucial to his achievement was Georges de La Tour (1593–1652). Known mostly to provincial patrons in his lifetime and largely forgotten after his death, he has since become among the best-known French painters of his time. He worked in the Duchy of Lorraine, where he was born and where he lived most of his life. Henry II, Duke of Lorraine, bought pictures from La Tour in 1623 and 1624. In 1639, he was in Paris and sold a painting of St. Irene tending the wounds of St. Sebastian to Louis XIII (lost); that year he was also made *Peintre Ordinaire du Roi* (Ordinary Painter to the King), a title that did not require residence in Paris; in fact he is frequently recorded in Lunéville. Other works were made for the Governor of Lorraine, the Marshal de la Ferté. By 1652, when La Tour died, the taste for candlelit scenes with dark backgrounds had ended and his work sank into oblivion. Only in the 1930s as French art historians began to explore the roots of nineteenth-century realism did scholars begin to appreciate him again. Fewer than forty paintings are generally accepted now as authentic but others are known from good copies, proof that La Tour was admired in his lifetime.

La Tour's life was not written either by a local historian or by André Félibien (1619–95), the first biographer of French painters. Because only two works are dated—the *Penitent St. Peter* (Cleveland Museum of Art) of 1645 and *The Denial of St. Peter* (Musée des Beaux Arts, Nantes) of 1650—establishing the chronology of his work is difficult, although a broad consensus has been reached. There are gaps in his residence records in Lunéville when he could have made a journey to Rome, Paris, or Utrecht. Another painter from Lorraine, Jean Le Clerc (c. 1587/8–1633), did visit Rome in the 1610s and returned to Nancy, the capital of the duchy, in 1620/21. There he produced some paintings that share the preference of Caravaggio's Northern followers for revealing the light source, whether a candle, lantern, or torch. Maybe that was all that La Tour needed to create his own far more powerful visual language. On the other hand, the monumentality of his single figures of penitent saints seems inconceivable without first-hand experience either of Caravaggio's Roman altarpieces or of work by other Northern admirers that captured more of their power than Le Clerc did. While some experts believe that La Tour made a trip to Rome, others have suggested that he traveled to Utrecht, where Hendrick ter Brugghen (see Fig. 5.5) and Gerrit van Honthorst (see Fig. 5.6) had been producing religious works for local Catholic clients as well as genre scenes of themes introduced by Caravaggio.

The combination of wine red and turquoise blue amid a grayish-brown overall color scheme in some of La Tour's early paintings is reminiscent of the distinctive palette of ter Brugghen, which suggests contact with the Utrecht school, but the finesse of La Tour's technique is the best argument for a visit to Utrecht. No one in Nancy or even Paris until Vouet's return late in 1627 could have exposed La Tour to the visual exuberance and sheer painterly skills that he could have seen there. La Tour's decision to live in Lunéville, a town far from the major centers of

4.23 Georges de La Tour, *The Cheat with the Ace of Diamonds*, c. 1630. Oil on canvas, 41¾ × 57½ in (106 × 146 cm). Louvre, Paris.

artistic patronage and success, suggests that he was insecure, happier as the proverbial big fish in a small pond than competing with Vouet and his school in Paris. Having found his style, La Tour closed his mind to developments elsewhere for he had sufficient support locally to make a good living. This isolation enabled him to concentrate on refining his art to produce works of almost abstract simplicity.

La Tour painted two versions of a cardsharp composition, *The Cheat with the Ace of Diamonds* (Fig. **4.23**) and *The Cheat with the Ace of Clubs* (Kimbell Art Museum, Fort Worth). There are only slight differences between them, mainly in the colors and details of the costumes, but the changes make the *Ace of Diamonds* a slightly more effective design and a more convincing narrative. The theme was introduced by Caravaggio (see Fig. 1.38), whose cheat also pulls cards from behind his back, but his all-male cast has now been integrated—the central figure is a woman, probably a courtesan, in a splendid brown velvet dress. Her red feathered toque and the servant's exotic yellow turban are stage clothes, as is the beret with a huge ostrich plume worn by the dupe. In Dutch genre painting, it is worn by actors playing a fool, an appropriate reading here too. Both dupes are expensively dressed. In the *Ace of Clubs*, the dupe looks ahead, a glimmer of satisfaction on his face as if pleased with his cards but, thus posed, he is likely to detect the fraudulent moves on the left. The dupe illustrated here is totally absorbed in his cards and will not spot his opponent on the left extracting the winning ace from his belt to add to the cards in his hand. The cheat's shadowed face and position on the left (sinister) side are further hints of his nefarious intent. His right hand stands out against the dark blue weskit of the servant. That the cheat and the lady are in cahoots is clear: the lady's hand reaching for the glass also seems to ask for the cheat's card. The servant eyes us warily: she knows what is going on but will not give the game away. This vain young man will soon lose his money.

Scholars date these paintings around 1630–35. La Tour's earlier works tend to reduce underlying forms into simple solids, without realizing the solid masses of the figures as forcefully as here. The lady's head is a smooth oval. The dupe's white satin sleeve has spherical folds enveloping his arm; his jaw line has vanished into the orb of his head. The later paintings are almost all night scenes, the figures illuminated by candlelight or a lantern: it was for his "nocturnes" that he was cited by the only French writer to mention him before 1900.

La Tour painted *The Repentant Magdalen* at least five times, three with the saint dressed in a loose white shift and a red skirt, seated in dark interiors illuminated by an oil lamp or candlelight. One has a mirror with a heavy silver frame of almost vulgar ostentation. Such possessions recall her legendary past as a courtesan whose earnings enabled her to buy such luxuries. The version shown here (Fig. 4.24) is rendered in a somber monochrome of dark browns, beige, and cream, its restraint forcing the viewer to focus on the sacrament of penitence, the Magdalene's chief role in seventeenth-century Catholic art. The simple frame of her mirror is discreetly ornamented with small silver mounts at the corners. Its surface is filled with a reflection of the skull on a thick book, which the saint touches with her left hand as she meditates, her chin supported on the palm of her right hand in the classic gesture of melancholy. Her mouth is open. Apparently she has just let out a sigh because the candle flame, almost completely obscured by the skull, leans to the left. In the utter stillness of this austere scene, La Tour captured that breath, though only an attentive observer will spot this detail.[4]

A skull and a prayer book are the usual attributes of penitent saints. The Magdalene also has an ointment jar because she anointed Christ's feet at the feast in the house of Simon. It may be the object in the dark behind the mirror on the left edge of the painting. The mirror, a symbol of vanity, recalls the Magdalene's past life, while the reflected skull shows that she has abandoned that life. She now meditates on her mortality and hopes for salvation through prayer. The flame of the candle, the only source of light in this dark picture, becomes a symbol of the light brought by God "when darkness was upon the face of the deep" and "God said, 'Let there be light'; and there was light" (Genesis 1: 2–3). Even the smoke from a candle was interpreted by contemporary theologians as "signifying renunciation of the mortal life and aspiration for the beyond."

The difference between earthly and divine light is used by La Tour in one of his most affecting night scenes to convey its message of Christ's divinity. *St. Joseph the Carpenter* (Fig. 4.25) shows Joseph bending over his awl as he drills a hole in a thick curved plank of wood. The young Christ Child sits in front of him, holding a candle whose tall flame illuminates the contours of Joseph's head and arms before fading into the darkness behind him. The head of Christ glows instead with an inner light far stronger than that of a candle. This is miraculous light, reminding the faithful of the divine nature of God's Son. Christ's hand partly conceals the candle's flame, possibly to suggest that these divine truths are only partially revealed to those still in this world. Like *The Repentant Magdalen* (see Fig. 4.24), *Christ with St. Joseph* is painted almost entirely in a warm monochrome of browns and creams. A little red is used on Joseph's head and for Christ's hand and his belt, whose slight flash of color above his left arm attracts our attention but subliminally, before we are aware of it. The painting also portrays a touching dialogue between "crabbed age and youth": the old man listens respectfully, pausing in his work as the young Christ speaks.

By 1650 many painters had adopted the new interpretation of Mary's husband as a saintly man happy to live in perpetual chastity in order to protect the Virgin Mary and her Son. The elderly Joseph in La Tour's painting is a relic of medieval mystery plays, in which he was mocked as a man too old to have fathered a child, though he is

4.24 Georges de La Tour, *The Repentant Magdalen*, c. 1640. Oil on canvas, 44½ × 36½ in (113 × 92.7 cm). National Gallery of Art, Washington, DC.

4.25 Georges de La Tour, *St. Joseph the Carpenter*, c. 1635. Oil on canvas, 53⅞ × 40⅛ in (137 × 102 cm). Louvre, Paris.

portrayed here as a dignified and gentle presence. The simplification of the forms is greater than in *The Repentant Magdalen*. Joseph's left leg is a brown shape and Christ's left leg looks as if it is made from a piece of polished wood. Only the creases in the sleeves of Joseph's shirt and his wrinkled brow show La Tour's earlier fondness for depicting textures. Now he has purified and refined his visual language, as Caravaggio did in his last works, removing anything not essential to a spiritual message painted for a viewer seeking inspiration for his faith.

Simon Vouet's Successors

The isolation of La Tour in Lorraine helps to explain the originality of his artistic language, and its limited influence. The paintings of peasant families attributed to Louis Le Nain (1600/10–1648) and his brothers Antoine (1600/10–1648) and Mathieu (1600/10–1677) are more puzzling. The Le Nain brothers came from Laon, a cathedral town to the north-east of Paris. They settled in Paris in a shared residence around 1630 while maintaining their connections with Laon. From 1641 onwards they signed and dated some of their works, though only with their last name. No paintings are dated after 1648, when all three were founder members of the French Academy (both Louis and Antoine died later that year). A group of paintings of better-dressed subjects was associated with the surviving brother Mathieu but recent scholarly opinion does not even accept

4.26 Louis Le Nain (?), *A Peasant Family*, c. 1640. Oil on canvas, 44½ × 62½ in (113 × 159 cm). Louvre, Paris.

4.27 (below) Louis Le Nain (?), *Landscape with Peasants*, c. 1640. Oil on canvas, 18 × 22½ in (46.5 × 57 cm). National Gallery of Art, Washington, DC. Samuel H. Kress Collection.

this division of their hands. They also produced more conventional religious works and an occasional mythology and allegory.

Their works are not rare, proving that they were appreciated both in the seventeenth century and later, but there are no recorded patrons of these images of the rural poor seated around a table (Fig **4.26**) or standing beside their farm buildings with the flat fields of northern France in the distance (Fig. **4.27**). Are these portraits of actual families or generic images of typical agricultural workers? These families do not look as if they could afford to commission portraits of themselves, let alone a fine glass with which to offer a visitor some wine, though one scholar has suggested that they may not have been as poor as they seem to us. The Le Nains always portrayed the worthy poor; their subjects look honest and hard working, not guilty of the bad behavior seen in Netherlandish images of peasants. Children are shown with particular empathy. The outdoor scene is remarkable among seventeenth-century images of the countryside for its simplicity; it is as much a portrait of this plain landscape as it is of its inhabitants.

The two best painters to emerge from Vouet's orbit did not go to Italy. Laurent de la Hyre (1606–56) did not even study with him, yet his idealizing elegance could not have existed without Vouet's synthesis of Raphael, Reni, and Veronese. Eustache Le Sueur (1616–55) did train with Vouet but soon muted the more extravagant elements of his master's style to emphasize Raphael instead. The term "Attic classicism" has been coined for their work, because its refinement recalls Greek art rather than the robust proportions of Roman art, though few antiquarians or artists would distinguish them at the time.

Le Sueur's *Sleeping Venus* (Fig. **4.28**) shows how he tamed the almost vulgar excesses of Vouet's plump female nudes with pale colors and an exquisitely polished finish. This Venus has a body similar to those of Vouet, especially the enormous but apparently boneless arms and tapering fingertips, but the nuanced delicacy with which her pale flesh is set off against the white sheets and huge pillow edged with pale blue stripes surpasses Vouet's attempts at such effects. Turning her body toward the viewer while throwing back her head and left arm, Venus signals her

availability, a message reinforced by the lighting which places her head and left arm in shadow, thus emphasizing the rest of her immaculately smooth skin. The fires of passion are represented by the plum red of the velvet curtain draped around her bed and Vulcan's forge in the background, where the god hammers out arms for Aeneas while she waits: this is the narrative pretext for this carefully staged moment of erotic theater. In the center of the painting, Cupid tells us to keep quiet. His ruddy flesh contrasts provocatively with the pale pinks of Venus' luxuriantly displayed body. It is a particularly seductive portrayal of a woman awaiting her lover, unrivaled in France for its sensuality until the next century.

4.28 Eustache Le Sueur, *Sleeping Venus*, c. 1638. Oil on canvas, 48 × 46 in (121.9 × 116.8 cm). Fine Arts Museum of San Francisco, CA.

Philippe de Champaigne

Vouet and his circle catered to aristocratic patrons keen to flaunt their wealth and status in their new town houses. The middle-class patrons of Philippe de Champaigne (1602–74) believed in restraint rather than ostentation. He was born in Brussels and trained there, settling in Paris in 1621. He had studied with the landscape painter Jacques Fouquières and knew the work of Rubens. Champaigne's refined technique and his subtle grasp of the evanescent colors of human flesh reveal his Flemish origins but otherwise his work could not be less Rubensian in its avoidance of drama, spatial complexity, and movement. His work found a sympathetic audience among Parisian magistrates and clergy and even to some extent at court, especially for his portraits. He was a founder member of the Academy of Painting in 1648. He produced altarpieces and private devotional images for many religious orders in Paris; in his later years he was closely associated with the Jansenist convent of Port Royal, where his two daughters took orders in 1655 and 1657.

The *Dream of St. Joseph* (Fig. **4.29**), painted around 1638 for the church of the Minims in Paris, shows Champaigne's preference for a simple setting that places all the emphasis on the figures: St. Joseph on the left, the robust angel flying down toward him—a rare Rubensian flourish—and the praying Virgin Mary in the right background. While the yellow robe of Joseph and the blue and red worn by the Virgin are traditional colors, Joseph's overgarment is usually a dull ocher and his undergarment gray-violet. The golden yellow over pale violet used here draws all attention to him. He is not the old Joseph of medieval tradition but a handsome man. La Tour (see Fig. 4.25) still retained the traditional image of an old man more like a grandfather than a potential father of Christ, probably in deference to conservative provincial patrons. Murillo's much later *The Two Trinities* (see Fig. 3.44) also shows the new Joseph, which had by then replaced the medieval type throughout Europe.

Champaigne, who dominated portrait production in Paris during his lifetime, rarely painted full-length portraits because his clients would have regarded it as unseemly ostentation. He usually painted a bust or, at most, a half-length image that includes the hands. Almost all of his sitters were male. The color schemes are austere: black clothes, white collars, and dark backgrounds with only the flesh tones of the face and hands relieving the monochrome palette. Apart from Cardinal Richelieu, of whom Champaigne painted several full-length portraits (e.g. National Gallery, London; Louvre, Paris), he used this grandest of formats only five other times. The portrait of *Omer Talon* (Fig. **4.30**) is arguably the finest of them. Talon, then fifty-four, was a distinguished lawyer who was president (*Premier Avocat*) of the Parlement in 1641. He played an important role during the civil turmoil of the Fronde (1644, 1648–9), offering sage counsel to Anne of Austria and her Minister, Cardinal Mazarin, as he tried to negotiate concessions between the Crown and the Parlement that could have prevented the violent confrontations that followed in 1651–2. Talon ordered his portrait toward the end of his second term of office,

4.29 Philippe de Champaigne, *Dream of St. Joseph*, c. 1638. Oil on canvas, 82¼ × 61¼ in (208 × 155 cm). National Gallery, London.

4.30 Philippe de Champaigne, *Omer Talon*, 1649. Oil on canvas, 88½ × 63½ in (225 × 161.5 cm). National Gallery of Art, Washington, DC.

possibly to assert his authority as he and other leaders in the Parlement argued against the newly enforced property taxes being levied against Parisian landlords by corrupt tax officials. These taxes, brutally enforced in the countryside during a period of poor harvests, had caused extreme privation, even starvation, and finally rebellion among the peasants. Fearing greater destruction of their crops and property, landowners and nobles petitioned the Crown to moderate its demands.

Talon comes across as a man of power and accomplishment in perfect control of himself. His direct gaze and his crimson wool robes, played off against the sweep of wine-red silk draped behind him, arrest the viewer's attention. Champaigne's meticulous surface finish and the perfectly calibrated composition become visual metaphors for the order and precision of the legal profession practiced by this exemplary representative. A low viewpoint puts us in our place, roughly level with Talon's knees, unable to see the surface of the table covered with a luxurious Turkish carpet, on which is displayed a gold table clock, a status symbol as well as a reminder of the brevity of life. The other devices used to communicate his high social rank—the column on a tall base and the cloth of honor—had been

French Painting and Printmaking

4.31 Philippe de Champaigne, *Mother Cathérine-Agnès Arnauld and Sister Cathérine de Ste. Suzanne Champaigne*, 1662. Oil on canvas, 65 × 90⅛ in (165 × 229 cm). Louvre, Paris.

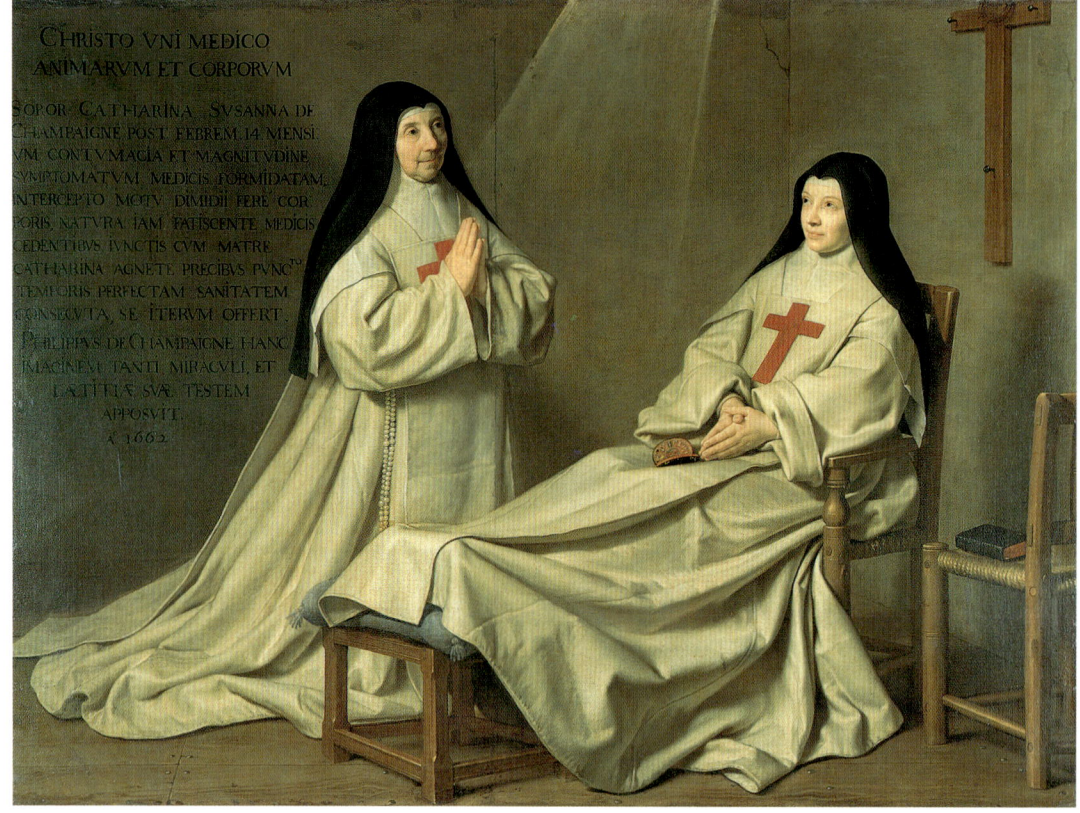

used by Anthony van Dyck and others before, but the way in which Champaigne rendered the various surfaces of stone, wool, silk, skin, and carpet lifts the portrait well beyond what might otherwise have been a conventional, even tedious, exercise. Given the political situation in Paris in 1649, could the shadow cast on the statue of Justice by the cloth of honor, an attribute usually associated with supreme rulers such as kings, symbolize the possible consequences of the Crown's failure to heed the advice of the Parlement's representatives?

Champaigne's most famous work is both a portrait and a religious painting: the ex-voto portrait of *Mother Cathérine-Agnès Arnauld and Sister Cathérine de Ste. Suzanne Champaigne* (Fig. 4.31) shows the artist's daughter seated on the right with her legs supported on a footstool and the Mother Superior of Port Royal kneeling in prayer beside her. Catherine had entered the convent of Port Royal in 1657 as a postulant. In 1660 she became paralyzed by an illness that was thought to be incurable; she was healed the following year, purportedly through the prayers of Mother Agnès and the other nuns. The bare walls of Catherine's cell carry an inscription that describes the illness and its miraculous cure and records the artist's gratitude to God for this outcome. He gave the painting to the convent soon afterwards. Its limited color scheme reflects the vows of poverty of this Jansenist order. Apart from the crimson cross on the women's heavy white robes and their pale flesh tones, the painting is executed entirely in neutral tones of beige, brown, gray, and black. The only furniture in the room apart from that supporting Catherine is a simple wooden chair with a woven rush seat and a wooden cross on the wall behind her. Three nails mark the places where Christ's palms and feet would have been attached as reminders of his sacrifice. Only the viewer realizes that a miracle has occurred, because a beam of light enters the windowless cell just behind Mother Agnès. Neither woman seems aware of it. Their serene facial expressions convey their complete faith in God. It is not clear whether Catherine knows that she is no longer paralyzed or is simply waiting to be healed, confident that it will happen. This miracle is therefore imperceptible. Nothing could offer a greater contrast to the awestruck faces raised to heaven seen in Italian images of saints in the ecstatic throes of visions (see Fig. 1.131). The

Jansenists of Port Royal were particularly opposed to such emotional displays of Christian faith which they associated above all with the Jesuit Order. Champaigne was completely in sympathy with their beliefs, as powerfully expressed in this painting.

Nicolas Poussin in Paris and Rome

The two most admired French painters of the seventeenth century, Nicolas Poussin (1594–1665) and Claude Lorrain, spent most of their working lives in Rome. Nevertheless they are part of the history of French seventeenth-century painting for both influenced artists in Paris once collectors there began to acquire their works after 1630 and Poussin was also sought out by French artists who went to Rome to complete their training.

Poussin was born near Les Andelys in Normandy, a small town about sixty miles (100 km) down river from Paris on the Seine. His father is said to have come from a prosperous family who lost their property during the Wars of Religion. His mother was illiterate despite being the daughter of a city official. Such parents would not seem likely to produce a son who would become a painter of such intellectual depth that art historians find in his work the most subtle commentaries not only on ancient history, philosophy, and epic poetry, but also on Catholic dogma and current politics. His parents must have given him a good education, hoping probably that he would become a notary or lawyer, for his knowledge of Latin, ancient history, and mythology impressed other artists when he reached Rome. He is said to have decided to become a painter after watching a mediocre artist, Quentin Varin (c. 1570–1634), at work in a local church in 1612.

Poussin's next decade is poorly documented but according to Bellori, who knew him, he studied in Paris. A friend with court connections gave him access to Italian art in the royal collections. Two attempts to reach Rome were thwarted: in Florence "some incident" obliged him to return to Paris; and, on the second occasion, he ran out of money in Lyons. Not until 1622 did he get a proper commission—six tempera paintings for the Jesuit College in Paris to celebrate the canonization of their founder saints, Ignatius of Loyola and Francis Xavier. The Italian poet Giovanni Battista Marino (1569–1625), who had been living in Paris since 1615, was impressed, and offered Poussin room and board and thus access to his library and art collection, mostly by Italian artists. Marino was then supervising the publication of his ambitious poem *L'Adone*, which elaborates in richly ornamented language stories found in Ovid's *Metamorphoses*. A small group of drawings by Poussin which illustrate Ovidian

4.32 Nicolas Poussin, *Orpheus in Hades*, 1622–23. Pen and ink wash, 7⅜ × 12½ in (18.9 × 32 cm). The Royal Collection, England, © 2004, Her Majesty Queen Elizabeth II.

4.33 Nicolas Poussin, *The Death of Germanicus*, 1627. Oil on canvas, 58¼ × 78 in (147.96 × 198.12 cm). William Hood Dunwoody Fund. Minneapolis Institute of Arts, Minneapolis, MN.

tales are said to have been made for Marino (Fig. 4.32). They are the only works made by Poussin before 1624 that survive in good condition.

It is important to appreciate the degree of determination and persistence that carried Poussin from Normandy to Rome, where he was still a novice painter in his early thirties. He left Paris just as his fortunes changed, completing an altarpiece depicting the death of the Virgin for Notre Dame in 1623 (lost since the Revolution, it has recently been found but in lamentable condition). Marino had preceded him, reaching Rome in 1623 in triumph after the publication of *L'Adone*. He told his friends at the Barberini court about Poussin's imminent arrival. Cardinal Francesco Barberini's secretary, Cassiano dal Pozzo (1588–1657), would become Poussin's most important patron for the next twenty years. Poussin is said to have spent some time in Venice on his way south; many of his less formal works of the 1620s suggest that he did so.

Poussin's hardships continued after he reached Rome in March 1624. Marino left for Naples where he died in 1625 and Cardinal Francesco left Rome for Paris on a diplomatic mission, taking Cassiano with him. After difficulty selling two large battle paintings, Poussin began making small mythological works with landscape settings in the Venetian style that had more appeal (see Fig. 4.36). He also began absorbing all that Rome had to teach him: he studied anatomy and perspective; made copies of the reliefs on Trajan's column and on sarcophagi and vases; and went to the Vatican to see Raphael's frescoes in the Stanze and such classical statues as the Belvedere torso, the Laocoön, and the Apollo Belvedere. His rare dated paintings from the 1620s show an astonishing degree of change and progress.

His first commission for the Barberini family, the *Sack of Jerusalem* (Jerusalem Museum, Israel), paid for in February 1626, is impressive and ambitious (the subject was unprecedented) but it is also full of awkwardly drawn figures and the perspective of the burning temple is faulty. His second, *The Death of Germanicus* (Fig. 4.33), finished a year later, is a masterpiece, followed quickly by another, *The Martyrdom of St. Erasmus* (see Fig. 4.34), in 1629. Beautifully staged and executed with lively brushwork and strong colors controlled with virtuoso aplomb, this prestigious commission for St. Peter's established Poussin as one of the best of a new generation of painters in Rome that included Pietro da Cortona and Andrea Sacchi. In September 1630 he married Anne-Marie Dughet, daughter of the French cook in whose home Poussin had found lodging.

The story of Germanicus would have been familiar only to the most highly educated Roman audiences at this time. Poussin apparently chose the subject himself, again one of many subjects that he introduced to the history of art. Germanicus (15 BC–AD 19), who acquired his name after leading successful campaigns against the Germanic tribes, was a Roman general, and the adopted son of the Emperor Tiberius. Following the orders of Tiberius, who was jealous of his son's growing reputation not only for military prowess but also for the nobility of his character, Germanicus was poisoned by the local ruler in Syria. His loyal soldiers stand around his bed swearing to avenge his death while he gestures weakly to his family on the right, whom he urged to "submit to cruel fortune" with dignity before bidding them farewell. Poussin isolates Germanicus by leaving the space in front of him open. The white pillow and sheets pull our eyes there first; then gradually we explore the reactions of the standing soldiers who fill the left half of the painting and then the smaller group of women and children on the right. The woman covering her eyes is Agrippina, his wife, and the child who stands beside her with his hand on her leg is the future Emperor Caligula. The colors they wear are quieter than the primary reds, blues, and gold of the men who represent different military ranks. They all respond with distress and compassion to their beloved leader's fate. The man on the left with his back to us is weeping, the man next to him touches his own face in a gesture of sympathy while others reach out toward their dying leader as if they would embrace him once more. His discarded armor lies on the ground at the foot of his bed.

Poussin later painted many works using the basic compositional format seen here—a rectangular picture field, a group of figures arranged in a loosely spaced frieze across the width of the canvas, and an appropriate setting whose forms accent the key figures. The convincing depiction of a range of *affetti*, that is, emotional responses to the event shown, was also to be a constant element in his work. The group of grieving men around the deathbed in *Germanicus* echoes a famous composition found on many Roman sarcophagi depicting the death of Meleager; the cloth hanging behind the group, however, is an addition that creates a more intimate setting and focuses our attention on the drama taking place within a spacious stone hall. Poussin's emphatic use of the three primary colors—blue for the drapery behind the dying hero, red on the cloak of the soldier beneath the lighted archway, golden yellow for the armor on the officer raising his hand as he swears to avenge this crime—will also become a characteristic trait. The officer swearing an oath, firmly erect in the middle of the canvas, just below the main vertical pilaster of the architectural setting, hints at the events that will follow—active revenge by the men, passive resignation by the women.

For a work that was not on public display but remained in Palazzo Barberini in Rome until 1958, where it was accessible only to visitors with letters of introduction, the *Death of Germanicus* had a surprisingly strong impact on later generations of artists. The theme of the hero on his deathbed gathered momentum during the next two centuries, as it was often chosen by artists for the "masterpiece" that would qualify them for membership in the academies of Paris and London, as well as by established painters. Jacques Louis David's *Death of Socrates* (1787, the Metropolitan Museum, New York) and Benjamin West's *Death of General Wolfe* (1771, National Gallery of Canada, Ottawa) are among the best-known examples.

4.34 Nicolas Poussin, *The Martyrdom of St. Erasmus*, 1628–29. Oil on canvas, 10 ft 6 in × 6 ft 1 in (3.2 × 1.86 m). Pinacoteca, Vatican Museums, Rome.

Poussin's *The Martyrdom of St. Erasmus* (Fig. 4.34) depicts the execution of Erasmus, Bishop of Antioch, by having his intestines wound around a windlass—as ordered, according to legend, around AD 303 by the Emperor Diocletian. The saint is a handsome man bound to a wooden trestle that displays his body at an angle to the viewer, his head and shoulders toward us, his gorgeous red and gold brocade cape filling the foreground. His white bishop's miter has been tossed onto it as a sign of the Romans' lack of respect for the Church. Little blood is visible around the slit in his stomach where an executioner grasps the emerging rope of intestine in both hands. The blood is represented symbolically instead by the executioner's and the saint's red robes. Both the executioner and the priest stare at the saint, urging him to change his allegiance to the pagan gods of antiquity represented by a golden statue of Hercules on the upper right. An assistant wearing blue behind the man in red leans over to watch the saint's reactions, astonished at his bravery and self-control. The man turning the windlass in the background looks up at the sky, as if aware of the two putti overhead who carry the martyr's crown of laurel and palm branch. They look down at the saint, pulling our gaze back to him. His ideally proportioned body represents his nobility of character. He stares up at the sky, withdrawn into his own thoughts as he ignores the harangue of the pagan priest. Attention is focused on the human drama, even though the center of the picture is occupied by the almost surgical depiction of the method of execution.

To the right of *The Martyrdom of St. Erasmus* in the central altar of St. Peter's north transept is Valentin de Boulogne's *The Martyrdom of Sts. Processus and Martinian* (Fig. 4.35). The two saints in Valentin's picture were guarding St. Peter in the Mamertine Prison near the Roman forum when they were converted to Christianity by his eloquence. Thrown into jail with Peter, these Roman soldiers were tortured by being stretched on a rack, the moment in their story shown by Valentin, before being beheaded. Processus is stretched out with his arms behind his head; Martinian's feet are next to Processus' left arm, his ribcage and face visible just to the right of his companion's ribs. They seem to be parallel to the picture plane but must be at a slight angle to account for the foreshortening of their figures. Valentin was an experienced painter by 1629 but he had never worked on this scale with so many figures. He does not marshal his figures as effectively as Poussin, whose design is echoed not only in Processus's pose but also in the circular movement that guides the viewer around the canvas, though counterclockwise instead of clockwise. A young soldier seen from behind in the right foreground snatches a long stick with which to beat the two victims. Just behind him is an official seated on a dais who shields his face with his hands, as if he cannot

4.35 Valentin de Boulogne, *The Martyrdom of Sts. Processus and Martinian*, 1628–29. Oil on canvas, 10 ft 6 in × 6 ft 1 in (3.2 × 1.86 m). Pinacoteca, Vatican Museums, Rome.

French Painting and Printmaking 277

bear to watch this spectacle. An angel like Caravaggio's bringing the palm to St. Matthew (see Fig. 1.44) leans down from a cloud to offer one to Processus; a younger angel waits behind with a second palm for Martinian. On the left is Lucina, a Christian woman believed to have comforted the saints and encouraged them to remain true to their faith. Processus's serene expression and the sympathetic gazes of Lucina and the angel all draw attention to the two saints' exemplary behavior, preferring painful deaths to rejection of their faith.

When Valentin's dark canvas with its color scheme of chocolate browns and inky blues was installed next to Poussin's brightly lit canvas full of red, blue, and cream, it was inevitable that they would be compared. The German artist and writer Joachim von Sandrart (1606–88), who was in Rome at the time, reported that their relative merits were much debated. The conclusion was that both were outstanding works but that Poussin's invention was superior as was his depiction of expression and feeling while Valentin's painting had greater naturalism, better union of tonal values and color harmony. Sandrart's account has been misread in the past to argue that Poussin's altarpiece was poorly received, thus explaining his failure to receive any other public commissions in Rome. The text states that both altarpieces were appreciated for their distinctive merits; both artists were also paid a bonus and Poussin was paid 50 scudi more than Valentin. When Bernini was in Paris in 1665, he told Paul Fréart de Chantelou that Guido Reni had accused him of praising Poussin's *St. Erasmus* excessively to Urban VIII. Bernini then told Guido that if he was a painter, he would have felt mortified by Poussin's achievement.

Poussin's evolution from subdued colors to a rich palette stressing primary colors can be seen by comparing his *Death of Adonis* of around 1626 (Fig. **4.36**) with his *Tancred and Erminia* of about 1635 (Fig. **4.37**). Though close in size, the grander proportions of the figures in the later picture make it seem much larger. The subject of both is frustrated love—Venus pours nectar on the dead body of her young lover, whom she failed to keep from the hunt she knew would kill him; Erminia desperately cuts off her hair to staunch the blood flowing from Tancred's battle wounds, which she thought had killed him. Both women gaze intently at their beloved, Venus in quiet resignation, Erminia with desperation because Tancred has just revived enough to moan and prove that he is still alive. Much of the earlier canvas is shown in half light and shadow that creates a mood of sadness. Its expansive setting and small figures distance us from the mourning Venus, whose face is small, her expression unclear. Erminia, by contrast, dominates the center foreground, though Tancred's magnificent

4.36 Nicolas Poussin, *Death of Adonis*, c. 1626. Oil on canvas, 22½ × 50⅜ in (57 × 128 cm). Musée des Beaux Arts de Caen.

body draped in golden yellow cloth and supported by his arms bearer, Vafrino, demands attention too. Tancred's shadowed head and shoulders frustrate our efforts to see if he is alive, making us experience what Erminia is feeling as she tries to save his life. Though the overall light in this work is more subdued than in most of Poussin's work of the 1630s, it is still lighter than in the earlier picture. The saturated lapis blue of Adonis' garment has become a lighter blue on Erminia, and the orange robe beneath him has become yellow on Tancred. Adonis has deep blue sandals, Tancred has white ones. Both works communicate a passionate romanticism unprecedented in Roman art. Even Guercino's *Erminia Discovering the Wounded Tancred* (see Fig. 1.73), painted roughly a decade earlier, looks rhetorical and melodramatic next to Poussin's carefully orchestrated narrative.

Poussin after 1630

After 1630, Poussin worked only for private clients, except for two altarpieces made in Paris in 1641–2. He also slowed down his rate of production and took more care over the preparation of his canvases and finish. Having found astute and influential patrons willing to let him paint novel subjects even before his reputation was established, Poussin retreated from the public arena and set about perfecting his painting for which he never again lacked clients. Between 1630 and 1631, Poussin completed two large paintings for Fabrizio Valguarnera, a Sicilian merchant who was laundering illicit funds by buying art. Poussin's testimony given during Valguarnera's trial in 1631, with that of some other artists working for Valguarnera, provides invaluable information about relations between artists and patrons as well as two rare dates for

4.37 Nicolas Poussin, *Tancred and Erminia*, c. 1635. Oil on canvas, 29⅝ × 39¼ in (75.5 × 99.7 cm). Barber Institute of Fine Arts, University of Birmingham, England.

Poussin's poorly documented production. Valguarnera visited Poussin's studio, saw there the unfinished *The Plague of Ashdod* (Fig. **4.38**) and asked the artist to finish it for him. Poussin then proposed a second purchase, a "giardino di fiori" (garden of flowers), which the patron called "Primavera" (Spring); today it is usually known as *The Realm of Flora* (Fig. **4.39**).

In other words, Poussin began the *Plague at Ashdod* without having secured a patron and, having found one, proposed a different, less gloomy subject. Unlike *The Plague*, *The Realm of Flora* cannot be connected with a single literary text, though the flower myths shown can be found in Ovid and passages of Marino's poetry conjure up garden images similar to the painting: the subject matter as presented here is, however, Poussin's invention. Both are large canvases but they are not the same size and were not conceived as pendants. Rather Poussin intentionally created for one patron two large, complex paintings of novel subjects whose mood and appearance are in complete contrast, in order to demonstrate his abilities to the Roman art world.

Their contrasting styles show that Poussin was already selecting the appropriate "mode" for each painting according to its subject. Poussin explained the modes in a letter to Paul Fréart de Chantelou (1609–1694), one of his most important patrons after 1640. The letter was written after Chantelou complained that Poussin had sent a better picture to a rival patron, Jean Pointel.

> *If you feel affection for the picture of* Moses Found in the Waters of the Nile *[now Louvre, Paris], which belongs to M. Pointel, is that a proof that I made it more lovingly than I did yours? Do you not see that, along with your own disposition, in the nature of the subject lies the cause of this effect, and that the subjects which I am treating for you have to be done in a different manner? All artifice in painting depends on this. . . .*

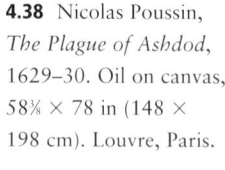

4.38 Nicolas Poussin, *The Plague of Ashdod*, 1629–30. Oil on canvas, 58¾ × 78 in (148 × 198 cm). Louvre, Paris.

Our wise ancient Greeks, inventors of all beautiful things, found several Modes by means of which they produced marvelous effects. This word "Mode" means actually the rule or measure and form, which serves us in our productions. This rule constrains us not to exaggerate by making us act in all things with a certain restraint and moderation [which] is nothing more than a certain determined manner or order, and includes the procedure by which the object is preserved in its essence. [. . .] the ancient sages attributed to each its own effects. Because of this they called the Dorian Mode stable, grave and severe, and applied it to subjects which are grave and severe and full of wisdom. And proceeding thence to pleasant and joyous things, they used the Phrygian Mode, in which there are more minute modulations than in any other mode, and a more clear-cut aspect. These two styles and no others were praised and approved of by Plato and Aristotle, who deemed the others superfluous; they considered this [Phrygian Mode] intense, vehement, violent, and very severe, and capable of astonishing people. I hope before another year is out to paint a subject in this Phrygian Mode. The subject of frightful wars lends itself to this manner. They [the ancients] also decided that the Lydian Mode lends itself to tragic subjects because it has neither the simplicity of the Dorian nor the severity of the Phrygian. The Hypolidian Mode contains a certain suavity and sweetness which fills the souls of spectators with joy; it lends itself to subjects of divine glory, and paradise. The ancients invented the Ionic, with which they represented bacchanalian dances and feasts in order to achieve a festive effect."[5]

4.39 Nicolas Poussin, *The Realm of Flora*, 1630–31. Oil on canvas, 4 ft 4 in × 5 ft 11 in (1.31 × 1.81 m). Staatliche Kunstsammlungen, Dresden.

Since Poussin does not connect any of his own works with a particular mode in this letter, it is not always easy to understand how he adapted these ancient modes derived from music and literature to his art. Is *The Martyrdom of St. Erasmus* in the Phrygian Mode, used for

French Painting and Printmaking

"pleasant and joyous things" but also for "intense, vehement, violent, and very severe" themes? Is *The Death of Germanicus* in the Lydian Mode, used for tragic subjects? In an earlier letter to another patron, Poussin says that he used a "soft" style for a picture of *Armida abducting Rinaldo* (Staatliche Museen, Berlin) and a "severe" style for a moral tale of treason punished, *Camillus and the School Master of the Falerii* (Louvre, Paris). Poussin's letter to Chantelou continues with a brief discussion of Virgil's poetry and how he used the sounds of words to suggest appropriate moods, so that "in the portions where he speaks of love, one finds that he has skillfully chosen such words as are sweet, pleasant and very delightful to hear; whereas, if he sings of a feat of arms or describes a naval battle or a storm, he chooses hard, rasping, harsh words, so that when one hears or pronounces them, they produce a feeling of fear."

The letter implies that Poussin adjusted the colors, lighting, settings, and visual rhythms of each work to produce more seductive or abrasive or somber effects, depending on the subject. He was not alone nor the first to vary his style to create different moods. Annibale's late *Pietà* (see Fig. 1.35) is painted in a limited color range of blues, violet, and browns with overcast light that creates an appropriately somber mood but his *Temptation of St. Anthony* (National Gallery, London) painted around the same time, is much brighter. Its clarity encourages the viewer to consider the saint's exemplary behavior.

The Plague of Ashdod was painted during a severe outbreak of the bubonic plague in Italy in 1629–31, an event, as noted earlier, when images

4.40 Nicolas Poussin, *The Birth of Venus*, 1638–40. Oil on canvas, 45 × 57¾ in (114.3 × 146.6 cm). George W. Elkins Collection. Philadelphia Museum of Art, Philadelphia, PA.

282 Chapter 4: France

of Saints Sebastian and Roch, or local patron saints, were commissioned to intercede with the Virgin for protection (see Fig. 1.67). Poussin instead used an Old Testament story about God's vengeance after the sacred ark of the Israelites was captured by the Philistines and placed in the Temple of Dagon (I Samuel 5–6). The statue of the false god has fallen over, its head and hands severed from its body. Rats are scurrying about the temple precinct. Men, women, and children are dying. The overcast sky and somber color scheme complement the mood of tragedy—no rich lapis blues, crimson, or gold, but instead more neutral colors like ocher, rusty browns, and blues toned down with gray. The Doric Order used on a large building in the right background was declared appropriate for tragic stage sets by Sebastiano Serlio in his *Architettura* of 1551. Poussin knew that text and a print based on a lost drawing by Raphael of *The Plague of Phrygia*, which also shows a man holding his nose against the stench of death while gently pushing the baby away from its dead mother's breast.

The Realm of Flora exudes instead the pale sunshine of an early spring day when its warmth seems to pull the flowers out of the soil. Four white horses pull the chariot of the sun god Apollo across a light blue sky. The blues, creams, and yellows that fill the sky set the tone for the entire painting, where garments of light blues, rose pink, gold, olive green, and warm orange clothe the beautiful young men and women who fill the garden and act out the myths that created the flowers associated with them. On the left Ajax commits suicide, though no one seems to notice: a carnation springs from his blood as it reaches the soil. Narcissus stares at his reflection in a vase, ignoring his beautiful companion. Behind him Clytie, leaning against a basket of her sunflowers, stares at Apollo overhead. On the right Smilax (bindweed) and Crocus embrace. Hyacinth touches the fatal wound in his head while contemplating the flowers named for him. Adonis nearby with his pair of elegant hunting hounds points to a wound in his leg whose blood produces a pretty blue flower (it should be but is not an anemone). The young woman wearing green and dancing in the center is Primavera or Spring, the season when flowers return after the chill of winter. A herm of Priapus, the fertility god often placed in gardens by the Romans, regards the scene with a knowing smile. The light colors and lyrical mood belie the assorted tragic stories represented here—Ajax's falling pose is echoed and balanced by the dancing pose of Primavera as if to let us know that this is only a story about a flower, not a human tragedy. The contrast in mood with *The Plague of Ashdod* could not be greater. The daylight clarity of Flora's kingdom, more typical of Poussin's art in the 1630s than in the previous decade, seems to announce his next phase.

A number of Poussin's most ambitious paintings of the 1630s have subjects that show figures in movement, a phase represented here by the painting known as *The Birth of Venus* of 1638–40 (Fig. **4.40**) made for Cardinal Richelieu. The subject of this assembly of sea gods and goddesses, nymphs, tritons, dolphins, and putti is unclear. While the identity of Neptune on the left with his trident and hippocamp-steeds is clear, that of the woman in the center is not. She has been called Amphitrite, Galatea, and Venus. The cupids who cavort above her toss roses, shoot arrows, and carry a blazing torch, all allusions to love and marriage. Neptune is not known to have had an affair with Venus, however, while Galatea was loved by Acis and Polyphemus, but not by Neptune. Amphitrite, on the other hand, was a sea nymph who resisted the advances of Neptune, fleeing as far as she could until persuaded to return to him by a dolphin, three of whom tow the scallop-shell craft bearing the central female figure. Still, if this is Amphitrite, why is Cupid riding toward her from the sky on the left in a golden chariot pulled by white doves, birds associated only with Venus? Love, marriage, and beauty are her realms. It seems most likely that Poussin has depicted the birth of Venus from the sea after all and Neptune is present only to escort her safely to shore. Even the artist's most literate spectators, who would have known that the ancient Greek painter Apelles depicted the newly born Venus rising from the sea wringing water from her hair, were puzzled about the subject. Bellori avoided the question altogether, calling the picture the *Triumph of Neptune*.

Confusion with the story of Galatea exists because Raphael's fresco in the Villa Farnesina in

Rome of that flirt riding her dolphin-powered shell was Poussin's major visual source (see Fig. 1.33). His putto in the center foreground is so close in pose and position to his twin in the fresco that Poussin presumably meant his audience to recognize the borrowing and to compare the two paintings. Like Raphael, Poussin creates a symmetrical composition of sea-borne figures but on a horizontal canvas, not a vertical fresco field. He also repeats poses in back and front views and uses a clockwise movement to direct our attention around the picture field. Raphael's design has been transformed into a much richer, more ambitious spectacle. The result is both a tribute to Raphael and a challenge: Poussin offers a more complex variation on the design by his Renaissance idol that some might even think superior.

The artificiality of this beautifully balanced ensemble resists being read as reality but it should be noted that Neptune and Venus are about to land. There is not enough water to support either the dolphin below the putto in the central foreground, however, or those behind him. The woman on the right with her back to us is reclining on a rock draped with a shot-silk cloth of cream and blue. Distracted by Neptune and Venus, the viewer may see her as part of the approaching sea-borne crowd. The color scheme emphasizes flesh tones, light blues, rose and peach pinks, a palette similar to that of the *Flora* without its greens, but the figures and animals all have greater mass. The foreshortened forms of the airborne cupids against the gray cloud are as brilliantly realized as those in any ceiling fresco by Poussin's Italian contemporaries.

Between 1638 and 1648, Poussin executed two sets of paintings illustrating the Seven Sacraments of the Roman Catholic Church, the first for Cassiano dal Pozzo (finished 1642) and the second for Paul Fréart de Chantelou, one of his two major patrons after 1640. Of the numerous works that Poussin made for Cassiano, the set of Sacraments was regarded then and now as the finest. Chantelou saw Cassiano's set and asked Poussin to make him copies; unable to find an artist capable of doing this to his standards, Poussin made him his own separate set between 1644 and 1648.

The Seven Sacraments were rarely depicted either in one work or as a unified series, except on medieval fonts and occasionally in early Netherlandish painting. Poussin used events in the New Testament to illustrate five of the Sacraments—*Baptism* is that of Christ by St. John; *Eucharist* is the "Last Supper," the event on which the sacrament of communion is based; *Marriage* is represented by that of the Virgin and Joseph; and *Ordination* is shown by Christ giving the keys to Peter as the first bishop of the Roman Catholic Church. For *Penance* Poussin chose the moment when the penitent harlot, always identified as the Magdalene, anointed Christ's feet with precious oils when he was dining with Simon the Pharisee (Luke 7: 36–50). Only the *Confirmation* and *Extreme Unction* could not be shown using stories in the life of Christ, so Poussin set them in the first decades of Christianity, showing Roman families converting to the Christian faith in the scenes of confirmation and being blessed by a Christian priest on their deathbeds in those of *Extreme Unction*. The *Baptism* from the first set is now in the National Gallery in Washington; *Penance* was destroyed in a fire, leaving five in the collection of the Duke of Rutland at Belvoir Castle in Leicestershire. All seven paintings in the second set are on permanent loan from the Duke of Sutherland to the National Gallery of Scotland in Edinburgh.

The first set brought together Poussin's and Cassiano's shared interest in the early history of the Catholic Church and in the minutiae of daily life in antiquity, Roman as well as Christian, in order to provide a historically accurate image of early Christian rituals. Cassiano had commissioned drawings of every kind of tool, ornament, furnishing, and clothing as well as the grander remnants of Roman civilization such as statues, reliefs, vases, and architectural fragments. The scene of *Extreme Unction* in the first set (Fig. 4.41) takes place in a simple room with wooden beams supporting the ceiling and no decoration except a circular stone molding on the wall behind the dying man's bed. This seems to be the room of an ordinary citizen of Rome shortly after Christian rites began to be practiced. To the right is a table with lion-shaped legs of a type seen on Roman reliefs, and, on it, vases and dishes of authentic design too. Everyone wears classical dress, though Roman garments were not dyed these bright colors. The priest who anoints the

4.41 Nicolas Poussin, *Extreme Unction*, c. 1638–40. Oil on canvas, 37½ × 47½ in (95.2 × 120.6 cm). Belvoir Castle, Leicestershire, England.

4.42 Nicolas Poussin, *Ordination*, c. 1638–40. Oil on canvas, 37⅝ × 47⅝ in (95.5 × 121 cm). Belvoir Castle, Leicestershire, England.

French Painting and Printmaking **285**

dying man wears a heavy ocher robe, his acolyte assistant a red one. These two notes of brighter color bracket the torso of the man whose family and friends have gathered around him, reacting in various ways to this inevitable moment. Their responses recall both *The Death of Germanicus* and Domenichino's *Last Communion of St. Jerome* (see Fig. 1.59), a work Poussin is known to have admired. The filtered light that enters the simple room is both a metaphor for the fading life of the man receiving unction and a device to create a suitably somber setting.

To contrast with the dark indoor scene of *Extreme Unction* from the first set, *Ordination* from the second set has been chosen (Fig. **4.43**). This was, in fact, the work that so provoked Chantelou's complaint to Poussin that it resulted in the famous letter about the Modes quoted earlier. Its majestic solemnity is entirely appropriate to its theme. Christ stands in the center, one raised arm holding the golden key of heaven that he will hand to Peter, who kneels before him. His other hand with a silver key points at the ground, or, as Elizabeth Cropper and Charles Dempsey argue, to the base of the pier with the letter E engraved at its summit. The twelve apostles are arranged, six to either side, but in groupings that avoid a monotonous symmetry. Apart from the kneeling St. Peter in his traditional yellow cloak over a blue garment, and Paul, wearing a rose-red robe over green who stands just behind Christ's right side, none of the apostles can be identified.

4.43 Nicolas Poussin, *Ordination*, c. 1646. Oil on canvas, 46 × 70 in (117 × 178 cm). National Gallery of Scotland, Edinburgh (on loan).

Emphatic primary colors assert themselves—a splendid yellow cloak on the apostle nearest us on the left, a crimson cloak on his counterpart on the right with brilliant white on the apostle behind him. Their positions mark the starting point of a diagonal line created by the receding lines of apostles to left and right that lead the viewer's eyes to Christ but also beyond him into the setting, which includes some prominent architectural structures—a bridge behind Christ, a cubic building with a pyramidal roof on the right, and, on the left, the pier with the letter E.

The E almost certainly stands for Ecclesia (Church in Latin), and so for the Church, now being established by Christ through Peter. Cropper and Dempsey provide additional support for this interpretation, arguing that the pier is a sort of funerary monument marking the burial place of Peter, which was the traditional site of both Old and New St. Peter's. Thus it is also the rock (*petrus*) on which the Church is founded according to the Latin words of St. Matthew's Gospel (16: 18): "Tu es Petrus et super hanc petram aedificabo ecclesiam meam." The buildings not only give the design a sense of balance and solidity that adds to the ceremonial mood of the event but may also represent buildings in ancient Rome around the Vatican described in Antonio Bosio's book *Roma sotterranea* (1632). The cubic structure may be the tomb of Scipio Africanus, and the bridge one that crossed the Tiber near the Castel Sant'Angelo, whose restored circular form can be detected behind the left end of the bridge. Every element in this carefully planned painting seems to carry a message but Poussin explained none of this symbolism to Chantelou in their correspondence.[6]

The setting for the first *Ordination* (Fig. 4.42) is a grassy path below a slope with a grove of trees—one for each apostle, as Verdi points out, with a dead tree on the right above the apostle furthest from Christ, who is probably Judas. The composition was inspired by Raphael's design for the Sistine Chapel tapestry, "Feed my Sheep", with Christ and Peter on the left and the apostles grouped to the right. Poussin breaks up Raphael's solid group of robed men and disposes the apostles in two casual groups spread across the width of the canvas. It looks as if they were strolling in the countryside when Christ stopped, told the

4.44 Nicolas Poussin, *Self-Portrait*, 1650. Oil on canvas, 38½ × 29⅛ in (98 × 74 cm). Louvre, Paris.

apostles that he had an announcement to make and asked St. Peter to approach. Paul may be the apostle just behind Peter wearing green over red, his traditional color combination, but he is not given the prominence that he normally enjoyed in depictions of the twelve apostles from medieval times onwards and that Poussin has restored to him in the second *Ordination*. The colors are more subdued and modulated in the first than in the second canvas. It is a beautiful picture, especially the landscape setting, but it lacks the powerful presence and more developed significance of the later interpretation.

While Poussin worked on the Sacraments for Chantelou, he did not neglect his other chief Parisian patron, Jean Pointel. Little is known about him except that he was a banker, that he visited Poussin in Rome in 1647, and that he had twenty-one works by Poussin in his home when he died in 1660. Poussin painted his only self-portraits for these two patrons, the first in 1649 for Pointel (Gemäldegalerie, Berlin), and the second in 1650 for Chantelou (Fig. **4.44**). Poussin looks approachable with a hint of a smile in Pointel's painting but has a stern, serious expression in that for Chantelou. Do these expressions portray two aspects of Poussin's character, or are they clues to the character of his relations with these two patrons? Unfortunately none of his letters to Pointel survives.

In 1648 Pointel asked Poussin to paint a picture that would rival Guido Reni's *Sewing*

French Painting and Printmaking **287**

4.45 Nicolas Poussin, *Rebecca and Eliezer at the Well*, 1648. Oil on canvas, 46½ × 78¾ in (118 × 199 cm). Louvre, Paris.

School (Hermitage, St. Petersburg), an image of the Virgin seated with eight companions busy with their needlework. He hoped especially for "different types of female beauty," something he had already obtained from the artist in his picture of the *Finding of Moses* (Louvre, Paris). Poussin chose the story of *Rebecca and Eliezer at the Well* (Fig. 4.45), as recounted in Genesis 24. Most artists showed Rebecca offering water to Eliezer at the well. Poussin depicted instead Eliezier's proposal of marriage on behalf of Isaac, the son of his master Abraham, after Rebecca has shown her kind nature by offering him water and also drawing some for his camels. As he offers her some jewelry and tells her that she has been chosen by the Lord, she puts her right hand on her heart and lifts the hem of her blue robe as if about to step back in surprise. The twelve women around her express reactions ranging from astonishment and jealousy to lack of awareness or interest. They too have been interrupted in their daily routine of gossip and fetching water in their vases. These allude to Agnolo Firenzuola's treatise *On the Beauty of Women* (1548), in which the ideal shape of a woman is described as a vase with a narrow neck and a swelling body that suggests both a slim neck rising from her shoulders and the narrow waist and small bosom rising above the hips "which should be quite pronounced." Presumably the vase beside Rebecca with handles that emerge from the curve of its body is Poussin's idea of a perfect shape, while the other vases, only one of which has the elegant neck described by Firenzuola, mark the women beside them as less desirable beauties. Bellori admired the pair of women helping each other to fill a vase. One of them is so transfixed by what is happening that she has let her vase overflow even though her friend touches her hand gently to tell her to stop.

Twelve women, twelve apostles—can *Rebecca and Eliezer* be seen as a kind of Old Testament companion to the *Ordination* that Poussin had just finished for the ungrateful Chantelou? The Church fathers interpreted the story of Rebecca as a prefiguration of the Annunciation to the

Virgin, and the Virgin Mary was constantly identified with the Church. The woman whose vase spills over and her companion, the most prominent in position and color in the painting apart from Eliezer and Rebecca, wear the colors traditionally worn by Sts. Peter and Paul, who from the early Middle Ages appear together with Christ as founders of Christianity. If so, then the message regarding the role of women in the Church's mission would seem to be to practice charity, in addition to obedience to commands from divine authority applicable to all the faithful. The domestic character of the buildings behind the women on the left contrasts with the temples and grand tombs behind the apostles in the *Ordination* and alludes to women's traditional sphere of activity. Finally the pier crowned with a globe on the right is, as has often been noted, a geometric replica of the women who stand beneath it. Like Domenichino, whose *Archery Contest of Diana and her Nymphs* (see Fig. 1.60) idealizes female beauty without any recourse to nudity, Poussin avoided hints of eroticism. His idea of beauty is of an elevated kind.

Poussin and Landscape Painting

Judging by his production before 1640, Poussin accepted the Italian theorists' scale of values that ranked landscape just above still-life but below genre scenes, which do include human beings. Poussin painted a number of small canvases in the 1620s where the small figures, usually of mythological subjects, animate the landscape rather than reduce it to background. In the 1630s he made a few more carefully constructed small landscapes with figures that supply scale rather than tell a story. Some of his landscape settings are so beautiful that they can distract the viewer's attention from the narrative. In the 1640s he extended his exploration of the possibilities inherent in landscape, creating some of the greatest landscape paintings of the seventeenth century, and indeed in the history of the genre. His reasons for gradually adopting this genre for some of his most moving philosophical and artistic statements were never articulated in his letters or mentioned by his biographers, who, except for Félibien, pay Poussin's landscapes little attention. The example of Claude may partly explain his

4.46 Nicolas Poussin, *Landscape with St. Matthew and the Angel*, 1639–40. Oil on canvas, 39 × 53⅛ in (99 × 135 cm). Staatliche Museen, Berlin.

4.47 Nicolas Poussin, *Landscape with St. John on Patmos*, 1640. Oil on canvas, 39½ × 53¾ in (100.3 × 136.4 cm). A.A Munger Collection. Art Institute of Chicago, Chicago, IL.

conversion, though their landscapes are very different in style and aim, and it was Claude who followed Poussin in introducing novel themes into his landscapes.

Poussin painted his *Landscape with St. Matthew and the Angel* (Fig. **4.46**) and also *Landscape with St. John on Patmos* (Fig. **4.47**) in 1639–1640 for Gian Maria Roscioli, chamberlain and secretary to Urban VIII. The two canvases were conceived as pendants with St. John on the right looking toward St. Matthew. Both paintings then have their largest tree masses on their outside edges and more open spaces on the inner sides, though the main features of the land in one do not flow seamlessly into the other. The river Tiber in the *Landscape with St. Matthew* seems to flow toward us and out of the picture on the right, while the sloping lines made by the banks of sandy hillocks behind St. John lead our eyes to the left past the saint and column drums and other blocks of masonry like those that fill the foreground of St. Matthew's setting.

While satisfactory as independent compositions—and conceived as such for each has its own central vanishing point—these landscapes reveal more subtleties in their design when studied as a pair. Poussin was familiar with Claude's use of similar compositional devices in his pendants, which often contrast a sea coast with an inland vista. In Claude's hands, the coast of the island of Patmos would probably have been in the foreground and the river behind Matthew far less prominent; the distant hills would have dissolved in a pale blue haze. For Poussin, however, the atmosphere is washed clean by a recent rainfall so that even distant features can be seen clearly. His clouds and trees are solid masses that allow no light to penetrate, unlike the feathery foliage of Claude, and his architectural fragments give weight, literal and metaphorical, to these scenes where they represent the decaying pagan religions of antiquity that will be replaced by Christianity. Both saints have been painted many times but Matthew never in a landscape setting when receiving the Gospel from an angel, and John on Patmos only in much earlier, more primitive Italian images, in which the island is so tiny that there is barely enough room for him to recline. Poussin's Patmos is a comfortable retreat with an expanse of sandy hillocks, some black oaks for shade, and a beautiful view to the distant coast of the mainland on the far left. The subjects, though not as rare as many others of Poussin, have been made original by their treatment.

St. Matthew and St. John seem isolated in a strip of foreground from the panoramas behind them; if they are covered up, it is easy to imagine the paintings without them. Poussin's next landscapes integrate the figures and their setting more completely and thereby vastly expand the significance of both. They are also on canvases as large as those of his history paintings. The *Landscape with a Man Killed by a Snake* (Fig. **4.48**), painted in 1648 for Pointel, leads the viewer from the horrifying spectacle of a young man trapped in the coils of a large snake in the left foreground, then to the man on the right fleeing in terror, and finally to an old woman in the center, who cannot see what has frightened the man but whose response reveals her state of alarm. Some men reclining in the shade on the left bank of the lake in the center of the painting have yet to react to these events. The landscape leads the viewer out to the glassy surface of the lake and beyond to a distant town and mountains whose peaks are just touched by a passing cloud. The degrees of perception of the dreadful event by these figures seem mirrored by the dark shadows on the left that creep toward the sunnier right side, where two boatmen have yet to realize what has happened. Félibien, who was in Rome in 1647–9 and so had an opportunity to discuss the work with Poussin, wrote later that it "should be regarded as one of the most beautiful landscapes that he painted." He especially admired the way that Poussin expressed the sense of terror of the figures, "feelings that few other painters have known how to portray so well."[7] Scholars have failed to find an ancient story or myth that could explain the event shown. Blunt proposed that the painting's theme may have been suggested by stories told about a marshy area south of Rome that was infested then and now with snakes (though not with boa constrictors, which is what the creature strangling the youth seems to be). The lake and buildings beyond are also reminiscent of Fondi, a town in this area.

As Richard Verdi has noted, "the theme of a serpent lurking in the grass to prey upon unsuspecting humanity occurs in a number of classical sources," where it "serves as a *topos* of the

4.48 Nicolas Poussin, *Landscape with a Man Killed by a Snake*, 1648. Oil on canvas, 47 × 78¼ in (119.4 × 198.8 cm). National Gallery, London.

omnipresence of death in the midst of peaceable nature." Snakes occur in other works of Poussin with this meaning, for example the snake who bites Eurydice in *Orpheus and Eurydice* (Louvre, Paris), and, even closer in theme to the painting reproduced here (see Fig. 4.48), the much smaller, earlier *Landscape with a Man pursued by a Snake* (Museum of Fine Arts, Montreal). Verdi has also explored Poussin's fascination with what he called "the tricks of fortune," the theme behind a pair of landscapes painted earlier for Pointel that contrast a violent storm with another landscape that Félibien called "calme & serein." Lightning that can strike suddenly and kill a man, as in *The Storm* (Musée des Beaux-Arts, Rouen), was already a common symbol of fortune in the sixteenth century, most famously in Giorgione's *Tempest* (Accademia, Venice). The serpent, of course, is traditionally associated with the temptation of Adam and Eve (Genesis 3:1–7). The man who flees the snake can therefore also be read as fleeing from sin. Thus Poussin's landscape with a few anonymous figures becomes a painting with a moral message as serious as those of his canvases with themes taken from the Bible or ancient history.

Poussin's Last Works

Poussin's last four paintings of the *Seasons* (Louvre, Paris), on which he worked from 1660 to 1664, were conceived as a *summa* of his goals as an artist. In his final years he worked on one more ambitious work, the *Apollo and Daphne* (Louvre, Paris), which he gave unfinished to Cardinal Camillo Massimi when he could no longer work. It too is a densely imagined and complex painting rather than a simple rendition of the myth most memorably treated in Bernini's spectacular marble group (see Fig. 1.89). His *Seasons* are even more complex, following neither the Northern precedent of illustrating cyclical agricultural practices nor the Italian one employing allegory. He gave each season a subject from the Old Testament: *Spring* has Adam and Eve in Paradise; *Summer* the meeting of Ruth and Boaz in his corn fields beside Bethlehem; *Autumn* the spies returning from the Promised Land with huge grapes (Fig. 4.49) and *Winter* the Deluge. Each season also depicts a time of day. Thus the lush spring landscape has a cool early morning sun just emerging behind a rocky mass on the left, summer has an early afternoon light on the wheat field awaiting harvest (the cast shadows are too long for noon) while autumn has the more subdued, grayish light of an October afternoon. Winter is painted in somber grays. A pale moon can be seen just above the horizon on the left while a flash of lightning reveals the sky covered with dark clouds. The four ages of man are also implied—youth in the paradise of spring, maturity in summer, the fruits of older age in autumn, and death amid the barren rocks and gray water in winter. Further intricacies have been teased out of these basic elements by Willibald Sauerländer, a medievalist who has argued that these four subjects are to be read as a prefiguration of events in the New Testament. Adam and Eve are not expelled from this paradise (the serpent is not shown), which may therefore prefigure the true paradise of the Christian Church with Adam as the coming Christ. The wheat of summer and the grapes of autumn would then refer to the bread and blood of Christ offered at the Eucharist and the deluge to the Last Judgment, where the sun rises over the ark of Noah, long associated with the Church and salvation. The traditional pagan deities of the seasons are also present—Apollo the sun god for spring, Ceres with her wheat stalks for summer, Bacchus' grapes for autumn and Pluto's dark underworld for winter. Yet, as Verdi noted in his sympathetic commentary, "the complex symbolism of these pictures is so completely absorbed into the theme and design of each that they appear remarkably uncomplicated in meaning."

Autumn, also known as *Spies Bringing Grapes from the Promised Land*, may be the last of the set to have been finished. Its surface has a rougher texture than that of the other three, showing more evidence of the trembling hand about which Poussin had complained in letters from the 1640s onwards. Looking at it, one can easily imagine him trying to steady his hand with a maulstick and making small jabs rather than strokes of paint with his brush. The lush foliage and burgeoning growth of *Spring* has given way to a less fertile terrain where grass grows in pockets of soil between rocks and only one old apple tree bears fruit. Two small trees on the left have already begun to drop their leaves. Patches

of light filtering through the clouds shine on a town below the slopes of a mountain in the distance and on some buildings on a rocky terrace on the right. The falling line of the clouds echoes that of the cliffs and slopes below them, gently directing our eyes left to follow the journey of the two men with their huge bunch of grapes and a branch of oranges as large as melons. Rising out of the grapes—or so it seems—is the ladder that supports a young woman picking apples in the tree. An allegorical engraving by Jerome Wierix of 1607, from which Poussin took the figures of the men with the grapes, shows Christ on the cross rising from the grapes, suggesting an interpretation of the apple tree as the Tree of Life with the apples as the fruit of paradise that awaits those who believe in Christ.

When the *Seasons* first reached Paris in 1665, they were discussed by the painters Charles Le Brun and Sebastian Bourdon, Michel Passart, a patron of both Poussin and Claude, and Loménie de Brienne, who recorded the comments. The writer thought that the *Deluge* was the best, as did Passart, but Le Brun preferred *Summer* by far and disliked *Spring* and *Autumn*; Bourdon voted for *Spring* as the best. The austere beauty of the *Deluge* (rarely called *Winter*) has probably had the greatest appeal in later centuries but the originality and grandeur of the entire group has long been recognized. French landscape painters in the later eighteenth century, when the Rococo fantasies of François Boucher and Jean-Honoré Fragonard had gone out of favor, turned frequently to Poussin's *Seasons* and his other large landscapes for inspiration. And Jean Baptiste Camille Corot, who loved Italy too, especially admired *Autumn*: "Voilà la nature!" he exclaimed.

Bernini was brought to see Poussin's second set of Sacraments by Chantelou in July 1665.

4.49 Nicolas Poussin, *Autumn (Spies Bringing Grapes from the Promised Land)*, 1660–64. Oil on canvas, 3 ft 9 in × 3 ft 7 in (1.18 × 1.16 m). Louvre, Paris.

French Painting and Printmaking

He spent a long time studying all of his host's paintings by Poussin; on seeing a copy of a *Bacchanal* made for Cardinal Richelieu, he exclaimed "O il grande favoleggiatore!" (Oh what a great story teller he is!). Chantelou kept the paintings of the Sacraments covered up and revealed them one by one to Bernini, starting with the *Confirmation*, which elicited the comment, "He is a great painter of history: what piety! What silence!" Bernini even got down on his knees to see those taken off the wall to be put in a better light. The experience, he said, was like listening to a great sermon. He spent over an hour, and finally declared: "Today you have caused me great distress by showing me the talent of a man who makes me realize that I know nothing. [. . .] In my opinion these pictures are equal to those of any painter in the world."[8] Poussin was by then too frail to paint. In October Jean Dughet, his brother-in-law, wrote to Chantelou to tell him that Poussin was close to death. One wonders whether Chantelou told Poussin how much Bernini had admired his works, even turning away from a small painting by Raphael to say that Poussin was his equal. Poussin would surely have been pleased.

One Italian painter, Salvator Rosa (1615–73), followed Poussin's example by painting large landscapes peopled with figures illustrating exemplary moral behavior and taken from literary sources rarely illustrated by painters. Indeed, Rosa depicted the Cynic philosopher Diogenes throwing away his bowl (*The Philosophers' Grove*, Palazzo Pitti, Florence, c. 1645) before Poussin used the story for his painting of around 1650 (Louvre, Paris), and returned to it in 1651 in a vertical canvas pointedly exhibited in public the following year before its sale to the Venetian ambassador. A Neopolitan, Rosa was a restless and ambitious man who was a gifted poet and playwright as well as painter. He first went to Rome when he was twenty and moved there in 1639 after more studies in Naples. He then spent a decade living near Florence and Siena (1640–49) before moving back to Rome. Much to Rosa's regret, his career was not marked by a series of major public commissions. Having established an early reputation for seascapes and craggy landscapes evocative of the splendid scenery around the coasts and mountains of Naples, Rosa found himself typecast as a landscape artist and had to struggle to receive commissions that he believed worthy of his talents.

Rosa's *Landscape with Mercury and the Dishonest Woodsman* (Fig. 4.50), which illustrates one of Aesop's fables, is a fine example of the wilder aspects of nature that Rosa preferred for his moral statements. Mercury had offered

4.50 Salvator Rosa, *Landscape with Mercury and the Dishonest Woodsman*, 1660. Oil on canvas, 49½ × 79½ in (125 × 202 cm). National Gallery, London.

an honest woodsman an ax of precious metal to replace one that he had lost. When the woodsman refused to recognize it as his lost ax, Mercury rewarded him with a golden ax. A dishonest woodsman then tried to get a golden ax from the god for himself, claiming he had lost one. However Mercury recovered his discarded ax of base metal, proving him a liar. In the painting we see Mercury in the water showing the dishonest woodsman his cheap ax. Behind them is a thick grove of trees that seem to explode toward us; a pleasant view toward a distant seacoast and blue mountains is visible on the left, while on the right several dead trees suggest the harsh fate awaiting those who try to trick the gods. Some Roman patrons, such as Don Lorenzo Onofrio Colonna, appreciated both Rosa's assertive dramas and Claude's gentler visions of the ancient world (see below), but never commissioned a landscape from Poussin. In the eighteenth century, however, British collectors admired Poussin, Rosa, and Claude, relishing the contrasts presented in their work.

Claude Lorrain and French Landscape Painting

Claude Gellée, called Claude Lorrain (c. 1600/5–82), is the other great French expatriate painter of the seventeenth century. Unlike Poussin, he never returned to France once his career in Rome was launched, and he never painted anything but landscapes. He was extremely successful, attracting the patronage of popes, cardinals, princes, and kings rather than the middle-class civil servants that collected Poussin's works. Together they transformed the genre of landscape in Rome, expanding the market from pleasant, escapist imagery to re-creations of the Roman *campagna* with mythological and historical inhabitants that added poetical and moral dimensions to the beautiful settings.

Claude, as he is called by English speakers, left Lorraine for Italy, reaching Rome around 1617. Employed as a cook by the landscape painter Agostino Tassi, Claude switched professions and began his training with Tassi, who specialized in illusionistic architecture (see Fig. 1.74) and scenes of boats in dock and coastal landscapes with travelers. Before 1629, the date of his first surviving painting, little is known of his life except that he returned to France in 1625–6 to assist Claude Deruet (c. 1588–1660) with the decoration of the Carmelite church in Nancy. According to Filippo Baldinucci, Claude fell from the scaffolding and decided to give up fresco painting as a result. True or not, he was back in Rome by Easter 1627 and never left except to make sketching trips to such picturesque sites as Subiaco, Tivoli, and the coast near Rome. Baldinucci also says that Claude studied for two years in Naples with Goffredo Wals (c. 1595–c. 1633), a fascinating but poorly documented landscape artist known from a small group of surviving works with circular formats, compositions of minimalist simplicity and extremely subtle lighting effects (Fig. 4.51). Since Claude became renowned for recording the distinct qualities of light at various times of day and for his control of a myriad of delicate observations of nature within a perfectly judged compositional structure, his contact with Wals was important. Tassi may have provided Claude with some of his favorite motifs but he was a crude painter compared with Wals, who was inspired by Elsheimer's exquisite landscapes (see Fig. 1.56).

4.51 Goffredo Wals, *Country Road with House*, c. 1625. Oil on copper, diameter 9⅝ in (24.5 cm). Fitzwilliam Museum, Cambridge, England.

4.52 Claude Gellée (Lorraine), *The Mill*, 1631. Oil on canvas, 24¼ × 33¼ in (61.6 × 84.5 cm). Seth K. Sweetser Fund. Museum of Fine Arts, Boston, MA.

The Mill (Fig. **4.52**), an exceptionally well preserved painting of 1631, shows how Claude took the coast and river scenes of Tassi with a few boats pulled into shore and transformed the theme by conjuring a misty dawn instead of his teacher's bland, neutral light. All the landscape elements are treated with such tender care that the paint seems breathed rather than brushed onto the canvas. How did Claude create effects like the two distant hills whose gray-blues differ only slightly but just enough to show that the larger one is many miles away? We can almost see the light changing as the sun rises on the left, catching the upper parts of the mill buildings on the right and the feathery trees behind them while leaving the trees that screen the dawn sky from us in a fuzzy dark green silhouette. The movement of the trees on both sides suggests a slight breeze. An artist sits in the foreground sketching a man milking his goat, while on the right another man loads planks onto a flat-bottomed barge. In the middle distance a man prepares to ferry a load of cattle to the far shore. Claude has distilled a moment in time so that we can contemplate the pleasures of a cool summer morning before the heat makes everyone drowsy. There are no exotic mountains or precipitous gorges such as those Bril liked to paint (see Fig. 5.66) and no Roman ruins, though a column drum and base provide seating for the artist and his companions.

Claude could not have painted such effects without studying them from life. There are hundreds of drawings by Claude of trees, waterfalls, shadowed groves seen against the sun, and views along the Tiber and lakes near Rome. They demonstrate how assiduously he observed the way sunlight falls on surfaces like ruined walls, grassy slopes, tree trunks, and boulders with water rushing past them, how it filters through the foliage of aspen and black oak and how it dissolves the forms of distant plains and hills. Though the majority were made in the 1630s and 1640s, Claude was still making nature studies in his sixties. The *Grotto of Neptune at Tivoli* (Fig. 4.53) is an especially dramatic example of a nature study drawn almost entirely with ink washes laid down with a brush rather than with a pen. The artist perched on the rocks has an even closer view of this site than we do. Though the brushwork may remind us of Chinese scroll paintings, Claude seems to have invented this technique on his own as a way of capturing evanescent effects quickly.

While Claude's judgment of tonal values and compositional masses was faultless, his lack of an early training with good teachers meant that he never really mastered either the human figure or the anatomy of the animals that fill his pastoral scenes, though quantities of studies of cows and sketches after ancient statues show that he tried to make up for his deficiencies. Even his trees have oddities if examined closely—the branches may be thicker some distance from the trunk than where they begin, and the trunks are too thin, especially in his later works, to survive a storm. He used to tell clients that they paid for the landscape and that he supplied the figures free. It was formerly thought that he had the figures done by collaborators, but this seems to have been rare. If they were not his own work, their forms would jump out of his carefully judged tonal harmonies. Once familiar, the idiosyncratic charm of his figures can seem preferable to the slick shepherds of his competitors. Carefully posed and painstakingly executed, their gestures and reactions to the stories they tell are utterly sincere and even moving. Claude never took short cuts. Every inch of his canvases is meticulously painted by him alone. Like Poussin, he had help only with chores like preparing the paint and stretching the canvases. Copyists and imitators never manage to capture the subtlety of Claude's paint surfaces, especially those of his magical distances.

The figures in Claude's paintings in the 1630s are usually peasants guarding livestock in the

4.53 Claude Gellée (Lorraine), *Grotto of Neptune at Tivoli*, c. 1640. Drawing, pen and brown ink, brown wash, 6¹¹⁄₁₆ × 9⁵⁄₁₆ in (170 × 237 cm). Teylers Museum, Haarlem, The Netherlands.

French Painting and Printmaking

countryside or men servicing ships in seaports but he painted the flight of the Holy Family to Egypt or their rest on the journey a number of times and an occasional mythological story too. For important patrons such as Louis XIII and Urban VIII—and Claude always had more prestigious clients than Poussin—he would do special subjects, for example the siege of the Protestant stronghold of La Rochelle in 1631 for the king (Louvre, Paris) and a view of the pope's summer palace at Castelgandolfo in 1639 for him (Fig. 4.54). He also made more elaborate versions of the seaports and country festivals for them than those painted for lesser patrons. Around 1640, more original subjects begin to appear—the flaying of Marsyas, Mercury and Aglauros, Samuel anointing David—and, for the port scenes, the arrival and departure of characters whose travels had never previously inspired pictures of these moments in their lives. Gradually the simple pastorals disappear too and Claude's range of subjects becomes as challenging and original as those of Poussin.

Claude was poorly educated. We know this from the *Liber Veritatis* (Book of Truth), an album in which he made a drawn record of all his work from about 1635 onwards with the name of the patron, or, in some cases, the city or country to which it was sent. These inscriptions, written in an awkward script, use a touching mixture of French and Italian ("quadro faict . . ."). Claude's decision to depict unusual stories from Ovid's *Metamorphoses* and Virgil's *Aeneid* was commendable because it challenged his limited skills at figure drawing and his poor education. While Poussin probably encouraged Claude to move from simple pastorals to grander themes and his patrons also proposed subjects to him, the desire to push his art to new levels of ambition had to come from Claude himself.

His *Trojan Women Setting Fire to their Fleet* of 1643 (Fig. 4.55) shows how he adapted the genre scenes of merchants and sailors conducting their business near moored ships (see Fig. 4.52) to a dramatic narrative taken from ancient history, in this instance Virgil's *Aeneid*. Tired of

4.54 Claude Gellée (Lorraine), *Lake Albano and Castelgandolfo*, 1639. Oil on copper, 12 × 14¾ in (30.5 × 37.5 cm). Fitzwilliam Museum, Cambridge, England.

wandering from port to port, the Trojan women took matters into their own hands by attempting to destroy the fleet so that they could settle down at last. The pale light and long shadows indicate that it is early morning. The center of the picture is dominated by a ship with furled sails whose interior is issuing plumes of gray smoke from different spots. The women on the shore in the foreground are small but their movements and gestures make us look at the boat on the left, which the women are about to board and set alight, and off to the right to the Trojan encampment to see how the Trojan men are reacting. The gray storm cloud taking shape on the right saved Aeneas by dousing the ships with rain before they were seriously damaged. In this case we know that the patron, Girolamo Farnese (1599–1668), chose the subject after returning from a very difficult diplomatic mission in Switzerland, seeing in the travails of Aeneas a learned parallel to his own difficulties. The commission inspired one of Claude's most beautiful seascapes: here and in other seacoasts and seaports he captured the textures of the surface of the water with astonishing realism.

Claude had painted seaports since the early 1630s but, as the decade proceeded, he included more numerous and more elaborate buildings to frame either side of the vista out to sea. They are variants of familiar Roman buildings, ancient and modern—the Villa Medici, Bramante's Tempietto, the Arch of Titus among others—as well as prominent forts and lighthouses, so that his port cities evoke Rome. They also depict harbors far grander than any that then existed in the Mediterranean. Was Claude inspired by Herodotus's description of the ancient port of Alexandria with its huge lighthouse, one of the legendary seven wonders of the world, to imagine and create his splendid seaport cities?

Before he painted the *Embarkation of St. Paula for Spain* (Prado, Madrid), he had not given his port scenes a subject. Intrigued by the idea that many famous people took sea journeys during their lives, he began to introduce their moments of departure into his repertoire: Cleopatra

4.55 Claude Gellée (Lorraine), *Trojan Women Setting Fire to their Fleet*, 1643. Oil on canvas, 41⅓ × 59⅞ in (105 × 152 cm). Fletcher Fund, 1955. Metropolitan Museum of Art, New York.

French Painting and Printmaking 299

4.56 Claude Gellée (Lorraine), *Embarkation of the Queen of Sheba*, 1648. Oil on canvas, 58½ × 76⅓ in (148.5 × 194 cm). National Gallery, London.

leaving for Tarsus (Louvre, Paris), St. Ursula and her ten thousand virgins embarking on their journey (National Gallery, London), Ulysses leaving the Phaeacians (Louvre, Paris) and, perhaps the most impressive of all, the *Embarkation of the Queen of Sheba* (Fig. **4.56**). Further it has a companion painting on the same scale, which reveals a vista between groves of magnificent tall trees across shaded meadows to a broad river and, beyond, to distant mountains whose forms are almost dissolved in haze (Fig. **4.57**). Claude's inscription on the painting identifies the subject as the marriage of Isaac and Rebecca, but the events shown do not illustrate any recorded moment in the biblical narrative; the young couple reclining in the central foreground watching the dancers performing on the right are presumably Isaac and Rebecca. Claude has paired a seaport with a landscape, a contrast he had offered in earlier pairs too, though on a smaller scale.

Claude's most spectacular light effects occur in his seaports, with the sun rising or setting just above the horizon creating a shimmering path below. The Queen of Sheba is embarking at dawn so the light is cool, the sky a pale lemony yellow shading to pale blue, and the sea a deep turquoise near the shore. Some large waves lead our eyes to a boat into which men are loading a large trunk. Its orange leather body is banded with dark green—such fancy luggage must belong to the queen. She can be seen on the steps of the palace on the right being greeted by two gentlemen. They will accompany her to the nearby barge where her companions await her. The barge will take all of them to the ship, now moored in deeper water, in which she will sail to meet Solomon. These practical details are not skimped by Claude, unlike Rubens whose depiction of the arrival of Marie de' Medici at Marseilles has little to do with reality (see Fig. **2.28**).

The long shadows cast by the trees in the companion painting imply that the dancing is taking place in the cool air of an early summer evening above the Tiber. Claude has flattered it here—it is not such a wide river even near its mouth—but the infinite depth suggested by the distant hills on the right and the glimpses of the broken aqueduct on the far left contribute to the evocative effect, as do the waterfall cascading over a cliff on the left and the watermill below. It is as if Claude wanted his patrons to associate the sound of water and its refreshing presence with an earthly paradise.

The *Embarkation of the Queen of Sheba* and the *Landscape with the Marriage of Isaac and Rebecca* were originally commissioned by Cardinal Camillo Pamphili around 1647. When he renounced that office and married, he was expelled from Rome by Innocent X (his uncle) and the formidable Donna Olympia (his mother) (see Fig. 1.94). Camillo then relinquished these paintings, which Claude sold to a French duke. This information is relevant because the subjects chosen both refer to marriage—the second obviously, the first less so. It was not the cardinal's future plans to which the paintings referred but symbolic marriages—of the soul to Christ and of Christ with the Church. Solomon and Isaac were both regarded as prefigurations of Christ, and both the Queen of Sheba and Rebecca as the soul, and the latter as the Church as well. Such an interpretation would be meaningful to a cardinal of the Catholic Church, who would have ensured that the commissioned artist was made aware of these readings. The elevated artistic language that Claude employed suggests that he wanted these paintings to convey more than the visual pleasures of an exotic voyage and a country festival. When Camillo Pamphili was forgiven, he quickly ordered a copy from Claude of the *Marriage* scene but its new companion is a *View of Delphi with a Procession* (Doria Pamphili collection, Rome). Both still belong to descendants of the family and can be seen in the family palace in the center of Rome. The landscape is known only as *The Mill*; Claude did not inscribe it with the identification he gave the first version, though the images are identical. Thus if we prefer to see only an ancient wedding celebration beside the Tiber on a late summer afternoon, Claude has given us permission to do so.

4.57 Claude Gellée (Lorraine), *Landscape with the Marriage of Isaac and Rebecca (The Mill)*, 1648. Oil on canvas, 58⅞ × 77½ in (149.2 × 196.9 cm). National Gallery, London.

French Painting and Printmaking 301

Claude outlived Poussin by seventeen years and was working, though slowly, until the end. His later works are almost ethereal—the tonal contrasts less emphatic, the colors softer, the figures, buildings, and trees taller and thinner. The *Landscape with the Nymph Egeria Mourning over Numa* (Fig. 4.58), painted in 1669 for Prince Lorenzo Onofrio Colonna, the artist's best patron, uses subdued light and color appropriate to a sad subject. Prince Colonna owned land near Lake Nemi, a volcanic lake with steep sides south of Rome, visible behind the figures. Ovid describes how Egeria went there to mourn for her husband Numa, one of the legendary early kings of Rome. Diana sent her nymphs to console her, though even they were unable to stop her tears. When she eventually died of grief, Diana turned her into a spring of water.

The patron's coat of arms featured a single column (*colonna* in Italian); Claude carefully included one in each of his nine works for the family. Here it is tucked into the right edge of the canvas high above the Temple of Diana on the lake shore below. The tree that soars above Egeria and her solicitous companions is a Roman umbrella pine but it is slimmer than any real specimen. Claude's earlier nature studies show accurately drawn examples of this tree, typical of this area, so these distortions are intentional. They alert anyone familiar with Rome and its environs that Claude's paintings depict another world, reminiscent of the Rome familiar to his seventeenth-century patrons but not a pedantic reconstruction of its ancient appearance. He is telling us a story and in the process is transporting us to his imagined ancient worlds, exactly as Virgil and Ovid themselves did in their descriptions of the Mediterranean landscape and its inhabitants, and their histories and mythologies. It is a journey that kings, popes, dukes, cardinals, bishops, and many less socially elevated patrons were delighted to take (countless readers still do). Claude's art influenced landscape painters in the Dutch Republic and France in the seventeenth century, and in France and England in the eighteenth. English garden designers began to replace the geometric parterres that were fashionable in the sixteenth and seventeenth centuries with broad lawns framed by huge shade trees leading to distant bridges, lakes, and temples. Such vistas

4.58 Claude Gellée (Lorraine), *Landscape with the Nymph Egeria Mourning over Numa*, 1669. Oil on canvas, 61 × 78⅓ in (155 × 199 cm). National Museum of Capodimonte, Naples.

are epitomized in Claude's evocations of dawn, early morning, afternoon shade, and the slowly failing light of a summer evening.

Claude's paintings were popular in Paris and French painters began to emulate his classical landscapes with subtle lighting, though they did not attempt his seaports with their more spectacular effects of sunrise and sunsets. Laurent de la Hyre (1606–56), though primarily a figure painter, produced several fine examples with figures reduced in scale, though not to insignificance. His delicate trees, misty distances, and fragments of ruined temples all evoke Claude's Rome (Fig. 4.59). The example here contrasts a lush grove of trees beside a pond with a pair of dead trees on the left cruelly silhouetted against the sky. Like Ruisdael's dead birch trees (see Fig. 5.71), the trees function as a *memento mori*, reminding the viewer of inevitable mortality amid the enduring beauty of this Virgilian paradise. Pierre Patel (*c*. 1605–76) produced elegant small paintings of classical landscapes whose ruins are chipped and invaded with plants. Philippe de Champaigne also produced an occasional landscape, though always with biblical figures. The Academy's disdain for the genre did not encourage French painters to take it as seriously as Poussin and Claude had, with the result that, with some exceptions, French landscape paintings rarely rise above the level of pleasant decoration.

Charles Le Brun and the Academy

Charles Le Brun (1619–1691) was the most influential artist in France during the last thirty years of his life but his reputation never extended much outside France except in the world of art academies. While his work remains largely unknown to the lay public (there is still no complete scholarly catalogue for him), a retrospective exhibition held at Versailles in 1963 began the process of reconstructing his career and considering anew his contribution to the education of artists in France and elsewhere. More recent studies have focused on his drawings and his *Conférence sur l'expression générale et particulière* (Lecture on General and Particular Forms of Expression), given before the Academy in 1688 and published in many editions from 1693 onwards.

The son of a sculptor and a mother whose family were renowned teachers of calligraphy to

the court and aristocracy, Le Brun was precocious, attracting the support before he was fifteen of Pierre Séguier (1588–1672), Chancellor of the Parlement from 1635 until his death. Le Brun's first teacher was François Perrier (1590?–1650), who had spent five years in Rome before returning to Paris in 1632, when he collaborated briefly with Simon Vouet on a decorative commission. Le Brun joined Vouet's workshop in 1634 as an assistant. His *Crucifixion of Christ with Angels* (Pushkin Museum, Moscow), painted for Séguier in 1637, is a very able essay in Vouet's elegant, Italianate manner. A similar style and familiarity with Vouet's working methods can also be seen in Le Brun's early chalk figure studies, although Le Brun's mastery of the male figure is far superior to that of Vouet; significantly, he continued to work from the model when making preparatory studies throughout his career. It was the work of Nicolas Poussin, however, that was to have the greatest impact on Le Brun's mature artistic persona.

In 1640 Poussin, whose first commissions for patrons in Paris had started arriving in the 1630s, left Rome, obedient to royal command, to devise a ceiling decoration for the Grande Galerie of the Louvre. When he returned to Rome in 1642, ostensibly to bring his wife back with him, the Louvre ceiling planned but not yet started, Le Brun accompanied him. He had by then

4.59 Laurent de la Hyre, *Landscape with Boy Playing a Flute*, c. 1645. Oil on canvas, 42⅛ × 52 in (107 × 132 cm). Musée des Beaux Arts, Lille.

successfully completed several public commissions in Paris as well as paintings and designs for engraved frontispieces for private clients. Le Brun's patron Séguier commissioned copies after Raphael, Giulio Romano, and Roman antiquities, but Le Brun also studied such painters as Annibale Carracci, Domenichino, Lanfranco, Pietro da Cortona, Sacchi, and Guercino. The first two of these artists would have been recommended to him by Poussin, to whose work Le Brun had unusual access: Poussin worked alone and allowed few visitors to distract him.

Le Brun's few surviving works from this phase show him developing an invigorated version of Vouet's style with figures whose convincingly rendered anatomy is proof of Le Brun's assiduous study of the human body. He also made other paintings where his admiration of Poussin's style almost goes beyond hero worship to become mindless imitation. Indeed his *Horatius Coclius at the Bridge* (Dulwich College Picture Gallery, London) was, according to his biographers, done deliberately in the style of Poussin to see if he could pass it off as a work by his admired exemplar. His mature style is, like that of his close contemporary Carlo Maratta in Rome, an intelligent synthesis of all the artists, ancient and modern, that he most admired, with Poussin and Raphael the most apparent of these models. An informed and conscious blend of the finest art of the past had for generations been the accepted goal of artists training in studios of most artists in Bologna, Florence, and Rome. Maratta would see that it became the goal of all young artists taught by the Accademia di San Luca in Rome from the 1660s onwards. Le Brun filled the same role in Paris but, because he enjoyed far greater political and financial support for these educational goals from the king, he was to be far more successful at instituting uniform aesthetic goals for the training of artists.

In 1656 Le Brun was hired by Nicolas Fouquet, Louis XIV's treasurer, to decorate his country estate at Vaux-le-Vicomte (see Fig. 4.5), whose completion was celebrated in August 1661. As discussed above, the team of architects and artists assembled by Fouquet and supervised by Le Brun were taken over by the king and employed at the Louvre and then at Versailles. Le Brun was installed in a handsome apartment in the château to supervise the decoration and paid lavishly as well. He more than met the artistic and administrative challenges, thus earning a position in the ranks of such outstanding artists as Rubens, Bernini, Cortona, and Wren, who were also able administrators.

At Vaux-le-Vicomte Le Brun was given the opportunity to design and execute several ceiling decorations that called on his familiarity with Roman achievements. That for the entrance hall (see Fig. 4.6) required a combination of architectural framework, architectural and sculptural elements in the painted frames surrounding the narrative scenes, and some allegorical figures (eight of the nine Muses) sitting on the entablature, smiling at the spectators below as they brandish their attributes. In the center of the ceiling, in a barely perceptible overhead illusion contained within a thick octagonal frame, Fidelity is transported to the realm of the Muses accompanied by Prudence, Virtue, Reason, and Clio, the Muse of epic history. The design shows that Le Brun, while aware of Cortona's spectacular ceiling frescoes in Rome (see Fig. 1.122) and Florence (see Fig. 1.125), chose not to follow their example of unifying the whole scheme with overlapping elements and compositional movement flowing between the various parts. Instead the various sections are neatly defined with emphatic borders that stress the overall symmetry of the plan while marking out sections of more complex decoration. Le Brun used a similar approach in 1661 for the Salon of Apollo in the Louvre and, his largest and most important decorative commission of all, the ceiling of the Galerie des Glaces at Versailles (see Fig. 4.10).

By 1660 Le Brun was the most powerful artist in Paris. Made *Premier Peintre du Roi* (First Painter to the King) in 1661 and director of the Académie Royale in 1663, he had administrative control of the training of all artists in Paris as well as the distribution of the most significant commissions awarded by Louis XIV and his court. Le Brun's position was comparable in some respects with that of Bernini during the papacies of Urban VIII and Alexander VII, though Le Brun exercised more influence. Other established Parisian artists, especially Pierre Mignard (1612–95), chafed at Le Brun's status but the king's response was to challenge both artists to outdo each other (the king always sided with Le Brun when the competing paintings were submitted to his judgment). Not until Le Brun's death in 1690 did Mignard enjoy the kind of opportunities that his rival had enjoyed for thirty years.

Le Brun's *Chancellor Séguier* (Fig. 4.60) is perhaps the grandest of equestrian portraits produced in the seventeenth century yet neither the circumstances nor date of its commission are known. Equestrian portraits of anyone except the monarch and the occasional duke are rare in France and elsewhere. This dignified procession of the chancellor on his white horse with eight pages has usually been linked to the triumphal entry into Paris of Maria Teresa of Austria, future bride of Louis XIV, in 1660. The painting makes no specific reference to that event, however, though the costume of the pages suggest that 1660–61 is the correct date. Séguier's influence was by then in decline but when the artist he had supported for so long finally became the king's *Premier Peintre*, he may have commissioned this image to draw his monarch's attention to his long and loyal service as chancellor, a position he had held for over a quarter of a century. This masterpiece was never engraved and virtually forgotten for three centuries. The artist himself is said to be portrayed as the page holding the parasol over his patron's head—the protector of the arts protected by the artist? Neither he nor Séguier look as old as they would have been in 1660 (Séguier would have been seventy-two, Le Brun forty-one) but by showing both men in their prime, Le Brun created an image of timeless authority proceeding calmly across the picture plane against a sky filled with clouds whose upper edges are tinted with rose as if from a setting sun.

Séguier does not need allegories of Fame in the sky or a river god representing the Seine in the foreground. His horse does not rear up so that he can demonstrate his exceptional horsemanship, controlling the powerful beast with one loosely held rein, a flattering conceit used by Velázquez, for example (see Fig. 3.32). The restraint of the color scheme and planar simplicity of Le Brun's composition mask the splendor of this retinue.

4.60 Charles Le Brun, *Chancellor Séguier*, 1660–61. Oil on canvas, 116⅛ × 140⅞ in (295 × 358 cm). Louvre, Paris.

Séguier's huge cloak and riding skirt are both made of brocade woven with gold thread, as is the cloth draped over his white horse, who eyes us warily. The pages wear costumes of blue silk edged with gold brocade ribbons or jackets and short breeches elaborately worked with gilt braid. Séguier wears the prestigious Ordre du St. Esprit and carries an elaborate gold tassel, an attribute of his office. Le Brun subtly draws attention to himself not only by placing himself in the foreground just behind his patron but also by letting the light fall on his white sleeve and shirt, the lightest tone in the picture.

Le Brun's once famous *The Queens of Persia at the Feet of Alexander the Great*, also known as *The Tent of Darius* (Fig. 4.61), was painted in 1660–61 at Fontainebleau at the request of Louis XIV, who liked to drop in unannounced to watch the painter at work. The choice of subject was significant. The king liked to imagine himself, like Alexander the Great, as the triumphant ruler of vast territories gained by both force and diplomacy while also fostering an image of magnanimity, long believed to be an important attribute of great leaders. The moment when the family of the defeated Persian king Darius were visited in their tent after their capture by Alexander the Great and his best friend Hephaestion had been chosen by painters before, for example by Veronese, to carry the same message for a powerful Venetian family. When Darius's mother mistook Alexander's friend (the warrior on the left in a red cloak) for the young king, this act was regarded as an unforgivable *faux-pas*, hence the anxious reactions of Darius's entourage. His mother is still prostrate before Hephaestion but his wife and son look up at Alexander with outstretched arms pleading for mercy. One of his daughters wipes tears away with the corner of her cloak, the other seems frozen in a gesture that suggests both terror and prayer. On the far right a eunuch bows down to the ground, rightly fearing for his life. The other figures in the tent are not so easy to see now as they were when the painting was finished but their facial expressions and gestures are easily legible variations of those in the foreground. The painting fulfills admirably Poussin's prescription for a serious history painting, namely that the moral significance of a depicted event should be comprehensible to any spectator who would take the time to "read" each face and gesture. Like Poussin's *Fall of Manna* (Louvre, Paris), no single figure or pair of figures dominates the composition. The viewer must look across the whole crowd, carefully reading the figures from left to

4.61 Charles Le Brun, *The Tent of Darius (The Queens of Persia at the Feet of Alexander the Great)*, 1660–61. Oil on canvas, 9 ft 8 in × 14 ft 9 in (2.98 × 4.53 m). Palace of Versailles.

right, to understand what has happened and to grasp the moral significance of Alexander the Great's sympathetic response to the family's breach of etiquette.

Every element of Alexander's pose was carefully considered, as Félibien explained in his description of the painting published two years after its completion:

The painter was not satisfied with representing in Alexander's face his youth, his gentle temperament, his valor and all other qualities that history has revealed and which he has incorporated into a faithful image. There are four different actions evident in his gestures. His compassion towards the princesses is apparent both in his bearing and the look in his eye. His open hand reveals his clemency and is a perfect expression of the mercy he shows to the entire court. His other hand resting on Hephaestion shows that the latter is his favorite or, rather, an incarnation of himself, and his left leg, which is pulled back, is a mark of the civility he shows towards the princesses. The painter did not have him bending forward any further because he is depicting him at the moment when he approaches the women, and it was not a Greek custom; moreover, he could not bend over much further due to a thigh injury he had sustained in the last battle.[9]

It would be hard to exaggerate the influence of this painting on later developments in France. *The Tent of Darius* was engraved in 1661, so that its composition could be studied by artists who did not have easy access to the king's gallery of paintings at the Tuileries, where it was first installed. Félibien's eloquent description drew attention to Le Brun's aesthetic goals, while the latter's position as *Premier Peintre du Roi* ensured that all ambitious young painters would attempt to emulate him. Some of the heads illustrating different emotional states in the publications of Le Brun's famous *Conférence sur l'expression générale et particulière* were based on those in this painting, for example that of the woman on the right edge with both hands raised, whose face expresses "*l'admiration avec étonnement*" (admiration with astonishment) (Fig. 4.62). The staging and acting of Le Brun's painting now seems stiff, lacking the spontaneity of genuine human emotion that modern viewers sense in the work of Caravaggio and Rembrandt, for example. Further, the incident portrayed depends on understanding the traditional ways of standing on ceremony and obeying the rules of court protocol. It is difficult for us to appreciate Le Brun's achievement but it would be a mistake to ignore it. It was not only part of Louis XIV's careful management of his public image but it also launched the career of Le Brun as the chief orchestrator of the Sun King's fabulous public persona at Versailles.

Le Brun followed up the success of *The Tent of Darius* by proposing to the king other paintings of events from the life of Alexander the Great. His first ideas were for such subjects as Alexander's clemency towards Timoclea, but he abandoned these intimate psychological themes for four vast canvases (the biggest are over 39 feet [12 meters] wide) depicting Alexander's victorious military achievements—the *Battle at the River Granicus*, the *Defeat of Darius at*

4.62 Charles Le Brun, "Admiration with Astonishment," from *The Expression of the Passions*, 1696. Engraving. British Museum, London.

French Painting and Printmaking

Arbela, the *Defeat of Porus*, and *The Triumphal Entry of Alexander the Great into Babylon* (Fig. 4.63). All were finished by 1668. While perhaps more impressive than moving to modern viewers, they still offer an opportunity to savor a vivid recreation of the ancient world: scenes of a Greek army surging across a river to confront the Persian enemy in hand-to-hand combat on horseback; Darius climbing down from his enormous gold chariot, now immobilized because all the horses pulling it have been killed; and the wounded Porus, the last ruler defeated by Alexander, brought to the victorious emperor who treats him gently and turns an enemy into a friend. Beautiful horses, sumptuous costumes, and armor for the principal characters, rippling muscles on the bodies of both victors and defeated soldiers—there is plenty of spectacle to enjoy while absorbing the subliminal message that Louis XIV is a monarch of comparable achievements and noble character.

This message is also conveyed in even more specific form in the famous Galerie des Glaces at Versailles, whose structure was begun in 1678 (see Fig. 4.10). It was Le Brun's task to design for the ceiling of this dazzling interior space images of Louis XIV's recent military and diplomatic triumphs.

The subjects of some of the variously shaped canvases mounted overhead give the flavor of this commission: the Assumption of Personal Rule by Louis XIV; Preparing to Fight on Land and at Sea; Deciding to Wage War against Holland in 1671; the Franche-Comté conquered a Second Time in 1674; the Capture of Ghent in Six Days in 1678; Holland Accepting Peace and Severing her Alliances with Germany and Spain. All the gods of Olympus rally round to help the king—Neptune calms the seas, Vulcan forges arms, Hercules brandishes his club, Minerva offers wise counsel, Apollo shines down on his endeavors, and so on. These gods and others play a similar role in Rubens's *Life of Marie de' Medici* (see Figs. 2.26–2.29), which Le Brun certainly knew, though his compositions and palette owe little to Rubens. On the contrary, these big canvases

4.63 Charles Le Brun, *The Triumphal Entry of Alexander the Great into Babylon*, 1662–68. Oil on canvas, 10 ft 2 in × 16 ft 8 in (3.1 × 5.1 m). Louvre, Paris.

could have benefited from some of Rubens's energy and fluent handling of this characteristic seventeenth-century blend of myth and reality.

Le Brun's scenes are a dutiful compilation of the elements demanded by the king and Colbert; they lack the imaginative power of his series celebrating the triumphs of Alexander the Great. The artist's original scheme illustrating the labors of Hercules, yet another flattering allusion to the king, was summarily dismissed after Louis signed the two Treaties of Nijmegen in 1678, and Le Brun had to prepare new designs in some haste while also working on the decorations of the Salon de la Paix and the Salon de la Guerre. These circumstances might explain the lack of inspiration or perhaps Le Brun delegated much of the execution to assistants, knowing that the paintings would be seen only from afar. They are now ignored by most visitors, enchanted instead by the mirrors in their gilded frames and the panorama seen through the tall windows of the magnificent garden vistas orchestrated by Le Nôtre.

Colbert, the artist's great supporter against his jealous rivals, died in 1685 so Le Brun's final years were affected by the politics of Pierre Mignard and his supporters at the Academy. As if to compensate for their attacks, a supporter of Le Brun, Nicolas de Largillière, submitted to the Academy as his *pièce de réception* in 1686 a superb full-length portrait (Fig. 4.64). The painter is seated in a high-backed chair upholstered in dark blue velvet, his lower body draped with a sumptuous dark crimson velvet cloak. He points to a *modello* of the scene in the Galerie des Glaces showing the conquest of the Franche-Comté on his easel behind him, his right hand directing our gaze to the figure of the king in it. Scattered about him are casts of antiquities, books, and an engraving of *The Tent of Darius*, anchored to a table on the right by a small bronze replica of the Borghese Warrior. Here at least Le Brun is in total command of his affairs and reputation.

By the time of his death, Le Brun had helped to place the visual arts at the heart of French politics. None of his successors had the same control or influence but the system he created and which the French Crown supported until the Revolution of 1789 produced hundreds of artists and craftsmen for another century. A steady stream of well-trained painters and sculptors emerged from the Academy system along with the occasional genius such as Antoine Watteau, who did not fit its rules but was accommodated nevertheless. The superb furniture, tapestries, porcelain, metalwork, and other crafts that the French produced in such abundance in the eighteenth century were made possible by the workshops started during Henry IV's restoration of Paris and expanded by the opportunities produced by Louis XIV's court and those of his successors at Versailles. Le Brun had as much—if not more—impact on the later history of French art as the director of the various royal workshops and the Academy than as a painter. The Academy was the model for all later art academies in Europe and America and so, ultimately, for the art schools and studio departments that flourish in colleges and universities throughout the world today.

4.64 Nicolas de Largillière, *Charles Le Brun*, 1686. Oil on canvas, 91⅓ × 73⅔ in (232 × 187 cm). Louvre, Paris.

French Painting and Printmaking

5 THE DUTCH REPUBLIC

Frans Hals, *Shrovetide Revellers*, c. 1615. Oil on canvas, 51¼ × 39¼ in (131.4 × 99.7 cm). Bequest of Benjamin Altman, 1913. Metropolitan Museum of Art, New York.

THE DUTCH REPUBLIC DID NOT EXIST as an independent political and territorial entity in the sixteenth century. When Charles V abdicated in 1554, he gave the seventeen provinces of the Netherlands to his son, Philip II of Spain. The seven northern provinces had been allowed a degree of autonomy until then by Spain, which had assumed control of this land as part of the Burgundian-Habsburg Empire in 1556. Philip then began to tax his new possessions heavily to shore up his gradually faltering economy. The decision that triggered organized opposition to Spanish rule, however, was the refusal of the Spanish Crown and its local surrogates to tolerate anything by way of religious dissent. Those who feared persecution for their beliefs as well as those opposed to Habsburg rule began moving to cities that would allow them to worship as they wished and run their business affairs without punitive tax rates. Antwerp was particularly affected: over half of its citizens chose to leave what had been the wealthiest city in the Netherlands when the Duke of Alva and his troops invaded in 1568. Much of its mercantile, intellectual, and artistic talent fled to towns in the northern provinces. Thus began the economic decline of the Spanish Netherlands and with it the transformation of the United Provinces into the Dutch Republic and the wealthiest country in seventeenth-century Europe. The Twelve Year Truce (1609–21) halted the fighting over the border between the independent northern provinces and those still under Spanish rule, gaining *de facto* recognition by the Spanish Crown that they no longer controlled the northern areas. Spain finally ceded all claims to this territory under the Treaty of Münster, signed in 1648.

Having wrested political and religious independence from the most powerful ruling dynasty of Europe, the seven northern provinces (Holland, Zeeland, Utrecht, Gelderland, Groeningen, Friesland, and Overijssel) became the United Provinces. Their ruling classes organized the administration of their military, political, and economic affairs using "Stadhouders" (literally town holders). These were elected military leaders who were in charge of each province, and who, with elected delegates to the States General, met regularly in The Hague to settle affairs of common concern. Thus the Republic was governed by soldiers, merchants, lawyers, and other influential citizens, not by hereditary aristocrats. Boards of regents drawn from the same groups also ran civic bodies. The House of Orange did, however, control the post of Stadhouder of Holland, the most prosperous province. Willem I, Prince of Orange (1533–84), a descendant of the Counts of Nassau and one of the leaders of the revolt against the Spanish Crown, was the first to hold the office. He had been Governor of the northern provinces of Holland, Zeeland, and Utrecht since 1564 when he was both Catholic and loyal to the Spanish Crown. After the revolt, he became a Calvinist and his military and political skills were crucial to the success of the rebellion, though he hoped eventually that the divided territories would be reunited. After he was assassinated in 1584, his sons Maurits (1567–1625) and Frederick Hendrick (1584–1647) held the post in succession. Their court at The Hague was, however, a modest affair compared with those of established European monarchies and of the Medici in Florence.

As the Dutch Republic had neither a large population nor many natural resources, its economic success after 1609 is extraordinary. It imported most of its grain and even the timber it needed to build its ships, which transported the goods that contributed to its wealth: finished wool and linen cloth, beer, bricks, cheese, herrings, even salt. Because they did not have to use most of their arable land to grow grain, the Dutch could use it for more profitable crops such as flax, hops, and tobacco. They grew luxury vegetables—the exotic new cauliflower, the famous carrots of Hoorn—instead of humbler root crops. They were also excellent breeders of livestock who raised the milk production levels of their dairy cattle far above those in the rest of Europe.

In addition to making and marketing these products, the Dutch were outstanding mapmakers and navigators. These skills combined with their exceptional abilities as designers and builders of boats were crucial to their control of trade to the Baltic (grain and timber) and to the Mediterranean and Far East. They were also able to move goods throughout their own territory and the adjoining countries on their extensive system of canals and up the Rhine and Meuse (Maas in Dutch). The Dutch East India Company was established in 1602 by the States General and the Dutch West India Company in 1621. The latter controlled the trade that took bricks to the Far East and brought back spices, silks, and porcelain. Dutch pride in the skills that earned them the highest per capita income in Europe is reflected in pictures of cattle at rest, of linen bleaching in the fields outside Haarlem, of imported luxury goods like parrots (see Fig. 2.55) and Venetian goblets in still-life paintings, of maps hanging on the walls of their rooms (see Fig. 5.61), and of every kind of ship from flat-bottomed barges to the three-masted "East Indiamen" which sailed as far as Australia.

The population of the United Provinces grew from roughly one and a half million in 1600 to almost two million by the end of the century. The most highly populated and urbanized province was Holland, which included the cities of Amsterdam, Haarlem, Leiden, Delft, Rotterdam, and The Hague. The population of Amsterdam had swollen from 30,000 in 1572 to over 100,000 by 1600 and 150,000 by 1650. Well-educated, industrious, ingenious, more tolerant of other religious beliefs than their European neighbors, and well defended from aggressors by their navy and by the rivers that formed natural boundaries between the Republic and the Spanish Netherlands, the citizens of the United Provinces prospered. Their surplus wealth enabled even the rural population to live decently, while the urban middle classes bought cheap imitations of what their social superiors owned, decorating their homes with fine furniture, Turkish carpets (collected only by the elite), and paintings by native and foreign artists.

Peter Mundy observed in 1640 when he visited the Republic:

All in generall [strive] to adorne their houses, especially the outer or street roome, with costly peeces, Butchers and bakers not much inferior in their shoppes, which are Fairly sett Forth, yea many tymes blacksmithes, Coblers, etts., will have some picture or other by their Forge and in their stalle.[1]

Mundy was not exaggerating by much. Michael Montias has estimated that over a million paintings were produced in the Dutch Republic in the seventeenth century. The numbers of works from this period still available for purchase by Dutch artists of all levels of accomplishment is proof of the vast growth in the production of these commodities and of their availability in the seventeenth century to anyone with some discretionary income. Competition was intense. Some excellent artists either gave up painting and took up other professions or took another job to provide a supplementary income. The landscape painter Meindart Hobbema (1638–1709) became a wine gauger for the Amsterdam customs and excise office in 1668, after which he painted rarely; Johannes Vermeer sold paintings by other masters to supplement his income; Jan Steen owned a tavern.

The growth in the popularity of portraits, landscapes, still-life images, and genre scenes was greater in Holland than anywhere else in Europe. Montias's statistics document the expansion of these genres at the expense of the traditional staples for private clients—religious paintings for private devotion and mythological and historical subjects for the reception rooms of more highly educated clients. Overtly Catholic images such as the Virgin and Child with saints and depictions of miracles were replaced for Calvinist clients by scenes from the Old Testament. Genre subjects, at first seemingly innocent of moral messages, often convey warnings against sin as well as the inevitability of death. Some were nevertheless celebrations of the pleasures of daily life, for example men playing skittles on a warm spring day (see Fig. 5.64) or a tasty snack of herring, bread, and beer.

Haarlem and the Creation of a Dutch National Style

The Flemish artists who dominate modern accounts of the artistic peaks in the fifteenth and sixteenth centuries, notably Jan van Eyck and Pieter Bruegel the Elder, worked mainly in what became the Spanish Netherlands after 1600. Several cities in the Dutch Republic had nevertheless produced excellent artists before 1600. Haarlem and Leiden could cite the achievements of Dieric Bouts and Geertgen Tot Sint Jans in the fifteenth century and of Lucas van Leyden and Maerten van Heemskerck (1498–1574) in the next. The dissolution of the Spanish Netherlands in the late sixteenth century had dire consequences for Haarlem. It was the first place attacked by the Duke of Alva when he tried to win back these territories after he had reasserted Spanish authority in the south. The Siege of Haarlem by the duke and his troops between December 1572 and July 1573 caused enormous hardship and left the population too poor to pay the ransom that would have prevented soldiers from sacking the city after its surrender. The duke's poorly paid troops had been pushed to their limits, however, and the campaign to capture the northern provinces for Spain soon petered out.

Haarlem recuperated slowly with the help of entrepreneurial immigrants from the south, including Protestants from France and Germany. Its population doubled between 1572 and 1622, when it reached 40,000. Its new Town Hall was ready for decoration in 1620. The new Weigh House, the Vleeshal (Meat Hall) on the square beside the great cathedral of St. Bavo, and a new tower for the Nieuwe Kerk (New Church), these last two by Lieven de Key, were visible proof of the city's recovery (see Fig. 5.16). They also provided opportunities to artists who supplied stained-glass windows, tapestries, and pictures honoring the city's heroic recent struggles to furnish them. The professional skills of the newcomers added to those of its residents in making beer and textiles, especially fine linen damask cloth. The Guild of St. Luke had fifty-eight painters on its registers in 1634 along with six sculptors and two architects. Among the artists were the still-life painter Pieter Claesz, the landscape painter Jan van Goyen, the portraitist Frans Hals, and Pieter Sanraedam, known for views of the Republic's old churches. Their range of specialties is representative of the paintings produced in Haarlem and elsewhere for the new Republic.

The Haarlem Mannerists

"Mannerism," or *maniera*, whose decline in Italy is described above, had its adherents in Haarlem too. The emphasis on male and female nudes in difficult poses that flaunt the artists' knowledge of human anatomy and understanding of foreshortening is often extreme in this last phase of the style. It dominates many of the paintings of Cornelis Cornelisz. van Haarlem (1562–1638), who never went to Italy but learnt about it from prints. Some were made by his fellow townsman Hendrick Goltzius (1558–1617), a far more significant figure who was the outstanding engraver of his age as well as a fine painter. His career spans work that is as ambitiously Mannerist as anything produced in Europe in this style to drawings and paintings that place him among the Dutch pioneers of the new naturalism. Goltzius went to Italy where, between 1590 and 1591, he visited Bologna, Florence, and Rome, sold his prints, and made drawings of such antiquities as the Apollo Belvedere, of which he made engravings after his return. The slight exaggeration of the swelling forms of Hercules' muscles is similar to—but less flamboyant than—the way in which Cornelisz treated human anatomy in his paintings.

Goltzius is now primarily valued as a printmaker. There were indeed no engravers then in the rest of Europe who surpassed his skills at manipulating the burin across the smooth metal surface of the plate to create the undulating lines whose varying widths modeled forms and created illusions of bulging muscle and pulsating movement simultaneously. His engravings after the paintings of Bartholomeus Spranger (1546–1611), the most influential artist north of the Alps working in a Mannerist style, helped to spread his influence to the Netherlands from Prague, where Spranger worked for the court of Rudolf II. Goltzius usually worked from drawings by Spranger, and was an excellent draughtsman himself—his portrait drawings and studies of trees and landscape are among the first natural and "unmannerist" works produced in Haarlem (Fig. 5.1). After returning from Italy, he gradually abandoned the exaggerated anatomy of Spranger's Mannerism and, after 1600, began to paint. Encouraged by his success as a portrait draughtsman, he painted several portraits before tackling more ambitious subjects such as *Vertumnus and Pomona* (Fig. 5.2).

The deities Vertumnus and Pomona were traditionally associated with gardens and ripening fruit, a connection made by the pruning scythe held by Pomona and the apples and pears beside her. As recounted in Ovid's *Metamorphoses*, Vertumnus, besotted with love for Pomona but rejected by her, tried courting her in various disguises, including that of an old woman, as depicted here. In this form, she unsuspectingly allowed him to approach and plead his cause and, as implied by her sympathetic gaze, he is about to be victorious. Transformed back into his real form as a splendid young god, he admits his deception and she accedes to his desires. For painters, the female nude had become a metaphor for art and beauty, whose impact is heightened here by its poignant contrast with the old body of Vertumnus. The deceit of artistic illusion offered to the viewer is underscored by Vertumnus' trick that allows him to win his love. That the artist, then about fifty-seven, identified with the disguised lover rendered harmless by his age and gender, seems inevitable as he created this vision of robust and alluring female beauty. Goltzius's rendition of areas such as Pomona's stomach, her sun-tanned hand, and knee are based on close observation of one of his models. The globular shape of her breasts seems, however, a deliberate distortion intended to emphasize the connection between this goddess and fruit, thus with fertility, as does the slight swelling of her stomach. The eccentric viewpoints and

5.1 Hendrick Goltzius, *View of the Dunes near Haarlem*, 1603. Drawing, pen and brown ink, 3½ × 6 in (9 × 16 cm). Museum Böymans Van Beuningen, Rotterdam.

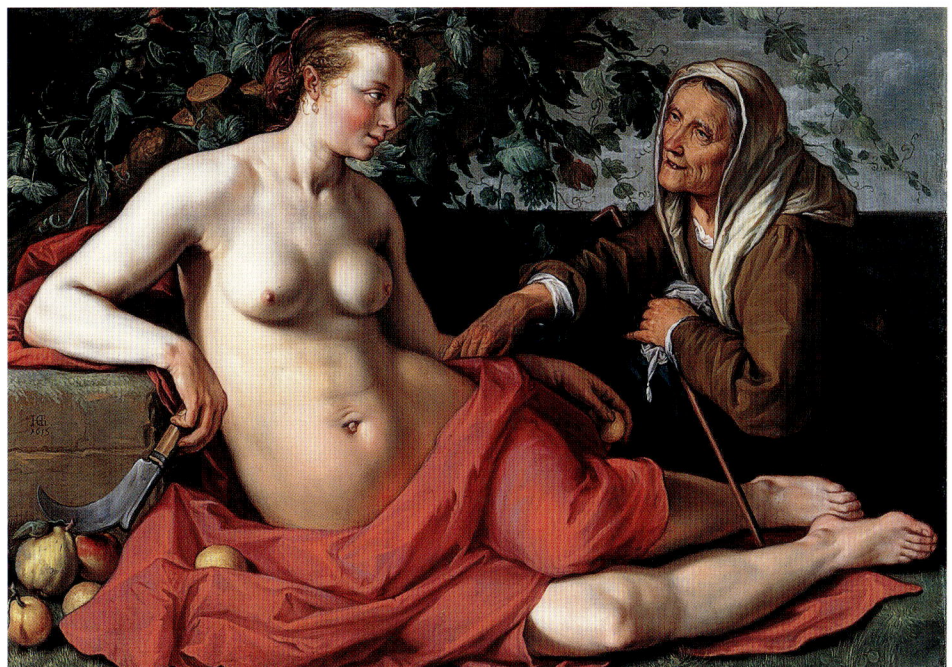

5.2 Hendrick Goltzius, *Vertumnus and Pomona*, c. 1615. Oil on canvas, 35½ × 41 in (90.4 × 104.2 cm). Fitzwilliam Museum, Cambridge, England.

tricky poses of Cornelisz. van Haarlem's paintings are gone. Hendrick Goltzius's picture proclaims the artist to be an enthusiastic supporter of art based on nature rather than on artificial conventions.

The Utrecht "Caravaggisti"

Goltzius left Italy too soon to see any public commissions by Caravaggio, whose work affected Dutch artists powerfully between 1610 and 1630. It was the next generation of artists who saw them and became enthusiastic emulators of his realism and dramatic chiaroscuro. None came from Haarlem. It was Utrecht, the most Catholic city in the Republic, whose artists introduced this new style, and who are therefore known as the Utrecht "Caravaggisti." The greatest was Hendrick ter Brugghen (1588–1629) and the most successful was Gerard van Honthorst (1592–1656), dubbed by the Italians Gherardo delle Notti (Gerard of the Nights).

Ter Brugghen's life is poorly documented. He was born in 1588, probably in The Hague where his father was working, but his parents were natives of Utrecht. The exact years of his apprenticeship with the city's leading artist Abraham Bloemaert (1566–1651) are unknown, as are those of the time he spent in Rome though he was probably in Italy from 1608 to 1614. He registered as a master painter in the local guild and married in 1616. Ten years later he could afford to move his family to a larger house near his brother's tavern in the town center. He died in the plague of 1629, leaving seven children and a pregnant widow. Rubens was later reported to have called ter Brugghen the best painter in the Seven Provinces; the artists most often in contention for that title are Rembrandt and Vermeer, both of whom admired ter Brugghen. He may also have been a formative influence on Georges de la Tour.

Ter Brugghen and his colleagues from Utrecht evidently had access to Caravaggio's private commissions as well as his public works, for they quickly picked up and used his novel themes such as cardsharps, fortune tellers, and musicians. The men seated around the table with St. Matthew in the scene of his *Calling* (see Fig. 1.41) became the starting point for many pictures of well-dressed young men gambling, drinking, flirting with loose women, and making music. Ter Brugghen painted many single figures of musicians or drinkers that monumentalize the figure and, like Caravaggio, play down or virtually ignore the setting. He never adopted the strong chiaroscuro typical of Caravaggio's mature work but kept his lighting muted, employing a distinctive color range based on soft browns relieved by plum,

5.3 Hendrik ter Brugghen, *The Concert*, 1626. Oil on canvas, 39 × 46 in (99.1 × 116.8 cm). National Gallery, London.

5.4 (right) Hendrik ter Brugghen, *Melancholia*, c. 1625. Oil on canvas, 26⅜ × 18⅜ in (67 × 46.5 cm). Art Gallery of Ontario, Toronto.

5.5 (opposite) Hendrik ter Brugghen, *St. Sebastian Tended by St. Irene*, 1625. Oil on canvas, 58¹⁵⁄₁₆ × 47¼ in (149.6 × 120 cm). Allen Memorial Art Museum, Oberlin College, OH.

rose red, and turquoise blue. He usually showed the light source for night scenes and portrayed the differences between light cast by a fire, a lantern, or candles. His masterful *The Concert* (Fig. 5.3), for example, has a candle in a metal stand in the foreground that sheds creamy light on the adjacent sleeves of the two musicians in the foreground while another candle on the wall defines the back wall of the room where they are performing.

Ter Brugghen's allegorical work, *Melancholia* (Fig. 5.4), shows a woman resting her head in her right hand and contemplating the skull she holds in her left. She could easily be mistaken for an image of the penitent Magdalene. The head-in-the-hand pose has a long association with Melancholy but the Magdalene adopted this pose too after her conversion and she is often shown with a skull (see Fig. 4.24). She usually wears red, however, not the whites and soft blues seen here. The dividers beside the prayer book are also often seen with images of Melancholy, for this was one of the four temperaments often associated both with mathematicians and artists: Ter Brugghen himself was said to suffer from melancholia. The fall of candlelight on the woman's skin and on the gauzy fabrics wrapped around her head and shoulders is observed with a sensitivity that even Vermeer might have envied and which he certainly admired.

One of ter Brugghen's finest religious paintings is *St. Sebastian Tended by St. Irene* of 1625 (Fig. 5.5). Earlier images of this martyr show him

erect with arrows in his chest, sometimes with a few of the Roman soldiers who failed to kill him after shooting him, sometimes in isolation in a landscape setting. While such images were still made after 1600 (see Fig. 3.14), a variant began to appear after 1586 when an influential theologian wrote about St. Irene rescuing and healing the wounded saint; she thus became a patron saint of nurses. Irene was regularly invoked whenever there was an outbreak of the plague, which did indeed occur in Utrecht in 1623–4. Sebastian's suffering was compared to that of Christ on the cross and his miraculous survival was interpreted as a parallel to Christ's resurrection. Ter Brugghen endorsed that connection by reminding the viewer of scenes of Christ's body being taken down from the cross, showing St. Irene and her companion untying Sebastian's stiff right arm and delicately extracting one arrow from his right side as she gently supports his chest with her other hand. The pallid gray skin suggests that he is barely alive. The collapsing body of the young man is placed on the edge of the pictorial space so that ter Brugghen could focus on physical details such as the soft modeling of the ribcage and the bony toes. When the painting was placed, as intended, on the altar of a private family chapel or on one in a local hospital, the knees of the saint would have been just above the viewer's eye level. The unusually low viewpoint is marked by the horizon of the landscape on the right. A pale dawn light just catches the contours of the land where a thin tree rises like a water spout, described with one bravura squiggle of olive-brown paint. One brilliant note of color is provided by the sumptuous red and gold brocade cloth on the left. It matches that of a cope with a pattern of pomegranates and thistles that belonged to David of Burgundy, a pre-Reformation bishop of Utrecht. The cope, which survived destruction by iconoclasts, became a symbol of the suppressed Catholic

5.6 Gerrit van Honthorst, *St. Sebastian*, c. 1620. Oil on canvas, 39¾ × 46 in (101 × 117 cm). National Gallery, London.

Church to local citizens; it appears in other religious paintings by ter Brugghen and Abraham Bloemaert.

Honthorst's painting of *St. Sebastian*, circa 1620 (Fig. **5.6**), both starkly confrontational and restrained, also shows the saint seated and bound to a tree trunk, but he is alone in a dark setting where only a few leaves catch the miraculous light that otherwise illuminates only his body. The tracks of dried blood on his right thigh tell us that he was standing when shot but sank down afterwards. His body is as smooth as polished marble, as if Honthorst were deliberately competing here with sculpture, perhaps the *St. Sebastian* by Bernini (the Thyssen-Bornemisza Collection, Lugano), who also posed the saint seated against a tree trunk, his right arm held back by ropes. There is a pedantic literalism about Honthorst's painting, however, that diffuses the elegaic mood evoked by ter Brugghen's saint.

Frans Hals and Dutch Portraiture

"The annals of the poor are brief." Thus begins Seymour Slive's splendid account of the life and works of Frans Hals, the portrait painter of Haarlem whose productivity and originality should have earned him enough to live comfortably throughout his long life. He was born around 1582/3 in Antwerp and fled that city with his family before its recapture by Spanish troops. He joined the Guild of St. Luke in Haarlem in 1610. In 1611 he married Annetje Harmansdr., who died four years later leaving him with two children. Hals gave her a mere pauper's burial; the records suggest that this was because he was a spendthrift, rather than lacking income. He was paid for his first militia company painting in 1616, proof of some solid professional success. He remarried in February 1617; his second wife, Lysbeth Reyniers, gave birth to their daughter nine days later. They had seven more children and she survived him by eight years. Most of Hals's sons became painters too but it has proved impossible to isolate their hands. The remaining documentation for Hals, apart from the dates on his paintings, concerns the births and deaths of his many children, occasional contract disputes, and assorted family debts, not all of his making.

5.7 Frans Hals, *Pieter Cornelisz. van der Morsch (Man with a Herring)*, 1616. Oil on canvas, transferred from panel, 34⁷⁄₁₆ × 27¼ in (87.5 × 69.2 cm). Carnegie Museum of Art, Pittsburgh, PA.

Like Rembrandt, however, he liked to collect art and sometimes had to surrender possessions to pay his bills. His last years were especially difficult. He was exempted from paying his dues to the guild after 1661 and was given a pension by the city from 1662 until his death.

Hals's first surviving work is a bust portrait of *Jacobus Zaffius* (Frans Halsmuseum, Haarlem) dated 1611, in which the confidently placed strokes of paint along the sitter's cheeks, nose, and beard already reveal the artist's distinctive touch. The portrait of *Pieter Cornelisz. van der Morsch* (Fig. **5.7**), in which the sitter is brandishing a herring in one hand and grasping a bundle of straw in the other, is even more daring. That any Dutch or Flemish artist should have left the traces of his brushstrokes so flamboyantly visible as Hals did was far bolder than a modern viewer may realize. His predecessors and peers all concealed their craft, smoothed over the rough paint edges, and left an isolated stroke only when its shape matched the form it was describing. Hals made the act of painting part of his content, forcing the viewer to consider the means by which he conjured up these engaging images of an alert but ageing archdeacon (Zaffius) and the mocking Pieter Cornelisz. playing the fool for his Leiden Rhetoricians' society. Hals's technique is most visible in portraits of single sitters because the

viewer is close enough to see the surface but will stand back from a group portrait in order to see the whole canvas. Up close the forms dissolve into a patchwork of overlapping strokes accented with a dark line here, a light flick there. Hals made this look easy, yet no one else in Haarlem dared to imitate him. Haarlemers must have admired Hals's technique because more of his portraits survive than by any of his neater rivals.

Hals varied the size and degree of apparent spontaneity in his brushstrokes according to the subject and area of the composition. While he mostly painted members of Haarlem's prosperous middle class, he also painted fishermen and boys, a few children playing recorders and lutes, and a few portraits of local eccentrics such as *Verdonck Waving a Jawbone* (National Gallery of Scotland, Edinburgh) and *Malle Babbe* (Fig. 5.8), a laughing old woman with a huge beer tankard and an owl perched on her shoulder.

5.8 (above) Frans Hals, *Malle Babbe*, c. 1630–33. Oil on canvas, 30⅞ × 26 in (78.5 × 66.2 cm). Staatliche Museen, Berlin.

5.9 (below) Frans Hals, Pieter van den Broecke, c. 1633. Oil on canvas, 28 × 24 in (71.2 × 61 cm). The Iveagh Bequest. Kenwood House, London.

The strokes in these works are much freer and more visible than those in most of his portraits, suggesting that Hals restrained himself when working for wealthy sitters who wanted a reasonable facsimile of their best lace collar or expensive embroidered sleeve. His *Pieter van den Broecke* (Fig. 5.9), for example, uses very small, disciplined descriptive strokes for the parts of the lace collar in full light and broad, long strokes for his right hand grasping a staff in the foreground. The artist knows that viewers will look past the hand to study the face and collar first; even the dangling tassel is more sketchily rendered than the collar's fringes edged with tiny triangles. The sitter was a widely-traveled trader who had been to West Africa, Arabia, Persia, and India; his journal of his time in West India displays the straightforward, confident character that Hals's portrait conjures up for us too. He wears a gold chain, his reward for services rendered to the East India Company in 1630: a valuable and prestigious tribute, it is painted with care. The dark strokes between his parted lips suggest that he is on the verge of speech in a way that is typical of Hals. The firm grasp of his staff, his left arm posed with elbow out and wrist on hip, all exude authority. Although he looks straight out of the painting, he regards the viewer kindly and his casually messy hair also makes him seem approachable. Its outer edges, like those of the contours of his shadowed left arm, are deliberately blurred as if dissolving into the background. There are no sweeping curtains or fancy furniture, just a glimpse of the chair back. Only the dim shadow on the right implies that a plain wall is nearby.

The differences between Hals and his contemporary portrait painters are apparent if his *Pieter van den Broecke* is set beside Thomas de Keyser's *Constantijn Huygens with his Page* (Fig. 5.10). In 1625, Huygens had been appointed secretary to the Stadhouder, Prince Frederick Hendrik of Orange, a position he retained in The Hague until 1650. He was therefore a man of considerable political and social standing throughout these important years of the young Republic. Though it is a full-length portrait of two people with an elaborate setting, de Keyser's panel painting is only slightly larger than Hals's canvas. His figures are thus well below life-size and cannot match the presence of Hals's confident trader, who is just under life-size. De Keyser (1596/7–1667), who was the leading portrait painter in Amsterdam until the arrival of Rembrandt, offers instead a careful description of Huygens's world. A page arrives with a message and the secretary turns, rather self-consciously, to tip him while holding a corner of the document on which he was working. There is a compass beneath his hand and an ink pot with a quill in it set precariously on a small pile of books. Behind it lies a *chitarrone*, more books, and a set of terrestrial and celestial globes. The tapestry hanging behind him and the Turkish carpet on the secretary's worktable were expensive possessions. The room, too, with its grand fireplace and high ceiling, also implies wealth and high social standing but of a more accessible kind than that conjured up by the huge column bases and swathes of drapery in van Dyck's portraits. If the setting depicts a room in Huygens's house,

5.10 Thomas de Keyser, *Constantijn Huygens with his Page*, 1627. Oil on oak, 36¾ × 27¼ in (92.4 × 69.3 cm). National Gallery, London.

Frans Hals and Dutch Portraiture 321

de Keyser must have been provided with a sketch of the room and had some of the objects transported to Amsterdam.

There is not a brushstroke out of place in de Keyser's carefully crafted painting but Huygens's personality remains an enigma. He is caught in mid-movement, yet he seems frozen rather than alive. Pieter van der Broecke has a more stable pose yet seems to shift his weight as we watch. Is it those blurred contours, that windblown hair, or the transitory facial expression that makes us believe he has just moved? After looking at any of Hals's portraits, we feel as if we have met and had a conversation with each sitter and gained a sense of their character: the portly *Claes van Voorhout* (Metropolitan Museum, New York), a brewer, evidently enjoyed his own beer; *Jasper Schade* (National Gallery, Prague) is nailed as a conceited fop; the steady gaze and firmly closed mouth of *Johannes Hoornbeek* (Musée des Beaux Arts, Brussels), who holds a book with his place in it marked by his thumb, suits an intellectual fully engaged in theological controversies.

Hals was as astute a judge of people as Rembrandt, and, unlike almost all of his peers, he was as good at endowing women with real personalities as he was his male patrons. Instead of women whose features have been homogenized into bland composites of the current ideal of female beauty, Hals portrayed them with what appears to be complete, even excessive, honesty. Double chins, large noses, eye sockets, and cheeks sunk with age are all recorded as skillfully as the smooth features of plain young women. These women let themselves be painted as they were—albeit in their finest clothes—rather than as they might have wished to be seen; such lack of pretense is more appealing than the parade of artificial beauties portrayed by Sir Peter Lely (see Fig. 6.7). Some of the younger women in fine clothes are newly married and seem a little unsure of their new role, for example *Aletta Hanemans* (Mauritshuis, The Hague). The older women seem more confident: Anna van der Aar, wife of the Haarlem historian and poet Pieter Schrevelius, who was sixty when Hals painted her, has a slightly raised eyebrow that conveys skeptical amusement (Metropolitan Museum, New York). The *Portrait of an Elderly Woman* (Fig. 5.11) has a hint of a smile. Her black dress spills out of her chair, which is larger than usual to accommodate her bulk. Her firm grip on the arm of the chair suggests however a certain reserve—"kind but firm" could be her motto. She represents a generation born during Haarlem's greatest turmoil, those who survived and prospered. Further clues to the governing beliefs of this appealing matriarch include her cap, which covers her hair completely, her black dress, and the "millstone" collar, which older Calvinist women retained after most younger women had stopped wearing them.

Among Hals's more ambitious works are his marriage and family portraits. That of *Isaac Massa and Beatrix van der Laen* (Fig. 5.12) seems to have captured a fleeting moment in the subjects' lives as well as any photograph. The brushwork contributes to this effect but in such a large picture, the viewer is not immediately aware of it, and, in this relatively early work of

5.11 Frans Hals, *Portrait of an Elderly Woman*, 1633. Oil on canvas, 40½ × 34 in (103 × 86.4 cm). National Gallery of Art, Washington, DC.

1622, Hals painted their heads, collars, and cuffs with care. It is the informality of their poses and expressions that gives the image its spontaneity. The couple seem to pause in the midst of an intimate family joke to let Hals paint them in the grounds of their country estate. Isaac Massa leans back and touches his chest as if to address the viewer, asking, "Am I not a lucky man to be married to such a lovely woman?" Beatrix rests her right hand—her marriage ring displayed on her forefinger—on his left arm, which he holds akimbo in an assertive gesture common to male portraiture. Her left hand rests in her lap but seems to gesture toward him. She leans forward slightly so that we (or the artist) can see her better while she smiles at us warmly. No classic beauty with her broad button nose, she looks at ease in her role as a young wife married to the entrepreneurial Massa (he traded with Russia and was widely traveled). She is even in the center of the painting, with her husband to one side—a compositional decision surely made by the artist in collaboration with Massa, who employed the landscape specialist Pieter Molijn (1595–1661) to provide the landscape setting.

As Rubens did in his portrait of himself with his new bride (see Fig. 2.14), which Hals may have seen when he visited Antwerp in 1616, Hals included some symbols familiar to a Dutch audience. The garden setting may show Massa's estate at Lisse, but here it is the garden of love. The ivy that meanders across the right foreground as well as clinging to the tree trunk on the left was associated with steadfast love, faithfulness, and fertility. The large thistle was also a symbol of fidelity. A glance at Rubens's portrait shows how carefully he established his status in relation to his wife and the greater formality of their poses. Isaac graciously gives pride of place to his wife, even though he retains his traditional position on our left. The bold asymmetry and welcoming, friendly expressions create

5.12 Frans Hals, *Isaac Massa and Beatrix van der Laen*, c.1622. Oil on canvas, 55⅛ × 65⅜ in (140 × 166 cm). Rijksmuseum, Amsterdam.

an immediate rapport between them and us; we can imagine chatting with them but might hesitate to approach Rubens and Isabella Brandt.

Hals's most challenging works were his five portraits of Haarlem's military companies, painted between 1616 and 1639. All have remained in the city but they no longer hang in the halls for which they were made. Since the early sixteenth century the members of such companies who commissioned a group portrait traditionally shared the cost equally among themselves. After the separation of the Netherlands in the late sixteenth century, the custom was revived, first in Amsterdam but soon in Haarlem too, where Cornelis Cornelisz. van Haarlem painted two in 1583 and 1599 (Fig. 5.13). By contrast with Cornelisz.'s stiffly posed assembly of officers crammed into a room that seems too small to contain them, Hals's *Banquet of the Officers of the St. George Civic Guard* of 1616 (Frans Halsmuseum, Haarlem) is on a large canvas. Hals put the three principal officers in front and posed them as if they were asked to turn around from the table, at which they are about to enjoy a meal, and face us. Three men, one with a flag, stand on the right, adding variety to the poses and levels of the heads. The remaining officers make an erratically spaced row across the middle ground, turning this way and that to engage a companion in conversation or to look out at the viewer. There is the impression of a momentary pause in the banquet, an annual function during which the company honored retiring officers.

The sitters in the *Haarlem Militia Company of St. George* (Fig. 5.14) from about 1627 are identifiable from documents that record their terms of office. Hals also painted a few of them on other occasions, so we know that the man seated behind the table in the center is indeed Jacob Olycan, one of a prosperous brewing family, eighteen of whom were portrayed by Hals. The chief officer in front of the table holding his glass upside down is Michiel de Wael, one of three captains and the owner of two popular taverns. Only the established citizens of Haarlem could join these companies and only its wealthiest members could be officers. Several members of this company went to the aid of Breda in 1625 when it was under siege by Spanish troops (an event painted by Velázquez; see Fig. 3.29).

Although the painting depicts a brief moment of shared conviviality, Hals never assembled everyone to plan his painting and their positions in it. He apparently worked directly onto the primed canvas, without even laying in some preliminary guidelines. (As Slive has pointed out, no composition studies survive for Rembrandt's *The "Night Watch"* either; see Fig. 5.33). Hals made no major adjustments to the composition, only small alterations to contour lines. He completed everything but the individual heads, for which the officers would come to his studio to pose when it was convenient.

5.13 Cornelisz. van Haarlem, *Banquet of the Officers of the St. George Civic Guard*, 1599. Oil on panel, 61⅝ × 87⅝ in (156.5 × 222 cm). Teylers Museum, Haarlem.

324   *Chapter 5: The Dutch Republic*

Hals's militia banquets can be seen as brilliant solutions to the "Last Supper" problem: everyone on the near side of the table must either be shown from the back or will have to join the rest of the party on the far side and face the spectator, an arrangement that would never have been adopted in real life. Hals had no theological messages to convey, only the superior status of the major officers, and he found a simple solution: he put the officers in front, but again turned around as if to face a photographer recording a special occasion. No one dominates; conversations continue quietly on left and right as the sitters allow Hals to complete his task. The artist is an undeniable presence because the subjects would never have taken these positions if he were not there. De Wael tells a servant to fill his glass again; we can almost hear the quiet murmur as they occupy themselves patiently before resuming their meal. The term "seeming realism" has been applied to Dutch images such as these, a useful phrase that reminds us of the artist's ultimate control over the final result.

While Hals usually made portraits, he did paint some genre subjects, among them children with baskets of fish at the sea shore or drinking and playing recorders. The fisher boys and girls are the first images of working children in Western European art: Hals rendered them with some of his most spectacular painterly effects and provided them with his only landscape backgrounds—scudding gray clouds, a few soaring gulls, a flash of sunshine on a patch of sea grass—in which the cold, salty atmosphere is almost palpable. The bold technique and life-size scale of these half-length paintings make them among Hals's most appealing images to a modern viewer for whom even the more relaxed demeanor of Hals's middle-class sitters is too formal. The most spectacular genre subject by Hals is, however, a theatrical scene, the *Shrovetide Revellers* (see p. 310). Only the width of a table separates the

5.14 Frans Hals, *Haarlem Militia Company of St. George*, c. 1627. Oil on canvas, 70½ × 101⅜ in (179 × 257.5 cm). Frans Hals Museum, Haarlem.

Frans Hals and Dutch Portraiture

viewer from a rowdy quartet in clothes that feature both exquisite lace and strings of sausages. The central figure is a woman in an elaborate dress—a superb wing collar with a wide border of starched bobbin lace, a delicately embroidered vest, skirt, and cape of brick-red silk, gray satin sleeves with cuffs in matching lace, and a coral necklace and bracelet. She is crowned with a laurel wreath and is holding up her right hand as if keeping time and trying in vain to exert some control over the boisterous men behind her. She is being embraced by Peeckelhaering (Pickle Herring), a regular actor's role at these Shrovetide parties along with Hans Wurst (Sausage), who leers down at her from our right and makes a lewd gesture. His clothes might look elegant, but no proper gentleman would have worn a gray woolen outfit trimmed in red, still less a sausage in his hat. Her clothes are also too flashy, even for a wedding gown. These are all costumes worn by actors: "she" may even be a man, as women seldom appeared on the stage at this time. Pickle Herring's garland of sausages has the requisite dried herrings, some root vegetables, and a pig's trotter. To his right another man makes a mocking gesture toward his eyes, as if to say all is not as it seems. A dish of sausages and pigs' feet sits in front of the young woman with some bread, a tankard of beer, a pot of mustard, and a set of bagpipes, then considered a noisy, crude musical instrument (and still so regarded by some). Its phallic connotations, which have a long history in Netherlandish art, are also appropriate here. All perform for us, facing the audience as if on a tiny stage the width of the canvas. For those familiar with the small genre scenes of drinking parties and indecent proposals produced by Hals's contemporaries in Haarlem, the scale of Hals's *Shrovetide Revellers* seems almost heroic. Was it made in order to tell potential patrons in Haarlem that he was capable of painting something besides sober men and women in black? If so, he had no takers and painted only one other similar work, the so-called *Yonker Ramp and his Sweetheart* of 1623 (Metropolitan Museum, New York), an up-to-date portrayal of the prodigal son wasting his inheritance on women and drink.

Hals's last two group portraits, of the *Regents of the Old Men's Almshouse* (Fig. **5.15**) and of the *Regentesses* (Frans Hals Museum, Haarlem), painted around 1664–5, may have been awarded in part as an act of charity for, to judge by the brushwork, the artist's sight was failing. Eugène Fromentin even declared in 1876 that Hals was "three-quarters dead" by 1660.[2] The change in

5.15 Frans Hals, *Regents of the Old Men's Almshouse*, c. 1664. Oil on canvas, 69½ × 100⅚ in (176.5 × 256 cm). Frans Hals Museum, Haarlem.

his technique between 1650 and 1660 is marked. Blotchy, almost incomprehensible when details are examined closely, the late brushwork produces a rough but powerful likeness of the men and women who administered the almshouse. While Hals's defenders have argued that his technique is a deliberate evolution from the more illusionistic yet precise descriptions of lace, embroidery, and facial features in his earlier work to a late style that discards all trivial detail for the essence of the sitter, this reading denies the social context in which he worked. If Hals had been free to discard almost all legible information about his sitters' social class and standing, which is conveyed primarily by costume, as well as treating their features with such freedom that their faces look unfinished, he would have done so. To admit that Hals could no longer paint as he wished and, more important, as most potential clients wished, is not to deny his achievements in these two late group portraits and the few late portraits of single sitters. Two of them—one being the *Portrait of a Man in a Slouched Hat* (Hessisches Landesmuseum, Kassel) and the other *Portrait of a Man* (Fitzwilliam Museum, Cambridge)—are among his most brilliant and moving canvases, in part because we can sense the struggle that he faced to create the image that both artist and patron sought through eyesight diminished by increasingly severe presbyopia.

The two almshouse group portraits are not as well preserved as Hals's earlier militia company portraits. Because they are more thinly painted, they have darkened over time so that white areas, such as the collar and shirt of the man on the right in the *Regents* portrait (see Fig. 5.15), draw attention to him and away from his companions. The men no longer smile and interact as they do in his earlier groups, but pose with gazes that place their thoughts elsewhere. If the man on the left with the book is the head regent, his status is not reinforced by either visual accents or his pose. Only the old servant behind them delivering a message is alert, as if the chance to be portrayed were a treat.

The mood in the portrait of the *Regentesses* is less somber. Three of the four women look at us; one even smiles. As in *Regents*, a servant enters from the right with a message. Her arrival triggers a descending diagonal of movement along the women's hands to the sitter at the left whose right hand acknowledges our presence. The woman on the right is the leader of this group. Her location beside the large ledger-book and her assertive pose are also markers of her higher status and authority. A large landscape painting on the wall behind them once offered a vista of the outside world but, like other elements of the setting, it is barely visible. Perhaps Hals could not control his paint as he once did, but his sense of his sitters' inner life is as perceptive and as effectively conveyed as it was in previous decades.

Town Planning and Architectural Developments in Haarlem and Amsterdam

Gerrit Berckheyde's *The Market Place and the Grote Kerk at Haarlem* (Fig. 5.16), painted in 1674, neatly summarizes the basic trends of architectural history in the Low Countries in the seventeenth century. It focuses on the huge church of St. Bavo, built in the fourteenth and fifteenth centuries in a plain Gothic style. To left and right are the step-gabled red-brick house façades typical of Dutch domestic architecture in the sixteenth and seventeenth centuries and, in the right foreground, the classical Doric portico of the Town Hall added to an older structure in 1633. The portico, which represents the new classical style, no longer exists but St. Bavo does, though no longer hemmed in by little shops along its flanks in the main square; some of the gabled houses have also survived. The very tallest of the step gables on the right next to the Grote Kerk is the Vleeshal or Meat Market, designed in 1602 by Lieven de Key (c. 1560–1627), the first Dutch designer to introduce Italian architectural motifs to the Republic. He had worked in England for several years before being appointed city architect of Haarlem in 1593. His updating of the traditional façade in this example is mostly limited to decorative elements like fans of stone over each window and the little obelisks perched on alternate gables. He also gave the building a grand central doorway with rusticated bands of stone and an emphatic keystone accent to the arched opening outlined with stone. These details

5.16 Gerrit Berckheyde, *The Market Place and the Grote Kerk at Haarlem,* 1674. Oil on canvas, 20⅜ × 26⅜ in (51.8 × 67 cm). National Gallery, London.

display some familiarity with Italian Renaissance architecture, though their piecemeal application here compared with his handling of detail in other major commissions suggests that these patrons insisted on a traditional design. Key never visited Italy and derived his notion of Italian styles from the buildings that he saw in England and from collections of engravings like those of Hans Vredeman de Vries (1527–1606). Vredeman's fantastic concoctions were extremely influential not only on the design of house façades, and in the decorative arts, especially furniture, but also on a clutch of artists who made small paintings of these impossible structures. They are the architectural equivalent of the contorted, outlandish poses that fill the late Mannerist paintings produced in Prague and Haarlem.

The shift from traditional building forms ornamented with details inspired by Italian Renaissance sources to buildings that depended on a fuller knowledge of ancient and modern Italian architectural models occurred slowly in the United Provinces. None of their architects visited Italy so their knowledge of Italian models was dependent on descriptions and engravings. Hendrick de Keyser (1565–1621) was a sculptor and stone mason who became the municipal architect of Amsterdam in 1595. His house façades, like Key's Vleeshal, recall the English Jacobean style soon swept aside by Inigo Jones's designs for the Banqueting House in Whitehall, London (see Fig. 6.9). Still de Keyser's designs made sensitive use of the classical orders and simplified the stepped gable while retaining the traditional materials of red brick with stone details. Between 1606 and 1614 he designed and built the Zuiderkerk in Amsterdam, one of the first new Protestant churches in the Republic. Then he improved on its awkward design with his Westerkerk (Figs. **5.17, 5.17a**), begun in 1620. The interior, which contrasts white wall surfaces and gray stone arches, string courses and pilasters marking the divisions between the groin-vaulted side bays and clerestory windows, recalls Filippo Brunelleschi's Florentine church interiors, which de Keyser did not know. Only the interruption of the central vista by the pews grouped around the large pulpit reminds visitors that this is not a Catholic church. Rembrandt was buried there.

The expansion of Amsterdam according to a plan that featured a series of semicircular canals with radiating roads connecting them was not the

5.17 Hendrick de Keyser, The Westerkerk, interior, Amsterdam, begun 1620.

5.17a (below) Hendrick de Keyser, The Westerkerk, plan, Amsterdam, begun 1620.

work of a cosmopolitan city planner but of the city carpenter, a certain Hendrick Staets. Laid out in 1613 and followed for the rest of the century, it is largely preserved today along with many of the later seventeenth- and eighteenth-century houses facing its narrow streets and canals. The three widest, the Herengracht, Keizergracht, and Prinsengracht, were occupied by the wealthier citizens, some of whom bought double or triple lots, making possible broad façades reflecting

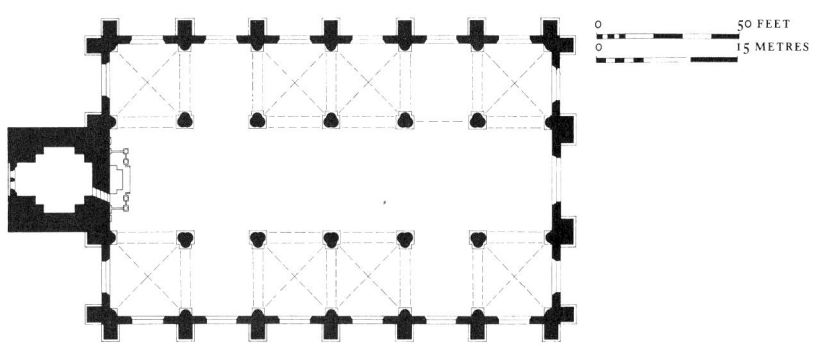

Town Planning and Architectural Developments in Haarlem and Amsterdam

classicizing models. Justus Vinckboons's Trippenhuis of 1662 (Fig. **5.18**) is an especially handsome surviving example with its eight grand Corinthian pilasters separating the tall window bays crowned by a rich acanthus scroll frieze and a triangular pediment filled with the weapons that produced the family fortune.

The Old Town Hall of Amsterdam was a charming mishmash of structures built and rebuilt after several fires in the fifteenth and sixteenth centuries. A portico supporting a single story with a steep pitched roof was attached to a crumbling tower and a house whose oddly distributed windows betrayed its makeshift history. Pieter Sanraedam preserved its appearance in a delicately toned painting made in 1657 (Fig. **5.19**), the Town Hall itself having been destroyed by fire in 1652. He had made a careful watercolor drawing of the building in 1641 and guessed that the city authorities might like to have a painted record of its appearance. They did—he received 400 guilders for it.

The difference between that odd assortment of buildings decorated with a whale rib and the huge palace that replaced it epitomizes the transformation of the city from a provincial backwater into a thriving center of European commerce. The new Town Hall (Figs. **5.20, 5.20a**), built between 1648 and 1655 to designs

5.18 (above) Justus Vingboons, Trippenhuis, façade, Amsterdam, 1662.

5.19 Pieter Jansz Sanraedam, *Amsterdam Town Hall before 1651*, 1657. Oil on panel, 25⅜ × 32⅝ in (64.5 × 83 cm). Rijksmuseum, Amsterdam.

5.20 Jacob van Campen, Royal Palace (former Town Hall), Amsterdam, 1648–55.

5.20a (below) Jacob van Campen, Royal Palace (former Town Hall), Amsterdam, plan, 1648–55.

by Jacob van Campen (1595–1657), was intended first of all to outdo in scale and prestige that of Antwerp, which was the most important building in the Renaissance style erected in the Netherlands in the sixteenth century when Antwerp reached its economic peak (see Fig. 2.1). Van Campen's building faces the Dam, the only large open space in a city where land was scarce: every square foot had to be reclaimed from the mud and every house supported by massive timber piles driven down to the bedrock below. This huge building has, however, no grand welcoming staircase. It is barely raised above eye level. Visitors enter it through seven arched openings in the center of the low, undecorated ground floor. The large spaces and impressive staircases found in comparable buildings in Italy or France do not belong here. The architect deliberately made entry difficult and access to the main floor diffused among four staircases located at the

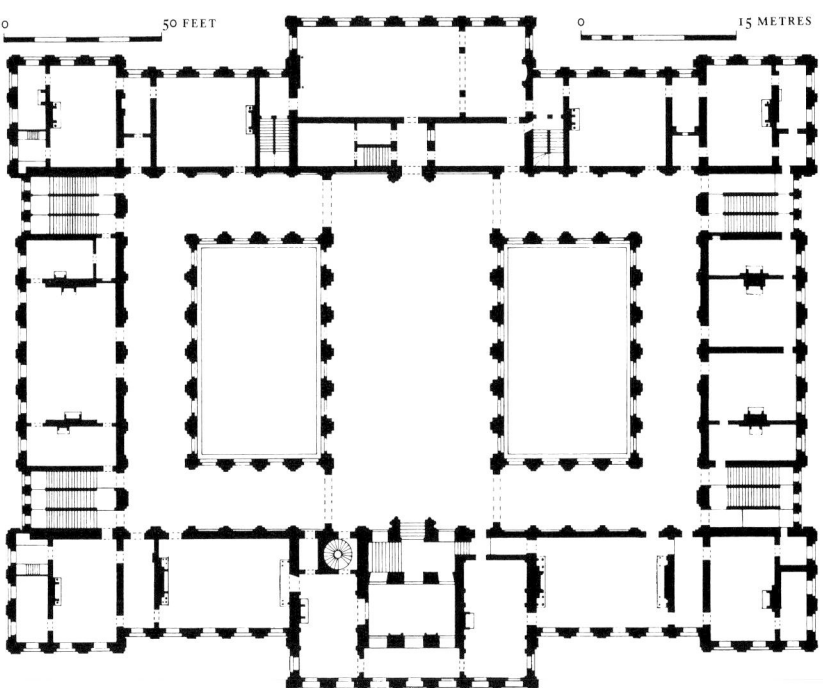

Town Planning and Architectural Developments in Haarlem and Amsterdam 331

sides so that the interior could be closed quickly and defended in case of war or rebellion.

The façade is twenty-three bays wide but the repetitive design is varied by a central block of seven bays that breaks forward from the main unit, an interruption echoed by the slight forward projection of three flanking bays on each side with their own peaked roofs. A pediment crowns the central block. Behind it is a circular tower on a square base that can be seen from afar by ships approaching the harbor. The two-story design actually encompasses two floors on each level, though the great central hall occupies the entire height of the building. Two rectangular courtyards on either side of the central hall serve as lightwells. It was the biggest building in Europe when it was completed, a proud symbol of Amsterdam's new wealth and power. The interior decoration, for which a team of Flemish sculptors and many of the city's best painters were employed to carve allegories and make huge canvases celebrating events in the early history of Dutch territories, was not finished until the 1660s.

While the exterior of the Town Hall is a pedestrian mass, van Campen's earlier design for the Mauritshuis in The Hague is a perfectly proportioned town house in Palladian style (Figs. **5.21, 5.21a**). It was made for Prince Johan Maurits van Nassau, a general who served as Governor of the Dutch colony in Brazil. Because the site was open on all sides—the house is surrounded by water at the end of an oblong canal fronting the royal palace—the architect was able to do more than plan room sequences around narrow staircases and design some decorations for the façade, as most architects had to when designing row houses in Dutch cities. Van Campen placed a staircase leading to the front entrance and a double staircase in the entrance hall giving access to the second floor. An ingenious symmetrical floor plan yields one large formal room accessed from the entrance hall and three rooms on either side, one more intimate and two of square plan, all well lit and each with its own fireplace. The lowest floor functions as a stylobate platform for the main structure, whose brick walls are articulated with unfluted Ionic limestone pilasters on all four sides. Their arrangement varies on the front and back façades, which each have a central pediment. That on the entrance façade frames a bay of three windows where stone replaces the brick and garlands decorate the spaces between the first and second floor, as they do on the brick bays to either side. Proportions are nicely judged throughout and details are sensitively placed. The result is a city residence as elegant as Palladio's Villa Rotonda.

5.21 (above) Jacob van Campen & Pieter Post, Mauritshuis, façade, The Hague, 1633–44.

5.21a (right) Jacob van Campen & Pieter Post, Mauritshuis, The Hague, plan, 1633–44.

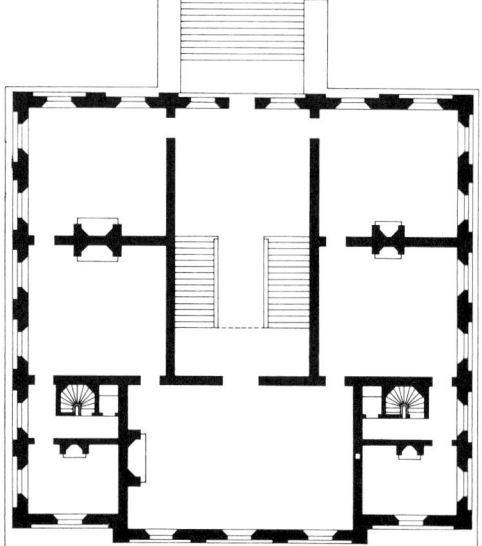

332   Chapter 5: The Dutch Republic

Painting in Amsterdam

Thou Amsterdam dost make Apelles' fame bend...
For thou art the Paragon of the world...
Italy thou defiedst, all that she had or has.

When this clumsy panegyric was penned in 1618, Amsterdam's artistic community was not worthy of such bombastic praise.[3] Haarlem's artists offered more depth and versatility in the first decades of the century and Utrecht's well-traveled admirers of Caravaggio also offered local collectors striking new imagery. Not until the 1630s, after Rembrandt had moved to Amsterdam from Leiden and established himself as the most exciting painter in the Dutch Republic, might such extravagant claims be made for the city's artistic achievements. Amsterdam was, however, the largest and most prosperous city in the Dutch Republic and thus offered artists many opportunities. Never invaded or sacked in the Republic's struggle for independence, it grew dramatically during the early years of the century, attracting Jewish and Protestant immigrants from Portugal, France, Germany, and the Spanish Netherlands. The population swelled from 60,000 to over 100,000. Its successful citizens commissioned portraits of themselves, their wives, and even their entire families. The various civic bodies—guilds, military companies, and syndics—ordered group portraits of their officers. Their fine new town houses and country estates needed architects as well as paintings to fill the walls of the reception rooms. Only sculptors lacked serious commissions, for the Dutch rarely ordered marble tombs for their churches or even a portrait bust. Skilled craftsmen could produce the carved decoration used in domestic settings. The team of sculptors who decorated the new Town Hall of Amsterdam after 1648 were all Flemish.

Talented artists worked in many small towns throughout the Republic but the wealth of Amsterdam was a magnet that gradually drew artistic talent from elsewhere. The innovations of Haarlem's painters in the first decades of the seventeenth century, who transformed portraiture, landscape painting, still-life, and genre scenes, were soon adopted in Amsterdam, though few competent specialists in these genres were active there before 1640. Only the portraits of Rembrandt and the history paintings of Rembrandt and his teacher Pieter Lastman had no competitors elsewhere. By the 1640s, however, the city might claim that its artists could best their rivals in the rest of the Republic, and even challenge the greatest artists of antiquity and Italy, as Theodore Rodenburgh declared in his awkward (and cleverly translated) poem quoted above. It is significant that to outperform the artists of classical antiquity and of Italy was an important goal.

The most important painter working in Amsterdam in the teens and twenties was Pieter Lastman (1583–1633), with whom Rembrandt studied for six months in 1623/4. Lastman was in Italy from 1601/2 to 1606. In Rome he discovered the work of Adam Elsheimer (see Figs. 1.55, 1.56), who was only five years older. Elsheimer's concentrated dramas on small copper supports, acutely observed and exquisitely detailed, were admired by many artists but Lastman modeled his art more closely on them than anyone else. He mostly preferred oak panels to the silvered copper used by Elsheimer; he also worked on a larger scale. What Lastman did adopt from his German exemplar were the richly costumed, crowded casts of characters, the vaguely Roman buildings and landscape settings, and the tenderly observed human reactions of his actors. All of these features were in turn admired, understood, and adapted by Rembrandt in his earliest surviving paintings. He was still adapting Lastman's compositions in the 1640s.

Lastman devoted his career to history paintings, a brave decision at the time. He never painted portraits or landscapes, for which there was a ready market, but chose subjects from the Bible and ancient history, sometimes quite rare themes that only highly educated or extremely devout patrons would have recognized. His *Abraham Dismissing Hagar and Ishmael* (Fig. 5.22) has fewer figures than most of his other paintings; it is a touching portrayal of the story told in the book of Genesis that focuses on the inner feelings of the protagonists. Abraham and his wife Sarah had entered into an agreement whereby their servant Hagar had borne a son, Ishmael, to Abraham as Sarah had for many years failed to conceive a child. When Sarah then

5.22 Pieter Lastman, *Abraham Dismissing Hagar and Ishmael*, 1612. Oil on oak panel, 19 × 28⅛ in (48.3 × 71.4 cm). Kunsthalle, Hamburg.

gave birth to a son, Isaac, she no longer tolerated the arrangement and insisted that Hagar and Ishmael be banished. Abraham's reluctant compliance is conveyed by his right hand laid on Ishmael's head; as Hagar makes her eloquent last pleas, she rests her left hand on her son's shoulder while Abraham listens in stoic silence. Ishmael has turned away, resigned to his fate. He clutches a flask, an allusion to a later moment in the story when he almost dies of thirst before an angel appears to show Hagar the location of a nearby spring of water. Sarah, holding her baby in her arms, watches from the left distance near an archway leading to the town. Behind Hagar is an expansive vista with a river, a bridge, and mountains, terrain into which she and her son will venture with bare feet. The weather does not look hospitable. Rembrandt was impressed. He made a drawing after the painting and had it in mind in 1637 when he made an etching of the same moment, concentrating on the figures, especially Abraham. Both Abrahams wear plump turbans and layers of rich fabrics, those in Lastman's painting decorated with deep embroidered borders. Lastman's chunky Ishmael is no perfect Italian child and Hagar is also homely rather than elegant. The lack of idealization of characters who could reasonably be shown as beautiful or handsome is another trait adopted by Rembrandt.

Rembrandt van Rijn and his School

Rembrandt's Early Years in Leiden

Rembrandt van Rijn was born on July 15, 1606 to a miller, Harmen Gerritszoon and his wife, Neeltgen van Zuytbroeck, the daughter of a baker in Leiden. The city, which had broken a four-month siege by the Spanish in 1574 by breaching the dykes that protected them and flooding their land, was the seat of the oldest Protestant university in Europe. It was founded right after the defeat of the Spanish forces and was a focus of civic pride in many disciplines. Rembrandt was listed in the registry of its matriculated students in 1620 when he was fourteen. This may mean only that he was a competent Latinist or it may mean that his parents intended him to follow a different career that required a university education, as Rubens's mother had also hoped for her son. Having studied with the Leiden painter Jacob van Swanenburg around 1619–22, Rembrandt was in Amsterdam from 1622–3, working in the studio of Pieter Lastman. He may well have received more "book learning" than most painters of his day. His choice of unusual subjects and of unexpected moments in familiar stories later on proves that Rembrandt was not only literate but a thoughtful close reader of the texts that inspired—in the full meaning of that overused word—his images.

The small *Tobit and Anna* (Fig. **5.23**) painted when the artist was only twenty, has been described by Gary Schwartz as "his first truly accomplished painting." Anna has brought her old blind husband a goat that she has been given. Instead of delight and praise, he accuses her of stealing it and insists she return it or give it away. She is upset and upbraids him for being more generous to strangers than to her. Distraught, he prays for death as Anna looks on in amazement at this turn of events. Only Lastman had depicted this moment before; other artists preferred Tobit's accusation of his wife instead. This was a more difficult subject than the more dramatic moments that precede it in the story as told in the Apocrypha. Rembrandt describes the reactions of both figures with ease: Anna's jaw is a little slack as she gazes at Tobit; he turns away from her, his blind eyes closed, his mouth barely open as he murmurs his pleas to God. Rembrandt also created a vivid picture of the daily life of this ageing couple caught in a domestic squabble motivated by Tobit's strict moral principles: the rendering of elaborate patterned fabrics on Tobit, tattered and patched; Anna's stole with bands of rose and blue, her gnarled hands clutching the young goat; the string of onions hanging beside the window; the basket hooked up on the wall behind her; other utensils stacked on shelves in the shadows behind.

The relatively bright colors and well-lit interior space of this painting soon disappear from Rembrandt's work. Even here, the light falls more fully on Tobit than on Anna in a manner not explicable by normal conditions. By 1627, Rembrandt was already adopting a more monochrome palette and using more dramatic light effects, sometimes in night scenes with candles and torches as the light source. His earliest self-portraits—a group of etchings of his head in a variety of expressive poses and small panels with his features partially concealed in pools of shadow (Fig. **5.24**)—also play with exaggerated contrasts of light and dark, his best-known

5.23 (left) Rembrandt van Rijn, *Tobit and Anna*, 1626. Oil on canvas, 15½ × 11⅞ in (39.5 × 30 cm). Rijksmuseum, Amsterdam.

5.24 (right) Rembrandt van Rijn, *Self-Portrait*, c. 1629. Oil on panel, 9¼ × 6⅝ in (23.4 × 17.2 cm). Staatliche Museen, Kassel.

Rembrandt van Rijn and his School

stylistic trait. Undoubtedly he was aware of the work of Utrecht painters such as ter Brugghen (see Figs. 5.3–5.5) as he sought to find a style less obviously modeled on that of Lastman.

By 1631, Rembrandt was ready to try his luck in Amsterdam. He and his studio companion, Jan Lievens (1607–74), had already attracted the attention of Constantijn Huygens (see Fig. 5.10), the Stadhouder's secretary, who described them around 1630 as young artists of exceptional promise. Of the two, "Rembrandt surpasses Lievens in the faculty of penetrating to the heart of his subject matter and bringing out its essence." Both, however, were "know-it-alls, and do not think it worth their while to sacrifice the few months that it would take them to visit Italy. This is plainly a touch of idiocy in intelligences that in other respects are quite exceptional."[4] Huygens, who had received a classical education, thought that a serious artist could not achieve greatness without visiting Italy and studying Michelangelo and Raphael as well as the monuments of ancient Rome. He knew that Rubens had done so, and had similar ambitions for Rembrandt and Lievens at the court of The Hague. They not only refused to follow his example but said that they could see plenty of Italian art in Amsterdam. Rembrandt collected Italian prints and did see a few important Italian paintings in local collections, but his knowledge of earlier art was quite limited compared with Rubens's.

Rembrandt in Amsterdam

Rembrandt launched his career in Amsterdam with two outstanding portraits, the first of *Nicolaes Ruts* (Fig. 5.25) and the other of *Marten Looten* (County Museum, Los Angeles), the latter signed and dated January 17, 1632. Both show the subjects in three-quarter view facing the spectator, their figures cut off slightly below the waist. Lootens's simple black clothes (he was a member of the Mennonite sect) are relieved only by a flat white collar and the piece of paper he holds with a message from the artist. Ruts stands in front of a wall subtly illuminated around his figure that gives full play to the irregular contours created by his sumptuous sable-lined sleeveless coat and fur-edged hat; his right hand, a little plump and a little arthritic, rests on a chair back close to us. Ruts, like Isaac Massa (see Fig. 5.12), had made money in the fur trade with Russia; by the time of his death in 1638, however, he was almost bankrupt. His daughter, who had married well, may have commissioned his portrait to display in her shop which sold furs and silks.

The *Anatomy Lesson of Dr. Nicolaes Tulp* (Fig. 5.26) confirmed Rembrandt's position as Amsterdam's best portraitist. Seven well-dressed men listen as Dr. Tulp holds up the tendons that move the thumb and forefinger with a surgical tool. The corpse of Aris Kint, who had been executed the day before for stealing a coat, fills the foreground, his feet in shadow next to a large anatomy textbook. Tulp was not only

5.25 Rembrandt van Rijn, *Nicolaes Ruts*, 1631. Oil on mahogany panel, 46 × 34⅜ in (116.8 × 87.3 cm). Frick Museum, New York.

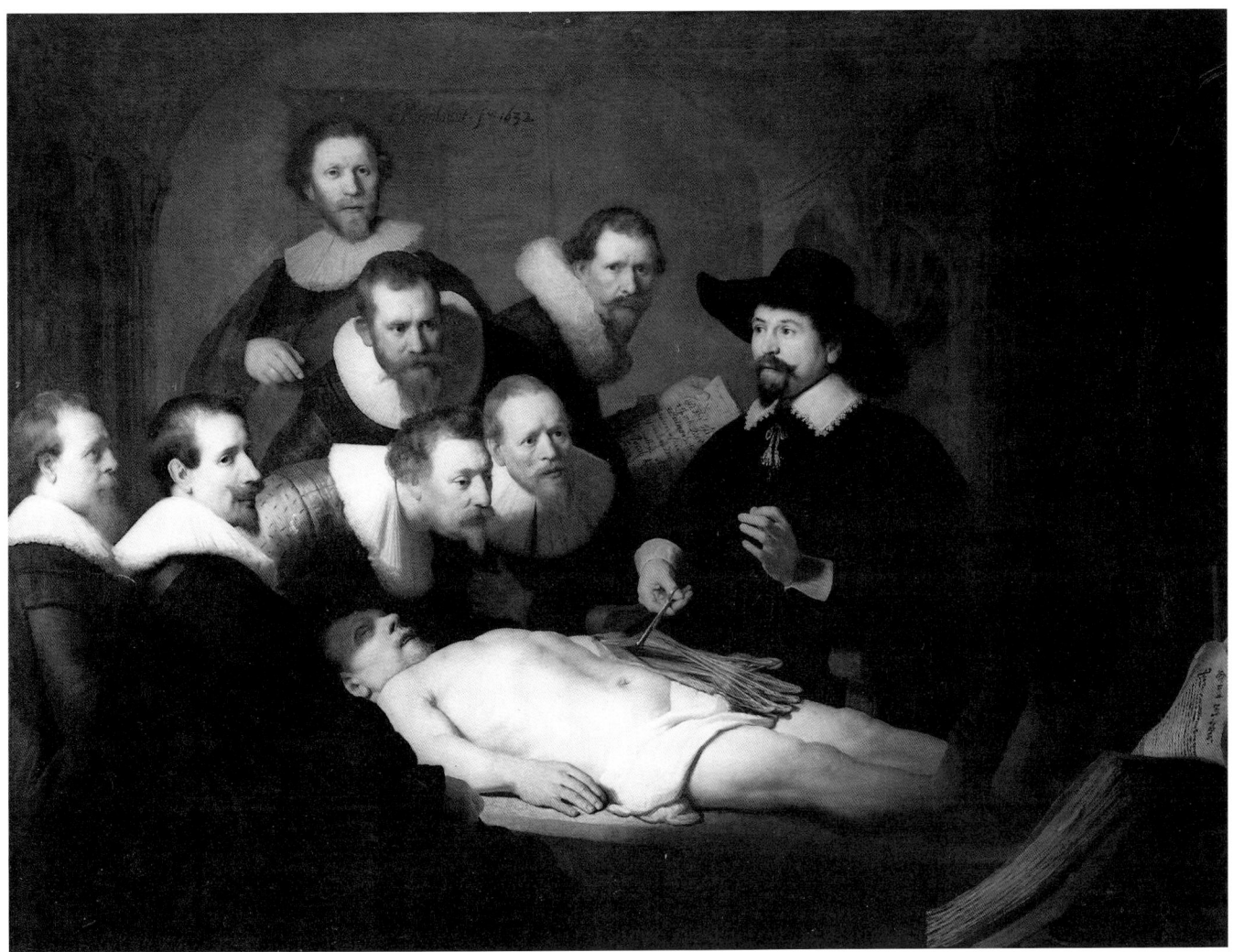

the prelector of the anatomy guild, but later also Burgomaster of Amsterdam; several of his predecessors also held both posts, so highly regarded were those who understood human anatomy. In this discipline at least, the newly established University of Amsterdam could rival that of Leiden's older establishment. The demonstration of Tulp recorded by Rembrandt was actually the second public dissection of January 1632, the previous one having been performed by a doctor dismissed soon afterwards because he was a Remonstrant.[5] Tulp's decision to record the dissection was made, according to Gary Schwartz, to publicize the caliber of Amsterdam's doctors.

Rembrandt's portrait of Tulp departs from convention in a significant way that reveals Tulp's other motives for ordering the picture. Dissections always began by opening the stomach and removing the organs, which decay more rapidly than the rest of the body. Thus by starting on the arm, as Tulp is doing, he emphasizes the human hand, a far more complex and versatile structure than those of apes or other closely related animal species. Tulp had in fact argued in his book that the human hand with its opposable thumb was proof of man's superior status in the great chain of being. Rembrandt, a painter whose hand could conjure up such images out of paint on a canvas or panel, surely agreed with Tulp's views for he signed his name prominently on the back wall. Even the concentration on the lecture is a departure from earlier group portraits of this kind, in which most of those present regard the viewer rather than the corpse of the dead criminal in the foreground. Tulp does not occupy the center of the picture either, as in earlier examples, but has the right third of the canvas to himself. Attendant members of the surgeons' guild, grouped on three

5.26 Rembrandt van Rijn, *Anatomy Lesson of Dr. Nicolaes Tulp*, 1632. Oil on canvas, 66⅔ × 85¼ in (169.5 × 216.5 cm). Royal Cabinet of Paintings, Mauritshuis, The Hague.

Rembrandt van Rijn and his School 337

levels to his right, peer down, around, and (in three cases) out of the group to the audience for whom the lesson is also clearly intended.

While portraits first made Rembrandt's reputation in Amsterdam and provided a steady source of income for most of his life, narrative subjects taken from mythology and the Bible had captured his imagination first and, for an ambitious painter, would always be the preferred category. His *The Artist in his Studio* (Fig. **5.27**) shows him standing back to look at his work, a canvas larger than anything he had painted so far, as if to announce that this was the scale on which he wanted to work. None of his religious or mythological works to date was as large as the *Anatomy Lesson* and few would be afterwards. Some time in the early 1630s, however, Huygens did obtain for Rembrandt a commission to paint two medium-sized panels for the Stadhouder depicting events from the Passion of Christ, the *Raising of the Cross* (see Fig. 5.29) and the *Descent from the Cross* (see Fig. 5.30). These are the subjects of the central panels of Rubens's two great triptychs in Antwerp completed a few years earlier (see Figs. 2.15 and 2.18). The coincidence was deliberate: Huygens saw Rembrandt as the Dutch artist equal to Rubens in potential; Rembrandt would now have a chance to demonstrate his gifts in a way that would allow connoisseurs to compare the two. Rembrandt had never seen Rubens's altarpieces but he knew their compositions from engravings by Lucas Vorsterman.

There are extensive differences between these works by the two giants of Netherlandish painting in the seventeenth century that can only partly be explained by the disparity in scale and function. Rubens's panels are over 15 feet (4.5 meters) high, those of Rembrandt just over 3 feet (0.9 meters) high. Rubens made his triptychs for public worship in large interior spaces. Rembrandt's paintings were displayed in the Stadhouder's private quarters in The Hague. Given the scale, Rembrandt knew that he could not emulate the drama and dynamism of Rubens's heroic renditions buttressed by quotations from famous ancient and modern Italian art. He needed a different approach. Instead of Rubens's muscular superman in a rhythmic *contrapposto* pose, Rembrandt cast Christ as a thin man in a pose as straight as the cross itself. His body would require no effort to lift; it is even turned away from us and made less impressive by the foreshortened three-quarter view. The raising of the cross is being assisted by the artist, who has put himself in the well-lit center of the canvas. A turbaned man on horseback directs the proceedings as shadowy figures push from behind and a man in contemporary armor pulls from the front. In the gloom behind them on the right the two thieves walk together, the bad one bowed over, the good one erect. The viewer's attention is drawn back again and again to the slim figure of Christ gazing heavenwards, the only fully lit figure in the painting, which he dominates far more completely than Rubens's Christ amid a crowd of muscular giants straining to lift him into position.

Rubens's dead Christ in his *Descent from the Cross* (Fig. **5.30**) is a paler, more relaxed version of the figure portrayed in the *Raising of the Cross* (Fig. **5.29**). Rembrandt's conception could hardly be less heroic: the dead Christ in the latter has collapsed and crumpled, his head dropped over his chest, his body kept upright only by his skinny right arm held by a man in blue on a ladder. The artist is holding Christ's legs, his own hands covered by the winding sheet as others assist in sliding the dead body slowly to the ground. As in Rubens's painting, the white shroud held up behind the corpse makes a

5.27 Rembrandt van Rijn, *The Artist in his Studio*, c. 1627–8. Oil on panel, 9¾ × 12½ in (24.8 × 31.7 cm). Zoe Oliver Collection, given in memory of Lillie Oliver Poor. Museum of Fine Arts, Boston, MA.

338   *Chapter 5: The Dutch Republic*

5.28 Rembrandt van Rijn, *Blinding of Samson*, 1636. Oil on canvas, 6 ft 8 in × 9 ft (2.06 × 2.76 m.) Städelsch Kunstinstitut, Frankfurt.

dramatic patch of light around it against the surrounding gloom. Instead of Rubens's bold diagonal shaft of white, however, Rembrandt uses a smaller, almost symmetrical triangle of cream cloth in the center of the canvas. The turbaned supervisor has dismounted and watches from the shadows on the right. The group of women around the fainting Virgin Mary can be made out only dimly in the left foreground. It is the patch of light falling on Christ and the artist, who stares intently toward Christ's unseeing eyes, that holds the viewer's attention. The awkward physicality of the artist's face pressed up against Christ's stomach forces us to think about what is happening. Rembrandt shows himself converting from persecutor to follower in these two paintings, possibly therefore as Longinus, the soldier who, according to legend (he is unnamed in the Gospels), became a Christian when he pierced Christ's side with his spear. As noted above, Rubens may have taken the same role in his own *Raising of the Cross*, where he seems on the verge of changing sides even as he helps to push up the cross, though he does not reappear in the *Descent from the Cross*. Rembrandt may have been aware of this piece of self-identification and for that reason decided to play a similar role in his two paintings. It is a far more prominent role than those he had assumed in some of his earlier narrative scenes, in which he appears more discreetly as part of a watching crowd.

The Stadhouder was pleased and commissioned three more paintings of Passion subjects from Rembrandt, the *Entombment*, *Resurrection*, and *Ascension* (all Altepinakothek, Munich). The artist did not deliver the *Ascension* until 1636 and the other two until 1639. The delays provoked some correspondence between the artist and Huygens; the letters from Rembrandt are the only ones by him to have survived. The artist

5.29 (left) Rembrandt van Rijn, *Raising of the Cross*, c. 1633. Oil on canvas, 37⅜ ×28 ⅜ in (96 × 72 cm). Alte Pinakothek, Munich.

5.30 (right) Rembrandt van Rijn, *Descent from the Cross*, c. 1633. Oil on canvas, 36⅜ ×27 ⅜ in (92 × 69.3 cm). Alte Pinakothek, Munich.

hoped to get 1,000 guilders for each picture but had to settle for 600 plus the cost of the frames.

Besides such negotiation, the letters mention a gift to Huygens from the artist, "a piece 10 feet long and 8 feet high [. . .] as a token of appreciation, which will be worthy of my lord's house."[6] Huygens evidently demurred for in a letter of January 1639 Rembrandt insisted, "sending this accompanying canvas against my lord's wishes, hoping that you will not take me amiss in this as it is the first token which I offer my lord." In a postscript, he added: "My lord hang this piece in a strong light and so that one can stand at a distance from it, then it will show at its best," which is how the artist himself studies his work in the little *The Artist in his Studio* (see Fig. 5.27). What did he send to Huygens? The usual suspect is the *Blinding of Samson* (Fig. **5.28**), whose measurements match the gift, though some have doubted that such a brutal image would have found favor with a patron who admired Italian art and classical restraint. If he did accept a large painting from the artist, there is no further record of it in his possession. When Rembrandt painted the *Blinding of Samson*, however, he intended to make his mark as an artist equal to Rubens by painting a dramatic subject on a scale that would allow him a fair chance to prove his case. For that reason alone, it would have been an appropriate gift to a patron who wanted to see how his protégé compared with the Flemish competition.

Rembrandt began by picking a different moment in the story of Samson as told in the Old Testament book of Judges. Artists usually showed Samson asleep and about to be shorn of his hair, the source of his phenomenal strength. Rembrandt shifted the emphasis from Delilah's seduction of Samson to its humiliating and gory consequences. Delilah flees from the tent clutching Samson's locks and the shears, but looks back at the man she has betrayed. The weakened hero is pinned on his back, his chest bared to the blade of a spear held by a soldier in an exotic deep red and apricot-orange costume. One soldier in armor holds Samson's right wrist in shackles while another uses an arm to keep him down as he plunges a dagger into his right eye. Samson grits his teeth, tenses his toes, and clenches his fist but he cannot dislodge his enemies. The futility of his efforts is made palpable by the force of the descending line of Philistines on the right. The details are made all the more telling through the juxtapositions of light against dark: the blade against Samson's chest; his clenched toes against Delilah's white sleeve; the soldier on the left against the daylight flooding into the tent. Like Caravaggio's *Judith and Holofernes* (Palazzo Barberini, Rome), which forces the viewer to confront the bloody reality of decapitation and makes all previous interpretations of the story look tame, Rembrandt's *Blinding of Samson* is a sensational and deliberately confrontational depiction of cruelty. He may well have had Caravaggio's provocative realism in mind as well as Rubens's heroics; Samson's pose was directly inspired by Rubens's *Prometheus Bound* (see Fig. 2.21) though Rembrandt avoided any hint of the superbly honed musculature of this source.

Rembrandt's Self-Portraits

Of the roughly seventy-five self-portraits that Rembrandt painted, etched, and drew between the late 1620s and his death in 1669, four are shown here: one small early example (see Fig. 5.24); *The Artist in his Studio* (see Fig. 5.27), the half-length *Self-Portrait at the Age of Thirty-Four* (see Fig. 5.31); and the late *Self-Portrait with Maulstick and Brushes* (see Fig. 5.40). No artist before or since has produced as many independent self-portraits nor displayed such variety in format, type, and medium. Why did he do them and who acquired them? There were none in his house when the contents were inventoried in 1657 after he was forced to declare bankruptcy; records of ownership during his lifetime are scant, though Charles I of England and Duke Cosimo II de' Medici had one each. This evidence suggests that the self-portraits were acquired or given by the artist to patrons, and that his reputation was such that he had no trouble getting rid of them. It was even worth his while to make a few etched self-portraits. Indeed, the sheer quantity of surviving self-portraits is alone proof of the artist's fame during his lifetime and afterwards.

The most important characteristic of these self-images is that—with one painted exception of 1632 (Glasgow Art Gallery and Museum) and a related etching made in 1631—Rembrandt never portrayed himself as most of his fellow artists did, as a respectable member of the upper classes wearing the black jacket and white collar that was the standard uniform for Dutch and Flemish male sitters in commissioned portraits before 1650 and for many years afterwards. Furthermore, Rembrandt's unruly mop of curly brown hair is either a halo of swirls around his pudgy face or it is partly concealed under berets of various sizes, by turbans, helmets, or a hat with a sweeping brim and a large feather stuck in the ribbon round its crown. None of this was conventional. His clothes often look like theatrical costumes rescued from a jumble sale, piled on in layers and held together with sashes and belts. Rembrandt painted himself in roles that had nothing to do with his own life, ranging from dignified oriental potentate or pathetic beggar to confident soldier, proud standard bearer, fierce ruler, and successful courtier draped with the gold chains then given by princes to their favorites. He even portrayed himself as St. Paul.

The apparent honesty with which Rembrandt recorded his own changing features as he aged implies an acceptance of the human condition which the creation of flattering images of himself or others would not. Rembrandt's great gifts as a narrative painter who could convey the full gamut of human behavior would seem to require a superior degree of self-knowledge that would be enhanced by repeated confrontation with his own persona. While some recent writers have sought to downplay this reading as too post-Freudian to make sense of a seventeenth-century Dutchman, others note that the Greek words for "Know thyself" were inscribed on the Temple of Apollo at Delphi. However we interpret Rembrandt's character, it is clear that he avoided conventional norms in his self-portraits. Only the earliest, informal examples can be explained as training exercises that enabled him to master facial expression and the effects of bright and half light on his features. The rest require other justifications.

When the second edition of Giorgio Vasari's *Lives of the Most Excellent Painters, Sculptors and Architects* was published in 1568, each artist's biography was preceded by a woodcut self-portrait. A few Northern European artists, for whom no such comprehensive account of their achievements had yet been compiled, had made self-portraits before then but the numbers increased markedly after 1550. In 1572 Domenicus Lampsonius, an Antwerp humanist, published a compilation of twenty-three engraved portraits of Northern artists. It was so popular that it was reprinted four times before 1600, and then reissued in an expanded Dutch edition of sixty-eight in 1610. Rembrandt probably owned both books for some of his more fanciful outfits of sixteenth-century fashions are based on these prints. His use of costume associated with great predecessors implied that he considered himself a legitimate successor also worthy of lasting fame.

By about 1630 the self-portrait had a well-established role in promoting and sustaining an artist's reputation in Europe, but most sixteenth- and seventeenth-century artists did not depict themselves in working clothes with the tools of their trade. To do so would be to associate them with the craft professions of the humbler classes. They presented themselves instead as perfect gentlemen relaxing with one ungloved hand in a setting that hinted at a princely lifestyle (see Fig. 2.2). Rembrandt, however, showed himself at his easel already around 1627 (see Fig. 5.27), then in an etching with his wife Saskia in 1635, in another of 1648 beside a window, and in several late portraits where he almost flaunts his rumpled work clothes, palette, and brushes (see Fig. 5.40). What is wrong, he seems to ask, with being an artist? Why pretend to be someone of such elevated social status that you never touch a brush or crayon?

While self-promotion explains in general why Rembrandt produced so many self-portraits, this motive does not explain their varied character. Some are classifiable as *tronies* (head studies, usually sporting exotic headgear), a popular category with Dutch collectors. Specialists cannot always decide if some of his portraits represent him or not but their owners may not have worried, happy to have an image that resembled the artist even if he was wearing an outmoded hat or gold chains that he did not possess. The famed chiaroscuro was there, the familiar head emerging from half light, while the eyes, scrutinizing the owner as if on the verge of speech, testified to Rembrandt's expertise in conveying the inner feelings of his subjects. These images are more than simple *tronies*, however. The beret, which became his trademark, was his own self-identifying choice of headgear, which was then imitated by some of his pupils. His costumes enabled him to hint at the roles of his characters in his history paintings while his skill at suggesting fur, silks, and glinting metal displayed his virtuoso techniques that could also be employed in either portraits or history paintings. Finally their variety provided evidence of his infinite capacity for *invenzione*. Thus Rembrandt's self-portraits are always about his art and are made to advance his reputation among his peers as well as with patrons. They are also about his bid for posthumous fame. No single example makes this point in more complex, multi-layered fashion than the *Self-Portrait at the Age of Thirty-Four* of 1640 (Fig. 5.31).

As has long been recognized, the composition with the artist's right arm resting on a ledge close to the viewer's space is taken from Titian's *Portrait of a Man* (National Gallery, London); formerly in Amsterdam, it is believed by some to represent the poet Ludovico Ariosto. The initials, T(iziano) V(ecellio), are inscribed on the stone ledge supporting the plump, padded blue silk sleeve of the costume. Both the direct gaze and the physiognomy support the identification as Titian, which Rembrandt may have guessed. The rendition of the sumptuous sleeve is offered to the spectator as proof of the artist's genius, a *dimostrazione d'arte*. Raphael had flaunted his skills similarly but in more subtle form in his portrait of *Baldassare Castiglione* (Louvre, Paris), which came up for auction in Amsterdam in 1639: it was bought by Alfonso Lopez, the owner of the Titian portrait, for 3,500 guilders. Rembrandt made a sketch of Raphael's portrait and noted the price beside it. The *Self-Portrait* of 1640 blends both images.

While the Titian portrait is remarkable for its splendid blue sleeve, the *Baldassare Castiglione* is equally remarkable for its austere, virtually monochrome palette of black, gray, beige, and white framing the skin tones of the sitter's face and hands. The neutral colors are enlivened by different textures: gray moleskin for the writer's sleeves that catches the light along their contours; matte black for his hat with its odd, jagged silhouette picked up by his stand-up collar and for the lower part of his sleeves; and striated white for a pleated shirt emerging from the body of his black jacket. Encased in a stable pyramid of luxurious, warm clothes, Castiglione faces left but turns his head toward the viewer. His gaze seems direct but is distant. Both men could hold these poses for a long time. Rembrandt used Titian's pose and Raphael's monochrome, altering both yet retaining enough of each to make his adoption clear to any connoisseur familiar with both paintings, as many were in Amsterdam in 1640.

Westermann sees here an example not merely of *aemulatio* (emulation), which all art students were taught to do, as were students of Greek and Latin, but also of the next stage of classical rhetorical training, *contaminatio*, "the seamless melding of the motifs and formal characteristics of several examples."[7] Chance had provided Rembrandt, who refused to go to Italy, with perfect examples of Venetian *colore* and Roman *disegno*. Both terms carry broader meanings than the words "color "and "drawing" or "design." The Venetian passion for rich color was also associated with greater naturalism and lack of drawn preparation; the numerous preparatory drawings made by Florentine and Roman artists before they began work testified to a more deliberate, intellectual approach that despised the unfiltered realism and rapid execution of the

5.31 Rembrandt van Rijn, *Self-Portrait at the Age of Thirty-Four*, 1640. Oil on canvas, 40¼ ×31 ½ in (102 × 80 cm). National Gallery, London.

Venetians. Rembrandt knew about these old rivalries from reading a Dutch translation of Vasari. His "seamless melding" of the two masterpieces and their transformation into an image of himself in sixteenth-century costume can be read both as a critique of the debate itself (for all great painting requires not only design and color, but also patience and passion) and as a declaration of himself as a Dutch painter whose work could hang beside theirs and hold its own. He challenges Titian and Raphael by reducing his palette to a range of browns from dark chocolate to beige while still achieving a mesmerizing image of calm reserve equal to that of both of his models. "Had I been alive when you were," his steady gaze and antiquated costume seem to say, "you would have had to reckon with me as an artist beyond criticism both in conception and drawing, and in the execution of my ideas as well." It is the most carefully executed of all Rembrandt's self-portraits. It is also much larger than the Titian or the Raphael. He set out to paint a masterpiece in all senses of that word and succeeded brilliantly.

Rembrandt in Amsterdam, 1639–42

Between 1639 and 1642 Rembrandt received several portrait commissions from wealthy and powerful members of Amsterdam society, for whom he created some of his finest work. Among them was the remarkable portrait of the Mennonite preacher *Cornelis van Anslo and his Wife* (Fig. 5.32), one of his largest portraits apart from the *Night Watch*. Mennonite preachers were chosen for their eloquence in interpreting the Bible. Anslo's abilities inspired Joost van der Vondel to write a quatrain, which Rembrandt inscribed on the verso of a study for his etched portrait of the preacher:

That's right, Rembrandt, paint Cornelis' voice!
His visible self is second choice.
The invisible can only be known through the word.
For Anslo to be seen, he must be heard.

The etching and the painted portrait, both made in 1641, would seem to respond to the

5.32 Rembrandt van Rijn, *Cornelis van Anslo and his Wife*, 1641. Oil on canvas, 67¾ × 82¼ in (172 × 209 cm). Staatliche Museen, Berlin.

poem's challenge to "paint Cornelis' voice." Anslo is alone in the print but turns as if to address someone outside the frame as he points to a passage in the Bible propped up in front of him. The painting depicts Anslo and his wife seated in his study, she totally absorbed in his words as he discourses about a passage in the open Bible placed on a small lectern on a table covered in carpets. The viewpoint is so low that both sitters seem to be on an elevated stage, perhaps to remind the viewer of Anslo's position above his congregation in a church pulpit. Light (that is truth) falls on the open book and on their faces as he speaks and she hears his voice. The contrast between their mood and the informality of Hals's *Isaac Massa and Beatrix van der Laen* (see Fig. 5.12) could hardly be greater yet both celebrate the ideal of marriage by showing a close bond between each couple.

The *Night Watch*, the convenient and evocative nickname of Rembrandt's most famous painting, has long replaced its correct descriptive title, the *Military Company of Captain Frans Banning Cocq* (Fig. 5.33). It was one of six group portraits of officers of military companies of musketmen completed by various artists between 1640 and 1643 for the company headquarters in Amsterdam. They were made for the spacious rectangular Groote Sael (Great Room) on the second floor of a new wing completed in 1636. It had six large windows in the long wall that faced the river Amstel and was the largest interior space in the city until the completion of the new Town Hall in 1648. Together these well-lit paintings represented most of the prominent citizens of the city portrayed by the best practitioners of portraiture in the Dutch Republic. Only Hals, who did not like working away from home, was omitted.

All of these painters were working on a larger scale than usual. Rembrandt rose to the challenge with ease, but the others produced dutiful likenesses, with each man in good light and careful attention to their rank and costume. The result is rows of heads and big ruffs. Rembrandt created a unified composition that holds the picture field together in its sweep. He put Banning Cocq and his Lieutenant, Willem van Ruijtenburch, in a patch of sunlight in the central foreground and left most of the other participants in half light and shadow. Descending lines of heads and arms from the groups of figures to left and right converge on the two principal officers and give the painting a focus that the others lack. Their arrangements look posed, that of Rembrandt almost natural. Further, he has enlivened the occasion with other participants—a man cleaning a musket and an old man clutching one, a dwarf running away from the main group on the left, a drummer on the right edge with a barking dog and, in a patch of sunlight, an attractive young woman with a white hen attached to her waist by its legs. The most brightly lit figure in the painting apart from Cocq and Ruijtenburch, she is a kind of mascot carrying chicken legs which appear on the company's coat of arms. Rembrandt's portrait is less formal, more entertaining, and livelier than those of the other five militia groups. Payment was not withheld, so Banning Cocq and his fellow officers must have been satisfied.

While always darker than the other military portraits with which it hung until the eighteenth century, Rembrandt's *Night Watch* does not take place at night. Still, there is some evidence that his subdued lighting was criticized, for he received fewer portrait commissions after 1642 than in the previous decade. Was it his use of chiaroscuro or did something else affect his patronage? Saskia died that year, leaving him to raise their only surviving child, Titus, on his own. Saskia was the niece of an art dealer, Hendrick van Uylenburgh, who became her guardian on the death of her parents. Rembrandt stayed with them when he first arrived in Amsterdam: Hendrick's connections helped him to launch his career. Saskia was also given a substantial dowry by her uncle when she married Rembrandt. Their first wills, made in 1636, left everything to the other. Her second will, however, made only ten days before her death, left everything she owned to Titus, not to her husband. Since their property was jointly owned, Titus, then nine months old, became joint owner of everything his father possessed. If he died without issue, her property would go to one of her sisters. Rembrandt was appointed guardian. Both the provisions of Saskia's will and Rembrandt's declining number of commissions suggest that he and the Uylenburgh family were no longer on good terms.

5.33 Rembrandt van Rijn, *The "Night Watch" (Military Company of Captain Frans Banning Cocq)*, 1642. Oil on canvas, 11 ft 8 in × 14 ft 4 in (3.59 × 4.38 m). Rijksmuseum, Amsterdam.

Studies of Rembrandt have encompassed the undeniably tragic aspects of his private life—the death of his first wife after eight years of marriage and the deaths of three of their four children in infancy. Titus, the only child of theirs who lived long enough to marry and sire a child himself, predeceased his father by a year. His daughter Titia, born after her father's death, lost her mother and grandfather the following year. Hendrickje Stoffels, Rembrandt's companion and common-law wife, who lived with him from 1649 onwards and bore him a daughter, Cornelia, in 1654, predeceased him too in 1663. These events used to provide an explanation for the gloom and darkness of Rembrandt's work, whether manifest in the solemnity of his sitters and protagonists or in his late self-portraits. The artist was believed to have achieved an admirable degree of equanimity in the face of these misfortunes, to which could be added a decline in his reputation after the completion of the *Night Watch* in 1642 and his subsequent bankruptcy.

Everything that had looked so promising in 1641—new house, a son, some major commissions—had become complicated and bleak by 1644. Saskia's death in 1642 and its concomitant financial complications was followed by Rembrandt's affair with Geertge Dircx, the nursemaid who had been hired to take care of Titus. Once we know how Rembrandt got rid of her and connived with Geertge's brothers to deprive her of any financial support and then of her freedom in the last years of her life, it is impossible to regard images such as Rembrandt's serene *Supper at Emmaus* (the Louvre, Paris), painted in 1648, as the uncomplicated emanation from the soul of a man of profound goodness.

Rembrandt's Landscape Prints and Drawings

Rembrandt made etchings throughout his career, some of exceptional scale, complexity, and accomplishment. He experimented with the medium in almost every imaginable way: how small could he make a complete portrait or landscape?; how dark could he make a print and still keep it legible?; how much detail did he have to provide?; could a print mimic a drawing and still find a public?; could he print on vellum as well as fine paper from Japan?; could he simply scratch a design onto a bare plate (dry point) and skip the application of wax and the acid bath?; how would this design look if it was more heavily inked or more cleanly wiped? Rembrandt's fascination with process and his intimate involvement in the creation and production of his prints makes them a far more personal expression of his artistic goals than those by any of his contemporaries except Hercules Seghers (*c.* 1590–1633/8). They were widely known and admired throughout Europe.

Among Rembrandt's twenty-seven landscape prints made between 1640 and 1653 some are in pure dry point or a mixture of dry point with etching, others are etched and reworked in different states. Among his first was a *View of Amsterdam* (Fig. 5.34) seen across marshy ground and the river Ij. A completely convincing image of the distant city, its churches flanking the windmill near the warehouses of the East India Company, is conveyed in a space barely two inches high and six inches wide. The upper two-thirds of the paper are blank except for a faint shadow of wiped printing ink to hint at the damp atmosphere of a dull day. Such effects were practiced first in drawings, as in his even more economically conceived study of *Het Molentje*—a popular inn situated beside a small windmill—seen across the Amstel (Fig. 5.35). He chose a long, narrow band of "oatmeal" paper about ten inches wide (the drawn frame is his) and then marked the horizon line halfway up the paper with just enough lines and dabs of wash to indicate the mill, some adjoining houses, a barge, a small boat, and another more distant mill on the left. The blank paper in the foreground

becomes an expanse of calm water, the unmarked sky that of an overcast day. Even when we know we are looking at paper and ink, the illusion is irresistible and utterly convincing.

The grandest and most ambitious of all Rembrandt's landscape prints is known, for obvious reasons, as the *Three Trees* (Fig. 5.36). It was made in 1643, the year after Saskia died, and was the only print he dated that year except one of a large pig tied up and awaiting slaughter. There is only one signed and dated painting from this year, *Bathsheba Bathing* (Metropolitan Museum, New York), which is not unanimously accepted as autograph. The *Three Trees* is technically his most complex landscape print for he used etching, dry point, and engraving with sulphur tint on the plate to capture the tonal effects he wanted. As his only major artistic statement of 1643, and furthermore one to which he devoted enormous

5.34 Rembrandt van Rijn, *View of Amsterdam*, c. 1640. Etching, 44 × 60 in (112 × 153 cm). Metropolitan Museum of Art, New York.

5.35 Rembrandt van Rijn, *Het Molentje (The Little Windmill)*, c. 1654. Pen, brown ink, and brown wash drawing, 3¼ × 8⅝ in (8.3 × 22.6 cm). Fitzwilliam Museum, Cambridge, England.

5.36 Rembrandt van Rijn, *Three Trees*, 1643. Etching, 8⅓ × 11 in (21.3 × 27.9 cm).

effort, this etching had to have personal significance. Further, the three trees are such a prominent element in the composition that to deny them meaning beyond the literal would be perverse. Placed on a rise, they inhabit the sky, dominating the otherwise flat terrain that stretches into such a distance on the left that church towers and windmills are reduced to small scratches. One popular interpretation is that they represent the three crosses on Golgotha used at Christ's crucifixion, the subject of a magnificent later etching by Rembrandt. Another reads the trees as emblems of fortitude, constancy, and humility, "the deep roots of virtue, victorious over tribulation, [. . . and] the capacity of prayer to nourish the soul."[8] The latter reading would suit Rembrandt's own circumstances, bereft of Saskia but facing the future as best he could. The storms on the left are moving away—or are they travelling toward us?—the viewer must decide. A tiny figure seated on the rise of land on the right faces into the clear skies with his back to the trees, an element that would seem to deny an association with the crucifixion. The artist's message may be that life continues. Those able to study the original in good light with a magnifying glass will find lovers in the underbrush on the lower right, a fisherman on the shore on the left, and a man and some animals in the fields behind him. Man is barely a speck in this universe; Fortune, long allegorized as a passing storm, is not always kind. Even spectators unaware of Rembrandt's particular circumstances in the year that this great print was made will sense the weight of its metaphorical language.

Rembrandt after 1642

A year later Rembrandt's mood had changed: a quick scatological sketch (Metropolitan Museum, New York) made his views about ignorant art critics pungently clear. He also painted a splendid interpretation of *Christ and the Woman Taken in Adultery* (Fig. 5.37). The woman, wearing white, kneels before Christ, who is dressed in a simple brown shift. The Pharisees presenting her to him, however, are resplendent in plum-red velvet and plumed hats; the temple setting behind them resembles a Wurlitzer organ. Were rumors already circulating about his relationship with Geertge and was the choice of subject a riposte by the artist? He also painted two touching images of the *Holy Family* in 1645 and 1646 (Hermitage, St. Petersburg, and Gemäldegalerie, Kassel), the latter with a painted, illusionistic frame partly obscured by a painted curtain drawn back to allow us to peer into the dark interior of Joseph's shop where Mary is comforting the infant Christ. While referring to Dutch collectors' practice of covering their best works in this fashion (see Fig. 5.50), the conceit is

5.37 Rembrandt van Rijn, *Christ and the Woman Taken in Adultery*, 1644. Oil on wood, 33 × 25¾ in (83.8 × 65.4 cm). National Gallery, London.

also an allusion to the competitive *trompe l'oeil* feats of Zeuxis and Parrhasius (see p. 370). Once again, Rembrandt draws attention to his genius by inviting us to compare his achievements with those of the greatest artists of the past.

Jan Six (1618–1700), who first encountered Rembrandt in 1645, was to prove a valuable new friend. Well-educated (his own Latin inscription on his portrait by Rembrandt declares that he "worshipped the Muses from youth"), wealthy, and a well-respected member of the city's elite, Six commissioned an etched portrait of himself from Rembrandt in 1647 (Fig. **5.38**) and a painted one in 1654 (Fig. **5.39**). He also lent the artist money interest free and bought three of his unsold paintings of the 1630s, among them a superb portrait of Saskia (Gemäldegalerie, Dresden). The etching portrays Six as a thoughtful man of learning. As he leans against an open window, he reads a pamphlet folded back along its spine. The contrast between bright sunlight around his upper body and the deep shadows of the interior space that takes up most of the print is meticulously exploited. Part of a painting half covered by a curtain on the left wall is just visible. A low chair in the left corner facing the window is piled with books, the top one open and hanging over the edge. Its pages offer the only real highlight in the left half of the print. The steel handle of a large sword with its

5.38 Rembrandt van Rijn, *Jan Six*, 1647. Etching, 9⅝ × 7½ in (24.4 × 19.1 cm). Rijksmuseum, Amsterdam.

5.39 Rembrandt van Rijn, *Jan Six*, 1654. Oil on canvas, 9⅝ × 7½ in (24.4 × 19.1 cm). Private Collection, Amsterdam.

scabbard and leather belt, the gentleman's essential accessory, catches some light. The precision with which Rembrandt worked the various dark tones that create the setting is extraordinary.

The painted portrait of *Jan Six* celebrates Rembrandt's technical virtuosity in a different way. It is a flamboyant display of spontaneous, rough brushwork that would have dazzled Hals and Velázquez. Six stands, a little over half-length, slightly off center, holding one of his gloves in his bare right hand. His gray overcoat has openings in the sleeves and front that can be closed with rows of buttons, marked with blobs and dashes of yellow paint. A crimson greatcoat is perched on his left shoulder, its collar edged with gold braid laid in with a few judiciously placed long strokes of ocher paint. Down its front marches a procession of blobs and horizontal strokes of yellow paint, laid in with calculated spontaneity. Six's white collar and the collar of his coat float above his shoulders on shadowed tones. He regards us calmly, his head at a slight angle, as if curious about our response to this painterly magic. In his two images of Six, Rembrandt seemed to be asking his contemporaries: rough or smooth, dark or light, fast or slow, precise or vague, in color or in black and white—how would you like me to create your portrait? The answer was increasingly smooth, light, precise, and in color. Even Six's own wife had her portrait (Staatliche Museen, Kassel) painted by the more fashionable Govert Flinck, who rendered her blue silk dress and the rose in her hand with the kind of detail that Rembrandt was avoiding by the mid-1630s.

The most impressive history paintings of Rembrandt's later years are large, boldly painted, and difficult to reproduce on a small scale; their mood is more introspective and meditative than those of the 1630s. People listening, watching, witnessing, thinking, and pondering their options appear over and over again in both paintings and prints: Bathsheba (1654; Louvre, Paris) holds the letter from King David inviting her to betray her husband as her servant washes her feet; Asenath, Joseph's wife, watches blind old Jacob blessing their sons but giving the privileged touch to the younger one (1656; Gemäldegalerie, Kassel); and Aristotle famously contemplates a bust of Homer (1653; Metropolitan Museum, New York).

Despite receiving such large commissions, Rembrandt was forced to declare bankruptcy in 1656. The documents do not fully explain why then, rather than before, Rembrandt could no longer put off paying for his handsome house in the Breestraat, on which he owed almost 10,000 guilders in capital, interest, and taxes by 1653. He seems to have made payments to his creditors rarely, preferring instead to acquire paintings and drawings by other artists, casts after antique and modern sculptors, prints by all the major European graphic artists, as well as exotic weapons and assorted curiosities. He even owned the skins of a lion and lioness. He sold some of his possessions in 1656 but he kept the proceeds, in retrospect a recklessly irresponsible act. The house and its contents were auctioned in 1658. One creditor was able to extract 4,180 guilders from the proceeds but most of the artist's debtors never received full payment. Others were forced to accept some of his paintings in lieu of cash. The inventory taken of the contents of Rembrandt's house in 1656 remains an invaluable source of information about his artistic tastes.

Rembrandt's self-portraits made after his bankruptcy and his move to smaller quarters are inevitably moving for viewers aware of his circumstances. Most have a roughly impasted surface, though none that would justify the anecdote told by Arnold Houbraken (author of a set of lives of Netherlandish painters published in 1718) about a painting "in which the colors were so heavily loaded that you could lift [the portrait] from the floor by the nose." It is impossible not to see Rembrandt's steady confrontation of his own ageing features as courageously direct about the fact of human mortality. Several show him at work and one in particular seems to have a particular message for posterity, the three-quarter-length *Self-Portrait with Maulstick and Brushes* (Fig. 5.40). Both format and scale are exceptional: only his portrait with Saskia (Gemäldegalerie, Dresden) and another late self-portrait of 1658 are larger. Rembrandt stands facing us, a confrontational presentation rarely used even for rulers; he holds his palette, maulstick, and brushes in his left hand as he pauses, gazing at himself (and now at us) before continuing to work on the canvas whose edge is just visible on the upper right. He even seems to have decided to stop work at this point for much of the coat and the lower regions are barely indicated. Behind him are two large circles whose diameters are blocked by Rembrandt's head and cut off by the canvas on both sides. Their meaning has been much debated but the connection with the story about Giotto drawing a perfect free-hand O as proof of his skills for a skeptical ruler is appealing. Rembrandt's painted circle is divided; had he put one behind himself, however, he would have looked like a god with a huge halo. Again, as with the London portrait of 1640, Rembrandt is challenging the hegemony that puts Italian artists at the summit of perfection while reminding his Dutch contemporaries of the genius in their midst. This genius does not, however, believe it necessary to face his public in his Sunday best. The rejection of his enormous painting, the *Conspiracy of the Batavians under*

5.40 Rembrandt van Rijn, *Self-Portrait with Maulstick and Brushes*, c. 1665. Oil on canvas, 43⅜ × 33½ in (111 × 85 cm). The Iveagh Bequest. Kenwood House, London.

Claudius Civilis, commissioned for the vast public corridor of the new Town Hall of Amsterdam in 1661, must have been a bitter blow (it survives only as a cut-down fragment: Nationalmuseum, Stockholm). The *Self-Portrait with Maulstick and Brushes* is not dated but is placed after 1661 by experts. In one of our early examples (see Fig. 5.24) and in this much later one, Rembrandt used the end of his brush to scrape lines into the wet paint, in the hair of the first and to mark lines of gathered cloth on the shirt of the later canvas. Traces of the artist's hand are invisible in the smooth surfaces of his rivals.

Among all the introspective images of Rembrandt's last decades, one more dramatic painting stands out. *Peter Denying Christ* (Fig. **5.41**), which is almost 6 feet (1.82 meters) wide, must have been a commissioned work destined for the space over the mantelpiece of a client with a large house. Schwartz has speculated that the patron was Jacob Trip, who not only owned a splendid house able to accommodate such a large canvas but bought portraits of himself and his wife from the artist in 1661. The subject was not rare but in earlier treatments by Dutch Caravaggesque artists, the saint was often pushed to one side and the crowd of carousing soldiers stressed instead. Here Peter fills the center of the canvas and receives the most light as he reacts to the young woman whose query elicits the first of his three denials of his association with Christ. As she asks, she holds up a candle to check her belief that he is the man she had seen earlier in Christ's presence. Light equals truth, but Peter turns away from her and it into the shadows, where Christ is dimly visible and looks back at his disciple. A Roman soldier below Peter pauses as if listening before taking another drink from a large water jar. The dramatic focus is on the saint caught in a moment of all too human weakness. The color

5.41 Rembrandt van Rijn, *Peter Denying Christ*, 1660. Oil on canvas, 60⅝ × 66½ in (154 × 169 cm). Rijksmuseum, Amsterdam.

scheme is limited to a monochrome of brown tones, except for the creamy white of Peter's robe, flesh tones, and the red vest worn by the "certain maid" who said, "This man was also with him" (Mark 14:67).

Rembrandt still received a few portrait commissions. In addition to the pair made for Jacob Trip in 1661, about fifteen other portraits of single sitters are known, as well as one family portrait (Herzog Anton Ulrich-Museum, Brunswick) and an impressive group portrait, the *Syndics of the Drapers' Guild* (Fig. 5.42). The syndics or *staalmeesters* (sample masters) checked the quality of the blue and black woolen cloth produced by local merchants and applied their seal to the samples that passed inspection. Though the guild had been in existence since the early fifteenth century, no portraits of the syndics, who served one-year terms, had been painted in the seventeenth century. As with the portrait of *Cornelis van Anslo and his Wife* (see Fig. 5.32), Rembrandt probably used a low viewpoint for this work because it was to be hung over a tall fireplace. Viewers may feel intimidated on finding themselves facing scrutiny by four of the five syndics, whose authority over them is implied by their elevated position. One is caught as he rises from his chair (Rembrandt originally had him standing). Only the syndic with the book who gestures as if addressing us averts his gaze. What event provoked the reactions of these soberly dressed men? Their duties were not carried out in a group so this is a manufactured moment. Schwartz proposed that the sitters asked to be shown looking directly at the spectator, as their predecessors were, in a well-lit room. The brighter setting may cater to the patrons' demands but the coordination of their gazes can be explained another way. What Rembrandt has captured is a common psychological response to the gaze of others: we will stare at someone whose attention is directed elsewhere, but we will glance away periodically while engaged in conversation with someone to avoid seeming too confrontational. Their expressions may be nothing more than the artist's way of creating some psychological tension to enliven what would otherwise be a static assembly. The asymmetry of the table's position is offset by that of the break in the wall behind the sitters, whose shifting head levels keep the spectator's eye glancing around the group. Their focus on us recalls that of the sitters in Velázquez's *Las Meninas* (see Fig. 3.38). It is surely part of this picture's power to hold our attention too: its meaning is only completed by our presence.

Rembrandt was active until the end. He painted two self-portraits in 1669 and a few others in that decade as well as a few moving history subjects. Perhaps the most haunting of these is *Lucretia* (Fig. 5.43); the virtuous woman killed herself after being raped by Sextus Tarquinius, son of the Roman tyrant king, Tarquinius Superbus, while her husband was absent on military duty. In an earlier version of this theme (1664; National Gallery of Art, Washington, DC) Rembrandt shows Lucretia just before she stabs herself; the later canvas shows her just after she has withdrawn the dagger from her heart. She faces us but her solemn gaze is distant, her thoughts elsewhere. The blood is already draining from her face as it stains her white shift. She pulls a bell cord to summon her husband and attendants to whom she will explain her decision to die a suicide rather than live in shame. Her death was soon avenged by her brother and husband who killed both Tarquins, ended their tyrannical monarchy, and established the Roman Republic.

Dutch humanists read the story as an allegory of the founding of their own Republic after the defeat of the Spanish Crown. Most Italian and Northern artists who painted or engraved this subject before Rembrandt—and it was popular—could not resist making it into a "sexy suicide" scene, even though Plutarch's text states explicitly that Lucretia carefully arranged her clothes so that her body would remain covered after her death. Titian exploited the erotic potential of the subject by showing the rape itself (Fitzwilliam Museum, Cambridge); others—even Artemisia Gentileschi (Palazzo Cattaneo-Adorno, Genoa)—emphasized Lucretia's allure by exposing the heroine's upper body as she prepares to stab herself. Rembrandt's Lucretia is covered up to the neck, her breasts so flat that they are barely detectable. She is a tragic heroine presented with such concentration and dignity that all frivolous reactions to her plight are swept aside. Only Rembrandt depicted her story in a way that forces viewers to confront not only Lucretia's virtue but also her mortality and their own. A much cited and discussed phrase in one of Rembrandt's letters to Huygens about the artist's efforts to express "the greatest and most natural emotion" (*die meeste ende die natureelste beweechgelickheijt*) may be only a common rhetorical trope, but the depth of feeling that centuries of Rembrandt's admirers find in images like this one testify to the artist's ability to make us believe in their psychological truth.

The political symbolism of the story does not seem to have been a motivating element for Rembrandt but rather the tragedy of the story itself. He must also, however, have remembered the plight of Hendrickje, who was accused of adultery in 1654 by the Reformed Church in Amsterdam a few months after she became pregnant by Rembrandt, and was banned from their services after their daughter Cornelia was born. He would not marry Hendrickje, it is thought, for fear of losing his share of Saskia's estate. Her blameless role in this predicament may have seemed to him to offer a moral parallel to the innocence of Lucretia. Depicting her as he did gave him a way to restore to the ancient heroine her status as an exemplary woman, a "type of virtue" and model of chastity and noble behavior, that she had had in medieval and Renaissance literary traditions but so rarely embodied in the visual arts. If Rembrandt believed that Hendrickje had been unfairly persecuted for bearing his child, as seems likely, he probably chose this story for reasons that must have intensified after her premature death.

Rembrandt's Artistic Heirs

Rembrandt died on October 4, 1669 and was buried in the Westerkerk four days later. Both he and Titus may have succumbed to the plague. Cornelia was fifteen. Titia, Titus's daughter, was barely seven months old. Rembrandt's true heirs were the many artists who had worked or studied with him since 1628 and worked in styles indebted to him. Among the first were Jan Lievens (1607–74) and Gerrit Dou (see Fig. 5.51) who had shared his studio in Leiden. Later pupils such as Govert Flinck (1615–60), Ferdinand Bol (1616–80), Nicolaes Maes (see Fig. 5.53), Carel Fabritius (1622–54), and Philips Koninck (see Fig. 5.69) became outstanding painters of portraits, narrative subjects, and landscapes in mid-century Amsterdam. Flinck was extremely successful, garnering commissions for group portraits and large history paintings that Rembrandt himself coveted and deserved, above all twelve huge canvases for the new Town Hall. Flinck died in 1660 before completing

5.42 Rembrandt van Rijn, *Syndics of the Drapers' Guild*, 1661–62. Oil on canvas, 75⅜ × 109⅞ in (191.5 × 279 cm). Rijksmuseum, Amsterdam.

5.43 Rembrandt van Rijn, *Lucretia*, 1666. Oil on canvas, 43⅜ × 36⁵⁄₁₆ in (110.7 × 92.28 cm). William Hood Dunwoody Fund. Minneapolis Institute of Arts, MN.

most of them; only then was the *Conspiracy of Claudius Civilis* assigned to Rembrandt, then to be rejected soon after it was installed. Flinck had adopted a modified version of his teacher's chiaroscuro and did not idealize his figures in his history paintings either but his more polished, detailed realism and richer color schemes were more appealing to Amsterdam's wealthy patrons than the increasingly somber and roughly painted canvases of Rembrandt. Bol's adjustments of Rembrandt's style replicate those of Flinck. Even the tragically short-lived Fabritius, who painted a brilliant *Self-Portrait* (Museum Boymans-van Beuningen, Rotterdam) in Rembrandt's rough style in the 1640s, preferred a smooth surface for his rare outdoor genre scenes made after settling in Delft in the early 1650s. Only Rembrandt's last pupil, Aert van Gelder (1645–1727), retained the deep chiaroscuro, the brown palette enriched with red, gold, and cream, and the heavily impasted surfaces of his master well into the next century.

Dutch Genre Painting before 1650

Art historians use the word "genre" in two ways: to refer to the type or kind of painting; still-life, landscape, portrait, history, and so on; but also—confusingly—for all images of daily activities that match no known biblical, historical, or mythological text. It began to be used in this second sense in France in the eighteenth century and slowly acquired its current dual meanings. The Dutch themselves listed such pictures in seventeenth-century inventories by more specific titles—a merry company, two smokers, a round picture of a bagpipe player, a drunken woman asleep, a kitchen scene—often without the name of the artist at all. It was not the most popular genre, comprising under 4 per cent of works in Delft and Amsterdam inventories in 1610–19 and only 10 per cent by the end of the century. Genre scenes were thus much less numerous than paintings classified as histories, which declined from 46.5 per cent in 1610–19 to 14.1 per cent by the 1680s. The most popular genre was landscape, which expanded from an already impressive 22.9 per cent in the 1610s to 38.7 per cent in the 1680s. Still-life and portraiture also gained somewhat at the expense of histories, but not to the degree that landscape painting did.

One type of still-life was the *vanitas*, a specialty of painters in Leiden but produced elsewhere in the Dutch Republic as well as in Flanders, France, and Spain. The example here by Pieter Claesz (c. 1597/8–1661) (Fig. **5.44**), who worked in Haarlem, has the classic elements displayed on a table set at the edge of our world: a skull weighing down some large, scholarly tomes; an elegant watch in a gold case; an empty, overturned glass; and an oil lamp whose flame has just been extinguished. A wisp of smoke rises heavenwards, a poignant metaphor of a life just ended. The artist chose a restrained color scheme of browns, fawns, and dull cream. Only the blue ribbon attached to the watch case brings a slight hint of color to this almost monochrome image. The strictest Calvinist can have had no qualms about looking at such an image. While its moralizing content is emphatically present, the image is so sensitively realized that we may find ourselves distracted for a moment by Claesz's artistry. The irregular seams of the skull bones that protect the brain, the large eye sockets, and the missing teeth have all been so tenderly painted in a filtered, warm light that its former owner's presence seems to linger there. The artist's skill both holds our attention and forces us to absorb the uncomfortable message of our own mortality.

While Dutch genre scenes offer historians a fund of information about daily life in the Dutch Republic—about costume, furniture, and house

5.44 Pieter Claesz, *Vanitas Still Life*, 1630. Oil on wood panel, 15½ × 22 in (39.5 × 56 cm). Royal Cabinet of Paintings, Mauritshuis, The Hague.

interiors; food and kitchen equipment; the consumption of tobacco and alcohol; musical performance, popular culture, courtship rituals, and so on—they were not conceived as documentary records and cannot be used as such. Scholars have begun to take more account than before of a wide range of contextual information, especially legal documents and literary evidence from both elite and popular culture, when interpreting these images. They have noted patterns and themes, exclusions as well as inclusions, that reveal the motives inspiring the production of particular categories. Moral instruction often lurks near the surface with the seven deadly sins—greed, lust, envy, pride, anger, covetousness, and sloth—as common targets. Jan Steen's famous messy households served to warn the wealthy families that owned these exceptionally large pictures about the evils of excess, or greed, which could so easily lead to lust and sloth. Terborch warned young ladies about the temptations offered by visiting soldiers (greed, lust). Pieter de Hooch (see Fig. 5.52) and Dou (see Fig. 5.51) celebrated the virtues of the good mother with her children in an immaculately kept home. Anyone asleep who should be awake may represent sloth (see Fig. 5.53); fat people represent greed, fighting peasants anger, rich folk primping before a mirror vanity, and so on. Owners could both condemn and enjoy these images of common human failings while aspiring to keep their houses in such immaculate order as those depicted by de Hooch and Dou.

Most genre scenes made before about 1640 depict either low-life or high-life characters. The poor are beggars, military conscripts, and boors squabbling in dingy taverns. The rich are young couples enjoying a banquet or making music together in garden settings, usually behaving with a fair degree of decorum. The pleasures of these indulged offspring of rich parents are brief. Moralizing inscriptions below engravings of such carefree parties or the addition of a skeleton visiting a couple absorbed in transitory delights make this message clear (Fig. 5.45). Pictures about passing pleasure—Shakespeare's "primrose way to the everlasting bonfire"—were produced throughout the century but later examples have fewer actors and their interactions are observed more closely.

More original and more significant for later developments was the introduction of domestic subjects. These paintings focus on the lives of families who were neither rich nor poor with women as the protagonists. Indeed women play a far more significant role in Dutch genre imagery than elsewhere in Europe, a phenomenon that would appear to correlate with their reputation among foreign visitors for being exceptionally competent, entrepreneurial, and—to those unused to such independence—domineering. Sir William Mountague commented thus after a visit in 1695:

Tis very observable here, more women are found in the shops and business in general than men; they have the conduct of the purse and commerce, and manage it rarely well, they are careful and diligent, capable of affairs, (besides domestick) having an education suitable, and a genius wholly adapted to it.[9]

5.45 Jan van de Velde II, *Death Surprising a Young Couple*, 1616. Etching, 7¾ × 6¹/₁₆ in (19.6 × 15.5 cm). Harris Brisbane Dick Fund, 1929. Metropolitan Museum of Art, New York.

Judith Leyster

Dirck Hals (1591–1656), the younger brother of Frans, who painted merry company subjects taking place indoors as well as in "gardens of earthly delight," introduced the theme of a woman alone with a letter that became popular after 1650, when it was used by Vermeer and others (see Fig. 5.58). Judith Leyster (1609–60) is remarkable for having both reinterpreted the theme of prostitution (see Fig. 5.46) and painted several of the earliest images of women at home with their children. Born and partly raised in Haarlem, she knew the work of Frans Hals well—and even sued him when he tried to take one of her students away from her studio to join his and won. She was the only Dutch artist to use some of his dashing brushwork to good effect in her own work, but she nearly always worked on a smaller scale and painted as many small group scenes as single figures. Sadly after her marriage in 1636 to another painter, Jan Meinse Molenaer (c. 1610–68), she seems to have virtually ceased painting. Only a watercolor of a tulip made in 1643 can be securely dated after 1636 (Frans Hals Museum, Haarlem). She may have stopped in order to avoid competing with him for he was also a genre painter. Assisting him with the accounts while caring for the household may have given them a better income. They had at least five children.

In Leyster's *The Proposition* (Fig. **5.46**), a woman sewing by candlelight is ignoring a man who has approached from behind and is touching her right arm and offering her a handful of coins. Is this an honest offer of marriage, as some have recently suggested, or an unwanted offer of sexual favors for payment? To anyone familiar with the usual treatment of "tempting offers" by Leyster's contemporaries, such as Dirck van Baburen, only the first reading may seem to make sense. Baburen's *Procuress* (Museum of Fine Arts, Boston), an image made famous by Vermeer's use of it in the background of two of his paintings, shows a buxom lass in a low-cut dress exchanging lascivious looks with a young man who holds up a single coin while an old woman next to them points to her empty palm— the price is not yet right! That the young woman is more than willing to accede to the young man's proposal is perfectly clear, as it is in all other images of this theme. By contrast, Leyster's woman is not dressed provocatively. Her blouse is pulled up tight around her neck, her skirts allow not even a glimpse of an ankle, and she pays her visitor no heed at all. She is engaged in precisely the sort of domestic work that all contemporary tracts insisted should occupy female "paragons of virtue" in idle moments. She is, however, alone rather than meeting her suitor in the presence of a chaperone, and does not welcome him at all.

The glow of coals in her foot warmer is just visible at the hem of her skirt. This tells us that she is not in fact "looking for love" but is either married or engaged to be wed. Placed under the skirt, the foot warmer—a little wooden box with holes pierced in the top into which square clay containers filled with hot coals were inserted— kept women warm in cold homes. However, foot warmers meant much more than that, as anyone

5.46 Judith Leyster, *The Proposition*, 1629. Oil on panel, 12⅛ × 9½ in (30.9 × 24.2 cm). Royal Cabinet of Paintings, Mauritshuis, The Hague.

5.47 Judith Leyster, *Boy Playing a Flute*, c. 1635. Oil on canvas, 28¾ × 24⅜ in (73 × 62 cm). Nationalmuseum, Stockholm.

who checks their role in Dutch genre scenes involving encounters between the sexes will quickly realize. When shown under the skirt, the lady is taken; halfway out with her foot on the warmer, she may be signaling that a suitor has a chance. If it is on the floor and empty, the coals now cold, she currently has no male companion. There is one on the floor behind Vermeer's *The Milkmaid* (see Fig. 5.56): empty, awaiting fresh coals, it signals that this virtuous woman engaged in domestic chores is single. Dou's *The Young Mother* (see Fig. 5.51) uses one to raise her left leg and make a more comfortable support for the baby she is about to feed. She is clearly not available.

Leyster painted several lively scenes of men and women making music together but the *Boy Playing a Flute* (Fig. 5.47), which has only one

Dutch Genre Painting before 1650   359

figure, is her masterpiece. The atmospheric rendering of the wall behind with its suggestive shadows and texture, even a nick just above the boy's right hand, creates a convincing space for the boy to recline a bit awkwardly on a broken-backed chair. That it is more than a picture of a boy playing a flute is indicated both by its size—it is one of her largest works—and by the prominent and beautifully painted violin and recorder hanging on the wall behind him. The boy's instrument is, according to Cynthia Rupprath, "a keyless cylindrical transverse flute (or *dwarsfluit*)," popular in the sixteenth century but now losing out to the recorder, which was more easily kept in tune. The better instrument hangs behind him along with the more prestigious violin (string instruments traditionally had a higher status than wind instruments; in antiquity, for example, the lyre of Apollo was ranked above the shepherd's pipe, and not just because it was the choice of a god). Thus the boy needs to give up his simple flute and make the wise choice between the instruments behind him. His musical progress will, we understand, offer a parallel to his intellectual and moral education. Instead of imitating the vulgar emotions of peasants, he will be trained in the subtle harmonics of strings tuned according to mathematical proportions accessible only to an educated mind. All elements in this exquisitely composed painting lead us to this conclusion: entering along the split in the boy's jacket, the eye is carried up to his hands, then by the tilt of the flute to his head, and by the red hat and angle of the boy's head to the violin and recorder. Their vertical forms block this movement and send us back down to begin another circuit. Then we may catch the broken chair slat and understand that its old wood is no longer a reliable support for the youth, who must get up to meet the new challenges represented symbolically behind him.

It would be nice to imagine that one of Leyster's sons posed for the picture, but none had been born by 1635, when it was probably made. The Dutch may have been more accepting of women with professional accomplishments than their contemporaries elsewhere, but expectations that even these exceptional women should still fulfill their traditional roles were powerful. Two other outstanding Dutch women painters—the two flower painters Maria van Oosterwyck (1630–93) and Rachel Ruysch (1664–1750)—made different choices. The former worked throughout her life and remained single. Ruysch continued to work after marrying a portrait painter, Juriaen Pool II (1666–1745). Although they had ten children, she never stopped producing her exquisite and exceedingly popular flower pieces (Fig. **5.48**). The reason in her case was surely economic: her work was sought after and well rewarded by wealthy and aristocratic patrons. Ruysch and Pool could afford the household help necessary to enable her to continue to work in a specialty in which she had become an international celebrity by the early eighteenth century. Leyster never had the kind of response that would have encouraged her to keep working. The inventory of their household goods taken after Molenaer's death in 1668 lists many works by both of them.

5.48 Rachel Ruysch, *Still-Life with Flowers and Fruit*, 1703. Oil on canvas, 33½ × 26 ⅝ in (85 × 68 cm). Gemäldegalerie, Vienna.

Dutch Genre Painting after 1650

One clear difference between the genre scenes produced in the early years of the century and those made after about 1640 is class: low-life characters are largely replaced by middle- and high-class protagonists. Pictures like the tavern fights of Adrien Brouwer almost vanish. Even the soldiers are better dressed. The intimate domestic genre subjects introduced by Judith Leyster and Dirck Hals were taken up with enthusiasm by Gerrard Dou in Leiden, Pieter de Hooch in Delft, Nicolaes Maes in Dordrecht, and Gerard Terborch (1617–81) in Deventer. This genre was also the raw material on which Vermeer wrought his magic. Women shopping, preparing food, embroidering and making lace, delousing their children's hair and teaching them to say grace, sweeping a courtyard, putting away clean linen, and checking the household accounts—gradually the whole sphere of women's domestic responsibilities became legitimate artistic subject matter. Some readers may object that the roles represented are traditional and limited, but their appearance alone is important because it signals recognition of the value of women's lives that artists had previously ignored. Perhaps it was the signing of the Treaty of Münster in 1648 that finally guaranteed peace in the Seven Provinces that allowed the Dutch to turn from military themes to the pleasures and comforts of a well-run home. Licit seems to replace illicit sex. Gentlemen are shown bowing deferentially at the entrance to the living rooms of beautifully dressed young women or offering them wine and listening to them playing a lute or harpsichord (see Fig. 5.50). Some, but not all, of these encounters depict illicit love, though so discreetly that a provocative ambiguity is created. Patrons now liked their moral lessons presented with a veneer of upper-class elegance.

Gerard Terborch's signature works did not emerge until the 1650s: he had traveled widely, visiting London, Germany, Italy, France, and Spain, eventually settling in Deventer in 1654, when he also got married. His earlier works are guardroom scenes, an emphatically male world, as were those of Metsu. *The Parental Admonition* (Fig. **5.49**) is typical of Terborch's mature work. Like Leyster's *Proposition*, it has been interpreted as both a proper and an improper encounter between the sexes. Is the older woman their chaperone or is she the madam? Is there a coin between the thumb and forefinger of the soldier? If not, what does his gesture mean? Is it significant that the toe of the boot on his crossed leg almost touches her skirt and that her form is framed by the red draperies of the bed behind her? The lady's back is turned, her face averted from us and from him. Her reactions to his proposal remain hidden. Their companion keeps her thoughts to herself, sipping her wine and pretending not to see what is going on. Terborch seems to have wanted the scene to be ambiguous, leaving it up to the viewer to decide whether this is a respectable proposal of marriage or a less savory offer. At all events, no current authorities believe it is a father scolding a daughter. Alison Kettering suggests that the gleaming white satin—Terborch's ability to depict this expensive fabric was much admired—is a metaphor for the skin of the woman that it conceals. Perhaps both Leyster and Terborch are saying that no sharp line can be drawn between lust and love.

5.49 Gerard Terborch, *The Parental Admonition*, 1654–55. Oil on canvas, 28⅛ × 24⅜ in (71.4 × 62.1 cm). Staatliche Museen, Berlin.

one with its richly carved gilt frame—the latest fashion—is a work by Metsu himself depicting a Twelfth Night feast. It is partly covered by a curtain, exposing enough to allow it to be identified and its boisterous mood to contrast with the genteel encounter in the foreground. The other painting shows a woodland scene. Pleasant landscapes like this appear in courtship scenes to suggest that the lover's suit will be successful. The woman wears a raspberry-red silk jacket and soft pink silk skirt; her solemn suitor is more soberly dressed in a gray jacket, though his stockings are blue. Metsu was particularly fond of warm oranges, crimsons, and rich browns. This work is lighter in tone and cooler in color than his most typical works, though the glimpse of red carpet on the right edge is almost as good as a signature.

Images that offer ideal models for correct female behavior were also popular. Dou's *Young Mother* (Fig. **5.51**) and de Hooch's *The Mother* (see Fig. **5.52**), for example, celebrate motherhood in a way seen previously only in images of the Virgin and Child. Dou's presentation of the beautiful young mother opening her fur-edged jacket to feed her baby is especially calculated to elevate this moment from mundane reality to iconic perfection. She wears expensive clothes that are in danger of being stained by the baby's

5.50 (above) Gabriel Metsu, *Man and Woman Seated by a Virginal*, c. 1658. Oil on wood, 15⅛ × 12⅝ in (38.4 × 32.2 cm). National Gallery, London.

5.51 (right) Gerrit Dou, *Young Mother*, 1660. Oil on panel, 19⅓ × 14¾ in (47.2 × 37.4 cm). Staatliche Museen, Berlin.

Gabriel Metsu (1629–67) was born in Leiden and trained there, probably with Dou. He joined the new Guild of Painters in 1648 and, after working in both Leiden and Amsterdam in the 1650s, settled permanently in the latter in 1657. Neither as finicky as Dou nor as obsessed with satin as Terborch, Metsu made a distinctive contribution in his small, beautifully painted scenes of courting couples, housewives shopping and preparing foods and lovers exchanging letters. His *Man and Woman Seated by a Virginal* (Fig. **5.50**) shows a well-lit interior in which a young woman hands a sheet of paper to her male companion, who offers her a toast with his slender "flute" glass. Two inscriptions on the virginal suggest that this is a moral household and not a thinly disguised brothel: "In thee do I put my trust; let me never be ashamed" and "Let everything that hath breath praise the Lord" (from Psalms, Vulgate: 30.2 and 70.1). On the wall behind them are two paintings. The larger

drool and—since it wears no diaper—other excretions too. Her red velvet-padded chair is worthy of a cardinal; a luxurious coverlet spills out of the baby's pretty wicker cradle; the chandelier overhead has even been compared to a crown. The huge tapestry curtain pulled back to reveal this moment of domestic bliss emphasizes its privileged, even miraculous character. Add to all this the extraordinary finesse of Dou's technique, "so (fine) as hardly to be distinguish'd from enamail," according to John Evelyn,[10] and his popularity in his lifetime is easy to understand. The dimly lit interior space with light falling on the key figures in a way inexplicable in real life is owed to Rembrandt, with whom Dou studied in his teens in Leiden, but Dou quickly differentiated himself from Rembrandt by always favoring meticulous finish. He inspired the term "fijnschilder" (fine painter) that became the specialty of other artists in Leiden, though none equaled Dou's obsessively refined surfaces. In purely financial terms, he was the most successful painter in the Dutch Republic.

De Hooch's *The Mother* (Fig. **5.52**) offers a useful contrast to Dou's artificiality by depicting the mother unlacing her bodice in a well-lit room without ostentatious accessories. The high ceiling and paintings indicate that the family is nevertheless comfortably situated, but the image conforms more closely with what we would have

5.52 Pieter de Hooch, *The Mother*, c. 1660. Oil on canvas, 36¼ ×39 ⅓ in (92 × 100 cm). Staatliche Museen, Berlin.

Dutch Genre Painting after 1650 **363**

seen in Delft in 1660 than Dou's interior would to the household of a wealthy Leiden doctor. This mother looks tenderly toward the cradle and extends her hand with the end of the lace to distract the baby, who has probably begun to cry to signal its hunger. A pet dog watches the mother. Often a surrogate for the absent lover in courtship scenes, here the dog calls attention to a man's red cloak hanging on a peg above, which presumably belongs to the husband. Their young daughter stands in the open doorway looking out into the world beyond. Only the rumpled bedclothes, where the mother may have been resting, hint at any disorder in this neat home. The perfectly calibrated geometry of the setting with the vista into the room beyond, and patches of sunlight on the walls and floor, makes this one of de Hooch's finest works. He was the first artist to show sunlight penetrating a domestic interior convincingly; it became one of his trademarks.

Nicolas Maes (1634–93), a native of Dordrecht who studied with Rembrandt in the early 1650s, painted mainly good housewives but also used them on occasion to illustrate vices. *The Idle Servant* (Fig. 5.53) has a more ambitious setting than usual with a view to a back room where two women chat. In the foreground the mistress, who has come to the kitchen to fetch a drink for the visitors, discovers her maid asleep and dirty dishes spread over the floor. Above the dozing girl a cat is making off with a small boiled chicken, an image often used to indicate a seduction. Here it may explain the servant's condition, exhausted after a late night. Her mistress points her out to us with an understanding smile instead of waking her with a reprimand: this moment of sloth is not apparently worth a tirade. The lighting and color scheme of warm browns and black, contrasted with the white apron and blouse of the principal figure and a little red on the sleeper, show the influence of Rembrandt but the execution is more precise, especially the splendid still-life of clay dishes on the tiled floor in the foreground. Other paintings by Maes of the 1650s include two depicting exemplary behavior—a woman scraping turnips watched by a child (National Gallery, London) and an old woman saying grace before eating a modest meal (Rijksmuseum, Amsterdam)—while a third shows a woman falling asleep instead of finishing her accounts (Saint Louis Art Museum). This last work, while alluding to the role many Dutch women played in their husbands' businesses, might imply that sloth is preferable to avarice or greed, the sins usually pilloried in pictures of people checking their finances. Each work has a format like a window into a world set parallel to the picture plane, the verticals and horizontals of walls, windows, doors, and tables skillfully arranged to frame the key figures in a convincing interior that, like those of de Hooch, conforms to what is known of Dutch homes of the period. After 1660 however, Maes stopped producing genre scenes and devoted himself to portraits, settling in Amsterdam in 1673 to be near his fashionable clients.

Emmanuel de Witte (c. 1617–92), who specialized in paintings of church interiors, painted one remarkable portrait that combines elements of genre, still-life, and urban scene. The result is

5.53 Nicolas Maes, *The Idle Servant*, 1655. Oil on oak panel, 27 9/16 × 21 in (70 × 53 cm). National Gallery, London.

5.54 Emanuel de Witte, *Adriana van Heusden and her Daughter at the New Fishmarket, Amsterdam*, 1662. Oil on canvas, 22½ × 25¼ in (57.1 × 64.1 cm). National Gallery, London.

an exceptional painting whose first owner had to sue the artist to obtain it (Fig. **5.54**). De Witte was born in Alkmaar but worked in Delft until 1654, when he moved to Amsterdam, where the painting was made around 1662. The artist was then living in the house of the notary, rent-free with meals and an annual salary thrown in, on condition that he hand over his entire production to him. When de Witte moved out in 1663, he took this painting and three others with him. They were then claimed in a lawsuit that dragged on for a decade. The notary died before the matter was resolved. It is not even clear if his widow, Adriana van Heusden, ever received the work, which shows her with her daughter shopping in the New Fish Market.

Marketing scenes that show well-dressed women negotiating with the vendors of assorted produce were not new but one that used such a setting for a portrait was a novelty. The patron's wife must have proposed the idea herself—certainly de Witte could offer her no precedents in his own work. Her persistence in trying to obtain it suggests that she was well aware of its originality and quality (she refused to accept a copy instead). Adriana van Heusden is shown fulfilling two of her approved domestic roles—careful marketing and educating her daughter about such duties. Her gesture and that of the fishwife suggest that some tough bargaining is going on: Adriana has turned away as if the fish available is either not to her taste or too expensive; the fishmonger's wife is trying to persuade her that the selection she is touching will suit her customer well. The billowing sails of ships in the harbor and other buildings are visible behind them, but the focus is on the stall with its canopy, the two women, and the shining fresh fish. Adriana's white overskirt tied around a fur-edged jacket resembles the costume worn by the mistress of the sleeping scullery maid in Maes's *The Idle Servant* (see Fig. **5.53**), also a genre scene about relationships between mistresses and those who serve them. Adriana's pride in the way she performed her duties must have inspired de Witte's rare departure from the conventional portraits of demurely seated women in dark clothes in a dim interior.

Dutch Genre Painting after 1650

Johannes Vermeer

The most admired Dutch painter of domestic genre scenes and, with Rembrandt, now the most popular Dutch artist of the century, is Johannes Vermeer (1632–75). That this should be the case is intriguing because his restrained introspective work offers far less narrative content and social comment than that of his contemporaries. Lawrence Gowing, one of Vermeer's many eloquent interpreters, observed that "simplicity is not a quality of genius in which we easily believe." The subtlety of Vermeer's visual language and its dense subliminal content challenges every critic and historian who has attempted to explain it. Marcel Proust already commented on Vermeer's "withdrawal and silence," declaring that "passion and suffering and sex are banished from his art."[11] How could an artist who appeals so deeply to us now have been forgotten after his death and only gradually been rediscovered in the twentieth century?

Hundreds, even thousands, of paintings survive by some productive Dutch seventeenth-century painters. Only thirty-six works at most are authoritatively accepted as by Vermeer. Early inventories and auction catalogues do not record many more than this, so while some have certainly been lost, the evidence suggests that he worked slowly and seldom produced more than two or three paintings a year. When the Frenchman Balthasar de Monconys paid a call in 1663, probably on the recommendation of Constantijn Huygens, he reported that Vermeer had nothing on hand for sale. Vermeer was only forty-three when he died twelve years later, leaving his wife and eleven children with heavy debts and some unsold paintings as assets, most of them by other artists. A baker, perhaps the one in whose house de Monconys saw one Vermeer in 1663, accepted two as security for a debt of 617 guilders for his estate in 1675, a high price for genre paintings (and a very big bread bill!). The earlier purchase had cost the baker 600 livres, presumably the French equivalent of guilders, which de Monconys thought excessive. Thus Vermeer seems to have insisted that he be well paid, demanding sums comparable with those of his most successful peers such as Dou and Frans van Mieris. He apparently received them from a few admirers able to afford them but the income was not sufficient to support his large family, even though he had additional income as an art dealer and from inherited real estate. His widow declared in 1676 that poor economic conditions in recent years had affected sales, hence the debts.

With few works in circulation to sustain his reputation, Vermeer's artistic identity became confused with those of more productive peers. *The Art of Painting* (see Fig. 5.61), Vermeer's most complex and personal artistic statement, disappeared after being auctioned off reluctantly by his widow in 1676. It reappeared in Vienna in 1813, the property of a saddle maker, who sold it for a small sum to Count Czernin, who thought he had bought a Pieter de Hooch. It was not identified as a Vermeer until 1860. In the 1930s and 1940s, the perception of Vermeer's style was so vague that crude forgeries by Hans van Meegeren fooled alleged experts. One was even bought by Hitler's Reichsmarschall Hermann Goering.

We do not know who taught Vermeer to paint. By 1656, when he painted *The Procuress* (Fig. 5.55), he was already a good observer of

5.55 Jan Vermeer, *The Procuress*, 1656. Oil on canvas, 56⅛ × 51⅛ in (143 × 130 cm). Staatliche Kunstsammlungen, Dresden.

light falling on the complex patterns and textures of a Turkish carpet and could integrate patches of crimson, green, and yellow into a bold grouping of figures close to the picture plane but flanked by other dark figures lurking in shadow. The frank treatment of the subject—the client embraces the girl from behind, one hand on her left breast, the other holding the coin above her open right hand—recalls much earlier works by such Utrecht artists as Dick van Baburen. Vermeer's mother-in-law Maria Thins, who was related to the Utrecht painter Abraham Bloemaert, owned Baburen's *Procuress* (Museum of Fine Arts, Boston) of 1622 but the sophistication of Vermeer's technique suggests that he spent long enough in Utrecht to study first hand the paintings of Bloemaert, who loved red and yellow. Vermeer's two other early works have large figures and history subjects—*Christ in the House of Martha and Mary* (National Gallery of Scotland, Edinburgh) and *Diana and her Companions* (Mauritshuis, The Hague). These choices imply an ambition to become a true history painter; their gorgeous colors also depart sharply from the prevailing moody browns of Rembrandt and his school. Then Vermeer took up genre subjects, possibly because of the phenomenal success of Dou in nearby Leiden or the appeal of Maes's sensitive adaptation of Rembrandt's history paintings to domestic genre themes. Several Delft artists were also using perspective in novel ways in views of church interiors or street scenes. Vermeer seems to have taken note of all these developments and then proceeded to transform domestic genre by sheer painterly genius, raising its emotional resonance and significance to levels never imagined by his contemporaries.

Only one other work by Vermeer is dated, *The Astronomer* of 1668 (Louvre, Paris). The chronology of his canvases depends on their relationship to these two fixed points: 1656, before his characteristic interior image had emerged; and 1668, by when it was long established. Experts agree that the most richly impasted works were made first and that his late works have an almost mechanical smoothness; undated works are dated approximately in sequence from more textured to less. *The Milkmaid* (Fig. 5.56), placed around 1658–60, exploits a variety of impasto effects to make palpable the rough crust of the bread, the glazed surfaces of the terracotta dish and jug being used by the servant, and the encrusted decoration on the blue stoneware jug beside her. These painterly delights bring the viewer straight into this woman's world, a bare-walled room filled with daylight from a window on the left. Utterly absorbed in her task of pouring fresh milk on bread to feed a child, she exemplifies womanly virtues of humility, modesty, and selfless dedication to the welfare of others. She is a sturdy woman whose bulk gives her symbolic role literal and metaphorical weight. Her hair is concealed beneath her white cap, her chest completely covered. A violet-gray apron covers part of her deep blue overskirt; her rolled-up sleeves also show that she is prepared to work. The foot warmer behind her does not imply anything here except her availability, a state hinted at too by the Cupid painted on the tile between it and her on the back wall. No Dutch artist had ever painted a servant with more empathy and dignity: not until Jean-Baptisie-Siméon Chardin took up such themes in France in the eighteenth century would she have any rivals.

This painting may have been a surprise to its first spectators in Delft for members of the lower classes were rarely singled out to exemplify virtue. The lighting is also used to create a far more powerful sense of dense form in atmospheric space than seen in any earlier Dutch painting, even that of Rembrandt. It is full of evidence of slow, disciplined observation of the fall of light. The wall is shadowed near the window wall but gradually lightens behind the maid, who casts a soft shadow on the tiled floor too. A small broken pane of glass lets a small patch of brighter light onto the adjacent frame. The basket on the wall is in half light but the metal basket hanging on the far wall just below it reflects the light back and casts such odd shadows on the wall that Vermeer must have studied them from life. The interior of the bread basket is lit but mainly hidden from view. Visible instead is the shadowed exterior, whose weave is marked by tiny glints of light seen through small openings.

A visual clue to Vermeer's motives for creating this meticulous record of light in a humble kitchen is provided by the servant's clothes.[12] Her sleeves are yellow with a violet lining, but their crumpled mid-section is green with yellow

5.56 Jan Vermeer, *The Milkmaid*, c. 1658–60. Oil on canvas, 17⅞ × 16 in (45.4 × 40.6 cm). Rijksmuseum, Amsterdam.

highlights. One of the attributes of Pittura (Painting) in Cesare Ripa's *Iconologia* was fabric with shot colors. The milkmaid's sleeves offer that attribute and—placed in the center of the painting—proclaim that servants did not wear clothes of such bright colors. The other three servants in Vermeer's paintings wear brown dresses; in works by contemporaries, servants wear a white blouse alone or with a dull-hued overblouse. Still, Vermeer's woman is not dressed like the mistress of the household either. The exceptional colors of her costume tell us that she plays two roles here. Her underskirt is red, a dull red but enough for her clothes to display all three primary colors. The green cuffs, her suntanned hands, and violet-gray apron and cuffs provide the three secondary colors. By displaying shot colors with the three primaries and their secondaries, this woman becomes an allegory of Pittura. The painting thus has a double message: this is a painting about the art of painting as well as an image of female virtue.

The Milkmaid was described as celebrated in 1719, certainly for the finesse of its execution rather than for its subject matter. Thus it has long been appreciated in both senses even if this clue to Vermeer's allegorical intentions has not been noted before. It would have been understood more easily in Delft in 1660 when everyone knew what sort of clothes a milkmaid wore, though only the better educated viewers who had read the Dutch translation of Ripa's book issued in 1644 might have remembered the attributes of Pittura. And how appropriate to this context it is to learn that another subtle painter, Pieter Sanraedam, lived in Haarlem on "sweet milk and white bread" street!

As *The Milkmaid* is an allegory of painting, so Vermeer's *Girl with a Pearl Earring* (Fig. 5.57) may be too. Her unconventional clothes have long puzzled scholars. Why is she wearing a turban and an oddly cut coat of a type not usually worn by women? They are, like the colors of the servant's dress in *The Milkmaid*, clues to the fact that she is more than a beautiful woman. Her turban is made of blue and yellow fabric, her lips are red—the three primary colors again—and her jacket is made of a fabric that shifts from bronze to dark green in the shadows. Her outsize pearl earring is a perfect symbol for light and dark (chiaroscuro), as is her illuminated image against the dense black background. This is a pure allegory, stripped to its essentials. It makes Frans van Mieris's *Allegory of Painting* (Getty Museum, Los Angeles), which includes every attribute suggested by Ripa—a palette and brushes in Pittura's hands, messy hair, a gold chain, and a medal inscribed *Imitatio*—look trivial and fussy. While the enduring fame of Vermeer's *Girl with a Pearl Earring* stems from its intrinsic beauty, its deeper allegorical meaning has doubtless contributed to its appeal, however subliminally.

Vermeer usually depicted the well-to-do, as did his fellow artists of these years. Most of his genre scenes portray one person. He avoided family scenes altogether, never painted a child except two with their backs to us playing in the foreground of the *Little Street* (Rijksmuseum, Amsterdam) and never included the elderly, except in *The Procuress* (see Fig. 5.55). When Vermeer's men pay calls on ladies, everyone is on their best behavior—there is a glass of wine,

5.57 Jan Vermeer, *Girl with a Pearl Earring*, c. 1665. Oil on canvas, 18⅜ × 15⅝ in (46.5 × 40 cm). Royal Cabinet of Paintings, Mauritshuis, The Hague.

some fruit, a little music expertly performed, but no gaming boards, plates of aphrodisiac oysters, or visible beds. The theme of letters—written, sent, received—attracted him six times, perhaps because human encounters are implied rather than shown. The earliest is *Woman Reading a Letter at an Open Window* (Fig. 5.58), in which Vermeer includes a pale yellow-green silk curtain on a rod, painted as if it has been drawn back to reveal the image to us. We cannot approach the woman because our access is blocked by a table covered with a rumpled Turkish carpet supporting a dish of fruit. Standing in pure profile before an open window, her hands holding both sides of the paper as she absorbs its text, this woman ignores us. Her face is expressionless, her chin a little withdrawn. Is the news good or bad? We cannot tell. Vermeer originally placed a painting of Cupid on the wall behind her. By covering it here, he made the image more reticent and ambiguous, a discreet portrayal of courtship. The curtain is a knowing allusion to the story of Zeuxis and Parrhasius, who, according to the legends passed on by Pliny, competed in ancient Greece for the title of best illusionist painter. When Zeuxis attracted a bird to his painted fruit, Parrhasius answered with a similar image covered by a painted curtain. When Zeuxis reached to pull it aside, he knew that he had lost the contest: he had fooled a bird but his rival had fooled a man. Dutch collectors did cover some of their paintings in this fashion (see Fig. 5.52) and Dutch humanists certainly knew the story that inspired other painted curtains over images. The dish of fruit makes the reference to Parrhasius clear.

The women who appear in Vermeer's work have never been identified, though naturally scholars have wondered whether his wife, Catharina Bolnes, served as his model. Vermeer converted to her Roman Catholic faith before they married in 1653. During the twenty-two years that they lived together, they had fifteen children, four of whom died in infancy. A yellow silk jacket edged with fur worn by several women in his paintings may be the one listed in the inventory of their possessions made after his death, and thus she may be the woman wearing it. A different yellow silk jacket edged with black whose sleeves are decorated with black bands appears in the *Woman Reading a Letter* and also in the *Officer and a Laughing Woman* (Frick Collection, New York), another relatively early work. It is worn too by the *Young Woman with a Water Jug* (Metropolitan Museum, New York), by the woman playing the harpsichord in *The Concert* (formerly Isabella Stewart Gardner Museum, Boston) and her counterpart at the virginals in the *Music Lesson* (Queen's Gallery, London). In this last work, the back view conceals the black sleeve piping which is visible, however, in the mirror reflection above her head. Similarly a fine white linen cape worn by the woman with the brass water jug partially conceals its distinctive decoration. Thus this item of clothing almost certainly belonged to Catharina too (her mother, Maria Thins, as an older woman, would have worn less ostentatious clothes). The features of the woman in all five paintings are close enough for a tentative identification with one model to be plausible. Rubens,

5.58 Jan Vermeer, *Woman Reading a Letter at an Open Window*, c. 1658. Oil on canvas, 32⅝ × 25⅜ in (83 × 64.5 cm). Staatliche Kunstsammlungen, Dresden.

370   *Chapter 5: The Dutch Republic*

5.59 Jan Vermeer, *Woman Holding a Balance (Woman Weighing Gold)*, c. 1665. Oil on canvas, 15⅞ × 14 in (40.3 × 35.6 cm). National Gallery of Art, Washington, DC.

Rembrandt, and Jordaens, among others, used their own wives as models in their paintings; it seems that Vermeer did too. Was she also the apparently pregnant model for the *Woman Holding a Balance* (Fig. 5.59)? The nose seems larger and the domed forehead higher here than in the other paintings, but this may simply be the angle and deep shadows that modify her features as well as the effect of her cap, which conceals her hair.

This painting was called *Woman Weighing Gold* in 1696 but the pans of her scales are empty. She is just preparing to weigh some coins and jewelry. Judgment awaits both herself and the new soul inside her, a message reinforced by the painting of the *Last Judgment* hanging on the wall behind her, indeed framing her, just as the bed frames the young woman in Terborch's *The Parental Admonition* (see Fig. 5.49). This time Vermeer depicted a darkened interior with little light filtering through the closed window and draperies. Its cool grays and soft black forms seem natural, unlike the golden browns of Rembrandt's interiors. A table set parallel to the picture plane projects from the wall, marking out the space between us and the woman quietly meditating on the meaning of her life. The small mirror opposite her invites self-reflection too. Are the pearls on the table there only to represent worldly goods or are we meant to recall associations of the pearl with wisdom, purity, even desire for the Kingdom of Heaven? Some scholars have suggested that the woman is meant to recall the Virgin Mary in her role as intercessor for Christian souls.

No viewer can mistake the mood and intent of this image as mere "genre," but the artist's subtlety invites various readings of his themes, maybe intentionally. Did Vermeer choose this serious subject after the deaths of some his own children? Nothing suggests a specific memorial, yet the symbolism and its somber yet serene

Dutch Genre Painting after 1650

5.60 Jan Vermeer, *View of Delft*, c. 1662. Oil on canvas, 38⅝ × 46¼ in (98.5 × 117.5 cm). Royal Cabinet of Paintings, Mauritshuis, The Hague.

presentation allows viewers familiar with the artist's life and Roman Catholic faith to find a personal message in this, his darkest painting. No work by Vermeer better illustrates his genius for transmuting themes used by predecessors to prate against sin into a universal image that transcends its origins to achieve the weight and power of history painting.

Vermeer demonstrated his artistic stature with majestic confidence when he painted his *View of Delft* (Fig. 5.60). It is unprecedented not only in his own work but also in the rich history of Dutch townscapes. It is his largest canvas, which suggests that it was a significant commission. Its first owner was Pieter Claesz van Ruijven (1624–74), the artist's best patron, who at his death owned twenty paintings by Vermeer. Why would he want to have such a large picture of his home town? On October 12, 1654, one of Delft's gunpowder magazines had exploded, devastating the north-east section of the city and killing hundreds, including the painter Carel Fabritius. Windows in the city's churches were blown out, thousands of roof tiles shattered, and doors slammed shut as far away as Haarlem. Egbert van der Poel (1621–64), who lost one of his own children in the disaster, found a ready market for small panels showing the blast and its consequences. Vermeer painted instead the south-west corner of Delft, the area furthest from the damaged streets, thus making the city seem whole again. The result is an image of Delft that stressed continuity and strength to its citizens. The sunlight on houses in the middle distance to the right draws the attention of viewers familiar with the city to its north-east quarter, the site of the explosion. It had been cleared by 1660 and the gunpowder storage sites still within the city walls moved to a new building just outside them. The city was moving on with its life.

The most striking difference between earlier painted and engraved or etched views of Dutch cities and Vermeer's *View of Delft* is the viewpoint. Vermeer has placed his easel on the second floor of a house opposite the harbor, too close to provide a complete panorama silhouette of the city used in all earlier paintings and engravings of Delft and other cities. These views miniaturize the distant city, reducing its landmarks to a few steeples and windmills. By moving closer, Vermeer monumentalized Delft. He also employed far stronger contrasts of light and shade than his predecessors had, though not than those of Jacob van Ruisdael (see Fig. 5.71). Vermeer, who used landscape paintings in the backgrounds of several of his paintings, was certainly aware of the work of this contemporary. He shows the bell tower of the Nieuwe Kerk just right of center and, in shadow in the right foreground, the twin towers of the Rotterdam Gate. The Schiedam Gate with a clock tower is the weightiest building in the left half of the painting. The boats moored on the far shore almost vanish into the shadows but the bulk of one on the right is defined by flickering accents of cream paint, like strings of miniature Christmas lights, that pick up the reflections along its side. The mortar between the bricks on the Rotterdam Gate is suggested by similar dabs of rough paint. Restorers have found sand mixed with roughly ground white lead in the underpaint of these passages. Thus these effects were not due to last-minute moments of inspiration but were carefully planned and prepared by this most assiduous observer of daylight. Whether he used a device such as a *camera obscura* when preparing this painting or others is almost beside the point. From its blurred information only a painter of Vermeer's disciplined acuity could have extracted such results. The reflections in the water of the two city gates were extended to the shoreline in the foreground in a late stage of the execution to a point that exaggerates reality but stabilizes the weight of the horizontal panorama above the water beneath its shifting cloud cover. It is worth remembering when looking at this painting that the light conditions it portrays are as momentary as the facial expressions of Frans Hals's subjects. This image, too, is a stopped moment in time.

Vermeer never sold *The Art of Painting* (Fig. 5.61) and his widow tried hard to keep it, giving it to her mother in a futile attempt to keep it out of the hands of her creditors. It is the largest of his domestic interiors, though the adjective "domestic" hardly seems appropriate. An artist in elegant black costume and beret is in the center, his back to the viewer.[13] His subject is a young woman dressed in a stiff blue fabric that creates large angular folds; her head is crowned with a laurel wreath. She clasps a bulky tome with her left arm while delicately balancing the trumpet in her right hand. She is dressed as Clio, the muse of history, and by implication the true subject of art but one that did not appeal to Vermeer's public. The map on the back wall, one of many that appear in Vermeer's interior views, all so distinctly depicted that they have been identified, is the largest ever published of the Netherlands. It shows them united (with North to the right) but with a significant crack along the

5.61 Jan Vermeer, *The Art of Painting*, c. 1666–67. Oil on canvas, 47¼ × 39⅓ in (120 × 100 cm). Kunsthistorisches Museum, Vienna.

division between the Spanish Netherlands and the Seven Northern Provinces. On the table is a plaster mask, some fancy multicolored cloths, and an open sketchbook with drawings, apparently the artist's preparatory studies for his painting. A chair can just be made out in the shadows of the left foreground. A splendid brass chandelier hangs from the rafters. Light falls onto the model and the painter from the window on the left, which is concealed by a massive tapestry pulled back as if to reveal the process of artistic transformation from nature into art. What does this all mean?

Nothing defines the setting as a seventeenth-century rather than an earlier scene except the date of the map, which was published after 1652. Like other maps of the time, it still shows the Netherlands as one country. Its control by the Habsburg monarchy in the sixteenth century is even hinted at by the eagle insignia in the upper part of the chandelier, and its division, as noted above, by the crease in the middle. Vermeer and his wife were Catholic. Did they wish that the division into Protestant North and Catholic South had never occurred? It seems unlikely that such a futile political agenda inspired the creation of this image. Rather the map serves to remind viewers of the achievements of all artists from this territory, past and present.

This also seems to be the message of the artist's costume. He is not Vermeer with his back turned, despite popular belief that this is the case. This artist represents all the artists of these territories, hence his oversized scale in this complex scenario. Clio was also understood to represent Fame, most of whose attributes she shares. The model is also Nature, which the artist must study carefully before he sets brush to canvas, along with ideal models (the mask representing *Imitatio*) and the texts on which great art depends. The sketchbook represents *disegno*, both the inspiring concept behind a painting and its careful study in drawings before the painting begins. That no drawings by Vermeer himself have been identified is irrelevant; their use in the Netherlands was widespread. The artist's black and white costume may stand for chiaroscuro, as can the pavement. His red stockings and her blue costume and yellow book give central focus yet again to the three primary colors. The uneven surface of the map on the back wall as well as the tapestry curtain offer virtuoso displays of Vermeer's ability to depict patterns and textured material in different light conditions. The curtain may be another nod to the legend of Zeuxis and Parrhasius. That neither Vermeer nor any other Dutch painter would have started with final details like Clio's wreath rather than the background and markings of the overall design only signals to the informed viewer that this is a symbolic, not a real, image of an artist at work.

Did Vermeer know Rembrandt's *Self-Portrait* of 1640 (see Fig. 5.31) or its etched version of 1639? That he knew the latter at least seems certain, and that he knew of the former likely, including its Italian sources. If Vermeer had those works in mind, then his *The Art of Painting* can also be read as a riposte to Rembrandt's self-promotion. Instead of offering his own image as proof that Dutch artists were as good as the great Italians of the previous century, Vermeer asks us look beyond the individual artist and his achievement to pay tribute to the power of Painting herself. Flemish artists since Jan van Eyck had excelled at depicting realistic interiors filled with daylight. Thus Vermeer draws attention not only to his own achievements but also to his predecessors in a specialty in which they could rightfully consider themselves superior to Italian artists. Even the map celebrates Dutch cartographers. The only surviving example of this one, the largest and most ambitious then made, lacks the images of cities seen in the borders in the painting: Vermeer preserved them for posterity.

Jan Steen

No Dutch artist offers a more vivid contrast with Vermeer than Jan Steen (1626–79). Instead of silence, Steen's paintings conjure up a world of clinking glasses and raucous laughter. Instead of one or two motionless figures, Steen's lively crowds of characters are caught in mid-action. And instead of a limited output that makes Vermeer's public hunger for more, Steen's cornucopia of productivity overwhelms his admirers with canvases that are not always executed with as much diligence as they deserved. His best works—and there are many that vie for the honor—are full of visual delights. He loved to create passages of flashy brushwork on the silk skirts of his wanton women that hark back to Hals, while his portrayals of Dutch interiors and their contents can rival the settings and still-life elements in the work of Terborch and Metsu.

Jan Steen, like Rembrandt and Dou, was born in Leiden of good middle-class stock: his parents and grandparents were grain merchants. The family, which was Catholic, also owned a brewery and property in Leiden. Jan, the oldest son, enrolled in Leiden University in 1646 when he was twenty, so had completed his studies at the Latin School, acquiring a better education than usual for a painter. He left shortly afterwards, however, and qualified as a master painter in 1648. A year later he married the daughter of the landscape painter Jan van Goyen and moved to The Hague. In 1654 the family moved to Delft, where Jan ran a tavern leased for him by his father until 1657. The next few years were spent back in Leiden and then in nearby Warmond (until 1660), followed by a decade in Haarlem (1661–70), where Steen painted many of his best pictures. He returned to Leiden in 1670, having inherited a house there, and opened a tavern in 1672. The second Anglo-Dutch War (1665–7) drained all discretionary income for such luxuries as art. When Steen remarried in 1673 (his first wife died in 1669), she continued to sell meat in the local market to help support their eight children. He was only fifty-three when he died. His constant moves suggest a search for a congenial city for his artistic output that he eventually found in Haarlem. He avoided Amsterdam, however, whose wealthy collectors would have been unlikely to respond to his comic vein of narrative painting.

Steen probably painted more self-portraits than anyone in the history of European painting. Unlike most of Rembrandt's, however, these were not isolated images of the artist. Instead he introduced "participant" images of himself as one of the characters in his own comic dramas, usually playing the leading role. He did paint one conventional half-length *Self-Portrait* (Rijksmuseum, Amsterdam) which in the context of his production is remarkable for its sobriety. A better clue to his artistic persona is his *Self-Portrait Playing a Lute* (Fig. 5.62). Seated facing us but with his right leg indecorously propped up on his left and wearing the costume of a comic actor, Steen strums an outsize lute and eyes us with a knowing smile as he entertains us with a song, probably one full of suggestive *double-entendres*. A huge pewter tankard rests on the table beside him; a great sweep of drapery behind him tells us that this is a staged comic performance. Steen has combined portrait and genre subject—he had Hals's half-length pictures of musicians in mind—to come up with a novel twist on the self-portrait of the artist as an accomplished gentleman unsullied by practicing a manual trade. Steen mocks the implied class elevation of prototypes such as Paul Bril's picture of himself playing a lute with an example of his landscape painting on the easel behind him (Rhode Island School of Design, Providence) and relishes the opportunity to ham it up for us while, of course, making the same points about his own impressive range of accomplishments.

5.62 Jan Steen, *Self-Portrait Playing a Lute*, c. 1661–63. Oil on wood, 21¾ × 17¼ in (55.3 × 43.8 cm). © Museo Thyssen-Bornemisza, Madrid.

Dutch Genre Painting after 1650

The titles of some of Steen's most popular works, for example *The Young Ones Chirrup as the Old Ones Sing*, *In Luxury Beware*, and the *Dissolute Household*, give an idea of their festive yet moralizing character even to those unfamiliar with them. His *Twelfth Night* (Fig. 5.63) is a lively variation of a theme better known from his paintings in Boston and Amsterdam. Significantly each one is unlike the others in format, setting, participants, and in the activities shown, ample evidence of Steen's capacity for artistic invention. The Feast of the Epiphany on January 6, known in the Netherlands as "Driekoningenavond" (Evening of the Three Kings), is still occasionally celebrated as Steen recorded it. One custom required all members of the family to play roles chosen by drawing titles from a hat, though that of the king might be settled by serving a cake with an almond or coin in it: the recipient of the coin became king for the evening. The other roles of fool, cook, musician, wine steward, and so on were then distributed. Suitable costumes, especially for the fool, would be found in the family's trunk of old clothes or invented from common household objects. In the example illustrated here, the king's paper crown has been awarded to a child who is being given a sip of wine. The announcement "The king drinks!" was the signal for everyone else to start indulging too. In Jordaens's depictions of this subject (see Fig. 2.50), the king is always an extremely fat old man. Steen surely knew of them and thus his choice of an innocent child for the role was deliberate. It makes for a lighter, less obviously judgmental mood than Jordaens's gross kings do. The pose of the woman in an orange weskit and gorgeous yellow silk skirt in the foreground reveals that she has already had a few drinks. She smiles indulgently at the "king"—her own child maybe—while her glass of wine rests precariously against the edge of the table. Her sloppy pose, loose jacket, and the exposed foot warmer are all blatantly suggestive though her companions ignore her. The egg shells scattered on the floor could also have erotic meaning beyond the prosaic fact that they were broken to make the batter for the waffles eaten at the feast. The "king's" train is held by an older child who wears a basket on his head. A "musician" behind him has a huge funnel for a hat. The three-branched

5.63 Jan Steen, *Twelfth Night*, 1668. Oil on canvas, 32⅓ × 42⅓ in (82 × 107.5 cm). Staatliche Museen, Kassel.

candle on the bench alludes to the three kings and was used for a children's dance that may have already been performed. Steen himself is the host with his wife at his side. He seems to enjoy both the violinist behind him and the raucous noises of the *rommelpot* (a type of friction drum) being played by the fool on the other side of the table. A more restrained group on the right keep themselves apart from the wilder folk on the left. No inscriptions warn of the dangers of *Luxuria* or excessive indulgence, nor does this picture include a basket of beggars' tools overhead, as Steen did elsewhere. Balancing the hilarity of the majority against the sobersides on the right, the artist seems to be saying that it is fine to celebrate this religious festival in one's own home amid family and friends, regardless of getting tipsy.

Many of Steen's genre scenes take place out of doors, unlike those of Dou, Metsu, Terborch, and Vermeer. Even Pieter de Hooch's outdoor scenes take place in enclosed courtyards that are still part of women's domestic world. The outside world portrayed by Steen gave men a bigger role—as quack doctors selling suspicious nostrums at village fairs, at gatherings beside inns, at festivities organized by military companies, at country festivals (*kermissen*), and at weddings. Still Steen's crowds always represent a wide range of ages, sexes, classes, and professions, as do most of his indoor gatherings that do not focus on relations between the sexes. Steen's world is all-embracing, one of many reasons for his persistent popularity, especially in the Netherlands. An especially appealing example of Steen's outdoor genre scenes is *Skittle Players Outside an Inn* (Fig. 5.64). On a wood panel only slightly over a foot (30 cm) high, the painting conjures up a warm spring day when the trees at last begin to leaf out and it is warm enough to sit on the ground with friends and for a child to run about shoeless. This is, it seems, just a picture of good folk enjoying a nice day outside the Swan Inn. Steen painted other quiet pictures of families saying grace and a touching interpretation of the *Supper at Emmaus* (Rijksmuseum, Amsterdam). He can be a serious as well as an entertaining artist. Steen's religious paintings are as original as his genre scenes, perhaps even more so because, unlike other Dutch artists who painted biblical subjects, he disdained obvious debts to Italian models. He used an idiosyncratic mixture of antique and modern dress; some of the humorous elements of his genre scenes are retained in ways that challenge the decorum his public would have expected for pictures of the *Worship of the Golden Calf* (North Carolina Museum of Art, Raleigh) or the *Wedding at Cana* (National Gallery of Ireland, Dublin). More so than his genre scenes, such works as *Samson and Delilah* (County Museum, Los Angeles) and the *Capture of Samson* (Wallraf-Richartz-Museum, Cologne) look like staged theatrical performances, especially when enormous silk draperies hang over the protagonists. Given his lifelong adherence to Roman Catholicism, Steen's religious paintings cannot be ignored in any balanced account of his achievement. Some are among his most ambitiously conceived and executed canvases. They were well represented in the important exhibition of his work held in Washington in 1996.

5.64 Jan Steen, *Skittle Players Outside an Inn*, c. 1660-3. Oil on wood, 13³⁄₁₆ × 10⅝ in (33.5 × 26.9 cm). National Gallery, London.

Landscape Painting before 1650

For cloudy skies and melancholy weather take up as much time as [sunny weather] yet are noething soe pleasant.
EDWARD NORGATE, *MINIATURA*, 1650[14]

The most popular kind of painting in the Dutch Republic was landscape. It replaced history as the major category in Dutch collections as its share grew from about 23 per cent in the 1610s to almost 40 per cent by the 1680s. The themes discussed by Wolfgang Stechow in his fundamental study show how thoroughly Dutch artists explored their newly won land: dunes, rivers and canals, beaches, winter scenes, seascapes, woodlands and forests, panoramas, night and evening scenes, and townscapes. Dutch artists also traveled and brought back sketches of the rocky terrain and rushing streams of Scandinavia, of the Rhine and Moselle valleys, and of Italian ruins and sunlight. Dutch landscape paintings are rarely uninhabited, even if the figures do little but provide scale; some scenes include people fishing, maneuvering ferries across a river, guarding livestock, or putting linen out to bleach in the sun.

Neither the climate nor the geography of the Netherlands would seem to offer temptations for a landscape painter. The terrain is mainly flat and the weather better known for rain than sunshine. The Flemish pioneers of landscape painting such as Joachim Patenir (d. 1524) and Herri met de Bles (active by 1535) made their reputations with panoramas taken from artificially high viewpoints; the vast expanse of land thus surveyed could include impressive if strange mountains, seacoasts, rivers, wooded slopes, fertile meadows, and sheltered valleys with towns and villages. Not even the Alps offered all these elements from one spot. They were imaginary compilations of the most appealing and spectacular aspects of European geography, assembled for the delight of the wealthy armchair traveler who could explore this world without facing any of the dangers and discomfort of a long journey. It is nearly always summer; some blue sky is shown even if there are clouds. These *Weltlandschaft* (world landscape) panoramas were also made in Germany by Albrecht Altdorfer (*c.* 1480–1538) and others, and developed and perfected in Flanders by Pieter Bruegel the Elder (*c.* 1525–69) in prints as well as in paintings. His influence was enormous well into the next century.

Early Tonal Landscape Painting

The shift from images of landscapes that patrons had rarely seen to pictures of their own countryside took place in Haarlem in the early seventeenth century. In 1603 Hendrick Goltzius made a remarkable drawing (see Fig. 5.1) that depicts an extensive view from foreground to distance; the viewpoint is well above ground level but the horizon, situated just above the halfway mark, is absolutely level. The coastal dunes west of Haarlem would have offered Goltzius an elevated site from which to make this meticulously observed record of flat farmland. The recession from foreground to distance is convincingly rendered without the aid of any landmarks such windmills or church towers. The panorama landscapes by Philips Koninck, painted over fifty years later, differ from Goltzius's little drawing in scale and medium but hardly at all in composition (see Fig. 5.69).

In the first decades of the century, Dutch draughtsmen and printmakers in Haarlem produced the most innovative landscapes. A number of such prints, for example Claes Jansz. Visscher's *Pleasant Places* of *c.* 1611–12, found a ready market, testifying to the popularity of scenes of villages, farmhouses, and country roads. The sales pitch on the title page told prospective buyers that "Here you may have a quick look at pleasant places, you art lovers who have no time to travel far." These art lovers were not offered the spectacular Alpine views that Pieter Bruegel designed for Antwerp engravers in the previous century; a muddy track with travelers, a sheep herder with a small flock moving toward some woods, and the occasional ruin was, it seems, enough. As Catherine Levesque has shown, however, these works, created thirty years after the turbulent struggle for independence from Spanish rule, contain some clear references to those events and the hard-won peace that followed.[15] The last of these "pleasant places" shows the *Huis ter Kleef* (Fig. 5.65), where the commander of the Spanish troops that laid siege to Haarlem in 1572–3 had his headquarters. Now a ruin with birds flying around its tallest structure, it serves as an architectural *memento mori* of events still vivid to many of Haarlem's older citizens. The whole series meant more than "pleasant places" to its intended audience. The scenes celebrate victory over Spain as well as the honest labors that sustain the new Republic. The flat ordinary "Dutchness" of this terrain was crucial to the formation of a new national identity for those who lived there.

The landscape paintings of Jan van Goyen (1596–1656) are typical of many produced between 1625 and 1650 in what is called the "tonal" phase of Dutch painting. In these decades bright local colors vanish from still-life, portraiture, genre, and religious subjects, and especially from landscape. Instead of the artificial contrasts of icy blue distances, cool green middle grounds, and brown foregrounds used by such Mannerist artists as Paul Bril (Fig. 5.66) that exaggerate the effects of aerial perspective (the fading of local colors as they recede), van Goyen and others managed to create convincing scenes through a limited palette of cream, beige, olive greens, grays, and browns. The sun shines through shifting clouds that allow little blue to show: an overcast sky with gray clouds is typical. As Edward Norgate observed, such conditions prevail as much as sun. Still earlier painters ignored them, except to depict an occasional storm. The flat horizon line that Goltzius placed almost halfway down the page (see Fig. 5.1) now descends further, giving more than three-quarters of the picture space to the sky in some cases. Van Goyen was especially adept at suggesting infinite depths with a sliver of land beneath layers of scudding gray clouds.

Van Goyen's paintings are often small and are painted on oak panels primed with a pale ground on which the image was almost as much drawn

5.65 Claes Jansz. Visscher, *"Huis te Kleef"*, from *"Pleasant Places"*, 1611. Engraving. Rijksmuseum, Amsterdam.

5.66 Paul Bril, *Fantastic Landscape*, 1598. Oil on copper, 8⅓ × 11½ in (21.3 × 29.3 cm). National Gallery of Scotland, Edinburgh.

Landscape Painting before 1650

as painted. The sky and clouds were laid in first over the priming layer. Sometimes a few lines of black chalk underdrawing can be detected under the lively scribble of strokes depicting dead oak trees, farmhouses, sandy dunes, and muddy riverbanks. The *Windmill by a River* (Fig. 5.67) shown here is small—just under a foot (30 cm) high—but there is a sense of infinite space stretching from the pale yellow of the dunes in the right foreground, where a windmill faces the distant shore, to the horizon as the terrain changes to soft greenish gray and then to pale bluish hues. The artist's VG monogram and date are concealed in the brown strokes of the left foreground, a favorite trick. The site is invented but based on the knowledge van Goyen acquired making hundreds of sketches as he traveled around the Republic. While he also painted views of particular towns sited on rivers, he was at his best conjuring up expanses of water with a few sailboats making their way up an estuary on a wet day with a good breeze (National Gallery, London). Clients and artists chose images of nature at its least rather than most attractive. The sunny pastorals of Italy may even have seemed decadent temptations to Calvinist patrons. This attitude could also explain why the only season depicted in its own right was winter, a theme that inspired painters from Hendrik Averkamp to Jacob van Ruisdael to create some of their best works (see Fig. 5.72).

Landscape Painting after 1650

As the Dutch economy flourished and its citizens built themselves larger town houses and country retreats, they had the space and income to acquire larger pictures. Landscape specialists responded, using canvas instead of the costlier oak panels for bigger paintings. The subtle tonal contrasts and grayed palette of the tonal phase gradually gives way to sunnier scenery. The later works of Salomon van Ruysdael (1600/3–70) reduce the cloud cover, use more greens and blues, and allow a few spots of bright local color on the costumes of figures in the foreground. Bartholomeus Breenbergh (1599/1600–1657)

5.67 Jan van Goyen, *Windmill by a River*, 1642. Oil on wood, 11⁵⁄₁₆ × 14⁵⁄₁₆ in (29.4 × 36.3 cm). National Gallery, London.

5.68 Jacob van Ruisdael, *Windmill by a Country Road*, c. 1650. Oil on wood panel, 19½ × 27 in (49.5 × 68.5 cm). Cleveland Museum of Art, Cleveland, OH.

returned from Italy and began painting views of the Roman campagna with crumbling ruins and ancient bridges bathed in the warm light of a late summer afternoon. The most obvious mark of a new stylistic approach, however, are bolder contrasts of light and shade that produce more solid forms than those of the tonal phase. Jacob van Ruisdael's *Windmill by a Country Road* (Fig. **5.68**) epitomizes these changes. Its horizon level is as low as that in van Goyen's view (see Fig. 5.67) but the mill is closer to us so that its dark shape and sails set on a small hill against the fading light, catch our attention along with the scruffy oak trees on either side. The panoramic vista of van Goyen has vanished, replaced by a less extensive but nevertheless typical Dutch rural view on the left.

Rembrandt painted only a few landscapes, all relatively small and idiosyncratic. The terrain usually does not look like Holland and the forceful chiaroscuro looks even more artificial than in his subject paintings. His prints and drawings of landscape subjects, which are more realistic, were more influential. These were known not only to those who frequented his popular studio in Amsterdam but also to artists elsewhere. Of these Philips Koninck (1619–88), who attended Rembrandt's studio in Amsterdam in the 1640s, made the most impressive use, especially in his bold panoramas that adopt the format pioneered by Goltzius (see Fig. 5.1) and then used by Rembrandt in prints (see Fig. 5.34) and drawings. In these large, almost square, paintings divided roughly equally into sky and land (Fig. **5.69**), Koninck presents a Dutch *Weltlandschaft*, a broad expanse of territory that can easily be imagined continuing beyond the frame. His use of a rough impasto mimics the texture of the dunes and paths depicted. None of Koninck's views has ever been identified. Apparently he intended them to be generic evocations of the territory of the Dutch Republic whose boundaries were finally settled by the Treaty of Münster in 1648. Raised paths on dunes in the foreground of the diagonal paths that carry our eyes toward the horizon imply that we are standing on this level just beyond the picture plane. When Thoré-Bürger saw Vermeer's *View of Delft* (see Fig. 5.60) for the first time in the 1850s, the sky reminded him of those by Koninck. In both the moving clouds explain the patches of light and shade on the scene before us.

Landscape Painting after 1650 381

5.69 Philips Koninck, *Landscape with a Hawking Party*, c. 1660. Oil on canvas, 52¼ × 63 in (132.7 × 160 cm). National Gallery, London.

The greatest Dutch landscape painter of the century was Jacob van Ruisdael (1628/9–82). He was precocious, technically brilliant, and versatile, producing masterpieces in every category of landscape made by his contemporaries except Italian views. Born in Haarlem, he probably began his training with his father, by whom only a few landscapes are known. Ruisdael then probably assisted his productive uncle, Salomon van Ruysdael, before emerging as an independent artist in his late teens (see Fig. 5.68). There are signed and dated paintings by Jacob from the age of seventeen until he was in his mid-twenties. After that he rarely dated his work, though he usually signed or monogrammed it. Pride in his precocious achievements would explain the flurry of dates in his early years, some of which predate his matriculation in Haarlem's Guild of Painters in 1648. He moved to Amsterdam in 1657 and seems to have lived there for the rest of his life, though he was buried in Haarlem. These are almost the only known facts of his career, despite extensive archival research. He must have led a blameless life and seems not to have married.

Several of Ruisdael's works have become national icons, none more so than the *Mill at Wyck near Duurstede* (Rijksmuseum, Amsterdam), postcards of which outsell everything else in that museum except Rembrandt's *Night Watch* and Vermeer's *Little Street*. His "Haarlempjes"—surprisingly small paintings with views of his birthplace seen from distant dunes across flat fields with the imposing mass of the church of St. Bavo dominating the skyline—have often been chosen to represent the artist in general surveys. Like the Koninck shown here (see Fig. 5.69), they suggest great distances and national identity with economy and distinction. It is not possible to encompass Ruisdael's varied achievements with a few works for his range was prodigious. He painted marshy woodlands, squalls ruffling the water of estuaries, mills with streams cascading past their wheels, grain fields ripening under a fitful sky, waterfalls between steep banks of fir trees, snow-dusted landscapes beneath inky skies, coast and beach scenes, and even some unusual views of Amsterdam. His two treatments of the *Jewish Graveyard* (Detroit Institute of

Arts, Detroit, and Staatliche Kunstsammlungen, Dresden) are also famous. Seymour Slive has discussed these masterpieces by Ruisdael eloquently in the exhibition catalogue of 1981, in his survey of Dutch seventeenth-century painting, and in his monograph on Ruisdael's paintings. For this book, some relatively unfamiliar examples of Ruisdael's production have been selected, to extend our appreciation beyond the famous—and easily accessed—works usually shown.

An outstanding example of Ruisdael's transformation of the ordinary into the extraordinary is the *View of Bentheim Castle* (Fig. 5.70). The castle survives, though somewhat altered, and still overlooks this small town on the border between the Netherlands and Germany. Ruisdael and another painter, Nicolas Berchem, visited the area, which had a more picturesque and varied terrain than that around Haarlem, in 1650. He made drawings of the castle (none of which have survived), the local half-timbered houses, and water mills, which he then used for paintings of these motifs after his return home. Several paintings feature the castle from different angles; others are of water swirling past wooden bridges, mill wheels, and old houses with patched walls and moss-covered roofs (e.g. National Gallery, London). In earlier Dutch landscapes, a single house or tree never occupies so much pictorial space and thus fades into the land; the viewer contemplates infinity rather than a particular motif within a larger scene. Ruisdael's early paintings use a lot of impasto so that the rough bark, bare twigs, and weathered planks seem almost palpable. This process of emphasizing the mass and thus the pictorial presence of his main motif was taken to new lengths, however, in *Bentheim Castle*. The real castle sits amid houses on a small rise of land amid flat fields: its elevated position in the painting is pictorial fiction. The result is so splendidly realized that the viewer believes the castle and town must have looked like this.

5.70 Jacob van Ruisdael, *View of Bentheim Castle*, 1653. Oil on canvas, 43½ × 56⅝ in (110.5 × 144 cm). National Gallery of Ireland, Dublin.

Landscape Painting after 1650 383

Ruisdael's fascination with Bentheim Castle as a subject, though never a topographically accurate one, implies that it must have had particular significance for him or for his patrons. To interpret a castle or fortress as a metaphor of refuge, hence of divine protection, would be an obvious response for Dutch Calvinists.[16] Several psalms make the analogy. Psalm 18 declares: "The Lord is my rock and my fortress and my deliverer," and Psalm 59 calls the Lord "my defense and refuge in the day of my trouble." The old hymn "A mighty fortress is our God," whose original words and music are by Martin Luther, takes its inspiration from these psalms. This reading would make sense of the storm clouds that cluster around the castle and the clear sky around the little windmill in the distance: emblem books include analogies between a man without God and windmills without wind, rendering both useless.

While scholars give varying degrees of emphasis to the symbolism that can be read into Ruisdael's landscapes, most agree that he used it more often than his peers. Dead birch trees with their distinctive silver-white bark peeling off occur frequently, usually decaying in the streams and rivers into which they have fallen. For Ruisdael they serve as Nature's equivalent of the skull in Vanitas paintings, reminders of the brevity of human life as well as of the natural cycle of birth, life, death, and decay. Both of the paintings of the *Jewish Graveyard* have them and so does the melancholy *Ruins of Egmond Castle* (Fig. 5.71) painted around 1655. A shattered brick tower forms the central motif, anchoring the painting with its vertical form reflected in the water that fills the foreground. Bands of gray clouds surge across the sky, leaving a few patches of blue visible at either side. A flicker of sun lights up the mortar and bricks at the base of the tower. A patch of grayish white in the right foreground draws attention to the stump of a dead birch tree. Otherwise the painting is executed in subtle variations of blue-green, green, and gray.

Egmond Castle, situated north of Haarlem near Alkmaar, had, like the Huis ter Kleef, been occupied by Spanish troops in the 1570s. After their defeat, the castle was deliberately destroyed so that it could not be used against the Republic again. Ruisdael made several drawings of the site from various angles and used them for the ruins

5.71 Jacob van Ruisdael, *Ruins of Egmond Castle*, c. 1655. Oil on canvas, 38¾ × 51⅛ in (98.5 × 130 cm). Mr and Mrs Potter Palmer Collection. Art Institute of Chicago, Chicago, IL.

in the two *Jewish Graveyard* canvases as well as in this painting, varying their appearance in each work. The ruins are actually on flat land so that the hills behind them here are invented, as is the position of the ruins at the edge of a river. This manipulation of motifs observed from nature to make them more impressive than they were is typical of Ruisdael's working method. His uncle had painted the ruins of Egmond in the distance on a sunny day where their significance is easily overlooked. In Ruisdael's canvas, the ruins of the castle are closer to us than the walls in Vermeer's *View of Delft* (see Fig. 5.60), and so have great physical presence as well as an almost tragic character enhanced by the overcast sky. No contemporary viewer would have looked at the severed tower and broken arches without remembering their history, or wondering about it if they had not heard the stories before. The human effort required to create these buildings and the reasons for their destruction recall heroic acts and lives lost, all important events in the history of Haarlem and the United Provinces. But life continues—a small flock of sheep graze on the far banks, guarded by a shepherd in a red jacket. This color, never worn by farm laborers, was used by the artist to ensure we would spot him and think about his role in this elegiac painting.

Another example of Ruisdael's ability to take a landscape subject that others had popularized and transform it is his interpretation of the winter landscape. The early ones by Hendrick Averkamp (1585/6–1634) are descended directly from those of Pieter Bruegel the Elder and his sons. Amid a few terracotta red brick buildings and elegant bare trees, crowds of figures in red, black, and brown outfits skate on the frozen water or play an early form of ice hockey: the mood is joyful despite the cold. Jan van Goyen and others continued the tradition, though the reds vanish during the tonal phase. Ruisdael, who turned to this theme in the late 1660s and early 1670s, offers only gray skies and a few small figures walking or dragging a loaded sled (Fig. 5.72). Winter, as Stechow noted, was associated with old age and the end of the day. The quietly meditative mood of this snow scene suits that association. Many of Ruisdael's snow scenes include a windmill or two: while indispensable in the Republic to drain the land and

grind wheat, windmills were also interpreted in emblem books as embodying the interdependence of man and God: as the windmill is powerless to work without wind, so, these texts argued, man needs God's spiritual guidance in this world and the next. The sails facing the heavens make this reading a probable one, especially when the mill is given emphasis in the painting, as it is here and, even more dramatically, in the *Mill at Wyck near Duurstede* (Rijksmuseum, Amsterdam). This small winter painting is a tour de force. Only slightly over a foot (30 cm) high, it is executed entirely in various shades of gray and white, yet, like Rembrandt's drawing of *Het Molentje* (see Fig. 5.35), it creates a spacious scene with restricted means. Two gulls are just visible against the clouds whose movement they evoke. A duck in the foreground is about to take flight. A man stands in the center of the canvas on the bluff of land supporting the house and mill staring across the frozen water to the distant shore. Only a painter of Ruisdael's gifts could encompass the range seen in the heroic vision of the *View of Bentheim Castle*, the contemplative melancholy of the *Ruins of Egmond Castle*, and the elegiac mood of the *Winter Landscape with Windmill*. Like Nicolas Poussin, he lifted the genre of landscape to levels above the sentimental and anecdotal and gave his imagery the moral weight of history painting.

5.72 Jacob van Ruisdael, *Winter Landscape with Windmill*, c. 1670. Oil on copper, 14⅝ × 18 in (37.2 × 45.8 cm). Frits Lugt Collection. Institut Neerlandais, Paris.

6 ENGLAND

Christopher Wren, St. Paul's Cathedral, London, exterior, 1675–1710.

BRITAIN'S TUDOR MONARCHS were not enterprising patrons of the visual arts. Their biggest expenditures were for new palaces and extensions to existing residences. Their interior decoration featured fancy plaster ceilings, elaborate carved wood screens, and tapestries, but few paintings. Most of the artists employed at court were foreigners of limited talent: even the post of Sergeant Painter required little but the application of appropriate coats of arms and emblems to royal possessions. The notable exception is Hans Holbein (1497/8–1543), one of the greatest German painters of the sixteenth century. He made two visits to England, working for other patrons before Henry VIII eventually hired him in 1536 because he was "very excellent in making Physiognomies." So very compelling are Holbein's aggressively frontal presentations of the king that they have defined his persona ever since. Portraits of Elizabeth I (1523–1603), who became queen in 1558, usually show her full-length in splendid clothes but she was never painted by an artist of Holbein's stature. She was not interested in hiring foreign artists, though she heard that "the Italians [. . .] had the name to be the cunningest and draw best."[1] Anthonis Mor (c. 1517/20–1576/7), after Titian the best court portraitist in Europe, paid a visit in 1564, when he painted *Mary Tudor* (Prado, Madrid). Federico Zuccaro (c. 1540–1609) followed in 1575, again invited for his skills at portrait painting, but only his drawn portraits of the queen and her favorite, Robert Dudley, Earl of Leicester, are known today (British Museum, London).

Britain's greatest contribution to the visual arts in the seventeenth century were made by her architects. In neither painting nor sculpture were native artists more than competent until mid-century except in the art of the miniature portrait. The first outstanding English master of that specialty was Nicholas Hilliard (c. 1547–1619). The son of a jeweler, from whom he received his training, he created small portraits that were worn like jewels, attached to necklaces or pinned into ladies' hair. The typical portrait is painted on an oval of vellum less than two inches high with the head and shoulders seen in three-quarter view against a background of lapis blue, the whole then set into a gold frame with a crystal cover. Despite the tiny scale, Hilliard could catch a convincing yet flattering likeness. A few of his portraits have larger formats allowing for a full-length figure. Of these, the elegant youth leaning against a tree amid a patch of thorny roses, his right hand touching his heart as he gazes out at us, suits to perfection the mood of Elizabethan lute songs about the torments of love (Fig. 6.1). Hilliard's own *Treatise concerning the Arte of Limning* is full of excellent practical advice to those who would follow his example, though he believed that only gentlemen should take up this profession. Isaac Oliver (by 1568–1617) and Samuel Cooper (1609-72) were the first of his many successors who had few rivals elsewhere.

6.1 Nicolas Hilliard, *Man Leaning Against a Tree Among Roses*, c. 1590. Oval, tempera on vellum, 5⅝ × 21¹³⁄₁₆ in (14.2 × 55.6 cm). Victoria and Albert Museum, London.

Portraits of the reigning monarch and favored members of court would remain the most reliable source of patronage for ambitious painters in Britain for the next two centuries. Genre scenes, still-life, and landscape painting did not find much favor, though there was some demand for topographical maps and views of estates, a minor genre that gave little scope for artistic imagination. Since the dissolution of the monasteries by Henry VIII and his assumption of control of the Church of England in the 1530s, all "Popish things" such as altarpieces and religious paintings of New Testament subjects ceased to be made except for private use by Catholic families. Only in the late seventeenth century did a market develop for large-scale decorative paintings with complex allegorical and historical content; for these, too, foreign artists were usually hired.

Anthony van Dyck (see pp. 174–182) and, briefly, Peter Paul Rubens (see pp. 145–174), were both brought to London in the 1620s on the initiative of Thomas Howard, 14th Earl of Arundel (1585–1646), as also were Gerrit van Honthorst from Utrecht and his fellow Caravaggio follower, Orazio Gentileschi. Arundel was among the first to visit Italy and bring back examples of art, ancient and modern, for his houses. He ordered full-length portraits of himself and his wife from Daniel Mytens (*c.* 1590–1647) showing galleries behind them full of ancient sculptures and recent paintings. He was especially fond of Titian, a taste he encouraged Van Dyck to develop when he accompanied Lady Arundel to Venice in 1623. The Duke of Buckingham, Charles's favorite, and several other members of his circle had also started serious art collections by 1625. When the Duke of Mantua ran into financial difficulties and put his entire collection of paintings up for sale in 1627, Charles I acquired it all, though Oliver Cromwell auctioned it off after the king's execution. Thus briefly Charles I owned Caravaggio's *Death of the Virgin* (see Fig. 1.48), bought by the duke on Rubens's advice after its Roman patrons rejected it. The wealth of European art of the sixteenth and seventeenth centuries in Britain today testifies to the energy, taste, and finances devoted to collecting by its "landed gentry" from the 1620s onwards.

English Painting

Van Dyck in England

Anthony Van Dyck's presence in London working for Charles I (1625–49) and his court from 1632 until his death in 1641 transformed British portraiture. Daniel Mytens (*c.* 1590–1647) who came from Delft, had been the favored artist at the court of James I (1566–1625), for whom he began working in 1620. In addition to the portraits of the Earl and Countess of Arundel mentioned above, he made fine full-length portraits of James and of Charles I, but left London for The Hague soon after Van Dyck's arrival, as few sought his services any longer. The delivery of Van Dyck's *Rinaldo and Armida* (see Fig. 2.47) to the court in 1629 had whetted the king's appetite. He considered Van Dyck to be on a par with Titian, an artist he admired deeply. Titian had served the Emperor Charles V and Philip II of Spain with portraits that, like Van Dyck's, outclassed those of his competition. A royal invitation was extended to Van Dyck in March 1632. He was in London by April 1 and was knighted three months later. It was a felicitous match of patron and artist.

Van Dyck painted Charles I many times in various formats, costumes, and situations: in his ermine robes with full regalia; riding out of a triumphal archway on a magnificent white horse with his riding master in attendance (see Fig. 6.3); dismounted from a different steed on the banks of the Thames (Louvre, Paris); seated on another superb horse in full armor; as a knight of the Order of the Garter; half-length with his queen, Henrietta Maria; with the queen and their two oldest children full-length; and bust-length from three different views (see Fig. 6.4). He painted the queen in various settings too, and the royal children, as well as many members of their circle. Van Dyck fixed for posterity an enduring image of the Caroline court and its doomed monarch, the greatest British royal patron of the visual arts to date, but a disastrous ruler.

Among the most frequently reproduced of these royal commissions is Van Dyck's *Le Roi à la chasse* (*The King at the Hunt*) of 1635 (Fig. **6.2**). There is no crown, scepter, orb, or suit of fancy armor; neither is there a vast, palatial setting curtained in silk embroidered with royal emblems. The king's identity is secured by the inscription on the rock in the right foreground, CAROLUS I REX MAGNAE BRITANNIAE, yet he is depicted simply as a wealthy gentleman surveying the boundaries of his estate. Contemporaries would, however, have associated hunting with the privileged life of the nobility. Dismounted, standing in profile but looking at us, the king seems to have been distracted from the view of the river Thames at Richmond by our arrival in his presence. His enormous horse bows his head as if doing the obeisance expected of the king's subjects. Poised, at ease, one glove on, the other off, this is the king as the perfect courtier. Outdoor settings were quickly adopted by Charles's friends for their portraits too. Other European nobility depended on their land for income and status but none so consistently advertised this relationship as the British aristocracy did.

In other portraits of Charles, Van Dyck provided the kind of propaganda image of royal power and status expected of a court painter. The most dramatic of all is *Charles I with Monseigneur de St. Antoine* of 1633 (Fig. **6.3**). Twelve feet high, this image filled a wall at the end of a long gallery in St. James's Palace in such a way that the king appeared to be riding into the room through a triumphal arch on his magnificent white horse. On the other walls were similarly authoritarian pictures of Roman emperors by Titian and Giulio Romano. The royal coat of arms on the left completes the message. The symbolism of the arch was obvious even to spectators who had never been to Rome. To it Van Dyck added that of the equestrian leader which originated for post-medieval artists with the bronze equestrian statue of Marcus Aurelius on the Capitoline hill in Rome. The splendid clothes of Monseigneur de St. Antoine, the king's riding master, and his presence here indicate his status at court, while the king's pose, erect and confident, is both a tribute to lessons mastered and proof of his right to rule.

Van Dyck's most intimate and poignant portrait of the king, *Charles I in Three Positions* (Fig. **6.4**), was made around 1635 to enable Bernini to carve a marble portrait bust of a sitter he could not see himself. To do this he needed close-up images of the king's head in profile, full-face, and in three-quarter view. The official portraits just described keep the king at some distance from the viewer. Here, however, we are face to face with him, a privilege shared by only a small circle of intimate courtiers, his family, and Van Dyck himself, for whom the work also presented a new version of an old challenge—whether painting was superior to sculpture or vice versa, the *paragone* much debated in sixteenth-century Italy. Would his portrait or that of Bernini, the greatest living sculptor, be judged the finer? Would the white marble somehow seem more life-like than the illusion of three-dimensional form in painted color on a flat surface? Van Dyck gave the king three different costumes (and three slightly different lace collars), thus relieving what could have become monotonous repetition, reserving the crimson doublet for the central portrait. The sky behind has some dark clouds, which should not be read

as perceptive political comment as Charles's serious political problems had not yet begun. Later writers, even in the seventeenth century, thought the king seemed a little melancholy, as if foreseeing his fate, but what Van Dyck intended to convey was an appropriate reserve. Charles wears the Order of the Lesser George on the blue ribbon round his neck: the badge of the Order of the Knights of the Garter is visible on his sleeve at the right edge of the painting. The king wore the former, a gold locket with an image of St. George and the Dragon, at all times, even on the day of his execution. Knowledge of that fate—the only English monarch to be executed in office—gives this image a special poignancy, for he was not a cruel or wicked leader, only inept. Bernini's marble bust was much admired when it arrived, along with futile hopes that such gifts might persuade Charles to become a Catholic. It was destroyed in 1698, when much of Whitehall Palace burnt to the ground.

6.2 (opposite) Anthony van Dyck, *Le Roi à la chasse (The King at the Hunt)*, 1635. Oil on canvas, 8 ft 11 in × 6 ft 11 in (2.75 × 2.14 m). Louvre, Paris.

6.3 Anthony van Dyck, *Charles I with Monseigneur de St. Antoine* (post-restoration), 1633. Oil on canvas, 12 ft × 8 ft 8 in (3.68 × 2.69 m). The Royal Collection, England, © 2004, Her Majesty Queen Elizabeth II.

6.4 Anthony van Dyck, *Charles I in Three Positions*, c. 1635. Oil on canvas, 33¼ × 39¼ in (84.5 × 99.7 cm). The Royal Collection, England, © 2004, Her Majesty Queen Elizabeth II.

English Painting

6.5 Anthony van Dyck, *Queen Henrietta Maria with Sir Jeffrey Hudson*, 1633. Oil on canvas, 86¼ × 53 in (219.1 × 134.8 cm). National Gallery of Art, Washington, DC.

Queen Henrietta Maria was French, Catholic, and very well connected as the daughter of Henry IV of France and Marie de' Medici. Her brother had become Louis XIII of France following their father's assassination in 1610; her sister Elizabeth married Philip IV of Spain. Charles, a shy man who was not temperamentally suited to be king, had just succeeded his father when their marriage took place in 1625. She had been given special permission by the pope to marry a Protestant with the understanding that she could raise her children in her own faith and protect Catholics in Great Britain. Privately, the pope hoped she would convert her husband. Marie de' Medici told her daughter to pray for this outcome daily.

Henrietta Maria was not happy in England. She did not speak English. Her faith was vilified and her circle of Catholic advisers aroused intense suspicion, but her sweet nature gradually won her some acceptance. She was comfortable with Van Dyck, a fellow Catholic with whom she could speak Italian. She is said to have sat for him twenty-five times. His portraits of her are as astutely sympathetic as they are flattering. She was small, with a narrow face, long nose, and prominent teeth, yet even the witness who drew attention to those 'disappointing' features, having seen her portraits, conceded that she had beautiful eyes and skin.

In Van Dyck's *Queen Henrietta Maria with Sir Jeffrey Hudson* (Fig. **6.5**) she is portrayed full-length in a blue silk hunting costume, accompanied by the knighted dwarf, whose wit and tiny, well-proportioned body made him a favorite at her court. The pet monkey's name was Pug. Their presence lightens the mood of this statuesque portrayal of the queen, whose crown rests on a ledge on the right edge of the canvas, nestling in the folds of a golden brocade drapery behind which appears the standard attribute of wealth and power, the base of a huge column. Behind her left side is an urn with a young orange tree, a plant that she had introduced along with other exotica to English horticulture. The contrast in height between the two figures makes the queen look taller than she was. A replica by the artist of this portrait was paid for in October 1633, when the queen gave birth to her third child, James, Duke of York (later James II). She was probably pregnant when the original was painted. She would not have posed for more than the head and hands, however, nor would it have been considered appropriate to do more than hint at her condition, but it may explain why her head and arms seem small for someone of her girth.

Portraits continued to dominate Van Dyck's production in his last decade. There were few opportunities to paint religious images in England for Charles's public was always alert for any signs of support for "Popish things." By now Van Dyck was chiefly known for his ability to render the high born and powerful in ways that made their status clear while also making them appear sympathetic. Even when he returned to Antwerp and Brussels for some months in 1634, he was mainly occupied doing portraits but a beautiful *Lamentation* (Alte Pinakothek, Munich) of that year shows that he had not lost his capacity to invent touching and original images of familiar Catholic subjects.

Van Dyck's *Self-Portrait with Sir Endymion Porter* (Fig. **6.6**) is an especially fine example of the friendship portrait. The artist's slightly bowed head and relaxed hands in earlier self-portraits convey both diffidence and eagerness to be accepted. Were his companion not present, Van Dyck would be seen to have gained confidence in

392   Chapter 6: England

the meantime. Indeed it is known that he lived ostentatiously with many servants. His pose is more erect than before as he gazes towards us but, beside the confident bulk of Sir Endymion in his white silk jacket, Van Dyck's dark form recedes into the setting, giving the limelight to his friend. Both sitters rest their hands on a rock, a symbol of the solidity of their friendship. The turbulent sky behind them may be a symbol of fortune, as it was in Venetian Renaissance portraits, suggesting that this relationship would survive whatever storms it encountered. Van Dyck also painted a portrait of Sir Endymion with his wife and children.

Sir Endymion had made his way at the courts of James I and Charles I on the strength of his personality and abilities. He was well read, good at languages, diplomatic, and good fun. Van Dyck met him first in 1621, when Porter worked for the Duke of Buckingham. As Groom of the Bedchamber for Charles I, Porter was employed buying art, including the collections of the Duke of Mantua in 1627. It was he who had brought Van Dyck the commission to paint *Rinaldo and Armida* in 1629 and encouraged the king to make him court painter.

As the political situation deteriorated, payments from the English court were becoming less reliable, so Van Dyck decided to move back to Antwerp. Then he heard that Louis XIII wanted someone to paint the ceiling of the Grand Galerie in the Palais du Louvre, and, seeing a chance to rival Rubens's Medici cycle, he went to Paris to try to capture the commission awarded soon after to Nicolas Poussin. Van Dyck returned to London, where by June 1641 his health was giving cause for alarm. His wife gave birth to a daughter on December 1. A week later Van Dyck was dead. He was buried in St. Paul's Cathedral, London. His widow inherited enough money to live comfortably and some valuable paintings, including important works by Titian.

Later Portrait Painters

Van Dyck established the conventions of British portraiture for the next two centuries, and thus of court portraiture throughout Europe. His immediate successors in England—William Dobson, Peter Lely, and Godfrey Kneller—reiterated his achievements but usually with less painterly skill and rarely with such tactful perceptions about their sitters' character. Cornelius Johnson (1593–1661), generally considered an able and sensitive portrait painter, was born in London but of Dutch parents. Details of his training are unknown. After working in London

6.6 Anthony van Dyck, *Self-Portrait with Sir Endymion Porter*, c. 1635. Oil on canvas, 46¾ × 56⅝ in (119 × 144 cm). Prado, Madrid.

6.7 Peter Lely, *Two Ladies of the Lake Family*, c. 1660. Oil on canvas, 4 ft 2 in × 5 ft 11 in (1.27 × 1.18 m). Tate, London.

for over twenty years, he took his family to the United Provinces in 1643, fearing for their safety during the impending civil war, and never returned. The best native-born portrait painter, William Dobson (1611–46), died young after only four years of recorded activity, though he left some memorably gutsy images, especially that of *Endymion Porter* (Tate Britain, London), which may be the first example of a British genre later dubbed "the swagger portrait."

Van Dyck's real successor was Sir Peter Lely (1618–80). Born in Soest, Westphalia, of Dutch parents, he trained in Haarlem and moved to London shortly after the death of Van Dyck in 1641. With little competition, Lely soon replaced Van Dyck among those seeking flattering "countenances" of themselves and their families. In 1647 he painted an impressive double portrait of *Charles I with James, Duke of York* (Syon House, London), which rivals Van Dyck at his best in spacious design, touching psychology, and appealing colors. When the Civil War ended, Lely was soon working for leading figures of the Commonwealth, including Oliver Cromwell; when the monarchy was restored in 1660, Lely had played his cards so well that his successes then continued uninterrupted. Ellis Waterhouse rightly described him as, "for the historian of painting, the most important figure working in England in the seventeenth century."

Lely's painting of *Two Ladies of the Lake Family* (Fig. **6.7**) displays a considerable range of skills, in particular that of rendering satin fabrics in various subtle colors, a vital accomplishment for portrait artists in the later seventeenth century. The sitter on the left wears a blue silk dress, her companion on the right a bronze silk that has yellowish highlights and whose hues are subtly emphasized by her satin stole of a cooler brown shade. Another splendid fall of dull red satin fills the right background. The blue-robed lady pretends to strum her guitar; the lady in brown arranges her arms in a gesture both vaguely protective and reminiscent of the ancient Venus Pudica. Neither seems aware of the other, unlike the sitters in Van Dyck's male "friendship" portraits (see Fig. 2.45). The result is gorgeous to look at but psychologically empty. Still, Van Dyck had treated two sisters in a similar mode in his *Lady Elizabeth Thimbleby and Dorothy, Viscountess Andover* (National Gallery, London) of about 1637, a work that Lely owned.

As usual outside the Dutch Republic in the seventeenth century, artists tended to homogenize

394 *Chapter 6: England*

women's features to accord with the current tastes about female beauty. Lely's portraits of women are all painted long oval faces, high foreheads, emphatically arched brows over eyes with drowsy lids, long straight noses, and neatly pursed lips. Low-cut gowns and corsets that pushed up the breasts were also the height of fashion. After seeing Lely's series of "Windsor Beauties" painted for the Duchess of York, Samuel Pepys noted in his diary: "good, but not like." Whether or not the identity of a Lely female portrait is recorded (nothing is known about the two Lake ladies, for example), this knowledge rarely adds to our appreciation of the woman's image. For male sitters, however, Lely provided details of individual physiognomies with more honesty and some accessories that hinted at their professional achievements. He adopted Van Dyck's use of outdoor rather than indoor settings, thus establishing a convention that prevailed for another century.

Lely added little to Van Dyck's achievements. Many mediocre portraits left his studio during his lifetime but as long as he himself was responsible for the work, the result was always well drawn, and, when the color schemes chosen by his sitters appealed to him, seductively colored. Success went to his head: Pepys reported after a visit to Lely's studio that "a mighty proud man he is, and full of state." He invested his considerable earnings in an important collection of Old Master paintings, including twenty-five works by Van Dyck, and a huge collection of Old Master prints and drawings. Lely was knighted barely a year before his death in 1680. His successor in terms of valuable commissions and rank at court was an Italian of obscure origins and training, Antonio Verrio (c. 1639–1707). He is dismissed today as a pompous mediocrity whose success as a decorative painter was mainly due to the lack of competition. The situation improved in the eighteenth century with the arrival of the Venetians Gianantonio Pellegrini (1675–1741) in 1708 and Sebastiano Ricci (1659–1734) in 1712. Not until Sir James Thornhill (1675/6–1734) reached maturity, however, did Britain have an artist better than Verrio for the large paintings now desired for the walls around the grand staircases of new country mansions. Thornhill did not go to Italy himself; having watched Verrio, Pellegrini, and Ricci at work, however, he could by 1707 offer British clients a decent version of Venetian wall decoration. He is chiefly associated with commissions for Greenwich Hospital (1708–27) and Hampton Court (1715), also being chosen in preference to Sebastiano Ricci to decorate the dome of St. Paul's Cathedral (see Fig. 6.15). He was, however, a follower, not a leader in the great European tradition of large-scale decorative painting.

Those who wanted portraits after 1680 turned to Godfrey Kneller (1646–1723), another foreign-trained import. Kneller was German—he was born in Lübeck—and trained in Amsterdam with Ferdinand Bol before going to Italy in 1672–5. There he studied, among much else, the portraits of Maratta (see Fig. 1.129) and Gaulli, though Bol remained the dominant source of his early style. Kneller had reached London by 1676, and by the time of James II's accession in 1685, was established enough for John Evelyn to refer to him as "the famous painter" in demand for portraying male and female clients. He was knighted in 1692. Pushed to produce at a prodigious rate and motivated by the rewards such industry offered, Kneller often depended on repetitious formulas that his many assistants could complete after he had sketched in the head. His impressive half-length portrait of the sculptor *Grinling Gibbons* (Fig. 6.8) has an unaffected

6.8 Sir Godfrey Kneller, *Grinling Gibbons*, c. 1690. Oil on canvas, 49¼ × 35⅛ in (125 × 90 cm). The State Hermitage Museum, St. Petersburg.

dignity. Kneller was better with male than female sitters, for whose standardized features he offered few compensations like sensuous treatments of skin and fabrics. The Kit-Kat Series (1707–17, National Portrait Gallery, London), forty-two paintings of the members of the Kit-Kat Club, all in relatively modest half-length format, show not only his skill at composing within limited space, but also astute judgement of male character. Achievements by British artists equal to their peers in the rest of Europe in the seventeenth century can be found mainly in architecture, and the work of Inigo Jones and Sir Christopher Wren.

Palladianism and Architectural Planning in London

to saie trew all the composed ornaments the wch Proceed out of ye aboundance of desseigners and wear brought in by Michill Angell and his followers in my oppignion do not well in sollid Architecture and ye fasciati of houses, but in gardens loggis stucco or ornaments of cimnies peeces or in the inner parts of houses thos compositiones are of necessity to be yoused. For as outwardly every wyse man carrieth a graviti in Publicke Places, whear ther is nothing els looked for, yet inwardly hath his immaginacy set on fire, and sumtimes licentiously flying out, as nature hir sealf doeth often tymes stravagantly, to delight, amase us sumtimes moufe us to laughter, sumtimes to contemplation and horror, so in architecture ye outward ornaments oft [ought] to be sollid, proporsionable according to the rulles, masculine and unaffected.

INIGO JONES, 1615

Inigo Jones

Inigo Jones (1573–1652) was the quiet catalyst for a revolution in the prevailing styles and materials of British architecture. His work will strike modern viewers familiar only with the multitude of derivations that can be found all over Britain and the Eastern United States as unexceptional. No one in Britain before him, however, had mastered the underlying principles of Roman and Italian Renaissance architecture as well as their decorative vocabulary and then used them with such assurance and restraint. He was a Londoner, the son of a tailor, who went to Italy first around 1605 after enjoying some success as a painter. On his return, he designed stage sets and costumes for the masques of Ben Jonson and others beloved by Queen Anne of Denmark. In 1613 Jones returned to Italy, this time in the company of Lord Arundel, and studied the villas and palaces of Andrea Palladio (1508–80) in Vicenza and the surrounding area as well as Roman antiquities there and in Rome. His self-confidence is revealed by a note made after meeting the elderly architect Vincenzo Scamozzi (1552–1616) in Venice: "This secret Scamozio being purblind under stood nott"! He returned in 1615 with first-hand knowledge of all the major architectural monuments of Rome and North Italy and a library of books on architecture, including his own well-annotated copy of Palladio's *Four Books of Architecture* (1570).[2]

Two of the three first buildings that he executed in his pure classically based style still survive—the Queen's House in Greenwich (begun 1616–18; finished 1629–38) and the Banqueting House (1619–22) in Whitehall (Fig. **6.9**), about halfway between Trafalgar Square and the Houses of Parliament. Henry VIII had moved his London residence from Westminster to York House, the home of Cardinal Thomas Wolsey, between the site of the Banqueting House and the Thames, when the cardinal fell from favor in 1529. The king preferred Wolsey's more luxurious accommodation to his own and set about expanding it. Whitehall Palace, as it became, was the principal London residence of the sovereign until it was destroyed by fire in 1698.

When the Banqueting House was built, it was taller than all of the surrounding red brick buildings. It must have looked like a wedding cake in a butcher's shop window. Now that all the surrounding offices of Whitehall are built on a much larger scale in materials and styles that imitate and harmonize with Jones's building, it no longer looks either original or important. The street façade, which is what the visitor first sees today, is seven bays wide with two ranges of tall windows set on a rusticated base with small square windows at street level. The three central bays are divided from each other by columns, the two outer bays by pilasters which are doubled at each end. It has Ionic order capitals on the first floor and Composite on the second, a progression from lightly ornamented to richer decoration used in Roman buildings and adopted by Italian Renaissance architects. The lower level of windows have alternating segmental (curved) and triangular pediments; the upper windows have flat pediments with garlands above them running the width of the façade, creating a frieze at the level of the capitals (in classical architecture, the frieze runs above them). This motif would become a favorite with Wren. The composition is completed by a balustrade at the roof line with thicker supports over the columns of the central bay. The wall surfaces between the pilasters and columns and the windows are rusticated but with smooth surfaces between the channels. The façade derives from Palladio's palace designs but these had an entrance in the center, whereas the Banqueting House is entered from the north (left) end. The slight emphasis on the central bays created by substituting columns for pilasters provides subtle variety to a simple repeated motif without making the visitor expect a door. Palladio's window bays were not as wide as these, a change that gives the Banqueting Hall a more stable appearance. Altogether the building conforms perfectly with Jones's principles in his statement of 1615 quoted above: " in architecture ye outward ornaments oft [ought] to be sollid, proporsionable according to the rulles, masculine and unaffected."

The interior is a large rectangular hall, which now has a platform at the far end where it is thought the king's throne faced visitors as they entered. The proportions are the double cube (110 feet by 55 feet) that Jones used elsewhere and which creates a static, barn-like interior space. Ionic half-columns on the main floor and Corinthian pilasters on the upper level frame all the window bays. A narrow balustrade for performing musicians runs around the entire perimeter between the two window levels supported on thick corbels decorated with acanthus scrolls. The ceiling still contains the nine canvases by Rubens that celebrate the life of James I with their heavy gilded wooden frames of alternating oval and rectangular shapes. Installed in 1635, it is his only ceiling decoration still in its original location. Charles I forbade the performance of masques in the Banqueting House after 1635 for fear that smoke from candles and lanterns would obscure the paintings, reserving it for the reception of ambassadors and similar ceremonies. That the Banqueting House survived both the

6.9 Inigo Jones, Banqueting House, Whitehall, London, 1619–22.

Palladianism and Architectural Planning in London

6.10 Edward Pierce, *Christopher Wren*, 1673. Marble. Ashmolean Museum, Oxford.

Great Fire of London in 1666 and the fire that destroyed Whitehall Palace in 1698 is a miracle. Holbein's largest painting of *Henry VIII* and Bernini's bust of *Charles I* were among many treasures lost. There is, however, one surviving tribute to the Bernini, Edward Pierce's portrait bust of *Christopher Wren* (Fig. 6.10). The cascading ringlets of Wren's wig and the drapery wrapped around his shoulders were both inspired by Bernini's lost masterpiece.

The Queen's Chapel at St. James's Palace (now Marlborough House Chapel) by Jones was the first ecclesiastical building in the classical style built in England (1623–7). Much of Jones's other work was either destroyed or planned but never built. His designs for Whitehall Palace suggest that his sense of scale and related masses were insufficient. The only surviving example of city planning by Jones is St. Paul's church in Covent Garden and the surrounding piazza, which was laid out on land given by Francis Russell, the 4th Earl of Bedford in 1630–38 to create the first planned open space surrounded by houses of a uniform design in England. Inspired by the Place des Vosges in Paris, such squares became one of the most attractive and characteristic features of London. Covent Garden retains the plan but not the appearance of the buildings that Jones designed. The church's interior was destroyed by fire in 1795 but its massive Roman character has been preserved. Its proportions were cribbed by Jones from "purblind Scamozio." After the Civil War began in 1642, funds for major buildings dried up. Jones's practice was continued after his death by his pupil and collaborator John Webb (1611–72), whose designs have sometimes been attributed to Jones. Together they ensured that "Gothick" would no longer be the dominant idiom for domestic, civic, and ecclesiastical buildings in Britain.

Christopher Wren

The word "architect" was introduced into English as early as 1563 by John Shute in his publication *The First & Chief Groundes of Architecture*, which depended very heavily on Sebastiano Serlio's *L'architettura* of 1537–51. Shute not only defined the term—"the art and trade to rayse up and make excellent edifices and buyldings," but also outlined the duties and necessary skills of the ideal architect: "For faith he [. . .] must be sharpe of understandinge and both quicke and apse to conceive the trewe Instructions and meaning of them that have written thereof." Shute required as well an excellent education in mathematics, music, physics, astronomy, and some familiarity with such ancient texts as those like Vitruvius. Wren's preparation for his career more than fulfilled these demands.

As the son of country rector in Wiltshire who became the Dean of Windsor in 1634, Wren had access to an excellent education. He studied classical languages, mathematics, and science, and was inventing scientific measuring devices in his teens. In 1649 he entered Wadham College, Oxford (BA 1651), where he went on to study astronomy, becoming the Gresham Professor of Astronomy in London in 1657 and Savilian Professor of Astronomy in Oxford four years later.

In 1661 Wren was asked to survey and to improve harbor fortifications in the city of Tangier. He refused this offer, accepting instead a commission from Gilbert Sheldon, Archbishop of Canterbury from 1663, for a theater in Oxford: the Sheldonian (1662–3) is still used for degree ceremonies. Its ingenious roof truss design demonstrated Wren's abilities as an engineer while the sources of the design, which adopted Serlio's picture of the Theater of Marcellus in Rome and sixteenth-century Italian church façades, revealed his familiarity with the standard source books about ancient and modern Italian architecture. He also designed chapels for Pembroke (1663–5) and Emmanuel (1668–73) Colleges in Cambridge.

Wren never went to Italy but did visit Paris in 1665, while Bernini was there working on plans for the east front of the Louvre. Wren later reported that "Bernini's Designs of the Louvre I would have given my Skin for, but the old reserv'd Italian gave me but a few Minutes View. [...] I had only Time to copy it in my Fancy and Memory." What he did see to his enormous advantage when designing St. Paul's Cathedral were two recently built churches with domes—Jacques Lemercier's church of the Sorbonne (1635–48) and the Val-de-Grâce by Lemercier and François Mansart (1645–62). What Wren knew of the Pantheon in Rome or Bramante's and Michelangelo's designs for the dome of St. Peter's was culled from engravings and published descriptions. Louis Le Vau's Collège des Quatre-Nations, still under construction in 1665, was another important architectural source for its sophisticated use of seventeenth-century Roman sources for the dome, façade, and concave wings transmuted into a purer classical idiom. Wren was impressed not only by the design but also by the urban planning involving the Square Court (Cour Carré) of the Louvre on the other side of the Seine: the Collège des Quatre-Nations and the Louvre were to be connected by a bridge that was never built (the Pont des Arts on that site was built later). Wren visited Versailles twice, toured the Louvre and the Tuileries and aimed to return with "almost all France on paper." He was also impressed by Paris's paved streets, its drains, and the numbers of houses and civic buildings made of stone and brick.

Shortly after returning from France, Wren offered the Commission responsible for the fabric of Old St. Paul's a design that would have incorporated a large dome over the crossing. Four months later St. Paul's was destroyed in the Great Fire along with eighty-seven city churches and thousands of homes and businesses in the City of London. Fifty-one of the churches were eventually rebuilt using designs by Wren along with four outside the city limits. St. James's, Piccadilly, though gutted in World War II, has been expertly restored. Twenty-five of the city's churches had been pulled down by 1939; nineteen more were destroyed by bombs between 1939 and 1945 and others damaged. Thirty survive to testify to Wren's fertile architectural imagination and his willingness to work in Gothic as well as Palladian and French seventeenth-century idioms, adapting them to the original foundations and, in a few cases, to the existing walls as well. The most important function of the interior was, in Wren's words, "in our reformed Religion" to allow "all who are present both [to] hear and see." A walking tour of some of the survivors with Nikolaus Pevsner as your guide is recommended: St. Benet Paul's Wharf, Upper Thames Street ("one of his most lovable exteriors, delightfully Dutch"); St. James Garlickhithe, Garlick Hill ("Square tower, pierced parapet and bulgy vases"); St. Margaret Pattens, Rood Lane ("The tower at the NW end crowned by one of the most remarkable of Wren's spires"); and St. Stephen Walbrook (Fig. 6.11), "the most majestic

6.11 Christopher Wren, St. Stephen Wallbrook, interior, 1672–87.

of Wren's parish churches." Its domed design (1672–7) gave Wren the chance to explore some of his ideas for St. Paul's on a smaller scale. The spires of Wren's churches also offer delicious contrasts: St. Bride's (Fig. 6.12), Fleet Street, with its tiers of small classical arcades; St. Augustine, Watling Street, with a square plan of several tiers of stone finished with an open metal spire of wilder character—volute scrolls supporting a little open tower topped with a tall onion dome; St. Mary Aldermary, Queen Victoria Street, with its perpendicular Gothic tower; St. Dunstan-in-the-East, Idol Lane, another Gothic essay, this time using flying buttresses to support the steeple; and, most elegant of all, St. Vedast (Fig. 6.13), Foster Lane (1697), the design of which recalls Borromini's ingenious use of curved surfaces in the superimposed pilasters flanking concave and convex window bays of decreasing size.

Wren offered a plan for the rebuilding of the city after the fire that would have made St. Paul's the focal point of two wide avenues, one extending east to the Royal Exchange, the other to the Tower of London, while other streets would radiate out from the Exchange. The scheme suggests that Wren had seen engravings of Sixtus V's plans for Rome in the 1580s, though no new monuments were proposed to orient the pedestrian. Even St. Paul's, set at the tip of the triangular wedge of land bounded by two long avenues, could be seen only by visitors approaching from the west. There was not time, money, or will to make drastic changes to the layout of London's streets so Wren's plans were never carried out. For St. Paul's he could, however, now urge a new building rather than partial revisions of the old structure to which Jones had added new exterior walls and a large Corinthian portico in the 1630s. These were memorably described by John Summerson as "a gallant attempt to make a Classical silk purse out of a Gothic sow's ear." Not until part of the repaired structure collapsed in 1668 did the authorities agree to this expensive solution. Abandoning the cathedral

6.12 (left) Christopher Wren, St. Bride's, steeple, 1670–84.

6.13 (right) Christopher Wren, St. Vedast, steeple, 1697.

may have been the only practical solution, but it was not an easy decision. Old St. Paul's was the largest cathedral in Britain, larger even than its replacement. It had long been in need of serious restoration: during the Civil War, it had been used to stable eight hundred horses.

Every one of Wren's designs featured a dome, which Evelyn said was "a forme of church-building not as yet known in England but of wonderfull grace." Even his pre-fire design substituted a dome with a lantern "and Spiring Top" for the old square tower and steeple. Wren also wanted a centrally planned church like that envisioned originally by Bramante and Michelangelo for New St. Peter's. The various stages of Wren's designs can be followed in drawings, a first model (only partly preserved) judged insufficiently "stately" and the Great Model, 13 feet (4.3 m) high, of 1673. Wren's most perfectly resolved design, it fulfilled his intent to produce a church "not to be exceeded in Magnificence, by any [. . .] in Europe." The main façade was a temple front like the Pantheon; a smaller dome over the nave added variety to the simple masses of the whole. The outer walls appear to be of one story only plus a base and attic, giving the dome maximum emphasis. Charles II approved; Wren was knighted and resigned his Oxford Chair in astronomy to focus on supervising the construction.

The clergy were not happy with the central plan. The short nave, so disliked by conservative elements in both the Roman and Anglican Church, would reduce the ceremonial grandeur of the processions integral to many of its services. The eight piers of the crossing and the adjacent structures would also have to be built all at once and not in stages as the money from the coal tax assessed to aid the rebuilding of London after the Great Fire filtered into the church coffers. The Warrant Design of 1675 accommodated these practical requirements. It had short transept arms one bay deep and a nave with two more bays than the choir, all with groin vaults. It also had a much smaller dome with a spire like St. Bride's. Wren however managed to get the king to agree to let him make "some Variations, rather ornamental than essential" at his own discretion. These proved to be significant: the executed nave and choir each have three bays, now with saucer

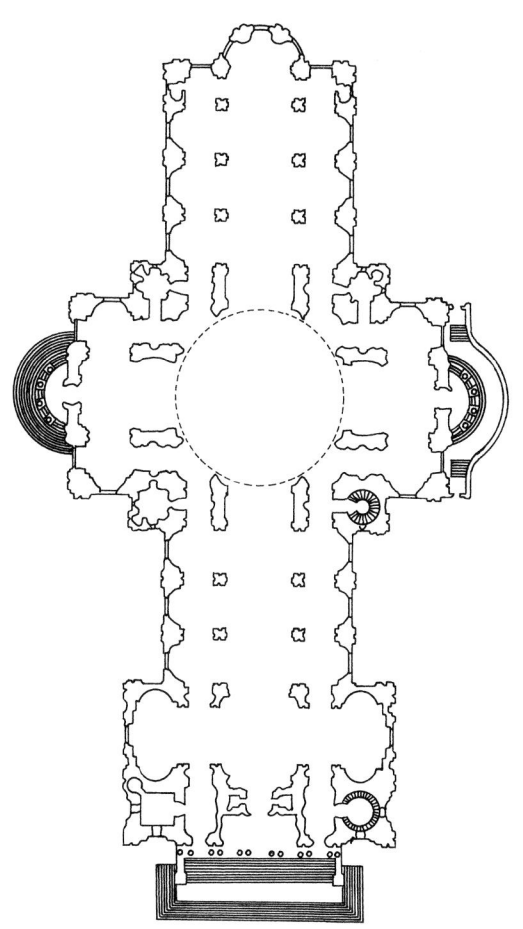

6.14 Christopher Wren, St. Paul's Cathedral, London, plan, 1675–1710.

domes, though the nave also has an additional larger bay at the entrance (Fig. **6.14**). The nave and transept are also wider, their aisles narrower, requiring complex adjustments in the crossing area to support the dome while retaining a visual impression of symmetry (see Fig. 6.15). All the supporting piers and walls were thickened and strengthened and the transept entrances redesigned. At a late stage, too, the west front was reworked with the twin towers that are an intrinsic feature of the present façade. Creation and approval of the design before the foundation stone was laid took nine years, the actual construction another thirty-four. As long as Wren could adapt and change the design, he did. Wren was seventy-six when the lantern of the dome was installed. Had he not lived to be ninety, the completion of all the interior and exterior finishing under his watchful eye might have had very different results. The final bill for construction and all the interior and exterior carvings, plaster decorations, the organ with a case carved by Grinling Gibbons, and the marvellous gilded wrought-iron railings by Jean Tijou amounted to £747,661 and 10 shillings. Wren's funeral tablet in the crypt declares, "Lector, si monumentum requiris, circumspice": Reader, if you seek a monument, look about you.

Understanding the vicissitudes of the cathedral's building history as well as the faith that Charles II and his successors had in Wren, are crucial aspects of appreciating the magnitude of his feat: completing this enormous structure according to one consistent, if evolving, vision, in less than forty years. The rebuilding of St. Peter's in Rome took a century and its decoration most of another. Wren's achievement took more than ideas about architectural forms: it took diplomacy, political skills, judgment when hiring all the masons and craftsmen who carried out his plans, and some luck. The fruitful relationship between Wren, several monarchs, and the bishops of St. Paul's during its building resemble those between Bernini and Popes Urban VIII and Alexander VII. All these patrons were amply rewarded for their faith in the artists they backed.

The final result is a building that betrays none of the hesitations, alterations, and compromises that were made along the way. The exterior walls have two stories with arched windows in each lower bay and windows with triangular pediments on the upper level. The rusticated surface between the paired pilasters flanking each bay recalls Jones's Banqueting House, as does the frieze of garlands over the lower windows that connects with the Corinthian capitals to create a continuous band of decoration. The window details are grander, as befits the scale of St. Paul's. The upper story screens the flying buttresses that support the nave and provides a strong visual platform for the dome (see p. 386). Its exterior design resembles neither its seventeenth-century predecessors nor Michelangelo's dome for St. Peter's, all of which have more sculptural elements that break up the spherical forms of the drum and dome. No prominent stone ribs or small windows break the pure half-sphere of Wren's executed dome, however, only slim vertical moldings that match the divisions of the window bays of the supporting drum. The drum immediately below the dome is ringed with square windows whose elegant frames owe something to Michelangelo's innovative designs. The larger drum below that level has a colonnade reminiscent of Serlio's elevation of Bramante's proposed dome for St. Peter's with the addition of a balustrade like that of his Tempietto beside San Pietro in Montorio. To vary the repetition of this basic design, Wren filled every fourth bay with a shell niche and a garland. In Summerson's words: "the effect is to introduce in the quick rhythm of the peristyle a series of slow beats which give the whole a monumental stability and a relationship to the static mass of the Cathedral below." The crowning element is a square lantern articulated with paired columns capped by a little dome with recessed corners surmounted by a globe and cross. The same symbols crown Bernini's Baldacchino (see Fig. 1.103). So much for popery!

The west façade, facing Ludgate Hill (see p. 386), also underwent important changes. For the Giant order and massive Pantheon-like portico of the Great Model, Wren substituted a two-story design with coupled rather than evenly spaced Corinthian columns for the central portico. There are six paired columns on the ground floor but only four smaller pairs above, creating a visual progression upwards to the triangular pediment with its carved relief of the conversion of St. Paul. A statue of the saint stands at its summit. The design produces a far more dramatic play of solids and voids than its classically inspired predecessor. The twin towers flanking the pediment recall those of Borromini's Sant'Agnese in Agone in Rome, especially the projecting pairs of columns on the second level above the roof line, but the base with a huge oculus is a bold departure from precedent and every detail has been changed.

The spacious nave of St. Paul's (Fig. **6.15**) with its arched bay openings and vista to the vast crossing area recall the interior of St. Peter's and its Roman sources. These both use barrel vaults to span the main area, whereas Wren has used a series of saucer domes, an innovation for which precedents are hard to find, except in early medieval churches. Michelangelo's dome is supported on four massive piers that fill the corners of the crossing space. The same area in Wren's cathedral is open because eight supporting piers share the lighter load of Wren's double dome (the upper one seen from the exterior is a wooden structure protected with lead). Paired fluted pilasters with Corinthian capitals decorate the piers of the crossing and the nave. Some visual sleight of hand was required above the level of the capitals in the crossing area, where eight arches of equal size help to distract the eye from the narrower openings between the piers at the angles: their forms rise behind the arches, visibly wider on one side than the other. This is the only element of the design that has attracted much criticism but the gain in spacious expanse for the nave, transepts, and choir are fine compensation. Coffers with rosettes ornament the soffits of all the arches; some garlands at capital level occur in the interior too but Wren wanted an interior without fussy decoration. Jones's "masculine and unaffected" was his taste too. When the authorities insisted towards the end of the building on adding a balustrade around the upper perimeter of the outside walls, he protested, muttering that "Ladies think nothing well without an edging." It was one of the few battles he lost. He also wanted the interior painted white with the exception of the main dome, for which he wanted mosaics or, if that was too costly, a geometric illusionistic painting. Thornhill's paintings of the life of St. Paul are at least executed in monochrome. St. Paul's remains the supreme achievement by Britain's greatest seventeenth-century artist. Wren's administrative abilities and restlessly fertile artistic imagination rank him with the other great administrative artistic geniuses of his age — Bernini, Cortona, and Rubens.

The "Gothik" manner was permanently reduced to the status of old-fashioned in Britain by Wren, who always described his style as "modern." Wren's most able assistant, Nicholas Hawksmoor (1661–1736), created a bold new idiom full of contrasted angular masses quite distinct from Wren's judiciously proportioned classical elements; his work is often labelled Baroque, as is that of the remarkable amateur Sir John Vanbrugh (1664–1726), whom Hawksmoor assisted with the design and construction of Castle Howard in North Yorkshire and Blenheim Palace in Oxfordshire. The arrival of Palladian models and classically inspired architecture in the United States later is rightly linked with the Neo-Palladianism of Richard Boyle, 3rd Earl of Burlington, and the taste of Thomas Jefferson, but Wren's influence was also notable. His modestly scaled city churches and those of his successors in London, especially James Gibbs (1664–1754), were replicated with variations up and down the east coast of America, in stone in the cities and in wood painted white in small towns. Domes with colonnaded drums modeled on that of St. Paul's became an important feature of many American civic buildings, starting with the Capitol Building in Washington, DC, designed in 1792 and imitated by state capitals throughout the United States. Wren's college buildings in Oxford and Cambridge were another fruitful source of inspiration when Harvard and Yale began building their own libraries, colleges, and residences. Wren thus helped to lay the foundations of ecclesiastic and civic architecture on both sides of the Atlantic for many generations.

6.15 Christopher Wren, St. Paul's Cathedral, London, interior, 1675–1710.

EPILOGUE

> *Baroque art . . . is at once essentially popular in its appeal to man's emotional and sensual nature, its reliance on visual display and outward splendor, and highly elitist in its courtly origins, its aristocratic patronage and sheer expensiveness.*
>
> JUDITH HOOK,
> The Baroque Age in England (1976)

The artistic achievements in the six countries discussed in this book continued well into the eighteenth century. Indeed, in many books the term Baroque covers both centuries, with the term Rococo representing the lighter, more curvaceous forms found in all the arts after 1700, but especially in painting, architectural interiors, and the decorative arts. There were, however, important territorial shifts as wealth and political power coalesced in different centers. In the seventeenth century, the greatest concentrations of patronage and thus of artistic talent were to be found in Italy, France, and the Dutch Republic. Only Italy and France continued to generate both talent and financial support for all major art forms after 1700. Even in the seventeenth century, the Dutch had neither the space nor the social requirements for huge palaces and large new churches, nor for self-glorifying sculptural monuments. Their painters, rather than architects or sculptors, had brought about their Golden Age of art. After 1700, however, the Dutch economy started to falter and Britain emerged as the major sea-trading nation of Europe, while gaining a measure of political détente with its rival upon the accession of William of Orange as King William III in 1688.

France under Louis XIV had threatened the political autonomy of England, Spain, Germany, and the Netherlands in the seventeenth century. French tensions with these nations persisted until the death of Louis XIV in 1715. The wars that he had waged with the Dutch Republic and, even more ruinously, with Spain had emptied the royal treasury and resulted in punitive levels of taxation on the middle classes and agricultural workers. Courtiers began to flee the oppressive ceremonials of court life at Versailles for Paris, especially after 1715. There wealthy aristocrats began to build elegant new residences whose more intimate spaces suited the *goût moderne*. They filled them with *boiseries*, tapestries, furniture inlaid with rare woods and gilded accessories, and decorative paintings celebrating frivolous mythological themes with no hint of tragic outcomes. Eighteenth-century Parisian collectors also admired Dutch painting, especially the exquisitely finished genre scenes of artists such as Gerard Terborch (see Fig. 5.49) and Gabriel Metsu (see Fig. 5.50). Their work in turn influenced French genre painters such as Jean-Baptiste-Siméon Chardin (1699–1779) and Marguerite Gérard (1761–1837), among others.

The paintings of Rubens had been ignored by several previous generations of French painters—even the cycle celebrating the life of Marie de' Medici in the Palais de Luxembourg (see Figs. 2.26–2.29). Only in the 1680s did Charles de la Fosse (1636–1716), Antoine Coypel (1661–1722), and later Antoine Watteau (1684–1721) succumb to Rubens's brilliant colorism. The critic Roger de Piles (1635–1721) was the catalyst for this significant change of taste in Paris away from the classicizing styles inspired by Poussin—and supported by Charles Le Brun during his long directorate of the Académie Royale (1663–1690)—and toward the rich colorism and freer paint handling of the artists associated with *colore*, especially Rubens. De Piles had championed his cause in *Conversations on the Knowledge of Painting* (1677), the *Dissertation on the Works of the most Famous Painters* (1681), and, most famously, in his *Catalogue of the Names of the Most Noted Painters, and their Degrees of Perfection in the Four Principal Parts of Painting* (in *Cours de peinture par principes*, Paris, 1708). Here fifty-eight painters from Francesco Albani to Taddeo Zuccaro were rated for their skills in composition, drawing, color, and expression.

Rubens and Rembrandt, for example, scored 17 out of 20 for color, whereas Raphael received only 12, although he outscored them in drawing (18 compared to 6 for Rembrandt and 13 for Rubens). A curious and fascinating document in the history of taste—Michelangelo has a lower total score (37) than Leonardo (49) and Otto van Veen (47)—it shows nevertheless that de Piles respected all four qualities in his preferred artists, even if some of his scores are hard to understand today.

Both La Fosse and Coypel had also spent formative years in Italy studying the work of Cortona, Gaulli, Correggio, and Veronese, as well as the officially approved curriculum of ancient sculpture, Raphael, Annibale Carracci, and Domenichino. Convinced by de Piles's advocacy of the works of Titian and Rubens, La Fosse and Coypel began to warm up their palettes. They also began to make use of the illusionism pioneered by Correggio, and the brilliant fusions of painting, sculpture, and architecture employed by Cortona and Gaulli in their Roman ceiling paintings. La Fosse's dome painting in the church of the Invalides in Paris is a loose variation on Correggio's dome fresco in San Giovanni Evangelista, Parma. Coypel's ceiling decoration for the nave of Jules Hardouin-Mansart's enormous chapel at Versailles was even more radical for France, the vaults seemingly opened up to a heavenly vision of rising and falling figures indebted to Gaulli's *The Glorification of the Holy Name of Jesus* in Il Gesù, Rome (see Fig. 1.133).

Eighteenth-century Spain did not manage to produce artists to rival her greatest seventeenth-century painters until Francisco Goya (1746–1826) launched his career. The Spanish court resumed its practice in the new century of importing experienced fresco painters from Italy, beginning with Luca Giordano who worked in the Escorial and Buen Retiro palaces (1692–1702), to be followed in 1753 by Corrado Giaquinto (1703–1765), who became Director of the Academy of San Fernando in Madrid as well as painting a ceiling in the new Royal Palace in Madrid. He was succeeded by Venice's greatest painter of the eighteenth century, Giovanni Battista Tiepolo (1699–1770), who resided in Madrid from 1762 until his death in 1770 and painted his last decorative masterpieces in the Palacio Real. The most significant impact of Spanish seventeenth-century art on the next century was in the export of brilliantly idiosyncratic adaptations of Italian church architectural styles to Spanish colonies in Central and South America.

Meanwhile the more peaceful conditions that prevailed in the Hapsburg territories and adjacent principalities and bishoprics of Central Europe after 1648, and that were more firmly established with the defeat of the Turks outside Vienna in 1683, meant that major architectural commissions could be undertaken in Prague, Vienna, Berlin, and Dresden. Gifted painters from those cities who had traveled to Italy or France to study could now return home and find challenging work. Many Italian painters in Rome, Bologna, and Venice also began to find steady patronage there too. Only in the eighteenth century would Central European and Austrian artists and architects come into their own to create some of the most splendid pilgrimage churches, and palace and park ensembles, anywhere in Europe. Even Italian artists undertook commissions for Austrian and Central European patrons; Tiepolo painted his most brilliant ceiling paintings for a minor but ambitious archbishop of Würzburg.

Venice had been a major artistic center in the later Renaissance, but after the deaths of Titian in 1576, Veronese in 1588, and Tintoretto in 1594, no painters had emerged from that city with sufficiently distinctive and original styles to sustain that tradition until almost a century later. Then suddenly artistic talents were abundant. Giovanni Battista Piazzetta (1683–1754), who trained in Bologna with Giuseppe Maria Crespi (1664–1747), was among the first, atypically preferring strong chiaroscuro for his powerful altarpieces, unlike the lighter tones and pastel hues favored by his contemporaries. Sebastiano Ricci (1659–1734) was the originator of a new, lighter style of painting in Venice that blended elements taken from the work of Correggio, Veronese, Cortona, and Luca Giordano. An excellent decorator, Ricci worked in Milan, Florence, and Vienna before going to England around 1712, and Paris a few years later, spreading the fashion for this revived Venetian painting everywhere he worked. Tiepolo, the last great Italian fresco painter, left evidence of his fluent brush, luscious colors, and witty imagination not only throughout northern Italy but also (as noted above) in the Bishop's Palace by Balthasar Neumann in

Würzburg (1750–1753) and in Madrid. Venice was producing great artists once more, but it could not afford to employ them much of the time. The Venetian economy had long been in decline, as other trade routes were directing ships away from Venice to Genoa, Amsterdam, and London. Only if Venetian artists were painting views of the city for tourists, as did Antonio Canaletto (1697–1758) and Francesco Guardi (1712–1793), or portraits of visiting English aristocrats—the specialty of the pastelist Rosalba Carriera (1675–1757)—could they earn a steady income.

By the middle of the seventeenth century Rome had begun to decline as a source of significant Church patronage of the arts, even though Alexander VII and his successors continued to build and decorate despite shrinking balances in the papal treasury. The popes no longer exerted the political or military influence that they had in the past. Major treaties such as that of Utrecht (1713), which divided up the vast territories of the Spanish Empire after the death of Charles II of Spain and had major implications for the Catholic faith, were now signed without papal intervention. Rome nevertheless remained an attraction throughout the eighteenth century for French artists funded by the Académie Royale in Paris to study the achievements of Italian art, and for English gentlemen on the Grand Tour. In Rome the latter could have their portraits painted by Pompeo Batoni (1708–1787), or later by one of two outstanding women portraitists, Elizabeth Vigée-Lebrun (1755–1842) or Angelica Kauffman (1741–1807)—full-length if they could afford it and with ancient Roman statues completing the setting.

English painters and sculptors played a minor role in the history of seventeenth-century artistic achievements in a European context, but they came into their own after 1700. Genre painting and political satire were both launched with panache and vigor by William Hogarth (1697–1764), who was also a splendid portraitist on the rare occasions that he was lured into that specialty. The portraits by Sir Joshua Reynolds (1723–1792), Thomas Gainsborough (1717–1788), and Joseph Wright of Derby (1734–1797) include memorable images of Britain's military leaders, actors and actresses, musicians, and country squires, as well as "milords and ladies" of all ranks. Gainsborough and Wright of Derby also made inroads into that continental specialty, landscape, so that English admirers of Claude, Poussin, and Rosa could now acquire for their collections examples of Gainsborough's feathery evocations of country roads at dusk, or Wright's magnificent moonlight views of Derbyshire and Italian coastal scenes with classical associations. Angelica Kauffmann even converted the British to history painting to such a degree that her elegant classical narratives found their way into decorative interiors by the architect Robert Adam (1728–1792), and even onto painted china.

Inigo Jones's devotion to Palladio and his ancient models, and Christopher Wren's more cosmopolitan tastes, were both taken up in the next century by outstanding architects. The Palladian tradition was continued, and even more firmly established, by Richard Boyle, Third Earl of Burlington (1694–1753), an architect of distinction and the patron of William Kent (1685–1748), who worked in the same vein. Nicolas Hawksmoor (1661–1736), who has been called the first professionally trained British architect, emerged from Wren's workshop (where he had assisted with the completion of St. Paul's Cathedral and Greenwich Hospital) to create several highly original London churches. He also collaborated with the brilliant and versatile amateur, Sir John Vanbrugh (1664–1726), on his designs for two of the grandest residences ever built in Britain—Castle Howard in Yorkshire (1699) and Blenheim Palace in Oxfordshire (1705–1724).

Blenheim Palace was built to reward John Churchill, Duke of Marlborough, for his victory over Louis XIV at Blenheim on the Danube, a major setback to the ageing king's pan-European ambitions. Vanbrugh promised Queen Anne that Blenheim would be both "a private habitation" and "a Royall and a National Monument . . . (of) Beauty, Magnificence and Duration." More a royal palace than a country residence, it is the only British building to which the adjective "baroque"—with all its connotations of vast scale, expenditure, and excess—can justifiably be applied.

NOTES

Introduction
1. Karel van Mander, *Her Schilderboek*, Haerlem (sic), 1604, fol. 219r. Quoted and translated by Robert A. Koch in *Joachim Patenir*. Princeton, NJ: Princeton University Press, 1968, p. 8.
2. From John Donne's *An Anatomy of the World: The First Anniversary*, 1611, 1.205.

Chapter 1: Italy
1. G. Paleotti as translated by D. Posner, *Annibale Carracci*. London: Phaidon Press, 1971, I, p. 36.
2. Abbot Grillo quote in L. von Pastor, *History of the Popes*. London, 1938, XX, p. 305.
3. H. Hibbard, *Carlo Maderno*. University Park, PA: Pennsylvania State Press, 1971, p. 5.
4. The grasshopper caricature by Bernini in the Museum der Bildende Künste, Leipzig, is illustrated by A. Sutherland Harris, *Selected Drawings by Gian Lorenzo Bernini*. New York: Dover Press, 1977, no. 100.
5. C.C. Malvasia's life of Annibale translated by Anne Summerscale. University Park, PA: Pennsylvania State Press, 1999, pp. 159–160.
6. John Rupert Martin, *The Farnese Gallery*. Princeton, NJ: Princeton University Press, 1965, p. 9.
7. Translation of G.P. Bellori from Hibbard, *Caravaggio*. New York: Harper and Row, 1983, p. 144.
8. See A. Weston-Lewis in *Orazio Gentileschi at the Court of Charles I*, ed. G. Finaldi. London: National Gallery Publications, 1999, p. 39–52.
9. W. Bissell, *Artemisia Gentileschi*. University Park, PA, and London: Pennsylvania State Press, 1999, p. 1.
10. R. Magurn, *The Letters of Peter Paul Rubens*. Cambridge, MA: Harvard University Press, 1955, pp. 53–54.
11. John Ruskin quoted by R. Spear, *Domenichino*. New Haven, CT, and London: Yale University Press, 1982, I, p. 118.
12. For Reni's boast, see C.C. Malvasia, *The Life of Guido Reni*, translated by C. and R. Enggass. University Park, PA: Pennsylvania State Press, 1980, p. 134.
13. Contemporary accounts cited by A. Emiliani, *Guido Reni, 1575–1642*. Washington, DC: National Gallery of Art, 1988–9, p. 276.
14. For Ludovico's words about the young Guercino, see D. Mahon, *Guercino*. Washington, DC: National Gallery of Art, 1992, pp. 14–15.
15. Scannelli is cited in English by S. Ebert-Schifferer in D. Mahon, *Guercino*. Washington, DC: National Gallery of Art, 1992, p. 76.
16. R. Wittkower, *Art and Architecture in Italy, 1600–1750*. Harmondsworth, England: Pelican History of Art, 1958, pp. 134–135.
17. F. Baldinucci, *The Life of Bernini*. University Park, PA, and London: Pennsylvania State Press, 1966, p. 15.
18. H. Hibbard, *Bernini*. Harmondsworth, England: Penguin Books, 1965, p. 137, citing J.M. Cohen's translation.
19. *Diary of John Evelyn*, ed. E.S. de Beer. Oxford: Clarendon Press, 1955, II, p. 261.
20. R. Wittkower, *Art and Architecture in Italy, 1660–1750*. Harmondsworth, England: Pelican History of Art, 1958, p. 167.

Chapter 2: Flanders
1. Cited by W. Stechow, *Rubens and the Classical Tradition*. Cambridge, MA: Harvard University Press, 1986, p. 26.
2. Rubens, P.P., *The Letters of Peter Paul Rubens*, trans. & ed. Ruth Saunders Magurn. Cambridge, MA: Harvard University Press, 1955; reprinted 1971, p. 67.
3. *Ibid.*, pp. 184–185.

Chapter 3: Spain
1. Document quoted by B. Proske, *Juan Martínez Montañés*. New York: Hispanic Society of America, 1967, p. 40.
2. A.E. Pérez Sánchez and N. Spinosa, *Jusepe de Ribera, 1591–1652*. New York: Metropolitan Museum of Art, 1992, pp. 164–165.
3. For Ribera's presence at the Accademia di San Luca, see J. Milicua, citing J. G. Hoogewerff in Pérez Sanchez and Spinosa. New York: Metropolitan Museum of Art, 1992, p. 13.
4. Edward Sullivan, "Ribera's Clubfooted Boy: Image and Symbol," *Marsyas*, 19 (1977–8), pp. 17–21.
5. G.B. Passeri, cited by R. Spear, *Domenichino*. New Haven, CT, and London: Yale University Press, 1982, I, p. 69.
6. J. Brown, *Francisco de Zurbarán*. New York: H.N. Abrams, 1973, p. 11.
7. J. Brown, *Painting in Spain, 1500–1700*. New Haven, CT, and London: Yale University Press, 1998, p. 124; and *Velázquez*. New Haven, CT, and London: Yale University Press, 1986, pp. 118–119.
8. *Ibid*, p. 247.

Chapter 4: France
1. A. Blunt, *Art and Architecture in France, 1500–1700*. Harmondsworth, England: Penguin, 1953; 2nd ed. 1973, p. 1.
2. The quotes by Henry IV about his plans for Paris come from Z. Wazbinski, "Simon Vouet et le cardinal Francesco Maria del Monte: une hypothèse sur le mécénat d'Henri IV à Rome," *Simon Vouet, Actes du colloque international*, Paris, 1992, p. 149 & 161. The translation is by Ann S. Harris.
3. N. de la Blanchardière, "Simon Vouet, Prince de l'Académie de Saint-Luc," *Bulletin de la Société de l'Histoire de l'art français*, 1972 (1973), pp. 88–89. The translation is by Ann S. Harris.
4. The significance of the moving flame was noted by N. Conisbee in *Georges de la Tour and his World*. Washington, DC: National Gallery of Art, 1996–1997, p. 105. He also included the quote below about candle smoke from Father Hesius, *Emblemata Sacrada de Fide, Spe, Charitate* (1636), p. 109.
5. The translation of Poussin's letter comes from E. Holt, *A Documentary History of Art*. New York: Anchor Doubleday, 1958, II, pp. 154–156.
6. E. Cropper and C. Dempsey, *Nicolas Poussin: Friendship and the Love of Painting*. New Haven, CT, and London: Yale University Press, 1996, pp. 138–144.
7. A. Félibien, *Entretiens sur les vies et sur les ouvrages des plus excellens peintres . . .*, Paris, 1685–8 (1725 ed.), pp. 63, 150–151.
8. P.F. de Chantelou, *Diary of the Cavaliere Bernini's Visit to France*. Princeton, NJ: Princeton University Press, 1985, p. 79.
9. The translation of Félibien's text of 1663 about Le Brun's *The Tent of Darius* is taken from Michel Gareau, *Charles Le Brun: First Painter to Louis XIV*. New York: H. N. Abrams, 1992, p. 199.

Chapter 5: The Dutch Republic
1. R.C. Temple, ed., *Travels in Europe, 1639–1647*, from *The Travels of Peter Mundy in Europe and Asia: 1608–1667*. London: The Hakluyt Society, 1907–36, Vol. 4, p. 70.
2. S. Slive, *Frans Hals*, London, and Frances S. Jowell, "The Rediscovery of Frans Hals," in *Frans Hals*. London: Royal Academy Publications, 1989, pp. 73–74, 367–368.
3. T. Rodenburgh poem quoted in *Pieter Lastman: The Man who Taught Rembrandt*. Zwolle: Waanders Uitgevers, 1991, p. 16.
4. Huygens' letters about Rembrandt and Lievens cited in G. Schwartz, *Rembrandt, His Life, His Paintings*. London: Phaidon, 1985, pp. 74, 76.
5. Remonstrants were Dutch followers of the Dutch theologian Jacob Arminius, whose critique of John Calvin's views on predestination (the Arminian Articles of Remonstrance of 1610) were officially condemned at the Synod of Dort in 1618. The Remonstrants consequently suffered some persecution from the more numerous Calvinists.
6. Rembrandt's letters to Huygens are in G. Schwartz, *Rembrandt, His Life, His Paintings*. London: Penguin Books, 1985, pp. 112–114.
7. M. Westermann, *Rembrandt*. London: Phaidon, 2000, p. 153.
8. On the three trees as emblems of fortitude, constancy, and humility, see A. Ziemba quoted by George Keyes in *Six Centuries of Master Prints: Treasures from the Herbert Greer French Collection*, ed. K.L. Spangenberg. Cincinnati, OH: Cincinnati Art Museum, 1993, p. 165.
9. Sir William Mountague, *The Delight of Holland; or a Three-Months' Travel about That and Other Provinces*. London, 1969, p. 184.
10. Evelyn's admiring comment on Dou is cited by S. Slive, *Dutch Painting, 1600–1800*. New Haven, CT, and London: Yale University Press, 1995, p. 102.
11. Proust on Vermeer is quoted by John M. Montias, *Vermeer and his Milieu: A Web of Social History*. Princeton, NJ: Princeton University Press, 1989, p. 199.
12. The interpretation offered here is the author's.
13. Experts are divided about the dating of the clothing worn by the artist, but it is at least not the usual costume seen in contemporary male portraits. Steen wears a more colorful, theatrical version in the *Self Portrait* illustrated here (see Fig. 5.62).
14. Edward Norgate, *Miniatura, or The Art of Limning*, edited with an introduction and notes by Jeffrey M. Muller and Jim Murrell. New Haven, CT, and London: Yale University Press, 1997, p. 85.
15. C. Levesque, *Journey through Landscape in Seventeenth-Century Holland: The Haarlem Print Series and Dutch Identity*. University Park, PA: Pennsylvania State Press, 1994, pp. 15, 53–54.
16. For the association of Bentheim Castle with Psalms 18 and 59 as well as other possible symbolic readings, see Nils Büttner and Gerd Unverfehrt, *Jacob van Ruisdael in Bentheim: Ein niederländischer Maler und die Burg Bentheim im 17 Jahrhundert*. Bielefeld: Museumsverein für die Grafschaft Bentheim, 1993.

Chapter 6: England
1. Quoted by J. Hook, *The Baroque Age in England*. London: Thames and Hudson, 1975, p. 15.
2. Jones's statement about architecture at the beginning comes from a notebook he kept in Italy; the comment about Scamozzi is a marginal note in his copy of Andrea Palladio's *Quattro libri dell'architettura* (*Four Books of Architecture*) that he took with him to Italy. See J. Summerson, *Architecture in Britain, 1530–1830*. Harmondsworth, England: Pelican History of Art, pp. 66–67.

TIMECHART

Politics and Religion		Painting	
1600	Marriage of Henry IV to Marie de' Medici.	1599–1602	Caravaggio; paintings for the Contarelli chapel, S. Luigi dei Francesi, Rome.
		1602	Birth of Philippe de Champaigne (d. 1674).
1603	Elizabeth I of England dies. James Stuart becomes king (James I).		
1605	Pope Clement VIII dies; Paul V becomes pope.	1604	Annibale Carracci finishes Farnese Gallery, Rome.
		1606	Birth of Rembrandt.
1607	Union of Navarre with France.		
1609	Bank of Amsterdam chartered.	1609	Founding of the Accademi dei Lincei. Death of Annibale Carracci (b. 1560).
1610	Assassination of Henry IV. Marie de' Medici regent.	1610	Deaths of Caravaggio (b. 1570/1) and Elsheimer (b. 1578).
1612	Death of Rudolf II of Hapsburg.		
		1613–14	Guido Reni: *Aurora*, ceiling fresco in Casino Rospiglioso, Rome.
1614	Majority of Louis XIII of France proclaimed.	1614	Vouet in Rome.
1615	Marriage of Louis XIII and Anne of Austria.		
1618	Thirty Years' War starts.	1617–18	Birth of Murillo (d. 1682).
		1619	Birth of Le Brun.
1620	Treaty of Angers; Marie de' Medici and Louis XIII end disputes.	1620	Rubens commissioned to decorate Church of the Jesuits, Antwerp.
1620	*Mayflower* pilgrims sail to America.		
1621	Gregory XV becomes pope.	1621	Guercino: *Aurora*, ceiling fresco, Casino Ludovisi, Rome.
1621	Philip III of Spain dies; Philip IV becomes king.	1622–5	Rubens: Gallery of Marie de' Medici in the Luxembourg Palace, Paris (now in Louvre).
1623	Urban VIII becomes pope.		
1624	Richelieu joins Council of Louis XIII.	1624	Arrival of Poussin in Rome.
		1624–5	Orazio Gentileschi in Paris.
1625	Charles I becomes king of England.	1625	Birth of Maratta (d. 1713). Rembrandt: *The Stoning of St. Stephen* (Lyons).
1627	Richelieu's Siege of La Rochelle. Founding of the Company of the Holy Sacrament.	1627	Return of Vouet to Paris.
1629	Richelieu appointed prime minister.	1629	Death of Ter Brugghen (b. 1588). Sacchi: *An Allegory of Divine Wisdom*, fresco, Barberini Palace, Rome.
		1629	Poussin: *Martyrdom of Saint Erasmus* (Vatican).
		1629–34	Rubens: ceiling of reception room, Whitehall, London.
		1630	Velázquez: *The Forge of Vulcan* (Prado).
1631	Marie de' Medici exiled; flees to Brussels.	1632	Death of Valentin in Rome (b. 1591).
		1632	Van Dyck in London. Birth of Vermeer (d. 1675).
1633	Louis XIII takes possession of Lorraine.	1633–7	Pietro da Cortona: *Glorification of the Rule of Urban VIII* (ceiling fresco, Great Hall, Barberini Palace, Rome).
1635	France declares war on Spain.	1635–6	Velázquez: *The Surrender of Breda* (Prado).
		1637	Van Dyck: *Portrait of Charles I* (Louvre).
1638	Birth of Louis XIV (d. 1715).		
		1640	Death of Rubens (b. 1577).
		1640–2	Poussin in Paris.
		1641	Death of Van Dyck (b. 1599).
1642	Death of Richelieu.	1642	Rembrandt: *Nightwatch* (Amsterdam). Ribera: *Club-Footed Man* (Louvre).
1642–48	English Civil War.		
1643	Death of Louis XIII. Anne of Austria regent. Mazarin becomes prime minister.		
1644	Innocent X becomes pope.		
		1646	Murillo: *Food of the Angels* (Louvre).
		1647–50	Le Sueur: Cabinet des Muses, Hôtel Lambert, Paris.

Architecture, Sculpture, Engraving		Literature, Philosophy, Music, Sciences	
1600	S. Maderno: Sta. Cecilia in Trastevere, Rome.	1600	Condemnation and execution of Giordano Bruno.
		1603	Shakespeare: *Hamlet*.
1605	C. Maderno begins St. Peter's façade.		
1605	Construction begins on the Place Royale (now Place des Voges), Paris.	1605	Cervantes: *Don Quixote* (Part 1).
1605–14	Equestrian statue of Henry IV on the Pont Neuf, Paris.	1606	Jonson: *Volpone*.
		1607	Monteverdi: *Orfeo*.
		1608	Birth of John Milton (d. 1674).
		1610	Galileo invents telescope.
1612	C. Maderno: façade of St. Peter's, Rome. S. de Brosse: Luxembourg Palace, Paris.	1613	Shakespeare: *Henry VIII*.
		1615	William Harvey discovers blood circulation.
		1616	Death of William Shakespeare.
1618	Bernini: bust of *Paul V*.	1620	Francis Bacon: *Novum Organum*.
1619–21	I. Jones: Banqueting Hall, London.	1620	Birth of John Evelyn (d. 1706).
		1621	Birth of Andrew Marvell (d. 1678).
1622	Bernini: *Apollo and Daphne*, Borghese Gallery, Rome.	1623	Birth of Blaise Pascal (d. 1662).
		1623	Giambattista Marino: *Adone*. Birth of Pascal (d. 1662). Campanella: *Civitas Solis*.
1624	Bernini: begins *Baldacchino*, St. Peter's, Rome.	1624	Birth of George Fox (d. 1691).
1624–6	Bernini: church of Sta. Bibiana.		
		1627	Birth of Robert Boyle (d. 1691).
1628–47	Bernini: tomb of Urban VIII at St. Peter's, Rome.	1628	Birth of John Bunyan (d. 1688).
1629	F. Duquesnoy: Sta. Susanna, Sta. Maria di Loreto, Rome.		
		1630	Tirso de Molina: *El burlador de Sevilla*.
1632	Bernini: *Cardinal Scipione Borghese* bust.	1632	Galileo: *Dialogo... sopra i due massimi sistemi del mondo*.
1633	F. Duquesnoy: *Saint Andrew*, St. Peter's, Rome. Callot: *Disasters of War*.	1633	Galileo tried and condemned in Rome by the Inquisition.
		1635	Founding of the Académie Française. Death of Lope de Vega (b. 1562).
1636	Sarrazin: Caryatids, Pavillon de l'Horloge, Louvre.	1637	Descartes: *Les Discours de la méthode*.
1638–41	Borromini: monastery of San Carlo alle Quattro Fontane, Rome.		
		1639	Birth of Racine (d. 1699).
1642–50	Borromini: Sant'Ivo alla Sapienza, Rome.	1642	Monteverdi: *Incoronazione di Poppea*.
1643–44	Bernini: *Triton Fountain*, Rome.	1643	Molière founds the Illustre Théâtre.
1645–52	Bernini: *Ecstasy of Saint Teresa*, Sta. Maria della Vittoria, Rome.		

Politics and Religion		Painting	
1648	Beginning of the Fronde.	1648	Founding of the Académie Royale de Peinture et de Sculpture, Paris. Deaths of Antoine Le Nain and Louis Le Nain.
1648	Peace of Münster; legal recognition of Dutch republic.		
1648	Treaty of Westphalia.		
1648	George Fox, founder of Quakers, begins preaching.	1649	Death of Vouet.
1649	Execution of Charles I of England.	1649–51	Velázquez in Rome, *Portrait of Innocent X* (Pamphili Gallery, Rome).
		1650	La Tour: *The Denial of St. Peter* (Nantes).
1652	Louis XIV returns to Paris.	1652	Death of La Tour (b. 1593).
1653	End of the Fronde.		
1653–8	Oliver Cromwell Lord Protector of England.		
1654	Coronation of Louis XIV.		
1655	Alexander VII becomes pope.		
		1656	Velázquez: *Las Meninas* (Prado).
1660	Marriage of Louis XIV to Maria Theresa of Austria.	c.1660	Jacob van Ruisdael: *Jewish Cemetary* (Dresden). Vermeer: *View of Delft* (The Hague).
1660	Charles II becomes King of England.		
1661	Death of Mazarin. Beginning of the reign of Louis XIV.	1662	Philippe de Champaigne: *Ex-Voto* (Louvre).
1664	New Amsterdam seized by the British, who rename it New York.	1664	Poussin: Series of the *Seasons* (Louvre).
		1664	Death of Zurbarán (b. 1598). Frans Hals: *Regents of the Old Men's Almshouse* (Haarlem).
1665	Charles II becomes King of Spain.	1665	Death of Poussin, Rome (b. 1594).
1665	Great Plague of London.	1665	Vermeer: *Artist in his Studio* (Vienna).
1666	Great Fire of London.	1666	Death of Guercino (b. 1591). Carreno de Miranda: *Founding of the Trinitarian Order* (Louvre). Death of Frans Hals (b. 1581/5).
		1666	Founding of the Académie de France, Rome.
		1666–8	Félibien: *Entretiens sur les vies et les ouvrages des plus excellents peintres.*
1667	Clement IX becomes pope.		
		1669	Death of Rembrandt.
1670	Clement X becomes pope.		
		1671	Lecture by Philippe de Champaigne at the Académie Royale, Paris, on Titian's *Virgin with Rabbit* (Louvre). Beginning of the quarrel between the Poussinists and the Rubenists.
1672	Louis XIV moves to Versailles.	1672	Valdés Leal: *Hieroglyphs of Our Last Days* (Selville).
1672–8	Dutch War.		
		1673	Death of Salvator Rosa (b. 1615).
		1674–9	Gaulli: ceiling of Gesù at Rome.
		1675	Sandrart: *Der Teuschen Academie.*
1676	Innocent XI becomes pope.		
1678–9	Treaties of Nijmegen (between United Provinces and France).		
		1679	Le Brun begins decoration of Galerie des Glaces, Versailles.
		1681	Baldinucci: *Notizie de' professori del disegno da Cimabue in quà.*
1682	Louis XIV moves French court to Versailles.	1682	Death of Claude, Rome.
1683	Deaths of Colbert (prime minister, 1661–1683) and Maria Theresa.		
		1684	Birth of Watteau (d. 1721).
1685	Revocation of the Edict of Nantes (1598).		
1685	James II become King of England.	1686	Largillierre: *Portrait of Le Brun* (morceau de réception for the Académie; Louvre).
1689	Alexander VIII becomes pope.		
1689	William III and Mary II King and Queen of England.		
1689	Peter the Great seizes power in Russia.	1690	Death of Le Brun. P. Mignard made Premier Peintre.
1691	Death of Louvois (principal minister, 1683–1691).		
1691	Innocent XII becomes pope.		
1692	Spanish Crown bankrupted.		
		1696	Birth of G.B. Tiepolo (d. 1770).
		1697	Birth of Hogarth (d. 1764) and Canaletto (d. 1768).
		1699	Birth of Chardin (d. 1779). Desportes: *Self-Portrait as a Hunter* (morceau de réception for the Académie; Louvre).
1700	Philip V becomes King of Spain.		

Architecture, Sculpture, Engraving		Literature, Philosophy, Music, Sciences	
1648–51	Bernini: *Fountain of the Four Rivers*, Piazza Navona, Rome.	1651	Hobbes: *Leviathan*.
1653–5	Borromini designs Sant'Agnese, Rome.	1653	Walton: *The Complete Angler*.
1654	Bernini begins *Vision of Constantine*.		
1656	Bernini begins work on Cathedra Petri.		
1657	Le Vau begins Vaux-le-Vicomte.	1657	Pascal: *Les Provinciales*.
1657–63	Bernini: square and colonnade of St. Peter's, Rome.		
1661	Le Vau begins Versailles.	1662	Royal Society founded in London.
1662	Le Vau begins the Collège des Quatre Nations, Paris. Founding of the Manufacture Royale des Gobelins.	1662	Death of Blaise Pascal.
		1664	Molière: *Tartuffe*.
1665	Bernini in Paris.	1665	Molière: *Don Juan*.
1666–70	Le Vau, Perrault, Le Brun: Louvre colonnade.	1666	Leibniz invents concept of binary code.
		1666	Newton invents differential calculus.
1667–9	Bernini: *Angel with Crown of Thorns*, S. Andrea delle Fratte.	1667	Racine: *Andromaque*. Milton: *Paradise Lost*.
		1668	Birth of François Couperin (d. 1733).
1668–78	Louis Le Vau & J.-H. Mansart: garden façade, Versailles.	1670	Spinoza: *Tractatus Theologico-Politicus*. Bossuet: *Oraison funèbre d'Henriette d'Angleterre*.
1671	Founding of Académie Royale d'Architecture.	1671	Beginning of Mme de Sévigné's correspondence with her daughter, the comtesse de Grignan.
1671–4	Bernini: *Blessed Ludovica*, S. Francesco, Rome.		
1671–8	Bernini: tomb of Alexander VII, St. Peter's, Rome.	1671	Milton: *Paradise Regained*.
		1673	Molière: *Le Malade imaginaire*.
		1674	Boileau: *L'Art poétique*.
1675–90	Girardon: tomb of Richelieu.	1674	Death of John Milton.
1675–1710	Christopher Wren: reconstruction of St. Paul's Cathedral, London.		
		1677	Death of Spinoza (b. 1632).
1678	J.-H. Mansart enlarges Versailles and builds Galerie des Glaces	1678	Birth of Vivaldi (d. 1743). Mme de La Fayette: *La Princesse de Clèves*.
1679	J.-H. Mansart & Charles Le Brun begin Galerie des Glaces, Versailles.	1680	Founding of the Comédie Française.
1682	Puget: *Milo of Croton*, Louvre. Creation of the Compagnie de Saint-Gobain.	1682	Newton formulates the law of gravity.
		1685	Birth of Johann Sebastian Bach (d. 1750).
		1687	Newton: *Principia Mathematica*.
		1688–97	Perrault: *Parallèle des Anciens et des Modernes*.
1689	J.-H. Mansart: chapel of Versailles.	1689	Purcell: *Dido and Aeneas*.
1689–93	Coysevox: tomb of Mazarin, Institut de France, Paris.	1689	Birth of Samuel Richardson (d. 1761).
		1690	Locke: *Essay Concerning Understanding*.
1694	Death of Pierre Puget.	1694	Birth of Voltaire (d. 1778). Dictionary of the Académie.

BIBLIOGRAPHY

This bibliography includes much of the significant recent literature in English on the subjects covered and less specialized books that can be recommended for further reading. Countries are listed alphabetically. Within each country, general studies are followed by studies on individual artists. If there is no reliable study in English on an artist discussed in the text, then recommended texts in other languages are listed.

GENERAL BACKGROUND

Art Theory and Practice
Bellori, Giovan Pietro, *Le vite de' pittori, scultori e architetti moderni*, ed. Evelina Borea with an introduction by Giovanni Previtali. Turin: G. Einaudi, 1976.
Bryson, Norman, *Looking at the Overlooked: Four Essays on Still-Life Painting*. Cambridge, MA, and London: Cambridge University Press, 1990.
Holt, Elizabeth G., ed., *The Literary Sources of Art History*. Princeton: Princeton University Press, 1947, Volume II (*Michelangelo and the Mannerists, The Baroque and the Eighteenth Century*). Reprinted as *A Documentary History of Art*, II, Doubleday & Co., 1958.
Mahon, Denis, *Studies in Seicento Art and Theory*. London: Warburg Institute, University of London, 1947.
Muller, Jeffry, ed., *Children of Mercury: The Education of Artists in the Sixteenth and Seventeenth Centuries*. Ex. cat. Providence, RI: Bell Gallery, Brown University, 1984.
Pevsner, Nicolas, *Academies of Art, Past and Present*. Cambridge, MA: Da Capo Press, 1940; reprinted New York, 1973.
Schneider, Norbert, *The Art of Still-Life: Still-Life Painting in the Early Modern Period*. Cologne: Benedikt Taschen, 1990.
Shearman, John, *Mannerism (Style and Civilization)*. Harmondsworth, England: Penguin Books, 1967.

Historical Background
Brown, Jonathan, *Kings and Connoisseurs: Collecting Art in Seventeenth-Century Europe*. Princeton, NJ: Princeton University Press, 1995.
Cochrane, Eric, *Italy 1530–1630*, ed. J. Kirshner. London & New York: Longman, 1988.
Elliott, J.H., *Europe Divided, 1559–1598*. New York: Harper and Row, 1968.
Harris, William V., *Ancient Literacy*. Cambridge, MA: Harvard University Press, 1989, pp. 3–24.
Michaelski, Sergiusz, *The Reformation and the Visual Arts: The Protestant Image Question in Western and Eastern Europe*. London: Routledge, 1993.
Reeves, Eileen A., *Painting the Heavens: Art and Science in the Age of Galileo*. Princeton, NJ: Princeton University Press, 1997.
Smith, Alan G.R., *Science and Society in the Sixteenth and Seventeenth Centuries*. London: Thames and Hudson, 1972.

CENTRAL EUROPE

Artists
Adam Elsheimer
Andrews, Keith, *Adam Elsheimer*. London: Rizzoli, 1977.
Sumowski, Werner, "The Artist in Despair," *Master Drawings*, Vol. XXXIII (1995), no. 2, pp. 152–15.

DUTCH REPUBLIC

General Studies
The recent literature on Dutch art is extensive and lively. What follows is only a sample. Readers anxious to learn more will find many tempting leads in the bibliographies of the books listed.
Ackley, Clifford S., *Printmaking in the Age of Rembrandt*. Boston, MA: Museum of Fine Arts; and New York: New York Graphic Society, 1980.
Alpers, Svetlana, *The Art of Describing: Dutch Art in the Seventeenth Century*. Chicago, IL: University of Chicago Press, 1983.
Baarsen, Reiner J., et al., *Netherlandish Art 1600–1700*. Amsterdam and New Haven, CT: Yale University Press, 2001.
De Jongh, Eddy, "The Iconological Approach to 17th-Century Dutch Art" in *The Golden Age of Dutch Painting in Historical Perspective*. Eds. Frans Grijzenhout and Henk van Veen. Cambridge, England: Cambridge University Press, 1999.
Franits, Wayne E., *Paragons of Virtue: Women and Domesticity in Seventeenth-Century Dutch Art*. Cambridge, England: Cambridge University Press, 1993.
Franits, Wayne E., ed., *Looking at Seventeenth-Century Dutch Art: Realism Reconsidered*. Cambridge, England: Cambridge University Press, 1997.
Fremantle, Katherine, *The Baroque Town Hall of Amsterdam*. Utrecht: Haentjens Dekker & Gumbert, 1959.
Harwood, Laurie B., with C. Brown and A. C. Steland, *Inspired by Italy: Dutch Landscape Painting 1600–1700*. Ex. cat. London: Dulwich College Picture Gallery, 2002.
Hellerstedt, Kahren Jones, *Gardens of Earthly Delight: Sixteenth- and Seventeenth-Century Netherlandish Gardens*. Ex. cat. Pittsburgh: The Frick Art Museum in association with Indiana University Press, 1968.
Hofrichter, Frima Fox, et al., *Haarlem: The Seventeenth Century*. Ex. cat. Rutgers, NJ: The Jane Voorhees Zimmerli Art Museum, State University of New Jersey, 1983.
Honig, Elizabeth A., "The Space of Gender in Seventeenth-Century Dutch Painting," *Franits*, 1997, pp. 187–201.
Kahr, Madlyn Millner, *Dutch Painting in the Seventeenth Century*. New York: Harper and Row, 1978.
Kenseth, Joy, et al., *The Age of the Marvelous*. Hanover, NH: Hood Museum of Art, Dartmouth College, 1991.
Kettering, Alison M., "Ter Borch's Ladies in Satin," *Franits*, 1997, pp. 98–115.
Levesque, Catherine, *Journey through Landscape in Seventeenth-Century Holland: The Haarlem Print Series and Dutch Identity*. University Park, PA: Pennsylvania State University Press, 1994.
Montias, J.M., *Artists and Artisans in Delft in the Seventeenth Century: A Socio-Economic Study of the Seventeenth Century*. Princeton, NJ: Princeton University Press, 1982.
Montias, J.M., "Socio-Economic Aspects of Netherlandish Art from the Fifteenth to the Seventeenth Century: A Survey," *Art Bulletin*, 72, 1990, pp. 359–73.
Mosby, Dewey, ed., *Gods, Saints and Heroes: Dutch Painting in the Age of Rembrandt*. Ex. cat. Washington, DC: National Gallery of Art, 1980.
North, Michael, *Art and Commerce in the Dutch Golden Age*. New Haven, CT, and London: Yale University Press, 1997.
Roodenberg, Hermann, "The 'hand of friendship': Shaking Hands and Other Gestures in the Dutch Republic," *A Cultural History of Gesture*, ed. Jan Bremmer and Hermann Roodenberg. New York: Cornell University Press, 1992, pp. 152–189.
Schama, Simon, *The Embarrassment of Riches: An Interpretation of Dutch Culture in the Golden Age*. New York: Alfred A. Knopf (distributed by Random House), 1987.
Spicer, Joaneath A., with Lynn Federle Orr, *Masters of Light, Dutch Painters in Utrecht during the Golden Age*. Ex. cat. San Francisco, CA: Fine Arts Museums of San Francisco; and New Haven, CT: Yale University Press, 1997–1998.
Spicer, Joaneath A., "The Renaissance Elbow" in *A Cultural History of Gesture*, ed. Jan Bremmer and Hermann Roodenberg. New York: Cornell University Press, 1992, pp. 84–128.
Sutton, Peter, et al., *Masters of Seventeenth-Century Dutch Genre Painting*. Ex. cat. Philadelphia, PA: Philadelphia Museum of Art, 1984.
Van Duersen, Arie T., *Plain Lives in a Golden Age: Popular Culture, Religion, and Society in Seventeenth-Century Holland*. Cambridge, England: Cambridge University Press, 1991.
Westermann, Mariët, *A Worldly Art: The Dutch Republic 1585–1718*. New York: Harry N. Abrams, 1996.

Artists
Gerrit Dou
Wheelock, Arthur K., ed., *Gerrit Dou, 1613–1675: Master Painter in the Age of Rembrandt*. Ex. cat. by Ronni Baer. Washington DC: National Gallery of Art; and New Haven, CT: Yale University Press, 2000.

Frans Hals
Slive, Seymour, *Frans Hals*. Kress Foundation Studies in the History of European Art, 3 vols. London and New York: Phaidon Press, 1970–1974.
Slive, Seymour, et al, *Frans Hals*, Ex. cat. London: Royal Academy of Arts, 1989.

Pieter de Hooch
Sutton, Peter C., *Pieter de Hooch*. London: Dulwich College Picture Gallery; and Hartford, CT: Yale University Press, 1998.

Pieter Lastman
Tümpel, Astrid, & Peter Schatborn, *Pieter Lastman: The Man who Taught Rembrandt*. Ex. cat. Amsterdam: Het Rembrandthuis, in association with Waanders Uitgevers, Zwolle, 1991.

Judith Leyster
Hofrichter, Frima Fox, *Judith Leyster: A Woman Painter in Holland's Golden Age*. Amsterdam: Doornspijk, 1989.
Welu, James A., Cynthia Kortenhorst von Bogendorf Rupprath, et al., *Judith Leyster: A Dutch Master and her World*. Ex. cat. Haarlem: Frans Hals Museum; and Worcester Art Museum in association with Yale University Press, 1993.

Rembrandt van Rijn
Adams, Ann Jensen, ed., *Rembrandt's "Bathsheba Reading King David's Letter."* Cambridge: Cambridge University Press, 1998.
Alpers, Svetlana, *Rembrandt's Enterprise: The Studio and the Market*. Chicago, IL: Chicago University Press, 1988.
Bal, Mieke, *Reading "Rembrandt": Beyond the Word-Image Opposition*. Cambridge, England, and New York: Cambridge University Press, 1991.
Chapman, H. Perry, *Rembrandt's Self-Portrait: A Study in Seventeenth-Century Identity*. Princeton, NJ: Princeton University Press, 1990.
Chong, Alan, and Michael Zell, eds. *Rethinking Rembrandt*. Zwolle: Waanders Uitgevers, 2002.
Clark, Kenneth, *Rembrandt and the Italian Renaissance*. New York: New York University Press, 1966.
Haak, Bob, *Rembrandt: His Life, His Works, His Time*. New York: Thames and Hudson, 1969.
Haverkamp-Begemann, E., *Rembrandt: The Nightwatch*. Princeton, NJ: Princeton University Press, 1982.
Heckscher, W.S., *Rembrandt's Anatomy Lesson of Dr. Nicolaus Tulp: An Iconological Study*. New York: New York University Press, 1958.
Held, Julius S., *Rembrandt Studies*. 2nd ed. Princeton, NJ: Princeton University Press, 1991.
Schama, Simon, *Rembrandt's Eyes*. New York: Alfred Knopf, 1999.
Schwartz, Gary, *Rembrandt: His Life, His Paintings*. New York: Penguin, 1985.
Slive, Seymour, *Rembrandt and his Critics, 1630–1730*. The Hague: M. Nijhoff, 1953.
Westermann, Mariët, *Rembrandt*. London: Phaidon Press, 2000.
White, Christopher, *Rembrandt as an Etcher: A Study of the Artist at Work*. 2nd ed. New Haven, CT: Yale University Press, 1999.
White, Christopher, and Q. Buvelot, eds., with Ernst van de Wetering et. al., *Rembrandt by Himself*. Ex. cat. London: National Gallery Publications; and The Hague: Royal Cabinet of Paintings, Mauritshuis, 1999.

Jacob van Ruisdael
Büttner, Nils, and Gerd Unverfehrt, *Jacob van Ruisdael in Bentheim: Ein niederländischer Maler und die Burg Bentheim im 17. Jahrhundert*. Ex. cat. Bielefeld: Museumsverein für die Grafschaft Bentheim,1993.
Slive, Seymour, *Jacob van Ruisdael*. Cambridge, MA: Harvard University Art Museums, in association with Abbeville Press, New York, 1982.
Slive, Seymour, *Jacob van Ruisdael: A Complete Catalogue of his Paintings, Drawings, and Etchings*. New Haven, CT, and London: Yale University Press, 2002.
Walford, John, *Jacob van Ruisdael and the Perception of Landscape*. New Haven, CT, and London: Yale University Press, 1991.

Pieter Saenredam
Schwartz, Gary, and Marten Jan Bok, *Pieter Saenredam: The Painter and His Time*. The Hague: Gary Schwartz, SDU Maarssen, 1990.

Jan Steen
Chapman, H. Perry, Wouter Th. Kloek, and Arthur K. Wheelock, Jr., *Jan Steen: Painter and Storyteller*. Washington, DC: National Gallery of Art, 1996; and Amsterdam: Rijksmuseum, 1996–1997.
Walsh, John, *Jan Steen: The Drawing Lesson*. Malibu, CA: J. Paul Getty Museum Publications, 1996.
Westermann, Mariët, *The Amusements of Jan Steen: Comic Painting in the Seventeenth Century*. Zwolle: Waanders Uitgevers, 1997.

Jan Vermeer
Arasse, Daniel, *Vermeer: Faith in Painting*. Princeton, NJ: Princeton University Press, 1994.
Blankert, Albert, Ben Broos, Arthur K. Wheelock Jr., and Jørgen Wadum, *Johannes Vermeer*. Ex. cat. Washington, DC: National Gallery of Art; The Hague: Royal Cabinet of Paintings, Mauritshuis; and New York: Rizzoli, 1995–1996.
De Jongh, Eddy, "On Balance," *Vermeer Studies*, eds. Ivan Gaskell and Michiel Jonker. *Studies in the History of Art*. Washington, DC: National Gallery of Art; New Haven, CT: Yale University Press, 1998, pp. 351–365.
Gowing, Lawrence, *Vermeer*. 2nd ed. New York: Harper and Row, 1970; 3rd ed., Berkeley and Los Angeles, CA: University of California Press, 1997.
Franits, Wayne E., ed., *The Cambridge Companion to Vermeer*. Cambridge, England: Cambridge University Press, 2002.
Montias, John Michael, *Vermeer and his Milieu: A Web of Social History*. Princeton, NJ: Princeton University Press, 1989.
Salomon, Nanette, "Vermeer and the Balance of Destiny," *Essays in Northern European Art Presented to Egbert Haverkamp-Begemann on his Sixtieth Birthday*. Amsterdam: Doornspijk, 1983, pp. 216–221.
Sluijter, Eric Jan, "Vermeer, Fame, and Female Beauty: The Art of Painting," *Vermeer Studies*, eds. Ivan Gaskell and Michiel Jonker, *Studies in the History of Art*. Washington, DC: National Gallery of Art; and New Haven, CT: Yale University Press, 1998, pp. 265–283.
Welu, James A., "Vermeer: His Cartographic Sources," *Art Bulletin*, Vol. LVII, 1975, pp. 529–547.
Wheelock Jr., Arthur K., *Vermeer: The Complete Works*. New York: Harry N. Abrams, 1977.
Wheelock Jr., Arthur K. *The Public and the Private in the Age of Vermeer*. Ex. cat. Osaka: Osaka Municipal Museum of Art; New York: Metropolitan Museum of Art; and London: Philip Wilson Publishers, 2000.
De Winkel, Marieke, "The Interpretation of Dress in Vermeer's Paintings," *Vermeer Studies*, eds. Ivan Gaskell and Michiel Jonker, *Studies in the History of Art*. Washington, DC: National Gallery of Art; and New Haven, CT: Yale University Press, 1998, pp. 327–340.

ENGLAND

General Studies
Hook, Judith, *The Baroque Age in England*. London: Thames and Hudson, 1976.
Summerson, John N., *Architecture in Britain, 1530 to 1830*. Harmondsworth, England: Pelican History of Art, Penguin, 1953; 3rd ed., 1958.
Waterhouse, Ellis K., *Painting in Britain, 1530–1790*. Harmondsworth, England: Pelican History of Art, Penguin, 1953; 4th ed., 1978.

Artists
Nicholas Hilliard
Auerbach, Erna, *Nicholas Hilliard*. London: Routledge & Kegan Paul, 1961
Brett, Edwina, *A Kind of Gentle Painting* (an exhibition of miniatures by Nicholas Hilliard and Isaac Oliver): Edinburgh, Scottish Arts Council, 1975.
Hilliard, Nicholas, *A Treatise on the Arte of Limning*, ed. R.K.R. Thornton and T.G.S. Cain. Ashington, England: Mid Northumberland Arts Group in association with Carcanet New Press, 1981.
Reynolds, Graham, *Nicholas Hilliard and Isaac Oliver*. London: Ministry of Education, Victoria & Albert Museum Handbooks, no. 2, 1947.

Sir Godfrey Kneller
Stewart, J. Douglas, *Sir Godfrey Kneller*. Ex. cat. London: National Portrait Gallery, 1971.
Stewart, J. Douglas, *Sir Godfrey Kneller and the English Baroque Portrait*. Oxford: Oxford University Press, 1983.

Sir Peter Lely
Baker, C.H. Collins, *Lely and the Stuart Portrait Painters*. London: P. L. Warner for the Medici Society, 1912.
Beckett, R.B., *Peter Lely*. London: Routledge & Kegan Paul, 1951.
Millar, Oliver, *Sir Peter Lely*. Ex. cat. London: National Portrait Gallery, 1978.

Sir Christopher Wren
Downes, Kerry, *The Architecture of Wren*. New York: Universe Books, 1982.
Jardine, Lisa, *On a Grander Scale : The Outstanding Life of Sir Christopher Wren*. New York: HarperCollins, 2002.
Jeffery, Paul, *The City Churches of Sir Christopher Wren*. London: Hambleden Press, 1996.
Saunders, Ann, *St Paul's: The Story of the Cathedral*. London: Collins & Brown, 2001.

FLANDERS

General Studies
Filipczak, Zirka Zaremba, *Picturing Art in Antwerp, 1550– 1700*. Princeton, NJ: Princeton University Press, 1987.
Gerson, H., and E.H. ter Kuile, *Art and Architecture in Belgium, 1600–1800*. Harmondsworth, England: Pelican History of Art, Penguin, 1960.
Held, Julius S., "Artis Pictoriae Amator: An Antwerp Patron and his Collection," in *Rubens and his Circle: Studies by Julius S. Held*, ed. A.W. Lowenthal, D. Rosand, and J. Walsh, Jr. Princeton, NJ: Princeton University Press, 1982, pp. 35–64.
Hellerstedt, Kahren Jones, *Gardens of Earthly Delight: Sixteenth- and Seventeenth-Century Netherlandish Gardens*. Ex. cat. Pittsburgh, PA: The Frick Art Museum, 1968.
Honig, Elizabeth Alice, *Painting and the Market in Early Modern Antwerp*. New Haven, CT, and London: Yale University Press, 1998.
Marrow, Deborah, *The Art Patronage of Marie de' Medici*. Ann Arbor, MI: University of Michigan Press, 1982.
Sutton, Peter, Marjorie E. Weisman, et al., *The Age of Rubens*. Ex. cat. Boston, MA: Museum of Fine Arts, 1993.
Vlieghe, Hans, *Flemish Art and Architecture, 1585–1700*. New Haven, CT, and London: Yale University Press, 1998.

Artists
Sir Anthony van Dyck
Brown, Christopher, *Van Dyck*. Ithaca, NY: Cornell University Press, 1983.
Verdi, Richard, *Anthony van Dyck: Ecce Homo and The Mocking of Christ*. Ex. cat. Princeton, NJ: Princeton University Art Museum; and Birmingham, England: Barber Institute of Fine Arts, 2002–2003.
Wheelock Jr., Arthur K. et al., *Anthony van Dyck*. Washington, DC: National Gallery of Art, 1991.

Jacob Jordaens
Jaffé, Michael, *Jacob Jordaens*. Ottawa: National Gallery of Canada, 1968.

Sir Peter Paul Rubens
Belkin, Kristin Lohse, *Rubens*. London: Phaidon Press, 1998.

Fletcher, Jennifer, *Peter Paul Rubens*. London: Phaidon Press, 1968.
Haeger, Barbara, "Rubens's *Adoration of the Magi* and the Program for the High Altar of St. Michael's Abbey in Antwerp." *Simiolus*, Vol. 25 (1997), pp. 45–71.
Held, Julius S., *Rubens: Selected Drawings*. London: Phaidon Press, 1959.
Held, Julius, et al., *Rubens and the Book: Title Pages by Peter Paul Rubens*. Ex. cat. Williamstown, VA: Chapin Library, 1977.
Jaffé, Michael, *Rubens: Catalogo Completo*. Milan: Rizzoli, 1989.
Martin, John R., ed., *Rubens: The Antwerp Altarpieces—The* Raising of the Cross *and the* Descent from the Cross. New York: Norton, 1969.
Muller, Jeffrey M., *Rubens: The Artist as Collector*. Princeton, NJ: Princeton University Press, 1989.
Rubens, P.P., *The Letters of Peter Paul Rubens*, translated and edited by Ruth Saunders Magurn. Cambridge, MA: Harvard University Press, 1955; reprinted 1971.
Saward, Susan, *The Golden Age of Marie de' Medici*. Ann Arbor, MI: University of Michigan Press, 1982.
Wedgwood, C.V., *The Political Career of Peter Paul Rubens*, "The Walter Neurath Lecture". London: Thames and Hudson, 1975.

FRANCE

General Studies
Ballon, Hilary, *The Paris of Henri IV: Architecture and Urbanism*. Cambridge, MA, and London: M.I.T. Press, 1991.
Blunt, Anthony, *Art and Architecture in France, 1500–1700*. Harmondsworth, England: Pelican History of Art, Penguin, Penguin, 1953; 2nd ed. 1973.
Burke, Peter, *The Fabrication of Louis XIV*, New Haven, CT, and London: Yale University Press, 1992.
Clark, Alvin L. Jr., *From Mannerism to Classicism: Printmaking in France, 1600–1700*. New Haven, CT: Yale University Art Gallery, 1987–1988.
Goldfarb, Hilliard T., ed., *Richelieu: Art and Power*. Ex. cat. Montreal: Montreal Museum of Fine Arts, 2002.
Harth, Erica, *Ideology and Culture in Seventeenth-Century France*. Ithaca, NY, and London: Cornell University Press, 1983.
Knecht, R.J., *The Rise and Fall of Renaissance France, 1483–1610*. Oxford: Basil Blackwell, 2001.
Ladurie, Emmanuel Le Roy, *The Ancien Régime: A History of France 1610–1774*, trans. Mark Greengrass. Oxford: Basil Blackwell, 1996.
Mérot, Alain, *French Painting in the Seventeenth Century*. New Haven, CT, and London: Yale University Press, 1995.
Ranum, Orest, *Paris in the Age of Absolutism*. University Park, PA: Pennsylvania State University Press, 2002.
Rosenberg, Pierre, *France in the Golden Age: Seventeenth-Century French Paintings in American Collection*s. Catalogue by Pierre Rosenberg, introduction by Marc Fumaroli. New York: Metropolitan Museum of Art; and Chicago, IL: Chicago Art Institute, 1982.
Wolfe, Michael, ed., *Changing Identities in Early Modern France*. Foreword by Natalie Zemon Davis. Durham, NC: Duke University Press, 1997.

Artists
Salomon de Brosse
Coope, Rosalys, *Salomon de Brosse and the Development of the Classical Style in French Architecture from 1565 to 1630*. University Park, PA, and London: Pennsylvania State Press, 1972.

Jacques Callot
Russell, H. Diane, with Jeffrey Blanchard and John Krill, *Jacques Callot: Prints and Drawings*. Washington, D.C.: National Gallery of Art, 1975.

Claude Gellée (Lorrain)
Kitson, Michael, "Landscape with the Nymph Egeria," 49th Charlton Lecture. Newcastle, England: University of Newcastle, 1968.
Kitson, Michael, *The Art of Claude Lorraine*. London: Hayward Gallery, 1969.
Kitson, Michael, *Claude Lorrain: Liber Veritatis*. London: British Museum, 1978.
Langdon, Helen, *Claude Lorrain*. Oxford: Phaidon Press, 1989.
Röthlisberger, Marcel, *Claude Lorrain: The Paintings*. New Haven, CT: Yale University Press, 1961.
Röthlisberger, Marcel, *Claude Lorrain: The Drawings*. Berkeley, CA: University of California Press, 1968.
Russell, H. Diane, *Claude Lorrain, 1600–1682*. Washington, D.C.: National Gallery of Art, 1982.
Wine, Humphrey, *Claude: The Poetic Landscape*. London: National Gallery Publications, 1994.

Georges de La Tour
Conisbee, Philip, et al., *Georges de la Tour and his World*. Washington, D.C.: National Gallery of Art, 1996–1997.
Nicolson, Benedict, and Christopher Wright, *Georges de la Tour*. London: Phaidon Press, 1974.

Charles Le Brun
Gareau, Michel, *Charles Le Brun, First Painter to King Louis XIV*. New York: Harry N. Abrams, 1992.
Montagu, Jennifer, *The Expression of the Passions: The Origin and Influence of Charles Le Brun's* Conférence sur l'expression générale et particulière. New Haven, CT, and London: Yale University Press, 1994.

Nicolas Poussin
Blunt, Anthony, *The Paintings of Nicolas Poussin*. 3 vols. London and New York: Phaidon Press, 1958.
Cropper, Elizabeth, and Charles Dempsey, *Nicolas Poussin: Friendship and the Love of Painting*. Princeton, NJ: Princeton University Press, 1998.
Dempsey, Charles, "The Textual Sources of Poussin's *Marine Venus* in Philadelphia." *Journal of the Warburg and Courtauld Institute*, Vol. XXIX, 1966, pp. 438–442.
Friedlaender, Walter, *Poussin*. New York: Harry N. Abrams, 1964.
Mérot, Alain, *Nicolas Poussin*. London and New York: Abbeville, 1990.
Pace, Claire, *Félibien's Life of Poussin*. London: A. Zwemmer, 1981.
Rosenberg, Pierre, with Nathalie Butor, *La Mort de Germanicus du Musée de Minneapolis*. Paris: Editions des Musées Nationaux, 1973.
Verdi, Richard, "Poussin and the 'Tricks of Fortune' ", *The Burlington Magazine*, Vol. CXXVI, 1982, pp. 681–685.
Verdi, Richard, *Nicolas Poussin: Tancred and Erminia*. Birmingham, England: Birmingham Museum and Art Gallery, 1992–1993.
Verdi, Richard, *Nicolas Poussin, 1594–1665*. London: Royal Academy of Arts in association with A. Zwemmer, 1995.

Simon Vouet
Crelly, William R., *The Painting of Simon Vouet*. New Haven, CT, and London: Yale University Press, 1962.

ITALY

General Studies
Blunt, Anthony, *Artistic Theory in Italy, 1450–1600*. Oxford: Clarendon Press, 1940; rev ed. 1960.
Boucher, Bruce, *Italian Baroque Sculpture*. London and New York: Thames and Hudson, 1998.
Brown, Beverly Louise, ed., *The Genius of Rome, 1592–1623*. London: Royal Academy of Arts, 2001.
Emiliani, Andrea, et al., *The Age of Correggio and the Carracci: Emilian Painting of the Sixteenth and Seventeenth Centuries*. Ex. cat. Washington, DC: National Gallery of Art; and New York: Metropolitan Museum of Art, 1986–1987.
Findlen, Paula, *Possessing Nature: Museums, Collecting, and Scientific Culture in Early Modern Italy*. Berkeley, CA: University of California Press, 1994.
Hammond, Frederick, *Music and Spectacle in Baroque Rome: Barberini Patronage under Urban VIII*. New Haven, CT, and London: Yale University Arts Museum, 1994.
Haskell, Francis, *Patrons and Painters: A Study in the Relations Between Italian Art and Society in the Age of the Baroque*. London, 1963; 2nd revised ed., New Haven, CT: Yale University Press, 1980.
Krautheimer, Richard, *The Rome of Alexander VII, 1655–1667*. Princeton, NJ: Princeton University Press, 1985.
Mahon, Denis, *Studies in Seicento Art and Theory*. London: Warburg Institute, University of London, 1947.
Montagu, Jennifer, *Roman Baroque Sculpture: The Industry of Art*. New Haven, CT, and London: Yale University Press, 1989.
Nussdorfer, Laurie, *Civic Politics in the Rome of Urban VIII*. Princeton, NJ: Princeton University Press, 1992.
Rice, Louise, *The Altars and Altarpieces of New St. Peter's: Outfitting the Basilica, 1621–1666*. Cambridge, England: Cambridge University Press, 1997.
Scott, John Beldon, *Images of Nepotism: The Painted Ceilings of the Palazzo Barberini*. Princeton, NJ: Princeton University Press, 1991.
Waddy, Patricia, *Seventeenth-Century Roman Palaces: Use and Art of the Plan*. Cambridge, MA, and London: MIT Press, 1990.
Wittkower, Rudolf, *Art and Architecture in Italy, 1600–1750*. Harmondsworth, England: Pelican History of Art, Penguin, 1958.

Artists
Gian Lorenzo Bernini
Baldinucci, F., *The Life of Bernini*, trans. C. and R. Enggass. University Park, PA, and London: Pennsylvania State Press, 1966.
Barcham, William L., *Grand in Design: The Life and Career of Federico Cornaro, Prince of the Church, Patriarch of Venice, and Patron of the Arts*. Venice: Venetian Institute of Science, Letters, and Art, 2001.
Chantelou, Paul Freart de, *Diary of the Cavaliere Bernini's Visit to France*, ed. and introduced by Anthony Blunt, annotated by George C. Bauer, trans. by Margery Corbett. Princeton, NJ: Princeton University Press, 1985.
Harris, Ann Sutherland, *Selected Drawings of Gian Lorenzo Bernini*. New York: Dover Press, 1977.
Hibbard, Howard, *Bernini*. Harmondsworth, England: Penguin Books, 1965.
Weston-Lewis, Aidan, ed., *Effigies & Ecstasies: Roman Baroque Sculpture and Design in the Age of Bernini*. Edinburgh: National Gallery of Scotland, 1998.
Wittkower, Rudolf, *Gian Lorenzo Bernini: The Sculptor of the Roman Baroque*. London: Phaidon Press, 1955. Reprinted 1966; 1981.

Francesco Borromini
Blunt, Anthony, *Borromini*. London: A. Lane, 1979.
Connors, Joseph, *Borromini and Roman Oratory, Style, and Society*. New York and London: MIT Press, 1980.

Michelangelo Merisi da Caravaggio
Gregori, Mina et al., *The Age of Caravaggio*. New York: Metropolitan Museum of Art and Electa/Rizzoli, 1985.
Hibbard, Howard, *Caravaggio*. New York: Harper and Row, 1983.
Kitson, Michael, *The Complete Paintings of Caravaggio*. New York: Harry N. Abrams, 1969.
Langdon, Helen, *Caravaggio: A Life*. London and New York: Farrar, Straus, & Giroux, 2000.
Puglisi, Catherine, *Caravaggio*. London and New York: Phaidon Press, 1999.
Moir, Alfred, *Caravaggio*. New York: Harry N. Abrams, 1982.
Spear, Richard, *Caravaggio and his Followers*. Cleveland, OH: Cleveland Museum of Art, 1971; 2nd ed., New York: Harper and Row, 1979.

Annibale and Ludovico Carracci
De Grazia Bohlin, Diane, *Prints and Related Drawings by the Carracci Family: A Catalogue Raisonné*. Washington, DC: National Gallery of Art, 1979.
Dempsey, Charles, *Annibale Carracci and the Beginnings of Baroque Style*. 2nd ed. Fiesole: Cadmo Press, 2000.
Feigenbaum, Gail, *Ludovico Carracci*. Ex. cat. Milan and New York: Electa/Abbeville; and Fort Worth, TX: Kimbell Art Museum, 1994.
Martin, J. Rupert, *The Farnese Gallery*. Princeton, NJ: Princeton University Press, 1965.
Posner, Donald, *Annibale Carracci: A Study in the Reform of Italian Painting around 1590*. London: Phaidon Press, 1971.
Summerscale, Anne, *Malvasia's Life of the Carracci: Commentary and Translation*. University Park, PA: Pennsylvania State Press, 1999.

Pietro da Cortona
Scott, John Beldon, *Images of Nepotism: The Painted Ceilings of the Palazzo Barberini*. Princeton, NJ: Princeton University Press, 1991.

Domenico Zampieri, called Domenichino
Richard E. Spear, *Domenichino*. 2 vols. New Haven, CT, and London: Yale University Press, 1982.

Francesco Duquesnoy
Lingo, Estelle, "The Greek Manner and a Christian Canon: Francesco Duquesnoy's *Saint Susanna*," *The Art Bulletin*, Vol. LXXXIV, 2002, pp. 65–93.

Artemisia Gentileschi
Bissell, R. Ward, *Artemisia Gentileschi*. University Park, PA: Pennsylvania State University Press, 1999.
Garrard, Mary D., *Artemisia Gentileschi: The Image of the Female Hero in Italian Baroque Art*. Princeton, NJ: Princeton University Press, 1989.
Harris, Ann Sutherland, "Artemisia Gentileschi: The Literate Illiterate, or Learning from Example", *Docere Delectare Movere: Affetti, Devozione e Retorica nel Linguaggio Artistico del Primo Barocco*. Rome: Edizioni de Luca, 1998, pp. 105–120.
Mann, Judith, and Keith Christiansen, *Orazio and Artemisia Gentileschi*. Ex. cat. New York: Metropolitan Museum of Art; St. Louis, MO: St. Louis Art Museum; and New Haven, CT: Yale University Press, 2002.

Orazio Gentileschi
Bissell, R.W., *Orazio Gentileschi and the Poetic Tradition in Caravaggesque Painting*. University Park, PA, and London: Pennsylvania State University Press, 1981.

Christiansen, Keith, and Judith Mann, *Orazio and Artemisia Gentileschi*. Ex. cat. New York: Metropolitan Museum of Art; St. Louis, MO: St. Louis Art Museum; and New Haven, CT: Yale University Press, 2002.
Finaldi, G., et al., *Orazio Gentileschi at the Court of Charles I*. London: National Gallery Publications, 1999.

Giambologna (Giovanni da Bologna; Jean de Boulogne)
Avery, Charles, and Anthony Radcliffe, *Giambologna, 1529–1608: Sculptor to the Medici*. Edinburgh: National Gallery of Scotland; and London: The Arts Council, 1978.

Giovanni Francesco Barbieri, called Guercino
Mahon, Denis, *Studies in Seicento Art and Theory*. London: Warburg Institute, University of London, 1947.
Mahon, Denis, *Guercino: Master Painter of the Baroque*, with contributions from Andrea Emiliani, Diane de Grazia, and Sybille Ebert-Schifferer. Ex. cat. Washington, DC: National Gallery of Art; and New Haven, CT: Yale University Press, 1992.
Mahon, Denis, and Nicolas Turner, *The Drawings of Guercino in the Collection of her Majesty the Queen at Windsor Castle*. Cambridge, England: Cambridge University Press, 1989.

Carlo Maderno
Hibbard, Howard, *Carlo Maderno and Roman Architecture 1580–1630*. University Park, PA, and London: Pennsylvania State University Press, 1971.

Mattia Preti
Spike, John T. with Michèle K. Spike, *Mattia Preti: Catalogo ragionato dei dipinti*. Florence: Centro Di, 1999.

Guido Reni
Colantuono, Anthony, *Guido Reni's Abduction of Helen: The Politics and Rhetoric of Painting in Seventeenth-Century Europe*. Cambridge, England: Cambridge University Press, 1997.
Hibbard, Howard, "Guido Reni's Painting of the Immaculate Conception," *Metropolitan Museum of Art Bulletin*, 1969, Vol. 2, pp. 18–32.
Pepper, D. Stephen, *Guido Reni*. New York: New York University Press, 1984.
Spear, Richard E., *The "Divine" Guido: Religion, Sex, Money, and Art in the World of Guido Reni*. New Haven, CT, and London: Yale University Press, 1997.

Salvator Rosa
Kitson, Michael, et al., *Salvator Rosa*. London: Hayward Gallery: and The Arts Council, 1973.
Scott, Jonathan, *Salvator Rosa*. New Haven, CT, and London: Yale University Press, 1995.

Andrea Sacchi
Harris, Ann Sutherland, *Andrea Sacchi*. London: Phaidon Press; and Princeton, NJ: Princeton University Press, 1977.

SPAIN

General Studies
Brown, Jonathan, *Images and Ideas in Spanish Seventeenth-Century Painting*. Princeton, NJ: Princeton University Press, 1978.
Brown, Jonathan, *The Golden Age of Painting in Spain*. New Haven, CT, and London, 1991. Revised and expanded as *Painting in Spain, 1500–1700*. New Haven, CT, and London: Pelican History of Art, Penguin, 1998.

Brown, Jonathan, and John H. Elliott, *A Palace for a King: The Buen Retiro and the Court of Philip IV*. New Haven, CT, and London: Yale University Press, 1980.
Elliott, J.H., *Spain and its World, 1500–1700*. New Haven, CT, and London: Yale University Press, 1989.
Jordan, William B., and Sarah Schroth, *Spanish Still-Life in the Golden Age*. Fort Worth, TX: Kimbell Art Museum, 1985.
Jordan, William B., and Peter Cherry, *Spanish Still-Life from Velázquez to Goya*. London: National Gallery Publications; and New Haven, CT: Yale University Press, 1995.
Rosenthal, E.E., *The Cathedral of Granada*. Princeton, NJ: Princeton University Press, 1961.
Trusted, Marjorie, *Spanish Sculpture: Catalogue of the Post-Medieval Spanish Sculpture in Wood in the Victoria and Albert Museum*. London: Victoria and Albert Museum Publications, 1996.
Webster, Susan Verdi, *Art and Ritual in Golden-Age Spain: Sevillian Confraternities and the Processional Sculptures of Holy Week*. Princeton, NJ: Princeton University Press, 1998.

Artists
Alonso Cano
Wethey, Harold E., *Alonso Cano: Painter, Sculptor, and Architect*. Princeton, NJ: Princeton University Press, 1955.

Juan Martínez Montañés
Proske, B.G., *Juan Martínez Montañés*. New York: Hispanic Society of America, 1967.

Bartolomé Esteban Murillo
Brown, J., *Murillo and his Drawings*. Princeton, NJ: Princeton University Press, 1976.
Gaya Nuno, J.A., *L'opera completa di Murillo*. Milan: Rizzoli, 1978.
Iniguez, Diego Angulo, et al., *Bartolomé Esteban Murillo, 1617–1682*. Madrid: Prado, 1982; and London: Royal Academy, 1983.

Jusepe de Ribera
Brown, Jonathan, *Jusepe de Ribera: Prints and Drawings*. Ex. cat. Princeton, N.J: Princeton University Press, 1973.
Felton, Craig M., and William B. Jordan, *Jusepe de Ribera, lo Spagnoletto: 1591–1652*. Seattle, WA: Washington University Press, 1982; and Fort Worth, TX: Kimbell Art Museum.
Pérez Sánchez, Alfonso E., and Nicola Spinosa, *Jusepe de Ribera, 1591–1652*. New York: Harry N. Abrams and Metropolitan Museum of Art, 1992.

Diego Velázquez
Brown, Jonathan, *Velázquez: Painter and Courtier*. New Haven, CT, and London: Yale University Press, 1986.
Harris, Enriqueta, *Velázquez*. Ithaca, N.Y, and Oxford: Cornell University Press, 1982.
Stratton-Pruitt, Suzanne L., ed., *The Cambridge Companion to Velázquez*. Cambridge, England: Cambridge University Press, 2002.

Francisco de Zurbarán
Baticle, Jeannine, *Zurbarán*. New York: Harry N. Abrams and Metropolitan Museum of Art, 1987–1988. Additional essays by Y. Bottineau, J. Brown, and A.E. Pérez Sánchez.
Brown, Jonathan, *Zurbarán*. New York: Harry N. Abrams, 1973; 2nd ed., 1991.

PICTURE CREDITS

Pictures have for the most part been supplied by the museums credited in the captions alongside the illustrations. Sources for illustrations not supplied by museums or collections, additional information, and copyright credits are given below. Numbers are picture numbers unless otherwise indicated.

0.1 © Araldo De Luca, Rome; 0.3 © Photo Josse, Paris; 0.6 © Paul M.R. Maeyaert; 1.2 © Quattrone, Florence / www.Photoarchive.it; 1.3 © Vincenzo Pirozzi, Rome / fotopirozzi@inwind.it; 1.4 © Fotomas Index, Kent; 1.5 © Vincenzo Pirozzi, Rome; 1.7 © RMN, Paris; 1.9 Ministero per i Beni e le Attività Culturali, Bologna; 1.10, 1.11 © Scala, Florence; 1.12 © CAMERAPHOTO Arte, Venice; 1.13 Ministero per i Beni e le Attività Culturali, Bologna; 1.14 Reproduced from the Collections of the Library of Congress Z62/62873; 1.15 © Fotografica Foglia, Naples; 1.17 Ministero per i Beni e le Attività Culturali, Bologna; 1.19 © British Museum, London; 1.20 © Photo Josse, Paris; 1.21 Soprintendenza P.S.A.D. Bologna, Archivio Fotografico; 1.22 © Alinari, Florence; 1.23 Ministero per i Beni e le Attività Culturali, Bologna; 1.24, 1.25, 1.26 © Vincenzo Pirozzi, Rome; 1.28 www.araldodeluca.com; 1.29 © Fotografica Foglia, Naples; 1.30 www.araldodeluca.com; 1.31, 1.32 www.bridgeman.co.uk; 1.33, 1.34 © Vincenzo Pirozzi, Rome; 1.35 © Fotografica Foglia, Naples; 1.36 Bildarchiv Preussicher Kulturbesitz, Berlin; 1.37 © Alinari, Florence; 1.39 © Quattrone, Florence; 1.40 © Vincenzo Pirozzi, Rome; 1.41 © Quattrone, Florence; 1.42 Canali Photobank, Milan; 1.43 Bildarchiv Preussicher Kulturbesitz, Berlin; 1.44 Canali Photobank, Milan; 1.45 © Vincenzo Pirozzi, Rome; 1.46 Bildarchiv Preussicher Kulturbesitz, Berlin; 1.47 © Alinari, Florence; 1.48 © Photo Josse, Paris; 1.49 © Scala, Florence; 1.50 © Vincenzo Pirozzi, Rome; 1.51 www.bridgeman.co.uk; 1.52 © Prado Museum, Madrid; 1.53 Bildarchiv Foto Marburg; 1.54 Gift of Mr Leslie H. Green. Photograph © 1984; The Detroit Institute of Arts; 1.56 © Artothek; 1.57 © Alinari, Florence; 1.58, 1.60 © Vincenzo Pirozzi, Rome; 1.61 By kind permission of the Photographic Archive of the Soprintendenza Speciale per il Polo Museale Romano; 1.62 © Fotografica Foglia, Naples; 1.63 © Vincenzo Pirozzi, Rome; 1.64 © Scala, Florence; 1.65 © Vincenzo Pirozzi, Rome; 1.66 © Scala, Florence; 1.67 Ministero per i Beni e le Attività Culturali, Bologna; 1.68 © Vincenzo Pirozzi, Rome; 1.69 © Photo Josse, Paris; 1.70 © Vincenzo Pirozzi, Rome; 1.73 © Alinari, Florence; 1.74 © Vincenzo Pirozzi, Rome; 1.75 Bildarchiv Preussicher Kulturbesitz, Berlin; 1.78 © Vincenzo Pirozzi, Rome; 1.79 © Araldo De Luca, Rome; 1.80 © Scala, Florence; 1.81, 1.82, 1.83 © Vincenzo Pirozzi, Rome; 1.84 © Alinari, Florence; 1.85 © Quattrone, Florence; 1.86 © Vincenzo Pirozzi, Rome; 1.87 © Alinari, Florence; 1.88 © Araldo De Luca, Rome; 1.89, 1.90, 1.91 © Vincenzo Pirozzi, Rome; 1.92 © 2004 Photo Pierpont Morgan Library / Art Resource / Scala, Firenze; 1.93 © Alinari, Florence; 1.94, 1.95 © Vincenzo Pirozzi, Rome; 1.96 © Alinari, Florence; 1.97, 1.98, 1.99, 1.100, 1.101 © Vincenzo Pirozzi, Rome; 1.103 Achim Bednorz, Cologne; 1.104, 1.105 © Alinari, Florence; 1.107, 1.108, 1.109, 1.110, 1.111 © Scala, Florence; 1.112 © Vincenzo Pirozzi, Rome; 1.113 © Araldo De Luca, Rome; 1.114, 1.115, 1.116, 1.117 © Vincenzo Pirozzi, Rome; 1.118 © Prado Museum, Madrid; 1.121, 1.122 © Vincenzo Pirozzi, Rome; 1.123 Photo © John Beldon Scott; 1.124 © Vincenzo Pirozzi, Rome; 1.125 © Quattrone, Florence; 1.126, 1.127, 1.128 © Vincenzo Pirozzi, Rome; 1.129 © Scala, Florence; 1.130, 1.131, 1.132, 1.133 © Vincenzo Pirozzi, Rome; 1.136 © Fotografica Foglia, Naples; 1.137 Toledo Museum of Art. Purchased with funds from the Libbey Endowment, Gift of Edward Drummond Libbey, 1961.30; 1.138 www.bridgeman.co.uk; 1.139 © Quattrone, Florence; 1.140 Bildarchiv Preussicher Kulturbesitz, Berlin; 2.0 © Arthothek; 2.1 © Paul M.R. Maeyaert; 2.6 © Prado Museum, Madrid; 2.11 © 2004, Photo Pierpont Morgan Library / Art Resource / Scala, Firenze; 2.12 © Alinari, Florence; 2.13 Photographie © Musée de Grenoble; 2.15 © IRPA–Brussels; 2.16 Reproduced from the Collections of the Library of Congress, Washington, DC. Z62/62870/62871/62872; 2.17 © IRPA–Brussels; 2.18 www.bridgeman.co.uk / Peter Willi; 2.19 © Scala, Florence; 2.20 © British Museum, London; 2.21 Philadelphia Museum of Art: Purchased with the W.P. Wilstach Fund; 2.23 © Paul M.R. Maeyaert; 2.26, 2.27, 2.28, 2.29 © Photo Josse, Paris; 2.30 © IRPA–Brussels; 2.37 www.bridgeman.co.uk; 2.39 © Prado Museum, Madrid; 2.40 www.bridgeman.co.uk; 2.41 © Alinari, Florence; 2.42 © Quattrone, Florence; 2.43 © Fotografica Foglia, Naples; 2.44 National Gallery of Art, Washington, DC. Widener Collection. Image © 2004 Board of Trustees, National Gallery of Art, Washington, DC; 2.45 © Vincenzo Pirozzi, Rome; 2.49 © IRPA–Brussels; 2.53 © Prado Museum, Madrid; 2.54 Rheinisches Bildarchiv, Cologne; 2.57 © Collectiebeleid Antwerpen; 3.0 © Fotografica Foglia, Naples; 3.1 Bildarchiv Foto Marburg; 3.2 Oronoz, Madrid; 3.3 © Paul M.R. Maeyaert; 3.4 Oronoz, Madrid; 3.5 www.bridgeman.co.uk; 3.7 Wadsworth Atheneum, Hartford. The Ella Gallup Sumner and Mary Catlin Sumner Collection Fund; 3.8, 3.9 © Fotografica Foglia, Naples; 3.10 Columbia Museum of Art, South Carolina, canvas 100 x 69". Gift of Samuel H. Kress Collection CMA 1962.19; 3.11 © Fotografica Foglia, Naples; 3.12 © Photo Josse, Paris; 3.13 The Metropolitan Museum of Art, Samuel D. Lee Fund, 1934 (35.73). Photograph © 1979 The Metropolitan Museum of Art; 3.14 © Fotografica Foglia, Naples; 3.15 The Art Institute of Chicago (Robert A. Waller Memorial Fund, 1954.15); 3.16 Wadsworth Atheneum, Hartford. The Ella Gallup Sumner and Mary Catlin Sumner Collection Fund; 3.17 © Prado Museum, Madrid; 3.18 Photographie © Musée de Grenoble; 3.21 Philadelphia Museum of Art: Purchased with the W.P. Wilstach Fund, 1900; 3.23 © Prado Museum, Madrid; 3.24 www.bridgeman.co.uk; 3.25 Oronoz, Madrid; 3.27, 3.28, 3.29, 3.30, 3.32, 3.33 © Prado Museum, Madrid; 3.34 Copyright The Frick Collection, New York; 3.36 © Alinari, Florence; 3.37 The Metropolitan Museum of Art, Fletcher Fund, Rogers Fund, and Bequest of Miss Adelaide Milton de Groot (1876–1967), supplemented by gifts from the friends of the Museum, 1971 (1971.86). 3.38 © Prado Museum, Madrid; 3.39 © Photo Josse, Paris; 3.40, 3.41 © Prado Museum, Madrid; 3.43 www.bridgeman.co.uk; 3.45 © Paul M.R. Maeyaert; 3.46 © Patrimonio Nacional, Madrid / photo Paul M.R. Maeyaert; 4.0, 4.1 © RMN, Paris; 4.2 Photothèque des Musées de la Ville de Paris; 4.3 A.F. Kersting, London; 4.5, 4.7 © Paul M.R. Maeyaert; 4.8 © Fotomas Index, Kent; 4.9, 4.10 © Paul M.R. Maeyaert 4.11 © Photo Josse, Paris; 4.12 © RMN, Paris; 4.13 Editions Photographiques Marius BAR, Toulon; 4.14 © RMN, Paris; 4.15 © Angelo Hornak, London; 4.16 © RMN, Paris–Le Mage / Blot; 4.17 © British Museum, London; 4.18 © Fotomas Index, Kent; 4.21 © Photo Josse, Paris; 4.23 © RMN, Paris; 4.24 National Gallery of Art, Washington, DC. Ailsa Mellon Bruce Fund. Image © 2004 Board of Trustees, National Gallery of Art, Washington, DC; 4.25, 4.26 © Photo Josse, Paris; 4.28 Fine Arts Museums of San Francisco, Museum Purchase, Mildred Anna Williams Collection, 1977.10; 4.30 National Gallery of Art, Washington, DC. Samuel H. Kress Collection. Image © 2004 Board of Trustees, National Gallery of Art, Washington, DC; 4.31 © Photo Josse, Paris; 4.36 Musée des Beaux Arts de Caen, Martine Seyve Photographe; 4.37 www.bridgeman.co.uk; 4.38 © Photo Josse, Paris; 4.41, 4.42 www.bridgeman.co.uk; 4.44, 4.45 © Photo Josse, Paris; 4.46 Bildarchiv Preussicher Kulturbesitz, Berlin; 4.47 The Art Insitute of Chicago (A.A. Munger Collection, 1930.500); 4.49 © RMN, Paris; 4.52 Museum of Fine Arts, Boston. Seth K. Sweetser Fund 44.72. Photograph © 2004 Museum of Fine Arts, Boston; 4.55 The Metropolitan Museum of Art, Fletcher Fund, 1955 (55.119). Photograph © 1975 The Metropolitan Museum of Art; 4.58 © Fotografica Foglia, Naples; 4.59 © RMN, Paris; 4.60 © Photo Josse, Paris; 4.61 © RMN, Paris; 4.62 © British Museum, London; 4.63, 4.64 © Photo Josse, Paris; 5.0 The Metropolitan Museum of Art, Bequest of Benjamin Altman, 1913 (14.40.605). Photograph © 2000 The Metropolitan Museum of Art; 5.4 AGO / Sean Weaver; 5.5 © Allen Memorial Art Museum, Oberlin College, Ohio. R.T. Miller Jr. Fund, 1953; 5.7 Carnegie Museum of Art, Pittsburgh; Acquired through the generosity of Mrs. Alan M. Scaife; 5.8 Bildarchiv Preussicher Kulturbesitz, Berlin; 5.9 © English Heritage Photo Library; 5.11 National Gallery of Art, Washington, DC. Andrew W. Mellon Collection. Image © 2004 Board of Trustees, National Gallery of Art, Washington, DC; 5.17, 5.18, 5.20 © Paul M.R. Maeyaert; 5.22 Courtesy Bildarchiv Preussicher Kulturbesitz, Berlin; 5.25 Copyright The Frick Collection, New York; 5.27 © 2004 Museum of Fine Arts, Boston, Massachusetts. All rights reserved / www.bridgeman.co.uk; 5.28 © Artothek / Joachim Blauel; 5.32 Bildarchiv Preussicher Kulturbesitz, Berlin; 5.34 The Metropolitan Museum of Art, Bequest of Mrs. H.O. Havemeyer, 1929. The H.O. Havemeyer Collection. (29.107.16); 5.36 © Fotomas Index, Kent; 5.39 www.bridgeman.co.uk; 5.40 © English Heritage Photo Library; 5.49 Bildarchiv Preussicher Kulturbesitz, Berlin; 5.51 Staatliche Museen zu Berlin–Preussischer Kulturbesitz Gemäldegalerie, foto Jörg P. Anders; 5.52 Bildarchiv Preussicher Kulturbesitz, Berlin; 5.59 National Gallery of Art, Washington, DC. Widener Collection. Image © 2004 Board of Trustees, National Gallery of Art, Washington, DC; 5.62 © Museo Thyssen-Bornemisza, Madrid; 5.71 The Art Institute of Chicago (Mr. & Mrs. Potter Palmer Collection 1947.475); 6.0 © Angelo Hornak, London; 6.1 Victoria & Albert Museum Picture Library; 6.2 © RMN, Paris; 6.5 Image © 2004 Board of Trustees, National Gallery of Art, Washington, DC; 6.6 © Prado Museum, Madrid; 6.7 © Tate, London 2004; 6.9, 6.11, 6.12, 6.13, 6.15 A.F. Kersting, London.

INDEX

Abbate, Niccolò dell' 244
Abduction of Helen, The (Reni, 1631) 69–70, **69**
Abraham 333–4
Abraham Dismissing Hagar and Ishmael (Lastman, 1612) 333–4, **334**
academies xvii
    Academia de Dibujos 236
    Academia de San Fernando 237
    Academy of Painting 270
    Accademia degli Incamminate 8, 9, 56
    Accademia di San Luca xvii, 125, 260, 304
    French Academy (Académie Royale; Royal Academy) xvii, 260, 267, 304, 309
Acevedo, Don Manuel de 205
administrative skills 106, 113, 125, 160, 260, 304, 403
"Admiration with Astonishment" (Le Brun, 1696) **307**
Adonis 278, 279, 283
Adoration of the Magi (Rubens, 1624) 168–9, **168**
Adoration of the Magi (Velázquez) 212
Adoration of the Magi (Zurbarán, 1638) 212–13, **212**
Adoration of the Shepherds (Jordaens, 1657) 182, 185–6, **186**
Adoration of the Shepherds (Maino, 1612–13) 218, **218**
Adoration of the Shepherds (Tibaldi, 1549) **4**
Adriana van Heusden and her Daughter at the New Fishmarket, Amsterdam (Witte, 1662) 365, **365**
Aeneas, Anchises, and Ascanius (Bernini, 1618–19) 86, **87**
Agucchi, Giovanni Battista 56, 57
Ajax 283
Alba, Duke of 144
Albani, Francesco 56, 120
Albert, Archduke 147, 152, 165, 195
Aldobrandini, Pietro 56, 57
Aldobrandini family 60
Aletta Hanemans (Hals) 322
Alexander VII: xiii, 6, 78, 82, 87, 107
Alexander the Great 306, 307–8
Alexander the Great with Diogenes (Puget, 1671–93) 243, 256
Algardi, Alessandro 93–6, 113
    Donna Olympia Maidalchini 93, **93**
    Pope Leo I Driving Attila from Rome 108, **109**
    St. Mary Magdalene 94, 97, **97**
    St. Philip Neri with an Angel 94–5, **94**
    Tomb of Leo XI Medici 94, 95–6, **95**
alla prima 35
allegories xvi
Allegory of Divine Wisdom, (Sacchi, 1629–30) 121–3, **121**
Allegory of the Four Corners of the World (Rubens, c. 1615) 162, **162**
Allegory of Painting (Mieris) 369
altarpieces 12–13, 21, 68
Altdorfer, Albrecht 378
Alva, Duke of 311, 313
Amphitrite 283
Amsterdam 312, 328–32, 333–4, 336, 344, 345
Amsterdam Town Hall before 1651 (Sanraedam, 1657) 330, **330**
Anatomy Lesson of Dr. Nicolaes Tulp (Rembrandt, 1632) 336–8, **337**
ancient art xxi
Andrew, St. 101
angels 38, 41, 65, 94, 110, 111, 216, 217, 270
Angels' Kitchen (Murillo) 232

Anna 335
Anne, St. 207
Annunciation, The (Reni, 1609–11) 65, **66**
Annunciation, The (Zurbarán, 1650) 216, **216**
Anslo, Cornelis van 344
anti-war images 258
Antonio Coppola (Bernini) 91
Antonio da Sangallo the younger 5
    Palazzo Farnese, façade **24**
Antwerp
    economy xii, 143
    Peeters 187
    riots 144
    Rubens 152–65
    still-life 188
    town hall 331
    van Dyck 174–6, 180
    war 165
Apollo 66, 90–1, 283
Apollo and Daphne (Bernini, 1623–24) 88, 90–1, **90**
Apollo and Daphne (Poussin) 292
Apollo Tended by Nymphs (Girardon) 256
apprentices xvii
Archangel Michael, The (Reni, 1635) **70**, 71
Archduke Leopold-Wilhelm in his Gallery in Brussels (Teniers, the Younger, 1651) 192, **193**
Archery Contest of Diana and her Nymphs (Domenichino, 1616) 60–1, **60**
architecture
    Dutch Republic 327–32
    England 396–403
    France 243–53
    Rome 4–7, 78–89
    Spain 196–7
Ariadne 28
Armida 181–2
Armida Abducting Rinaldo (Poussin) 282
art, economics of xii–xiii
"art collection" paintings 186, 189, 191–2
art collectors 192, 248
Art of Painting, The (Vermeer, c. 1666–67) xvi, 366, 373–4, **373**
Artist in his Studio, The (Rembrandt, c. 1627–28) 338, **338**
artists xvi, xvii
    "As the Old Sing, so the Young Pipe" (Jordaens, c. 1640–45) 184–5, **185**
Ascension (Rembrandt) 339
Assereto, Gioacchino 234
Assumption of the Virgin (Bernini, Pietro) 108
Assumption of the Virgin (Carracci, Annibale, 1601) 31, **31**, 42, 43
Assumption of the Virgin (Lanfranco, 1625–28) 64, **64**
Astronomer, The (Vermeer) 367
astronomy xiii–xiv
Aurora 66, 74
Aurora (Guercino, 1621) 74, **75**
Aurora (Reni, 1614) 66, **67**
Autumn (Poussin, 1660–64) 292–3, **293**
avenues 78
Averkamp, Hendrik 380, 385

Baburen, Dirck van, *Procuress* 358, 367
Bacchanal of the Andrians (Titian, 1523–25) 114, **115**, 222
Bacchus 28, 36
Bacchus (Caravaggio, 1595–96) 36–7, **36**
Bacchus and Ariadne (Titian) 114
Baciccio, Il *see* Gaulli, Giovanni Battista

Baglione, Giovanni 45
Baldacchino (Bernini, 1624–33) 79–80, 99–100
Baldacchino, St. Peter's, Duquesnoy 96
Baldassare Castiglione (Raphael, c. 1514–15) xv–xvi, xv, 342–3
Baldinucci, Filippo 295
Balen, Hendrick van 174
Banquet of the Officers of the St. George Civic Guard (Cornelisz. van Haarlam, 1599) 324, **324**
Banqueting House (Jones, 1619–22) 396–8, **397**
Baptism (Poussin) 284
Barberini, Antonio 71
Barberini, Antonio, the Younger 121, 123
Barberini, Maffeo *see* Urban VIII
Barberini family 275
Barbieri, Giovanni Francesco *see* Guercino
Barcham, William 108
Barocci, Federico 21, 47, 159
    Presentation of the Virgin at the Temple 22, **22**
Baroque art xxi
Baroque classicism xxi
Baschenis, Evaristo xx
Batista de Toledo, Juan 196
Batoni, Pompeo 133
Beheading of St. John the Baptist, The (Caravaggio, 1608) 47, 48, **48**
Bellori, Giovanni Pietro xix, xxi, 37, 41, 64, 123, 125–6, 273, 288
Bentivoglio, Ezio 178
Bentivoglio, Guido 178
Berchem, Nicolas 383
Berckheyde, Gerrit, *Market Place and the Grote Kerk at Haarlem, The* 327, **328**
Bernini, Gian Lorenzo 86–92, 113
    Aeneas, Anchises, and Ascanius 86, **87**
    Alexander VII: 78
    Antonio Coppola 91
    Apollo and Daphne 88, 90–1, **90**
    Baldacchino 79–80, 99–100
    Cardinal Scipione Borghese bust 91–2, **91**
    Cardinal Scipione Borghese sketch 92, **92**
    caricature 17
    Cathedra Petri 71, 102, 106–8, **107**
    Cattedra Petri 71
    Charles I, bust 391, 398
    David 88, **89**, 90
    Ecstasy of St. Teresa 108–11, **110**
    Four Rivers Fountain 111–13, **111**
    Francesco d'Este, Duke of Modena 92–3, **93**
    Gaulli 127, 129, 131, 132
    Louvre plans 250
    Palazzo Barberini façade 80, **80**
    Pope Paul V: 91, **91**
    Poussin xxi, 278, 293–4
    Rape of Proserpine 88, **88**
    Sant'Andrea al Quirinale 84, 130
    sculptures 85–6
    St. Longinus 100, 101, **101**
    St. Peter's 6, 79
    Sta. Bibiana 97, **97**
    Tomb of Alexander VII: 102, 104, **106**
    Tomb of Urban VIII: 102, 104, **104**
    Triton Fountain 111, **112**
    Urban VIII: 87, 99
    Vision of Constantine, The 102, **102**
    Wren 399
Bernini, Pietro 87, 88
    Assumption of the Virgin 108
Berrettini, Pietro *see* Pietro da Cortona

Berruguete, Alonso 198
Besse, Pierre de 206
Bimbo, Bartolomeo del xx
Birth of Venus, The (Poussin, 1638–40) 283–4, **283**
Bitter Drink (Brouwer, c. 1630) xvi, 189, **191**
Bles, Herri met de 378
Blinding of Samson (Rembrandt, 1636) 339, 340–1
Bloemaert, Abraham 315, 367
Blunt, Anthony 243, 291
body, concepts of xv–xvi
Bol, Ferdinand 354, 356, 395
Bolgi, Andrea, *St. Helena* 100, 101
Bologna 1, 7, 56–77, 94, 134
Bologna, Giovanni da *see* Giambologna
Borghese, Scipione 61, 65, 66, 86, 92
Borngässer, Barbara 196
Borromini, Francesco xxi, 78–84
    Casa dei Filippini 83–4, **84**
    Palazzo Barberini façade **80**
    San Carlo alle Quattro Fontane 80–2, **81**, **82**
    Sant'Ivo alla Sapienza 82–3, **83**
Bosch, Hieronymus, *Table Top with the Seven Deadly Sins* 189
Bosio, Antonio 286
Boucher, Bruce 113
Boulogne, Jean de *see* Giambologna
Bourdon, Sebastian 293
Bouts, Dieric 313
Boy with a Club Foot (Ribera, 1642) 206, **206**
Boy Playing a Flute (Leyster, c. 1635) 359–60, **359**
Boyle, Richard, Earl of Burlington 403
Bracciolini, Francesco 120
Braham, Allan 227
Bramante 5
Brandt, Isabella 154, 171
Brandt, Jan 154
Breda 223
Breenbergh, Bartholomeus 380–1
Brienne, Loménie de 293
Bril, Paul xix, 379
    Fantastic Landscape 379, **379**
Broecke, Pieter van den 321
Brosse, Salomon de 246
    Luxembourg Palace, garden façade **247**
    Luxembourg Palace, plan **247**
Brosses, President de 111
Brouwer, Adriaen 188–9
    Bitter Drink xvi, 189, **191**
Brown, Jonathan 213, 222, 223, 224
Brueghel, Jan, the Elder 159, 160, 186, 189
    Still Life with Bouquet of Flowers 143, **143**, 186–7
Brueghel, Pieter, the Elder 172, 189, 313, 378
Buckingham, Duke of 388
Buoncompagni, Pietro 94
Burgundy, Dukes of 243
Butcher's Shop, The (Carracci, Annibale, c. 1580) 7–8, **8**

Calderón de la Barca, Pedro 195, 223
Calling of St. Matthew, The (Caravaggio, 1599–1600) 38–9, **38**
Calling of Sts. Peter and Andrew (Domenichino) 62
Calling of Sts. Peter and Andrew (Jordaens, c. 1618) 183–4, **183**
Callot, Jacques xiii, 258
    Fan with the Festival of St. James on the Arno 258, **259**
    Great Miseries of War, The 258, **259**
    Pillage of a Farmhouse **259**
    View of Pont Neuf, Paris 245, **245**
Calvaert, Denis 56, 64
Calvinists 144
Cambiaso, Luca 201
Camerino (Carracci, Annibale, 1595–97) 25–6, **25**
Camillus and the School Master of the Falern (Poussin) 282
Campen, Jacob van
    Mauritshuis 332, **332**
    Royal Palace (former Town Hall), Amsterdam 331–2, **331**

Cano, Alonso 200, 216–17
    Christ's Descent into Limbo 227
    Granada Cathedral, façade 196–7, **196**
    St. John the Evangelist's Vision of Jerusalem 217, **217**
Capture of Samson (Steen) 377
Caracciolo, Giovanni Battista 134
    Immaculate Conception with Sts. Dominic and Francis of Paola 134
Caravaggio, Michelangelo Merisi da xxi, 3, 34–49
    Bacchus 36–7, **36**
    Beheading of St. John the Baptist, The 47, 48, **48**
    Calling of St. Matthew, The 38–9, **38**
    Cardsharps, The 35–6, **35**
    Conversion of St. Paul 31, 42, 43, **43**
    Crucifixion of St. Andrew, The 134, **135**
    Crucifixion of St. Peter 31, 42
    David with the Head of Goliath 48–9, **49**
    Death of the Virgin 46–7, **46**, 388
    Entombment of Christ 1, 21, 47
    Flagellation 134
    followers 50–6
    Inspiration of St. Matthew, The (1st version) 41–2, **41**
    Inspiration of St. Matthew, The (2nd version) 42, **42**
    Madonna of the Rosary 182
    Martyrdom of St. Matthew 39, 41, **41**
    Penitent Magdalene 37
    Rest on the Flight into Egypt 37–8, **37**
    Seven Acts of Mercy 134
    Victorious Cupid 44–5, **44**
Cardi, Ludovico *see* Cigoli, Ludovico
Cardinal Bernardino Spada (Reni, 1630–31) 68, 69, 179
Cardinal Guido Bentivoglio (van Dyck, 1622–27) 69, 178–9, **178**
Cardinal Mazarin (Coysevox, 1689–93) 256, 257–8, **257**
Cardinal Richelieu (Girardon, 1694) 256–7, **257**
Cardinal Richelieu (Warin) 256
Cardinal Roberto Ubaldini (Reni) 69
Cardinal Scipione Borghese (Bernini 1632)
    bust 91–2, **91**
    sketch 92, **92**
Cardsharps, The (Caravaggio, c. 1594) 35–6, **35**
caricature 17
Caricature Heads (Carracci, Annibale, c. 1590) 17, **17**
Carlton, Sir Dudley 160
Carracci, Agostino 7, 8, 9, 24, 30
    Crucifixion, after Tintoretto **156**
    Domenichino 56
    Lanfranco 63
    Last Communion of St. Jerome 20–1, **21**
    Mystic Marriage of St. Catherine (after Veronese) 13, **14**
    Story of the Founding of Rome 20
Carracci, Annibale xix, 7–8, 9–10, 14, 17, 21
    Assumption of the Virgin 31, **31**, 42, 43
    Butcher's Shop, The 7–8, **8**
    Camerino 25–6, **25**
    Caricature Heads 17, **17**
    Choice of Hercules, The 25, 26, **26**
    Crucifixion with Saints 9
    Domenichino 57
    Galleria Farnese 27–31, **27**, **28**, **29**
    Jupiter and Juno, Galleria Farnese **29**
    Landscape with the Flight into Egypt xix, 33–4, **33**
    Landscape with River and Bridge 32–3, **33**
    Lanfranco 63
    Madonna with St. Matthew 13, 15, **15**, 16, 19
    Mystic Marriage of St. Catherine 14, **14**
    Pietà 32, **32**, 282
    Pietà with Virgin and Saints 10, 12, **12**
    Resurrection of Christ, The 18–19, **18**
    Rome 24–34, 56, 63
    sacra conversazione 181
    Story of the Founding of Rome 19, **19**, 20
    Study of Reclining Boy 7

Carracci, Ludovico 7, 9, 14, 21
    Conversion of St. Paul 9, **10**
    Family of Beggars 7
    Madonna degli Scalzi 16, **16**, 17, 19
    Madonna dei Bargellini 13, **13**, 16, 19
    Reni 64
    Story of the Founding of Rome 20, **20**
    studio 94
    Virgin and Child with Saints Joseph and Francis 72
Carracci family 3, 7–21
Carracci succession 56–77
Carreño de Miranda, Juan 241
Caryatids on the Pavillon de l'Horloge (Sarrazin & Guèrin, 1641) 254–5, **254**
Casa dei Filippini (Borromini) 83–4
Cassava Plant with Caterpillar and Butterflies (Merian, 1705) **xiv**
Cassiano dal Pozzo 274
Castillo, Juan del 232
Cathedra Petri (Bernini, 1657–66) 71, 102, 106–8, **107**
Catherine, St. 14, 76–7, 207
Catholic Church 1
Catholics xi, xii
Cavallino, Bernardo 134–5
    Judith with the Head of Holofernes 135, **136**
    St. Cecilia in Ecstasy 135
Cecilia, St. 58–9, 98
ceiling decoration, Italy 31
Cenci, Beatrice 98
Cerasi, Tiberio 31, 42
Cervantes, Miguel de 195
Cesari, Giuseppe d'Arpino 21–2, 38, 120
    Coronation of the Virgin 23, **23**
Champaigne, Philippe de 269–73, 303
    Dream of St. Joseph 270, **270**
    Mother Cathérine-Agnès Arnauld and Sister Cathérine de Ste. Suzanne Champaigne 272–3, **272**
    Omer Talon 270–2, **271**
Chancellor Séguier (Le Brun, 1660–61) 305–6, **305**
Chantelou, Paul Fréart de 280, 284, 287, 293–4
Charles I, of England 147, 174, 181, 182, 388–9, 391, 392, 397
Charles I, bust (Bernini) 391, 398
Charles I with James, Duke of York (Lely) 394
Charles I with Monseigneur de St. Antoine (van Dyck, 1633) 389, **391**
Charles I in Three Positions (van Dyck, c. 1635) 92, 389, 391, **391**
Charles II, of England 401, 402
Charles II, of Spain 140, 240
Charles V, of Spain 143, 201
Charles Le Brun (Largillière, 1686) 309, **309**
Cheat with the Ace of Clubs, The (La Tour) 265
Cheat with the Ace of Diamonds, The (La Tour, c. 1630) 265, **265**
Chiesa Nuova (Longhi, 1575–1606) **152**
Chiesa Nuova (Rughesi, 1575–1605) 84, **84**
Chigi, Agostino 30
Chigi Chapel 126
Chigi, Fabio *see* Alexander VII
children 201, 232, 233–4, 325
Choice of Hercules, The (Carracci, Annibale, 1597) 25, 26, **26**
Christ, Jesus 9, 12–17, 18–19, 23, 32, 37, 39, 47, 50, 62, 63, 72, 76–7, 129, 155–7, 158, 159, 176, 183, 184, 199, 209, 212, 214, 234, 266–7, 286, 352
Christ of Clemency (Montañés, 1603–6) 198–9, **199**
Christ on the Cross (Pacheco) 209
Christ Crowned with Thorns (van Dyck, c. 1620) 175–6, **175**
Christ in the House of Martha and Mary (Vermeer) 367
Christ and the Woman Taken in Adultery (Rembrandt, 1644) 348, **348**
Christopher Wren (Pierce, 1673) 398, **398**
Christ's Descent into Limbo (Cano) 227
Cigoli, Ludovico (Cardi) xiv, 159
    Descent from the Cross 159, **159**

city planning 4–7, 78–84, 102, 243–8, 327–32, 398
Claes van Voorhout (Hals) 322
Claesz, Pieter 313
   Vanitas Still Life xx–xxi, 356, **356**
classical art xxi
Claude Lorrain (Claude Gellée) 273, 289, 295–303
   Embarkation of the Queen of Sheba 300, **300**, 301
   Grotto of Neptune at Tivoli 297, **297**
   Lake Albano and Castelgandolfo 298, **298**
   Landscape with the Marriage of Isaac and Rebecca (The Mill) 300, **300**, 301
   Landscape with the Nymph Egeria Mourning over Numa 302, **302**
   Mill, The 296, **296**, 301
   patrons 295, 298
   Trojan Women Setting Fire to their Fleet 298–9, **299**
Clement VIII: 114
Clement IX: 129
Clement IX (Gaulli, 1667–68) 129, **129**
Clement X: 126
clients *see* patrons
Cobaert, Jacob 41
Coello, Claudio 241
   Sagrada Forma 241, **241**
Cointrel, Matteu 38
Colbert, Jean-Baptiste xiii, 250, 255, 309
Colonna, Don Lorenzo Onofrio 295, 302
commissions 114
Commodi, Andrea 113
Concert, The (ter Brugghen, 1626) 316, **316**
Concert, The (Vermeer) 370
Concino, Concino 165
Conférence sur l'expression générale et particulière (Le Brun) 303
Confirmation (Poussin) 284, 294
Conspiracy of the Batavians under Claudius Civilis (Rembrandt) 352
Constantijn Huygens with his Page (Keyser, 1627) 321–2, **321**
Conventi, Giulio Cesare 94
Conversion of St. Paul (Caravaggio, c.1601) 31, 42, 43, **43**
Conversion of St. Paul (Carracci, Ludovico, 1587–89) 9, **10**
Conversion of St. Paul (Michelangelo, 1542–45) 9, **11**
Cooper, Samuel 387
Copernicus, Nicolaus xiv
Cornaro, Federico 108
Cornelis and Lucas de Wael (van Dyck, 1621–22) 180, **180**
Cornelis van Anslo and his Wife (Rembrandt, 1641) 344–5, **344**
Cornelisz. van Haarlam, Cornelis 313, 324
   Banquet of the Officers of the St. George Civic Guard 324, **324**
Coronation of Marie (Rubens) 167
Coronation of the Virgin (Cesari, 1592–1614) 23, **23**
Coronation of the Virgin with Four Saints (Reni) 64
Corot, Jean Baptiste Camille 293
Correggio 10
Cortona, Pietro da xxi, 6, 21, 78, 113–20, 123–5
   Glorification of the Reign of Urban VIII: 119–20, **119**
   Martyrdom of St. Lawrence 117, **117**, 119
   Medici Prince Taken from Venus by Minerva 124–5, **124**
   Puget 255
   Rape of the Sabine Women 116, **116**
   Santa Maria della Pace 79
   Santi Luca e Martina 84
   St. Peter Damian Offering the Rule of the Camaldolese Order to the Virgin 117, **117**
   Sta. Bibiana Refusing to Sacrifice to Pagan Idols 113, **114**
   studio 125
   Triumph of Bacchus 114, **115**
Cosimo II de' Medici 74
cosmology xiii–xiv
Cotán, Juan Sánchez 215
Council of the Gods (Rubens) 168

Council of Trent 3
Country Road with House (Wals, c. 1625) 295, **295**
Coysevox, Antoine 256–8
   Cardinal Mazarin 256, 257–8, **257**
Cromwell, Oliver 388, 394
Cropper, Elizabeth 286
Crowning with Thorns (Titian, c. 1542–44) 176, **176**
Crucified Christ (Velázquez) 199
Crucifixion (Carracci, Agostino, after Tintoretto, 1589) 156
Crucifixion (Tintoretto) 155
Crucifixion, The (Zurbarán, 1627) 209, **209**
Crucifixion of Christ with Angels (Le Brun) 303
Crucifixion with Saints (Carracci, Annibale) 9
Crucifixion of St. Andrew, The (Caravaggio, 1607) 134, **135**
Crucifixion of St. Peter (Caravaggio) 31, 42
Crucifixion of St. Peter (Reni, 1604–5) 65, **65**
Crucifixion with the Virgin, St. John, and Another Figure (Ribera) 203
Cupid 44
Cybo, Alderano 126
Cyclops 28

daily life, scenes of xviii
Damian, St. Peter 117
Daniele da Volterra 159
Daphne 90
David 48–9, 90
David, Jacques Louis, *Death of Socrates* 275
David (Bernini, 1623–24) 88, **89**, 90
David with the Head of Goliath (Caravaggio, c.1609–10) 48–9, **49**
Death of Adonis (Poussin, c. 1626) 278, **278**
Death of General Wolfe (West, 1771) 275
Death of Germanicus, The (Poussin, 1627) **274**, 275
Death of Henry IV and the Proclamation of Marie de' Medici as Regent (Rubens, 1622–25) 167, **167**
Death of Socrates (David, Jacques Louis, 1787) 275
Death of St. Anne (Sacchi, 1649) **122**, 123
Death of St. Francis Xavier (Gaulli, 1676) 130, **130**
Death Surprising a Young Couple (Velde II, 1616) 357, **357**
Death of the Virgin (Caravaggio, c. 1601–2) 46–7, **46**, 388
Deigo de Avedo (Velázquez) 226
Déjeuner sur l'herbe (Manet, 1863) 146
del Monte, Francesco Maria 34–5, 120, 122
Delft 372–3
Delilah 340
Deluge (Winter) (Poussin) 292, 293
Dempsey, Charles 45, 286
Deruet, Claude 295
Desastres de la Guerra, Los (Goya) 258
Descent from the Cross (Cigoli, 1608) 159, **159**
Descent from the Cross (Rembrandt, c. 1633) 338–9, **340**
Descent from the Cross (Rubens, 1611–12) 154, 158, **158**, 338
Destitute Artist with His Family (Elsheimer, c. 1605) 55, **55**
Diana 28, 60–1
Diana and her Companions (Vermeer) 367
Dircx, Geertge 346
disegno 374
Disputation on the Holy Sacrament (Raphael) 126
Dobson, William 393, 394
   Endymion Porter 394
Domenichino (Domenico Zampieri) 21, 34, 56–63, 94, 134
   Archery Contest of Diana and her Nymphs 60–1, **60**
   Calling of Sts. Peter and Andrew 62
   Last Communion of St. Jerome 59–60, **59**
   St. Cecilia Distributing Alms 58, **59**
   Treasury Chapel, San Gennaro 205
   Vault of the Tribune 61–2, **62**
   Virgin and the Unicorn, The 31, 57, **57**
domestic subjects 357
Donna Olympia Maidalchini (Algardi, c.1650) 93, **93**
Dou, Gerrit 354, 357, 361
   Young Mother, The xviii, 359, 362–3, **362**

drawing 236–7, 296–7, 314, 343, 347, 381
Drawing Academy, A (Sweerts, c. 1650) **xvii**
Dream of St. Joseph (Champaigne, c. 1638) 270, **270**
Dream of St. Romuald (Sacchi) 123
Drinkers, The (Velázquez, c. 1628) 221–2, **221**
Drunken Silenus (Ribera, 1626) 203–4, **203**
Duquesnoy, François 96–7
   St. Andrew 100, **100**, 102
   Sta. Susanna 96–7, **96**
   Vryburch Monument 96, **96**
Dutch Republic xii, xviii, 311–85
dwarves 225–6, 392
Dyck, Anthony van *see* van Dyck, Anthony

Eastern Europe xi, xii
Ecce Homo (Reni, c. 1640) 71–2, **71**
economics of art xii–xiii
Ecstasy of St. Teresa (Bernini, 1645–52) 108–11, **110**
Edict of Nantes 243
education xvi
Education of Marie de' Medici, The (Rubens, 1622–25) 166–7, **166**
Egeria 302
Einden, Ferndinand van den 136
Elena Grimaldi, Marchesa Cataneo (van Dyck, 1623) 179, **179**
Elijah (Ribera, 1638) 206, **206**
Elizabeth I: 387
Elsheimer, Adam xix, 53, 55–6
   Destitute Artist with His Family 55, **55**
   Flight into Egypt, The xiv, 55–6, **56**
Embarkation of the Queen of Sheba (Claude, 1648) 300, **300**, 301
Endymion Porter (Dobson) 394
England xi, xii, 176–7, 387–403
Ensor, James 193
Entombment (Rembrandt) 339
Entombment of Christ (Caravaggio, 1603–4) **1**, 21, 47
Equestrian Portrait of Conde-Duque de Olivares (Velázquez, 1638) 225, **225**
equestrian portraits 305
Equestrian Statue of Philip IV (Tacca, 1634–40) 198, **198**
Erasmus, St. 277
Erminia 74, 278, 279
Erminia Discovering the Wounded Tancred (Guercino, 1618) 73–4, **73**
Escorial Madonna (Virgin of the Rosary) (Murillo, c. 1650–55) 234, **234**
Eucharist (Poussin) 284
Europe in 1648: **2**
Evelyn, John 113, 363, 395
exploration xiii
Expression of the Passions (Le Brun, 1696) 307
Extreme Unction (Poussin, c. 1638–40) 284, **285**
Eyck, Jan van 313
   Marriage Portrait of Giovanni Arnolfini and Giovanna Cenami 231

Fabritius, Carel 354, 372
   Self-Portrait 356
Family of Beggars (Carracci, Ludovico, c. 1580) 7
Fan with the Festival of St. James on the Arno (Callot, 1619) 258, **259**
Fantastic Landscape (Bril, 1598) 379, **379**
Farnese, Girolamo 299
Farnese, Odoardo 24, 26, 57
Farnese, Ranuccio 63
Farnese family xii, 14, 24, 104
Farnese Hercules (Goltzius, 1617) 24, **25**
Feast of Herod, The (Preti, c. 1665) 136, **138**
Feast of Herod, The (Rubens, c. 1639) 136, 138, **139**
Félibien, André 264, 291, 307
Felicity of her Reign (Rubens) 166
female beauty 288–9
Fernández, Gregorio 200
Ferri, Ciro 125
Finding of Moses, The (Gentileschi, Orazio, 1633) 51–2, **51**
Finelli, Giuliano 91

Index   419

Finis Gloriae Mundi (Valdéz Leal, 1670–72) **xx**
Fiorentino, Rosso 159
First School of Fontainebleau 244
Flagellation (Caravaggio) 134
Flanders 143–93
flesh painting, Rubens 161
Flight into Egypt, The (Elsheimer, 1609) xiv, 55–6, **56**
Flinck, Govert 350, 354, 356
Florence 1, 123–5, 134
Floris, Cornelis, Town Hall, Antwerp **144**
flower paintings 186–7
Fontainebleau 243–4
Fontana, Carlo 126
Fontana, Domenico 4–5
Fontana, Lavinia 52
Fortune Teller, The (Vouet, c. 1620) 50, 260–1, **261**
Fountain of the Turtles (Porta) 111
fountains 111
Fouquet, Nicolas 248, 250, 255, 304
Fouquières, Jacques 270
Four Ages of Man, The (Valentin, c. 1620) 50, 263–4, **263**
Four Rivers Fountain (Bernini, 1648–51) 111–13, **111**
Fourment, Hélène 171
"Fraga Portrait, The" (*Philip IV of Spain*) (Velázquez, 1644) 226, **227**
France xiii, 243–309
Francesco, Cardinal 71
Francesco d'Este, Duke of Modena (Bernini, 1652–53) 92–3, **93**
Francis I: 243, 244
Francis Xavier, St. 130
Franciscans 9
Francisco Leczano (Velázquez) 226
Frans Synders (van Dyck) 176
French Academy (Académie Royale; Royal Academy) xvii, 260, 267, 304, 309
frescoes 21, 57, 63
Fromentin, Eugène 326

Galatea 28, 283
Galatea (Raphael, c. 1512) **30**
Galerie des Glaces, Versailles (Hardouin-Mansart & Le Vau, 1678) 252–3, **253**
ceiling (Le Brun, 308–9)
Galileo Galilei xiv, 122
Galleria (Giordano, 1682–85) 139–40, **140**
Galleria Farnese (Carracci, Annibale, 1595–1600) 27–31, **27, 28, 29**
garden designers, English 302
Garzoni, Giovanna xx
Gaulli, Giovanni Battista (Il Baccicio) 127–33
 Clement IX 129, **129**
 Death of St. Francis Xavier 130, **130**
 Glorification of the Holy Name of Jesus, The 132–3, **132**
 Pietà 129, **129**
 Temperance and Chastity 131, **131**
Geest, Cornelis van der 154
Gelder, Aert van 356
Genoa xi, 1, 134, 255
genre painting xviii–xxi, 186–93, 356
 Dutch Republic 265, 313, 325, 326, 356–78
 Murillo 232, 233–4
 Spain 200–1
 Velázquez 218
Gentileschi, Artemisia 51, 52–3
 Judith and her Handmaid with the Head of Holofernes 53, **55**
 Susanna and the Elders 52–3, **52**
Gentileschi, Orazio 50–2, 53, 134, 388
 Finding of Moses, The 51–2, **51**
 Public Felicity Triumphant over Dangers 247
 Rest on the Flight into Egypt, The 50–1, **50**
geography xiii–xiv
Germanicus 275
Gesù, Il xii, 132–3
Giambologna (Jean de Boulogne) 85, 86, 198
 Neptune Fountain 85, **86**
 Rape of the Sabine Woman 85, **86**

Giaquinto, Corrado 141, 232
Gibbons, Grinling 401
Gibbs, James 403
Giordano, Luca 138–9, 232
 Galleria 139–40, **140**
 St. Michael Vanquishing the Devil 140, **141**
Giovanni da Bologna *see* Giambologna
Girardon, François 256–8
 Apollo Tended by Nymphs 256
 Cardinal Richelieu 256–7, **257**
Girl with a Pearl Earring (Vermeer, c. 1665) 369, **369**
Giulio Romano 244
Giustiniani, Marchese 42, 43–4
Glorification of the Holy Name of Jesus, The (Gaulli, 1676–79) 132–3, **132**
Glorification of the Reign of Urban VIII (Cortona, 1633–39) 119–20, **119**
Glory of St. Dominic (Reni) 65
Goliath 48–9
Goltzius, Hendrick 313–14
 Farnese *Hercules* 24, **25**
 Vertumnus and Pomona 314–15, **315**
 View of the Dunes near Haarlem 314, **314**, 378
Gonzaga, Vincenzo, Duke of Mantua 147, 152
Goudt, Hendrick 55
Gowing, Lawrence 366
Goya, Francisco 141, 232
 Desastres de la Guerre, Los 258
Goyen, Jan van 313, 379–80, 385
 Windmill by a River 380, **380**
Granada Cathedral, façade (Cano) 196–7, **196**
Great Fire, London 399
Great Miseries of War, The (Callot, 1633) 258, **259**
Gregory, St. 152
Gregory XV: 61, 74
Grinling Gibbons (Kneller, c.1690) 395, **395**
Grotto of Neptune at Tivoli (Claude, c. 1640) 297, **297**
Guercino (Giovanni Francesco Barbieri) 21, 72–7
 Aurora 74, **75**
 Erminia Discovering the Wounded Tancred 73–4, **73**
 Guiseppe Gaetano Righetti (?) Presented to the Virgin by Four Saints 72–3, **72**
 Mystic Marriage of St. Catherine, The (1620) 76–7, **76**
 Mystic Marriage of St. Catherine, The (1650) 77, **77**
 Susanna and the Elders 74
Guérin, Gilles, Caryatids on the Pavillon de l'Horloge 254
Guevara, Don Diego de 200
Guicciardini 143
Guild of St. Luke 313, 319
Guiseppe Gaetano Righetti (?) Presented to the Virgin by Four Saints (Guercino, c. 1616–17) 72–3, **72**

Haarlem 313–15, 319, 324, 327–8, 378
Haarlem Militia Company of St. George (Hals, c. 1627) 324–5, **325**
Haecht, Willem van 189
 Picture Gallery of Cornelis van der Geest 191–2, **192**
Hals, Dirck 358
Hals, Frans xix, 175, 188, 313, 319–27
 Aletta Hanemans 322
 Claes van Voorhout 322
 Haarlem Militia Company of St. George 324–5, **325**
 Isaac Massa and Beatrix van der Laen 322–4, **323**
 Jacobus Zaffius 319
 Jasper Schade 322
 Johannes Hoornbeek 322
 Malle Babbe 320, **320**
 Pieter Cornelisz. van der Morsch 319, **319**
 Pieter van den Broecke 320, 321, 322
 Portrait of an Elderly Woman 322, **322**
 Portrait of a Man 327
 Portrait of a Man in a Slouched Hat 327
 Regentesses 326, 327
 Regents of the Old Men's Almshouse 326, **326**
 Shrovetide Revellers **311**, 325–6
 Verdonck Waving a Jawbone 320
 Yonker Ramp and his Sweetheart 326

Hardouin-Mansart, Jules
 Galerie des Glaces, Versailles 252–3, **253**
 Versailles, garden façade and lake 252, **252**
 Versailles, plan **251**
Haro, Gaspar de 226
Harvey, William xv
Hawksmoor, Nicholas 403
Head of the Farnese Hercules (Rubens, 1606–8) 148, **149**
Healing of the Paralytic at the Pool of Bethesda (Murillo) 238
Hearing (Ribera) 202
Heem, Jan Davidsz de 188
 Still Life with Parrots **191**
Heemskerck, Maerten van 313
Helen 70
Helena, St. 101
Hélène Fourment in her Wedding Dress (Rubens, 1630–31) 171, **171**
heliocentrism xiv
Henri IV Receives the Portrait of Marie de' Medici (Rubens, 1622–25) **166**, 167
Henrietta Maria 392
Henry II: 264
Henry IV: xiii, 165, 167, 195, 243, 244, 254, 260, 309
Henry VIII: xi, 387, 388
Hercules 25–6, 124
Herod 138
Herodias 138
Herrera, Francisco de 236
Herrera, Juan de 196
Heusden, Adriana van 365
Hibbard, Howard 87, 100
Hilliard, Nicholas 387
 Man Leaning Against a Tree Among Roses 387, **388**
history paintings 356
Hobbema, Meindart 312
Holbein, Hans 387
Holland 312
Holy Family (Rembrandt, 1645) 348
Holy Family (Rembrandt, 1646) 348
Holy Family with St. John the Baptist (Jordaens, c. 1620) 183, **183**
Holy Family with Sts. Anne and Catherine of Alexandria, The (Ribera, 1648) 207, **208**
Holy Family with the Young St. John the Baptist and his Parents (Rubens, 1630–32) 170, **171**
Honthorst, Gerrit van 264, 315, 388
 St. Sebastian **318**, 319
Hooch, Pieter de 357, 361
 Mother, The 362, 363–4, **363**
Horatius Coclius at the Bridge (Le Brun) 304
Hôtel de la Vrillière (Mansart, 1635–38) 248, **248**
Houbraken, Arnold 351
Houses of Parliament (Jones) 396
Howard, Thomas, Earl of Arundel 176, 177, 388, 396
Hudson, Sir Jeffrey 226, 392
Huis ter Kleef (Visscher, 1611) 378–9, **379**
Huygens, Constantijn 321, 336, 339, 340
Huyssens, Pieter, St. Charles Borromeo, Antwerp 163, **163**
Hyacinth 283

Iconologia (Ripa) xvi
Idle Servant, The (Maes, 1655) 364, **364**
Ildefonso Altar open (Rubens, 1630–32) 170, **170**
illusionist painting 370
Immaculate Conception (Pacheco, 1616–17) 219, **220**
Immaculate Conception (Ribera, 1637) 205–6, **205**
Immaculate Conception (Velázquez, 1618) 210, 218, 219, 220, 236
Immaculate Conception of the Escorial (Murillo, c. 1660–65) 234, **234**, 236, 239
Immaculate Conception with Sts. Dominic and Francis of Paola (Caracciolo) 134
In Ictu Oculi (Valdéz Leal, 1670–72) 240, **240**
indecency 1
Infante Don Carlos (Velázquez, 1629) 220, **220**
Innocent X: xiii, 93, 113
Innocent X (Velázquez, 1650) 178, 228, **228**

Inspiration of St. Matthew, The
    1st version (Caravaggio, 1602) 41–2, **41**
    2nd version (Caravaggio, 1602) 42, **42**
Ireland xi
Irene, St. 318
Isaac Massa and Beatrix van der Laen (Hals, c. 1622) 322–4, **323**
Isabella, Infanta 147, 152, 165, 169, 170, 195
Isabella Brandt (van Dyck) 176
Italy xi, xii, 1–141, 176–80, 228, 243, 260

Jacobus Zaffius (Hals) 319
James I: 388
Jan Six (Rembrandt, 1647) 349–50, **349**
Jan Six (Rembrandt, 1654) 350, **350**
Jansenists of Port Royale 273
Jasper Schade (Hals) 322
Jefferson, Thomas 403
Jerome, St. 20, 59, 204–5
Jesuits 133, 144, 163, 180, 205
Jesus Christ *see* Christ, Jesus
Jewish Graveyard (two paintings) (Ruisdael) 382–3, 384, 385
Johannes Hoornbeek (Hals) 322
John, St. 48, 126, 217
Johnson, Cornelius 393–4
Jones, Inigo 396–8
    Banqueting House 396–8, **397**
    Houses of Parliament 396
    Queen's Chapel, St. James's Palace 398
    Queen's House 396
    St. Paul's church, Covent Garden 398
Jordaens, Jacob 160, 172, 182–6, 193
    Adoration of the Shepherds 182, 185–6, **186**
    "As the Old Sing, so the Young Pipe" 184–5, **185**
    Calling of Sts. Peter and Andrew 183–4, **183**
    Holy Family with St. John the Baptist 183, **183**
    King Drinks, The 184, **184**
Joseph 37, 50, 183, 207, 266–7, 270
Juan de Pareja (Velázquez, 1650) 228, **229**, 239
Judgment of Paris, The, (Raimondi, after Raphael, c. 1510) 146, **147**
Judgment of Paris, The, (Rubens, 1599) 146, **146**
Judgment of Paris, The, (Rubens, c. 1635) 146, **147**
Judith 53, 135
Judith and her Handmaid with the Head of Holofernes (Gentileschi, Artemisia, c. 1625) 53, **55**
Judith with the Head of Holofernes (Cavallino, c. 1650) 135, **136**
Julius II: 5
Julius II (Raphael) 129, 178, 228
Juno 146
Jupiter 172
Jupiter and Juno, Galleria Farnese (Carracci, Annibale, 1595–1600) 29
Justin of Nassau 223

Kepler, Johannes xiv
Kettering, Alison 361
Key, Lieven de 313, 327–8
    Vleeshal (Meat Market) 327
Keyser, Hendrick de 328
    Westerkerk, The 328, **329**
Keyser, Thomas de, *Constantijn Huygens with his Page* 321–2, **321**
King Drinks, The (Jordaens, c. 1655) 184, **184**
Kit-Kat Series (Kneller, 1707–17) 396
Kneller, Godfrey 393, 395–6
    Grinling Gibbons 395, **395**
    Kit-Kat Series 396
Koninck, Philips 354, 378, 381
    Landscape with a Hawking Party 381, **382**

la Hyre, Laurent de 269, 303
    Landscape with Boy Playing a Flute 303, **303**
La Tour, Georges de 264–7
    Cheat with the Ace of Clubs, The 265
    Cheat with the Ace of Diamonds, The 265, **265**
    Repentant Magdalen, The 265–6, **266**
    St. Joseph the Carpenter 266–7, **267**, 270
la Vrillière, Louis Phélipeaux de 70, 248

Ladies of the Lake Family (Lely, c. 1660) 394, **394**
Lady Elizabeth Thimbleby and Dorothy, Viscountess Andover (van Dyck) 394
Lake Albano and Castelgandolfo (Claude, 1639) 298, **298**
Lamentation (van Dyck) 392
Lampsonius, Domenicus 342
Landscape with Boy Playing a Flute (la Hyre, c. 1645) 303, **303**
Landscape with the Flight into Egypt (Carracci, Annibale, 1603–4) xix, 33–4, **33**
Landscape with a Hawking Party (Koninck, c. 1660) 381, **382**
Landscape with a Man Killed by a Snake (Poussin, 1648) 291, **291**
Landscape with a Man Pursued by a Snake (Poussin) 292
Landscape with the Marriage of Isaac and Rebecca (The Mill) (Claude, 1648) 300, 301, **301**
Landscape with Mercury and the Dishonest Woodsman (Rosa, 1660) 294–5, **294**
Landscape with the Nymph Egeria Mourning over Numa (Claude, 1669) 302, **302**
landscape painting xviii, xix–xx, 32
    Dutch Republic 313, 356, 378–85
    France 295–303
    Poussin 289–92
    Rubens 172
    Spain 201
Landscape with Peasants (Le Nain, Louis? c. 1640) 268, 269
Landscape with Philemon and Baucis (Rubens, c. 1625) 172, **172**
landscape prints, Rembrandt 346–8, 381
Landscape with River and Bridge (Carracci, Annibale, c. 1595) 32–3, **33**
Landscape with St. John on Patmos (Poussin, 1640) 290–1, **290**
Landscape with St. Matthew and the Angel (Poussin, 1639–40) 289, 290
Landscape with a View of Het Steen in the Early Morning (Rubens, c. 1636) 172, **173**, 174
Lanfranco, Giovanni 60, 61, 62, 63–4, 134
    Assumption of the Virgin 64, **64**
    Virgin and Child with Saints Charles Borromeo and Bartholomew 63, **63**
Laocoön (Maderno, Stefano, 1630) 98, **98**
Largillière, Nicolas de 253
    Charles Le Brun 309, **309**
Last Communion of the Apostles (Ribera) 207
Last Communion of St. Jerome (Carracci, Agostino, c. 1590) 20–1, **21**
Last Communion of St. Jerome (Domenichino, 1614) 59–60, **59**
Last Judgement (Michelangelo, 1536–41) 3, 45, **45**
Lastman, Pieter 333, 334
    Abraham Dismissing Hagar and Ishmael 333–4, **334**
Lawrence, St. 117, 119
Le Brun, Charles 186, 303–9
    administrative skills 304
    "Admiration with Astonishment" **307**
    Chancellor Séguier 305–6, **305**
    Conférence sur l'expression générale et particulière 303, **307**
    Crucifixion of Christ with Angels 303
    Expression of the Passions 307
    Galerie des Glaces, ceiling xiii, 308–9
    Horatius Coclius at the Bridge 304
    Louis XIV: 304, 306, 307
    Louvre, east façade 251, **251**
    Poussin 303, 304
    Poussin's Seasons 293
    Salle des Muses, Vaux-le-Vicomte 250, **250**, 304
    Tent of Darius, The (Queens of Persia) 306–7, **306**
    Triumphal Entry of Alexander the Great into Babylon 308, **308**
    Versailles 304
    Vouet 303
Le Clerc, Jean 264
Le Nain, Antoine 267

Le Nain, Louis 267
    Landscape with Peasants 268, 269
    Peasant Family, A **268**, 269
Le Nain, Mathieu 267
Le Nain brothers 267, 269
Le Sueur, Eustache 269
    Sleeping Venus 269, **269**
Le Vau, Louis 248
    Galerie des Glaces, Versailles 252–3, **253**
    Louvre, east façade 251, **251**
    Vaux-le-Vicomte 248–50, **249**
    Versailles, garden façade and lake 252, **252**
    Versailles, plan **251**
Lely, Sir Peter 322, 393, 394–5
    Charles I with James, Duke of York 394
    Ladies of the Lake Family 394, **394**
Leo X: 5
Leonarda da Vinci 243
Leoni, Leone 197
Leoni, Pompeo 197
Leopold-Wilhelm, Archduke 192, 231
Levesque, Catherine 378
Leyden, Lucas van 313
Leyster, Judith 358–60
    Boy Playing a Flute 359–60, **359**
    Proposition, The 358, **358**
Lievens, Jan 336, 354
lighting 53, 73, 75, 129, 266, 316, 335, 367
literacy xvi
Little Street (Vermeer) 369
Lives of the Most Excellent Painters, Sculptors and Architects (Vasari) 341
Longhi, Martino, the Elder, Chiesa Nuova 152
Longinus, St. 100, 101, 157
Lopez, Alfonso 342
Lorraine 264
Louis XIII: xiii, 165, 167, 246, 260, 298
Louis XIV: xiii, 186, 309
    Le Brun 304, 306, 307
    Royal Academy xvii
    Vaux-le-Vicomte 250
    Versailles 244, 251–3
Louis XIV (Rigaud, 1701) 254, **254**
Louvre 243, 250–1
    east façade (Le Vau, Perrault and Le Brun, 1667–70) 251, **251**
Low Countries 143
Lucretia (Rembrandt, 1666) 353–4, **355**
Ludovisi, Alessandro (later Gregory XV) 74
Ludovisi, Ludovico 74, 94
Luis de Góngora (Velázquez) 220
Lunéville 264
Luxembourg Palace 246–7
    garden façade (Brosse) **247**
    plan (Brosse) **247**

Maderno, Carlo
    Palazzo Barberini façade 80, **80**
    Santa Susanna, façade 6, **6**
    Sant'Andrea della Valle 6
    St. Peter's 6, 79
Maderno, Stefano
    Laocoön 98, **98**
    Sarrazin 254
    Sta. Cecilia 98–9, **98**
Madonna dei Bargellini (Carracci, Ludovico, 1587) 13, **13**, 16, 19
Madonna of the Rosary (Caravaggio) 182
Madonna of the Rosary (van Dyck, 1624–26) 177, **177**
Madonna degli Scalzi (Carracci, Ludovico, c. 1590) 16, **16**, 17, 19
Madonna with St. Matthew (Carracci, Annibale, 1588) 13, 15, **15**, 16, 19
Madrid 220–7, 228–32, 234
Maes, Nicolaes 354, 361, 364
    Idle Servant, The 364, **364**
Magdalene *see* Mary Magdalene, St.
Magi (three kings) 168, 212
Magnani, Lorenzo 19
Maids of Honor, The (Las Meninas) (Velázquez, 1656–57) 229, **230**, 231

Index **421**

Maino, Juan Bautista
   Adoration of the Shepherds 218, **218**
   Recapture of Bahia, The 223–4, **223**
Malle Babbe (Hals, c. 1630–33) 320, **320**
Malvasia, Carlo Cesare 70
Man Leaning Against a Tree Among Roses (Hilliard, c. 1590) 387, **388**
Man and Woman Seated by a Virginal (Metsu, c. 1658) 362, **362**
Mancini, Giulio 202
Manet, Edouard 232
   Déjeuner sur l'herbe 146
Mannerism 3–4, 313
Mansart, François 247–8, 250
   Hôtel de la Vrillière 248, **248**
Mantua 148, 149
Mantua, Duke of 388
maps xiv
Maratta, Carlo 125–7
   Accademia di San Luca xvii, 304
   Portrait of Clement IX Rospigliosi 129, **129**
   St. John the Evangelist Explaining the Doctrine of the Immaculate Conception to Sts. Gregory, Augustine and John Chrysostom 126–7, **127**
   Triumph of Clemency 126, **126**
Marchesa Brigida Spinola Doria (Rubens, 1606) **150**, 151
Margaret of Hungary 200
Margaret of Parma 143
Margaretha de Vos (van Dyck) 176
Margarita, Infanta 231
Mariana of Austria, Queen 228, 241
Marie de' Medici 70, 147, 165–8, 243, 244, 246–7, 254, 260
Marie de' Medici, Queen of France, landing in Marseilles (Rubens, 1622–25) 167, **167**
Marino, Giovanni Battista 273, 274
Market Place and the Grote Kerk at Haarlem, The (Berckheyde, 1674) 327, **328**
Marriage (Poussin) 284
Marriage Feast at Cana, The (Murillo, c. 1665–75) 237–8, **237**
Marriage of Louis XIII and Anne of Austria (Anonymous) **246**
Marriage Portrait of Giovanni Arnolfini and Giovanna Cenami (Eyck) 231
Martinian, St. 277
Martyrdom of St. Erasmus, The (Poussin, 1628–29) 275, **276**, 277, 278
Martyrdom of St. Lawrence (Cortona, 1646) 117, **117**, 119
Martyrdom of St. Matthew (Caravaggio, 1599–1602) 39, 41, **41**
Martyrdom of St. Peter Martyr (Titian) 19
Martyrdom of St. Philip (Ribera) 208
Martyrdom of Sts. Processus and Martinian (Valentin, 1628–29) 263, 277–8, **277**
Maruscelli, Paolo 84
Mary *see* Virgin (Mary)
Mary Magdalen, St. 37, 97, 266
Mary Tudor (Mor) 387
Massa, Isaac 323
Massimi, Camillo 292
Matthew, St. 39, 41–2
Mauritshuis (Campen & Post, 1633–44) 332, **332**
Mazo, Juan Bautista del 232
Medici family 85, 139, 258
Medici Prince Taken from Venus by Minerva (Cortona, 1641–42) 124–5, **124**
Meegeren, Hans van 366
Melancholia (ter Brugghen, c. 1625) 316, **316**
Mena, Juan Gomez de 196
Mena, Pedro de 200
Meninas, Las (The Maids of Honor) (Velázquez, 1656–57) 229, **230**, 231
Mercury 28, 146, 172, 294–5
Merian, Maria Sibylla xiv
   Cassava Plant with Caterpillar and Butterflies xiv
Metsu, Gabriel 361, 362
   Man and Woman Seated by a Virginal 362, **362**
Michael, St. 71, 140

Michelangelo Buonarotti
   Conversion of St. Paul 9, **11**
   Last Judgment 3, 45, **45**
   nudes 1
   Palazzo Farnese, façade **24**
   St. Peter's dome 5
   Tomb of Giuliano de' Medici 3, **3**
Miel, Jan, *Urban VIII Visiting Il Gesù, Rome* xiii
Mieris, Frans van, *Allegory of Painting* 369
Mignard, Pierre 304, 305, 309
Milan xi, 1, 78, 134, 243
Milkmaid, The (Vermeer, c. 1658–60) 359, 367, **368**, 369
Mill, The (Claude, 1631) 296, **296**, 301
Mill at Wyck near Duurstede (Ruisdael) 382, 385
Milo of Crotona (Puget, 1670–82) 255–6, **256**
Minerva Defending Peace from Mars (Rubens, 1629) 169, **169**
miniature portraits 387
Miracles of St. Francis Xavier (Rubens, 1618–19) 165, **165**
mirrors 253
Mochi, Francesco, *St. Veronica* 100, **101**
Molenaer, Jan Meinse 358
Molentje, Het (The Little Windmill) (Rembrandt, c. 1654) 347, **347**
monasteries, dissolution xii
Monconys, Balthasar de 366
Montañés, Juan Martínez 195, 198–200, 218
   Christ of Clemency 198–9, **199**
   Penitent St. Jerome, The 199–200, **200**
Montias, Michael 312, 313
moods xv–xvi
Mor, Anthonis 387
   Mary Tudor 387
Moretus, Balthasar 145
Moses 51–2
Mother, The (Hooch, c. 1660) 362, 363–4, **363**
Mother Cathérine-Agnès Arnauld and Sister Cathérine de Ste. Suzanne Champaigne (Champaigne, 1662) 272–3, **272**
Mountague, Sir William 357
Mundy, Peter 312
Murillo, Bartolomé Esteban 195, 232–9, 240
   Angels' Kitchen 232
   Healing of the Paralytic at the Pool of Bethesda 238
   Immaculate Conception of the Escorial 234, **234**, 236, 239
   Marriage Feast at Cana, The 237–8, **237**
   Self-Portrait 232, **236**, 237
   Two Boys Eating a Pie 201
   Two Trinities, The 238, **239**, 270
   Virgin of the Rosary (Escorial Madonna) 234, **234**
   Young Beggar, The 232–3, **233**
Music Lesson (Vermeer) 370
Mystic Marriage of St. Catherine (Carracci, Agostino, 1582, after Veronese) 13, **14**
Mystic Marriage of St. Catherine (Carracci, Annibale, c. 1586) 14, **14**
Mystic Marriage of St. Catherine, The (Guercino, 1620) 76–7, **76**
Mystic Marriage of St. Catherine, The (Guercino, 1650) 77, **77**
Mystic Marriage of St. Catherine (Veronese, c. 1565) 13
Mytens, Daniel 388
mythological themes 114

Naples 1, 62, 63, 134–41, 201, 206, 208
Narcissus 283
narrative subjects, Rembrandt 338
Nassau, Johan Maurits van 332
Neptune 283, 284
Neptune Fountain (Giambologna, 1566) 85, **86**
Neri, St, Philip 94–5
Netherlands 311
Nicolaes Ruts (Rembrandt, c. 1631) 336, **336**
night pictures 53
"*Night Watch", The (Military Company of Captain Frans Banning Cocq)* (Rembrandt, 1642) 345–6, **346**

Noort, Adam van 146, 182
Norgate, Edward 379
nudes
   female 226–7, 269, 314
   male 1
nymphs 60–1

Officer and a Laughing Woman (Vermeer) 370
official art 167
Old Woman Cooking Eggs (Velázquez, 1618) 218, **219**
Oliva, Paolo 132
Olivares 216, 217, 225
Oliver, Isaac 387
Omazur, Nicolas 237–8
Omer Talon (Champaigne, 1649) 270–2, **271**
Onate, Conde 69
Oosterwyck, Maria van 360
Ordination (Poussin, c. 1638–40) 284, **285**, 286–7
Ordination (Poussin, c. 1646) 286, **286**
Orpheus and Eurydice (Poussin) 292
Orpheus in Hades (Poussin, 1622–23) **273**, 274
Osuna, Duke of 203
Ovid 28, 302, 314

Pacheco, Francisco 199, 209, 210, 217, 236
   Christ on the Cross 209
   Immaculate Conception **219**, 220
Pala della Pesta (Reni, 1631) 66, **67**, 68
Palais du Luxembourg *see* Luxembourg Palace
Palazzo Barberini, façade (Maderno, Bernini and Borromeo, 1628–33) 80, **80**
Palazzo Farnese 24–31
   façade (Antonio da Sangallo the younger and Michelangelo, 1530s–1550) **24**
Palazzo Pitti 123–5
Paleotti, Gabriele 3
palette 161, 170–1, 203, 217, 278
Palladianism 396
Pallas Athena 124
Pamphili, Giambattista *see* Innocent X
Pamphili family 112, 131
Pan 28, 124
papacy xii–xiii
Parental Admonition, The (Terborch, 1654–55) 361, **361**
Paris 243–8, 399
Paris (Greek mythology) 28, 146
pasos 197
Passart, Michel 293
Passeri, G.B. 90
Patel, Pierre 303
Patenir, Joachim 378
patrons xvi, 85
   Claude 295, 298
   England xii, 388, 389
   France 243, 246, 260
   Italy xiii
   Jordaens 182
   Rubens 147, 163
   Spain 200, 201
   Titian 201, 221, 388
   Vouet 260
Paul III: 24
Paul V: 5
Pavillon de l'Horloge, Louvre 254, **254**
Peace of Vervins 243
Peasant Family, A (Le Nain, Louis? c. 1640) 268, **269**
Peeters, Clara 187–8
   Still-Life with Colander and Artichokes 187–8, **187**
Pellegrini, Gianantonio 395
Penance (Poussin) 284
pendants 290
Penitent Magdalene (Caravaggio) 37
Penitent St. Jerome, The (Montañés, 1609–13) 199–200, **200**
Pepys, Samuel 395
Perrault, Claude, Louvre, east façade 251, **251**
Perrier, François 303
Perseus Liberating Andromeda (Puget) 256
Pesaro Altarpiece (Titian, 1519–26) 13, **13**, 15, 181

Peter, St. 62, 184, 211, 352
Peter Denying Christ (Rembrandt, 1660) 352–3, **352**
Pevsner, Nikolaus 399
Philip II: 143, 195, 196, 197, 200, 201, 243, 311
Philip III: 147, 197
Philip IV: 147, 169, 174, 195, 197, 212, 220–1
Philip IV (Velázquez, c. 1635) 224, **224**
Philip IV of Spain (The "Fraga Portrait") (Velázquez, 1644) 226, **227**
Philip Prosper, Prince 228
piazza, St. Peters 102
Piazza Navona 112
Picture Gallery of Cornelis van der Geest (van Haecht, 1628) 191–2, **192**
Pierce, Edward, *Christopher Wren* 398, **398**
Pietà (Carracci, Annibale, c. 1599–1600) 32, **32**, 282
Pietà (Gaulli, 1667) 129, **129**
Pietà with Virgin and Saints (Carracci, Annibale, 1585) 10, 12, **12**
Pieter Cornelisz. van der Morsch (Hals, 1616) 319, **319**
Pieter van den Broecke (Hals, c. 1633) **320**, 321, 322
Pietro da Cortona *see* Cortona, Pietro da
Pillage of a Farmhouse (Callot, 1633) **259**
Piranesi, Giovanni Battista, *View of the Piazza and Basilica of St. Peter's* 5
Place Royale 246, **246**
Place des Vosges 246, **246**
plague xv, 135, 215
Plague of Ashdod, The (Poussin, 1629–30) 280, **280**, 282–3
Plantin, Christopher 143
Pleasant Places (Visscher) 378–9
Pluto 88
Poel, Egbert van der 372
Pointel, Jean 280, 287
politics xi–xii
Pomona 314
Pont-Neuf 245
Pool II, Juriaen 360
Pope Leo I Driving Attila from Rome (Algardi, 1646–53) 108, **109**
Pope Paul III Farnese and his Nephews (Titian, 1545) 178–9, **179**
Pope Paul V (Bernini, c. 1618) 91, **91**
Porta, Giacomo della
  Fountain of the Turtles 111
  Tomb of Paul III: 103, **103**
Porter, Sir Endymion 393
portrait busts 91–3
Portrait of Clement IX Rospigliosi (Maratta, 1669) 129, **129**
Portrait of the Duke of Lerma (Rubens, 1603) 148, **148**
Portrait of an Elderly Man (van Dyck, 1618) 174–5, **174**
Portrait of an Elderly Woman (Hals, 1633) 322, **322**
Portrait of a Man (Hals) 327
Portrait of a Man (Titian) 342
Portrait of a Man in a Slouched Hat (Hals) 327
portraits xvi, xviii, xix
  Champaigne 270
  Dutch Republic 313, 319–27
  England 388, 389–96
  equestrian 305
  France 270
  full-length 178, 179, 270
  miniature 387
  Raphael 180
  Rembrandt 338
  Reni 68
  Rubens 151, 171–2, 221
  self- xviii, 341–4, 351, 375
  Spain 200
  Titian 151, 178, 221, 388
  van Dyck 177, 178, 179, 180, 221, 389–93
  Velázquez 220, 224–6, 228
Posner, Donald 36
Post, Frans xiv
Post, Pieter, Mauritshuis 332, **332**
Pourbus, Frans, the Younger 247

Poussin, Nicolas 113, 260, 273–94
  Apollo and Daphne 292
  Armida Abducting Rinaldo 282
  Autumn 292–3, **293**
  Baptism 284
  Birth of Venus, The 283–4, **283**
  Camillus and the School Master of the Falern 282
  Confirmation 284, 294
  Death of Adonis 278, **278**
  Death of Germanicus, The **274**, 275
  Deluge (Winter) 292, 293
  Eucharist 284
  Extreme Unction 284, **285**
  Landscape with a Man Killed by a Snake 291, **291**
  Landscape with a Man Pursued by a Snake 292
  Landscape with St. John on Patmos 290–1, **290**
  Landscape with St. Matthew and the Angel **289**, 290
  landscapes 289–92
  Le Brun 303, 304
  Marriage 284
  Martyrdom of St. Erasmus, The 275, **276**, 277, 278
  modes (moods) 280–1
  Ordination 284, **285**, 286–7
  Ordination (c. 1646) 286, **286**
  Orpheus and Eurydice 292
  Orpheus in Hades **273**, 274
  Penance 284
  Plague of Ashdod, The 280, **280**, 282–3
  Realm of Flora, The 280, **281**, 283
  Rebecca and Eliezer at the Well 288–9, **288**
  Sack of Jerusalem 275
  Seasons 292–3
  Self-Portrait 287, **287**
  Spring 292, **293**
  Storm, The 292
  Summer 292, 293
  Tancred and Erminia 278–9, **279**
Pozzo, Andrea, *Triumph of the Missionary Efforts of the Jesuits* 133
Pozzo, Cassiano dal 113, 284
Presentation of the Virgin at the Temple (Barocci, c. 1594) 22, **22**
Presentation of the Virgin in the Temple (Vouet, 1641) 261, **262**, 263
Preti, Mattia 135–6
  Feast of Herod, The 136, **138**
  Virgin and Child with Sts. Francis Xavier and Rosalia 136, **137**
Primaticcio, Francesco 244
Primavera 283
prints 258, 314, 346–8
Procaccini, Giulio Cesare 234
Processus, St. 277
Procuress (Baburen) 358, 367
Procuress, The (Vermeer, 1656) 366–7, **366**, 369
Prometheus Bound (Rubens, 1618) 159–60, **161**
Proposition, The (Leyster, 1629) 358, **358**
Proserpine 88
Protestants xi, xvi
Proust, Marcel 366
Public Felicity Triumphant over Dangers (Gentileschi, Orazio) 247
Puget, Pierre 255–6
  Alexander the Great with Diogenes **243**, 256
  Milo of Crotona 255–6, **256**
  Perseus Liberating Andromeda 256
  Town Hall doorway, Toulon 255, **255**

Queen Henrietta Maria with Sir Jeffrey Hudson (van Dyck, 1633) **392**, 392
Queen's Chapel, St. James's Palace (Jones) 398
Queen's House (Jones, 1616–38) 396
Queens of Persia at the Feet of Alexander the Great, The (Tent of Darius) (Le Brun, 1660–61) 306–7, **306**

Raggi, Antonio 133
  St. Charles Borromeo: statue 82
Raimondi, Marc'Antonio, *Judgment of Paris, The* (after Raphael) 146, **147**
Rainbow Landscape, The (Rubens, 1636–37) 172, **173**

Raising of the Cross (Rembrandt, c. 1633) 338, **340**
Raising of the Cross (Rubens, 1610–11) 154–7, **155**, 157, 159, 338
Rape of Proserpine (Bernini, 1621–22) 88, **88**
Rape of the Sabine Woman (Giambologna, 1580–82) 85, **86**
Rape of the Sabine Women (Cortona, 1631) 116, **116**
Raphael Sanzio 30
  Baldassare Castiglione xv–xvi, **xv**, 342–3
  Disputation on the Holy Sacrament 126
  Galatea 30
  Julius II: 129, 178, 228
  portraits 180
  Self-Portrait with his Fencing Master 180
  Sistine Madonna 16–17, **16**
  St. Michael 71
realism xxi
Realm of Flora, The (Poussin, 1630–31) 280, **281**, 283
Rebecca and Eliezer at the Well (Poussin, 1648) 288–9, **288**
Recapture of Bahia, The (Maino, 1634–35) 223–4, **223**
Regentesses (Hals) 326, **327**
Regents of the Old Men's Almshouse (Hals, c. 1664) 326, **326**
religion xi–xii
religious commissions 114
religious dissent 311
religious wars xi
Rembrandt van Rijn xix, 333, 334–54, 381
  Anatomy Lesson of Dr. Nicolaes Tulp 336–8, **337**
  Artist in his Studio, The 338, **338**
  Ascension 339
  Blinding of Samson **339**, 340–1
  Christ and the Woman Taken in Adultery 348, **348**
  Conspiracy of the Batavians under Claudius Civilis 352
  Cornelis van Anslo and his Wife 344–5, **344**
  Descent from the Cross 338–9, **340**
  Entombment 339
  history paintings 350–1
  Holy Family (1645) 348
  Holy Family (1646) 348
  Huygens 336, 339, 340
  Jan Six (1647) 349–50, **349**
  Jan Six (1654) 350, **350**
  landscape painting 381
  landscape prints 346–8, 381
  Lucretia 353–4, **355**
  Molentje, Het (The Little Windmill) 347, **347**
  narrative subjects 338
  Nicolaes Ruts 336, **336**
  "Night Watch", The (Military Company of Captain Frans Banning Cocq) 345–6, **346**
  Peter Denying Christ 352–3, **352**
  portraits 338
  pupils 354
  Raising of the Cross 338, **340**
  Resurrection 339
  Self-Portrait 335, **335**
  Self-Portrait at the Age of Thirty-Four 342–4, **343**
  Self-Portrait with Maulstick and Brushes 351, **351**, 352
  self-portraits 341–4, 351
  Supper at Emmaus 346
  Syndics of the Drapers' Guild 353, **354**
  Three Trees 347–8, **348**
  Tobit and Anna 335, **335**
  View of Amsterdam 347, **347**
Renaissance xxi
Reni, Guido 21, 56, 58, 64–72, 134
  Abduction of Helen, The 69–70, **69**
  Annunciation, The 65, **66**
  Archangel Michael, The **70**, 71
  Aurora 66, **67**
  Cardinal Bernardino Spada 68, **69**, 179
  Cardinal Roberto Ubaldini 69
  Coronation of the Virgin with Four Saints 64
  Crucifixion of St. Peter 65, **65**
  Ecce Homo 71–2, **71**
  Glory of St. Dominic 65
  Pala della Pesta 66, **67**, 68

Repentant Magdalen, The (La Tour, c. 1640) 265–6, **266**
Rest on the Flight into Egypt (Caravaggio, c. 1594–95) 37–8, **37**
Rest on the Flight into Egypt, The (Gentileschi, Orazio, c. 1610) 50–1, **50**
Resurrection (Rembrandt) 339
Resurrection of Christ, The (Carracci, Annibale, 1593) 18–19, **18**
retablos 197, 213
Ribalta, Francisco 201–2
  Vision of the Father Simon, The 202
Ribera, Jusepe de 62, 134, 135, 138, 195, 201–8
  Boy with a Club Foot 206, **206**
  Crucifixion with the Virgin, St. John, and Another Figure 203
  Drunken Silenus 203–4, **203**
  Elijah 206, **206**
  Hearing 202
  Holy Family with Sts. Anne and Catherine of Alexandria, The 207, **208**
  Immaculate Conception 205–6, **205**
  Last Communion of the Apostles 207
  Martyrdom of St. Philip 208
  San Gennaro Emerging Unharmed from the Furnace 195, 206–7
  Sight 202
  Smell 202, 203
  St. Jerome with the Angel of Judgment 203, 204–5, **204**
  St. Sebastian 208, **209**
  Taste 202–3, **202**
  Touch 202
Ricci, Sebastiano 395
Richelieu, Cardinal xiii
Rigaud, Hyacinthe 253
  Louis XIV: 254, **254**
Rinaldo 181–2
Rinaldo and Armida (van Dyck, 1629) 181–2, **181**, 388, 393
riots, Flanders 144
Ripa, Cesare, *Iconologia* xvi
Rizi, Francisco 241
Rockox, Nicolas 154
Rodenburgh, Theodore 333
Roi à la Chasse, Le (The King at the Hunt) (van Dyck, 1635) 389, **391**
Rojas, Pablo de 198
"*Rokeby Venus, The*" *(Venus and Cupid)* (Velázquez, 1648) 226–7, **227**
Roldán, Luisa 200
Roldán, Pedro 200
Rome
  architecture 4–7, 78–89
  Carracci succession 56–77
  city planning 4–7, 78–84, 102
  Claude 295
  Le Brun 303–4
  painting 21–34, 113–33
  papal patronage 1
  Poussin 273, 274
  restoration 5
  Vouet 260
Rosa, Salvator 294
  Landscape with Mercury and the Dishonest Woodsman 294–5, **294**
Roscioli, Gian Maria 290
Rosso, Giovanni Battista (Rosso Fiorentino) 243–4
Royal Academy *see* French Academy
Royal Palace (former Town Hall), Amsterdam (Campen, 1648–55) 331–2, **331**
Rubens, Jan 145
Rubens, Peter Paul xxi, 21, 145–74, 193
  administrative skills 160
  Adoration of the Magi 168–9, **168**
  Allegory of the Four Corners of the World 162, **162**
  Antwerp 152–65
  assistants 160, 161
  Caravaggio's *Death of the Virgin* 46
  collaborators 159, 160
  Coronation of Marie 167

Council of the Gods 168
Death of Henry IV and the Proclamation of Marie de' Medici as Regent 167, **167**
Descent from the Cross 154, 158, **158**, 338
diplomat 165, 169
Education of Marie de' Medici, The 166–7, **166**
England 388, 397
Feast of Herod, The 136, 138, **139**
Felicity of her Reign 166
flesh painting 161
Head of the Farnese Hercules 148, **149**
Hélène Fourment in her Wedding Dress 171, **171**
Henri IV Receives the Portrait of Marie de' Medici **166**, 167
Holy Family with the Young St. John the Baptist and his Parents 170, **171**
house 154, 159, **160**
Ildefonso Altar open 170, **170**
Italy 148–52
Jordaens 182
Judgment of Paris, The (1599) 146, **146**
Judgment of Paris, The (c. 1635) 146, **147**
landscape painting 172
Landscape with Philemon and Baucis 172, **172**
Landscape with a View of Het Steen in the Early Morning 172, **173**, 174
Marchesa Brigida Spinola Doria 150, 151
Marie de' Medici, Queen of France, landing in Marseilles 167, **167**
Minerva Defending Peace from Mars 169, **169**
Miracles of St. Francis Xavier 165, **165**
patrons 147, 163
Portrait of the Duke of Lerma 148, **148**
portraits 151, 171–2, 221
Prometheus Bound 159–60, **161**
pupils 159
Rainbow Landscape, The 172, **173**
Raising of the Cross 154–7, **155**, **157**, 159, 338
Self-Portrait 145
Self-Portrait with Isabella Brandt 154, **154**
Serra 74
St. Gregory of Nazianus 163, **163**
St. Gregory (Pope) Surrounded by Saints, Worshipping the Miraculous Image of the Virgin and Child 152, **153**
Study after Laocoön 149, **149**
Study for Portrait of Brigida Spinola Doria 151, **151**
technique 170–1
Thomas Howard, 2nd Earl of Arundel and Surrey 172
Transfiguration, The 150, 151
van Dyck 174
Velázquez 221
women 162
Rudolf II: xi
Rughesi, Fausto, Chiesa Nuova 84, **84**
Ruijven, Pieter Claesz van 372
Ruins of Egmond Castle (Ruisdael, c. 1655) 384, **384**
Ruisdael, Jacob van 380, 382–5
  Jewish Graveyard (two paintings) 382–3, 384, 385
  Mill at Wyck near Duurstede 382, 385
  Ruins of Egmond Castle 384, **384**
  View of Bentheim Castle 383, **383**
  Windmill by a Country Road 381, **381**
  Winter Landscape with Windmill 385, **385**
Rupprath, Cynthia 360
Ruskin, John 63
Russell, Francis, Earl of Bedford 398
Ruts, Nicolaes 336
Ruysch, Rachel 360
  Still-Life with Flowers and Fruit 360, **360**
Ruysdael, Salomon van 380, 382

Sacchetti, Giambattista 232
Sacchetti, Marcello 113–14
Sacchetti family 113
Sacchi, Andrea xviii–xix, 120–3, 125
  Allegory of Divine Wisdom 121–3, **121**
  Death of St. Anne 122, **123**
  Dream of St. Romuald 123
  Urban VIII Visiting Il Gesù, Rome xiii

Sack of Jerusalem (Poussin) 275
sacra conversazione 181
sacraments 284
Sagrada Forma (Coello, 1685–90) 241, **241**
Salerno, Luigi xx
Salle des Muses, Vaux-le-Vicomte (Le Brun, 1657–61) 250, **250**, 304
Salome 138
Samson 340–1
Samson and Delilah (Steen) 377
San Carlo alle Quattro Fontane (Borromini, 1638–67) 80–2, **81**, **82**
San Gennaro Emerging Unharmed from the Furnace (Ribera, 1641–43) 195, 206–7
Sandrart, Joachim von 278
Sanraedam, Pieter Jansz 313
  Amsterdam Town Hall before 1651: 330, **330**
Santa Maria, Vallicella 6, 21–3
Santa Maria della Pace 78
  (Pietro, 1656) **79**
Santa Susanna, façade (Maderno, Carlo 1593–1603) 6, **6**
Sant'Andrea al Quirinale (Bernini) 84, 130
Sant'andrea della Valle 6, 60, 61–2
Santi Luca e Martina (Pietro) 84
Sant'Ivo alla Sapienza (Borromini, 1642–50) 82–3, **83**
Sarrazin, Jacques 254–5
  Caryatids on the Pavillon de l'Horloge 254–5, **254**
Saskia (Rembrandt's wife) 345
Sauerländer, Willibald 292
Scamozzi, Vincenzo 396
Scannelli, Francesco 75
Schwartz, Gary 335, 337, 352
Scotland xi
Scott, John Beldon 122
sculptors 85, 87
sculpture
  France 254–8
  Italy 85–112
  Spain 197–200
Seasons (Poussin) 292–3
Sebastian, St. 208, 318
Sebastián de Morra (Velázquez, c. 1645) 226, **226**
Second School of Fontainebleau 244
Secularization Act, Spain 213
Séguier, Pierre 303, 304, 305
Self-Portrait (Fabritius) 356
Self-Portrait (Murillo, c. 1670–75) 232, **236**, 237
Self-Portrait (Poussin, 1650) 287, **287**
Self-Portrait (Rembrandt, c. 1629) 335, **335**
Self-Portrait (Rubens, 1638–40) 145
Self-Portrait (Steen) 375
Self-Portrait (van Dyck) 174
Self-Portrait (Vouet, 1618–19) 260, **260**
Self-Portrait at the Age of Thirty-Four (Rembrandt, 1640) 342–4, **343**
Self-Portrait with his Fencing Master (Raphael) 180
Self-Portrait with Isabella Brandt (Rubens, 1609–10) 154, **154**
Self-Portrait with Maulstick and Brushes (Rembrandt, c. 1665) 351, **351**, 352
Self-Portrait Playing a Lute (Steen, c. 1661–63) 375, **375**
Self-Portrait with Sir Endymion Porter (van Dyck, c. 1635) 392–3, **393**
self-portraits xviii, 341–4, 351, 375
Serapion, St. 210
Serra, Jacopo 74, 152
Seven Acts of Mercy (Caravaggio) 134
Seville 208, 209, 210, 215, 217–20, 237
Sfondrato, Cardinal 65
Sheldon, Gilbert 398
Sheldonian (Wren) 398
Shrovetide Revellers (Hals, c. 1615) 311, 325–6
Shute, John 398
Sight (Ribera) 202
Siloé, Diego de 196
Sint Jans, Geertgen Tot 313
Sistine Madonna (Raphael, 1515–16) 16–17, **16**
Six, Jan 349
Sixtus V: 4, 78

424 *Index*

Skittle Players Outside an Inn (Steen, c. 1660–63) 377, 377
Sleeping Venus (Le Sueur, c. 1638) 269, **269**
Slive, Seymour 319, 383
Smell (Ribera) 202, 203
snakes 292
Snyders, Frans 159, 160, 176, 186, 188
 Still-Life with Poultry and Venison 188, **189**
Spada, Cardinal 69
Spain xi, xii, 140–1, 195–241
Spanish Armada 195
Spanish Discalced Trinitarians 81
Spanish Netherlands xii, 311, 313
Spear, Richard 71
Spinola, Ambrogio 223
Spinola, Brigida 151
Spranger, Bartholomeus 314
Spring (Poussin) 292, 293
St. Andrew (Duquesnoy, 1629–40) 100, **100**, 102
St. Augustine (Wren) 400
St. Bavo, Haarlem 327
St. Benet Paul's Wharf (Wren) 399
St. Bonaventure at the Council of Lyons (Zurbarán) 211
St. Bride's (Wren, 1670–84) 400, **400**
St. Cecilia Distributing Alms (Domenichino 1612–14) 58, 59
St. Cecilia in Ecstasy (Cavillino) 135
St. Charles Borromeo, Antwerp (Huyssens, 1615) 163, **163**
St. Charles Borromeo, statue (Raggi) 82
St. Dunstan-in-the-East (Wren) 400
St. Gregory of Nazianus (Rubens, 1621) 163, **163**
St. Gregory (Pope) Surrounded by Saints, Worshipping the Miraculous Image of the Virgin and Child (Rubens, 1606–7) 152, **153**
St. Helena (Bolgi) 100, 101
St. James Garlickhithe (Wren) 399
St. Jerome with the Angel of Judgment (Ribera, 1626) 203, 204–5, **204**
St. John the Evangelist Explaining the Doctrine of the Immaculate Conception to Sts. Gregory, Augustine and John Chrysostom (Maratta, 1686) 126–7, **127**
St. John the Evangelist's Vision of Jerusalem (Cano, 1635–38) 217, **217**
St. Joseph the Carpenter (La Tour, c. 1635) 266–7, **267**, 270
St. Longinus (Bernini, 1629–38) 100, 101, **101**
St. Margaret Pattens (Wren) 399
St. Mary Aldermary (Wren) 400
St. Mary Magdalene (Algardi, 1629) 94, 97, **97**
St. Michael (Raphael) 71
St. Michael Vanquishing the Devil (Giordano, c. 1663) 140, **141**
St. Paul's Cathedral 399
 (Wren, 1675–1710) 387, 400–3, **401**, **403**
St. Paul's church, Covent Garden (Jones) 398
St. Peter Damian Offering the Rule of the Camaldolese Order to the Virgin (Cortona, 1629) 117, **117**
St. Peter's (New) xii, 4, 5–6, 79, 95, 99–108
St. Peter Nolasco's Vision of the Crucified St. Peter (Zurbarán, 1625) 211, **211**
St. Philip Neri with an Angel (Algardi, 1638) 94–5, **94**
St. Sebastian (Honthorst, c. 1620) 318, 319
St. Sebastian (Ribera, 1651) 208, **209**
St. Sebastian Tended by St. Irene (ter Brugghen, 1625) 316, **317**, 318
St. Serapion (Zurbarán, 1628) 210–11, **210**
St. Stephen Wallbrook (Wren, 1672–87) 399–400, **399**
St. Vedast (Wren, 1697) 400, **400**
St. Veronica (Mochi) 100, 101
Sta. Bibiana (Bernini, 1624–26) 97, **97**
Sta. Bibiana Refusing to Sacrifice to Pagan Idols, (Cortona, 1626) 113, **114**
Sta. Cecilia (Maderno, Stefano, 1600) 98–9, **98**
Sta. Susanna (Duquesnoy, 1629–33) 96–7, **96**
Stadhouder 338, 339
Staets, Hendrick 329
Stanzione, Massimo 135
statues, Spain 197

Stechow, Wolfgang 378
Steen, Jan 313, 357, 374–7
 Capture of Samson 377
 Samson and Delilah 377
 Self-Portrait 375
 Self-Portrait Playing a Lute 375, **375**
 Skittle Players Outside an Inn 377, **377**
 Twelfth Night 376–7, **376**
 Wedding at Cana 377
 Worship of the Golden Calf 377
still-life xviii, xix, xx, 186–93, 313, 356
Still Life with Bouquet of Flowers (Brueghel, Jan, c. 1607) 143, **143**, 186–7
Still-Life with Colander and Artichokes (Peeters, 1613) 187–8, **187**
Still-Life with Flowers and Fruit (Ruysch. 1703) 360, **360**
Still Life with Lemons, Oranges, and a Rose (Zurbarán, 1633) 215, **215**
Still Life with Parrots (Heem, 1640–45) **191**
Still-Life with Poultry and Venison (Snyders, 1614) 188, **189**
Stoffels, Hendrickje 346
Storm, The (Poussin) 292
Story of the Founding of Rome (Carracci c. 1590) 19–20, **19**, **20**
 Carracci, Agostino 20
 (Carracci, Annibale, c. 1590) 19, **19**, 20
 (Carracci, Ludovico, c. 1590) 20, **20**
Strozzi, Bernardo 234
studios xvii
Study after Laocoön (Rubens, 1600–5) 149, **149**
Study for Portrait of Brigida Spinola Doria (Rubens, 1606) 151, **151**
Study of Reclining Boy (Carracci, Annibale, c. 1580) 7
subjects xviii–xxi
Sullivan 206
Summer (Poussin) 292, 293
Summerson, John 400
Supper at Emmaus (Rembrandt) 346
Surrender of Breda (Velázquez, 1634–35) 212, **222**, 223, 224
Susanna 53, 96–7
Susanna and the Elders (Gentileschi, Artemisia, 1610) 52–3, **52**
Susanna and the Elders (Guercino) 74
Swanenburg, Jacob van 334
Sweerts, Michael, *Drawing Academy, A* xvii
Syndics of the Drapers' Guild (Rembrandt, 1661–62) 353, **354**

Table Top with the Seven Deadly Sins (Bosch) 189
Tacca, Pietro 197–8
 Equestrian Statue of Philip IV: 198, **198**
Talon, Omer 270–1
Tancred 74, 278, 279
Tancred and Erminia (Poussin, c. 1635) 278–9, **279**
Tassi, Agostino 74, 295
Taste (Ribera, c. 1615) 202–3, **202**
taxation 195–6, 232, 311
Temperance and Chastity (Gaulli, 1666–71) 131, **131**
Teniers, David, the Elder 189
Teniers, David, the Younger 189, 192
 Archduke Leopold-Wilhelm in his Gallery in Brussels 192, **193**
Tent of Darius, The (Queens of Persia) (Le Brun, 1660–61) 306–7, **306**
ter Brugghen, Hendrick 264, 315–16
 Concert, The 316, **316**
 Melancholia 316, **316**
 St. Sebastian Tended by St. Irene 316, **317**, 318
Terborch, Gerard 357, 361
 Parental Admonition, The 361, **361**
Teresa, St. 108, 110–11
Thins, Maria 367
Thomas Howard, 2nd Earl of Arundel and Surrey (Rubens) 172
Thornhill, Sir James 395
Three Trees (Rembrandt, 1643) 347–8, **348**
Tibaldi, Pellegrino 201
 Adoration of the Shepherds 4

Tiepolo, Giambattista 141, 232
Tijou, Jean 402
Tintoretto, *Crucifixion* 155, **156**
Titian (Tiziano Veccellio) 178
 Bacchanal of the Andrians 114, **115**, 222
 Bacchus and Ariadne 114
 Crowning with Thorns 176, **176**
 Martyrdom of St. Peter Martyr 19
 patrons 201, 221, 388
 Pesaro Altarpiece 13, **13**, 15, 181
 Pope Paul III Farnese and his Nephews 178–9, **179**
 Portrait of a Man 342
 portraits 151, 178, 221, 388
 sacra conversazione 181
 Worship of Venus 114
Tobit and Anna (Rembrandt, 1626) 335, **335**
Tomb of Alexander VII (Bernini, 1628–37) 102, 104, **106**
Tomb of Giuliano de' Medici (Michelangelo, 1519–33) 3, **3**
Tomb of Leo XI Medici (Algardi, 1634–44) 94, 95–6, **95**
Tomb of Paul III (Porta, 1549–75) 103, **103**
Tomb of Urban VIII (Bernini, 1628–37) 102, 104, **104**
Touch (Ribera) 202
Town Hall, Amsterdam 330–2
Town Hall, Antwerp (Floris, 1561–66) 144
Town Hall doorway, Toulon (Puget, 1656–57) 255, **255**
town planning *see* city planning
trade xii, 143, 144
training xvii, 232, 236, 260, 304, 309
Transfiguration, The (Rubens, 1605) 150, 151
Treaty of Münster 311
Trip, Jacob 352, 353
Trippenhuis (Vingboons, 1662) 330, **330**
Triton Fountain (Bernini, 1642–43) 111, **112**
Triumph of Bacchus (Cortona, c. 1626–29) 114, **115**
Triumph of Clemency (Maratta, 1673–75) 126, **126**
Triumph of the Missionary Efforts of the Jesuits (Pozzo, Andrea) 133
Triumphal Entry of Alexander the Great into Babylon (Le Brun, 1662–68) 308, **308**
Trojan Women Setting Fire to their Fleet (Claude, 1643) 298–9, **299**
tronies 342
Tulp, Nicolaes 336–7
Twelfth Night (Steen, 1668) 376–7, **376**
Twelve Year Truce 165, 311
Two Boys Eating a Pie (Murillo, 1665–75) 201
Two Trinities, The (Murillo, c. 1680) 238, **239**, 270

United Provinces 311–12
Urban VIII: 61, 74
 astrology xiv
 Bernini 87, 99, 103, 104
 Claude 298
 patronage xii
 reaction to *Glorification of the Reign of Urban VIII*: 119
 Reni 71
 Sacchetti 114
Urban VIII Visiting Il Gesù, Rome (Sacchi & Miel, 1639–41) xiii
urban planning *see* city planning
Utrecht "Caravaggisti" 315–19
Uylenburgh, Hendrick van 345

Valdéz Leal, Juan de 236, 239–40
 Finis Gloriae Mundi xx
 In Ictu Oculi 240, **240**
Valentin de Boulogne 263–4
 Four Ages of Man, The 50, 263–4, **263**
 Martyrdom of Sts. Processus and Martinian 263, 277–8, **277**
Valguarnera, Fabrizio 279–80
van Dyck, Anthony xix, 151, 160, 172, 174–82, 193
 Antwerp 174–6
 Cardinal Guido Bentivoglio 69, 178–9, **178**
 Charles I with Monseigneur de St. Antoine 389, **391**
 Charles I in Three Positions 92, 389, 391, **391**
 Christ Crowned with Thorns 175–6, **175**

Cornelis and Lucas de Wael 180, **180**
Elena Grimaldi, Marchesa Cataneo 179, **179**
England 176–7, 388–93
Frans Synders 176
Isabella Brandt 176
Italy 176–80
Lady Elizabeth Thimbleby and Dorothy, Viscountess Andover 394
Lamentation 392
Madonna of the Rosary 177, **177**
Margaretha de Vos 176
Portrait of an Elderly Man 174–5, **174**
portraits 177, 178, 179, 180, 221, 389–93
Queen Henrietta Maria with Sir Jeffrey Hudson 392, **392**
Rinaldo and Armida 181–2, **181**, 388, 393
Roi à la Chasse, Le (The King at the Hunt) 389, **391**
Rubens 174
Self-Portrait 174
Self-Portrait with Sir Endymion Porter 392–3, **393**
Velázquez 221
Virgin and Child with Sts. Paul, Peter, and Rosalie 180–1, **180**
van Haecht, Willem *see* Haecht, Willem van
Vanbrugh, Sir John 403
vanitas xx, 356
Vanitas Still Life (Claesz, 1630) xx–xxi, 356, **356**
Varin, Quentin 273
Vasari, George, *Lives of the Most Excellent Painters, Sculptors and Architects* 341
Vault of the Tribune (Domenichino, 1625–28) 61–2, **62**
Vaux-le-Vicomte (Le Vau, 1657–61) 248–50, **249**
Veen, Otto van 146
Vega, Lope de 195
Velázquez, Diego 169, 195, 217–32
  Adoration of the Magi 212
  Crucified Christ 199
  Deigo de Avedo 226
  Drinkers, The 221–2, **221**
  Equestrian Portrait of Conde-Duque de Olivares 225, **225**
  Francisco Leczano 226
  Immaculate Conception 210, 218, **219**, 220, 236
  Infante Don Carlos 220, **220**
  Innocent X: 178, 228, **228**
  Italy 228
  Juan de Pareja 228, **229**, 239
  Luis de Góngora 220
  Madrid 220–7, 228–32
  Meninas, Las (The Maids of Honor) 229, **230**, 231
  Old Woman Cooking Eggs 218, **219**
  Philip IV: 224, **224**
  Philip IV of Spain (The "Fraga Portrait") 226, **227**
  portraits 220, 224–6, 228
  Sebastián de Morra 226, **226**
  Seville 217–20
  Surrender of Breda 212, **222**, 223, 224
  Venus and Cupid (The "Rokeby Venus") 226–7, **227**
Velde II, Jan van de, *Death Surprising a Young Couple* 357, **357**
Venice xi, xii, 1, 134, 149
Venus 124, 146, 227, 269, 278, 283, 284
Venus and Cupid (The "Rokeby Venus") (Velázquez, 1648) 226–7, **227**
Verdi, Richard 291, 292
Verdonck Waving a Jawbone (Hals) 320
Verhaecht, Tobias 146
Vermeer, Johannes (Jan) 312, 366–74
  Art of Painting, The xvi, 366, 373–4, **373**
  Astronomer, The 367
  Christ in the House of Martha and Mary 367
  Concert, The 370
  Diana and her Companions 367
  Girl with a Pearl Earring 369, **369**
  Little Street 369
  Milkmaid, The 359, 367, 368, 369
  Music Lesson 370
  Officer and a Laughing Woman 370
  Procuress, The 366–7, **366**, 369
  View of Delft 372–3, **372**
  Woman Holding a Balance 371–2, **371**
  Women Reading a Letter at an Open Window 370, **370**
  Young Woman with a Water Jug 370
Veronese, Paolo 13, 14, 181
Veronica, St. 100
Verrio, Antonio 395
Versailles 244, 251–3
  garden façade and lake (Hardouin-Mansart & Le Vau, 1669–85) **252**
  Le Brun 304
  plan (Hardouin-Mansart & Le Vau, 1667) **251**
  sculpture 256
Vertumnus 314
Vertumnus and Pomona (Goltzius, c. 1615) 314–15, **315**
Victorious Cupid (Caravaggio, c. 1602) 44–5, **44**
View of Amsterdam (Rembrandt, c. 1640) 347, **347**
View of Bentheim Castle (Ruisdael, 1653) 383, **383**
View of Delft (Vermeer, c. 1662) 372–3, **372**
View of the Dunes near Haarlem (Goltzius, 1603) 314, 378
View of the Piazza and Basilica of St. Peter's (Piranesi, c. 1751) 5
View of Pont Neuf, Paris (Callot, 1629) 245, **245**
Villiers, George 51
Vingboons, Justus, Trippenhuis 330, **330**
Virgil 302
Virgin (Mary) 12–17, 22–3, 32, 46, 50, 63, 68, 73, 76–7, 117, 127, 129, 181, 183, 206, 207, 212, 214, 216, 220, 234, 236
Virgin and Child with Saints Charles Borromeo and Bartholomew (Lanfranco, c. 1616) 63, **63**
Virgin and Child with Saints Joseph and Francis (Carracci, Ludovico) 72
Virgin and Child with Sts. Francis Xavier and Rosalia (Preti, 1656–59) 136, **137**
Virgin and Child with Sts. Paul, Peter, and Rosalie (van Dyck, 1629) 180–1, **180**
Virgin and Christ in the Holy House of Nazareth (Zurbarán, c. 1631–40) 213–14, **213**
Virgin of the Rosary (Escorial Madonna) (Murillo, c. 1650–55) 234, **234**
Virgin and the Unicorn, The (Domenichino, 1603–04) 31, 57, **57**
Vision of Constantine, The (Bernini, 1654–70) 102, **102**
Vision of the Father Simon, The (Ribalta, 1612) 202
Visscher, Claes Jansz.
  Huis ter Kleef 378–9, **379**
  Pleasant Places 378–9
visual themes, expansion of xviii–xix
Vleeshal (Meat Market) (Key) 327
Vos, Cornelis de 172, 182
Vouet, Simon 134, 260–3, 303
  Fortune Teller, The 50, 260–1, **261**
  Presentation of the Virgin in the Temple 261, **262**, 263
  Self-Portrait 260, **260**
Vries, Hans Vredeman de 328
Vryburch Monument (Duquesnoy, 1629) 96, **96**

Wael, Cornelis and Lucas 177, 180
Wales xi
Wals, Goffredo 295
  Country Road with House 295, **295**
Warin, Jean 256
  Cardinal Richelieu 256
Wars of Religion 244
Waterhouse, Ellis 394
waterschilders 182
Watteau, Antoine 193, 309
Webb, John 398
Wedding at Cana (Steen) 377
Weltlandschaft (world landscape) 378, 381
West, Benjamin, *Death of General Wolfe* 275
Westerkerk, The (Keyser) 328, **329**
Westermann, Mariët 343
Weston-Lewis, Aidan 52
Whitehall Palace 396
Willem I, Prince of Orange 311–12
Windmill by a Country Road (Ruisdael, c. 1650) 381, **381**
Windmill by a River (Goyen, 1642) 380, **380**
Winter Landscape with Windmill (Ruisdael, c. 1670) 385, **385**
Witte, Emmanuel de 364–5
  Adriana van Heusden and her Daughter at the New Fishmarket, Amsterdam 365, **365**
Wittkower, Rudolf 125
Woman Holding a Balance (Vermeer, c. 1665) 371–2, **371**
women 162, 226–7, 322, 357, 361, 395
  see also nudes
Women Reading a Letter at an Open Window (Vermeer, c. 1658) 370, **370**
Worship of the Golden Calf (Steen) 377
Worship of Venus (Titian) 114
Wren, Christopher 398–403
  administrative skills 403
  Sheldonian 398
  St. Augustine 400
  St. Benet Paul's Wharf 399
  St. Bride's 400, **400**
  St. Dunstan-in-the-East 400
  St. James Garlickhithe 399
  St. Margaret Pattens 399
  St. Mary Aldermary 400
  St. Paul's Cathedral 387, 400–3, **401**, **403**
  St. Stephen Wallbrook 399–400, **399**
  St. Vedast 400, **400**

Yonker Ramp and his Sweetheart (Hals) 326
Young Beggar, The (Murillo, c. 1650) 232–3, **233**
Young Mother, The (Dou, 1660) xviii, 359, 362–3, **362**
Young Woman with a Water Jug (Vermeer) 370

Zampieri, Domenico *see* Domenichino
Zuccaro, Federico 146, 201, 387
Zurbarán, Francisco de 195, 199, 208–17, 223
  Adoration of the Magi 212–13, **212**
  Annunciation, The 216, **216**
  Crucifixion, The 209, **209**
  St. Bonaventure at the Council of Lyons 211
  St. Peter Nolasco's Vision of the Crucified St. Peter 211, **211**
  St. Serapion 210–11, **210**
  Still Life with Lemons, Oranges, and a Rose 215, **215**
  Virgin and Christ in the Holy House of Nazareth 213–14, **213**